CHILDREN'S RIGHTS AND SUSTAINABLE DEVELOPMENT

Children often fare the worst when communities face social and environmental changes. The quality of food, water, affection and education that children receive can have major impacts on their subsequent lives and their potential to become engaged and productive citizens. At the same time, children often lack both a private and public voice, and are powerless against government and private decision-making. In taking a child rights-based approach to sustainable development, this volume defines and identifies children as the subjects of development, and explores how their rights can be respected, protected and promoted while also ensuring the economic, social and environmental sustainability of our planet.

CLAIRE FENTON-GLYNN is a lecturer in law at the University of Cambridge. Her research lies in the field of human rights and the protection of children. Dr Fenton-Glynn's first book, *Children's Rights in Intercountry Adoption* (2014) was awarded the Inner Temple Book Prize for New Authors, as well as the University of Cambridge Faculty of Law's Yorke Prize.

TREATY IMPLEMENTATION FOR SUSTAINABLE DEVELOPMENT

Over the past three decades, a series of international treaties have entered into force to address pressing global concerns of social and economic development and environmental protection. On climate change, biodiversity and biosafety, desertification, agriculture and seeds, and trade and investment liberalisation, new regimes have been established to implement global commitments related to sustainable development, many with nearly universal membership. Successful domestic implementation of these international treaty regimes is one of the most significant challenges facing international law today. Although much has been written on the content and form of treaty law, there is relatively little that examines the transition from international legal theory and treaty texts to domestic regulation and practice.

This series of books addresses this need and provides a serious contribution to ongoing global debates by conducting a detailed analysis of how myriad new treaty regimes that cover the future's most pressing concerns can be made to work in practice.

Series Editors

Marie-Claire Cordonier Segger
Markus Wilheim Gehring

Volumes in the Series

Sustainable Development, International Aviation, and Treaty Implementation
edited by Armand de Mestral, Paul Fitzgerald, and Tanveer Ahmad (2018)

NAFTA and Sustainable Development
edited by Hoi L. Kong, L. Kinvin Wroth (2015)

Legal Aspects of Implementing the Cartagena Protocol on Biosafety
edited by Marie-Claire Cordonier Segger, Frederic Perron-Welch, and Christine Frison (2013)

Sustainable Development, International Criminal Justice, and Treaty Implementation
edited by Sébastien Jodoin, Marie-Claire Cordonier Segger (2013)

Children's Rights and Sustainable Development

INTERPRETING THE UNCRC FOR FUTURE GENERATIONS

Edited by
CLAIRE FENTON-GLYNN
University of Cambridge

CAMBRIDGE
UNIVERSITY PRESS

University Printing House, Cambridge CB2 8BS, United Kingdom

One Liberty Plaza, 20th Floor, New York, NY 10006, USA

477 Williamstown Road, Port Melbourne, VIC 3207, Australia

314-321, 3rd Floor, Plot 3, Splendor Forum, Jasola District Centre, New Delhi - 110025, India

103 Penang Road, #05-06/07, Visioncrest Commercial, Singapore 238467

Cambridge University Press is part of the University of Cambridge.

It furthers the University's mission by disseminating knowledge in the pursuit of education, learning and research at the highest international levels of excellence.

www.cambridge.org
Information on this title: www.cambridge.org/9781316643464
DOI: 10.1017/9781108140348

© Cambridge University Press 2019

This publication is in copyright. Subject to statutory exception and to the provisions of relevant collective licensing agreements, no reproduction of any part may take place without the written permission of Cambridge University Press.

First published 2019
First paperback edition 2022

A catalogue record for this publication is available from the British Library

Library of Congress Cataloging in Publication data
NAMES: Fenton-Glynn, Claire, editor.
TITLE: Children's rights and sustainable development : interpreting the UNCRC for future generations / edited by Claire Fenton-Glynn, Lecturer, Faculty of Law.
DESCRIPTION: Cambridge [UK] ; New York, NY : Cambridge University Press, 2019. | Series: Treaty implementation for sustainable development
IDENTIFIERS: LCCN 2018045890 | ISBN 9781107193024 (hardback) | ISBN 9781316643464 (pbk.)
SUBJECTS: LCSH: Children (International law) | Sustainable development–Law and legislation. | Convention on the Rights of the Child (1989 November 20) | Children–Legal status, laws, etc. | Children's rights.
CLASSIFICATION: LCC K639 .C4825 2019 | DDC 341.4/8572–dc23
LC record available at https://lccn.loc.gov/2018045890

ISBN 978-1-107-19302-4 Hardback
ISBN 978-1-316-64346-4 Paperback

Cambridge University Press has no responsibility for the persistence or accuracy of URLs for external or third-party internet websites referred to in this publication, and does not guarantee that any content on such websites is, or will remain, accurate or appropriate.

Contents

List of Figures		*page* ix
List of Tables		xi
List of Contributors		xiii
List of Abbreviations		xxi

PART I A CHILDREN'S RIGHTS APPROACH TO SUSTAINABLE DEVELOPMENT   1

1 Introduction   3
   Claire Fenton-Glynn

2 Children's Rights and Sustainable Development from a "Law and Development" Perspective   12
   Wouter Vandenhole

PART II FUNDAMENTAL RIGHTS   31

3 Reimagining Children's Rights through the Prism of Sustainable Development: Implications for Educating Children and Young People   33
   Julie M. Davis

4 The Right to Participate in Domestic Law and Policy Development   52
   Holly Doel-Mackaway

5 What Course without Evils? Rare Diseases, Children's Right to Health and the Sustainable Development Goals   78
   Octavio Luiz Motta Ferraz

6	Gender Equality, Children's Rights and Sustainable Development *Amanda Kron*	114
7	Children with Disabilities, Human Rights and Sustainable Development *Paul Harpur and Michael Ashley Stein*	139

PART III CHILDREN AND THE ENVIRONMENT — 165

8	Intergenerational Equity and Children's Rights: The Role of Sustainable Development and Justice *Sumudu Atapattu*	167
9	Children's Rights and the Environmental Dimension of Sustainable Development *Ellen Desmet*	192
10	Children's Rights and Climate Change *Karin Arts*	216
11	Inclusion of Indigenous Children's Rights: Informing Water Management in Canada *Carissa Wong*	236

PART IV CHILDREN'S RIGHTS IN A GLOBALISED WORLD — 259

12	Children's Rights, International Trade Law and Economic Globalisation *Sébastien Jodoin and Candice Pollack*	261
13	Present Needs and Future Prospects: Exploring the Policy Conundrum of Working Children in Developing Nations *Jenny Driscoll*	283
14	Advancing the Right to Play in International Development *Tara Collins and Laura H. V. Wright*	306
15	Rapid Development and the Child's Future Right to the City *Liam Magee, Amanda Third and David Sweeting*	337
16	Healthy Diet as a Global Sustainable Development Issue: Reasons, Relationships and a Recommendation *Lucia A. Reisch and Wencke Gwozdz*	361

	PART V CONCLUDING OBSERVATIONS	385
17	The Future Research Agenda: Where to from Here? *Claire Fenton-Glynn*	387
Index		399

Figures

3.1	Five dimensions of rights for early childhood education in light of the challenges of sustainability	*page* 38
5.1	Levels of resource allocation decisions	88
5.2	Out-of-pocket expenditure on drugs as percentage of total out-of-pocket expenditure by family income	104
5.3	Evolution of expenditure with medicines, Ministry of Health, 2004–2009, in millions R$	105
5.4	Infant mortality by household income per capita quintiles, by region	107
16.1	Percentage of childhood overweight and obesity	364
16.2	Draft for a global convention on healthy diets	383

Tables

5.1 Infant mortality rate, by region – Brazil – 1990/1991/2000/2005 *page* 107
5.2 Proportion of women in fertile age (15 to 49 years) by schooling years, by region – Brazil – 1991/2000/2005   108
5.3 Infant mortality rate by years of schooling of the mother, by region – Brazil – 1990/2000/2005   108

Contributors

Claire Fenton-Glynn, University of Cambridge Claire Fenton-Glynn is a lecturer in law at the University of Cambridge, and a fellow of the Centre for International Sustainable Development Law. She has a BCL from Oxford University and a PhD from University of Cambridge, focusing on children's rights. Dr Fenton-Glynn's research focuses on the application of international children's rights instruments in domestic law contexts, with a particular focus on parenthood, birth registration and alternative care.

Karin Arts, ISS Karin Arts is Professor of International Law and Development at Erasmus University Rotterdam's International Institute of Social Studies based in The Hague, the Netherlands. One of her main fields of work is that of human rights– and child rights-based approaches to development. She is a member of the Editorial Board of the *Netherlands Quarterly of Human Rights*, the Human Rights Committee of the Dutch Advisory Council on International Affairs, the Supervisory Board of the Dutch national UNICEF Committee, and part of the team that generates the annual KidsRights Index. For publications and other details, see www.iss.nl/en/people/karin-arts.

Sumudu Atapattu, University of Wisconsin Sumudu Atapattu is the director of Research Centers and International Programs at the University of Wisconsin Law School. She teaches seminar classes on International Environmental Law and Climate Change, Human Rights and the Environment. She is the Executive Director of the UW-Madison Human Rights Program, Lead Counsel for Human Rights at the Center for International Sustainable Development Law and affiliated faculty at the Raoul Wallenberg Institute for Human Rights. Her publications include *Human Rights Approaches to Climate Change: Challenges and Opportunities* (2016), co-editor, *International Environmental Law and the Global South* (2015), *Human Rights and Environment: Key Issues* for Routledge (with Andrea Schapper, forthcoming) and co-editor, *The Cambridge Handbook on Environmental*

Justice and Sustainable Development (forthcoming). She holds an LLM and a PhD from the University of Cambridge and is an Attorney-at-Law of the Supreme Court of Sri Lanka.

Tara Collins, Ryerson University Tara Collins is Associate Professor in the School of Child & Youth Care at Ryerson University in Toronto, Canada. She is also Program Faculty with Ryerson's graduate programs on Immigration and Settlement Studies, Early Childhood Studies and Policy Studies. She has a PhD from the University of London and has worked on international human rights since 1996. Her professional experience includes work for universities in Canada, South Africa, and Ireland; Canadian federal government (Department of Foreign Affairs and CIDA) and Parliament and a non-governmental organization. Research interests include child and youth participation, child protection, monitoring, play and rights-based approaches. She supports several civil societal organizations and networks working in Canada and internationally.

Julie M. Davis, Queensland University of Technology Julie M. Davis is a professor attached to the School of Early Childhood and Inclusive Education, Queensland University of Technology, Australia. Julie's academic interests lie in early childhood education for sustainability (ECEfS) and systems approaches to embedding EfS into teacher education. Her work is grounded in developing pedagogical practices that encourage young children's participation as active citizens in the present while foregrounding intergenerational equity. Julie edited the world's first textbook for early childhood preservice educators, *Young Children and the Environment: Early Education for Sustainability* (2010, 2015), with the latter translated into Chinese (2018). She also co-edited the first research text in ECEfS published in 2014, with a second volume in preparation in 2018–2019.

Ellen Desmet, Ghent University Ellen Desmet is the first holder of the Chair in Migration Law, established at Ghent University in October 2016. She teaches Belgian, European and international asylum and migration law, as well as legal anthropology and coordinates the migration branch of the Human Rights and Migration Law Clinic. Her PhD from the University of Leuven concerned indigenous rights and nature conservation, including fieldwork in Peru. She then held positions at the Children's Rights Knowledge Centre, the Law and Development Research Group of the University of Antwerp and the Human Rights Centre of Ghent University. Ellen's research interests include asylum and migration law, human rights – with a focus on children's rights and indigenous rights – and legal anthropology.

Holly Doel-Mackaway, Macquarie University Holly Doel-Mackaway is an academic at the Macquarie University Law School. Her research focuses on children and the law, particularly the legal relationship between children and the state. Holly's work explores the interpretation and implementation of article 12 of the

Convention on the Rights of the Child that requires states to ensure children and young people have the opportunity to express their views about matters affecting them and consider these views in decision-making processes. Prior to becoming an academic, Holly worked as a children's rights lawyer with UNICEF, and Save the Children and managed a child-protection policy division within the NSW Department of Community Services.

Jenny Driscoll, King's College London Jenny Driscoll practised as a Family Law barrister in London for more than a decade, specialising in child protection, before moving to King's College London where she is a senior lecturer. Her academic interests are at the intersection of children's rights and child protection. Jenny was an academic adviser for the UK Alternative Civil Society Report to the UN Committee on the Rights of the Child. Current research projects include an ESRC-funded project on the role of schools in safeguarding and Leverhulme-funded study of the interaction between formal and informal child protection arrangements in Uganda. Her book *Transitions from Care to Independence* was published in 2017.

Octavio Luiz Motta Ferraz, King's College London Octavio Luiz Motta Ferraz is a reader in Transnational Law and co-director of the Transnational Law Institute at the Dickson Poon School of Law at King's College London. He is a former senior research officer to the UN Special Rapporteur for the right to health and has published extensively on social and economic rights, including the right to health. His book *Health as a Human Right: 30 Years of the Right to Health in Brazil* is forthcoming.

Wencke Gwozdz, Copenhagen Business School, Justus-Liebig-University Giessen Wencke Gwozdz holds a chair in consumer research at the Faculty of Agriculture, Nutritional Sciences and Environmental Management at Justus-Liebig-University Giessen in Germany and is a professor in Sustainable Consumption at Copenhagen Business School in Denmark. She holds a doctoral degree in economics and social sciences from University of Hohenheim (Germany). As a consumer researcher, her focus is on sustainable consumption, health behavior and consumer policy. In particular, her research is centered on obesity, clothing consumption and subjective well-being. Method-wise, she is specialized on quantitative methods and in particular on survey data analyses and field experiments.

Paul Harpur, University of Queensland Paul Harpur is an internationally recognised disability rights scholar who has tenure at the TC Beirne School of Law at the University of Queensland, holds a prestigious international distinguished fellowship with the Burton Blatt Institute at Syracuse University, is a 2019 Fulbright Futures Scholar and is a special advisor with IRIQ Law. Dr. Harpur has received research funding from domestic and international sources, advised the International Labour Organization, as well as a number of governments and commercial entities and sits on a range of boards. His monograph is published with Cambridge University Press and he has other journal articles and book chapters with publishers across the world. Outside his transformational work as a scholar and lawyer, Dr. Harpur is a former Paralympian.

Sébastien Jodoin, McGill University   Sébastien Jodoin is an Assistant Professor in the Faculty of Law of McGill University, where he directs the Law, Governance & Society Lab. He is also a member of the McGill Centre for Human Rights and Legal Pluralism and an Associate Member of the McGill School of Environment. Sébastien holds a PhD in environmental studies from Yale University, an MPhil in international relations from the University of Cambridge, an LLM in international law from the London School of Economics and BCL and LLB degrees from McGill University.

Amanda Kron, UN Environment Programme   Amanda Kron works as Legal Advisor at the Crisis Management Branch of UN Environment Programme (UN Environment) since 2015. She holds an LLM from Uppsala University (Sweden) with a specialization in international law. Prior to joining UN Environment, Amanda served as research assistant at the International Law Commission, and as Programme Coordinator for Human Rights at the Centre for International Sustainable Development Law. In addition, Amanda serves as member and Swedish representative of the International Law Association Committee on the Role of International Law in Sustainable Natural Resource Management for Development.

Liam Magee, Institute for Culture and Society   Liam Magee is Senior Research Fellow at the Institute for Culture and Society, Western Sydney University. A former software developer, much of his work is centred on the relationship of digital infrastructures to social practice and city life, and he has studied and been actively involved in practices of urban community mapping, open source movements, hackathons, living labs, gaming and participatory design. With colleagues, he is currently examining how developments in artificial intelligence are reworking institutional and social conditions in the Australiasian region. His most recent book is *Interwoven Cities* (2016).

Candice Pollack, AGEWELL National Innovation Hub-APPTA   Candice Pollack holds a Bachelor of Laws and a Bachelor of Civil Law from McGill University (2015) and was called to the New Brunswick Bar in June 2016. She completed her articles with the NB Office of the Child and Youth Advocate where she developed resources to support the implementation of the UN Convention on the Rights of the Child and empowered young people to participate in the decisions affecting them. In 2017, Candice took on the position of Manager and In-House Counsel for the AGEWELL National Innovation Hub: Advancing Policies and Practices in Technology and Aging. Candice continues to support the children's rights discourse as a volunteer with NB Champions for Child Rights and the Canadian Student Association for Children's Rights.

List of Contributors

Lucia A. Reisch, Copenhagen Business School Lucia A. Reisch is a behavioral economist and full professor for consumer research and policy at the Copenhagen Business School in Denmark. She has published more than 400 publications and disseminations in her main research areas: consumer, health and sustainability policy, empirical research into consumer behaviour (in particular sustainable consumption) as well as behaviourally based regulation. As academic policy consultant, she chairs the Advisory Council for Consumer Affairs of the German Federal Ministry of Justice and Consumer Protection (since 2014) and is a long-time member of the German Council for Sustainable Development as well as of the German Bioeconomy Council. She serves on several boards (e.g., Stiftung Warentest, Berlin; Robert Bosch Foundation, Stuttgart; Stockholm School of Economics, Stockholm). She has been elected lifelong member of the German Academy of Technical Sciences and serves as editor-in-chief of the *Journal of Consumer Policy*.

Michael Ashley Stein, Harvard University Michael Ashley Stein is the co-founder and Executive Director of the Harvard Law School Project on Disability, and a Visiting Professor at Harvard Law School since 2005. Considered one of the world's leading experts on disability law and policy, Dr. Stein participated in the drafting of the UN Convention on the Rights of Persons with Disabilities; works with disabled peoples' organizations and non-governmental organizations around the world; actively consults with governments on their disability laws and policies; advises a number of UN bodies and national human rights institutions and has brought landmark disability rights litigation globally. Professor Stein has received numerous awards in recognition of his transformative work, including the inaugural Morton E. Ruderman Prize for Inclusion; the inaugural Henry Viscardi Achievement Award and the ABA Paul G. Hearne Award. His authoritative and path-breaking scholarship has been published worldwide by leading journals and academic presses and has been supported by fellowships and awards from the American Council of Learned Societies, the National Endowment for the Humanities and the National Institute on Disability Rehabilitation and Research, among others. Dr. Stein holds an Extraordinary Professorship at the University of Pretoria's Centre for Human Rights, is a visiting professor at the Free University of Amsterdam and teaches at the Harvard Kennedy School of Government. He earned a JD from Harvard Law School (where he became the first known person with a disability to be a member of the Harvard Law Review) and a PhD from Cambridge University. Professor Stein previously was Professor (and Cabell Professor) at William & Mary Law School, taught at New York University and Stanford law schools and was appointed by President Obama to the US Holocaust Memorial Council.

David Sweeting, Urban Platform Studio David Sweeting is the founder and director of The Urban Platform Studio – an advisory, project management and research consultancy focused on developing innovative solutions for urban challenges in Asia Pacific. David has worked extensively on social, neighbourhood and urban planning projects in low-income urban communities across Asia Pacific (PNG, Thailand, India, Indonesia, Bangladesh, Cambodia and Nepal). He previously worked for World Vision International as Urban Technical Specialist and Save the Children as Urban Strategy Advisor and Innovation Lead, and has consulted for RMIT University Global Cities Program, UCL Development Planning Unit, Baan Mankong Housing Program and Save the Children International. He is the 2016 Dunlop Fellowship recipient in the Asialink Business Leaders Program and currently serves as Research Associate with the Institute of Culture and Society, Western Sydney University.

Amanda Third, Institute for Culture and Society Amanda Third is Principal Research Fellow in Digital Social and Cultural Research in the Institute for Culture and Society. Her research focuses on the socio-cultural dimensions of young people's technology use, with particular emphases on the intergenerational dynamics shaping technology practice, and vulnerable young people's technological engagements.

Wouter Vandenhole, Law and Development Research Group, University of Antwerp Wouter Vandenhole holds the chair in human rights and the UNICEF chair in children's rights at the faculty of law of the University of Antwerp since 2007. Vandenhole serves on the editorial board of several international journals and has taken up management functions in European research and teaching networks. His research interests include children's rights, human rights, in particular economic, social and cultural rights, and the relationship between human rights law and development. For some years now, he has focused on transnational human rights obligations, that is, the human rights obligations of new duty-bearers, and in particular on companies. More recently, he started to explore the conceptual implications of sustainable development for human rights law.

Carissa Wong, Centre for International Sustainable Development Law Carissa Wong is a lawyer with an environmental rights and collaborative law practice that facilitates early engagement in the impact assessment process and provides alternatives to litigation in environmental and natural resource disputes. She has worked and published extensively in the field of water resources management and indigenous customary law. She is also an Associate Fellow at the Centre for International Sustainable Development Law and coordinated the launch of its Voices of Future Generations Children's Book Series: www.vofg.org, in partnership with the United Nations, to celebrate the twenty-fifth Anniversary of the Convention on the Rights of the Child.

Laura H. V. Wright, Right to Play Laura H. V. Wright is a research associate and child participation and protection advisor with organizations, such as the International Institute for Child Rights and Development Leadership Team, Right To Play and the ResiliencebyDesign Research Lab, Royal Roads University. She is a doctoral candidate at the University of Edinburgh and holds a Master of Education, University of Toronto and Master of Arts, Royal Roads University. Her work with children, youth and adults has spanned the Middle East, Asia, East Africa, West Africa, Europe and North America. Laura is active in Canadian and international working groups and boards on child rights, play and participation to support collaboration and transformation across sectors and disciplines.

Abbreviations

CEDAW:	United Nations Convention on the Elimination of All Forms of Discrimination against Women
CFS:	child-friendly spaces
CRBAD:	child rights-based approach to development
CRBASD:	child rights-based approach to sustainable development
CRIA:	Child Rights Impact Assessment
CRPD:	United Nations Convention on the Rights of Persons with Disabilities
CWDs:	children with disabilities
ESD:	education for sustainable development
HRBAD:	human rights-based approach to development
ICCPR:	International Covenant on Civil and Political Rights
ICESCR:	International Covenant on Economic, Social and Cultural Rights
ICJ:	International Court of Justice
ICPD:	Programme of Action of the International Conference on Population and Development
ILO:	International Labour Organization
MDGs:	Millennium Development Goals
SDGs:	Sustainable Development Goals
SRHR:	sexual and reproductive health rights and services
UDHR:	Universal Declaration on Human Rights
UHC:	Universal Health Coverage
UNCRC:	United Nations Convention on the Rights of the Child
UNEP:	United Nations Environment Programme
UNESCO:	United Nations Educational, Scientific and Cultural Organization
UNFCCC:	United Nations Framework Convention on Climate Change
UNFPA:	United Nations Population Fund
UNGA:	United Nations General Assembly

UN Women:	United Nations Entity for Gender Equality and the Empowerment of Women
VCLT:	Vienna Convention on the Law of Treaties
WCED:	World Commission on Environment and Development
WHO:	World Health Organisation
WTO:	World Trade Organisation

PART I

A Children's Rights Approach to Sustainable Development

1

Introduction

Claire Fenton-Glynn

In 1973, Hilary Rodham said that "[t]he phrase 'children's rights' is a slogan in search of a definition".[1] For many years, much the same could be said about sustainable development. Widely accepted as a desirable policy objective, its very essence has been contested, meaning all things to all people. The idea of sustainable development is "fraught with contradictions",[2] and the same phrase is used to mask widely divergent mechanisms, tools and objectives. In recent years, with the introduction of the Sustainable Development Goals (SDGs), the concept has started to move beyond merely a catchphrase, to provide a more concrete understanding of its aims and objectives and how it should translate into practice. Nevertheless, these goals have not gone unchallenged, and the precise confines of the concept of sustainable development is still open to widely diverging interpretations.

In 1987, the Brundtland Report famously defined *sustainable development* as "[d]evelopment that meets the needs of the present without compromising the ability of future generations to meet their own needs".[3] But development must be about more than meeting basic needs. As Fukada-Parr and Ely Yamin have argued, development should concern the expansion of capabilities and the realisation of rights: this means that people should not only be passive beneficiaries of progress but also active agents who can voice their concerns and claim entitlements.[4] As such, this book will view sustainable development through a rights-based lens – what are

---

[1] H. Rodham, "Children under the Law" (1973) 43(4) *Harvard Educational Review* 487.
[2] M. R. Redclift, *Sustainable Development: Exploring the Contradictions* (London: Methuen, 1987), 438.
[3] World Commission on Environment and Development, "Our Common Future" (UN Doc. A/42/427, 1987), www.un-documents.net/our-common-future.pdf.
[4] S. Fukada-Parr and A. Ely Yamin, *The Power of Numbers: A Critical Review of MDG Targets for Human Development and Human Rights: Overview* (2013), 7, www.worldbank.org/content/dam/Worldbank/document/Gender/Synthesis%20paper%20PoN_Final.pdf.

the rights of the current generation, and how can they be implemented while not compromising the rights of future generations?

Even this simple definition is imperfect. In contrasting the rights of present children with those of future generations, it creates a conflict between the two sets of interests and fails to recognise that development also gives rise to conflicts even within current generations, where the needs of one group are met at the expense of another. Patterns of development can displace burdens not only in time but also in place, pushing them onto other parts of the world, or other sections of society. This is particularly the case for children, who are often less visible, and less able to assert their rights.

The question then becomes: how do we harmonise these interests and balance competing claims? Governments need to make choices about what actions to fund, what activities to support and how to support them, and a human rights-based approach gives them the framework to do this. It provides a structure by which we can assess policy choices and resource allocation, and challenges existing apparatus of power and decision making.

While a rights-based approach to sustainable development is not new, this volume seeks to view sustainable development through the somewhat narrower lens of a children's rights perspective. In particular, it will consider how the UN Convention on the Rights of the Child (UNCRC) and the language of rights can help children access the means to secure sustainable livelihoods. In doing so, it views children as not merely the beneficiaries of development but also active agents of change, whose rights are fundamental not only to our future but to our present also.

This volume uses the UNCRC and the SDGs as its starting point, but they are most certainly not the end point. The aim of the volume is to show ways in which the UNCRC can be used to ensure sustainable, equitable and child-friendly development, but equally, to identify areas in which its provisions do not go far enough to protect and advance children's rights. It does not attempt to work through each right under the UNCRC systematically, but instead identifies particular challenges to children's rights that have emerged in light of increasing development and globalisation and examines how these correlate with existing legal frameworks.

Part I of this volume provides the background to a children's rights approach to sustainable development. In addition to this introduction, Wouter Vandenhole (Chapter 2) presents an examination of how legal scholarship on children's rights can engage with the "law and development" field, and vice versa. He widens the discussion beyond traditional concepts of children's rights-based approaches to development (CRBAD) to children's rights-based approaches to *sustainable* development (CRBASD), including the key concepts of the intergenerational principle, the precautionary principle and common but differentiated responsibility. Drawing on an analysis of the evolution of the field of law and development, he identifies three areas in which it can be instructive for CRBASD: the importance of normativity, the complexity of social engineering through law and the need for localised and bottom-up approaches. In turn, he indicates areas in which CRBASD can contribute to law and development studies, namely by further broadening the understanding of development beyond the economic; by further broadening law and development scholarship beyond economic law research; and by initiating and stimulating debates within human rights and/in/for development scholarship on the conceptual relationship between children's rights and human rights law, and engagement with sustainable development law.

Part II moves on to consider how children's rights can be conceptualised in the context of sustainable development. In doing so, it highlights the strengths and weaknesses of the UNCRC and the ways in which children's rights theory has evolved since it was drafted almost 30 years ago. Julie M. Davis (Chapter 3) argues that the UNCRC is an outdated instrument, reflective of the image of the child and societies of the drafting period, and needs to be rearticulated, revised and significantly updated. She proposes instead a reconceptualised rights framework that young people are capable social actors who have a right to participate in decision making and action taking about sustainability matters and suggests that education holds the key to the necessary shifts in thinking, values and practice required for this transition. While this new framework begins with the rights drawn from the UNCRC, it also augments these rights with additional dimensions concerning recognition of active/agentic participation, collective rights, intergenerational rights and bio/ecocentric rights. Furthermore, Davis argues that there needs to be a significant shift in awareness, values and practices to change our currently unsustainable patterns of consumption and production, and that mainstream approaches to education are inadequate for dealing with the challenges that sustainable development imposes. She suggests that current educational paradigms are based in neoliberal individualism, market-based scientism, competitive outcomes and reductionist specialisms, and should be replaced with whole-of-systems, relational learning and critical, restorative and participative alternatives. Overall, she argues for a dramatic reorientation in educational thinking and practice, creating new values, ideas and institutions that support just, equitable and sustainable futures.

Chapter 4 focuses on the right of children to participate in decision making concerning them under article 12 of the UNCRC, and in light of SDG 16, which is dedicated to the promotion of peace and inclusive societies and building effective and accountable institutions. Holly Doel-Mackaway identifies children's participation in relevant law and policy making as a necessary component of democracy and of good governance, and that it is linked to upholding the rule of law and therefore essential for sustainable development. In analysing this right, Doel-Mackaway emphasises that participation is one of the foundational rights, which has the potential to positively impact on the implementation of the comprehensive body of children's rights, through providing an avenue for children and young people to inform and influence laws and policies relevant to their lives. She undertakes a detailed analysis of the right to participation under article 12, identifying different interpretations of this right according to the Vienna Convention on the Law of Treaties, and develops a template to assist states to better understand the meaning of this article, and how to involve children and young people when developing laws and policies concerning sustainable development.

In Chapter 5, Octavio Luis Motta Ferraz examines the children's right to health, and the SDG to achieve access to quality essential health-care services for all, in light of the "rights-resources dilemma". Using the rare genetic disease of Epidermolysis Bullosa as a case example, he explores the challenge of how to achieve this goal within limited resources in an efficient and equitable manner. In doing so, he recognises that any plausible interpretation of the right to health will allow for justified exclusions of certain treatments, and questions whether courts are able to hold the state to account in this task. Ferraz argues for a robust procedural revue of decision making, and the close engagement of courts with public health expertise in the field of priority setting, to ensure a just application of children's right to health.

The final three chapters in this section focus on groups of children who are particularly vulnerable in their capacity to exercise their rights. Chapter 6 analyses the ability of girl children to access their rights under the UNCRC and the effect that this has on sustainable development. Amanda Kron highlights the synergies between gender equality, and economic, social and environmental sustainability, and emphasises the double discrimination faced by adolescent girls by virtue of their age and gender. She examines the disadvantage that gender inequality creates for both girls *and* boys, and how this has been reflected in the Millennium Development Goals (MDGs) and SDGs. Focusing in particular on early and child marriage, she shows how this harmful practice directly inhibits sustainable development and children's right to health, education and participation, and presents major obstacles to achieving sustainable development for all. Kron then turns her attention to sexual and reproductive health and rights, and demonstrates how available, affordable, accurate and age-appropriate services are linked to achieving the right to the highest attainable standard of health and access to education. Finally, Kron emphasises that for these rights to be effectively respected and upheld, the cooperation of both state and non-state actors is crucial. She highlights the role of community leaders, religious leaders, as well as other influential political or social figures in conveying key considerations and acting as translators between the global and the local, as well as training and education efforts to ensure a stable shift of norms, practices and expectations.

In Chapter 7, Paul Harpur and Michael Ashley Stein examine the rights of children with disabilities (CWDs) in the context of sustainable development, with a particular focus on the right to education. They emphasise that the deprivation of the right to education of CWDs has broader implications for poverty and development, as it reduces prospects for future financial independence, and increases long-term social and financial costs to the state. Harpur and Stein analyse the rights of CWDs under the UNCRC, showing that while it requires significant efforts from states for CWDs within their own borders, it compels far less when promoting the rights and objectives of the Convention in development initiatives. In light of this, Harpur and Stein look to the Convention on the Rights of Persons with Disabilities (CRPD), which provides a standalone international cooperation and development clause, and signals a dramatic sea change from the limited protection historically provided to CWDs by international human rights laws. They emphasise the importance of not siloing advocacy to a single convention and argue that the implementation of SDG-based programmes must be effected in a manner conducive to realising UNCRC rights to education, but also consider the rights of CWDs under the CRPD.

Part III considers the environmental dimension of sustainable development, and how children's rights have been conceived and acknowledged within this. In Chapter 8, Sumudu Atapattu examines the intergenerational equity principle, and how this concept shapes the implementation of children's rights approaches to sustainable development. She notes that children are disproportionately affected by decisions taken by adults with regard to development but lack a voice at the table to influence these decisions. In this light, she considers whether there is a legal obligation to ensure that the next generation will be able to exercise their rights, focusing in particular on the conservation of natural resources, climate change and the environment. She identifies a gap in protection from the UNCRC in this respect, despite the concept being recognised on an international level at the time of drafting, but shows how other instruments at a national, regional and international level can be used to ensure that the intergenerational equity principle is respected. In Chapter 9, Ellen Desmet analyses how environmental concerns have been taken up in international children's rights law and policy, and, conversely, whether and how children and their rights are recognised within sustainable development policy agendas, with a focus on environmental issues. Noting the limited consideration of the environment in the UNCRC, she suggests that the UNCRC may not be well equipped to address the increase in nature and severity of environmental challenges. Moreover, when considering the main children's rights policy agendas at the United Nations focusing specifically on environmental challenges, she argues that the predominant images are of children as vulnerable beings, and a protectionist approach is apparent. Desmet argues that this image of children as future citizens, vulnerable beings and "resources" can also be seen in reviewing the sustainable development documents over the past decades, but that a shift has occurred in more recent instruments to a more nuanced understanding of children as participants and bearers of rights. She concludes by considering the recognition of children and their rights in the 2030 Sustainable Development Agenda, concluding that although there are some positive indications, ultimately the role of children in environmental issues, especially as actors, is not duly acknowledged.

Chapter 10 focuses on climate change, sustainable development and children's rights. Karin Arts highlights the impact that climate change has on children's rights – both now and the future – and argues that given the concrete risks, climate change interventions are mandatory, and must be rights based. She provides an overview of the way in which children's rights under the UNCRC are implicated by climate change, arguing that the large majority of provisions have a potential role to play and may be seriously affected by climate change. Arts then goes on to examine the work of the Committee on the Rights of the Child in this area, noting the striking lack of consideration in Concluding Observations by the Committee, as well as General Comments. She argues that the international community must step up its response to climate change, and the integration of children's rights in this agenda. In particular, she notes that at the level of multilateral human rights and environmental diplomacy, children are still marginally involved at best, and child participation requires support and facilitation structure and straightforward objectives to be (come) meaningful for all concerned. Finally, Arts emphasises the importance of generating and analysing disaggregated data, impact assessment of policies and other concrete interventions, as well as awareness raising and education of the impact of climate change, to effectively address the multifaceted challenges posed by this growing problem.

Carissa Wong (Chapter 11) considers the relationship between the rights of indigenous children and the fulfilment of the promise of sustainable development. Focusing on Canada as a case example, she argues that government policies have undermined the ability of indigenous knowledge keepers to pass on their understanding of the environment and attacked the relationship between indigenous peoples and natural resources. She suggests that this is particularly important in the context of water management, as indigenous law upholds the spirit and sacredness in nature that would support a more eco-centric, precautionary approach to water. Wong poses that by ensuring children's rights to receive information and ideas of all kinds, to be educated to respect their own and diverse cultural identities, values and religions and to express their views in matters that affect them, the UNCRC supports children's participation in the practice of indigenous law in Canada. This involves the right to learn respect for all living things, to internalise an eco-centric precautionary principle and to uphold the principle of progress as renewal. Furthermore, she argues that the UNCRC protects the right of a child to receive information about his or her natural environment, to life-wide equality and legal agency and to act as a duty bearer. Finally, she emphasises the importance of multi-stakeholder participation, rehabilitation, restoration and relationship building, seen in indigenous law, to ensure a more sustainable and adaptive management process for the sustainable use of water in Canada.

In Part IV, authors analyse children's rights in an increasingly globalised world, focusing on topics ranging from trade liberalisation, child labour and developing urban environments, to the right to play and the global obesity epidemic.

In Chapter 12, Sébastien Jodoin and Candice Pollack explore the relationship between children's rights and economic globalisation and consider whether and how the liberalisation of international trade has affected the rights of children.

They analyse the synergies and conflicts between the intersecting treaty regimes of the UNCRC and World Trade Organisation (WTO) and discuss the implications of the pursuit of mutual complementarity and the recognition of concurrent responsibilities. They argue that as a general matter, the liberalisation of international trade should not be seen as incompatible with the promotion and protection of the rights of children but that a children's rights-based approach must be at the heart of the negotiation and implementation of trade agreements. Using child labour as an example, Jodoin and Pollack consider whether trade measures adopted for the purposes of eradicating this practice could be found to be WTO compliant. In this respect, they examine the legality of banning goods produced through child labour, and conditioning access to preferential trade treatment on the basis of whether a developing country has adopted reasonable measures to enforce the prohibition on child labour. They conclude by examining two instruments that could be used to protect the rights of children in the context of an expanding global market: children's rights impact assessments and non-state market-driven certification programmes, demonstrating the opportunities for the promotion of children's rights in the arena of international trade.

Jenny Driscoll (Chapter 13) focuses on child labour, challenging the work/education dichotomy and arguing for a more nuanced and context-specific approach to determining what is in the best interests of the child. She argues that the principle of sustainable development – meeting the needs of the present without compromising the future – is as applicable to the life trajectory of the individual working child and the welfare of their family and community, as it is to global development. The chapter considers three issues: the relationship between poverty reduction and children's work at the national, regional and international level; the extent to which children can and should contribute to family income and community activities through paid and unpaid work when that work may have the potential to undermine both the developmental aims of the society in which they grow up and their own future prospects; and whether the International Labour Organisation's (ILO's) abolitionist agenda is congruent with the aims of the SDGs. In doing so, Driscoll provides insight into how concerns as to the immediate well-being of children can and should be balanced against considerations of their future prospects.

Chapter 14 examines the right to play in the context of international sustainable development. Tara Collins and Laura Wright suggest that play is often wrongly conceived as less important by individuals and organisations and argue that it should instead be seen as an integral element in sustainable development, as it is instrumentally important in supporting children's healthy development and well-being in the present and future, as well as having intrinsic value as part of childhood. They rely upon three main influences for its conceptual framework – children's rights, sociology of childhood and an anticolonial discursive framework – and evaluate the right to play in international development and humanitarian settings. They argue that providing opportunities for play hones innate play skills, which are critical resources that can support children's self-determination by preparing them for what life delivers, as well as helping them to develop coping mechanisms and skills for their own well-being and developing self-protection skills. They further suggest that play empowers children to meet challenges, and that the skills acquired through play contribute to children's meaningful participation in decision-making processes. These skills in turn play an integral part in supporting the actualisation of sustainable development in many areas, including gender equality, good health and well-being, education and peace and justice.

In Chapter 15, Liam Magee, Amanda Third and David Sweeting explore the intersections between discourses on child-friendly cities and sustainable development and the realities of rapidly expanding informal urban settlements. The authors take a capabilities approach to children's rights, which acts to enrich, extend and strengthen understandings of the UNCRC, allowing these rights to be translated into practical actions. In doing so, they consider how the city develops, unfolds and expands sustainably over time. Sustainable development then can be seen as a process of continued remaking of the city as a space where actual capabilities are exercised in the present, and potential capabilities are anticipated, and planned for, for the future. From this premise, the authors consider five provocations that might orient how the child's future rights to the city might be framed: "Complex Participation", "Multiplicitous Cartographies", "Open Development", "Organised Serendipity", and "Live Laboratories". They argue that a child-friendly city sees itself through the eyes of children, and children must feel that they can talk to the city and have an effect on its systems of structures and power. Children's agency must be acknowledged and mobilised, and they must feel that the city continues to develop its capabilities to house and nurture them. In conclusion, they caution against "child-friendly" becoming an empty adjective and argue that a more attenuated definition of sustainability and sustainable development is required to take stock of the complex and chaotic conditions of rapidly developing cities, and how these concepts must necessarily be negotiated and rearranged around the pivotal figure of the child.

In Chapter 16, Lucia A. Reisch and Wencke Gwozdz examine how and why healthy diets and health supporting environments are basic preconditions for children to develop and a fundamental right of all children. Noting the imperative in article 24 of the UNCRC to "combat malnutrition" and provide "adequate nutritious food", the authors emphasise that states have an obligation to act to combat obesity and ensure that all children have access to food that is not only sufficient in quantity but in quality also. They argue that childhood obesity has become a major factor jeopardising the sustainable development of societies, in a social, economic and ecological perspective, and this is particularly true for low- and middle-income countries. In terms of social sustainability, Reisch and Gwozdz highlight that obesity threatens social cohesion, equity and fairness, as it is closely linked to deteriorating health, reduced mobility, stigma, lower socio-economic status, income inequality and premature mortality resulting in an overall poorer quality of life. Obesity also has consequences for economic sustainability, and the ramifications of obesity on health-care systems and labour markets are severe. Finally, they argue that obesity is closely connected to ecological unsustainability because current food production and consumption are characterised by an excessive use of energy and water. To combat this, the authors argue that national and international efforts to protect children's health from environmental threats should extend their area of application to create health-supporting environments and empower children to make healthier food choices.

It is hoped that this book will contribute to a greater understanding of how children's rights are affected by, and can affect, sustainable development. It shows that the UNCRC has great potential to respect, protect and enhance the rights of children, but that it should be seen as a work in progress – a foundational framework rather than the final word on children's rights. In light of new and emerging challenges, it must be interpreted in a dynamic manner, and child rights advocates must be willing to move beyond the text to a broader understanding of the rights of children in our developing world.

2

Children's Rights and Sustainable Development from a "Law and Development" Perspective

Wouter Vandenhole

There is a long-standing, albeit not always very visible, tradition of law and development studies. In an early period, American law and development scholarship strongly drew on economic modernisation theory and was characterised by naïve legal instrumentalism (i.e., the belief that the introduction of modern law would allow states to turn traditional societies into modern ones).[1] In parallel, there was a strand in French literature that argued in favour of a new branch of (international) law, that is development law, with as its ultimate goal the realisation of the right to development.[2] After a period of crisis, law and development interventions and literature re-emerged somewhat in the 1990s, this time with a strong governance/rule-of-law agenda.

This chapter introduces the main threads of the law and development field and examines how legal scholarship on children's rights-based approaches to sustainable development (CRBASD) can engage with the law and development field, and vice versa. In particular, it seeks to identify learning point in both fields.

CRBASD as an area of study is still very much under construction. This edited volume will contribute to the way it is perceived by others, and the way scholars self-identify with it. But because it is not yet an established area of study, its contours and distinctive characteristics are not always clear. And there may be inherent tensions in bringing together an anthropocentric approach (children's rights) with a field that challenges and arguably seeks to decentre to some extent the human being from the

---

[1] D. M. Trubek and M. Galanter, "Scholars in Self-Estrangement: Some Reflections on the Crisis in Law and Development Studies in the United States" (1974) 4 *Wisconsin Law Review* 1062, 1073–1074.

[2] H. Sanson, "Le droit au développement comme norme métajuridique en droit du développement", in M. Flory, A. Mahiou and J. Henry (eds.), *La formation des normes en droit international du développement: Table Ronde franco-maghrébine Aix-en-Provence, 7 et 8 octobre 1982* (Paris: Editions du CNRS, 1984), 61–69.

notion of development (sustainable development law).³ Therefore, it has been challenging at times to spell out how CRBASDs map onto law and development scholarship, and in particular to outline how CRBASDs may contribute to that scholarship.

This chapter has no ambition to authoritatively write up the history of the law and development field. It does not offer a systematic review of the field and may be to some extent impressionistic. The observations are based also at least partly on participant observation over the last twenty years.

LAW AND DEVELOPMENT STUDIES

For a long time, economic development theories ignored or rejected the importance of institutions for development. In a broad understanding, law is also an institution. Hence, the relevance of law for development was hardly given attention.⁴ In the last two decades, the importance of institutions for development has been acknowledged and now seems to meet a general consensus:⁵

> Beginning in the early 1990s, an institutional perspective on development has become increasingly prominent in development thinking, captured in the mantra "institutions matter", or "governance matters". This perspective views the quality of a country's domestic institutions as a major determinant of its development prospects. The idea that institutions matter for development has both a theoretical and empirical genesis ...⁶ According to this perspective, lawyers – who often conceive of themselves as institutional designers – should become important contributors to the development enterprise.⁷

Two caveats are in place. First, although institutional theories of development only gained prominence in the 1990s, the legal dimensions of development have been studied in law and development studies since the 1960s. That institutional dimension was therefore not completely absent before the 1990s, at least not within the legal discipline. Second, law and development studies have been selective in the way they have studied the role of law in development. Often, there has been a one-sided focus on economic and commercial law and on these legal aspects and

---

³ So rather than to argue for reconcilability and seek to make tensions invisible, as mainstream law and development scholarship has arguably done with economic growth and environmental protection (see, e.g., M. J. Trebilcock and M. M. Prado, *Advanced Introduction to Law and Development* [Cheltenham, UK: Edward Elgar, 2014], 13) it may be more fruitful to make tensions between children's human rights and sustainable development visible and to analyse them.
⁴ Ibid., 17.
⁵ Ibid., 27 and 31.
⁶ Ibid., 32.
⁷ Ibid., 33.

institutions that matter for *economic* development. In what follows, I will develop both points in more detail.

Moments of Orthodoxy

As said, law and development studies fit into the strand of development theory that takes institutions, including the law, seriously. Different classifications of law and development studies can be made. Trubek's and Santos's classification has been guided by what represented the *orthodoxy* at certain periods. They have identified three "moments", that is periods "in which law and development doctrine has crystallized into an orthodoxy that is relatively comprehensive and widely accepted".[8] These three moments are (1) law as an instrument of the state; (2) law as an instrument of the market and (3) law as a regulator of the market. During Moment 1 – "Law and the Developmental State" (1950s–70s) – law was seen as an instrument of state intervention in the economy.[9] During Moment 2 – "Law and the Neoliberal Market" (1980s–90s) – law was primarily seen as the foundation for market relations. It was not to regulate but to serve the market.[10] So in both moments, legal instrumentalism prevailed,[11] that is the idea that law can be used as part of social engineering, as an instrument of the state or market forces. In the (emerging) Moment 3 (1990s–today), the law has become a regulator of the market, and a complementary to the market (in particular to incorporate the social). Also, development has been redefined beyond economic growth, and more attention is paid to local contexts and diversity.[12] Trubek and Santos refrain from giving Moment 3 a name, but an appropriate one could be "Law and the Regulated Market".

It is important to note that this classification in three moments is guided by orthodox thinking in three fields, that is that of development economics, international development practice, and economic law. First, these moments may therefore be silent on or even silence any critique or heterodoxies that existed. Moreover, legal research in other fields than economic law, in particular when it has not been picked up by development economics or practice, is ignored as well. Second, and most likely closely related to the first point, these moments mainly look at knowledge production in the North, to the neglect of new ideas and insights that have been generated in the Global South. Third, the focus is very much on the

---

[8] D. M. Trubek and A. Santos, "Introduction: The Third Moment in Law and Development Theory and the Emergence of a New Critical Practice", in D. M. Trubek and A. Santos (eds.), *The New Law and Economic Development: A Critical Appraisal* (Cambridge: Cambridge University Press, 2006), 2.
[9] Ibid., 5.
[10] Ibid., 5–6.
[11] Ibid., 9.
[12] Ibid., 6–9.

role of law in *economic* development,[13] much less on human or sustainable development.[14] Human development has been defined as being "about expanding the richness of human life, rather than simply the richness of the economy in which human beings live. It is an approach that is focused on people and their opportunities and choices".[15] Human development and the human development index has featured prominently in the UN Development Programme's annual *Human Development Report*.[16] Sustainable development has been defined as "[d]evelopment that meets the needs of the present without compromising the ability of future generations to meet their own needs".[17] Both concepts seek to move beyond a purely economic understanding of development.

Schools of Critique

My categorisation focuses not so much on consensus moments, but rather on *dissidence and critique*, first on the American law and development movement of the 1960s and its legal instrumentalism (described by Trubek as Moment 1), but later also on the neo-liberal orthodoxy (described by Trubek as Moment 2) and other mainstream thinking.[18] Inevitably, that introduces many more ideas that were produced in the South. Its interest is primarily with *human* rather than economic development.

In 2001, Vandenhole identified four schools or types of critique on the initial (mainly American) law and development doctrine and its legal instrumentalism:[19]

---

[13] Whereas Moment 3 is characterised by a reconceptualisation of development beyond the economic, Trubek and Santos put "economic development" firmly in the volume's title, and they acknowledge that that reconceptualisation may be more a matter of rhetoric than reality (ibid., 15).

[14] Although I favour as a matter of principle the use of the word *development* without further qualifications of *economic*, *human* and *sustainable* (see W. Vandenhole, "Human Rights Law, Development and Social Action Litigation in India" (2002) 2 *Asia-Pacific Journal on Human Rights and the Law* 136, 142), it is useful in the context of this chapter to use qualifiers.

[15] UN Development Programme, "About Human Development", http://hdr.undp.org/en/humandev.

[16] UN Development Programme, "Human Development Reports", http://hdr.undp.org/en/content/explore-human-development-reports-1990–2014.

[17] World Commission on Environment and Development, "Our Common Future" (UN Doc. A/42/427, 1987), www.un-documents.net/our-common-future.pdf, 27.

[18] By focusing primarily on the critique of the mainstream paradigms of law and development doctrines, Vandenhole therefore seems to fundamentally disagree with Trubek and Santos who argue that what "marks the Third Moment as more unsettled than the prior two periods of orthodoxy is the simultaneous presence of critique" (Trubek and Santos, "Introduction: The Third Moment", 8). Trubek and Santos qualify their statement some pages later, where they argue that the "critique of law and development orthodoxy has a long history" (ibid., 13).

[19] Which he labels as "naïve", see W. Vandenhole, "Mensenrechten en ontwikkeling: Een rechtstheoretische studie van de bijdrage van mensenrechten tot ontwikkeling, met een case-study van 'Social Action Litigation' in India" (unpublished PhD thesis, University of Leuven, 2001), 73.

law in alternative development, anthropological critique, ideological critique, and what could be called *normative legal instrumentalism*. Law in alternative development originated in the self-criticism of the American law and development movement and sought to offer a nonstatist perspective. It mainly focused on bottom-up and people-centred development and shifted emphasis to appropriate legal environments and legal resources. Human rights were considered important legal resources because "they empower the rural poor to participate in [their] struggles and demand protection of their basic interests".[20] Law in alternative development did not question law's ability to contribute to human-centred development, but insisted on the need to approach law differently, that is mainly by empowering the poor so that they can use the law.[21]

Griffiths's anthropological approach builds on the notion of semi-autonomous social fields[22] (and hence acknowledges legal pluralism) and seeks to study how certain legal rules function in concrete processes of change and interaction. Griffiths challenged that legal rules (can) cause the envisaged social change and questioned that state law can have a significant contribution to development. Von Benda-Beckmann has emphasised that law is the subject of social struggle (who makes and interprets law?) and that law is an important tool in struggles. The extent to which law can be mobilised as a resource in struggles will be mainly determined by the economic and political situation of the ones who seek to mobilise law.[23] Some of the human rights scholarship in legal anthropology and on localising human rights may be said to belong to this school too. For example, case studies on the limits of human rights protection for indigenous peoples have flagged three clusters of limitations, related to the notion of human rights, state conceptions, and indigenous representations.[24] In a localising perspective, human rights are seen as normative references that form part of a struggle for social justice.[25]

---

[20] C. Dias, "Rural Development, Grassroots Education and Human Rights: Some Asian perspectives", in K. E. Mahoney and P. Mahoney (eds.), *Human Rights in the Twenty-First Century: A Global Challenge* (Dordrecht, The Netherlands: Martinus Nijhoff, 1993), 707.

[21] Key writings of this critique include: C. Dias, "The Legal Resources Approach", in A. Eide et al. (eds.), *Food as a Human Right* (Tokyo: The United Nations University, 1984); J. Paul and C. Dias, "Alternative Development: A Legal Prospectus" (1982) 1 *Third World Legal Studies* 284.

[22] As coined by Moore, see S. F. Moore, "Law and Social Change: The Semi-Autonomous Social Field as an Appropriate Subject of Study" (1973) 7 *Law and Society Review* 719.

[23] Key writings of this critique include: J. Griffiths, "Recht en ontwikkeling" (1983) 9(2) *Recht en Kritiek* 175; F. Von Benda-Beckmann, "Introduction: Understanding Agrarian Law in Society", in F. Von Benda-Beckmann and M. van der Velde (eds.), *Law as a Resource in Agrarian Struggles* (Wageningen, The Netherlands: Agricultural University, 1992).

[24] S. Deklerck et al., "Limits of Human Rights Protection from the Perspective of Legal Anthropology", in E. Claes, W. Devroe and B. Keirsbilck (eds.), *Facing the Limits of the Law* (Berlin: Springer, 2009), 391–397.

[25] S. E. Merry, *Human Rights, Gender, and New Social Movements: Contemporary Debates in Legal Anthropology* (October 2006), www.ciesas.edu.mx/proyectos/relaju/documentos/Merry_Sally.pdf, 16; see also K. De Feyter, "Localising Human Rights", in W. Benedek, K. De Feyter

Central to the anthropological critique is the attention paid to context and unexpected consequences for the relevance of (human rights) law.

Within the ideological critique, two strands can be discerned: one inspired by left liberalism, and one inspired by (neo)Marxism. Both have in common that they do not take for granted law's potential to contribute to development, but the extent to which they question that potential varies. The critical attitude towards the social emancipatory potential of law is mainly grounded in studies of the colonial period, which have demonstrated how law was crucial in colonial control and dominance. Both also emphasise that law is not neutral, but rather ideological (as reflected in the rule of law, human rights) and legitimates political power. A central element in the social emancipatory potential of the law is the extent to which it legitimises power through the rule of law. However, the more radical strand has emphasised that human rights are historically and socially situated. Some argue that law can contribute to challenge the status quo (anti-hegemonic), but that it does not offer a counter-hegemonic ideology for radical transformation.[26] Others attribute to the law merely a normative consolidating role.[27] Yet others see a more active role for the law in bringing about social change and define the law as struggle or a site of struggle. However, the law cannot be relied upon as the only site of struggle.[28] De Gaay Fortman's emphasis on human rights as battleground beyond the law resonates with this analysis.[29] They also disagree on the potential of strategic social action litigation.[30]

Normative legal instrumentalism fully embraces the power-critical and power-constraining elements of formal law, such as the rule of law and human rights, in any mobilisation of the law, as inherent to the law.[31] Here too, it has been acknowledged that local variants of the rule-of-law minimum need to be carved

---

and F. Marrella (eds.), *Economic Globalisation and Human Rights* (Cambridge: Cambridge University Press, 2007).

[26] I. Shivji, "The Rule of Law and Ujamaa in the Ideological Formation of Tanzania" (1995) 4(2) *Social and Legal Studies* 147, 167, 169.

[27] Y. Ghai, "The Role of Law in the Transition of Societies: The African Experience" (1991) 35(1) *Journal of African Law* 8, 17–20.

[28] R. Dhavan, "Means, Motives and Opportunities: Reflecting on Legal Research in India" (1987) 50(6) *Modern Law Review* 725, 745; R. Dhavan, "Law as Concern: Reflecting on Law and Development", in Y. Vyas et al. (eds.), *Law and Development in the Third World* (Nairobi: Faculty of Law, University of Nairobi, 1994), 44–47.

[29] B. de Gaay Fortman, *Political Economy of Human Rights: Rights, Realities and Realization* (London: Routledge, 2011).

[30] Dhavan, "Means, Motives and Opportunities", 47 is rather pessimistic, Baxi rather optimistic (U. Baxi, "Law, Democracy and Human Rights", in R. Kothari and H. Sethi (eds.), *Rethinking Human Rights* (New York: New Horizons Press, 1989), 102–103. Vandenhole, "Mensenrechten en ontwikkeling", 91–105.

[31] Ibid., 108–110. Key writings of this strand include R. Martin, "Re-Thinking 'Law and Development'" (1985) 23 *Journal of Modern African Studies* 133; B. Tamanaha, "The Lessons of Law-and-Development Studies" (1995) 89 *The American Journal of International Law* 470.

out, in other words a simple legal transplant will not do.[32] A great deal more recent scholarship on human rights-based approaches to development may be counted to this strand of normative legal instrumentalism,[33] although there will be seldom explicit (self)identification with the law and development field.

A Third Way: International Law of Development

A different tradition of law and development scholarship emerged in French scholarship.[34] Rather than to study the relationship between law and development in practice, it coined the notion of international law of development ("le droit du développement").[35] Hence, the focus was on the elaboration of new substantive norms. For some, the international law of development was a new field of international law, similar to social law in domestic law.[36] For others, the international law of development was rather an attempt to renew public international law as such, so as to allow for economic sovereignty for the recently decolonised states.[37] All in all, the majority of international law of development scholarship has been concerned with technical questions. An exception is Chemillier-Gendreau, who mainly

---

[32] Tamanaha, "The Lessons of Law-and-Development Studies", 476.
[33] See, e.g., U. Jonsson, *Human Rights Approach to Development Programming* (Nairobi: UNICEF, 2003); M. Scheinin and M. Suksi (eds.), *Human Rights in Development Yearbook 2002: Empowerment, Participation, Accountability and Non-Discrimination: Operationalising a Human Rights-Based Approach to Development* (Leiden, The Netherlands: Martinus Nijhoff, 2005); P. Gready and J. Ensor (eds.), *Reinventing Development? Translating Rights-Based Approaches from Theory into Practice* (London: Zed Books, 2005); S. Hickey and D. Mitlin (eds.), *Rights-Based Approaches to Development: Exploring the Potential and Pitfalls* (Sterling, UK: Kumarian Press, 2009); B. A. Andreassen and G. Crawford (eds.), *Human Rights, Power and Civic Action: Comparative Analyses of Struggles for Rights in Developing Countries* (London: Routledge, 2013); P. Gready and W. Vandenhole (eds.), *Human Rights and Development in the New Millennium: Towards a Theory of Change* (London: Routledge, 2014).
[34] With some buy-in from anglophone scholarship, see F. Snyder and P. Slinn (eds.), *International Law of Development: Comparative Perspectives* (Abingdon, UK: Professional Books, 1987); J. Paul, "The United Nations and the Creation of an International Law of Development" (1995) 36 *Harvard International Law Journal* 307.
[35] M. Virally, "Vers un droit international du développement" (1965) *Annuaire Français de Droit International*, 3–12; M. Flory, *Droit international du développement* (Paris: Presses universitaires de France, 1977); J. Bouveresse, *Droit et politiques du développement et de la coopération* (Paris: Presses universitaires de France, 1990); K. De Feyter's *World Development Law: Sharing Responsibility for Development* (Antwerp, Belgium: Intersentia, 2001) may be considered in some respects to belong to this tradition too.
[36] B. Stern, "Le droit international du développement, un droit de finalité?", in Flory et al. (eds.), *La formation des normes en droit international du développement*, 44; N. Terki, "Normes 'nouvelles' du droit international et pratique nationale: l'exemple algérien", in Flory et al. (eds.), *La formation des normes en droit international du développement*, 316.
[37] P. Buirette-Maurau, *La participation du Tiers-Monde à l'élaboration du droit international* (Paris: Librairie générale de droit et de jurisprudence, 1983); J. Henry, "L'imaginaire juridique d'une société mutante", in Flory et al. (eds.), *La formation des normes en droit international du développement*, 33.

saw a mission for the international law of development as declaratory law ("droit déclaratoire"), that is (soft) law that reflects new and desirable social realities.[38]

The declaratory nature of the international law of development may be at its height in attempts to construct the right to development as the normative guiding principle of the international law of development.[39] Recent attempts to redesign the duty-bearer side of human rights law may belong to this strand of scholarship too.[40]

Lessons learnt within the international law of development may be most relevant for current attempts to elaborate international sustainable development law. They largely share the same ambitions: not only to create a new subfield of international law but also to renew international law from within.

LESSONS LEARNT IN THE LAW AND DEVELOPMENT FIELD THAT ARE OF RELEVANCE TO CRBASD

Children's rights-based approaches to development (CRBAD), as part of a broader movement of human rights-based approaches to development (HRBAD),[41] arose fairly in isolation of mainstream law and development studies. To the extent that they have a legal component, they can be considered to be part and parcel of that field of studies though, as suggested in the preceding text. In the next section, I will examine what CRBASD may contribute to law and development studies. Here, I examine what CRBASD can learn from law and development studies.

CRBAD typically do not explicitly refer to sustainable development but are quite clear on how they define development, that is as the full realisation of all human rights of children. In other words, the outcome of CRBAD is human development, which can be defined in this case as increased human rights enjoyment by children, and the process is guided by international children's rights standards, and directed to children's rights promotion and protection.[42] Central features of most human

---

[38] M. Chemillier-Gendreau, "Droit du développement et effectivité de la norme", in Flory et al. (eds.), *La formation des normes en droit international du développement*, 278.

[39] See for more recent work B. A. Andreassen and S. P. Marks (eds.), *Development as a Human Right: Legal, Political, and Economic Dimensions* (Cambridge, MA: Harvard School of Public Health, 2006); M. E. Salomon, "Legal Cosmopolitanism and the Normative Contribution of the Right to Development" (September 2008), http://papers.ssrn.com/sol3/papers.cfm?abstract_id=1272582; K. De Feyter, "Towards a Framework Convention on the Right to Development" (April 2013), http://library.fes.de/pdf-files/bueros/genf/09892.pdf.

[40] See, e.g., W. Vandenhole and W. Benedek, "Extraterritorial Human Rights Obligations and the North-South Divide", in M. Langford et al. (eds.), *Global Justice, State Duties: The Extraterritorial Scope of Economic, Social and Cultural Rights in International Law* (Cambridge, MA: Cambridge University Press, 2013), 332–363.

[41] I define children's rights as children's *human* rights, i.e., a subset of human rights that specifically applies to children. See W. Vandenhole, "Children's Rights from a Legal Perspective: Children's Rights Law", in W. Vandenhole et al. (eds.), *The Routledge International Handbook of Children's Rights Studies* (London: Routledge, 2015), 27.

[42] I restate here the Office of the High Commissioner for Human Rights' definition of *HRBAD* as a "conceptual framework for the process of human development that is normatively based on

rights-based approaches (HRBAs) can be summarised in the acronym PANEN, that is participation, accountability, non-discrimination, empowerment and normativity (the latter has sometimes also been referred to as linkage to human rights).[43] These features are equally characteristic of CRBAD.

HRBAD have been criticised for being a donor-led initiative[44] that detracts from key discussions on global inequalities and responsibilities,[45] with little traction on the ground, and with conceptual weaknesses such as its abstract nature and inflexibility, and its neglect of issues of power and change.[46] Hickey and Mitlin have listed pitfalls on four axes: conceptual, organisational and strategic, political and ideological.[47] Tobin has pointed out seven challenges: the contested nature of human and children's rights; the contested content of these rights; the competing nature of rights claims; the marginal status of rights-based approaches; the inevitability of political resistance or irrelevance; the potential for disciplinary resistance; and the need to navigate institutional and organisational culture.[48]

Tobin has also critiqued the UNCRC Committee's four general principles approach for lacking a solid conceptual underpinning.[49] In addition to the best interests and the right to life, survival and development, he has put forward two new

---

international human rights standards and operationally directed to promoting and protecting human rights" (OHCHR, *Frequently Asked Questions on a Human-Rights Based Approach to Development Cooperation* [2006], www.ohchr.org/Documents/Publications/FAQen.pdf, 16).

[43] Another acronym to define HRBA, used by the Food and Agricultural Organization, is PANTHER: it adds transparency and the rule of law, and human dignity substitutes linkage to human rights (see www.fao.org/righttofood/about-right-to-food/human-right-principles-panther/en/). The UN Development Group (UNDG) has come up with six clusters of human rights principles: universality and inalienability; indivisibility; inter-dependence and inter-relatedness; non-discrimination and equality; participation and inclusion; and accountability and the rule of law (UNDG, *Guidance Note: Application of the Programming Principles to the UNDAF* [2010], archive.undg.org/wp-content/uploads/2014/12/GuidanceNote-Application-Programming-Principles-UNDAF-2010.pdf, 24). The European Commission, for its part, has identified five "guiding working principles": applying all rights; participation and access to the decision-making process; non-discrimination and equal access; accountability and access to the rule of law; and transparency and access to information (see European Commission, Commission Staff Working Document, *A Rights-Based Approach, Encompassing All Human Rights for EU Development Cooperation* (Doc. no. 9489/14, 5 May 2014).

[44] See D. Mitlin and S. Hickey, "Introduction", in Hickey and Mitlin, *Rights-Based Approaches to Development*, 9.

[45] A. Cornwall and C. Nyamu-Musembi, "Putting the 'Rights-Based Approach' to Development into Perspective" (2004) 25 *Third World Quarterly* 1415, 1423.

[46] Andreassen and Crawford, *Human Rights, Power and Civic Action*; Gready and Vandenhole, *Human Rights and Development in the New Millennium*; W. Vandenhole and P. Gready, "Failures and Successes of Human Rights-Based Approaches to Development: Towards a Change Perspective" (2014) 32 *Nordic Journal of Human Rights* 291.

[47] S. Hickey and D. Mitlin, "The Potential and Pitfalls of Rights-Based Approaches to Development", in Hickey and Mitlin, *Rights-Based Approaches to Development*.

[48] J. Tobin, "Understanding a Human Rights-Based Approach to Matters Involving Children: Conceptual Foundations and Strategic Considerations", in A. Invernizzi and J. Williams (eds.), *The Human Rights of Children: From Visions to Implementation* (Farnham, UK: Ashgate, 2011).

[49] Ibid., 71.

principles as specific express principles of a CRBA: the principle of due deference and the principle of evolving capacities. The principle of due deference is the "requirement to respect parents and guardians in the exercise of their responsibilities for the care of the child".[50] The principle of evolving capacities, which is explicitly mentioned in article 5 UNCRC, refers to the fact that "[a]t different stages in their lives, children require different degrees of protection, provision, prevention and participation".[51] In sum, whereas there is discussion (albeit too little) on which principles exactly guide CRBAD, key principles of sustainable development law seem to be completely missing.[52] Key principles of sustainability development law that are absent from CRBAD include the intergenerational principle, the precautionary principle and common but differentiated responsibility.[53] I therefore have coined the acronym CRBASD, so as to distinguish it from the ordinary CRBAD.

In sum, HRBAD in general as well as CRBA(S)D face a number of conceptual critiques and practical challenges. To understand and address these, law and development studies may be instructive on a number of counts.

The *general* lessons that can be drawn from law and development studies are fivefold. First, a more comprehensive understanding of development, beyond economic growth or development, is needed. Second, a shift in perspective is warranted, away from or beyond the state as the key actor, towards social action groups and the legal strategies that these adopt. Third, the role of law in structural change should not be overestimated: legal strategies are not the only ones, and not necessarily the most important strategies in effecting structural change. Fourth, notwithstanding the limited potential of legal strategies, their relevance should not be ignored: the power critical aspects of law (normativity), as well as the potential of legal strategies for mobilisation and legitimation of structural change can be mobilised in broader struggles. Fifth and finally, the inherent limitations and risks of legal strategies, and in particular also of litigation, should be kept in mind: legal strategies will only allow for incremental change; they may be disempowering and individualising; law is a site of struggle; and a legal victory does not necessarily contribute to structural change.[54]

---

[50] Ibid., 72.

[51] G. Van Bueren, *Child Rights in Europe: Convergence and Divergence in Judicial Protection* (Strasbourg, France: Council of Europe Publishing, 2007), 37.

[52] Whereas sustainable development is often explained as a notion with three aspects or dimensions, i.e. social, economic and environmental, sustainable development *law* is more appropriately defined through the prism of six principles, i.e. common but differentiated responsibility; precautionary principle; intergenerational equity; good governance; subsidiarity; and the integration principle.

[53] For a more in-depth analysis of the relationship between human rights law and sustainable development law, see V. Bellinkx and W. Vandenhole, "Normative Guidance for Energy Governance: Sustainable Development and Human Rights" (2017) 8 *Journal of Human Rights and the Environment* 2, 254.

[54] For a more elaborate account, see Vandenhole, "Mensenrechten en ontwikkeling", 111–118. Some limits have been explored in more detail in W. Vandenhole, "The Limits of Human

In what follows, I spell out the relevance of some of these general lessons learnt for CRBASD as an area of study *in particular*. I group them together under three headings: the importance of normativity; the complexity of social engineering through law; and the need for bottom-up and localised approaches.

The Importance of Normativity

An important insight both in mainstream law and development scholarship and in some of its critiques has been that legal rules should not be detached from key normative principles such as the rule of law and human rights.

CRBASD is inherently normative because it is about the human rights of children (as codified also in legal instruments). Normativity is indeed one of its core principles. For this reason, CRBASD is less likely to be subjected to outright political instrumentalisation.

However, content-wise, the normativity of CRBASD may be rather weak or even absent on key principles of sustainable development law such as those of intergenerational justice, the precautionary principle and common but differentiated responsibility. Moreover, environmental concerns beyond those in the interest of human beings may be difficult to incorporate. Therefore, the *substance* of CRBASD's normative framework needs to complement the intergenerational principle, the precautionary principle and the principle of common but differentiated responsibility. Moreover, environmental concerns beyond the anthropocentric ones have to be incorporated (integration principle) if CRBASD is to speak meaningfully to sustainable development. Whereas reconciliation may be possible, it will not come without deep-seated tensions and dilemmas. Rather than to downplay these tensions and dilemmas, they should be identified and debated from a critical perspective. Such critical reflection acknowledges the deliberative character of CRBASD and opens up avenues for transformation and emancipation.[55]

Acknowledging Complexity in Social Engineering through Children's Rights Law

The critique on mainstream law and development, in particular the one voiced by the anthropological approach, has emphasised the complexity of using law to

Rights Law in Human Development", in Claes et al. (eds.), *Facing the Limits of the Law*, 364–374. See for similar analyses in particular about the need to situate human rights law strategies in "combination strategies", P. Gready and J. Ensor, "Introduction", in P. Gready and J. Ensor (eds.), *Reinventing Development? Translating Rights-Based Approaches from Theory into Practice* (London: Zed Books, 2005), 9.

[55] D. Reynaert et al., "Introduction: A Critical Approach to Children's Rights", in W. Vandenhole et al. (eds.), *Routledge International Handbook of Children's Rights Studies* (London: Routledge, 2015), 9–11.

bring about development. It has flagged that legal reforms often have unintended consequences, and seldom the intended once. Causality is extremely difficult to prove.

In more recent work on *human rights*-based approaches to development, this critique has been echoed. There is also little empirical evidence that law "works", that is to say that it brings about the intended effects.[56] More research is needed on "what the transformative potential of human rights law is, and what can be learned more generally from social change theories".[57] Gready and Ensor have pointed out that "[h]ow structural change might be achieved requires much greater clarification, both conceptually and practically".[58] A theory of change underpinning CRBASD is needed. "Such a theory should be grounded as much as possible in empirical evidence, spell out how it conceptualizes change (causation; influences; directions of change) and which actors and institutions it deems instrumental in bringing about social change; and clarify how power is understood".[59] In other words, CRBASD should explicitly engage with questions of power and change, empirically and conceptually.

Authors have also cautioned against any naïve mobilisation of human rights law for human development, by pointing out the limits of human rights law in development. These limits have to do with the nature of mainstream human rights law (such as its focus on the individual and on state sovereignty) and with the ideology of the liberal state. In addition, questions of legitimacy arise. The lessons drawn on HRBADs and human rights law in development are equally relevant to CRBASD.

First, conceptually, human rights law is ill-suited to satisfactorily address issues of human development for it takes an individualised approach to fundamentally structural problems: "The individual approach of human rights law sits uneasily with the structural and collective challenges which human development poses. Human development cannot be addressed adequately in a fractured and individualised manner."[60] Individualism becomes even more problematic in a context of sustainable development because the concern with intergenerational equity and with non-anthropocentric considerations adds additional layers of complexity.

Second, "[l]ifting the veil of formal equality between individuals and states appears to be a common challenge nationally and internationally to increase the relevance of human rights law for human development. While such an undertaking

---

[56] P. Gready and W. Vandenhole, "What Are We Trying to Change? Theories of Change in Development and Human Rights", in Gready and Vandenhole (eds.), *Human Rights and Development in the New Millennium*, 7–8.
[57] Vandenhole and Gready, "Failures and Successes of Human Rights-Based Approaches to Development", 294.
[58] Gready and Ensor, "Introduction", 27.
[59] Vandenhole and Gready, "Failures and Successes of Human Rights-Based Approaches to Development", 294–295 (footnotes omitted).
[60] W. Vandenhole, "The Limits of Human Rights Law in Human Development", in Claes et al. (eds.), *Facing the Limits of the Law*, 364.

threatens one of the longstanding principles of law, it may even have a more profound implication, in that it touches upon one of the underpinning ideological values of human rights law and liberalism".[61] In sustainable development law, the principle of common but differentiated responsibility is the challenge *par excellence* to the formal equality of states. CRBASD is therefore bound to be confronted with serious political opposition whenever it seeks to challenge that sovereign equality. However, insisting on the sovereign equality of states becomes less and less tenable as realities play out very differently.

Third, "human rights law ... can only meaningfully contribute to human development in a certain legal context, *ie* that of the rule of law. In light of the fragility, subversion or absence of the rule of law in a high number of third world countries, this is probably the most serious limit the human rights community is to acknowledge. Moreover, as a minimum, social justice is to be accepted as a fundamental value in society."[62] This ideological anchorage of human rights law in the liberal state is also implicitly pre-supposed in CRBASD. Where the rule of law is by and large irrelevant for the legitimacy of political power, CRBASD is bound to remain marginal too.

CRBASD strongly relies on children's rights law as its normative anchor. Given the conceptual and ideological constraints of children's rights law as the human rights law applicable to children, CRBASD is very unlikely to become "an autonomous vector of structural societal change".[63] This is not to downplay the importance of CRBASD but to invite a more realistic and thought-through understanding of its limits and potential.

No Simple Legal Transplants: Bottom-Up and Localised Approaches

Until recently, children's rights standard-setting has been a top-down exercise. States conclude treaties, reflecting more often than not a political compromise, which are then to be implemented on the ground. Discrepancies between the children's rights norms adopted among states and realities on the ground are seen as an implementation gap, which can be remedied through more and better implementation. The norms are seldom questioned. Children's rights litigation too, be it at the UN or the regional level, is often initiated by international organisations; cases may have been chosen mainly for their symbolic value or for their anticipated success.

In recent years, this top-down approach has been challenged. A range of approaches and methodologies has been proposed to draw attention to daily realities and the way human rights (also of children) are received by ordinary people on the ground. As a minimum, a bottom-up approach allows for a better response to

---

[61] Ibid., 356.
[62] Ibid.
[63] Ibid., 374.

cultural or local challenges in implementation. However, it does not necessarily question the substance of children's rights norms. In a more radical understanding, bottom-up and localised approaches see human rights primarily as struggle rather than as pre-conceived legal rules.[64] In the latter approach, a threefold shift takes place: "Whereas [a bottom-up and localised approach] does not exclude the use of human rights legal tools and norms, it does introduce a different starting point (local struggles, not international norms), a different prioritisation (processes rather than outcomes) and a different end-goal (change in power relations rather than the implementation of international standards)".[65] A localising children's rights perspective challenges the understanding of children's rights: children's rights are not so much a legal regime but rather normative references that form part of a struggle for social justice.[66]

It may not be too difficult to reach consensus on the point that CRBASD needs to take a localised and bottom-up approach. In fact, two of its principles, participation and empowerment, seem to foreclose a top-down approach. However, how radical the turn to localisation needs to be may be less straightforward because the more radical the approach taken is, the more likely it gets dragged into the highly sensitive universality debate on children's rights.[67] In some more politically informed understandings of HRBAD, universality has been explicitly included as one of the key principles that informs the approach,[68] so that the space for localisation of the *substance* of norms seems extremely limited. Whereas Merry starts from a top-down perspective in standard-setting but looks into how "grassroots individuals take on human rights ideas",[69] De Gaay Fortman understands upstream approaches as those that "arise from people's own convictions on concrete freedoms and entitlements relating to their human dignity", although he considers downstream and upstream perspectives on human rights as constituting "two sides of what is basically one process".[70] De Feyter too sees space for localising not only human rights action but also the *substance* of human rights norms, albeit only "for the further interpretation and elaboration of human rights norms",[71] not so much for challenging universal norms. Hanson and Nieuwenhuys may take the most radical turn to reconceptualising children's rights, also in *law*. They argue that "law always

---

[64] W. Vandenhole, "Localising Children's Rights", in M. Liebel, *Children's Rights from Below: Cross-Cultural Perspectives in Studies in Childhood and Youth* (Basingstoke, UK: Palgrave Macmillan, 2012), 80.
[65] P. Gready and W. Vandenhole, "What Are We Trying to Change?", in Gready and Vandenhole (eds.), *Human Rights and Development in the New Millennium*, 14.
[66] Merry, *Human Rights, Gender, and New Social Movements*, 16.
[67] For an introduction to the universality debate from a localising children's rights perspective, see Vandenhole, "Localising Children's Rights", 81.
[68] See note 44.
[69] S. E. Merry, *Human Rights and Gender Violence: Translating International Law into Local Justice* (Chicago: University of Chicago Press, 2006), 180.
[70] de Gaay Fortman, *Political Economy of Human Rights*, 13.
[71] De Feyter, "Localising Human Rights", 68.

represents an unstable translation of ideas of right and wrong that exist in the real world and are based on lived experiences. From this follows that children's rights are not merely the product of deliberations that are fixed in international legislation but that many of their underlying ideas already exist before they are translated into legal principles". With a theoretical framework built around the concepts of living rights, social justice and translations, they seek to capture "the complexities of children's rights as an open-ended endeavour that is responsive to the world that the young construct as part of their everyday life".[72]

The main lesson for CRBASD is that a more sophisticated understanding is needed of how the normative framework of children's rights in relation to sustainable development continues to be created and re-interpreted "in complex fluxes between different beliefs and perspectives on rights, their codification and the unstable interpretations given to these codified forms".[73] This will require a greater understanding of the principle of normativity in particular.

LESSONS OFFERED BY CRBASD FOR LAW AND DEVELOPMENT SCHOLARSHIP

As stated in the preceding text, CRBASD is still very much an area of study under construction. This section is therefore rather tentative and exploratory. Notwithstanding the somewhat premature character of the exercise, I feel it is important to make the lessons learnt assessment in both directions, that is not only on what can be learnt from law and development but also how the law and development field can learn from CRBASD.

(Re)defining Development: Beyond the Economic

Within law and development, a purely economic understanding of development has been abandoned. There is meanwhile acknowledgement of the so-called human and environmental dimensions of development. However, it is not at all clear to what extent mainstream law and development scholarship is willing or able to really integrate these additional dimensions in their work. For example, recent books originating from law and development scholarship still feature "economic development" in the title,[74] or have it as their primary focus.[75]

---

[72] K. Hanson and O. Nieuwenhuys, "Living Rights, Social Justice, Translations", in K. Hanson and O. Nieuwenhuys (eds.), *Reconceptualizing Children's Rights in International Development: Living Rights, Social Justice, Translations* (Cambridge: Cambridge University Press, 2013), 3.

[73] Ibid., 6.

[74] See, e.g., D. M. Trubek and A. Santos (eds.), *The New Law and Economic Development: A Critical Appraisal* (Cambridge: Cambridge University Press, 2006).

[75] See, e.g., Trebilcock and Prado, *Advanced Introduction to Law and Development*.

Article 6 UNCRC on the right to life, survival and development implicitly refers to human development through the use of the notions of "survival and development".[76] Scholarly work on CRBAD clearly moves beyond an understanding of development in purely economic terms and focuses on human development, but it has so far not engaged so much with sustainable development law and its principles.[77] The UNCRC does contain references to environmental pollution (article 24 UNCRC, right to health) and the natural environment (article 29 UNCRC, educational objectives), but does not at all engage with the principles of sustainable development law.

CRBASD reminds of need for comprehensive understanding of development, including the sustainable development dimension. Sustainable development law inserts principles such as intergenerational justice and the integration principle into the analysis.[78] These principles are all the more important with regard to children because they are the adults of tomorrow and because they seem to be more vulnerable to environmental impacts than adults are. Hence, the sustainable development principles need to be mainstreamed in CRBASD but also in law and development scholarship more generally.

Even more importantly, CRBASD is inherently characterised by a tension between the anthropocentric, here-and-now, individualistic focus of children's rights (law) and the non-anthropocentric, intergenerational and arguably more collective DNA of sustainable development law. Rather than pursuing an easy quick fix for these tensions, the continued discussion and analysis of these tensions will allow CRBASD to mature in a more sophisticated and practically relevant manner. This deliberative approach to CRBASD may in turn help mature the broader field of law and development studies in continuing the debate on tensions between the economic, social/human rights and environmental dimensions of development.

Broadening Law and Development Scholarship beyond Economic Law?

So far, law and development scholarship seems to have been confined by and large to those studying economic development, or the role of legal institutions in economic development.

Scholarship on CRBASD, to the extent that it is willing to engage with mainstream law and development scholarship and/or labels itself as law and development

---

[76] M. Nowak, *Article 6: The Right to Life, Survival and Development* (Leiden, The Netherlands: Martinus Nijhoff, 2005), 14.

[77] See, e.g., C. Apodaca, *Child Hunger and Human Rights: International Governance* (London: Routledge, 2010). For an exception and some engagement with the integration and intergenerational justice principles, see K. Arts, "A Child Rights Perspective on Climate Change", in M. A. M. Salih (ed.), *Climate Change and Sustainable Development: New Challenges for Poverty Reduction* (Cheltenham, UK: Edward Elgar, 2009).

[78] See note 53.

scholarship, may contribute to (re-)opening the debate on identity of and self-identification with law and development scholarship. A fundamental choice may have to be made between either becoming part of law and development scholarship or keeping a critical distance from it, for fear of co-optation. Whatever the outcome would be, this choice would require a debate between pros and cons for (not) self-identifying with the law and development field, ultimately also on the quintessential question whether there are good reasons for maintaining that field.

One view is that the label of law and development scholarship should not be left to mainstream scholarship with its preponderance towards economic development and market-friendly approaches, but should also be claimed by other types of law and development scholarship (on HRBAD, human rights in development, sustainable development, global justice) that has so far remained rather invisible, and that has been undertaken more often than not in the margins of the mainstream (mainly critiquing that mainstream scholarship).[79] The largely invisible and marginal nature of research that could be characterised as law and development scholarship too may be attributable to an intertwined dynamic of self-identification and perception. Scholars studying human rights (of children) in development more often than not do not self-identify themselves as law and development scholars. Moreover, both mainstream law and development scholarship and outsiders to that field tend to consider human rights in development scholarship as not being part of that discipline, or at least not being at the core of it. A similar dialectic may be found in sustainable development (law) scholarship.

A diametrically opposed view could be that a critical distance is to be kept from law and development scholarship to avoid co-optation or identification with the dominant school of law and development scholarship. The risks of being identified with naïve legal instrumentalism or a market-friendly approach in claiming the law and development label may be such that CRBASD scholarship decides to stay away and to create its own scholarly community, possibly as part of a broader human rights and/in/for development research community.

Either way, the construction of a new subfield of CRBASD will (re)invigorate the debate on identity of and self-identification with law and development scholarship.

Initiating and Stimulating Debates within Human Rights and/in/for Development Scholarship

Three debates within human rights and/in/for development scholarship may be initiated or stimulated through the construction of CRBASD as an area of study. First, alternative law and development scholarship has evolved in two opposing

---

[79] A good example of this is S. Adelman and A. Paliwala (eds.), *Law and Crisis in the Third World* in African Discourse Series (London: Hans Zell, 1993), which sought to stimulate debate about law and development by critiquing what was called "liberal law and development theory" (vii).

directions: whereas some have mainly focused on the potential and limits for law in development, others have primarily sought to create a legal sub-discipline in international law (international development law, world development law). The former is more about socio-legal research, the latter more about legal theory. In human rights (law), these two strands can be found in work on the right to development, on one hand, and on the potential and pitfalls of the human rights-based approach to development, on the other. CRBASD scholarship faces the same question: should it primarily focus on the integration of the sustainable development principles into its self-definition, or should it pursue the elaboration of a new subfield of international law, that is sustainable development law?

Second, the relationship between children's rights and human rights may require further clarification. In this chapter, I have brushed the question more or less aside by submitting that children's rights law is human rights law in relation to children. Others may argue, however, that children's rights law scholarship is or ought to be distinct or at least distinguishable from human rights scholarship, to do fully right to the uniqueness and specificity of children. This volume seems to adhere to the latter position. In the conceptual elaboration of CRBASD, the discussion on the intergenerational equity principle and possibly the integration principle will stir the debate on the need and appropriateness of a separate field of children's rights and development.

Third, CRBASD scholarship will necessitate children's rights and human rights and/in/for development scholarship to seriously engage with sustainable development scholarship. This engagement will force children's rights and human rights and/in/for development scholarship into a greater self-understanding of its strengths, weaknesses, opportunities and threats.

CONCLUSIONS

In this chapter, I have sought to situate CRBASD as an academic area of study, in law and development scholarship, to engage in a mutual learning exercise. I have been confronted with at least two complicating factors. First, mapping and defining law and development scholarship can be undertaken in myriad ways. I have offered two systematisations but without any ambition of offering a systematic review of the field: one that is informed by consensus moments in scholarship and practice (as developed by Trubek and Santos) and one that rather draws on the heterodoxies and critiques within the field. Second, CRBASD is still very much a field under construction, so that it is not always clear what the basic paradigms, principles and schools of thought within this field (will) look like.

Building on that mapping exercise of law and development scholarship, I have identified areas for learning between both "fields". Law and development studies may be instructive for CRBASD in at least three respects: first, to value the importance of normativity; second, to acknowledge the complexity of social engineering through children's rights law; and third, to assess the nature and extent of a localised and bottom-up approach.

CRBASD, in turn, may also contribute to law and development studies in at least three respects: by further broadening the understanding of development beyond the economic; further broadening law and development scholarship beyond economic law research; and initiating and stimulating debates within human rights and/in/for development scholarship on the direction to be taken (socio-legal studies on potential and pitfalls or elaborating a new subfield), the conceptual relationship between children's rights and human rights law, and engagement with sustainable development law.

A thread throughout the chapter is that the prevalence of uncertainty, tensions and debate is a strength rather than a weakness of the field of children's rights and sustainable development. Avoiding closure and taking a critical (in the sense of deliberative and emancipatory) approach will allow the field to mature and to enrich mainstream law and development studies.

PART II

Fundamental Rights

3

Reimagining Children's Rights through the Prism of Sustainable Development

Implications for Educating Children and Young People

Julie M. Davis

INTRODUCTION

The Big Issues

Concepts of social justice and children's rights have been familiar companions to many education theorists, researchers and practitioners, particularly in early education, over long periods of time.[1] Indeed, the majority of the literature often valorises these concepts[2] because of the important contributions of children's rights research as a driving force for the upgrading of the status of children in society.[3] The UN Convention on the Rights of the Child (UNCRC)[4] in particular, has been placed at the absolute centre of discussions often framing and/or motivating theory, research or practice. Rarely though is the UNCRC the actual object of analysis or discussion.[5] Instead "it has been allowed to define rights for children".[6] Like some researchers, for example Veerman,[7] I argue that the UNCRC is outdated, reflective of the image of the child and societies of the drafting period. Things have changed since then. We live in times of increasing insecurity and uncertainty where calls for

---

[1] See, e.g., J. Dewey, *Democracy and Education: An Introduction to the Philosophy of Education* (New York: Macmillan, 1916).
[2] Z. Mevawalla, "The Crucible: Adding Complexity to the Question of Social Justice in Early Childhood Development" (2013) 14 *Contemporary Issues in Early Childhood* 290.
[3] A. Quennerstedt, "Children's Rights Research Moving into the Future – Challenges on the Way Forward" (2013) 21 *International Journal of Children's Rights* 233.
[4] UN General Assembly (UNGA), *Convention on the Rights of the Child* (UN Doc. A/RES/44/25, 20 November 1989), 1577 UNTS 3.
[5] D. Reynaert, M. Bouverne-de Bie and S. Vandevelde, "A Review of Children's Rights Literature since the Adoption of the UN Convention on the Rights of the Child" (2009) 16 *Childhood* 518.
[6] Quennerstedt, "Children's Rights Research Moving into the Future", 233.
[7] P. E. Veerman, "The Ageing of the UN Convention on the Rights of the Child" (2010) 18 *International Journal of Children's Rights* 585.

the world's peoples to live more socially, economically and environmentally sustainable lives are becoming more urgent. The UNICEF report, *Sustainable Development Starts and Ends with Safe, Healthy and Well-Educated Children*, for example, states that it is increasingly recognised that a sustainable world requires a significant shift in awareness, values and practices to change our currently unsustainable patterns of consumption and production.[8] This same report argues that children's needs and rights are interdependent with sustainable development.

Education holds the key to the necessary shifts in thinking, values and practice required for these transitions.[9] However, the foundations of much of our current discourses about children, education and social issues are outdated. My starting point in this chapter is that the UNCRC is an historical and political artifact, requiring interrogation and updating, and not a document that sets children's rights "in stone".[10] First, however, I briefly discuss the role and relationship of education in (and for) sustainable development, before returning to the particular place of children's rights in early education.

Education for Sustainable Development

The field of Education for Sustainable Development (ESD) is generally recognised as having its formal beginning in the 1970s, with international documents, such as the Tbilisi Declaration of 1978, designating "environmentally-educated teachers" as "the priority of priorities".[11] Since this time, the education sectors have been engaged in a number of environmental and sustainability agendas – the establishment of professional associations for teachers with an interest in Environmental Education/Education for Sustainability (EE/EfS), research societies, conferences and journals for educators working in this space, and the establishment of a myriad of school-based programs. The UN Decade of Education for Sustainable Development (UNDESD) (2005–2014) saw UNESCO lead a range of national and international initiatives that scaled up or brought new entrants to existing programs such as Sustainable Schools (Australia), Green Schools (United States, China and elsewhere), Foundation for Environmental Education (FEE) schools (many European countries), Eco-schools (United Kingdom and New Zealand) and Eco-kindergartens (New Zealand). In the wake of the UNDESD, a new suite of educational activities and initiatives are now underway. An emphasis on engaging

---

[8] UNICEF, *Sustainable Development Starts and Ends with Safe, Healthy and Well-Educated Children* (2013), www.unicef.org/socialpolicy/files/Sustainable_Development_post_2015.pdf.
[9] S. Sterling, *Sustainable Education: Re-Visioning Learning and Change* (Devon, UK: Green Books, 2001); UNESCO, *UN Decade of Education for Sustainable Development (2005–2014)* (2005), www.unesco.org/education/tlsf/extras/img/DESDbrief.pdf.
[10] Cf. N. Bobbio, *The Age of Rights* (Cambridge: Polity Press, 1996).
[11] UNESCO-UNEP, "Environmentally Educated Teachers: The Priority of Priorities?" (1990) 15 (1) *Connect* 1.

educators more fully in ESD, focusing particularly on children and youth engagement, are strong themes in the post-UNDESD policy/action environment (cf. the Global Action Programme on Education for Sustainable Development).

Recent efforts in ESD, originally led and dominated by science and geography educators, emphasise that ESD is for all sectors of education – from early education to higher education – indeed for all sectors of society. It is also recognised that ESD requires a dramatic shift away from how education is currently framed and practiced – in other words, mainstream approaches to education are inadequate for dealing with the challenges that sustainable development imposes. Current educational paradigms are increasingly based in neoliberal individualism, market-based scientism, competitive outcomes and reductionist specialisms rather than whole-of-systems, relational learning, and critical, restorative and participative alternatives.[12] Many educators across a wide range of subfields consider such contemporary approaches to education to be woefully inadequate for enabling learners to understand and deal with the realities, uncertainties and complexities of a bewildering array of local, regional and global issues – related to economic instability, climate change, population migrations, inequalities, loss of biodiversity, rapid resource consumption and urbanisation, to name a few.

ESD, however, is about creating fundamental changes in how we think, teach and learn. While there is ongoing discussion and debate about what particular form or nomenclature should apply (e.g., EE, ESD, EfS, sustainable education) what *is* generally agreed upon is that each of these types of ESD implies a dramatic "reorientation" or transformation in educational thinking and practice through which education becomes transformative for sustainable living.[13] That is, it helps to create new values, ideas and institutions that support just, equitable and sustainable futures and addresses the systems and ideologies that create the problems. Key characteristics of such education include teaching and learning that is learner- rather than teacher-centred; collaborative and transactional learning rather than learning that is focused on the individual; emphasises cognitive, social, affective and skills-based learning rather than emphasising mostly cognitive objectives; and supports problem-solving and solution-seeking rather than learning facts and subject-specific content. Embedded within such transformative approaches are, for example, educator competencies aimed at helping learners understand the root causes of unsustainable development; connecting learners to their local and global

---

[12] See, e.g., H. Kopnina, "Neoliberalism, Pluralism, Environment and Education for Sustainability" (2014) 1 *Horizons of Holistic Education* 93; M. McKenzie, "Education for Y'all: Global Neoliberalism and the Case for a Politics of Scale in Sustainability Education Policy" (2012) 10 *Policy Futures in Education* 165; S. Sterling, "An Analysis of the Development of Sustainability Education Internationally: Evolution, Interpretation and Transformative Potential" in J. Blewitt and C. Cullingford (eds.), *The Sustainability Curriculum: The Challenge for Higher Education* (London: Earthscan, 2004).

[13] Sterling, "An Analysis of the Development of Sustainability Education Internationally".

spheres of influence; understanding the basics of systems thinking; recognising the interconnectedness of social, political, environmental and economic dimensions of human development; and understanding the interdependent nature of relationships between, for example, present and future generations, rich and poor, and between humans and nature/environment.[14]

RETHINKING SOCIAL JUSTICE AND CHILDREN AND YOUNG PEOPLES' RIGHTS IN EDUCATION/EARLY EDUCATION

Working with the ideas and principles of ESD outlined in the preceding text prompts this writer, as a teacher educator and researcher in Early Childhood ESD, to apply critique and analysis, not only to current educational practices that have been "captured" by neoliberalism but also those taken-for-granted values that many do see as transformative, and that represent a new wave of interest in social justice and human/children's rights. Here, I focus on early childhood education (ECE), which has a long history of concern for social justice and equity.

There is a considerable body of literature concerning social justice in ECE and its potential to recognise how power operates through political, economic and social systems and practices and how it might challenge stereotypes and oppressive practices, particularly in relation to gender, class and race.[15] Additionally, ECE offers a range of settings that enact children's rights, the most universally accepted articulation of children's rights being the UNCRC. Ideas articulated in the UNCRC underpin the work of many ECE educators and advocates, with the UNCRC being the foundational document for the Code of Ethics (2006) of Australia's largest professional association for early childhood educators, Early Childhood Australia, and its recently published *Supporting Young Children's Rights – Statement of Intent* (2015–2018). Nevertheless, as other authors have stated, the UNCRC is a product of its time.[16] I wish, however, to emphasise that I am not arguing for lessening the universalisation of children's rights across the globe; instead, I argue for greater amplification of thinking about children's rights if education is to make a lasting contribution to sustainability.

---

[14] UN Economic Commission for Europe and Sustainable Development, *Learning for the Future: Competencies for Education for Sustainable Development* (2012), www.unece.org/fileadmin/DAM/env/esd/ESD_Publications/Competences_Publication.pdf.

[15] S. Wong, "A 'Humanitarian Idea': Using a Historical Lens to Reflect on Social Justice in Early Childhood Education and Care" (2013) 14 *Contemporary Issues in Early Childhood* 311.

[16] S. Sheridan and I. Pramling Samuelsson, "Children's Conceptions of Participation and Influence in Pre-School: A Perspective on Pedagogical Quality" (2001) 2(2) *Contemporary Issues in Early Childhood* 169; S. Tomanovic, "Family Habitus as the Cultural Context for Childhood" (2000) 11(3) *Childhood: A Global Journal of Child Research* 339; D. Berthelsen, "Participatory Learning: Issues for Research and Practice", in D. Berthelsen, J. Brownlee and E. Johansson (eds.), *Participatory Learning in the Early Years: Research and Pedagogy* (New York: Routledge, 2009).

My starting point is a reimagining of how rights and justice can be formulated in response to the challenges confronting humanity in the twenty-first century and beyond. My core argument is that educators conceptualise rights, exemplified by the UNCRC with its origins in the social practices of liberal democracies post–World War II, far too narrowly.

While the ambitious, but aspirational, goals of the UNCRC remain important, twenty-first-century societies are already vastly different from those that framed the Universal Declaration on Human Rights (UDHR)[17] and the UNCRC in the twentieth century. Socio-political, economic and environmental dynamics have dramatically shifted; we live in a connected world with global movements of people, goods and services. Concurrently, the world appears fragmented and vulnerable with weakened economies, rising social tensions, uncontrolled human migrations and fears about global pandemics, food security and terrorism.[18] Such complex social, political, economic and environmental changes demand new responses, including challenges to our foundational, "rock solid" pillars such as the UNCRC that currently shapes and guides thinking about children's rights.

A REIMAGINED RIGHTS FRAMEWORK: NEW DIMENSIONS FOR NEW TIMES

Prompted by the challenges of sustainability, I have developed a revised children's rights framework that may offer educators a contemporary way of working with rights with sustainable development in mind. This framework was first presented in chapter 1 of Davis and Elliott, *Research in Early Childhood Education for Sustainability: International Perspectives and Provocations* in 2014.[19] Here, I provide an abbreviated and modestly updated version, illustrated in Figure 3.1.[20]

In brief, the first dimension of this reconceptualised rights framework remains the foundational and aspirational view of children and young peoples' rights drawn from the UNCRC. The second dimension expands child participation rights – an emergent area within the UNCRC – but calls for active/agentic participation to be the norm. The third dimension explores collective rights, including the rights of indigenous people and groups often marginalised by dominant perspectives, as an extension to thinking about children's/human rights. The fourth dimension considers intergenerational rights, while the fifth dimension expands beyond human rights, considering the rights of all living beings and the nonliving attributes of

---

[17] UNGA, *Universal Declaration of Human Rights* (UN Doc. A/810, 10 December 1948).
[18] Centre for Strategic and International Studies, *Critical Questions for 2013: Global Challenges* (25 January 2013), www.csis.org/analysis/critical-questions-2013-global-challenges.
[19] J. Davis, "Examining Early Childhood Education through the Lens of Education for Sustainability", in J. Davis and S. Elliott (eds.), *Research in Early Childhood Education for Sustainability: International Perspectives and Provocations* (Oxford: Routledge, 2014).
[20] Ibid., 23.

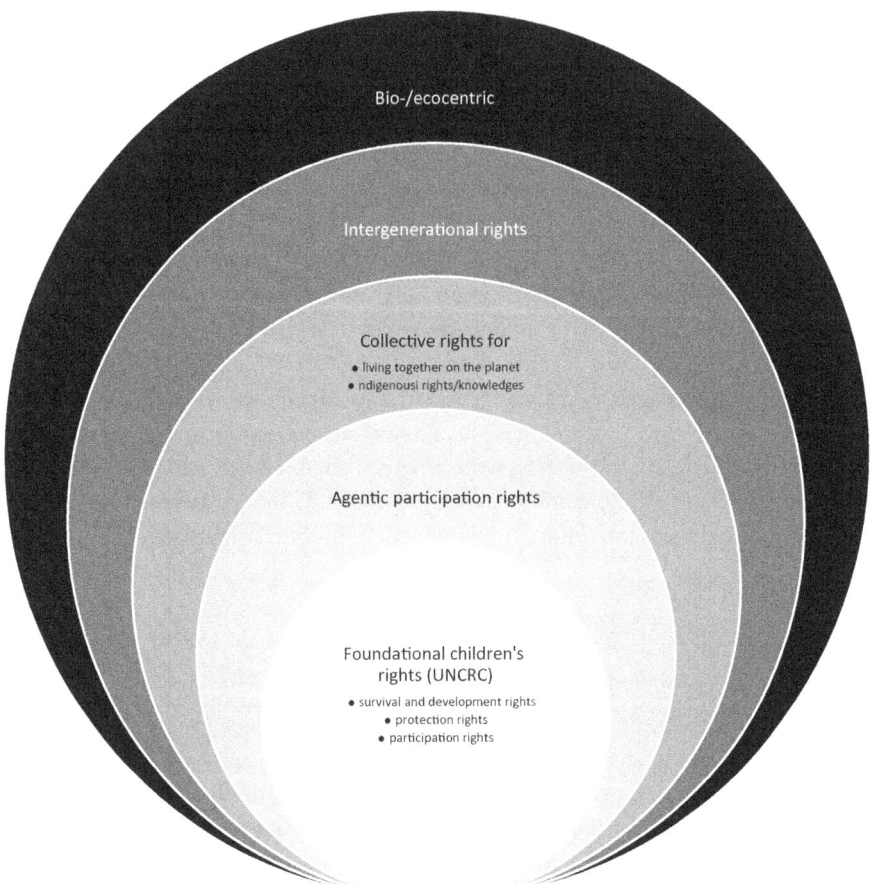

FIGURE 3.1 Five dimensions of rights for early childhood education in light of the challenges of sustainability

nature/natural environments. It is important to recognise that these five dimensions are not mutually exclusive. Boundaries overlap and seep into each other. I contend, though, that all dimensions require consideration and enactment if sustainability is to be realised. For elaboration purposes, however, each dimension is addressed here separately.

Dimension 1: Children and Young Peoples' Rights as Formulated in the UNCRC

One response to World War II was an attempt by the international community to entrench peace, rights and freedoms. Consequently, the UDHR was adopted by the UN General Assembly in December 1948. Arguably the foundation of international human rights law, the UDHR has inspired a rich body of legally binding international human rights treaties, covenants and conventions. The UDHR represents "the universal recognition that basic rights and fundamental freedoms are inherent to all human beings, inalienable and equally applicable to everyone, and that every one of us is born free and equal in dignity and rights."[21] In 1976, the International Covenant on Civil and Political Rights and the International Covenant on Economic, Social and Cultural Rights came into force, developing further most of the rights enshrined in the UDHR and effectively making them binding on nations that ratified them. These Covenants set out everyday human rights such as the right to life, equality before the law, freedom of expression and the right to work, social security and education.

Over time, international human rights treaties have become more specialised, such as the UNCRC, the world's most ratified human rights treaty. In 1989, world leaders resolved that people under eighteen years of age required a special convention, recognising that children and young people often require special or additional care and protection that adults do not. Thus, the UNCRC became the first legally binding international legal instrument to encompass a broad range of civil, cultural, economic, political and social rights for children. In so doing the Convention went beyond the protective rights focus of earlier children's rights documents, such as the earlier Declaration of the Rights of the Child (1959).[22] The UNCRC's recognition of children as "holders" of human rights and not simply having rights to "protection" significantly extended on earlier ideas of children's rights that focused on protecting the child because of their perceived physical and mental immaturity, and potential vulnerability. Over time, the UNCRC has become the starting point for much of the discussion and implementation of children's rights – including within ECE – around the globe.[23]

The guiding principles of the UNCRC are captured in forty articles that revolve around: rights to life, survival and development; non-discrimination and protection; and participation rights as summarised in the following text.

- *Survival and development rights* include the right to adequate food, shelter, clean water, formal education, primary health care, leisure, recreation and play, cultural activities and information about rights.

---

[21] United Nations, *The Foundation of International Human Rights Law* (undated), www.un.org/en/sections/universal-declaration/foundation-international-human-rights-law/index.html.

[22] G. MacNaughton, P. Hughes and K. Smith (eds.), *Young Children as Active Citizens: Principles, Policies and Pedagogies* (Newcastle, UK: Cambridge Scholars Publishing, 2008).

[23] See, e.g., Australian Human Rights Commission and Early Childhood Australia, *Supporting Young Children's Rights: Statement of Intent (2015–2018)* (2015), www.humanrights.gov.au/sites/default/files/supporting_young_children_rights.pdf; J. Bennett, "A Comparative Analysis of Provision Made in National Curricula to Strengthen Children's Democratic Participation in Early Childhood Centres", in MacNaughton et al. (eds.), *Young Children as Active Citizens*; Sheridan and Pramling Samuelsson, "Children's Conceptions of Participation and Influence in Pre-school"; Wong, "A 'Humanitarian Idea'".

- **Protection rights** include protection from abuse, neglect, exploitation and cruelty, the right to special protection in times of war, and protection from abuse in the criminal justice system.
- **Participation rights** include the right to express opinions and be heard in matters affecting their social, economic, religious, cultural and political life. Participation rights help bring about the realisation of all UNCRC rights and prepare children and young people for active societal roles.[24]

Dimension 2: Children and Young Peoples' Rights as Agentic Beings

The UNCRC's inclusion of participation rights as preparation for children's active role in society is my starting point for introducing Dimension 2 as a separate dimension in this new children's rights framework. As mentioned previously, having a voice, being heard and listened to are fundamental rights constituted in the UNCRC. Two points of critique of this aspect of the Convention can be made. The first relates to how children and young people are viewed in society; the second concerns how participation is viewed, that is whether it is agentic participation.

Since the UNCRC was initially presented in 1989, there has been considerable discussion and revisioning of children's participation rights, encompassing issues of identity, autonomy, freedom of choice, expression of thoughts and views and involvement in decision-making.[25] As MacNaughton, Hughes and Smith observe, contemporary research to do with young children now generates images of children who:

- Can construct and communicate valid meanings about the world and their place in it;
- Are capable social actors with a right to participate in social, cultural and political worlds and to contribute valid and useful ideas;
- Know the world in alternative (not inferior) ways to adults; and
- Have perspectives and insights that help adults better understand children's experiences.[26]

Such images are of children as visible, social, active players in their various contexts;[27] they are seen as human beings rather than human becomings. As Reynaert,

---

[24] UNICEF, *United Nations Convention on the Rights of the Child (UNCRC)* (2005), www.unicef.org/crc/index_30177.html.

[25] D. Berthelsen, J. Brownlee and E. Johansson (eds.), *Participatory Learning in the Early Years: Research and Pedagogy* (London: Routledge Research in Education, 2009); Sheridan and Pramling Samuelsson, "Children's Conceptions of Participation and Influence in Pre-School"; S. Tomanović, "Young People's Participation within the Family: Parents' Accounts" (2000) 8 *International Journal of Children's Rights* 151.

[26] MacNaughton et al. (eds.), *Young Children as Active Citizens*, ix.

[27] W. A. Corsaro, *The Sociology of Childhood* (Thousand Oaks, CA: Pine Forge Press, 1997); J. Nimmo, "Young Children's Access to Real Life: An Examination of the Growing Boundaries

Bouverne-de-Bie and Vandevelde comment, the academic children's rights discourse since the adoption of the UNCRC "has been preoccupied with highlighting the childhood image of the competent child",[28] a reaction against images of the incompetent child requiring protection because of their vulnerability. Indeed, the UNCRC as it stands today is often described as a contemporary, transformative instrument that guides policy on children.

Nevertheless, changing the imagery of children – even when backed by policy – is not enough to ensure their agentic participation. Use of the UNCRC as a cornerstone for children's participatory rights needs to be more than something to preach about, but rather something to enact. I argue that, as it stands, the UNCRC offers relatively limited guidance about agentic participation for young children and that children and young peoples' participation requires radical reformulation because many of the current ideas about participation and agency now seen outmoded. Indeed, it is in professional circles, such as paediatrics and health promotion, that we see stronger calls for children's participation, especially in light of climate change threats. As Strazdinis and Skeat state in their Australian responses report about young peoples' participation in climate change, many people were well informed about the likely human impacts of climate change, and agreed that children and young people would be adversely affected, but were concerned about the lack of involvement of children and young people in crucial policy decisions and agreed that urgent measures are necessary to address this.[29] Others, such as Coady, comment that children may be "active" psycho-socially without being demonstrable "social actors", and they may be psycho-socially active and social actors without necessarily being "agentic" in the political sense of being able to significantly influence their situation or being deeply listened to.[30]

Contemporary ways of thinking about rights necessitate recognition of children's capacities now to make a difference, especially within the context of the dynamic and complex challenges of unsustainability that will be exacerbated into the future. Consequently, viewing children as citizens with rights obliges recognition of children as social actors and agents of change able to make contributions that create better conditions for their childhoods now and in the future.[31] As UNICEF states

---

between Children in Child Care and Adults in the Community" (2008) 9 *Contemporary Issues in Early Childhood* 3.

[28] Reynaert et al., "A Review of Children's Rights Literature", 520.

[29] L. Strazdinis and H. Skeat, *Weathering the Future: Climate Change, Children and Young People and Decision Making* (Canberra: Australian Research Alliance for Children and Youth, 2011).

[30] M. Coady, "Beings and Becomings: Historical and Philosophical Considerations of the Child as Citizen" in MacNaughton et al. (eds.), *Young Children as Active Citizens*, 2.

[31] A. Smith, "Children's Rights and Early Childhood Education: Links to Theory and Practice" (2007) 32 *Australian Journal of Early Childhood* 1; L. Daniels-Simmond, "Early Childhood Professions' Beliefs and Practices Regarding the Rights of Young Children to Express Views and to Be Heard" (unpublished PhD thesis, Texas Women's University, 2009); UNICEF,

"partnering with children and young people empowers them to exercise their right to participate, raise awareness of issues that matter to children, and can lead to appropriate and innovative community solutions".[32]

I argue that images of children's *participation* – as well as images of children – require reformulation, as current conceptualisations of participation, and their attendant practices, are outmoded for the dynamic, complex and challenging times in which we live. As Strazdinis and Skeat identified, for example, many participatory attempts are top-down, more concerned with process than product and tend to replicate existing patterns of power and privilege. Overall, children remain largely invisible through tokenistic and poorly executed approaches to their participation.[33] Further, as noted, it is in professions such as paediatrics and public health,[34] rather than in education, that calls for children's agentic participation, especially in light of climate change and other environmental threats, are being made. Early childhood educators, too, need to see active participation as offering agency to young children so that they can make contributions that create better conditions for both present and future childhoods.[35]

Dimension 3: Collective Rights

This reimagined children's rights framework also includes a new dimension related to collective rights. Collective rights differ from individual rights. Rather than focusing on the individual independent of social groupings, the focus of collective human rights is on the rights of social groups. In contrast to the liberal proposition of the isolated human being, the idea of collective human rights begins with the view of humans (and, of course, children) as they really are, as social beings.[36] The UN Regional Information Centre for Western Europe asserts that existing human rights treaties, including the UNCRC, are poor vehicles for maintaining and supporting collective rights, such as those aimed at creating the conditions necessary for a common sustainable existence, or for recognising the rights of marginalised groups[37]

Sustainable Development Starts and Ends with Safe, Healthy and Well-Educated Children (2013), www.unicef.org/socialpolicy/files/Sustainable_Development_post_2015.pdf.

[32] Ibid., 15.

[33] Strazdinis and Skeat, *Weathering the Future*.

[34] S. Meucci and M. Schwab, "Children and the Environment: Young People's Participation in Social Change" (1997) 24 *Social Justice* 1; P. E. Sheffield and P. J. Landrigan, "Global Climate Change and Children's Health: Threats and Strategies for Prevention" (2011) 119 *Environmental Health Perspectives* 291.

[35] Daniels-Simmond, "Children's Rights and Early Childhood Education"; UNICEF, *Sustainable Development*.

[36] W. F. Felice, *Taking Suffering Seriously: The Importance of Collective Human Rights* (Albany: State University of New York Press, 1996).

[37] J. Kirk Boyd, *2048: Humanity's Agreement to Live Together* (San Francisco, CA: Berrett-Koehler Publishers, 2010).

who ought to be an integral part of sustainable communities.[38] This is because most treaties reflect an individualist concept of rights and rights-holders, and, in the case of early education, the changing image of childhood has had a strong focus on individualisation and children as autonomous human beings.[39] This highlighting of autonomy and individualism has, however, been a case for strong debate due to its possible distortion of the social conceptualisation of childhood. Taking this argument into the realm of participation in sustainable development, a focus on children's participatory rights from an individualistic perspective undermines notions of collective rights.

While there are many public campaigns and educational programs proclaiming that individuals can "fix the planet" if they recycle, save water, turn off the lights and so forth, the reality is that sustainability issues are collective in origin, for example, human-induced climate disruptions, overuse of non-renewable energy, human migrations, food and water security, biodiversity and species losses. The problems and their solutions are a complex mix of the national, international and global, and require collective responses. Focusing on individual rights in the era of large-scale, global challenges seems obtuse, especially as there is already strong evidence that individuals have poor responses to issues requiring collective answers.

A well-known example of this reluctance is "The Tragedy of the Commons", a cautionary tale that refers to the depletion of a common pasture shared among herdsmen who act independently according to individual self-interest, despite understanding that their desire to maximise individual benefit, rather than serving the collective interest, will result in the depletion of the common resource and its eventual collapse.[40] While no single act of consumption contributes much to the overall problem, the result of all individual actions is a collectively inferior outcome in which the commons can no longer sustain ongoing consumption.[41] The Tragedy of the Commons concept has disastrous implications for any commonly held resource when the individual cost of degrading it is lower than the cost of conserving and protecting it. As Nash comments, "[T]he enduring nature of the tragedy of the commons arises from its pervasive and continuing, if not mounting, relevance in the ways we utilize and interact with our environment."[42] In many ways, it is averting a global commons tragedy that sustainability seeks to address.

---

[38] United Nations Regional Information Centre for Western Europe (UNRIC), *Individual vs. Collective Rights* (2012), www.unric.org/en/indigenous-people/27309-individual-vs-collective-rights.

[39] Reynaert et al., "A Review of Children's Rights Literature".

[40] G. Hardin, "The Tragedy of the Commons" (1968) 162 *Science* 1243.

[41] J. Hickman and S. Bartlett, "Global Tragedy of the Commons" (2001) *Synthesis/Regeneration: A Magazine of Green Social Thought* 24.

[42] H. Nash "Tragedy of the Commons" in H. S. Schiffman and P. Robbins (eds.), *Green Issues and Debates: An A-to-Z Guide* (Thousand Oaks, CA: Sage Publications, 2011), 473.

Another relevant aspect to discussions about individual versus collective rights concerns how groups such as children, women, indigenous and the poor and destitute are represented within existing rights frameworks. Here, I limit discussion to indigenous people's rights and representation because of recognised links between indigenous/First Nations peoples' perspectives and environmental sustainability issues in many places across the globe. Specific rights for indigenous peoples made their international debut in 1957 with the adoption of the Indigenous and Tribal Populations Convention, later strengthened in 1966 when the UN General Assembly adopted the International Covenant on Civil and Political Rights.[43] The 1980s saw some UN agencies and international environmental organisations advocate for the recognition of the value of indigenous/traditional knowledges, particularly in bioconservation management, for example, the World Conservation Strategy 1980. In 1982, a UN Working Group with the mandate to draft the Declaration on the Rights of Indigenous Peoples was established, approved only in 2007. This Declaration recognises that "respect for indigenous knowledge, cultures and traditional practices contributes to sustainable and equitable development and proper management of the environment".[44]

Other initiatives, all proclaimed in 1992, that connect indigenous rights with environment and sustainability concerns include the Earth Summit, the Earth Charter, Agenda 21, the Convention on Biological Diversity, and the Treaty on Environmental Education for Sustainable Development and Global Responsibility. While generally assessed as giving inclusive and committed attention to indigenous perspectives/knowledges, a common critique is that many of these conventions view indigenous/traditional knowledges instrumentally, perceiving them as utilitarian in value and a resource to be documented, codified, decontextualised, universalised and widely applied.[45] Despite this criticism, however, these conventions do appear to have facilitated a revitalisation of aboriginal languages, epistemologies and pedagogies that recognise the importance of the land, privilege indigenous voices and involve elders in indigenous education.[46] Such revival and sharing also strengthens connections to what many Western scholars call a "sense of place", a feeling of connectedness to a particular geographical area with deep feelings of relatedness leading to shared responsibility for both the non-human world as well as for the humans who cohabit these common spaces. For these reasons, both

---

[43] S. Shava, "The Representation of Indigenous Knowledges", in R. B. Stevenson et al. (eds.), *International Handbook of Research on Environmental Education* (New York: Routledge, 2013).

[44] UNGA, *United Nations Declaration on the Rights of Indigenous Peoples* (UN Doc. 61/295, 13 September 2007), 2.

[45] Shava, "The Representation of Indigenous Knowledges", 384.

[46] G. Lowan-Trudeau, "Indigenous Environmental Education Research in North America", in R. B. Stevenson et al. (eds.), *International Handbook of Research on Environmental Education* (New York: Routledge, 2013), 404.

indigenous scholars[47] and non-indigenous authors[48] make robust claims for the inclusion of indigenous voices within contemporary environmental and sustainability scholarship, and I include this as an aspect of a reconceptualised framework for children's rights, in particular, within an education agenda that calls for redefinition of human rights from individual rights towards collective rights that bring people together for the common, shared purpose of long-term survival.

Dimension 4: Intergenerational Rights – Thinking for Future Generations

An extension of collective rights is intergenerational rights; hence, this is the next dimension in my new children's rights framework. Sustainability is about more than just the rights of current generations to strive for happy, healthy and secure lives. At the heart of the concept of sustainable development is fairness and justice for all, including for future generations. The injustice of current generations expending the resources and capital of the next, leaving the planet less equipped to meet the needs of future generations, is at the core of the oft-quoted definition of sustainable development, from *Our Common Future*, also known as the Brundtland Report (1989), that defines *sustainable development* as "development that meets the needs of the present without compromising the ability of future generations to meet their own needs".[49] As Beder observes,

> Although future generations do not yet exist, it is reasonably certain that they will exist and they will require clean air and water and other basic physical requirements for life. And although it is not known who the individuals of the future will be – they are not individually identifiable – they have rights as a group or class of people, rather than individually, and we can have obligations and duties towards them.[50]

A pertinent extension of intergenerational justice is the concept of the "chain of obligation". Howarth argues that a chain of obligation stretches from the present into the indefinite future, and unless we guarantee conditions favourable to the welfare of future generations, "we wrong our existing children in the sense that they will be unable to fulfil their obligation to their children while enjoying a favourable way of life themselves".[51] Leaving a sustainable world for the next generation is

---

[47] See, e.g., ibid.; Shava, "The Representation of Indigenous Knowledge", 384.
[48] See, e.g., M. G. Miller, "Intercultural Dialogues in Early Childhood Education for Sustainability: Embedding Indigenous Perspectives", in J. Davis and S. Elliott (eds.), *Research in Early Childhood Education*, 63; I. Dunn and J. Ritchie, "Making Eco-Waves: Early Childhood Care and Education Sustainability Practices in Aotearoa New Zealand" (2014) 24 *Children, Youth and Environments* 123.
[49] World Commission on Environment and Development (WCED), "Our Common Future" (UN Doc. A/42/427, 1987), www.un-documents.net/our-common-future.pdf, 8.
[50] S. Beder, "Intergenerational Justice", in Schiffman and Robbins (eds.), *Green Issues and Debates*, 309.
[51] R. B. Howarth, "Intergenerational Justice and the Chain of Obligation" (1992) 1 *Environmental Values* 133.

beneficial not only to their own future well-being but also because it qualitatively strengthens the moral and ethical position of our children towards their children.

Dimension 5: Biocentric/Ecocentric Rights

The final dimension in this augmented framework of children's rights centres on biocentric and ecocentric rights. To frame this discussion, I start with the "Anthropocene". While not official geologic nomenclature, the term has been adopted by some leading scientists, scholars, commentators and organisations (e.g., the Geological Society of London) and serves to mark the extent to which human activities have had a significant global impact on land use, ecosystems and biodiversity. The Anthropocene was coined in the early 1980s by ecologist Eugene F. Stoermer and popularised by Nobel Prize–winning atmospheric chemist, Paul Crutzen, who regards the influence of human behaviour on the earth's atmosphere as so significant as to constitute a new geological epoch.

In denoting the Anthropocene, the most significant causal factor is Anthropocentricism – literally, "human-centredness" – a perspective that regards humans as the most important entity on the planet. Rowe comments that anthropocentricism translates into a belief that human well-being is our central consideration.[52] Biocentrism, however, regards humans as just one of many biological species, and assigns inherent value to non-human organisms. Biocentrism holds that all living beings are equally valuable. Ecocentrism goes one step further, also assigning value to the earth's nonliving systems and processes, thus stressing that humans are reliant on the earth's entire ecosystem, including elements (such as carbon, air and water and their interdependent cycles), landscapes and environments such as river catchments. To some extent, ecocentrism equates with Lovelock's Gaia Hypothesis in which the earth is considered a living organism whose biological and physical parts are inextricably linked into a self-regulating system.[53] While somewhat controversial, the Gaia hypothesis draws attention to the interconnections of biological and geological processes on a planetary scale.[54] Whether one accepts the idea of Gaia, an advantage of adopting a biocentric or ecocentric approach is that the value judgements underlying the discourse of human and environmental questions become framed differently. Rowe notes, "[W]hen humans stop being the only measure of value, the scope of the debate is expanded."[55] Taken together, biocentrism and ecocentrism offer another dimension for revising rights in ECE.

While there are pros and cons on both sides of the anthropocentric versus bio/ecocentric debate, these positions do not necessarily need to be polarised, with

---

[52] B. M. Rowe, "Anthropocentrism versus Biocentrism", in Schiffman and Robbins (eds.), *Green Issues and Debates*.
[53] J. Lovelock, "Gaia: The Living Earth" (2003) 426 *Nature* 769.
[54] N. Vedwan, "Social Learning" in Schiffman and Robbins (eds.), *Green Issues and Debates*, 310.
[55] Rowe, "Anthropocentrism versus Biocentrism", 31.

recent debate moving towards recognition of the interconnectedness of the two positions.[56] It is increasingly recognised that human survival and well-being demand a healthy earth[57] and, if the overall objective of a bio/ecocentric position is to protect biodiversity and the environment for its own sake, then humans must also be protected as an integral component of that diversity. Such blurring between anthropocentrism and bio/ecocentricism has become evident in several recent jurisdictions including the adoption of the "Rights of Nature" in Ecuador's Constitution that recognises the inalienable rights of ecosystems to exist and flourish, gives people the authority to petition on the behalf of ecosystems and requires the government to remedy violations of these rights. In similar vein, Bolivia recently enacted a Framework Law for Mother Earth and Holistic Development to Live Well (October 2012) that states:

> Mother Earth is the living dynamic system made up of the indivisible community of all living systems and living beings, interrelated, interdependent and complementary, which share a common destiny. Mother Earth is considered sacred; it feeds and is a home that contains, sustains and reproduces all living things, ecosystems, biodiversity, societies and the individuals that compose them.

Anthropocentrism has dominated human versus environment debates for decades. Now, however, there appears to be a movement across a range of disciplines towards defining a bio/ecocentric approach to environment and sustainability matters.

REFRAMING CHILDREN'S RIGHTS: IMPLICATIONS FOR EARLY EDUCATION

So far, in this chapter I have outlined an expanded way of thinking about children and young people's rights. However, using a framework in early education such as I have proposed has implications for how society at large responds to these ideas. Here I offer some thoughts specifically related to ECE, my particular field of interest.

In relation to rights, a continuing focus on the centrality of rights in early education is vital, however this focus must be tempered by acknowledgement of the limitations of the UNCRC as it currently exists. ECE as an education field has embraced the UNCRC. In Australia, *Belonging, Being and Becoming: The Early Years Learning Framework for Australia* provides that early childhood educators are to "reinforce in their daily practices the principles laid out in the

---

[56] Ibid.
[57] See, e.g., WCED, "Our Common Future; World Health Organisation, *First International Conference on Health Promotion* (Ottawa, ON, 21 November 1986); B. Petterson and P. Tillgren (eds.), *The Sundsvall Conference on Supportive Environments* (Stockholm: Karolinska Institute, 1992).

UNCRC".[58] The National Curriculum for the Swedish Preschool has also been inspired by the principles of the UNCRC.[59] Nevertheless, my position is that relying on the UNCRC as the foundation for our rights work is too narrow for dealing with sustainability issues. With its World War II origins emphasising the rights of the individual and child protection, and even with updates that strengthen participation rights, the UNCRC is silent on collective rights, intergenerational rights and the rights of non-humans to live and thrive on the planet, and needs to be rearticulated, revised and significantly updated.

Thus, we need to take a holistic, "common worlds" standpoint. As Taylor and Giugni comment, the ethics and politics of living together requires a centralising framework that has the power to promote ideas about living sustainably.[60] This framework must consider individual children's rights as well as collective human rights *and* the rights of the non-human, not as separate elements of the early childhood curriculum but as integral, connected parts of a systemic approach. A truly just and caring society respects all life and, without such recognition, our human universe/sphere is artificially narrowed and puts at risk all living futures.

In relation to ECE practice, just as the UNCRC is an inadequate vehicle in the age of unsustainability, so too are some current practices in ECE. Yes, we must continue to connect/reconnect children's learning with the natural world as core business. ECE has a long history of supporting children's interactions with/in nature, tracing back to Froebel's original conception of the kindergarten, a "garden for children" where children were educated in close harmony with nature and, more recently, Malaguzzi's idea of the environment as the "third educator". Malaguzzi was the thinker and founder behind the noted Reggio Emilia education movement that has influenced ECE internationally throughout the past twenty years.[61] However, we must recognise that such mainstay practices no longer suffice. Unsustainability demands that we extend beyond simply emphasising children's nature connections and that we must embrace new modes of learning and interactions with nature underpinned by understandings that humans are a part of nature, not removed from or superior to it. Bone, for example, asks for a focus on "the animal" in ECE, proposing animals as the "fourth educator".[62] Gandhi is

---

[58] Department of Education, Employment and Workplace Relations (DEEWR), *Belonging, Being and Becoming – The Early Years Learning Framework for Australia* (2009), https://docs.education.gov.au/system/files/doc/other/belonging_being_and_becoming_the_early_years_learning_framework_for_australia.pdf, 5.

[59] The Swedish National Agency for Education, *Curriculum for the Pre-School, Lpfö 98* (Stockholm: The Swedish National Agency for Education, 2010).

[60] A. Taylor and M. Giugni, "Common Worlds: Reconceptualising Inclusion in Early Childhood Communities" (2012) 13 *Contemporary Issues in Early Childhood* 108.

[61] L. Gandini, "Education and Caring Spaces", in C. Edwards, L. Gandini and G. Forman (eds.), *The Hundred Languages of Children* (Greenwich, CT: Ablex, 1998), 177.

[62] J. Bone, "Love and Creatureliness in the Preschool" (Paper presented at the 19th Reconceptualising Early Childhood Education Conference, Politics of Care: Sharing Knowledges, Love and Solidarity, University of East London: 25–29 October 2011); J. Bone, "The Animal as

reputed to have observed that the sign of a great nation and its moral progress can be judged by the way its animals are treated.[63] A truly just and caring society respects all life and without such recognition our human universe/sphere is artificially narrowed and puts at risk all living futures. Such considerations may be useful in overcoming "biophobia" that some commentators[64] show increasing concern about and as a way of advancing children's recognition of the fact that they live in a multispecies world and are dependent upon these non-human species and environments for their own health, well-being and indeed survival. We need, then to incorporate bio/ecocentric rights into early childhood practice.

Further, there needs to be wide-ranging discussion and debate about what linking a common world/biocentric worldview rights framework might look like in early education for different communities, in different countries, and in the broad range of early educational contexts. For example, good work in embedding indigenous/First Nations perspectives in ECE is being undertaken in Australia and New Zealand by using the UNCRC to embed indigenous and Maori perspectives into ECE curricula and to strengthen early childhood educators' capacities to working authentically and inclusively with indigenous and Maori families and communities.[65] Such efforts are, however, only a starting point in the development of a comprehensive rights-based approach to early education in the age of unsustainability. Researchers from Japan,[66] for example, call for better nuancing of early childhood ESD that respects different national-cultural-historical perspectives so that a diversity of thinking and practices are supported rather than seeking to impose a universal approach.

Finally, roles for children and young people participating as "agents of change" for sustainability require deeper consideration. At the broadest level, education for sustainability is about creating change, focused on rethinking and remaking educational programs and pedagogies to support sustainable societies. It draws on critical[67] and transformative education approaches[68] that support social critique of the

---

Fourth Educator: A Literature Review of Animals and Young Children in Pedagogical Relationships" (2013) 38 *Australasian Journal of Early Childhood* 57.

[63] R. Bennon, "Research Guide for Animal Welfare and Animal Rights" (1984) 4 *Legal Reference Services Quarterly* 3.

[64] P. H. Kahn Jr., "Developmental Psychology and the Biophilia Hypothesis: Children's Affiliation with Nature" (1997) 17 *Developmental Review* 1; R. Louv, *Last Child in the Woods: Saving Our Children from Nature Deficit Disorder* (Chapel Hill, NC: Algonquin Books of Chapel Hill Press, 2008).

[65] Miller, *Intercultural Dialogues in Early Childhood Education*; Dunn and Ritchie, "Making Eco-Waves".

[66] See, e.g., M. Inoue, "Perspectives on Early Childhood Environmental Education in Japan: Rethinking for a Sustainable Society", in Davis and Elliott (eds.), *Research in Early Childhood Education*, 63.

[67] J. Habermas, *Knowledge and Human Interests* (Boston, MA.: Beacon, 1971).

[68] German Advisory Council on Global Change, *Factsheet 5: Research and Education: Drivers of Transformation* (Berlin: WBGU and German Government, 2012); J. Mezirow, "Transformative Learning as Discourse" (2003) 1 *Journal of Transformative Education* 58.

thinking and practices that contribute to unsustainability and require transformative teaching and learning practices where educators support children and young people as agents of change around sustainability issues. Critical and transformative pedagogies encourage problem-solving, participating, and decision-making and having choices, that is, they give children the power to do things.[69] They offer participatory, action-based learning focused on real-life issues of relevance and importance to children. Relying on the UNCRC limits such an education. For example – article 12 recognises that children have the right to express an opinion. However, several authors[70] comment that the right to have an opinion is generally exercised for the limited purposes of learning and that when attention *is* given to participation, it is often restricted to the *learning processes – how and what to learn* – less frequently addressing any right to participation in processes, for example, school management. Yet, under the guidance of the UNCRC, schools have a duty to involve children in all matters that affect them. There should be no discretion to ignore a child's view simply because he/she is young. Applying this to ECE, I make the case for far greater participation by young children in managing their learning, their learning environment, as well as changing their environment. They must also be supported to act on their ideas and concerns. There are a growing number of case studies in ECE illustrating agentic participatory processes "in action" where preschoolers contribute to policy development and decision-making and are encouraged to put sustainability measures into place. One example involves children and staff of the Raglan Childcare and Education Centre, New Zealand, who, after visiting the community-driven recycling depot, designed and displayed wearable art made from recycled materials. The children also engaged in permaculture gardening that produced seedlings sent home to families that, in due course, came back to the centre as fully grown produce.[71] Further examples, reporting on topics as diverse as working with local indigenous community members, exploring the economics and ethics of battery hen farming, engaging in water conservation and inviting the wider community to protect local habitats and species can be found in *Young Children and the Environment: Early Learning for Sustainability* and *Research in Early Childhood Education for Sustainability: International Perspectives and Provocations*.[72]

---

[69] G. MacNaughton and G. Williams, *Techniques for Teaching Young Children: Choices in Theory and Practice* (Frenchs Forest, NSW: Pearson Education Australia, 3rd ed., 2009).

[70] See, e.g., A. Osler and H. Starkey, "Children's Rights and Citizenship: Some Implications for the Management of Schools" (1998) 6 *International Journal of Children's Rights* 313.

[71] Dunn and Ritchie, "Making Eco-Waves".

[72] J. M. Davis (ed.), *Young Children and the Environment: Early Learning for Sustainability* (Melbourne: Cambridge University Press, 2010); J. M. Davis (ed.) *Young Children and the Environment: Early Learning for Sustainability*, 2nd ed. (Melbourne: Cambridge University Press, 2015); Davis and Elliott (eds.), *Research in Early Childhood Education*.

CONCLUSION

Sustainability is a global issue urgently needing to be addressed. Failure to tackle this "wicked problem"[73] will have dire consequences with children and future generations being the worst affected parties. It is *their* present and *their* futures most at stake from unsustainable development, as evidenced by climate change, growing inequalities, mass migrations, food and energy security and economic instability. This chapter argues that a fundamental revisioning of how we constitute rights is vital if we are to have any hope of living sustainably. The UNCRC can no longer be regarded as the premier vehicle for children's rights as it is an outdated, limited document formulated in the last century before conversations about sustainability had even begun. Inevitably, reliance on its articles leads to outdated policies and practices that cannot even begin to address the challenges of the changed world in which we live today. In particular, I have framed my arguments about the UNCRC within ECE where it has been the cornerstone for thinking and practice in early education. I argue that ECE's reverence of the UNCRC has inevitably resulted in its weak capability to respond to the contemporary issues of sustainability that are shaping the current and future lives of young people.

Instead, I argue in this chapter for a multidimensional rights approach, applicable to adults as well as to children and young people. While acknowledging that the UNCRC continues to have value as an aspirational document for advancing children's rights, the chapter calls for far stronger *agentic* rights as advocated for by those who understand that children and young people are capable social actors who have a right to participate in decision-making and action-taking about sustainability matters. I also argue that even an agentic model of rights is not enough. Greater focus on collective, intergenerational and bio/ecocentric rights is necessary. A "common worlds" framework of rights has so much more to offer in terms of guiding how educators think and practice in these times of complexity, uncertainty and rapid change.

---

[73] H. W. J. Rittel and M. M. Webber, "Dilemmas in a General Theory of Planning" (1973) 4 *Policy Sciences* 155.

4

The Right to Participate in Domestic Law and Policy Development

Holly Doel-Mackaway

INTRODUCTION

Children and young people can act as powerful agents of social change including playing a pivotal role in achieving sustainable development.[1] The purpose of this chapter is to discuss how children's participation in designing child-related law and policy at the national level can play a vital role in working towards sustainable development. Domestic legislation and policy governs a vast range of matters affecting children and young people, yet they are rarely afforded the opportunity to be involved in designing these initiatives at the national level.[2] This is despite the fact that "there is abundant evidence from across the world that points to the extent to which children can play a more significant role as agents of change".[3]

This chapter discusses the potential for children and young people to actively shape relevant laws and policies in ways that transcend, for example, merely expressing "a view" about proposed legislation. This chapter seeks to add to the body of literature that conceptualises children and young people "as active and competent citizens" and "agents of change" with the potential to make powerful contributions toward achieving sustainable development – if they are afforded the opportunity.[4]

The chapter outlines the evolution of children's participation before and during the drafting of the UN Convention on the Rights of the Child (UNCRC),[5]

---

[1] Some of this work is reproduced from Holly Doel-Mackaway's unpublished PhD. A book based on the PhD will be published by Routledge in 2019. B. Percy-Smith and D. Burns, "Exploring the Role of Children and Young People as Agents of Change in Sustainable Community Development" (2013) 18(3) *Local Environment* 323.

[2] B. Bennett Woodhouse, "Enhancing Children's Participation in Policy Formation" (2003) 45 *Arizona Law Review* 751, 751–752.

[3] Percy-Smith and Burns, "Exploring the Role of Children and Young People", 324.

[4] Ibid., 325.

[5] UN General Assembly (UNGA), Convention on the Rights of the Child (UN Doc. A/RES/44/25, 20 November 1989) 1577 UNTS 3.

with focussed attention on the significance of the process involved in drafting article 12. An initial discussion about the linkages between sustainable development and children's participation in law and policy making is followed by an analysis of the meaning of article 12 and the manner in which the Vienna Convention on the Law of Treaties (VCLT)[6] requires states to interpret the provision. Given the widespread non-application of article 12 in legislative development processes internationally, this section provides a basis upon which states can understand and apply article 12 in their respective jurisdictions. The suggested method to do this is through the establishment of an "interpretive community" where children and young people (along with other stakeholders) are invited to participate in the interpretation and implementation of human rights treaty provisions and consequently participate in the way child-related legislation and policy is designed and implemented.

Creating a Sustainable World with Children and Young People

Part of creating a sustainable world is creating sustainable governance structures and legal systems that cater for, include and appropriately respond to all citizens across the lifespan. The Committee on the Rights of the Child (UNCRC Committee), the body responsible for monitoring State Party compliance with the UNCRC, has made it clear that:

> Children should be consulted in the formulation of legislation and policy ... and involved in the drafting, development and implementation of related plans and programmes.[7]

The active participation of children and young people in law and policy formation is relevant to achieving Goal 16 of the Sustainable Development Goals (SDGs). Goal 16 is "dedicated to the promotion of peaceful and inclusive societies for sustainable development, the provision of access to justice for all, and building effective, accountable institutions at all levels".[8] The UN General Assembly has made it clear that "democracy, good governance and the rule of law, as well as an enabling environment at the national and international levels, are essential for sustainable development".[9]

Children and young people's participation in relevant law and policy-making processes is a necessary component of democracy and good governance, linked to upholding the rule of law and therefore essential for sustainable development.

---

[6] UN International Law Commission, Vienna Convention on the Law of Treaties (23 May 1969) 1155 UNTS 331.
[7] UNCRC Committee, "General Comment No. 12 (2009) on the Right of the Child to be Heard" (UN Doc. CRC/C/GC/12, 1 July 2009), [122].
[8] www.un.org/sustainabledevelopment/peace-justice/.
[9] UNGA, "Transforming Our World: The 2030 Agenda for Sustainable Development" (UN Doc. A/RES/70/1, 21 October 2015), [9].

The implications of this are wide reaching and provide an avenue for children and young people to inform and influence laws and policies relevant to their lives such as matters relating to health, education, gender equality, violence against children, poverty and discrimination.[10]

Respecting children's views and taking account these views in decision-making processes are essential steps in facilitating children's participation: a foundation concept that runs throughout the text of the UNCRC. Article 12 of the UNCRC requires states to "assure" children who are "capable of forming [their] own views the right to express those views freely in all matters affecting the child" and that such views be "given due weight in accordance with the age and maturity" of the child. Thus, all State Parties to the UNCRC (every country apart from the United States) are duty bound to ensure people under the age of eighteen have the right to contribute to decision-making processes about "all matters affecting" them, and for these contributions to be considered in decision-making processes. Thus, article 12 of the UNCRC provides for children's right to participate in the process of making child-related law and policy and imposes a duty on State Parties to fulfil this right. This chapter examines the nature and scope of article 12 and articulates how State Parties are duty bound to include children and young people in law and policy development under this provision. This chapter also establishes that article 12 imposes a duty on states to involve children and young people in the development of laws and policies likely to affect them.

THE EVOLUTION OF CHILDREN'S PARTICIPATION RIGHTS

> Historically, the embryonic development of children not merely as citizens, but as active citizens of the world, participating in helping develop global legislation regarding their own autonomy, began with the drafting of the CRC.[11]

The introduction of the UNCRC provided the foundation for a global movement acknowledging children as individuals and holders of human rights, rather than "mini-persons with mini-human rights".[12] The rights articulated in the UNCRC fundamentally altered, and progressed,[13] the relationship between children and

---

[10] A. Minujin and M. Ferrer, "Assessing Sustainable Development Goals from the Standpoint of Equity for Children" (2016) 32(2) *Journal of International and Comparative Social Policy* 98, 107.

[11] G. Van Bueren, "Acknowledging Children as International Citizens: A Child-Sensitive Communication Mechanism for the Convention on the Rights of the Child", in A. Invernizzi and J. Williams (eds.), *The Human Rights of Children: From Visions to Implementation* (Farnham, UK: Ashgate, 2011), 117.

[12] M. de Boeur-Buquicchio, "Celebrating Children's Rights: A Council of Europe Wish", in J. Zermatten, A. Panayotidis and J. Connors (eds.), *18 Candles: The Convention on the Rights of the Child Reaches Majority* (Sion, Switzerland: Institut International des Droits de L'enfant, 2007), 15.

[13] A. Parkes, *Children and International Human Rights Law: The Right of the Child to Be Heard* (New York: Routledge, 2013), 27.

young people and the state because the UNCRC "brought about a qualitative transformation in the status of children as the holders of rights".[14] The UNCRC defined a new status for children and "marked the beginning of a universal rights-based approach toward the child",[15] one that perceives children as holders of rights rather than protection being available to children through adult rights, namely parental rights. The UNCRC is a key milestone positively altering children's legal, social and political status.

The UNCRC is the most highly ratified human rights treaty, globally enjoying near universal ratification with 196 State Parties. Somalia ratified the UNCRC on 1 October 2015, and South Sudan acceded to the UNCRC on 30 April 2015, leaving the United States as the only country that has not ratified the instrument.[16] Given the near global ratification of the UNCRC it is now the most appropriate legal instrument and "unavoidable starting point for any discussion of the legal rights of children".[17] When the UNCRC came into force it represented a "new vision for children" and provided, for the first time, a body of legally enforceable rights for children.[18] However, despite near universal ratification of the UNCRC, domestic implementation and enforceability of the rights it contains remain underdeveloped. Tobin says, "Although the CRC has attained almost universal ratification, its incorporation into domestic law remains the exception rather than the norm", consequently, the rights provided for in the UNCRC "are rarely enforceable in domestic courts".[19]

Children's right to participate in all matters affecting them – the principle articulated in article 12 – is the lynchpin of the UNCRC,[20] and lies at the heart of the provisions contained in the treaty.[21] Children's right to participate in matters affecting them is described by the UNCRC Committee as one of the four foundational principles of the Convention,[22] along with the right to non-discrimination, the right to life and development and the best interests of

---

[14] P. Alston and J. Tobin, "Laying the Foundations for Children's Rights: An Independent Study of Some Key Legal and Institutional Aspects of the Impact of the Convention on the Rights of the Child" (UNICEF Innocenti Research Centre, 2005), ix.
[15] Parkes, *Children and International Human Rights Law*, 5.
[16] The United States is the only country that has not ratified the UNCRC despite signalling its intention to ratify by formally signing the UNCRC on 16 February 1995.
[17] D. Archard, *Children: Rights and Childhood*, 3rd ed. (London and New York: Routledge, 2015), 107.
[18] I. Byrne, "Participation: The Forgotten 'P' in the Convention on the Rights of the Child" (2003) 14 *Interrights Bulletin* 45, 45.
[19] J. Tobin, "Judging the Judges: Are They Adopting the Rights Approach in Matters Involving Children?" (2009) 33(2) *Melbourne University Law Review* 580, 581, 620.
[20] M. Freeman, "Whither Children: Protection, Participation, Autonomy?" (1994) 22(3) *Manitoba Law Journal* 307, 319.
[21] J. Tobin, "Understanding a Human Rights Based Approach to Matters Involving Children: Conceptual Foundations and Strategic Considerations", in Invernizzi and Williams (eds.), *The Human Rights of Children*, 61.
[22] UNCRC Committee, "General Comment No. 12 (2009)", 5.

the child.²³ In the words of the UNCRC Committee, article 12 "establishes not only a right in itself, but should also be considered in the interpretation and implementation of all other rights".²⁴ Thus, article 12 is a right as well as an enabling principle that facilitates the fulfilment of other rights contained in the UNCRC.²⁵ Importantly, the rights emanating from article 12 have "pushed the boundaries beyond protection and provision rights to those of participation".²⁶ Thus, the introduction of the UNCRC shifted the children's rights movement away from a focus on protecting and providing for children to a focus on children as active agents with the right to participate in decision-making.²⁷

The development of the UNCRC was a remarkable achievement in the history of children's rights. The text did more than stipulate a catalogue of children's rights, it set in motion a new way of conceptualising children and the position children hold in global society. As Cantwell explains:

> Welfare, development and protection were established once and for all as human rights issues. And out of this, among other things, emerged the child participation ethic now so fundamental to rights-based work.²⁸

The UNCRC Committee recognises that children have a right to participate in UN processes and in 2014 produced the "Working Methods for the Participation of Children in the Reporting Process of the Committee on the Rights of the Child" (UN Committee's Working Methods).²⁹ This provides detailed guidance on how the UNCRC Committee involves children and young people in their activities, and also provides State Parties with guidance about how to involve children and young people in any participation activity.

The development of the UNCRC not only provided an international human rights legal instrument but also a global mechanism for children's rights education

---

²³ The UNCRC Committee outlined the four general principles contained in the UNCRC in 1991, see: UNCRC Committee, "General Guidelines Regarding the Form and Content of Initial Reports to Be Submitted by States Parties under Article 44, Paragraph 1(a) of the Convention" (UN Doc. CRC/C/5, 1991).
²⁴ UNCRC Committee, "General Comment No. 12 (2009)".
²⁵ H. Van Beers et al., "Creating an Enabling Environment: Capacity Building in Children's Participation" (Save the Children Sweden, Viet Nam 2000–2004, 2006). See also Parkes, *Children and International Human Rights Law*, 276.
²⁶ K. E. M. Tisdall, "Is the Honeymoon Over? Children and Young People's Participation in Public Decision-Making" (2008) 16(3) *International Journal of Children's Rights* 343, 343.
²⁷ B. Milne, *The History and Theory of Children's Citizenship in Contemporary Societies* (Dordrecht, The Netherlands: Springer, 2013), 241 citing P. Adams et al., *Children's Rights: Toward the Liberation of the Child* (New York: Praeger, 1971), 30.
²⁸ N. Cantwell, "Words That Speak Volumes", in J. Zermatten, A. Panayotidis and J. Connors (eds.), *18 Candles: The Convention on the Rights of the Child Reaches Majority* (Sion, Switzerland: Institut International des Droits de L'enfant, 2007), 29.
²⁹ UNCRC Committee, "Working Methods for the Participation of Children in the Reporting Process of the Committee on the Rights of the Child" (UN Doc. CRC/C/66/2, 16 October 2014).

and awareness raising.[30] Most notably, the UNCRC provided a platform for "innovative collaboration for children both in civil society and at the intergovernmental level, as well as between the two".[31]

The Rights of the Child before the UNCRC

Prior to the UNCRC coming into force there were a range of instruments that sought to recognise and improve children's status at the international level. The Geneva Declaration on the Rights of the Child[32] adopted in 1924 by the League of Nations was a statement of principles regarding the welfare of the child "recognising the economic, social and psychological needs of the child".[33] The 1924 Declaration did not place binding legal obligations on State Parties, and did not include reference to children's participation rights.[34] Thirty-four years later the United Nations adopted the 1959 Declaration on the Rights of the Child,[35] which consisted of ten principles including the right to name, nationality, adequate nutrition, housing, medical care, education and recreation, among others.[36] Like the 1924 Declaration, children's participation rights were not included in the 1959 Declaration. The 1959 Declaration was a significant step in the lead up to placing children's rights on the international agenda; however, it was not sufficiently influential in galvanising support to include children's rights in mainstream human rights discourse and practice.[37]

In 1978 Poland submitted a draft resolution for a children's convention (which was largely based on the 1959 Declaration)[38] to the UN Commission on Human Rights (UNCHR) at its 34th session. Like the 1924 and 1959 declarations, this document did not include a provision relating to children's right to participate in decision-making.[39] However, Poland's 1978 initiative sparked a series of preliminary consultations with UN member states, and international agencies, culminating in the UNCHR's decision in 1979 to set up an open-ended ad hoc Working Group to explore the question of a convention on children's rights.[40]

---

[30] N. Cantwell, "Are Children's Rights Still Human?", in Invernizzi and Williams (eds.), *The Human Rights of Children*, 37.
[31] Ibid., 41.
[32] League of Nations, Declaration of the Rights of the Child (26 September 1924) OJ Spec, Supp. 21.
[33] Parkes, *Children and International Human Rights Law*, 50.
[34] Ibid.
[35] UNGA, Declaration on the Rights of the Child (UN Doc. A/4354, 20 November 1959).
[36] Parkes, *Children and International Human Rights Law*, 50.
[37] Cantwell, "Are Children's Rights Still Human?", 38.
[38] Parkes, *Children and International Human Rights Law*, 50.
[39] Cantwell, "Are Children's Rights Still Human?", 37. See also Parkes, *Children and International Human Rights Law*, 50.
[40] Cantwell, "Are Children's Rights Still Human?"

Cantwell highlights the pre- and post-UNCRC rights climate for children. He says, "[I]t is clear that the general perception in the run-up to the drafting of the CRC was that children's issues did not fall within the scope of human rights."[41] Rather, children's rights prior to the drafting of the UNCRC were implemented in a sporadic, inconsistent manner, largely based on notions of "charity" and "doing good" for children – not on the basis of a legal duty to recognise and implement rights.[42] The consequence of this was that "children's issues and human rights were ... two rather different worlds".[43] Hilary Clinton's (then Rodham) 1973 assessment that "children's rights is a slogan in search of definition" summarised the context for children's rights in the 1970s – an emerging, yet undeveloped, area of thought, law and practice.[44] Clinton identified the need for a theory of children's rights and for the legal status of children to change "by extending more adult rights to children and by recognizing certain unique needs and interests of children as legally enforceable rights".[45]

In the 1970s, prior to the drafting of the UNCRC, "children's liberationist" scholarship emerged calling for states to acknowledge and protect children's rights.[46] This body of thought was based on evolving notions of the meaning and nature of "childhood",[47] and a rejection of persistent attitudes based on sentimentality and non-inclusion of children in the human rights framework.[48]

Drafting Article 12 of the UNCRC

A Working Group drafted the UNCRC from 1979 to 1989, and this process involved lively – often highly conflictual – debates about which rights should be included and excluded, and the nature and form of the provisions. Cantwell details numerous occasions when the Working Group could not reach consensus about the content of the UNCRC, and notes that at times the inability to agree on the text threatened to terminate the drafting process.[49]

During the drafting, the difficulty of designing a document representing the rights of children globally, which encompassed international cultural perspectives

---

[41] Ibid., 38.
[42] Ibid.
[43] Ibid., 39.
[44] H. Rodham, "Children under the Law" (1973) 43(4) *Harvard Educational Review* 487, 487.
[45] Ibid.
[46] Ibid.; Milne, *The History and Theory of Children's Citizenship in Contemporary Societies*; R. Farson, *Birthrights* (London: Collier Macmillan, 1974); J. Holt, *Escape from Childhood* (Harmondsworth, UK: Penguin, 1975); S. Firestone, *The Dialectic of Sex: The Case for Feminist Revolution* (London: Jonathon Cape, 1970).
[47] Milne, *The History and Theory of Children's Citizenship in Contemporary Societies*.
[48] Cantwell, "Are Children's Rights Still Human?", 38; Alston and Tobin, "Laying the Foundations for Children's Rights"; J. Eekelaar, "The Emergence of Children's Rights" (1986) 6(2) *Oxford Journal of Legal Studies* 161.
[49] Cantwell, "Words That Speak Volumes", 25.

regarding children's lives, was almost insurmountable.[50] These difficulties were however eventually overcome, and ten years after the Working Group was formed the UNCRC opened for signature in 1989 and came into force in 1990.

Freeman notes that, despite the importance placed on including children's participation rights in article 12, children were not involved in the drafting process.[51] He suggests the non-participation of children produced flaws in the text of the UNCRC as it did not, and still does not, encompass the full range of issues important to children and young people.[52] Tobin agrees, "[T]he drafting process was dominated by Western States and completely excluded children."[53] Arce concludes that the Working Group's Western-centric, paternalistic view of childhood – reflected in the text of the UNCRC – "conceives children not only as weaklings, but also as ignorant, private, needy, dependent, developing, innocent, [and] incompetent", and it was these conceptualisations that prevented children from participating in the drafting of the text.[54] The non-participation of children in the drafting of the UNCRC was not an oversight, according to Arce, but indicative of the philosophical perspective on childhood held by the Working Group at the time.[55]

By contrast, Van Bueren, one of the original drafters of the UNCRC and member of the Working Group, details her first-hand experience of being present when children spoke to the Working Group during the drafting process.[56] She notes children's participation "was more *ad hoc* than structured, and occasional rather than comprehensive",[57] yet she attributes significance to these contributions because "for the first time the global community … acknowledged the value not only of children speaking on their own behalf but also, as citizens of the world, speaking on behalf of their fellow children globally".[58]

There may have been ad hoc or indirect contributions from children in the drafting process, however, there are no records in the formal drafting history that children contributed to forming the text of the UNCRC.[59] Van Bueren's reflections indicate minimal participation by children and suggest the drafting process of the UNCRC was the first time any international instrument had been influenced by children.[60]

---

[50] Ibid.
[51] M. Freeman, "The Future of Children's Rights" (2000) 14 *Children and Society* 277, 282.
[52] Ibid.
[53] J. Tobin, "Children's Rights in Australia: Confronting the Challenges", in M. Castan and P. Gerber (eds.), *Contemporary Perspectives on Human Rights Law in Australia* (Rozelle, NSW: Thomson Reuters, 2013), 297.
[54] M. Cordero Arce, "Maturing Children's Rights Theory" (2015) 23(2) *International Journal of Children's Rights* 283, 297.
[55] Ibid.
[56] Van Bueren, "Acknowledging Children as International Citizens", 118, see note 2.
[57] Ibid., 118.
[58] Ibid., 117.
[59] Freeman, "The Future of Children's Rights", 282.
[60] Van Bueren, "Acknowledging Children as International Citizens", 117.

ARTICLE 12 OF THE UNCRC

When the UNCRC came into force in 1990 this marked the first point in history where State Parties became duty bound under international law to "assure" children's right to express their views and to give these views "due weight" in decision-making processes affecting the child.[61] Children and young people had the right to freedom of expression before the UNCRC came into force under article 19 of the International Covenant on Civil and Political Rights[62] and other international instruments. However, through article 12 and other associated provisions, the UNCRC provides a specific mandate to State Parties to respect, and give due weight to, children and young people's views in decision-making processes. The participation rights set out in article 12 are supported by other rights in the instrument, namely the rights to freedom of expression;[63] freedom of thought, conscience and religion;[64] and the right to access appropriate information.[65] These rights are also linked to the three other foundational principles of the UNCRC of non-discrimination, best interests and survival and development. Article 12 of the CRC sets out the principle of children's participation as follows:

1. State Parties shall assure to the child who is capable of forming his or her own views the right to express those views freely in all matters affecting the child, the views of the child being given due weight in accordance with the age and maturity of the child.
2. For this purpose, the child shall in particular be provided the opportunity to be heard in any judicial and administrative proceedings affecting the child, either directly, or through a representative or an appropriate body, in a manner consistent with the procedural rules of national law.

The word *participation* is used widely, even though the text of the UNCRC does not specifically refer to this word. The UNCRC Committee describes children's participation as "ongoing processes, which include information-sharing and dialogue between children and adults based on mutual respect, and in which children can learn how their views and those of adults are taken into account and shape the outcome of such processes".[66]

A growing body of literature asserts that children and young people are capable of forming, and freely expressing their own views about matters as complex as laws

---

[61] Ibid.
[62] UNGA, International Covenant on Civil and Political Rights (UN Doc. A/6316, 19 December 1966) 999 UNTS 85.
[63] Art. 13, UNCRC.
[64] Art. 14, UNCRC.
[65] Art. 17, UNCRC.
[66] UNCRC Committee, "General Comment No. 12 (2009)".

and policies that are likely to affect their lives.[67] However, globally, children and young people's views are rarely sought and given "due weight" in the development of legislation and policy.[68] State Parties are duty bound under article 12 of the UNCRC to involve children and young people in law and policy-making process and failure to do so is a breach of State Parties' international human rights law duty. The following provides a template for interpreting article 12 of the UNCRC using the VCLT and offers an analysis of states duties under article 12 of the UNCRC. Analysis concludes that state duties extend to involving children and young people in decision-making processes, including legislative and policy development about matters affecting them. It is hoped that the following will assist State Parties to better understand the meaning of article 12 and provide instruction about how to involve children and young people when developing laws and policies likely to affect them.

Interpreting Article 12

There are various rules for the interpretation of treaties including the "textual approach, the restrictive approach, the teleological approach, and the effectiveness approach".[69] The VCLT only supports the textual approach, as does the jurisprudence of the International Court of Justice (ICJ).[70] Thus, in this analysis the textual approach is the favoured method for interpreting article 12 of the UNCRC.

Interpretations of international human rights law may evolve over time. The ICJ, while supporting the textual approach outlined in the VCLT, has determined that within the parameters of the VCLT "an international instrument has to be interpreted and applied within the framework of the entire legal system prevailing at the time of the interpretation", rather than the time of drafting or adoption.[71] This approach permits some latitude in the interpretation of treaty provisions thereby loosening what commentators refer to as the "straightjacket" of article 31(1) of the VCLT.[72] Nevertheless, the appropriate starting point to determine the meaning

---

[67] Tisdall, "Is the Honeymoon Over?"; U. Kilkelly, "Using the Convention on the Rights of the Child in Law and Policy: Two Ways to Improve Compliance", in Invernizzi and Williams (eds.), *The Human Rights of Children*, 208; A. Invernizzi and B. Milne, "Are Children Entitled to Contribute to International Policy Making? A Critical View of Children's Participation in the International Campaign for the Elimination of Child Labour" (2002) 10 *International Journal of Children's Rights* 403.

[68] Ibid.

[69] J. Crawford, *Brownlie's Principles of Public International Law* (Oxford: Oxford University Press, 2012), 379.

[70] Ibid.

[71] *Legal Consequences for States of the Continued Presence of South Africa in Namibia (South West Africa) Notwithstanding Security Council Resolution 276 (1970)* (Advisory Opinion) [1971] ICJ Rep 16, [53].

[72] J. Tobin, "Seeking to Persuade: A Constructive Approach to Human Rights Treaty Implementation" (2010) 23 *Harvard Human Rights Journal* 1, 3; J. Weiler, "Prolegomena to a Meso-Theory of Treaty Interpretation at the Turn of the Century" (paper presented at the IILJ

of a treaty provision is the framework provided in the VCLT, and this is the approach adopted in the following text.

Article 26 of the VCLT states: "Every treaty in force is binding upon the parties to it and must be performed by them in good faith." The VCLT sets out a three-part framework for assessing the meaning of a treaty. The first step to determine the meaning of a treaty provision is to apply the *general rule* provided by article 31(1). The general rule stipulates that "[a] treaty shall be interpreted in good faith in accordance with the ordinary meaning to be given to the terms of the treaty in their context and in the light of its object and purpose." Thus, in accordance with the principles of "indivisibility, interdependence and interconnectedness of all human rights" the meaning of separate provisions in the UNCRC "can only be understood when they are read and interpreted in conjunction with the other rights protected in the Convention".[73] After the general rule has been applied, article 32 of the VCLT states: "Recourse may be had to supplementary means of interpretation, including the preparatory work of the treaty ... in order to confirm the meaning resulting from the application of article 31."

Article 32(a) and (b) of the VCLT further provides that supplementary materials may be referred to if the ordinary meaning under article 31 is "ambiguous or obscure" or "leads to a result which is manifestly absurd or unreasonable". Thus, the VCLT permits reference to the drafting history of the treaty, and statements from UN monitoring bodies, such as the UNCRC Committee, to determine the meaning of a provision where the application of the general rule is unclear. Further, to determine the rules of international law, the ICJ, under article 38(1)(d) of the *Statute of the International Court of Justice*, can refer to the "teachings of the most highly qualified publicists" (leading academics of international law) as a legitimate subsidiary means of interpretation.[74]

The following examines the meaning and scope of article 12 of the UNCRC from these three perspectives: the "ordinary meaning" of the text, in accordance with the VCLT; the history of drafting the UNCRC, in particular, the deliberations that took place when drafting article 12; and an analysis of the contemporary meaning according to the UNCRC Committee and other authorities' interpretation of, and recommendations about, children and young people's participation in law and policy-making according to article 12 of the UNCRC.

Meaning of Article 12

Ascertaining the meaning and scope of article 12 of the UNCRC is not an easy undertaking – a difficulty that is not peculiar to the UNCRC, as most international

---

International Legal Theory Colloquim: Interpretation and Judgment in International Law, NYU Law School, 14 February 2008).

[73] L. Lundy, "'Voice' Is Not Enough: Conceptualising Article 12 of the United Nations Convention on the Rights of the Child" (2007) 33(6) *British Educational Research Journal* 927, 932.

[74] *Statute of the International Court of Justice*, art. 38(1)(d).

human rights laws are "invariably vague and ambiguous" leading to interpretation and implementation problems.[75] Interpretations of rights evolve over time, and within jurisdictions. Statements from the UNCRC Committee about article 12 reflect and provide evidence about these developments: these statements are discussed in the following text.

There is no single or correct way to interpret and implement article 12 of the UNCRC.[76] Children's participation will be understood and applied differently across and within jurisdictions, and these interpretations will develop over time. However, it is possible to ascertain some meaning from the text and understand the rights that the text affords children and young people, as well as the duties the text imposes on states. The following examination of the scope and meaning of article 12 is provided to demonstrate that article 12 places a duty on states to engage children and young people in law and policy development. The result of this examination presents a preferred meaning of article 12 in relation to the duty on states to involve children and young people in law and policy development.

Applying the VCLT formula is not without difficulty given the complexity of the requirement in article 31 to take as the first test the "ordinary meaning" of the terms of a treaty, in their context and in light of the object and purpose of the treaty. To this end, the "object and purpose" of the UNCRC, its preamble, the deliberations of the Working Group when drafting the treaty and comments from bodies such as the UNCRC assist with the interpretation of article 12.

The ordinary meaning of article 12 articulates a specific right in and of itself and is also instructive in relation to how the other rights contained in the UNCRC are to be implemented. Parkes says:

> Article 12 operates as both a substantive right as well as a procedural right. It has been acknowledged that article 12 is substantive as it recognises that children are entitled to be actors in their everyday lives and have a right to contribute to any decisions affecting them.[77]

Article 12 is a substantive right because it provides a basis for children's agency and contributions to decisions about their lives. Article 12 is also, however, a procedural right. This arises "from the fact that children are empowered to challenge and to take action in promoting and protecting their rights, including all of the other rights of the child recognised under the UNCRC".[78]

Four extracts of text from article 12 in the following text are relevant to children and young people's right to participate in law and policy-making. The meaning of these elements of article 12 was discussed by the Working Group when drafting the provision and have been discussed since by the UNCRC Committee in various

---

[75] Tobin, "Seeking to Persuade", 1.
[76] Ibid.
[77] Parkes, *Children and International Human Rights Law*, 54.
[78] Ibid.

contexts. Ascertaining the meaning of the following elements of article 12 of the UNCRC is the aim of this section. These sections are:

(i) "shall assure to the child";
(ii) "who is capable of forming his or her own views";
(iii) "the views of the child being given due weight in accordance with the age and maturity of the child" and
(iv) "the right to express those views freely in all matters affecting the child".

"Shall Assure to the Child"

Application of the general rule under article 31(1) of the VCLT requires that the meaning of the words "shall assure" should be interpreted in accordance with the "context" as well as the "object and purpose" of the UNCRC.

The UNCRC established a universally agreed set of standards and obligations to protect children's human rights globally, and the object and purpose of the UNCRC is the realisation of rights for all children everywhere, and at all times.[79] This indicates that the scope of article 12 should be read widely, and the wording of the provision, by virtue of the words "shall assure", emphasises the legal duty of State Parties to fulfil the participatory rights of all children. The ordinary meaning of the words "shall assure" refer to the duty of states to provide each child "capable of forming his or her own view" the opportunity to express his or her views and the obligation to give these views consideration in decision-making.

Moreover, the drafters made it clear they intended article 12 would establish a binding duty on states. The proposal submitted by Poland to the UN Commission on Human Rights at its 36th session[80] included a specific reference to children's participatory rights, article 7, which later became the basis of article 12.[81] It said:

> The State parties to the present Convention *shall enable* the child who is capable of forming his own views the right to express his opinion in matters concerning his own person, and in particular, marriage, choice of occupation, medical treatment, education and recreation.[82]

This marked the first time the United Nations had been asked to consider children's participation rights. A range of iterations of this proposal were considered by the Working Group during their deliberations. Each iteration carried implications for the development of children's participatory rights. The development of children's

---

[79] UNCRC, preamble.
[80] Parkes, *Children and International Human Rights Law*, 28.
[81] Ibid.
[82] UN Economic and Social Council, "Question of a Convention on the Rights of the Child" (UN Doc. E/CN.4/1349, 17 January 1980), art. 7.

participation rights during the drafting process is demonstrated by the Australian member's amendment to the Polish proposal, which read as follows:

> The States parties to the present Convention *shall assure* to the child the right to express his opinion in matters concerning his own person, and in particular marriage, choice of occupation, medical treatment, education and recreation. In all such matters *the wishes* of the child shall be given due weight in accordance with his age and maturity.[83]

Notably, the Australian representative successfully petitioned for the inclusion of stronger language – "shall assure" rather than "shall enable" – a recommendation that was accepted by the Working Group and included in the text of article 12.[84] This suggests that the intended meaning of the words "shall assure" when the provision was drafted was designed to place a binding duty on State Parties to provide children and young people with the opportunity to express their views on matters affecting them.

This interpretation is supported by reference to other supplementary sources – particularly the UNCRC Committee. In its General Comment No. 12, the Committee defined the "literal" meaning of the words "shall assure" as:

> [A] legal term of special strength, which leaves no leeway for State parties' discretion. Accordingly, State parties are under strict obligation to undertake appropriate measures to fully implement this right for all children. This obligation contains two elements in order to ensure that mechanisms are in place to solicit the views of the child in all matters affecting her or him and to give due weight to those views.[85]

"Capable of Forming His or Her Own Views"

Achieving uniform interpretation of this phrase has proved to be challenging and controversial across jurisdictions. In particular, states often conflate children's ability to form views, and the weight to be given to these views. Lundy provides insight into the ordinary meaning of the words "capable of forming his or her own views" noting that "while there may be an element of uncertainty about what constitutes the capacity to form a view" the right to express these views is not connected to "the age and maturity of the child".[86] Under article 12 the "age and maturity of the child" is relevant only to determining the "due weight" of these views in the decision-making process (discussed in the following text).[87] Thus, "[C]hildren's right to express their

---

[83] UN Economic and Social Council, "Report of the Working Group on a Draft Convention on the Rights of the Child" (UN Doc. E/CN.4/L.1575, 17 January 1981), [74] (emphasis added).
[84] Parkes, *Children and International Human Rights Law*, 29.
[85] UNCRC Committee, "General Comment No. 12 (2009)", [19(a)(i)].
[86] Lundy, "'Voice' Is Not Enough", 935.
[87] Ibid.

views is not dependent upon their capacity to express a mature view; it is dependent only on their ability to form a view, mature or not".[88]

The UNCRC Committee has cautioned State Parties not to unduly limit the operation of article 12 through inappropriate application of these qualifications.[89] The UNCRC Committee asserts the rights provided by article 12 apply to children of all ages[90] and State Parties are obliged to assess children's capacity to form views in the widest possible manner.[91] In General Comment No. 7, "Implementing Child Rights in Early Childhood", the UNCRC Committee said young children "make choices and communicate their feelings, ideas and wishes in numerous ways, long before they are able to communicate through the conventions of spoken or written language".[92]

The UNCRC Committee, in their General Comment on the Right to Be Heard stated that the words "capable of forming his or her own views" "should not be seen as a limitation, but rather as an obligation for State parties to assess the capacity of the child to form an autonomous opinion to the greatest extent possible".[93] The UNCRC Committee guides states to begin with the presumption that children have the capacity to form their own views, and recognise children's right to do so.[94] Importantly, the UNCRC Committee says states must refrain from requiring children to prove their capacity to form their views, and instead "assess the capacity of the child to form an autonomous opinion to the greatest extent possible".[95]

These comments from the UNCRC Committee support the idea that children's participatory rights do not commence when a child becomes verbal, or when a child becomes verbally competent. Rather, the UNCRC Committee asserts in the preceding statement that children's ability to participate in decision-making arises well in advance of the onset of verbal skills.

The UNCRC Committee supports the idea that children should participate in the development of laws and policies that may affect them. The General Comment No. 19, "On Public Budgeting for the Realisation of Children's Rights (art 4)", says that states should "regularly hear children's views on budget decisions that affect them, through mechanisms for the meaningful participation of children at the national and subnational levels".[96] In this comment the UNCRC Committee further elaborates states' responsibility to fund the meaningful participation of

---

[88] Ibid.
[89] UNCRC Committee, "General Comment No. 7 (2005) on Implementing Child Rights in Early Childhood" (UN Doc. CRC/C/GC/7, 1 November 2005), [14].
[90] Ibid.; UNCRC, art. 12.
[91] UNCRC Committee, "General Comment No. 12 (2009)", [20].
[92] UNCRC Committee, "General Comment No. 7 (2005)", [14].
[93] UNCRC Committee, "General Comment No. 12 (2009)", [20].
[94] Ibid.
[95] Ibid.
[96] UNCRC Committee, "General Comment No. 19 (2016) on Public Budgeting for the Realisation of Children's Rights (Art 4)" (UN Doc. CRC/C/GC/19, 20 July 2016), [52], [53].

children in child-related law and policy development "[i]n particular, States should consult with children who face difficulties in making themselves heard, including children in situations of vulnerability".[97]

Giving the Views of the Child "Due Weight"

Once a child has expressed their views, article 12 requires states to give these views "due weight". While the ordinary meaning of "due weight" may be unclear,[98] looking to the context of the treaty as a whole, and its object and purpose, provides further guidance. The scope of article 12 is wide, and the participation rights it provides are linked to other provisions in the UNCRC. As stated earlier, children's participation rights are situated as one of the four foundation principles of the Convention.[99] Therefore, the ordinary meaning of the words "due weight" suggest these words should be interpreted to mean a degree of influence in proportion to the maturity of the child.

While there is not a large body of information about the deliberations that took place when the Working Group was drafting the words "due weight", more light can be shed by looking at other supplementary sources that have been produced since the Convention's ratification.

The UNCRC Committee in their General Comment on the Right to Be Heard clarify the meaning of the words "due weight" in article 12.[100] The UNCRC explains that this element of article 12 "stipulates that simply listening to the child is insufficient; the views of the child have to be seriously considered when the child is capable of forming her or his own views".[101] With reference to the word "maturity", the UNCRC Committee states that a child's biological age alone does not "determine the significance of a child's views".[102] Maturity, in this context, "refers to the ability to understand and assess the implications of a particular matter".[103] The UNCRC states that an assessment of a child's capacity to form a view needs to be done on a "case-by-case" basis.[104]

Under article 12 the "age and maturity of the child" is relevant to determining the "due weight" of these views, that is the degree to which children's views should influence decisions about matters affecting the child. The "due weight" children and young people's views should be afforded in relation to law and policy-making is not articulated in article 12, and an examination of the UNCRC Committee

---

[97] Ibid. [52].
[98] Lundy, "'Voice' Is Not Enough", 937.
[99] UNCRC Committee, "General Guidelines Regarding the Form and Content of Initial Reports to be Submitted by States Parties under Article 44, Paragraph 1(a) of the Convention".
[100] UNCRC Committee, "General Comment No. 12 (2009)", [28].
[101] Ibid.
[102] Ibid., [29].
[103] Ibid., [30].
[104] Ibid., [29].

statements about this appear to be confined to a model where State Parties "should consult" with children.

Article 12 however, provides a basis for much more than children's right to be consulted about matters affecting them – this provision opens opportunities for children to be active decision makers, not only participants in decision-making.[105] Freeman asserts restricting children's role in decision-making to consultation is inconsistent with the intentions of the framers of the UNCRC.[106] Furthermore, Tobin suggests Archard's interpretation of the UNCRC, which asserts adults "retain final authority over children", is "neither a necessary nor persuasive interpretation of this instrument".[107] Tobin argues that the wording of article 12 is sufficiently open, such that, under the provision sufficiently mature children are afforded not only the opportunity to participate in decision-making processes, but that their views must be given due weight in the final decision.[108] This interpretation of article 12 has the potential to enhance children's participatory rights in relation to child-led initiatives, and in relation to children as active decision makers, rather than being restricted to participants in decision-making. Tobin's and Freeman's views accord with Lundy's child rights-based approach to matters involving children and her four interconnected elements required to implement meaningful children's participation under article 12: "Space, Voice, Audience and Influence".[109] Lundy's model likewise transcends the "consultation" paradigm and positions children and young people as agents in decision-making processes.

The analysis required by the VCLT to assess the meaning of the words "due weight" concludes that states are required to assure children and young people not only have the opportunity to express their views about matters relevant to them (as demonstrated in the preceding text) but that these views must influence decisions about matters affecting children and young people. Further, that the presumption that children have the capacity to form views should be the starting point for states.

"In All Matters Affecting the Child"

The phrase "in all matters affecting the child" may at first appear uncomplicated, but this could potentially cover any matter in relation to children. Such an interpretation is likely to produce an "unreasonable", "absurd" and impractical result[110] because it is hard to imagine many matters that would not in some way relate to children.

---

[105] J. Tobin, "Understanding Children's Rights: A Vision beyond Vulnerability" (2015) 84(2) *Nordic Journal of International Law* 155.
[106] M. Freeman, "The Value and Values of Children's Rights", in Invernizzi and Williams (eds.), *The Human Rights of Children*, 26–34.
[107] J. Tobin, "Justifying Children's Rights" (2013) 21 *International Journal of Children's Rights* 395, 432 citing Archard, *Children: Rights and Childhood*, 66.
[108] Ibid.
[109] Lundy, "'Voice' Is Not Enough", 927.
[110] *Vienna Convention on the Law of Treaties* art. 32(b).

However, the *travaux preparatoires* of the UNCRC can help narrow down that scope. In the original draft written by Poland, this was framed as the right of children to express their "opinion in matters concerning his own person, and in particular, marriage, choice of occupation, medical treatment, education and recreation".[111] At this early drafting stage the Working Group focused on providing children with the right to express their views about "matters concerning his own person".[112] In doing so, the Working Group contemplated restricting children's participatory rights to the private sphere.

The Danish delegation favoured the inclusion of parents and guardians in children's participatory rights emphasising increased influence on decision-making and responsibility as children grow older. Again, the text, by virtue of the words "person of the child" and "personal matters", emphasised the private realm in which children's participatory rights were being considered by the Working Group. The Danish delegation submitted the following wording for article 12:

> Parents or other guardians have the right and duty to decide in matters concerning the person of the child. But the child shall as soon as possible, have an influence in such matters. As the child gets older, the parents or the guardian should give him more and more responsibility for personal matters with the aim of preparing the child for the life of a grown-up."[113]

The recommendations from the Australian and Danish representatives focussed on matters relevant to children's private domain. The suggestion from the US delegate sought to broaden the ambit over which "matters" the child was able to express their views under article 12.[114] The US representative proposed the following wording:

> The states parties to the present Convention shall enable the child who is capable of forming his own views the right to express his opinion effectively and non-violently in matters concerning his own person and in particular, religion, political and social beliefs, matters of conscience, cultural and artistic matters, marriage, choice of occupation, medical treatment, education, travel, place of residence, and recreation."[115]

The comments from the US delegation suggest that matters beyond the child's private sphere were considered when drafting the text. However, the expanded list of matters proposed by the United States was expressed in relation to children's private realm by the words "in matters concerning his own person". The text suggests that the proposed list was not intended to provide a right for children to express their views about "religion, political and social beliefs, matters of conscience, cultural and

---

[111] UN Economic and Social Council, "Question of a Convention on the Rights of the Child".
[112] Ibid.
[113] UN Economic and Social Council, "Report of the Working Group on a Draft Convention on the Rights of the Child", 13–14.
[114] Ibid.
[115] Ibid.

artistic matters" in relation to public decision-making, only in relation to how these matters relate to the child's "own person".

After much debate, and several years of deliberation, the "list of matters" to which article 12 would apply was abandoned in favour of wording stating that a child who is capable of forming their own views has the right to express those views in "*all* matters affecting the child".[116] The Working Group stated that the "various circumstances in which a child may express himself or herself should not be subject to the limits of a list".[117] This suggests the drafters of the UNCRC intended the provision to evolve over time that these words "were not static, but were by definition evolutionary".[118]

The final wording of article 12 reflected the decision by the drafters of the UNCRC to settle on the broad wording "all matters" with a qualifying statement "affecting the child", not "children".[119] The wording of article 12 intentionally left the scope of what "matters" the article encompassed wide so as not to provide "a normative list of the matters concerned".[120] Yet the choice of the Working Group to refer to "the child", rather than "children" in article 12, further suggests the provision was designed to apply to the individual circumstances of a child's life.

The later suggestion by the United States to include the word "all" before the word "matters" such that article 12 then read "all matters affecting the child" was accepted.[121] The insertion of the word "all" significantly altered the legal effect of the provision. The UNCRC Committee has linked the words "all matters affecting the child" with the object and purpose of the UNCRC, and the "principle, which highlights the role of the child as an active participant in the promotion, protection and monitoring of his or her rights".[122]

Moreover, statements from the UNCRC Committee state that the "matters" referred to in article 12 extends to providing children with a right to participate in public decision-making. In 1999, the UNCRC Committee stressed the need to progress children's rights "from lip service to political action" calling for governments to "consult and involve children more actively in decision-making ... at the local, regional and national levels".[123] This call to action accentuated the

---

[116] Parkes, *Children and International Human Rights Law*, 51–54; UNCRC, art. 12.
[117] Parkes, *Children and International Human Rights Law*, 52.
[118] *Legal Consequences for States of the Continued Presence of South Africa in Namibia (South West Africa) Notwithstanding Security Council Resolution 276 (1970)* (Advisory Opinion) [1971] ICJ Rep 16, [53].
[119] Cantwell, "Are Children's Rights Still Human?", 55.
[120] Ibid.
[121] UN Economic and Social Council, "Report of the Working Group on a Draft Convention on the Rights of the Child", 13–14.
[122] UNCRC Committee, "General Comment No. 5 (2003) on General Measures of Implementation for the Convention on the Rights of the Child" (UN Doc. CRC/GC/2003/5, 27 November 2003), [12].
[123] UNCRC Committee, "Tenth Anniversary of the Convention on the Rights of the Child Commemorative Meeting: Achievements and Challenges", UN Doc. excerpted from

requirement under article 12 that child participation be embedded in the formulation of government decisions and policies "on an everyday basis" not only as "one-off events or symbolic gestures".[124] Thus, in 1999 the UNCRC made it clear that children and young people's involvement in local, national, regional and international decision-making is within the meaning of the words "all matters" in article 12 of the UNCRC. Ten years later, in 2009, the General Assembly further developed this imperative through the adoption of a resolution on children's rights urging all states to:

> [S]trengthen the participation of children and adolescents in planning and implementation relating to matters that affect them, such as health, environment, education, social and economic welfare and protection against violence, abuse and exploitation.[125]

Adding to this, in 2009 the UNCRC Committee issued a General Comment on the Right to Be Heard, in which the Committee reiterated the expansive application of the words "all matters" in article 12 emphatically stating that the drafters "rejected a proposal to define these matters by a list limiting the consideration of a child's or children's views".[126] This General Comment provides clear guidance to State Parties as to how to implement article 12 of the UNCRC.[127] Included in this statement are several specific references to the role children can play in the development of law and policy affecting them. For instance, when discussing the role of State Parties to protect children from rights violations, the UNCRC Committee said:

> The Committee notes that the voices of children have increasingly become a powerful force in the prevention of child rights violations ... Children should be consulted in the formulation of legislation and policy related to these and other problem areas and involved in the drafting, development and implementation of related plans and programmes.[128]

The UNCRC Committee has also made clear that "State parties should carefully listen to children's views wherever their perspective can enhance the quality of solutions".[129] Furthermore, the UNCRC Committee elaborates and specifically references children's involvement in the creation of law in the following statement: "The views expressed by children may add relevant perspectives and experience and

---

CRC/C/87, Annex IV 22nd Session (30 September–1 October 1999, 7 December 1999), [278] and [280].
[124] Ibid., [278].
[125] UNGA, "Rights of the Child" (UN Doc. A/RES/63/241, 13 March 2009), [11].
[126] UNCRC Committee, "General Comment No. 12 (2009)", [27(iv)].
[127] Ibid.
[128] Ibid., [122].
[129] Ibid., [27].

should be considered in decision-making, policy-making and preparation of laws and/or measures as well as their evaluation".[130]

These statements by the UNCRC Committee were made in the context of defining both the ambit of children's participatory rights, and states duties to protect these rights.[131] This, combined with the fact that the framers of article 12 left the wording of the provision somewhat open, and the fact that states understanding of the right has evolved, presents a body of evidence supporting article 12 as a foundation for children's right to participate in legislative and policy development. Interpretations of article 12 have changed over time and will continue to change as states increase their compliance with their duties under article 12.

The analysis of the meaning of article 12 was carried out in this chapter against a three-tiered analysis looking first, as the VCLT requires, to the "ordinary meaning" of the text; then drawing insights about the meaning from the history of drafting process of the UNCRC; and lastly, through an analysis of the UNCRC Committee's and other authoritative sources' interpretation of, and recommendations about, article 12.

So far, this chapter sought to increase knowledge about the nature of article 12 of the UNCRC and draw attention to state duties arising from this provision. It is hoped that State Parties will commit to interpreting and implementing article 12 of the UNCRC in the way in which this chapter envisages and take steps to engage children and young people in domestic law and policy development. The conclusion of this chapter presents a mechanism for how State Parties could engage children and young people in this way through a national "interpretive community".

A MECHANISM FOR CHILDREN AND YOUNG PEOPLE TO PARTICIPATE

Pursuing children and young people's involvement in law and policy development is a necessary and vital means by which to fulfil state duties under article 12 of the UNCRC, as well as progress the achievement of Goal 16 of the SDGs.[132] The evolution of children's participation rights before and since the adoption of the UNCRC places a duty on governments and alters the relationship between the State and children and young people. Before the UNCRC came into force there was no binding legal duty on states to ensure children and young people were heard and their views taken into consideration. However, the post-UNCRC climate places a duty on states to renegotiate their relationships with children and young people and ensure children and young people's participation rights are enjoyed.

One element of the post-UNCRC relationship between children and the State that remains undeveloped is the involvement of children and young people in the

---

[130] Ibid., [12].
[131] Ibid.
[132] See note 8.

development of child-related laws and policy frameworks. The involvement of children and young people in this way has wide-ranging positive implications for sustainable development. To achieve sustainable development, children and young people must have input into, and influence, the legal frameworks within which they live. Agyeman and colleagues define sustainable development as:

> The need to ensure a better quality of life for all, now and into the future, in a just and equitable manner, whilst living within the limits of supporting ecosystems.[133]

Children's active participation in decision-making about matters affecting them is taking place across a myriad of different fields and settings[134] – in the home, in the community, in education and health-care settings, just to name a few. Children and young people's participation in law and policy development is just one of the many settings where State Parties are duty bound to facilitate children and young people's participation. Children and young people's participation in child-related law and policy development is a right within the democratic process and is fundamental to achieving sustainable international development, yet this practice is largely absent in the mechanics of governmental decision-making processes globally. The goal is to move beyond a consultation paradigm – practices that are widely considered to be tokenistic because children and young people's views are sought but do not necessarily influence eventual decisions made. The challenge is to engage children and young people in meaningful, not tokenistic, ways that lead to embedding children and young people's views in eventual laws and policies that are likely to affect them.

To support children and young people's role in sustainable legal and policy development governments must do more than hold children's parliament events or establish children's councils. Governmental participation endeavours must be underpinned by a genuine commitment to perceiving and treating children and young people as citizens in their own right, complete with the requisite skills and rights to participate in civic decision-making processes. However, perceiving children and young people as agents of change is not necessarily a view that is shared across State Parties to the UNCRC. It is for this reason that this chapter has outlined

---

[133] J. Agyeman, R. Bullard and B. Evans (eds.), *Just Sustainabilities: Development in an Unequal World* (Cambridge, MA: MIT Press, 2003), 5.
[134] J. Tobin, "Beyond the Supermarket Shelf: Using a Rights Based Approach to Address Children's Health Needs" (2006) 14(3) *International Journal of Children's Rights* 275; J. Skattebol et al., "Making a Difference: Building on Young People's Experiences of Economic Adversity" (Social Policy Research Centre, UNSW, 2012); Bennett Woodhouse, "Enhancing Children's Participation"; S. Tomanovic, "Negotiating Children's Participation and Autonomy within Families" (2003) 11(1) *International Journal of Children's Rights* 51; M. A. Powell and A. B. Smith, "Children's Participation Rights in Research" (2009) 16(1) *Childhood* 124; M. Couzens, "Exploring Public Participation as a Vehicle for Child Participation in Governance: A View from South Africa" (2012) 20(4) *International Journal of Children's Rights* 674; E. Barratt Hacking, R. Barratt and W. Scott, "Engaging Children: Research Issues around Participation and Environmental Learning" (2007) 13(4) *Environmental Education Research* 529.

exactly how article 12 of the UNCRC mandates all State Parties to engage children and young people in decision-making processes.

One model for the involvement of children and young people in law and policy development is through the establishment of an "interpretive community".[135] This model reflects Agyeman and colleagues' definition of *sustainable development* provided in the preceding text with a focus on justice and equity for children and young people, positioning them as active agents capable of inputting into and influencing the legal frameworks governing their lives. Membership of an "interpretative community" includes children and young people and other citizens along with government and civil society and collectively they decide, for example, how international treaties will be applied in the context of that particular jurisdiction giving regard to factors such as the cultural context of that place.

This model is proposed as a meaningful, non-tokenistic mechanism to facilitate participation "which directly support[s] the active roles of young people in sustainable change processes" and avoids "tokenistic approaches to participation based simply on 'having a say', and instead this mechanism acknowledges the importance of young people's participation as citizens".[136] An interpretive community model draws on the work of Fish, later developed by Johnson and then Tobin.[137] It is appropriate for governments to lead the establishment of an interpretive community given that they are the primary duty bearers responsible for ensuring citizens enjoy human rights. The creation of an interpretive community is a formal, ongoing and politically entrenched means for children and young people (and a range of other groups of people) to participate in the development of relevant laws and policies likely to affect them.

The preceding discussion regarding article 12 and the VCLT set out a basic starting point for how states should interpret the provision. The practical implications of how this should be operationalised in specific states can be negotiated and evaluated within an interpretive community. There are many ways an interpretive community may be established and operate. The appropriate method will vary from state to state yet the independence of an interpretive community is paramount and may, for example, be established as an independent advisory body established by a statute that is associated with (or operates under the umbrella of) an independent human rights institution.

---

[135] I have discussed this elsewhere see: H. Doel-Mackaway, "'Just Ask Us. Come and See Us': The Participation of Aboriginal Children and Young People in Law and Policy Development" (unpublished PhD Thesis, Macquarie University, 2016), section 8.2.3.

[136] Percy-Smith and Burns, "Exploring the Role of Children and Young People", 326 and 324.

[137] S. E. Fish, *Is There a Text In This Class? The Authority of Interpretive Communities* (Cambridge, MA, and London: Harvard University Press, 1980); I. Johnstone, "Treaty Interpretation: The Authority of Interpretive Communities" (1990) 12 *Michigan Journal of International Law* 371; I. Johnstone, "The Power of Interpretive Communities", in M. Barnett and R. Duvall (eds.), *Power in Global Governance* (Cambridge: Cambridge University Press, 2004) vol. 98, 185; Tobin, "Seeking to Persuade".

The value of an interpretive community is that it overcomes the typical situation operating across most jurisdictions where "the only interpreters of the law are domestic officials who are institutionally and politically predisposed to positions that favour their government or state".[138] This method of interpretation generally excludes children and young people from the process of interpreting and deciding on how international treaties will be applied in practice. An interpretive community "provides an opportunity to balance and mediate the interests of State actors with the interests of non-State actors"[139] and expands the democratic process by including children and young people.

The means by which children's rights are interpreted in states, and the importance attributed to the participatory rights provided for by the UNCRC, clearly have a significant bearing on how children and young people enjoy their rights. To achieve sustainable development, children and young people must be afforded the opportunity to express their views about how their rights are interpreted and applied in practice, rather than government representatives deciding on how children's interests will, or will not be, interpreted and applied.

Within the interpretive community disagreements about the nature and method of implementation of children's rights will occur due to "the diverse and potentially conflicting interests within the relevant interpretive community when attributing a meaning to human rights standards".[140] Dworkin suggests the inevitable process of debate then disagreement about the meaning of a particular human right can be resolved and shared understandings about treaty provisions reached over time through "conventions of description, argument, judgment and persuasion as they operate in this or that profession or discipline or community".[141] This approach does not, however, depend on reaching consensus among the interpretive community about all matters; instead, the process emphasises listening to and considering dissonant views. It is important, though, that a certain level of consensus is achieved in the interpretive community for the implementation of human rights to progress.[142]

The purpose of an interpretive community, as a vehicle for the implementation of human rights standards, is linked to achieving the SDGs, in particular Goal 16 given that the focus of this goal on "building effective, accountable institutions at all levels".[143] In the context of sustainable development, this requires making sure that children are involved in deciding how best to implement the SDGs through membership of an interpretive community whose role it is to deliberate

---

[138] Johnstone, "The Power of Interpretive Communities" in Barnett and Duvall, Power in Global Governance, 189.
[139] Doel-Mackaway, "Just Ask Us. Come and See Us", section 7.5.1.
[140] Tobin, "Seeking to Persuade", 10.
[141] R. Dworkin, "Law as Interpretation" (1982) 60 *Texas Law Review* 527, 562.
[142] Tobin, "Seeking to Persuade".
[143] See note 8.

and decide on implementation strategies for child-related laws and policies in accordance with the UNCRC.

CONCLUSION

Children and young people comprise more than 30 per cent of the world's population, and their participation in the design of laws and policies affecting them is required at international law and necessary for sustainable international development. This chapter shows that article 12 of the UNCRC imposes a legal duty on State Parties to seek and take into consideration children and young people's views in legislative and policy formation; and further that such involvement is a means by which to achieve sustainable development. However, this requirement and the legal basis of this duty at international law are little understood by State Parties globally. The analysis of the meaning of article 12 provided in this chapter concludes that states are required to assure children and young people have the opportunity to express their views about matters relevant to them, and that these views must influence the decisions made. This conclusion supports the presumption that children have the capacity to form views and this premise is the appropriate starting point for states when implementing article 12 of the UNCRC.

The drafting history of the UNCRC produced an instrument that is reflective of a time in history where children's rights were an emerging area of thought and practice.[144] Since then, however, interpretations of article 12 have evolved, and this evolution is reflected in guidance to states emanating from the UN Committee, and other treaty-monitoring bodies. Legislation and policy that is likely to affect children and young people is a "matter affecting" children and young people and falls within the scope of the meaning of article 12. Thus, children and young people must be involved in the process of designing laws and policies that will affect their lives. Furthermore, the involvement of children and young people in national law and policy development supports sustainable development, in particular the achievement of Goal 16 of the SDGs.[145]

Despite the almost universal ratification of the UNCRC, and the centrality of children's participation rights within this instrument, the voices of young people remain largely silent in law and policy development processes globally. The involvement of young people in the design, development and review of legislation and policy pertaining to them is infrequently attempted, and the efficacy of these efforts varies widely in jurisdictions where this is undertaken. The non-involvement of children and young people in the development of legislative and policy provisions relating to them is a breach of State Parties' international law responsibilities to

---

[144] Cantwell, "Are Children's Rights Still Human?", 41–42.
[145] UNGA, "Transforming Our World", [9].

"assure" children and young people enjoy the "right to express their views", and have these views considered, about matters affecting them.[146] The challenge is how to reverse children and young people's non-participation in lawmaking and demonstrate the instrumental value and contribution their involvement in these processes could make toward achieving sustainable international development. For children to experience their human rights, "far more than law itself is required ... to be effective the legal enforcement of human rights ... must mobilise the supportive elements and/or processes present within the social routines of everyday life".[147] The UNCRC Committee has made it clear that "[l]istening to children should not be seen as an end in itself, but rather as a means by which States make their interactions with children and their actions on behalf of children ever more sensitive to the implementation of children's rights."[148]

Children and young people – if afforded the opportunity – can play a vital role as active agents for sustainable development with respect to legislative and policy initiatives likely to affect them. The involvement and consideration of children and young people's views about these initiatives offers State Parties a mechanism to enhance their compliance with the UNCRC, advance children's participation rights and, in doing so, contribute to sustainable international development.

---

[146] UNCRC, art. 12.
[147] A. Woodiwiss, "The Law Cannot Be Enough: Human Rights and the Limits of Legalism", in S. Meckled-Garcìa and B. Çalı (eds.), *The Legalization of Human Rights: Multidisciplinary Perspectives on Human Rights and Human Rights Law* (London and New York: Routledge, 2006), 36–37.
[148] UNCRC Committee, "General Comment No. 5 (2003) on General Measures of Implementation for the Convention on the Rights of the Child" (UN Doc. CRC/GC/2003/5, 27 November 2003), [12].

5

What Course without Evils?

Rare Diseases, Children's Right to Health and the Sustainable Development Goals

Octavio Luiz Motta Ferraz

INTRODUCTION

Epidermolysis Bullosa (EB) is a genetic disease that causes the skin to be extremely fragile, being easily injured by minor mechanical friction or trauma and causing painful blisters.[1] Because EB skin is not able to heal properly, chronic open wounds and extensive scarring develop, with irreversible damage, disability and disfigurement accruing over a lifetime. These include decreased mobility owing to the pain and the extensive scaring; constriction of the mouth or throat; and fusion of the fingers and toes ("mitten" deformities). For some types of EB, the internal mucosa is also affected, for example the esophagus, stomach, intestines, upper airway, bladder and genitals. As a result, nutrition can be compromised, resulting in osteoporosis and general inability to thrive. A type of skin cancer, squamous cell carcinoma, is also a common occurrence and major cause of death in some forms of EB.

Given that there is no cure to EB, treatment is currently restricted to the management of its symptoms, that is, prevention of injuries and blisters, caring for blistered skin, treatment for infection, treatment for nutritional problems and surgery to minimise the problem of fingers and toes fusion. Such preventive and palliative measures are hard enough to be successfully implemented in adults, let alone in children. The very act of birth is a painful bruising experience for babies, and avoiding injury is obviously particularly difficult for children, who have a natural urge to run around, jump and climb in their playing activities. The term *Butterfly Children* is often used to describe younger patients as their skin is as fragile

---

[1] I presented this chapter at the London Bioethics Colloquium at King's College London in September 2016. I am grateful to all the participants, in particular to Annette Rid and Jonathan Montgomery for invaluable comments. I am also thankful to Felipe Guimarães Assis Tirado for his invaluable assistance in editing the footnotes.
Aeschylus, *Agamemnon*, 1.211, cited in G. Calabresi and P. Bobbit, *Tragic Choices* (New York: W. W. Norton & Company, 1978), 18.

as a butterfly's wings (*Cotton Wool Babies* and *Crystal Skin Children* are also used, the latter particularly in South America).[2]

To make the situation of EB patients even more poignant and difficult, the prospects for development of curative treatment are not good and access to the existing palliative care, especially in developing countries, is very restricted.[3] Both are related to the fact that EB affects only a small number of individuals compared to the general population, which puts it among what the public health literature calls "rare diseases".[4] Rare diseases often face higher hurdles in the development of medical knowledge and treatment arrangements, as commercial incentives for treatment development are low, *per capita* costs of whatever treatment is available are often very high (making their funding in public health systems of developing countries particularly challenging) and health professionals in general practice are not used to dealing with them.[5]

What ought to be done to improve this difficult situation of EB patients? An instinctive and visceral response would likely say "everything that is possible!" including massive investment in research to find a cure to EB and, at a minimum, the provision to all EB patients of the palliative medical care currently available as described in the preceding text. "No EB patient should go without treatment!" One could even add that this is no less than what the *right to health*, recognised in several international law treaties and domestic constitutions and legislation around the world, requires. Moreover, as EB affects children particularly badly, one could also invoke the Convention on the Rights of the Child, which recognises, in article 24, "the right of the child to the enjoyment of the highest attainable standard of health and to facilities for the treatment of illness and rehabilitation of health".[6]

---

[2] www.debra-international.org/epidermolysis-bullosa.html; www.nhs.uk/conditions/Epidermolysis-bullosa/Pages/Introduction.aspx; www.niams.nih.gov/health_info/epidermolysis_bullosa/epidermolysis_bullosa_ff.asp.

[3] www.orpha.net/consor/cgi-bin/Education_AboutRareDiseases.php?lng=EN.

[4] There is no internationally recognised single and specific criterion to determine what is a rare disease. Different criteria are therefore to be found in different countries and are often set in legislation or regulation aimed at the development of treatment for rare diseases. In the United States, the Orphan Drug Act of 1983 uses an absolute number, i.e., diseases affecting less than 200,000 people; in the EU Orphan Medicinal Products Regulation of 2000 it is <5 in 10,000 individuals in the population and the disease has also to be life threatening and/or chronically debilitating. See P. Stolk, M. J. C. Willemen and H. G. M. Leufkens, "Rare Essentials: Drugs for Rare Diseases as Essential Medicines" (2006) 84 *Bull World Health Organ* 745, 751 (defending the creation of a Rare Diseases Model List in the fashion of the Essential Medicines Model List of the WHO, and proposing seven criteria for inclusion in that list, excluding cost criteria).

[5] Treatments in this situation are usually called "orphan drugs", i.e., drugs that are not developed by the pharmaceutical industry for economic reasons but that respond to a public health need (www.orpha.net/consor/cgi-bin/Education_AboutOrphanDrugs.php?lng=EN).

[6] UN General Assembly (UNGA), *Convention on the Rights of the Child* (UN Doc. A/RES/44/25, 20 November 1989) 1577 UNTS 3. The right to health is also recognized in article 12 of the International Covenant on Economic, Social and Cultural Rights and several other treaties

This was, incidentally, the response given recently by the judiciary in Brazil when EB patients filed lawsuits demanding treatment that was then not available in the Unified Health System (SUS,[7] the Brazilian underfunded version of the NHS). Based on articles 6 and 198 of the Federal Constitution of 1988, which recognises "health as a right of everyone and a duty of the state", several state courts, backed by solid jurisprudence from the Supreme Federal Tribunal (STF), ordered the government to provide treatment to EB patients that was being refused on grounds of lack of resources. In one of these cases, in the northeastern state of Bahia, one of the less developed in Brazil, and where the prevalence of EB is particularly high compared to other states, the government is currently forced to provide treatment to forty-four EB patients through judicial orders, which generates a significant expenditure not originally planned by that state's Department for Health.[8]

Many will see in this case of judicially mandated treatment for EB just another example of the positive role that the right to health can have when the courts are willing to assertively enforce it on the face of state omission. This is even more so, some may argue, as EB affects predominantly children, a group that deserves priority in the protection of their interests due to their greater vulnerability. Although I am obviously sympathetic with the plight of children suffering from EB and instinctively pleased with the outcome of their judicial battle, I am concerned about the simplistic justification often given by courts in Brazil to ground their decisions in such cases.

In previous work I have analysed the growing phenomenon of right-to-health litigation and criticised a model emerging in some countries (mostly in Latin America, and particularly in Brazil) where courts adopt an extremely expansive (and simplistic) interpretation of the right to health as a right to any health treatment a patient may need, whatever its costs (we could call it "a right to everything"). As I tried to show in these studies, such a model, as well as being irrational in completely disregarding the intractable but unavoidable need of any society to prioritise when allocating the limited resources of the health system, may also, and often does, increase rather than diminish the health inequities that the right to health, properly interpreted, is supposed to combat. This is due to a combination of reasons, including unequal access to courts and some types of health interventions often claimed in right-to-health litigation (often not prioritarious from any

---

and national constitutions. UNGA, *International Covenant on Economic, Social and Cultural Rights* (ICESCR) (UN Doc. A/6316, 16 December 1966) 992 UNTS 3.

[7] Acronym of the Portuguese full title, Sistema Único de Saúde.
[8] As well as the lawsuits and judicial decisions I will cite in this article, all publicly available in electronic format on the Internet, I have conducted several interviews in the state of Bahia, Brazil, with a judge, public prosecutors, public defenders ("state attorneys"), state managers and employees in the health department, doctors and claimants in November 2014 within a project funded by the World Bank. I will refer more specifically to some of these interviews in the text and notes.

plausible perspective). Litigation under this simplistic model, I argued, will rarely be an equitable means of distributing the limited resources of a health system.[9]

In the unavoidable context of limited resources to spend on health faced by any country, but particularly low- and middle-income ones, prioritisation is indispensable and the right to health cannot therefore be interpreted, simplistically, as a right to every treatment available. On the contrary, any plausible interpretation of the right to health will allow for justified exclusions of certain treatments.[10] The intractable challenge (unduly avoided in the simplistic model just mentioned) is to come up with legitimate criteria to determine which treatments can and cannot be justifiably refused to individuals without disrespecting their right to health.

The health community, that is public health experts, health economists, administrators, doctors and nurses face this agonising challenge on a daily basis. It is called *priority setting* in technical parlance, or *rationing* in more blunt but politically sensitive language. The World Health Organization (WHO), whose constitution was the first international document to recognise the right to health in 1946,[11] has a specific programme (WHO-CHOICE) to help countries in this difficult task.[12] The express goal of the health community is to achieve what is now referred to as "universal health coverage" (UHC), proposed by the WHO and now part of the Sustainable Development Goals (SDG) (Goal 3), that is to "achieve access to quality essential health-care services and access to safe, effective, quality and affordable essential medicines and vaccines for all".[13] The challenge is how to achieve this goal within limited resources in an efficient and equitable manner.

Are courts able to hold the state to account in this intractable task? And if so, how? These are the issues I discuss in this chapter making use of the EB litigation case in Brazil as a useful concrete illustration of the complexity of the task. As I shall suggest in the end, the Brazilian courts decisions to order the state to provide EB patients with the treatment they needed, however expensive in per capita terms, may perhaps

---

[9] This is because the sole criteria for access to treatment in litigation under this model is access to justice, which is strongly limited in many countries to those with awareness and material resources. See O. Ferraz, "The Right to Health in the Courts of Brazil: Worsening Health Inequities?" (2009) 11(2) *Health and Human Rights* 33; O. Ferraz, "Harming the Poor through Social Rights Litigation: Lessons from Brazil" (2010) 89 *Texas Law Review* 1643; O. Ferraz, "Health Inequalities, Rights, and Courts: The Social Impact of the Judicialization of Health", in A. E. Yamin and S. Gloppen (eds.), *Litigating Health Rights: Can Courts Bring More Justice to Health?* (Cambridge, MA: Harvard University Press, 2011).
[10] B. Rumbold et al., "Universal Health Coverage, Priority Setting, and the Human Right to Health" (2017) 390(11095) *Lancet* 712.
[11] Preamble: "The enjoyment of the highest attainable standard of health is one of the fundamental rights of every human being without distinction of race, religion, political belief, economic or social condition." The Constitution was adopted by the International Health Conference held in New York from 19 June to 22 July 1946. Constitution of the World Health Organization, New York (22 July 1946) in force 7 April 1948.
[12] www.who.int/choice/en/.
[13] www.who.int/universal_health_coverage/en/.

be justified as a vindication of their right to health. To ground that conclusion, however, one cannot simply refer to the right to health recognised in the Brazilian constitution or international treaties such as the Convention on the Rights of the Child mentioned previously, as Brazilian courts have been doing. This, as already shown, is a simplistic interpretation of the right to health as a "right to everything" that perniciously ignores the inevitable need to prioritise health resources. What one needs to show to justify the decision to grant EB patients treatment is why, faced with so many other important health needs of its population, Brazilian health authorities ought nonetheless to have prioritised the needs of EB patients.

This is not an easy task, and perhaps not even one that courts are capable or legitimated to pursue. I want to explore, however, how courts ought to go about in this attempt in a legitimate manner, that is one that is not open to the challenges of lack of institutional capacity and legitimacy traditionally levelled against social rights adjudication.

The remainder of the chapter proceeds as follows. In "The Rights-Resources Dilemma: Defining the Content of Social Rights", I discuss in some detail the basic premises of the exercise to highlight its tremendous complexity, too often overlooked by the legal community. I call it the *rights-resources dilemma*. It can be summarised in the following question: who should we treat when resources are limited, as they always are? In "The Right to Health in the Courts" I look critically at how courts have so far inadequately responded to the rights-resources dilemma and suggest what a more adequate response would look like. I argue that an adequate response would need to fall into what I call a *robust procedural review approach* of the type developed by Norman Daniels in his influential "accountability for reasonableness" framework and that, to do that well, courts will need to engage closely with public health expertise in the field of priority setting. In "Universal Health Coverage and the Right to Health" I briefly introduce what I regard as a crucial public health concept that the legal community ought to familiarise itself with, that of UHC (promoted by the WHO[14] and included among the new SDGs).[15] I then discuss a seminal recent report, also by the WHO, recommending priority-setting criteria in the path towards UHC, *Making Fair Choices on the Path to Universal Health Coverage*.[16] I suggest that it could be used by courts as an important aid in understanding the complexity of priority setting and in clarifying the basic and essential principles of cost-effectiveness and equity. In "The Right to Health in Brazil" I explore how this expert knowledge

---

[14] UHC is defined by the 2005 World Health Assembly as "access to key promotive, preventive, curative and rehabilitative health interventions for all at an affordable cost, thereby achieving equity in access", World Health Assembly, *Sustainable Health Financing, Universal Coverage and Social Health Insurance* (WHA, Res. 58.33, 2005).

[15] Goal 3: "Ensure healthy lives and promote well-being for all at all ages"; Goal 3.8: "Achieve UHC, including financial risk protection, access to quality essential health care services and access to safe, effective, quality and affordable essential medicines and vaccines for all."

[16] T. Ottersen et al., "Making Fair Choices on the Path to Universal Health Coverage: Final Report of the WHO Consultative Group on Equity and Universal Health Coverage" (WHO, 2012), www.who.int/choice/documents/making_fair_choices/en/.

developed in the public health domain may help in holding states to account in their duty to guarantee the right to health within the procedural framework defended in "The Right to Health in the Courts". I use Brazil as an illustrative example. Lastly, in "Rare Diseases and Children", the concluding one, I go back to the EB case in Bahia and discuss how children's entitlement to treatment for rare diseases may perhaps be justified within this framework.

THE RIGHTS-RESOURCES DILEMMA: DEFINING THE CONTENT OF SOCIAL RIGHTS UNDER RESOURCE SCARCITY AND MORAL-POLITICAL PLURALISM, *OR* WHO SHOULD WE TREAT WHEN RESOURCES ARE LIMITED, AS THEY ALWAYS ARE?

The Resources Conundrum

Resource scarcity presents important theoretical and practical challenges for the definition of the so-called *positive* duties of the state, that is duties to act to guarantee the civil, political, social and economic rights of its citizens. The costs of maintaining physical security, protecting private property, funding the electoral system, providing education and health and so forth at an optimal level will always exceed the resources available in any given society, both those privately held (i.e., held by individuals and companies) and, even more so, those held publicly (i.e., held by the state from taxes and other state income). It is always possible to increase the protection of personal security and property rights, for instance, by enhancing the number of police officers on duty, improving street lighting, investing in better equipment and so forth. It is always possible to increase the political participation of citizens in the political affairs of their country by increasing the number of poll stations, investing in programmes of political education, providing more public financing for political parties and so forth. It is always possible to improve education and health by increasing the number of teachers, nurses and doctors; improving their working conditions; investing in facilities and equipment; and so forth. I could, of course, go on and exhaust all the space of this chapter providing further examples of actions and measures that a state could, in principle, adopt to improve these and all the other areas (parks, national security, arts, environment, infrastructure, etc.) that the modern state is involved in financing mostly through the taxes collected from society. But my point, I hope, is already made. A state can always improve the quality of a public service or benefit provided to the citizen by increasing the amount of resources invested in that particular area,[17] but cannot, however rich, provide all public services and benefits to the population at their potential highest available standard at the same time.

---

[17] It can also, of course, do that by improving the efficiency of the service, i.e. doing more with the same amount of resources. But efficiency gains have limits, often very stringent, whereas improvements from more investment are often unlimited or much less stringent.

The richer the country, the higher its capacity, *in principle*, to provide a higher standard of public services and benefits to its population. But to provide the highest available standard in all areas and at the same time is never possible, not even *in principle*.[18] Health alone would consume all the resources of even the richest country and that would still not suffice to provide the whole population with the highest available standard of health. To see this vividly all one needs to do is imagine the aggregate cost of providing all expensive technology in treatment and equipment that continuously appears in the market to the whole of the population that may benefit – even if slightly – from it.[19] When one considers all the other areas previously mentioned in which the modern state is expected to invest, this becomes so obvious that no further argument would seem to be necessary.

Once this is understood, let us call it the *fact of scarcity*, the inadequacy of interpreting any social right, let alone health, as a right to the satisfaction of an individual's needs, irrespective of costs, becomes clear. As it is simply impossible to guarantee that high standard to everyone, it can only be guaranteed to some at the cost of others, in which case we are not talking of universal rights any longer, but of privileges, that is, private benefits, which are the antithesis of rights. As we shall see later, this is unfortunately how most Brazilian courts have been interpreting the right to health since its recognition in the 1988 Constitution. I call this the *needs-based interpretation of social rights*.

Rights and Scarcity

It follows from the discussion on scarcity in the preceding text that the content of any social right has to be determined within the necessarily limited resources available to the state. This is expressly recognised, of course, in the international and most domestic laws related to social rights, as, for instance, in article 4 of the International Convention on the Rights of the Child:

> States Parties shall undertake all appropriate legislative, administrative, and other measures for the implementation of the rights recognized in the present Convention. *With regard to economic, social and cultural rights, States Parties shall undertake such measures to the maximum extent of their available resources* and, where needed, within the framework of international co-operation. (emphasis added)

---

[18] It is important to emphasise the expression "in principle" because another important condition, which we will discuss further in the following text, is the political ability and willingness of a state to invest in public services, something that varies significantly from country to country.

[19] F. S. Vieira and I estimated the costs of doing this with only three new drugs for two diseases that affect a mere 1 per cent of the Brazilian population. It would cost around 4 per cent of Brazilian GDP. O. Ferraz and F. S. Vieira, "Direito à saúde, recursos escassos e equidade: os riscos da interpretação judicial dominante" (2009) 52 *Dados* 1 223, 251.

These drugs featured constantly in right to health cases in Brazil. See also the debate on the costly hepatitis C drug: S. Iyengar et al., "Prices, Costs, and Affordability of New Medicines for Hepatitis C in 30 Countries: An Economic Analysis" (2016) 13 *Plos Medicine* 5.

The inescapable fact of scarcity presents intractable problems for the task of defining the content of social rights. They are mainly related to the intractability of the following broad questions: (1) How should the phrase "maximum available resources" be interpreted?[20] (2) How should the state allocate its "maximum available resources" (however this is defined), given all those competing needs discussed previously, in a way that respects the social rights of all the citizens?

To help us apprehend in its full extent the difficulty of the task, let us break down these two broad questions into more specific ones. The expression "maximum available resources" can give rise to several different potential interpretations. In its most literal meaning, it refers to the amount of resources a government has available to spend in a certain fiscal year given the revenue it has managed to collect through taxes, fees, profits from companies it controls, loans, international aid, and so forth. It is often called "general government revenue" in the specialised literature and can be consulted in the so-called national accounts in transparent countries. Not surprisingly, countries vary significantly in their general government revenue because they vary in their endowment of natural resources; level of economic development; fiscal, industrial and economic policies; and so forth, that is in all variables that determine the general government revenue. To give a couple of concrete examples, let us look first at France and Italy, two European countries with a similar level of economic development yet a significant difference in general government revenues. In 2015, whereas France had a total revenue of EUR 1,166,276 billion Italy's was significantly lower at EUR 827,780.[21] Italy had therefore almost 25 per cent less available resources than France according to this measure. So, if we interpret "maximum available resources" in this empirical and neutral manner, that is as whatever a state collected as revenue in a given year, we will be forced to conclude that different countries, even of similar levels of economic development such as France and Italy, should have significant different levels of obligation to fulfil social and economic rights. That seems inadequate, as it leaves too much leeway for the state to determine the scope its own human rights obligations. Yet, what is the alternative? It seems hard to come up with a normative, non-arbitrary number as the level of total government revenue that a country ought to achieve to fulfil its obligation of using its "maximum available resources". Even if we use more relative indicators such as, for instance, general government revenue as percentage of GDP, how are we to say what exact percentage a state ought to attain? Is Mexico, the lowest Organisation for Economic Co-Operation and Development (OECD) country in terms of this indicator, at 23.7 per cent in violation of its human rights

---

[20] The same phrase is present in article 2 of the ICESCR, see note 6; the expression is also present in some domestic constitutions, such as the Constitution of the Republic of South Africa, 1996, arts. 25, 26 and 27.
[21] OECD, *National Accounts of OECD Countries, General Government Accounts* (2016), www.oecd-ilibrary.org/economics/national-accounts-of-oecd-countries-general-government-accounts-2016_na_gga-2017-en.

obligations? Is Norway, at 54.8 per cent, the highest among OECD countries, going beyond its obligations? Should the average of the OECD, about 40 per cent, be used as a benchmark?[22]

This brief and oversimplified discussion is nonetheless sufficient, in my view, to demonstrate the intractability of answering the first question, that is of how the phrase "maximum available resources" should be interpreted so we may move towards a more concrete definition of the *content of social rights*.[23] It is not surprising, under such indeterminacy, that so many are sceptical of the very idea of social rights, believing that they are not "real" rights, but rather hortatory statements to pressurise countries to improve the general socio-economic conditions of their population.[24] Once we look in more detail into the difficulties of answering the second question raised previously, this scepticism becomes even more understandable. To recall, how should the state allocate its "maximum available resources" (however this is defined), given all those competing needs of society, in a way that respects the social rights of all the citizens?

So that we can proceed in our inquiry, let us assume that "maximum available resources" is the same as general government revenue ("total revenue" for simplicity). Let us assume, further, that the total revenue of a particular state is 40 per cent of its GDP and that most of it is acquired through taxes.[25] I will call this the "supermacro level of resource allocation" for reasons that will become clear in the following text. The supermacro level determines the aggregate distribution of resources between government and society, that is the percentage of income that the state appropriates from society and the percentage it leaves in private hands through the traditional mechanism of taxation.[26]

Let us move then to the next complicated question we need to tackle: how ought the state allocate this resulting revenue from the super-macro allocation, that is its "maximum available resources", to fulfill social rights?[27]

---

[22] https://data.oecd.org/gga/general-government-revenue.htm#indicator-chart.
[23] Alicia Yamin's suggestion of using the human development index as "leading" or "background" indicators of economic and social rights compliance is interesting but does not go far enough in specifying the content of these rights (A. Yamin, "Reflections on Defining, Understanding, and Measuring Poverty in Terms of Violations of Economic and Social Rights under International Law" [1997] 4[2] *Georgetown Journal on Fighting Poverty* 273). See also, A. Kendrick, "Measuring Compliance: Social Rights and the Maximum Available Resources Dilemma" (2017) 39(3) *Human Rights Quarterly* 657.
[24] See Neier and Roth, for instance, for a credible discussion by two leading human rights activists about the difficulties of operationalizing social rights in the traditional manner followed for civil and political rights. A. Neier, "Social and Economic Rights: A Critique" (2006) 13(2) *Human Rights Brief* 1; K. Roth, "Defending Economic, Social and Cultural Rights: Practical Issues Faced by an International Human Rights Organization" (2004) 26(1) *Human Rights Quarterly* 63.
[25] A plausible assumption as 35 per cent of GDP is the approximate average tax revenue among OECD countries (https://stats.oecd.org/Index.aspx?DataSetCode=REV).
[26] This is of course, again, also a simplification, as there are many other ways in which the state influences the distribution of resources in a society.
[27] Note that I am simplifying the debate once more, as for us to know the actual supermacro distribution of resources among individuals in the population we need to disaggregate the tax

I will distinguish here between *macro, meso and micro* decisions, even if it simplifies, again, the much more complex scenario. *Macro-decisions* are those taken at the level of the whole government budget in the allocation of its total revenue (the supermacro level mentioned previously) into the large areas of government such as social security, health, education, justice, environment, agriculture, security, sports, culture, and so forth. They are often proposed by the executive and approved by the legislature in Western democracies, forming what is often called the *government's budget*. *Meso-decisions* are those taken at the level of each department in the allocation of the total budget among the several fixed expenses (capital and human resources), programmes and actions to be implemented. In health that includes a complex array of decisions such as how much to spend in the recruiting and training of health personnel (doctors, nurses, technicians), in the acquisition of health equipment, in the implementation of health prevention programmes, in each of the broad areas of medicine (cardio-vascular, oncology, infectious, neurology), and so forth. *Micro-decisions* are taken within each programme and action and often involve the distribution of services among individuals. In health, for instance, think of the difficult decision faced by many health departments around the world about whom, among several individuals with similar needs, should have priority in the access of a certain scarce health resource, such as renal dialysis, hip replacement surgery and organ transplant.

The difficulties are similar to that we saw previously at the "supermacro" level of total revenue. How much should a government devote to each of its departments? Is there a minimum that, say, health and education should receive before the government can invest in sports venues, cultural events or advertising (macro level)? Should new cancer drugs be allocated aditional resources when junior doctors or nurses are demanding a raise in their pay (meso level)? Which patients should have priority in the use of the limited machines of the renal dialysis unit in a local hospital (micro level)? See Figure 5.1.

---

revenue (35 per cent in our example) into the different groups and their specific contributions. The tax revenue does not tell us, for instance, if it is progressive or not, i.e., if it falls more heavily on those who are richer in society. This can be measured in several ways and I cannot discuss it in any detail here. One of the most interesting indicators is the decrease in the pre-tax (GINI coefficient). GINI is one of the most used indicators of inequality. It ranges from 0 to 1, 0 representing a perfectly equal society, where everyone has exactly the same income, and 1 representing the most unequal, where one person has 100 per cent of society's income. In all countries there is a reduction of pre-tax GINI through taxation and redistribution, but that varies significantly from country to country, ranging from about 45 per cent in Denmark and Sweden, to about 8 per cent in South Korea in OECD countries (the United States has a 17 per cent reduction). (See M. Roser and F. Ortiz-Ospina, "Income Inequality" [2017], https://ourworldindata.org/income-inequality/.) Comprehensive historical data is available from the OECD (https://stats.oecd.org/Index.aspx?DataSetCode=REV) and the World Bank (http://data.worldbank.org/indicator/SI.POV.GINI).

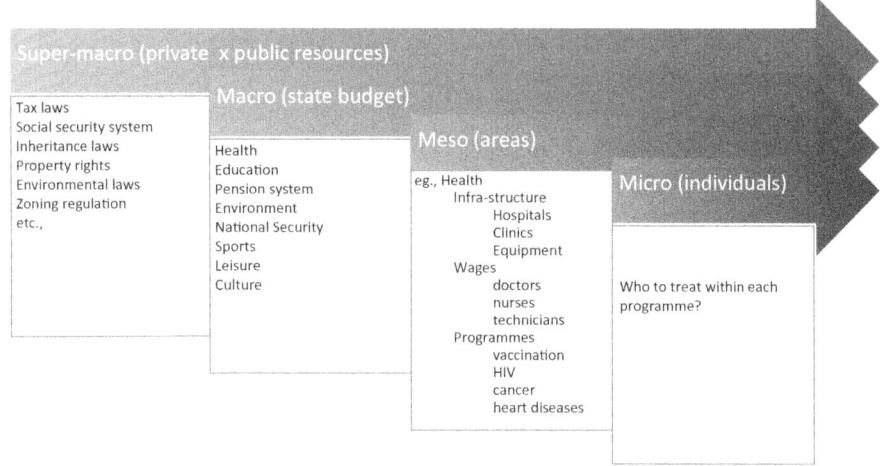

FIGURE 5.1 Levels of resource allocation decisions

There is no precise answer to any of these questions on which a reasonably extensive consensus can be formed. On the contrary, in any modern pluralistic society people will tend to disagree significantly about them depending on their political and moral views. If we think of the political-moral spectrum as a line running from a left, radical egalitarian point to a right, radical libertarian one, the closer one is to the right the less in favour one will be of any substantive government investment in any social service apart from law and order, that is policing, national security and courts. The closer to the left, the opposite will be true, that is people will tend to favour large-scale government investment in welfare systems such as health, education, housing, social security and so forth. Along the middle section of this spectrum several intermediate positions will be found.[28] This inevitable divergence of opinion, which we could call the "fact of pluralism" following John Rawls,[29] is the major challenge, in my view, that arises when human rights that entail positive duties on the state are incorporated in the legal system. Decisions that had hitherto been the quintessential stuff of politics[30] at all levels of resource distribution and allocation (supermacro, macro, meso and micro) are now expected to comply with the standards that rights are supposed to impose when understood in their traditional conception. Yet rights seem to provide no precise answers to

---

[28] I am aware that people's moral and political views do not fall that neatly into the simplified spectrum I set in the text merely as an illustrative device of the point that in a pluralistic society people will tend to fiercely disagree about the size and shape of government and public services.
[29] See J. Rawls, *Political Liberalism*, 6th ed. (New York: Columbia University Press, 2005).
[30] Issues that have traditionally been decided in democratic systems through continuous and permanent political battles, in the best scenario, and through raw power, lobbying and corruption in the worst.

any of these difficult distributive and allocative questions (more on this in "The Rights-Resources Dilemma".

A brief more concrete and recent real-life example illustrates vividly the nature and magnitude of the challenge. The major of London, Sadiq Khan, promised during the election campaign in 2016 that he would add a second police officer at each of the 629 wards of the city, which was the case then in only 100 wards.[31] The cost of these additional 500 and something officers would add up to several million pounds a year only in direct salary costs. Where would these resources come from? There are only a limited set of options: higher revenue (through, e.g., higher taxes), extra borrowing or reallocation from other areas. Whatever the option, or combination of options chosen, the point is that, as already noticed previously, any decision of a government that implies costs, and most of them do, is a complex exercise in allocating the limited resources available among a myriad of potential destinations. That is, they have what economists call *opportunity costs*. The amount spent to enhance policing in wards could have been spent elsewhere, for instance in the improvement of parks, other leisure facilities, arts and so forth.[32] Do the human rights to life, personal security and property that London citizens have help in finding an answer to these difficult allocative decisions? Is there an exact number of police officers per ward required by these rights? The answer seems to be in the negative.

Note that the complexity of the question results not simply, nor even mainly, from the empirical difficulty in knowing what exact number of police officers would be required to make Londoners completely safe. There might even be an approximate adequate, scientifically based answer to this question. Criminologists may well carry out studies that identify the ideal number of policemen per population required so that crime is fully prevented or is reduced to very low levels. But that would not imply that *there is therefore a right* to such numbers of policemen and a corresponding duty on the state to fund them. As already noted, the state has a myriad of other duties, rights related and not, that compete for the same limited resources. A zero-crime society, well apart from its dystopianism, would not be sustainable without significant losses in other areas where society's resources are also needed. The complexity of the question stems primarily from the difficulty of setting with reasonable precision the content of all these positive duties a society has. This is essentially a normative problem, not an empirical one, although the empirical difficulty compounds the normative problem. In other words, diffrent individuals will inevitably disagree about where resources should be allocated (the fact of

---

[31] www.mayorwatch.co.uk/sadiq-khan-announces-extra-dedicated-offers-for-every-london-ward/.
[32] As already mentioned, the decisions that set the exact amounts to be spent in each area are traditionally taken through the political process. In the present case, the Major's Budget, approved by the London Assembly (www.london.gov.uk/sites/default/files/2016-17finalmayors budget.pdf).

pluralism mentioned previously), and this disagreement is compounded, though not created, by a significant level of empirical uncertainty.

The Rights-Resources Dilemma

This intractability of the task of defining the content of resource-dependent rights leads to what we could call the *rights-resources dilemma*. Human rights, at least in their traditional conception widely accepted in most Western legal systems and in the international arena, are supposed to impose reasonably strong limits and guidance on what the state can and cannot do, and also what it ought to do for the citizens. In a rights-respecting democratic regime, the state should therefore not be totally free to allocate its limited resources in whatever way it sees fit, not even when backed by a strong electoral mandate. If rights are taken seriously, to use Ronald Dworkin's influential phrase, states must go about the task of allocating their resources at all levels (supermacro, macro, meso and micro) in a manner that respects rights.[33] Yet it seems impossible to determine, in our extremely complex societies, with their multitude of resource-dependent areas and diversity of opinions among citizens, with a minimum degree of precision and in a non-arbitrary manner how the myriad allocative decisions that lead to the specific levels of public services and benefits enjoyed by each citizen ought to be taken.

In the field of health, on which we shall focus from now on, where life is often directly at stake and the goods involved are particularly costly (especially when medical innovations are in question), the problem assumes even more dramatic contours. How much resources ought society to allocate to the protection of the health of its members in light of all the other resource-dependent actions and services on which it may want to invest (the macro level)? How ought health resources be allocated among areas, interventions and individuals (the meso and micro levels)?

If there are no right, that is reasonably precise answers to these questions, as I suggested, the important question that follows is this: what role, if any, does the recognition through law that health is a human right ought to play in this conundrum?

I have already mentioned one possible answer: that given by the sceptics. The right to health, or any social right, is not a "real" right, they would say. It does not possess a reasonably determinate content that can serve as a clear guide to what the state has to do, enabling thus accountability, political and legal (i.e., through courts). It is rather a generic hortatory statement of a generic goal that a decent society should pursue yet

---

[33] The phrase is the title of his seminal book and also of one of the chapters within it. See R. Dworkin, *Taking Rights Seriously* (London: Duckworth, 1977). As Dworkin properly states, when societies and their governments take rights seriously they accept that "it would be wrong to interfere [with someone's rights], or at least that some special grounds are needed for justifying any interference" (188).

whose precise contours are far from being sufficiently clear to enable the sort of strong accountability we expect rights to introduce in a political system. They are at best a different kind of right, aspirational, programmatic, whose legalisation, that is inclusion in constitutions or legislation, does not turn them into fully enforceable norms.[34]

This sceptical response raises several interesting theoretical and practical debates on the concept of a "real" right, the plausibility of calling rights what looks much closer to goals, and the actual effectiveness of "goal-like rights" in the advancement of individuals well-being. I cannot pursue them here.[35] Instead, I will now critically analyse the responses given by courts in some countries that have been grappling with the rights-resources dilemma on a regular (often daily) basis ever since social rights have been legally recognised in international and domestic law.

THE RIGHT TO HEALTH IN THE COURTS

The right to health is now constantly invoked in debates on how to allocate scarce resources among health needs, and the inevitable disputes that emerge from such debates are currently the object of thousands of lawsuits across the world, a phenomenon often called the *judicialisation of health*.[36] This judicialisation of the intractable matter of allocation of scarce resources is an inevitable corollary of the legalisation of the right to health (i.e., its legal recognition in constitutions and ordinary laws). Once the right to health is legalised, those who have the possibility to use lawyers and courts to enhance their access to health services and benefits will likely do so. Legalisation leads to judicialisation. How should courts respond when called to get involved in the intractable rights-resources connundrum discussed in the previous section of this chapter?

Inadequate Responses: A Right to Everything and a Right to Nothing

Judges have by and large responded in two different, almost opposite ways to these attempts of citizens to challenge in courts the allocative decisions of health authorities.[37] Many have refused to engage in any strong review of allocative

---

[34] For a classic discussion of this idea in the American context see L. G. Sager, "Fair Measure: The Legal Status of Underenforced Constitutional Norms" (1978) 91(6) *Harvard Law Review* 1212.
[35] For a good discussion, see J. W. Nickel, "Goals and Rights: Working Together?", in M. Langford, A. Sumner and A. E. Yamin (eds.), *The Millennium Development Goals and Human Rights: Past, Present and Future* (New York: Cambridge University Press, 2013).
[36] For a comprehensive treatment of the issue see A. Yamin and S. Gloppen, (eds.), *Litigating Health Rights: Can Courts Bring More Justice to Health?* (Cambridge, MA: Harvard University Press, 2011), 435.
[37] I have discussed these two approaches in more detail in O. Ferraz, "Between Abdication and Usurpation: Social Rights in the Courts of Brazil, India and South Africa", in O. Vilhena, U. Baxi and F. Viljoen (eds.), *Transformative Constitutionalism: Comparing the Apex Courts of Brazil, India and South Africa* (Pretoria: Pretoria University Law Press, 2013).

decisions made by politicians and public health officials on grounds that courts lack legitimacy, or institutional capacity, or both to interfere with the health budget. Such deferential approach persists even in countries where the right to health has been expressly recognised in the constitution, leading many rights' activists to complain of an alleged abdication of judges of their duty to protect this and other social rights.[38] A common response is that although constitutionalisation does indeed deal to a certain extent with the legitimacy problem, neutering blunt separation of powers objections to judicial interference, it does however not solve the difficulties mentioned earlier of determining the exact amount of resources that should be devoted to health. Under such conditions of indeterminacy and political disagreement, strong judicial interference would risk not only displacing government's presumptively legitimate (as democratically supported) choices but also diverting resources from some individuals to others without appropriate justification.

The United Kingdom offers a good illustration of this approach. The following and often-quoted passage from the famous Child B case sums up this position:

> I have no doubt that in a perfect world any treatment which a patient, or a patient's family, sought would be provided if doctors were willing to give it, no matter how much it costs, particularly when a life was potentially at stake. It would however, in my view, be shutting one's eyes to the real world if the court were to proceed on the basis that we do live in such a world. It is common knowledge that health authorities of all kinds are constantly pressed to make ends meet. They cannot pay their nurses as much as they would like; they cannot provide all the treatments they would like; they cannot purchase all the extremely expensive medical equipment they would like; they cannot carry out all the research they would like; they cannot build all the hospitals and specialist units they would like. Difficult and agonising judgments have to be made as to how a limited budget is best allocated to the maximum advantage of the maximum number of patients. That is not a judgment which the court can make. In my judgment, it is not something that a health authority such as this authority can be fairly criticised for not advancing before the court.[39]

---

[38] D. Bilchitz, "Giving Socio-Economic Rights Teeth: The Minimum Core and Its Importance" (2002) *South African Law Journal* 119.

[39] *R v Cambridge Health Authority* [1995] 2 All ER 129, whose leading opinion was given by Tom Bingham, who went on to become Lord Chief Justice in 1996 and Senior Law Lord in 2000. The other judges in that case were Sir Stephen Brown P and Simon Brown LJ. See also the South African case: *Soobramoney v Minister of Health (Kwazulu-Natal)* (CCT32/97) [1997] ZACC 17; 1998 (1) SA 765 (CC); 1997 (12) BCLR 1696 (27 November 1997), citing Child B, and stating: "The provincial administration which is responsible for health services in KwaZulu-Natal has to make decisions about the funding that should be made available for health care and how such funds should be spent. These choices involve difficult decisions to be taken at the political level in fixing the health budget, and at the functional level in deciding upon the priorities to be met. A court will be slow to interfere with rational decisions taken in good faith by the political organs and medical authorities whose responsibility it is to deal with such matters."

Other courts have taken a totally different approach, seeing in the constitutionalisation of the right to health and other social rights a sufficient mandate to interfere strongly with these traditional health policy issues without much fear of acting illegitimately or inexpertly. On the contrary, and often using a strong rhetoric against alleged political omission, administrative incompetence and corruption, they have granted claimants requests for health resources such as treatments, medicines, equipment and so forth without much regard (or any in many cases) to the reasons presented by health authorities not to provide them in the public system. The courts rationale in these cases is very often based exclusively on the right to health recognised in the constitution, domestic laws or international treaties, interpreted in a very expansive way as a right to any health benefit needed by an individual. Perhaps the most prominent examples of this approach can be found in some South American courts, and the most extreme is perhaps to be found in Brazil. The following extract from a leading Brazilian case decided in the SFT provides a good summary of this approach, which I call the *needs-based interpretation* of the right to health:

> The right to health – as well as a fundamental right of all individuals – represents an inextricable constitutional consequence of the right to life ... The interpretation of a programmatic norm cannot transform it into a toothless constitutional promise ... Between protecting the inviolability of the right to life, an inalienable fundamental right guaranteed by the Constitution itself (art. 5°, caput) or ensuring, against this fundamental prerogative, a financial and secondary interest of the state, I believe – once this dilemma is established – ethical and legal reasons impose on the judge one single and possible option: unswerving respect for life.[40]

Both approaches seem to me understandable but problematic. The deferential approach does seem to deprive the idea that health is a human right from much, if not all of its meaning. As I argued in the preceding text, the concept of rights implies at least some reasonably determined boundaries around individual interests that ought to be respected, protected or provided to everyone in society. When all that courts have to say when dealing with a right-to-health claim is that government should have ample discretion to determine how to allocate its limited resources, the idea of a right to health is playing little, if any role. However, when courts do the exact opposite, simply ignoring government's decisions and imposing their own, often with no regard to the resource limitation conundrum and the perennial problem of unequal access to justice that plagues to a lesser or greater extent all judicial systems, the idea of a right to health is not being honoured either. On the

---

[40] PET 1.246-SC and RE 271.286 AgR- RS (2000), quoting Min. Celso de Mello decision on the ARE 730.741/SP.
  My translation from the Portuguese. Full text, in Portuguese, available at the STF website: www.stf.jus.br/portal/processo/verProcessoPeca.asp?id=133345682&tipoApp=.pdf.

contrary, an inegalitarian form of privilege is being implemented, rewarding some (those with better access to courts, often the better off) and leaving most behind.[41]

Is there any way out of this conundrum?

More Adequate Responses

Important attempts have been made to deal with the rights-resource dilemma in a better manner than the two extreme inadequate responses discussed in the previous section. We can classify them into two categories: procedural or substantive, depending on where they fall in the spectrum between those two extremes as defined in the following text.

What I call "procedural" responses see courts as capable of exercising a legitimate and important role in guaranteeing the fairness of the *process* of decision making in the allocation of health resources. Rather than interfering with the substantive outcomes of resource allocation decisions (e.g., whether a certain treatment ought to be financed, or a certain patient ought to receive a certain treatment), courts should limit themselves to making sure that these decisions are made through a *fair process*. Procedural approaches follow naturally from the recognition that there are no right and precise answers to the difficult priority-settting questions that inescapably follow from the fact of scarcity discussed in the subsection "The Rights-Resources Dilemma: Defining the Content of Social Rights". Although not developed with courts in mind, but rather health authorities in charge of allocating health resources, Norman Daniels's well-received framework of "accountability for reasonableness" is perhaps the best argued and most detailed version of a procedural approach.[42] As he convincingly argues, given the facts of scarcity and pluralism discussed, reasonable disagreement about how to solve "conflicts among claimants within and across rights"[43] is inevitable and requires, thus, a procedural rather than a

---

[41] See, for a more detailed discussion, the works cited in note 9.

[42] In his excellent book, Syrett provides a defence of accountability for reasonableness as a legitimate and robust framework for the involvement of courts in health allocation decisions. K. Syrett, *Law, Legitimacy and the Rationing of Health Care: A Contextual and Comparative Perspective* (New York: Cambridge University Press, 2007). Also, N. Daniels et al., "Role of the Courts in the Progressive Realization of the Right to Health: Between the Threat and the Promise of Judicialization in Mexico" (2015) 1(3) *Health Systems & Reform* 229: "the courts should, where they have the discretion, *focus on promoting an equal right to health care for all*, which requires a broad view of the entire health system and a *focus on the fairness of allocation implications for different populations*" (233).

[43] Daniels rather plausible point is that, because different reasonable principles of distributive justice will necessarily lead to different and reasonable conflicting answers, i.e. people will reasonably disagree on what the correct one is, the solution can only be procedural (N. Daniels, *Just Health: Meeting Health Needs Fairly* [New York: Cambridge University Press, 2008], 328) I cannot engage here in a deep analysis here of Daniels's rich and complex proposal and the criticisms it has attracted. For a good discussion, see A. Rid, "Justice and Procedure: How Does 'Accountability for Reasonableness' Result in Fair Limit-Setting Decisions?" (2009) 35(1) *Journal of Medical Ethics* 12.

substantive solution, that is a "systematic rationale" to "address the underlying moral disagreements among reasonable people".[44] It requires, at a minimum, "the careful collection of evidence for interventions, the thorough review of arguments for establishing particular priorities, the involvement of all relevant stakeholders in the process, and transparency for all aspects of the process, including the rationales for the priorities adopted".[45] Lawyers will immediately identify the proximity of many of these elements (transparency, rationality, participation, justification) with the procedural legal safeguards ("due process") present in the administrative law in most democratic legal systems.[46]

Such a procedural accountability role is neither trivial nor easy to perform, unlike some critics often assume. Done well, it could potentially promote a significant improvement in the quality of decision making in health, especially in less developed countries where administrative bodies often lack in experience and expertise. Yet this approach, focused on the procedure rather than the substantive outcome, does fall way short of what many people believe ought to be a strong protection of rights. For them, the procedural model (sometimes called the *administrative model*)[47] relegates social rights norms to a second-class position, no different from any other norm in administrative law.[48]

As much as the requirements of transparency, participation and rationality go way beyond the deferential end of the spectrum of accountability, they are still "only" procedural, that is, they do not guarantee any particular substantive benefit to the right-holder. This is what motivates many to search for a more sustantive approach, that is one capable of giving the right to health some substantive content, even if not as expansive as the one I have already criticised, which is currently popular in some Latin American countries.

Substantive Approaches

In an attempt to move beyond procedural approaches and justify a more substantive content for social rights in general and the right to health in particular, many have argued for what is often referred to as a *minimum threshold* or a *minimum core* approach. The idea is that, whatever the complexities entailed by the issues I discussed previously (scarcity and disagreement), there are minimum levels of

---

[44] Ibid., 328.
[45] Ibid., 300.
[46] Daniels highlights this: "Accountability for reasonableness provides a systematic rationale for key elements of fair process in what is commonly thought to be part of a rights based approach" (ibid., 328) See also Syrett, *Law, Legitimacy and the Rationing of Health Care*, 266.
[47] C. Sunstein, "Social and Economic Rights? Lessons from South Africa" (Coase-Snador Working Paper Series in Law and Economics, 2001),
  http://chicagounbound.uchicago.edu/cgi/viewcontent.cgi?article=1454&context=law_and_economics.
[48] See Bilchitz, "Giving Socio-Economic Rights Teeth", 119.

education, health, housing and so forth that everyone should be able to enjoy and states are under a duty to guarantee.

The initial appeal of this approach seems clear. It fits better the prevalent idea of rights as substantive limits to what the state may do (and benefits it ought to provide) to individuals. It also seems to strike a more plausible balance between the "empty" deferential approach and the expansive unrealistic approach criticised previously.

Under the minimum core approach, society still has ample scope to disagree about how to allocate limited resources, but must comply at least with a minimum core. If it falls short, a violation of social rights obtains. Above that threshold, it is free to allocate its resources through the usual political mechanisms. The minimum threshold seems to allow our interests in health, education, housing, food, water and so forth to operate in the traditional manner of rights.[49] It imposes constraints on what can be done to individuals in the interests of others and society as a whole.

Yet although the minimum core approach seems at first rather plausible, it suffers from several significant conceptual and pragmatic difficulties. First, although the minimum threshold is supposed to solve the resource scarcity problem, its very determination is itself affected by it. This is because determining the minimum core will not escape intractable decisions about how to allocate limited resources among different areas and needs. Focusing on a minimum core rather than on an ideal level may, of course, simplify somewhat the task, especially in more developed societies where resources are more plentiful.[50] Yet, once one starts to think about what that minimum should contain it becomes clear that the exercise is still very complex, especially in low- and middle-income countries where resources are more limited, and especially in some fields like health where one is often dealing with tragic choices between life and death.

Imagine a middle-income country like Brazil or South Africa that has included social and economic rights to health, housing and education in its constitution. It must determine the minimum threshold of all these rights at the same time. Should the minimum include only primary education, or primary and secondary education? Should there be a minimum curriculum to be covered by all state schools? Should there be a minimum amount of sports and music activities, which require a certain amount of physical resources like fields, special classrooms, teachers and equipment? The same exercise has to be done for housing and health, and any other social right recognised in the legal system.

For the minimum threshold to fulfil the role that is expected of it, all these questions must be answered contemporaneously and in light of the available resources in the relevant community and also, it is important to emphasise, other

---

[49] Or, as expressed by K. Young in an insightful article: "With the minimum core concept as its guide, economic and social rights are supposed to enter the hard work of hard law" ("The Minimum Core of Economic and Social Rights: A Concept in Search of Content" [2008] 33 *Yale International Law Journal* 113, 114).

[50] See J. King, *Judging Social Rights* (Cambridge: Cambridge University Press, 2012), 37.

interests not formally recognised as rights but on which that community is willing to invest, for example parks, sports, culture and so forth. Some will believe that the parks of the community are in a poor state and ought to receive more resources for improvement and maintenance. Others will want better trained and paid teachers for the schools. Others will regard that more hospitals should be built and/or the existing ones should be better equipped. Yet others will complain that there are not enough police officers in their area. We seem to be back, thus, with the problem that the minimum core was supposed to solve, that is, determining its content will involve that same intractable exercise of resource allocation along those four dimensions (supermacro, macro, meso and micro) in a context of scarcity and political disagreement.[51]

Once these difficulties are taken on board, the procedural approach discussed in the preceding text starts to look like the only plausible one. The crucial point is this. Under such complex circumstances of resource scarcity and moral-political pluralism about how resources ought to be allocated, politically accountable institutions rather than courts seem to provide more legitimate frameworks to adopt substantive answers. Law and courts may still be able to provide the procedural safeguards for the political decision-making process to be fair, but it becomes rather suspect as a legitimate means of imposing substantive outcomes different from those arrived at through technical and political institutions, especially when they follow those procedural safeguards.[52]

---

[51] The same point seems to have been made by Young: "Without this clarity, the concept cannot supply a predetermined content to economic and social rights, rank the value of particular claims, or set the level and criteria of state justification required for a permissible infringement. Indeed, I suggest that it is unlikely that the concept will ever offer the relative determinacy required for these three tests. Yet it can assist as an object of interpretive agreement-or disagreement-around claims for socioeconomic protection" ("The Minimum Core of Economic and Social Rights", 116). Some also claim that the language of the minimum core reinforces neoliberalism (ibid., 174).

[52] That does not mean that judicial review is automatically undemocratic. My view on this perennial debate is that democracy does not imply any predetermined and unique set of institutions and practices. It requires institutions and practices that implement as well as possible its underlying value of political equality, but those can vary in form, power division and combination. The ultimate aim is that the decisions that affect everyone are taken through a procedure that respects the political equality of all citizens (i.e., their equal right to participate in those decisions) and their other individual rights. The right to equal political participation is better protected through an institutional design that allows individuals to elect representatives with whom they identify to an assembly that discusses and enacts rules that the whole collectivity is bound to follow. This is the usual function of parliaments in Western democracies. The legitimacy of judicial review will depend on whether it improves the overall legitimacy of the political system of a particular society by correcting the failures, not by simply overruling, the decisions of the representative assembly when they fail to respect political equality or other individual rights. For a good discussion on this see J. Waldron, *Law and Disagreement* (New York: Oxford University Press, Clarendon Press, 1999), 344 and R. Dworkin, *Justice for Hedgehogs* (Cambridge, MA: Harvard University Press, 2011), 379 ff.

It is true that procedural review cannot provide as assertive a protection to social rights as we have become used to expect when civil and political rights are at stake, as political bodies continue to have significant freedom to determine their policies in health, education, housing and so forth. But I believe that many of those who reject the procedural approach underestimate somewhat both the capacity of political and administrative bodies to interpret and implement in good faith their constitutional duties and the potential of procedural judicial review to provide meaningful accountability.[53] Procedural judicial review of the decision-making process of allocation of scarce resources can help improve the fairness of that process, which is by no means an irrelevant role for courts. To do it well and effectively, however, courts ought to become more familiar with the work of public health and other experts who have been grapppling with this difficult task and trying to develop principles to deal with it for a long time.

In "Universal Health Coverage and the Right to Health" I briefly discuss the idea of UHC and a recent WHO report on principles of priority setting that, in my view, ought to be closely studied by lawyers and judges involved in right-to-health adjudication.

UNIVERSAL HEALTH COVERAGE AND THE RIGHT TO HEALTH

As we have seen previously, the idea of a right to health was firstly recognised, in the international realm, in the constitution of the WHO in 1946. Since then, it has performed a leading role in advancing the goal of improving the health of the world population through research, technical support and standard setting. It is a little surprising, therefore, how little engagement one finds in right-to-health adjudication with the work of the WHO, other public health bodies and public health literature. This is particularly troubling given the difficulties we have discussed in determining the content of the right to health. Rather than tap into the rich literature and expertise developed by those engaged in the daily grind of health systems around the world, judges have by and large either taken a hands-off approach, refraining from any engagement as if it was not in their remit to interfere with health policy, or have taken the arrogant attitude of interfering assertively without paying much or any regard to the opinion of public health experts (see "The Right to Health in the Courts").

If the right to health is to serve any positive role in the advancement of health conditions in the population through the procedural review framework defended in the preceding text, lawyers and courts must start to engage in earnest with the literature and expertise developed in the realm of public health, in particular

---

[53] This is an empirical and highly contextual issue, as different countries vary significantly in the quality and performance of their institutions, their levels of corruption and so forth. All the same, many supporters of substantive judicial review of social rights seem to overlook this point. See Bilchitz, "Giving Socio-Economic Rights Teeth".

the recent yet crucial idea of UHC and the growing corpus of work developing around criteria for the prioritisation of resources in the path toward UHC.

UHC expresses, in more technical and practical terms, what the right to health ultimately aims to achieve. It aims to extend to everyone (universally) the best possible package of goods and services (coverage) available within the limited resources. As stated by the WHO, where the concept of UHC was developed and put forward, UHC is "by definition, a practical expression of the concern for health equity an the right to health".[54]

But even if UHC and the right to health do not correspond perfectly,[55] these debates are at the minimum extremely relevant for the intractable task of finding a more precise and substantive determination of the content of the right to health. It is therefore regrettable and surprising, I insist, that so few legal discussions on the content of the right to health engage with this rich and sophisticated literature on health resources prioritisation.

The recent report of the WHO Consultative Group on Equity and Universal Health Coverage, *Making Fair Choices on the Path to Universal Health Coverage*,[56] is perhaps the most relevant for those involved in the adjudication of the right to health.

The report, co-authored by a interdisciplinary group of experts including doctors, philosophers and lawyers, and led by Norwegian public health experts Trygve Ottersen and Ole Norheim, departs from the same premises I have highlighted earlier, that is that resources are scarce and that individuals disagree about the correct (i.e., fairest) way of distributing these resources among the myriad health needs of the relevant population. They start by expressly acknowledging, thus, the importance of robust and fair procedures for making these hard decisions, endorsing, that is, Norman Daniels's accountability for reasonableness approach also discussed, which requires transparency, reasonableness, participation and rewiewability.

As the report makes clear, however, the leeway left for decision-making authorities is not as large as usually assumed. This is due to further limitations embedded in the very concept of UHC, which has, as we shall see, a strong egalitarian component. National authorities have three main clear responsibilities in their effort towards

---

[54] World Health Organization, *Positioning Health in the Post-2015 Development Agenda* (2013), www.who.int/topics/millennium_development_goals/post2015/WHOdiscussionpaper_October2012.pdf. See also the WHO, *Health Systems Financing: The Path to Universal Coverage* (2010), www.who.int/whr/2010/en/ (accessed on 23 August 2017). The first explicit reference to "universal coverage" by the WHO appears in one of the reports to the 58th General Assembly in 2005, entitled *Sustainable Health Financing, Universal Coverage, and Health Social Security*. See J. C. de Noronha, "Universal Health Coverage: How to Mix Concepts, Confuse Objectives, and Abandon Principles" (2013) 29(5) *Cadernos de Saúde Pública* 847.

[55] For a critical analysis of the similarities and differences between the right to health and UHC see G. Ooms et al., "Great Expectations for the World Health Organization: A Framework Convention on Global Health to Achieve Universal Health Coverage" (2014) 128(2) *Public Health* 173.

[56] Ottersen, "Making Fair Choices on the Path to Universal Health Coverage".

UHC: *to expand priority services, to expand the access to these services and to reduce the financial burden of the population, that is out-of-pocket payments.* As the report makes clear:

> [I]n each of these dimensions, countries are faced with a critical choice: Which services to expand first, whom to include first, and how to shift from out-of-pocket payment toward prepayment? A commitment to fairness – and the overlapping concern for equity – and a commitment to respecting individuals' rights to health care must guide countries in making these choices. For fair progressive realization of UHC, the three critical choices and the trade-offs between the dimensions must be carefully addressed.[57]

The report then goes on to specify in more detail what a commitment to fairness and equity involves and reach rather determinate principles that restrict significantly the range of acceptable decisions open to the authorities. The authors of the report put forward three main overarching principles for prioritisation towards UHC:

1. Priority services ought to be chosen according to cost-effectiveness, priority to the worse off, and financial risk protection.
2. Priority services should be first extended to everyone before other services are covered.
3. Particular care should be taken so as disadvantaged groups (such as low-income groups and rural populations) are not left behind.

These principles are still rather generic, of course, and therefore open to interpretation, for example about what should be regarded as cost-effective, how to define the worse off and how to determine financial burden. Yet, once these are defined (and it is the duty of the decision-making authorities to define and publicise these in light of the principles of reasonableness, transparency and participation), the three principles become specific enough and provide important guidance for the priority-setting decisions to be taken by health authorities.[58] To highlight this, the authors suggest a set of five of what they call "unacceptable trade-offs", that is allocative decisions that would fall foul of the three overarching principles reccomended. Here are the decisions that the report would consider unaceptable in light of its three main principles:

1. To expand coverage for low- or medium-priority services before there is near universal coverage for high-priority services;
2. To give high priority to very costly services whose coverage will provide substantial financial protection when the health benefits are very small compared to alternative, less costly services;

---

[57] Ibid., x.
[58] Unless, of course, one interprets reasonableness in a more substantive manner, but then the framework would cease to be simply about procedural fairness and become substantive.

3. To expand coverage for well-off groups before doing so for worse-off groups when the costs and benefits are not vastly different;
4. To first include in the universal coverage scheme only those with the ability to pay and not include informal workers and the poor and
5. To shift from out-of-pocket payment toward mandatory prepayment in a way that makes the financing system less progressive.[59]

The WHO report has, expectedly, generated controversy and an interesting debate that I cannot pursue here.[60] It is, moreover, only a report, that is, despite the expertise of its authors and the respectability of the organisation that has sponsored it, it has no direct normative force. But it is this sort of literature that can and should be used, in my view, to help courts to play a more meaningful and credible role when involved in the difficult task of adjudicating the right to health. It provides judges with crucial insight into the administrative realm of priority setting and offer important tools for them to review more robustly the fairness of that process.

I will now attempt to illustrate how this might work using right-to-health litigation in Brazil as an example.

THE RIGHT TO HEALTH IN BRAZIL

We have already seen how the prevalent interpretation of the right to health in Brazil as a "right to everything" is inadequate as it simply ignores, with potential and likely pernicious effects, the need to prioritise health resources. Here I suggest what in my view would be a legitimate and robust approach to be taken by Brazilian courts, inspired by Daniels's accountability for reasonableness framework, UHC and the WHO report discussed in the previous section. For that I must give a little more detailed information about the Brazilian constitutional system.

The Brazilian constitution of 1988, nicknamed the "Citizen Constitution" ("Constituição Cidadã"), not only included a comprehensive list of so-called civil liberties (art. 5) that had been curtailed during the two decades of military rule (1964–1985), but also an extensive list of social and economic rights such as health, education, social security and assistance (art. 6), and a long list of labour rights including a minimum wage (arts. 7 ff). It also puts beyond doubt its social egalitarian nature right from the preamble and the first four articles, dedicated to what it names the "Fundamental Principles".[61] Article 3 is particularly relevant for the interpretation of

[59] Ottersen, "Making Fair Choices on the Path to Universal Health Coverage", xii.
[60] Rumbold et al., "Universal Health Coverage, Priority Setting, and the Human Right to Health".
[61] "We, the representatives of the Brazilian People, convened in the national constituent assembly to institute a democratic state for the purpose of ensuring the exercise of **social** and individual rights, liberty, security, well-being, development, *equality* and justice as supreme values of a fraternal, pluralist and unprejudiced society, founded on social harmony and committed, in the internal and international orders, to the peaceful settlement of disputes,

all constitutional norms, as it sets out the fundamental objectives of the Brazilian Republic. For our purposes, it is important to highlight subsections I and III, emphasising the aims of creating a "free, just and solidary society" (I) and of eradicating poverty and substandard living conditions and of *reducing social and regional inequalities* (III).[62] The same aims are repeated in the specific chapters of the Constitution that deal with the economic system.[63] In the specific field of health, article 196 formulates the right to health in the following manner:

> Article 196. Health is a right of all and a duty of the state and shall be guaranteed by means of social and economic policies aimed at reducing the risk of illness and other hazards and at the *universal and egalitarian access* to actions and services for its promotion, protection and recovery.[64] (emphasis added)

All of these constitutional terms and expressions are, of course, open to interpretation and, as such, disagreement about their actual meaning. What does a just and solidary society look like? What does egalitarian access to health actions and services mean beyond the prohibition of obvious discrimination? Yet despite the open and contested nature of these terms, they clearly impose certain limits on what can be regarded as valid and legitimate interpretations of the constitution. The principles suggested in the *Making Fair Choices* WHO report seem to me to express rather well the egalitarian spirit of the Brazilian constitution and offer an important guide in the interpretation of the "universal and egalitarian access" clause inserted in article 196.[65]

It is difficult to argue, for example, that extending the provision of costly medicines that add at best a few weeks at the end of the lives of urban and relatively well-off patients in their sixties, seventies and eighties is an allocative choice that would respect the right to health within any plausible interpretation of article 196 trascribed

---

promulgate, under the protection of God, this Constitution of the Federative Republic of Brazil" (Constitution of the Federative Republic of Brazil [1988]) (emphasis added).

[62] Art. 3 The fundamental objectives of the Federative Republic of Brazil are:
 I – to build a free, just and solidary society;
 II – to guarantee national development;
 III – to eradicate poverty and substandard living conditions and to reduce social and regional inequalities;
 IV – to promote the well-being of all, without prejudice as to origin, race, sex, colour, age and any other forms of discrimination.

[63] Art. 170 establishes that private property serves a "social function" (III) and repeats "reduction of social and regional inequalities" as an aim of the economy (VII).

[64] My translation.

[65] Although some fear that it does the opposite, corroding the right to health recognised in the Brazilian Constitution. The fear seems to be that the language of "coverage", as opposed to "access" or "use" favours market solutions such as health insurance "moving quickly towards transforming human health into a commodity and liquidating the principle that health needs should determine access to and use of health services rather than the ability to pay" (de Noronha, "Universal Health Coverage", 849)

previously when basic health services are lacking for a large portion of the population. It goes clearly against the unnaceptable trade-offs 1 and 3 of the WHO report.

To illustrate this point let us compare two well-established programmes of the Brazilian public health system: the Programa Saúde da Família (Family Health programme, hereafter PSF) and the Política de Assistência Farmacêutica (Pharmaceutical Assistance Policy, hereafter PNM).

The PSF provides a broad range of primary care services through local family health teams, including at least one physician, one nurse, one nurse assistant, and four community health agents (*agentes comunitários de saúde*, ACS). Each team is assigned to a designated geographical area and is responsible for enrolling and monitoring the health status of up to 3,500 people; providing primary care, health promotion and education services; and making referrals to other levels of care.[66] As of 2009, 27,324 PSF teams covered 98 million people (50 per cent of Brazil's population).

The PNM was approved in 1998[67] and consolidated in 2004[68] and aims at offering equitable access to pharmaceutical assistance to the whole population.[69] In terms of financing, it is divided into three components: basic, strategic and specialised.[70] This division is roughly based on cost and public health criteria, which also determines, to some extent, the primary responsibility for funding (The Federal Government is in exclusive charge of the strategic programmes such as tuberculosis, hanseniasis, malaria, and AIDS, whereas the basic component – mostly drugs for primary care – and the specialised – high-cost drugs – are negotiated among the Federal Government, states and municipalities).[71]

Although the basic component should be available free at the Basic Units of Health (rough equivalent to general practitioner surgeries in the United Kingdom) across the country, it is known that a significant portion of the population faces difficulties in

---

[66] Brazilian Ministry of Health, "Programa saúde da família" (2002) 2(7) *Revista Brasileira de Saúde da Família* 17D. As cited in L. J. Monahan et al., "Impact of the Family Health Program on Gastroenteritis in Children in Bahia, Northeast Brazil: An Analysis of Primary Care-Sensitive Conditions" (2013) 3 *Journal of Epidemiology and Global Health* 175.

[67] Brazil, Ministry of Health, Portaria n° 3.916/GM/MS, de 30 de outubro de 1998, http://bvsms.saude.gov.br/bvs/saudelegis/gm/1998/prt3916_30_10_1998.html.

[68] Brazil, Ministry of Health, Resolução n° 338, de 06 de maio de 2004, http://bvsms.saude.gov.br/bvs/saudelegis/cns/2004/res0338_06_05_2004.html. See also Brazil, Decreto n° 7.508, de 28 de junho de 2011 establishing, in art. 28, that the guarantee of universal and egalitarian access to medicines require that "prescriptions must be in accordance with Rename [the national medicines list] and the Protocolos Clínicos e Diretrizes Terapêuticas [PCDT, Clinical Protocols] … and have been prescribed within the state health system facilities", www.planalto.gov.br/ccivil_03/_ato2011-2014/2011/decreto/d7508.htm.

[69] For a good overview see F. Vieira, "Pharmaceutical Assistance in the Brazilian Public Health Care System" (2010) 27(2) *Revista Panamericana de Salud Pública* 149.

[70] Brazil, Ministry of Health, Portaria n° 204, de 29 de janeiro de 2007, http://bvsms.saude.gov.br/bvs/saudelegis/gm/2007/prt0204_29_01_2007_comp.html.

[71] Ibid.

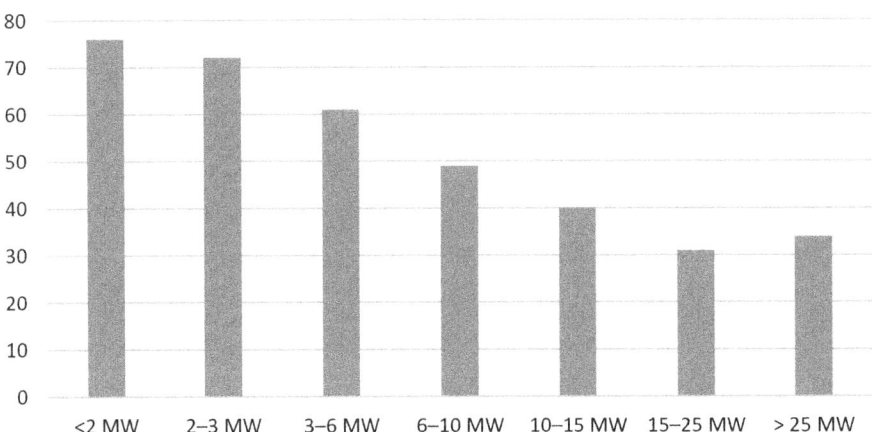

FIGURE 5.2 Out-of-pocket expenditure on drugs as percentage of total out-of-pocket expenditure by family income
Source: Pesquisa de Orçamentos Familiares (Family Budgets Survey), IBGE 2008, as reported by Medici[72]

accessing these medicines and end up paying for them out of pocket.[73] It is also known that out-of-pocket expenses with health affect more the low-income population as it consumes a higher percentage of their income, and out-of-pocket expenses with medicines as a percentage of total out-of-pocket expenses with health also follow a regressive economic gradient, that is, the lower the family income the higher the percentage of their health budget they spend on drugs, as Figure 5.2 shows.[74]

---

[72] See A. Medici, "Medicamentos Excepcionais e Prioridades de Saúde no Brasil" (*Instituto de Direito Sanitário Aplicado*, 12 September 2010), www.idisa.org.br/site/documento_4062_0_medicamentos-excepcionais-e-prioridades-de-saude-no-brasil.html. The minimum wage in Brazil is a constitutional right (art. 7, IV) and updated through ordinary legislation. In 2008 it was R$415,00 reais, just less than US$200.

[73] The government has indirectly admitted the lack of availability by introducing the programme Farmácia Popular, which offers discounted or co-payment (not free) medicines through a partnership with private pharmacies. See V. Paniz, "Acesso a medicamentos em população assistida por diferentes modelos de atenção básica nas regiões Sul e Nordeste do Brasil" (unpublished PhD thesis, Universidade Federal de Pelotas, 2009),
www.epidemio-ufpel.org.br/uploads/teses/Tese%20Vera%20Paniz.pdf, 224. See also L. C. F. de Oliveira, M. M. A. Assis and A. R. Barboni, "Pharmaceutical Assistance in the Basic Units of Health: From the National Drug Policy to the Basic Attention to Health" (2010) 15(3) *Revista Ciência & Saúde Coletiva* 3561. The paper claims that "the greater part of Brazilian municipalities, especially the poorest, suffer with low availability and discontinuity in the offer of essential medicines in the ABS unities [primary care units]".

[74] See L. P. Garcia et al., "Brazilian Family Spending on Medicines: An Analysis of Data from the Family Budget Surveys, 2002–2003 and 2008–2009" (2013) 29(8) *Cadernos de Saúde Pública* 1605.

What Course without Evils?

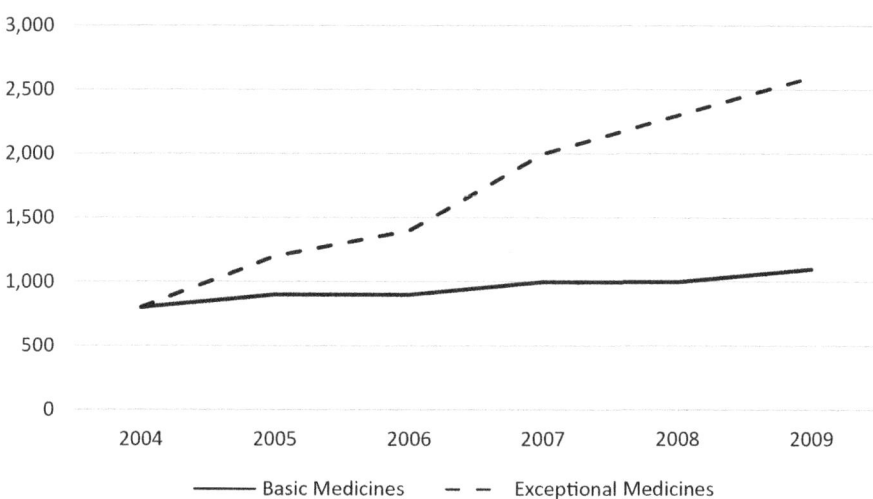

FIGURE 5.3 Evolution of expenditure with medicines, Ministry of Health, 2004–2009, in millions R$
Source: Medici[75]

If we accept the egalitarian principles of priority setting recommended in the WHO report as valid guides in the determination of the "universal and egalitarian access" clause of the constitutional right to health in Brazil, it seems that extending the PSF to 100 per cent of the Brazilian population, that is universalising it, and guaranteeing universal access to the basic and strategic, that is essential component of medicines should receive priority over extending the provision of high-cost drugs of the so-called specialised component. Yet the very opposite has been happening. Whereas the basic and strategic components have also seen some important increase in their budget, the specialised component has shot up much faster and now consumes more than double the amount of resources of the two other components combined.[76] The evolution of expenditure with medicines is particularly troublesome from an egalitarian perspective from 2004 onwards, as in that year the specialised (high cost) component and the two others combined had exactly the same expenditure (Figure 5.3).

This seems to me a clear example of what the WHO report describes as an unacceptable trade-off when making choices in the allocation of scarce resources

---

[75] Medici, "Medicamentos Excepcionais e Prioridades de Saúde no Brasil".
[76] For an analysis of the 2003–2007 period, in which specialized medicines went up 254 per cent (see F. Vieira, "Gasto do Ministério da Saúde com medicamentos: tendência dos programas de 2002 a 2007" [2009] 43[4] *Revista de Saúde Pública* 674).

within the idea of UHC, and would represent a violation of the right to health interpreted in light of these principles.[77]

This particular example within the field of pharmaceutical assistance is not an isolated case of "unacceptable trade-offs" in the Brazilian public health budget. When one considers the budget as a whole, it is clear that expenditure with medicines has grown significantly as a percentage of total health expenditure. From 2002 to 2007, for instance, it has almost doubled, from less 5.39 per cent to 10.70 per cent of the total budget. This is also significant in absolute terms, as we are talking of an increase of more than 3 billion reais, about US$1.5 billion in the average of that period.

The opportunity costs are therefore very significant, and our question is whether, from the perspective of the right to health, these resources ought not to be spent elsewhere, for instance, in the extension of the PSF mentioned earlier.[78] Again, when one looks at the health indicators of the country this seems another clear example of an "unacceptable trade-off", or a violation of the right to health as I am suggesting. As well as extending basic medical assistance to the population, one of the most important things that the PSF is aimed at achieving is the reduction of infant mortality in the country, which is still high, especially in the poorest regions of Brazil. It is particularly bad in the Northeast, at 38.9 deaths per thousand live births, roughly double that of the regions of the South and Southeast (see Figure 5.4).

Within every region in Brazil there is also a strong social gradient in infant mortality, with strong correlations with mothers' level of education and family income. Again, the Northeast is the worse, and infant mortality was as high as 56,7 in the poorest 20 per cent families in that region (see Tables 5.1, 5.2 and 5.3).

The egalitarian conception of the right to health interpreted through the prioritisation principles discussed previously would again, in my view, allow us to

---

[77] As they put it: "[M]any people find it unfair if some parts of the population do not have affordable access to even highly cost-effective services targeting very severe conditions, while other parts of the population are covered for very costly services that provide only limited benefits. Examples in the former category of services are antibiotics for pneumonia, skilled birth attendance, malaria treatment, and secondary prevention of stroke and myocardial infarction. An example in the latter category of services may be costly, experimental chemotherapy without proven benefits" (Ottersen, "Making Fair Choices on the Path to Universal Health Coverage", 7). Andre Medici, a Brazilian health economist, makes a similar point: "the decisions regarding allocation of resources for exceptional [non-essential] medicines should be conditioned on the previous coverage of unmet needs for essential and strategic medicines" (Medici, "Medicamentos Excepcionais e Prioridades de Saúde no Brasil", my translation from the original in Portuguese).

[78] Ottersen, "Making Fair Choices on the Path to Universal Health Coverage": "Healthy life years is not a perfect measure of health benefits, but it can nevertheless be very useful in comparing all types of health services. Moreover, the difference between health services are often so great that even an imperfect measure is highly valuable" (13). For a critical analysis of the underfunding of the PSF in Bahia, see M. R. Rosa and T. C. Coelho, "What the Expenses with the Family Health Program in a Municipality of Bahia Shows?" (2011) 16(3) *Revista de Ciência & Saúde Coletiva* 1863.

TABLE 5.1. *Infant mortality rate, by region – Brazil – 1990/1991/2000/2005*

Region	1990	1991	2000	2005	Relative diference (%)
Brazil	53,7	50,6	35,1	28,8	−46,4
North	52,9	49,9	34,1	28,3	−46,5
Northeast	87,3	81,6	50,9	38,9	−55,4
Centre-East	41,0	38,7	26,2	22,6	−44,8
Southeast	36,6	34,7	25,3	19,2	−47,5
South	35,2	33,3	22,0	18,1	−48,8

Source: Brazilian Institute of Geography and Statistics[79] (IBGE)

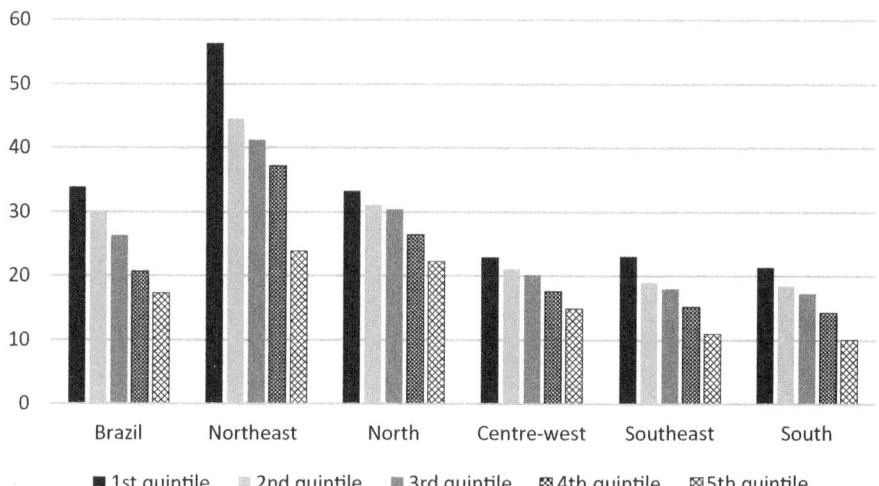

FIGURE 5.4 Infant mortality by household income per capita quintiles, by region
Source: Brazilian Comission on the Social Determinants of Health, 2008[80]

condemn the decisions to allocate so much resources to high-cost medicines when basic attention provided by the PSF is still lacking for so many families in the country.[81]

Here are thus a few examples of how Brazilian courts (and courts elsewhere, with appropriate contextual adjustments) could exercise a more legitimate and robust

---

[79] Ibid., 96.
[80] Censos Demográficos, 1991–2000 e Pesquisa Nacional por Amostra de Domicílios (PNAD) (Instituto Brasileiro de Geografia e Estatística, 2005), 98.
[81] One could argue that, even more than the PSF, basic sanitation and water provision, still lacking for a high percentage of the Brazilian population, should be the priority. I agree, but here we are talking about macro allocation among departments, as sanitation and water provision are in the purview of the Ministry of Planning and not the Ministry of Health in the Brazilian system.

TABLE 5.2. *Proportion of women in fertile age (15 to 49 years) by schooling years, by region – Brazil – 1991/2000/2005*

2005	<4 schooling years (%)	4 to 7 (%)	8 (%)
Brazil	12.3	24.8	62.9
North	16.1	26.8	57.0
Northeast	20.3	28.0	51.7
Centre-East	8.4	25.1	66.4
South	8.4	25.1	66.4
Southeast	8.4	22.1	69.4

Source: Brazilian Institute of Geography and Statistics[82] (IBGE)

TABLE 5.3. *Infant mortality rate by years of schooling of the mother, by region – Brazil – 1990/2000/2005*

Region	Total (%)	<4 schooling years (%)	4 to 7 (%)	>8 (%)	Ratio (%)
Brasil	28.8	39.9	25.8	18.4	2.1
Nordeste	38.9	56.2	31.9	20.3	2.7
Norte	28.3	37.5	24.9	18.7	2.0
Centro-Oeste	22.6	33.5	21.7	16.7	2.0
Sudeste	19.2	30.2	21.2	13.7	2.2
Sul	18.1	29.2	18.3	13.3	2.2

Source: Brazilian Institute of Geography and Statistics[83] (IBGE)

role in holding the state accountable in its constitutional duty to guarantee the right to health. Rather than force the state to provide any health benefit that a claimant may need according to his or her doctor ("the right to everything"), or to wash its hands from any involvement in health policy decisions ("the right to nothing"), it should review the fairness of the process of decision making followed by state health authorities, ensuring that it is transparent, reasonable and participatory. Under reasonableness, it should make sure that decisions follow appropriate criteria of priority setting, in particular those of efficiency and equity discussed previously. In most cases, it is hoped, health authorities will pass the test of fairness. When they do, or when it is not clear that they didn't (many cases will be of that sort given the complexity of the task) the judiciary should leave their decision standing. When they don't, the judiciary is legitimated in holding them to account.[84] It has, however, to engage in earnest with public health expertise to do it well.

[82] Ibid., 98.
[83] Brazil, Minstry of Health, "As causas sociais das iniquidades em saúde no Brasil" (2008), http://cmdss2011.org/site/wp-content/uploads/2011/07/relatorio_cndss.pdf.
[84] The precise remedies to be used are open to debate and contextual variation. They range from less interfering declaratory orders to more assertive injunctions. For a good discussion, see

I turn now, in the final section of this chapter, to the problem with which I started, that is that of rare diseases with a very high per capita treatment cost affecting children. How does the framework proposed deal with this highly complex case?

RARE DISEASES AND CHILDREN: A SPECIAL CASE?

In this concluding section I want to explore how the argument developed in the previous sections might work in a more complex scenario, perhaps the most complex, that is that of so-called rare diseases, using as a guide the case study of EB with which I started this chapter.

We have already seen how serious and debilitating the symptoms of EB are, particularly for children. Even with the best palliative care available, their lives are significantly restricted; without it their suffering is unbearable. Yet their small numbers and the enormous costs of the available treatment make their contemplation in the health budget extremely unlikely, especially in middle-income countries where so many other needs, also basic, compete for the same limited resources. Both the cost-benefit of funding their treatment and their political clout, two important determinants in the allocation of scarce health resources, will be too low.

Is this also a case in which the decisions of the political and technical organs not to fund treatment may be described as "unacceptable trade-offs", that is a violation of the right to health understood in the egalitarian vein proposed in this chapter?

Note that here, unlike in the examples I gave in the previous section, we are not in the presence of a blunt inegalitarian allocation. The needs of EB sufferers are potentially competing with equally important needs of vulnerable groups who, as we saw, still lack some of the most basic services and care. In such circumstances, can EB sufferers make a plausible right-to-health claim that their needs ought to be prioritised?

An interesting argument to that effect in favour of children's social and economic rights in general has been recently made by Aoife Nolan. Although accepting that, in general, the political branches are better placed to make allocative decisions that determine the special and economic entitlements of citizens due to their representativeness of their views (the same argument I made in the preceding text), she persuasively argues that this does not apply to children's rights because they cannot use the democratic process to advance their rights like other groups can.

Judicial review in the case of children's social rights would, therefore, not be interfering with democratic and legitimate decisions, but rather bolstering the democratic process by reinforcing rights of political participation and protecting

---

M. Tushnet, *Weak Courts, Strong Rights: Judicial Review and Social Welfare Rights in Comparative Constitutional Law* (Princeton, NJ: Princeton University Press, 2009).

the rights of minorities who are vulnerable to neglect or oppression (an argument famously made, in another context, by Alexander Bickel).[85] As Nolan puts it:

> As children cannot assume that the legislature and executive will protect their rights, the courts' role as "guardians of the constitution" is of greater significance to them than to others in society who can make their own voices heard through the democratic system[86]

A similar, though more general argument was made by Rosalind Dixon to justify stronger protection of social and economic rights when the political process suffers from what she calls "blind spots" and "burdens of inertia". As she persuasively puts it, legislatures and administrations may for different reasons (including lack of representativeness as highlighted by Nolan) simply fail to see (blind spots) or fail to act (inertia) on behalf of some groups in society. "Such omissions and delays – that are not driven by resource constraints or supported by principled forms of justification – will clearly have profound significance for the legitimacy of the system of constitutional ordering".[87]

Now, if this line of argument is valid, the children in question in the EB case seem to qualify *a fortiori*, as they are not only vulnerable for being children and therefore lacking full representation in the democratic process, but also for being sufferers of a rare disease, and therefore being small in numbers and suffering from an inordinately costly condition. Their voices are likely to be completely drowned out by the majority. The EB case seems therefore to epitomise the argument from exclusion that Nolan and Dixon persuasively make for justifying the legitimacy of judicial review in some social and economic rights' cases.

The problem, however, is that the mere identification of failures of representativeness in the political process does not tell us much about whether the substantive outcome of that process is also vitiated. The fact that a certain group hasn't been heard in the debates that led to allocative decisions does not tell us whether, had they been heard but nonehteless lost, there would still be a problem with the outcome of the process. Being heard, that is having the opportunity to take part in the debate is certainly an important step, but it does not guarantee any outcome. If this is all that can be done, their right to health seems, again, too weak.

Can we go any further towards stronger protection? Can we say that EB children and other rare diseases sufferers are entitled not only to take part in the discussion but also that some level of resources ought to be necessarily devoted to the

---

[85] A. Bickel, *The Least Dangerous Branch: The Supreme Court at the Bar of Politics*, 2nd ed. (New Haven, CT: Yale University Press, 1986).
[86] A. Nolan, *Children's Socio-Economic Rights, Democracy and the Courts* (Oxford: Hart Publishing, 2011), 182.
[87] R. Dixon, "Creating Dialogue about Socioeconomic Rights: Strong-Form Versus Weak-Form Judicial Review Revisited" (2007) 5(3) *International Journal of Constitutional Law* 391, 403–404.

protection of their interests? The dilemma here, and this is what I believe make so many balk at the idea of strong social rights, is that protecting the interests of one vulnerable group may come at the cost of disadvantaging other vulnerable groups, especially in low- and middle-income countries where resources are more limited. That risk is not present, I hope to have shown, in the blunt inegalitarian examples discussed in the previous section, but it is here.

I would like to emphasise here another important point I made earlier. The procedural safeguards of accountability are crucial to guarantee the transparency and rationality of the difficult decisions to be taken in the prioritisation of health needs. When that model is followed, we acquire crucial information about the cost-effectiveness of unavailable treatments (e.g., treatment for EB patients), its comparison with the cost-effectiveness of other treatments offered in the system and also its overall budgetary impact. As I mentioned earlier, this is still lacking in many systems, for reasons that range from incompetence and omission to lack of resources and adequate information.

There has been no such analysys, for instance, in the case of EB treatment.[88] EB sufferers have therefore not had the benefit even of those basic procedural guarantees. They would have a strong case, therefore, to claim that their right to health entitles them at least to an appropriate analysis of the relative priority of their treateation.

While such analysis is not carried out by the competent authorities, however, they may well use the information available to try and make a substantive case for their right to treatment as well.

According to the Secretariat for Health of the state of Bahia, the treatment of the forty-four patients that have EB has a monthly cost of R$1.4 million, which adds up to R$16,800,000 a year (around US$7 million in 2014). This is a per capita expenditure of around US$160,000.[89] The per capita GDP of Brazil in that year was US $15,951.221.[90] EB treatment was therefore about ten times GDP per capita per year. This is clearly not what is regarded as cost-effective or highly cost-effective by the WHO cost-effectiveness criteria (<3 and <1 GDP per capita, respectively).[91]

---

[88] M. F. Drummond, "Challenges in the Economic Evaluation of Orphan Drugs" (2008) 14(2) Eurohealth 16.

[89] If we use purchasing power parity we would need to consider the conversation rate of 0.735 in 2014. http://data.worldbank.org/indicator/PA.NUS.PPPC.RF?end=2015&locations=BR&start=2002.

[90] http://data.worldbank.org/indicator/NY.GDP.PCAP.PP.CD?end=2015&locations=BR&start=2002.

[91] For a critical analysis of cost-effectiveness, see www.who.int/bulletin/volumes/93/2/14-138206/en/. On the demand side, decision-makers are offered the results of cost-effectiveness analyses that neither distinguish between programme options with widely divergent ICERs nor account for budget constraints. Decision-makers may therefore tend to dismiss cost-effectiveness analyses and revert to political or organizational interests as decision criteria. On the supply side, the availability of global cost-effectiveness thresholds undercuts the incentive of investigators to generate the nuanced, context-specific information that

However, given the low number of individuals affected by EB, the aggregate budgetary impact of their treatment is not that high. Indeed, as a percentage of the total health budget of the state of Bahia for 2015 (R$4,581,663,905.17) it adds up to less than 0.37 per cent, and as a percentage of the health budget of the federal government for 2015 (R$109,000,000,000) it amounts to less than 0.0015 per cent.[92] But this, alone, is not sufficient to determine whether EB ought to be funded. All we know so far is that its per capita cost is high, but its aggregate impact on the budget seems not to be so high given the low number of individuals suffering from the disease. To be able to make a properly informed priority analysis we would need to have information about all health interventions currently and potentially available in the Bahian health system. This is unfortunately far from being available at present.

We can, however, use for illustration a health programme that has been introduced recently by the Federal Ministry of Health, namely HPV vaccination of girls between the ages of nine and thirteen, which is currently seen as a cost-effective programme to prevent cervical cancer, the second most common cancer among women in Brazil, whose incidence rate is two to three times higher in Brazil (19.2 per 100,000 women every year) than in North America and Europe.[93] It is also a cost-effective programme, with a per capita cost way below (less than ten times) the GDP per capita. In terms of aggregate impact, however, it is much higher. The Brazilian government has spent R$1.1 billion in the past three years to purchase 32 million doses of the vaccine. Given that immunisation is reached with two doses, the total number of girls that can benefit from this programme is 16 million, at a cost of R$68.75 per capita.[94] The aggregate yearly cost is therefore around R$370 million, or about 0.34 per cent of the federal budget.

This information is far from sufficient for us to form a well-grounded conclusion of whether treatment for EB should be prioritised in the Brazilian health system. It does give us an indication, however, of its comparative cost-effectiveness and budgetary impact. It is certainly not a clear-cut case as the blunt inegalitarian ones discussed in the previous section, yet perhaps one that could be made in favour of EB patients with more complete information.

---

decision-makers need. See also www.ncbi.nlm.nih.gov/pmc/articles/PMC4209096/ and www.ncbi.nlm.nih.gov/pmc/articles/PMC2810517/.

[92] If we take the estimate of 600 EB sufferers in the whole of Brazil and assume that their treatment would cost the same as in Bahia in per capita terms, we are taking about R$230 million per year, or 0.21 per cent of the federal health budget.

[93] http://bmcinfectdis.biomedcentral.com/articles/10.1186/1471-2334-12-250.

[94] It is estimated that there are 124,900 girls in Bahia in that age bracket. The aggregate cost in the state of Bahia is therefore R$8.586.875,00, i.e. 0.2 per cent of that state's budget. The great irony is that, due to low take-up (about 14 per cent), there is a huge surplus of vaccines in Bahian health surgeries. www.dsvc.com.br/2016/destaques/vacinas-contra-hpv-na-bahia-mais-de-1249-mil-meninas/; http://g1.globo.com/bahia/noticia/2016/07/sesab-aponta-que-apenas-25-das-meninas-tomaram-vacina-contra-hpv.html; www.brasil.gov.br/saude/2016/04/campanha-incentiva-meninas-a-procurar-vacinacao-contra-hpv.

CONCLUSION

I have argued in this chapter that the right to health (similar to any human right when their corresponding positive duties are at stake) faces significant difficulties to operate in the traditional manner of legal rights, that is as imposing reasonably clear and substantive duties on the state that can be strongly enforced by courts in case of breach.[95] This is because the state action required to guarantee the right to health is often elusive and open to debate, due mainly to its strong dependence on limited resources that the state has to allocate among a myriad of competing needs, health and non-health related. In this scenario of resource scarcity and inevitable disagreement in the community about how these resources should be allocated (the "fact of pluralism"), it is an intractable challenge to reach a reasonably precise definition of the content of the right to health (or of any right when the positive and resource-dependent duties are at issue, it is always important to re-emphasise).

This important difficulty lends credibility to the view that these rights are different, if not in nature, at least in the way they operate. Rather than impose a substantive prohibition or mandate on the duty holders (most often the state), they rather impose constraints on the process through which decisions are made on what actions will be taken and how resources will be allocated. These procedural constraints are far from negligible. They can provide significant strength to the right to health and other rights, yet not the strength that we have become accustomed to in the operation of civil liberties and other rights, especially in countries that follow the American originated practice of strong judicial review.[96]

But I also argued that, especially in highly unequal societies, in particular lower- and middle-income countries, where large portions of the population lack basic needs, including health services and care, and where the right to health and other social rights have been expressly included in the constitution as an egalitarian right (i.e., a right to "universal and egalitarian access" to health resources), priority-setting principles developed in the public health and bioethics literature can help strengthen that right. Some allocative decisions are so bluntly against the egalitarian spirit of social and economic rights that one can confidently claim that they are incorrect, that is, they violate the right to health or, to use the terminology of the WHO report *Making Fair Choices on the Path to Universal Coverage*, they strike an "unacceptable trade-off" that no decent society should admit.

---

[95] Unlike some rights whose primary corresponding duties are negative (i.e. impose omissions on others) and comparatively clearer, such as the traditional civil liberties (freedoms of speech, religion), the rights not to be tortured and not to be enslaved, which can operate as absolute (or almost absolute) trumps what the state can do to individuals.

[96] The "archetypal model of strong-form judicial review associated with judicial review in the United States" (Dixon, "Creating Dialogue about Socioeconomic Rights", 418).

6

Gender Equality, Children's Rights and Sustainable Development

Amanda Kron

INTRODUCTION

The right to non-discrimination, under article 2 of the UN Convention on the Rights of the Child (UNCRC), is not only a right in and of itself, it is one of the guiding principles of the Convention, providing the means by which other substantive articles are interpreted and perceived. Article 2 requires that State Parties respect and ensure that the rights of children are respected, protected and promoted without discrimination of any kind, irrespective of the child's or his or her parent's or legal guardian's race, colour, sex, language, religion, political or other opinion, national, ethnic or social origin, property, disability, birth or other status. While all these grounds are of vital importance, this chapter will focus on the issue of gender discrimination, and gender equality, and its impact on sustainable development.

Limited access to education, gender-based violence, early and forced marriages and the denial of sexual and reproductive health rights and services (SRHR) represent some of the greatest challenges pertaining to children's rights that the international community must overcome to ensure sustainable and inclusive development for girls as well as boys. In particular, access to SRHR has been highlighted as a crucial vehicle for enabling adolescent girls and boys to live healthy and fulfilling lives and has been shown to have a close connection to sustainable development, as will be discussed in the following text.[1]

First, this chapter examines the disadvantages that gender inequality creates for girls and boys, including limited access to education, gender-based violence, early

---

[1] This chapter is written in the author's personal capacity, and the contents of the chapter do not necessarily reflect the views of United Nations Environment Programme. Cf. C Barroso, "Beyond Cairo: Sexual and Reproductive Rights of Young People in the New Development Agenda" (2014) 9(6) *Global Public Health: An International Journal for Research, Policy and Practice* 599, 639: "There is now widespread recognition of the link between sexual and reproductive health and development".

and forced marriages and denied SRHR, and how these interact with sustainable development. Second, access to remedies and justice that do not require parental or spousal consent will be analysed. Third, the progress, prospects and challenges in implementing gender equality will be examined, including the possibilities provided by the use of gender disaggregated data, and the importance of not embedding gender stereotypes and inequalities when striving for more inclusive development. Lastly, some conclusions and observations on the future will be provided.

THE CHALLENGE AHEAD: THE IMPORTANCE OF GENDER EQUALITY FOR SUSTAINABLE DEVELOPMENT

The UN Entity for Gender Equality and the Empowerment of Women (UN Women) has found that there is growing evidence of the synergies between gender equality and economic, social and environmental sustainability.[2] As noted and emphasised in the work leading up to the adoption of the 2030 Agenda for Sustainable Development (Agenda 2030), gender equality is instrumental to, and a precursor for upholding, all the rights contained in the agenda as well as the Sustainable Development Goals (SDGs).[3] Specifically, Agenda 2030 states that:

> Realizing gender equality and the empowerment of women and girls will make a crucial contribution to progress across all the Goals and targets. The achievement of full human potential and of sustainable development is not possible if one half of humanity continues to be denied its full human rights and opportunities. Women and girls must enjoy equal access to quality education, economic resources and political participation as well as equal opportunities with men and boys for employment, leadership and decision-making at all levels ... The systematic mainstreaming of a gender perspective in the implementation of the Agenda is crucial.[4]

In addition to the 2030 Agenda, both the Beijing Platform for Action and the Programme of Action of the International Conference on Population and Development (ICPD) recognise the importance of women and girls' rights in relation to sustainable development imperatives such as economic development and health.[5] The empowerment of women and girls has been deemed "essential to expand economic growth and promote social development".[6]

---

[2] UN Entity for Gender Equality and the Empowerment of Women, *World Survey on the Role of Women in Development 2014: Gender Equality and Sustainable Development* (2014), www.unwomen.org/-/media/headquarters/attachments/sections/library/publications/2014/unwomen_surveyreport_advancei6oct.pdf?vs=2710.
[3] See, e.g., UN General Assembly (UNGA), "Transforming Our World: The 2030 Agenda for Sustainable Development" (UN Doc. A/RES/70/1, 21 October 2015), [20].
[4] Ibid.
[5] See "The Right to the Highest Attainable Standard of Sexual Health".
[6] United Nations, *Gender Equality: Why It Matters* (undated), www.un.org/sustainabledevelopment/wp-content/uploads/2016/08/5_Why-it-Matters_GenderEquality_2p.pdf.

It has been noted that adolescent girls "are doubly discriminated due to age and gender".[7] The impact of gender inequality on sustainable development and children's rights manifests itself in a number of ways. This impact stems from laws, policies and practices, or the lack thereof, that directly or indirectly affect the rights of children.

This can be seen in a number of different areas, including education, participation, property rights and violence against women and children. However, this chapter will focus on one specific area of gender discrimination that has a significant impact on sustainable development: the continued use of harmful practices against girl children.

The right to health is a critical part of achieving sustainable development for boys and girls.[8] Article 24(1) of the UNCRC recognises the right of the child to the enjoyment of the highest attainable standard of health, and article 24(3) calls for State Parties to take all effective and appropriate measures with a view to abolishing traditional practices prejudicial to the health of children. As will be outlined in greater detail in the following text, preventing unintended pregnancy and reducing adolescent childbearing through universal access to sexual and reproductive health-care services is critical to further advances in the health of girls.[9] The SDGs contains several targets on sexual and reproductive health and rights. SDG 5.1 calls upon the international community to "reduce the global maternal mortality ratio to less than 70 per 100,000 live births" by 2030, while SDG 5.2 calls for the end of "preventable deaths of newborns and children under 5 years of age, with all countries aiming to reduce neonatal mortality to at least as low as 12 per 1,000 live births and under-5 mortality to at least as low as 25 per 1,000 live births". Moreover, SDG 5.6 provides that by 2030, universal access to sexual and reproductive health-care services should be ensured, "including for family planning, information and education, and the integration of reproductive health into national strategies and programmes".

One particularly grim aspect of the way in which girls are disadvantaged, is through what has been termed "harmful practices", such as child, early and forced marriages and female genital mutilation, which SDG 5.3 aims to eliminate. The Committee on the Rights of the Child has on numerous occasions referenced the child's right to the highest attainable standard of health as prescribed by article 24 of the UNCRC, and in connection noted that this right is severely compromised by these harmful practices.[10] The Committee has also, together with the Committee on

---

[7] Every Woman Every Child, *Technical Guidance for Prioritizing Adolescent Health* (2017), www.unfpa.org/publications/technical-guidance-prioritizing-adolescent-health, 36.
[8] See, e.g., Every Woman Every Child, *The Global Strategy for Women's, Children's and Adolescent's Health 2016–2030* (2015), www.who.int/life-course/partners/global-strategy/en/, 38.
[9] See "The Importance of Sexual and Reproductive Health and Rights".
[10] UNCRC Committee, "General Comment No. 15 (2013) on the Right of the Child to the Enjoyment of the Highest Attainable Standard of Health (art. 24)" (UN Doc. CRC/C/GC/15, 17 April 2013), [9].

the Elimination of Discrimination against Women, expressed concern about the use of these practices "to justify gender-based violence as a form of 'protection' or control of women and children".[11]

The next section will focus on the harmful practice of child, early and forced marriage, and consider how ensuring SRHR can serve to mitigate harmful practices more broadly.

Elimination of Harmful Practices: Child, Early and Forced Marriages

The organisation "Girls Not Brides", a partnership of more than 500 civil society organisations, was launched to bring child marriage to the attention of the international community, and to raise awareness and call for laws and policies striving for the end of this harmful practices. Together with its partners, the organisation has demonstrated that more than 650 million women alive today were married as children.[12]

While the UNCRC does not explicitly mention child marriage, it does oblige State Parties to take "all effective and appropriate measures with a view to abolishing traditional practices prejudicial to the health of children".[13] In a recent General Comment, written in conjunction with the Committee on the Elimination of Discrimination Against Women (CEDAW Committee), the Committee on the Rights of the Child went into depth on the harm to health caused by child marriage, such as early and frequent pregnancy and childbirth, resulting in higher than average maternal morbidity and mortality rates.[14] CEDAW is more explicit, requiring that marriage must be entered into with the free consent of the intending spouses, and that all unions where either party is under 18 shall be regarded as illegal and void.[15] This reflects the fact that, as the CEDAW Committee has noted,

---

[11] CEDAW Committee and UNCRC Committee, "Joint General Recommendation No. 31 / General Comment No. 18 (2014) on Harmful Practices: (UN Doc. CEDAW/C/GC/31-CRC/C/GC/18, 4 November 2014), [6]. See also CEDAW Committee, "General Recommendation No. 19 (1992) on Violence against Women" (UN Doc. A/47/38, 1993), [11]; UNCRC Committee, "General Comment No. 9 (2006) on the Rights of Children with Disabilities" (UN Doc. CRC/C/GC/9, 27 February 2007), [8], [10] and [79]; and UNCRC Committee, "General Comment No. 15 (2013)", [8] and [9].

[12] Girls Not Brides, Child Marriage around the World (undated), https://www.girlsnotbrides.org/where-does-it-happen/. See also United Nations Children's Fund, Child Marriage: Latest trends and future prospects, UNICEF, New York, 2018, https://data.unicef.org/wp-content/uploads/2018/07/Child-Marriage-Data-Brief.pdf.

[13] UNGA, *Convention on the Rights of the Child* (UN Doc. A/RES/44/25, 20 November 1989) 1577 UNTS 3, article 24(3).

[14] CEDAW Committee and UNCRC Committee, "Joint General Recommendation No. 31", [22].

[15] UNGA, *Convention on the Elimination of All Forms of Discrimination against Women* (UN Doc. A/RES/34/180, 18 December 1979) 1249 UNTS 13, article 16.

the right to get married freely and with consent is indispensable to ensure dignity and equality of all women and girls as human beings.[16]

The UN Human Rights Council (HRC) recognised in 2013 that "the persistence of child, early and forced marriage contributes to impairing the achievement of the Millennium Development Goals and sustainable and inclusive economic growth and social cohesion" and decided to convene a high-level panel discussion on the topic of early and forced marriage, which was convened on 23 June 2014.[17] In addition, the HRC requested a report from the Office of the High Commissioner for Human Rights on child, early and forced marriage, which outlines the impacts of forced, early and child marriages on human rights, such as access to education, and emphasises the importance of harmonising domestic laws on marriage.[18] The report notes that the impact on the realisation and enjoyment of girls' rights can be wide ranging. Significant age and power differentials can undermine the agency and autonomy of girls, who may also face physical, psychological, economic and sexual violence, and restrictions on their movement, as well as conditions that meet international legal definitions of slavery and slavery-like practices such as servile marriage, sexual slavery, child servitude, child trafficking and forced labour.[19] It is also associated with a range of poor health and social outcomes, and can pose significant obstacles to ensuring educational, employment and other economic opportunities.[20]

As noted in several reports by the UN Population Fund (UNFPA), adolescent mothers are less likely to have access to education than their peers who do not have children at that age.[21] Early and frequent pregnancies and forced continuation of pregnancy are all common in child marriages.[22] In particular, the UNFPA report

---

[16] CEDAW Committee, "General Recommendation 21 (1994) on Equality in Marriage and Family Relations", in "Report of the Committee on the Elimination of Discrimination against Women Thirteenth Session" (UN Doc. A/49/38, 12 April 1994), [16].

[17] UN Human Rights Council, "Strengthening Efforts to Prevent and Eliminate Child, Early and Forced Marriage: Challenges, Achievements, Best Practices and Implementation Gaps" (UN Doc. A/HRC/RES/24/23, 27 September 2013).

[18] Office of the United Nations High Commissioner for Human Rights (OHCHR), "Preventing and Eliminating Child, Early and Forced Marriage" (UN Doc. A/HRC/26/22, 2 April 2014).

[19] Ibid., [21].

[20] Ibid., [23–24]. See also K. G. Santhya and S. J. Jejeebhoy, "Sexual and Reproductive Health and Rights of Adolescent Girls: Evidence from Low- and Middle-Income Countries" (2015) 10 (2) *Global Public Health* 189, 200: "[A]lthough research from the developing world on the social and economic impact of adolescent childbearing is thin ..., evidence from developed countries suggest that early childbearing is associated with poor educational and economic outcomes for the mother and child".

[21] See UN Population Fund (UNFPA), *Giving Girls Today and Tomorrow: Breaking the Cycle of Adolescent Pregnancy* (2007), www.unfpa.org/sites/default/files/pub-pdf/giving_girls.pdf.

[22] OHCHR, "Preventing and Eliminating Child, Early and Forced Marriage", [23]. See also e.g., UNICEF, *A Profile of Child Marriage in Africa* (2015), www.unicef.org/media/files/UNICEF-Child-Marriage-Brochure-low-Single(1).pdf: "In Mozambique, the likelihood a young woman already had three or more children is seven times higher for those who had married by age 15".

"Marrying Too Young" outlines how working against child, early and forced marriage contributes to the Millennium Development Goals (MDGs) and sustainable development more generally.[23] It also highlights that in cases of child and/or forced marriage, in particular where the husband is significantly older than the wife, and where girls have limited education, the girls generally have limited decision-making power in relation to their own lives. Child marriage also contributes to higher rates of school dropout, especially among girls, forced exclusion from school and an increased risk of domestic violence, in addition to limiting the enjoyment of the right to freedom of movement.[24] Being denied education in turn means that these girls are not given the opportunity that education can provide in terms of self-fulfilment and the realisation of additional rights, as well as losing out on any information about SRHR that may be provided. Thus, the lack of access to quality education creates a vicious cycle in which several of the girls' rights are affected, and where it becomes even more difficult for these girls to be aware of their rights and becoming informed defenders of their own rights and dignity. For this and other reasons, child marriage in particular was deemed responsible for slowing down progress on six out of the eight MDGs.[25]

While many parents hope and believe that marriage presents a way out of poverty for their daughters, the reality is sadly often the opposite.[26] Girls that are married as children are more prone to suffer abuse and violence by their husbands, and a number of their human rights to education and health are severely affected.[27]

---

[23] UNFPA, *Marrying Too Young: End Child Marriage* (2012), www.unfpa.org/sites/default/files/pub-pdf/MarryingTooYoung.pdf, 13.

[24] CEDAW Committee and UNCRC Committee, "Joint General Recommendation No. 31", [22].

[25] Girls Not Brides, *Post-2015 Advocacy Toolkit* (2015), www.girlsnotbrides.org/wp-content/uploads/2015/01/GNB-Post-2015-Advocacy-Toolkit-January-2015.pdf. Cf. also UNFPA, *Marrying Too Young*, which turns the question on its head and demonstrates how eliminating child, early and forced marriages can lead to greater implementation of six of the MDGS; Goal 1 to eradicate extreme poverty and hunger, Goal 2 to achieve universal primary education, Goal 3 on promoting gender equality, Goal 4 on reducing child mortality, Goal 5 on improving maternal health and Goal 6 on combatting HIV/AIDS, malaria and other diseases.

[26] UNFPA, *Marrying Too Young*, 12. See also OHCHR, "Preventing and Eliminating Child, Early and Forced Marriage", [17]: "Empirical evidence shows poverty and insecurity as one of the root causes of child, early and forced marriage".

[27] UNFPA, *State of the World Population 2014: The Power of 1.8 Billion: Adolescents, Youth and the Transformation of the Future* (2014), www.unfpa.org/sites/default/files/pub-pdf/EN-SWOP14-Report_FINAL-web.pdf, 9. See also OHCHR, "Preventing and Eliminating Child, Early and Forced Marriage", [22], referencing Special Representative of the Secretary-General on Violence against Children and Plan International, *Protecting Children from Harmful Practices in Plural Legal Systems* (2012). See also Plan International, *A Girl's Right to Say No to Marriage: Working to End Child Marriage and Keep Girls in School* (2013), https://plan-international.org/publications/girls-right-say-no-marriage. See also UN Educational, Scientific and Cultural Organization (UNESCO), *International Guidelines on Sexuality Education: An Evidence Informed Approach to Effective Sex, Relationships and HIV/STI Education* (2009), http://unesdoc.unesco.org/images/0018/001832/183281e.pdf, 2: "These efforts recognize that all

Child, early and forced marriages also have a particularly detrimental effect on SRHR because these girls often lack access to information about and to protection against pregnancy and disease. In addition, the age difference between spouses can also make it difficult for girls to ask for safer sex practices or family planning.[28] Moreover, child and early marriages are linked to complications in pregnancy and childbirth due to the early pregnancies.[29] Out of the 287,000 maternal deaths worldwide in 2010, it is estimated that most of them could have been prevented.[30]

Thus, child, early and forced marriages directly inhibit sustainable development and children's right to health, right to education and right to participation, and present major obstacles to achieving sustainable development for all, particularly women and girls.[31] One of the most efficient ways to break the cycle of poverty and provide vehicles for sustainable development is to give young women education and agency.[32] Education has also been found to be a deterrent of child marriages: girls with no education are three times more likely to be married before the age of 18 as compared to those who receive a secondary education or higher.[33] The importance of education for sustainable development is underlined by SDG 4, namely target 4.1 ("By 2030, ensure that all girls and boys complete free, equitable and quality primary and secondary education leading to relevant and effective learning outcomes"); target 4.2 ("By 2030, ensure that all girls and boys have access to quality early childhood development, care and pre-primary education so that they are ready for primary education"); target 4.5 ("By 2030, eliminate gender disparities in education and ensure equal access to all levels of education and vocational training for the vulnerable, including persons with disabilities, indigenous peoples and children in vulnerable situations"); and target 4.7 ("By 2030, ensure that all learners acquire the knowledge and skills needed to promote sustainable development, including, among others, through education for sustainable development and sustainable lifestyles, human rights, gender equality, promotion of a culture of peace and non-violence, global citizenship and appreciation of cultural diversity and of culture's contribution to sustainable development").

---

young people need sexuality education, and that some are living with HIV or are more vulnerable to HIV infection than others, particularly adolescent girls married as children".

[28] UN Children's Fund, *Ending Child Marriage: Progress and Prospects* (2014), www.unicef.org/media/files/Child_Marriage_Report_7_17_LR.pdf.

[29] UNFPA, *State of the World Population 2014*, 9.

[30] UNFPA, OHCHR and Danish Institute for Human Rights, *Reproductive Rights Are Human Rights* (2014), www.ohchr.org/Documents/Publications/NHRIHandbook.pdf, 15.

[31] Regarding the connection to sustainable development, see e.g., UNGA, "The Future We Want" (UN Doc. A/RES/66/288, 11 September 2012), 238; UNFPA, *Marrying Too Young*, ch. 1: "Child Marriage: A Violation of Human Rights and Deterrent to Development".

[32] Cf. UNCRC Committee, "General Comment No. 4 (2003) on Adolescent Health and Development in the Context of the Convention on the Rights of the Child" (UN Doc. CRC/GC/2003/4, 1 July 2003), [38].

[33] UNFPA, *Marrying Too Young*, 34.

The CEDAW Committee has emphasised the importance of registering births and marriages to facilitate monitoring and supporting the effective implementation and enforcement of laws on the minimum age of marriage.[34] In accordance with article 7(1) of the UNCRC, every child has the right to be registered immediately after birth, the right to a name as well as the right to acquire a nationality. Registration facilitates access to the child's other rights under national and international law, such as, for example, the right to education. Moreover, data collection and demonstrating progress in relation to other objectives for sustainable development, for example in relation to the work to eliminate poverty, relies upon effective registration. To meet this obligation, states are urged to "establish national civil registration that is free, universal and accessible for the birth registration of all children and to ensure that all marriages are registered by a competent authority".[35] As part of the 2030 Agenda, SDG 16.9 also provides that by 2030, legal identity should be provided for all, including birth registration.

Providing for health services, comprehensive sexual education and improved agency all contributes to the fulfilment of children's rights and sustainable development. The next section of this chapter will go into further detail on the importance of SRHR in realising sustainable development and combatting child marriage.

THE IMPORTANCE OF SEXUAL AND REPRODUCTIVE HEALTH AND RIGHTS

Investments in adolescent health and wellbeing bring a triple dividend of benefits now, into future adult life, and for the next generation of children.[36]

Sexual and reproductive health and rights are closely connected to the realisation of sustainable development for three key reasons. First, SRHR contributes to reducing poverty. For instance, it has been demonstrated that investments in health and education are important pathways for promoting economic growth and human well-being,[37] as well as developing more prosperous societies through protecting rights to health and education for women and girls.[38] Second, SRHR promotes women's rights and gender equality. For instance, fulfilling and respecting the rights of girls to make choices relating to their own bodies, and providing them with education and supporting their agency to this end, strengthens their opportunities to

---

[34] OHCHR, "Preventing and Eliminating Child, Early and Forced Marriage", [15].
[35] Ibid.
[36] G. C. Patton et al., "Our Future: A Lancet Commission on Adolescent Health and Wellbeing" (2016) 387 *Lancet* 2423, 2424.
[37] D. E. Bloom, M. Kuhn and K. Prettner, *The Contribution of Female Health to Economic Development* (Vienna: Vienna University of Technology, 2015). See also Patton, "Our Future", 2424.
[38] Deliver for Good, *Ensure Equitable and Quality Education at All Levels* (undated), http://womendeliver.org/wp-content/uploads/2016/09/Deliver-for-Good-Card-6.pdf.

fulfil their rights to participation and freely expressing their own desires and wishes. Third, SRHR supports strengthening health systems and saving lives.[39] Implementing SRHR requires safe and well-equipped health facilities, which in turn reduces maternal as well as child mortality.[40]

The importance of SRHR has also been given a prominent place within the 2030 Agenda, as part of SDG 5. SDG target 5.6 stipulates that countries shall: "Ensure universal access to sexual and reproductive health rights as agreed in accordance with the Programme of Action of the International Conference on Population and Development and the Beijing Platform for Action and the outcome documents of their review conferences." This corresponds to different provisions on the right of the child to the highest attainable standard of health as per article 24(2) of the UNCRC.

A commonly used definition of SRHR stems from the 1994 ICPD and the subsequent Programme of Action, and will serve as the basic structure for the discussions herein.[41] The definition provides that all couples and individuals have the right to decide freely and responsibly the number, spacing and timing of their children and have the information and means to do so; the right to the highest attainable standard of sexual health; and the right to make decisions concerning reproduction free of discrimination, coercion and violence. This definition is particularly useful as it provides a good overview of both the participatory and substantive rights that girls and boys are entitled to, and the hurdles that must be overcome in securing these rights. In the following, the foundations and aspects of the three parts of the definition will be analysed.

All Couples and Individuals Have the Right to Decide Freely and Responsibly the Number, Spacing and Timing of Their Children and Have the Information and Means to Do So

The first part of the definition provides a right to family planning, which has roots in early human rights instruments and declarations. For instance, article 10 of CEDAW provides a right to family planning and sexual education. In addition,

---

[39] See, e.g., UNFPA, *Sexual and Reproductive Health for All: Reducing Poverty, Advancing Development and Protecting Human Rights* (2010), www.unfpa.org/sites/default/files/pub-pdf/uarh_report_2010.pdf and UNFPA, OHCHR and Danish Institute for Human Rights, *Reproductive Rights Are Human Rights*, 17. Cf. also UNFPA, "Report of the International Conference on Population and Development" (UN Doc. A/CONF.171/13, 18 October 1994), Chapter I, Resolution 1, Annex, principles 4–6 and section 3.16; and UNGA, "2005 World Summit Outcome" (UN Doc. A/RES/60/1, 24 October 2005), [57(g)].

[40] See, e.g., United Nations, "Framework of Actions for the Follow-Up to the Programme of Action of the International Conference on Population and Development Beyond 2014" (UN Doc. A/69/62, 12 February 2014), [24]: "The achievement of universal access to sexual and reproductive health and rights will depend on strengthening health systems by expanding their reach and comprehensiveness in a holistic manner".

[41] UNFPA, *Programme of Action Adopted at the International Conference on Population and Development Cairo, 5–13 September 1994* (2004), www.unfpa.org/sites/default/files/event-pdf/PoA_en.pdf, [7.3].

the 1974 World Population Conference and the Cairo World Population Plan of Action, which followed from it, provide that "all couples and individuals have the basic right to decide freely and responsibly the number and spacing of their children and to have the information, education and means to do so".[42]

Regarding access to information, it is important that family planning services and education efforts are provided at a low cost to be available to all.[43] In this regard, the Committee on the Rights of the Child encouraged states to involve adolescents "in the design and dissemination of information through a variety of channels beyond the school, including youth organizations, religious, community and other groups and the media", and speaks specifically to "safe and respectful ... sexual behaviours".[44]

It is also worth highlighting that the definition speaks about couples, and *all* individuals, including all genders. A challenge in terms of providing health services for men has been that a number of communities view seeking health services as something unmanly, which makes boys and men shy away from seeking help, putting themselves and the people around them at risk.[45]

The Right to the Highest Attainable Standard of Sexual Health

As noted, the UNCRC provides that every child has the right to "the highest attainable standard of health".[46] This provision echoes the right contained in article 12 of the ICESCR, which the Committee on Economic, Social and Cultural Rights (CESCR Committee) and the Office of the High Commissioner for Human Rights (OHCHR) have determined includes access to education and information on sexual and reproductive health.[47] A more detailed outline of the international legal norms and instruments that provides the foundation for this right will follow in "International Law".

The Right to Make Decisions Concerning Reproduction Free of Discrimination, Coercion and Violence

As discussed previously, harmful practices such as child, early and forced marriages can impact the ability of children to make decisions free of discrimination, coercion and violence, including decisions on reproduction.[48] Access to SRHR has been

---

[42] Ibid., [14(f)].
[43] See, e.g., UNFPA, *State of the World Population 2014*, 17.
[44] UNCRC Committee, "General Comment No. 4 (2003)", [26].
[45] See, e.g., V. Magar, "Gender, Health and the Sustainable Development Goals" (2015) 93(743) *Bulletin of the World Health Organization*: "Many communities view taking action on health as unmanly, reducing men's willingness to seek health services".
[46] UNCRC, article 24(1).
[47] UN Committee on Economic, Social and Cultural Rights, "General Comment No. 14 (2000) on the Right to the Highest Attainable Standard of HEALTH" (UN Doc. E/C.12/2000/4, 11 August 2000), [11].
[48] See, e.g., UNFPA, OHCHR and Danish Institute for Human Rights, *Reproductive Rights Are Human Rights*, 23.

highlighted as a crucial vehicle for enabling adolescent girls and boys to live healthy and fulfilling lives, and the ICPD recognised the significance of such rights to ensure both health and development.[49] At the ICPD Beyond 2014 Conference, held 20 years after the original conference had taken place, the linkages between sexual and reproductive health and rights, gender equality and sustainable development were once again emphasised, as these rights "are essential for all people, *particularly women and girls*, to achieve dignity and to contribute to the enrichment and growth of society, to innovation and to sustainable development" (emphasis added).[50]

Sexual and reproductive rights are also closely linked to autonomy and the right to privacy. Ensuring gender- and age- appropriate sexual and reproductive rights services contributes to the realisation of a number of related rights in the UNCRC. For instance, such services and education can serve as a vehicle to better implement laws for the protection of children against, for example, molestation, by ensuring that children know the names of their body parts and can articulate things that might have been done to them.[51] In this manner, knowledge and awareness about ones' rights can safeguard against exploitation and serves as an instrument for agency.

Moreover, SRHR are linked to the right to the highest attainable standard of health and access to education, which are both featured in UNCRC provisions as outlined in the preceding text. As noted by UNESCO, access to education is not just a right in and of itself, but also the precursor to realise other rights.[52] In addition, the Commission on the Status of Women in their 2016 outcome document "notes with concern the lack of progress in closing gender gaps in access to, retention in, and completion of secondary education, which is key to the achievement of gender equality and the empowerment of women and girls and the realization of their human rights and fundamental freedoms, as well as enabling other positive social and economic outcomes".[53]

Access to water and sanitation, which is critical for children's health and well-being, has been linked to supporting children's right to education through the importance of providing safe spaces for girls and boys. Many young girls are kept from school from the time that they start menstruating, due to lack of proper sanitation facilities or out of fear for harassment or assault, particularly if the way

---

[49] See "The Right to the Highest Attainable Standard of Sexual Health".
[50] UN Secretary-General, "Framework of Actions for the Follow-Up to the Programme of Action of the International Conference on Population and Development Beyond 2014" (UN Doc. A/69/62, 12 February 2014), [24].
[51] See, e.g., C. Buni, "The Case for Teaching Kids 'Vagina,' 'Penis,' and 'Vulva'", *The Atlantic*, 15 April 2013, www.theatlantic.com/health/archive/2013/04/the-case-for-teaching-kids-vagina-penis-and-vulva/274969/.
[52] UNESCO, *Connect with Respect: Preventing Gender-Based Violence in Schools* (2016), http://unesdoc.unesco.org/images/0024/002432/243252E.pdf.
[53] UN Women, *Women's Empowerment and the Link to Sustainable Development: 2016 Commission on the Status of Women Agreed Conclusions* (2016), www.unwomen.org/-/media/headquarters/attachments/sections/csw/60/csw60%20agreed%20conclusions%20conclusions%20en.pdf?vs=4409.

to the school and/or sanitary facilities is far and out of the way.[54] Through providing safe transportation and appropriate sanitation infrastructure, including menstrual hygiene management facilities and products, schools can be made more inclusive and gender-sensitive.[55]

International Law

Article 24 of the UNCRC stipulates a right to highest attainable standard of health. The African Charter on Human and Peoples' Rights (ACHPR) provides a similar provision in its article 16, stipulating that every individual "shall have the right to enjoy the best attainable state of physical and mental health" and calling upon states to take "necessary measures" to protect the health of their people.[56] In the European context, article 8 of the European Convention for the Protection of Human Rights and Fundamental Freedoms (ECHR) on respect for private life and family life has been used to provide for personal autonomy and SRHR. For instance, in *A, B and C v Ireland* before the European Court of Human Rights, the Court decided that one of the plaintiffs had the right to information about whether she was able to have an abortion under article 8 of the ECHR.[57]

As regards access to information, a number of international instruments provide for a right to information, which is vital for the fulfilment of SRHR. To begin with, article 5 of the UNCRC speaks to the "evolving capacities" of children and adolescents to make decisions based on the information he or she is entitled to seek out and receive in accordance with article 13 of the Convention. Article 17 of the UNCRC guarantees children's right to information more broadly, and is generally interpreted as covering a right to information on SRHR.[58] Likewise, the ICCPR provides that the right to information covers information of "all kinds" and many regional treaties also provide for a right to access to information.[59] CEDAW provides for a right to "access to specific educational information to help to ensure the health and well-being of families, including information and advice on family planning",[60]

---

[54] UNFPA, *State of the World Population 2016* (2016), www.unfpa.org/swop, 38.
[55] Deliver for Good, *Ensure Equitable and Quality Education at All Levels* (undated), http://womendeliver.org/wp-content/uploads/2016/09/Deliver-for-Good-Card-6.pdf.
[56] Organisation of African Unity, *African Charter on Human and Peoples' Rights* (OAU Doc CAB/LEG/67/3 rev. 5, 27 June 1981) 21 ILM 58 (1982).
[57] European Court of Human Rights, *A, B and C v. Ireland (Application no. 25579/05)*, Grand Chamber Judgment, Strasbourg (16 December 2010). See also UNFPA, OHCHR and Danish Institute for Human Rights, *Reproductive Rights Are Human Rights*, 107.
[58] OHCHR, *Information Series on Sexual and Reproductive Health and Rights: Adolescents* (2015), www.ohchr.org/Documents/Issues/Women/WRGS/SexualHealth/INFO_Adolescents_WEB.pdf.
[59] ICCPR article 19; Council of Europe, *European Convention for the Protection of Human Rights and Fundamental Freedoms* (1950) ETS 5, article 10; Organisation of American States, *American Convention on Human Rights* (1969), article 13; *African Charter on Human and People's Rights*, article 9.
[60] CEDAW, article 10(h).

while the Convention on the Rights of Persons with Disabilities guarantees accessible information for persons with disabilities.[61]

International Platforms, Declarations and Strategies to Ensure SRHR for All

The Beijing Platform for Action and the Commission of the Status of Women

The Beijing Platform for Action in 1995 was an important starting point for the discourse on women and girls' human rights. The Platform was endorsed by the General Assembly in 1996,[62] and contains twelve specific areas of concern. One of the areas listed relates to the girl child specifically.[63] Under this area, the mandate is to

> (e) Enact and strictly enforce laws to ensure that marriage is only entered into with the free and full consent of the intending spouses; in addition, enact and strictly enforce laws concerning the minimum legal age of consent and the minimum age for marriage and raise the minimum age for marriage where necessary.[64]

It should be noted that the document also contains several references to sustainable development and gender equality more broadly, highlighting that "eradication of poverty based on sustained economic growth, social development, environmental protection and social justice requires the involvement of women in economic and social development, equal opportunities and the full and equal participation of women and men as agents and beneficiaries of people-centred sustainable development".[65] The document also notes how "sustainable development will be an elusive goal unless women's contribution to environmental management is recognized and supported".[66]

As a result of the Beijing Conference, the mandate of the Commission on the Status of Women (CSW) was expanded to serve as the main body for monitoring and reviewing progress and challenges in the implementation of the Beijing Declaration and Platform for Action, as well as mainstreaming a gender perspective into

---

[61] CRPD, article 4(h).
[62] See UNFPA, OHCHR and Danish Institute for Human Rights, *Reproductive Rights Are Human Rights*, 22; UNGA, "Follow-Up to the Fourth World Conference on Women and Full Implementation of the Beijing Declaration and the Platform for Action" (UN Doc. A/RES/50/203, 23 February 1996).
[63] See UN Commission on the Status of Women, "Political Declaration on the Occasion of the Twentieth Anniversary of the Fourth World Conference on Women" (UN Doc. E/CN.6/2015/L.1, 9 March 2015), [5].
[64] United Nations, "Report of the Fourth World Conference on Women" (UN Doc. A/CONF.177/20/Rev.1, 4–15 September 1995), [274 (e)].
[65] Ibid., Chapter I, Resolution 1, Annex I, [16].
[66] Ibid., [251].

all activities by UN institutions.[67] The CSW, which meets annually and has done so since it was established under the UN Economic and Social Council in 1946,[68] has developed a number of important resolutions and working documents pertaining to the rights of women and girls.

International Conference on Population and Development and Cairo Programme of Action

In 1994, the ICPD, together with its Cairo Programme of Action, made clear that reproductive rights are not a new set of rights, referring to domestic legislation and international instruments providing for the constellation of rights and freedoms that makes up SRHR.[69] Adopted by consensus, the framework provided a strong call for adopting a gender perspective in all processes of policy formulation and implementation and in the delivery of services, especially in sexual and reproductive health.[70] In fact, the ICPD has been termed a "landmark agreement" because of its rights-based approach, which explicitly recognised that reproductive rights also belong to young people.[71]

The ICPD outcome document provides a number of direct linkages to sustainable development and the right to development, for instance noting that "the right to development must be fulfilled so as to equitably meet the population, development and environment needs of present and future generations".[72] Moreover, the Programme of Action placed "poverty eradication [and] sustained economic growth in the context of sustainable development ..., human resource development and the guarantee of all human rights, including the right to development as a universal and inalienable right and integral part of fundamental human rights" as its

---

[67] UN Economic and Social Council, "Follow-Up to the Fourth World Conference on Women" (UN Doc. E/RES/1996/6, 22 July 1996).
[68] UN Economic and Social Council, "Commission on the Status of Women" (UN Doc. E/RES/11(II), 21 June 1946).
[69] UNFPA, OHCHR and Danish Institute for Human Rights, *Reproductive Rights Are Human Rights*, 21.
[70] UNFPA, *Programme of Action*, [46]. The Programme of Action was later endorsed by the General Assembly; see UNGA, "Report of the International Conference on Population and Development" (UN Doc. A/RES/49/128, 8 February 1995).
[71] Women Deliver, *Respecting, Protecting, and Fulfilling Our Sexual and Reproductive Health and Rights: A Toolkit for Young Leaders* (2015), http://womendeliver.org/wp-content/uploads/2016/04/A_Toolkit_for_Young_Leaders.pdf, 11. See also Centre for Reproductive Rights, *Substantive Equality and Reproductive Rights: A Briefing Paper on Aligning Development Goals with Human Rights Obligations* (2014), www.reproductiverights.org/sites/crr.civicactions.net/files/documents/Equality_Guide_Reduced_size.pdf, 10: "For the first time in an international consensus document, states agreed that reproductive rights are human rights that are already recognized in domestic and international law, and that reproductive health should be an essential aspect of development programs."
[72] UNFPA, *Programme of Action*, Principle 3.

objective.[73] The programme focused on modifying consumption and production patters to foster "sustainable resource use and preventing environmental degradation".[74]

Importantly, the Cairo Programme of Action recognised the particular vulnerabilities of young people and adolescents in terms of SRHR and that "information and services should be made available to adolescents to help them understand their sexuality ... combined with the education of young men to respect women's self-determination and to share responsibility with women in matters of sexuality and reproduction" was "uniquely important for the health of young women and their children, for women's self-determination and, in many countries, for efforts to slow the momentum of population growth".[75] One of the four issues that emerged for consideration at the ICPD Beyond 2014 Conference was "the right to integrated and quality SRHR services, education and information, including comprehensive sexuality education (CSE) for adolescents, particularly adolescent girls".[76] Another issue of particular importance was the international recognition of sexual rights.[77]

In 2012, the Commission on Population and Development adopted what has been termed a "landmark resolution" on adolescents and youth, "reaffirming that development is a central goal in itself and that sustainable development in its economic, social and environmental aspects constitutes a key element of the overarching framework of United Nations activities", and urging governments to protect "the human rights of adolescents and youth to have control over and decide freely and responsibly on matters related to their sexuality, including sexual and reproductive health".[78] Girard has noted that this 2012 session of the Commission was "a first opportunity to generate momentum on SRHR".[79] This important resolution was followed by a similar declaration in a meeting in Bali the same year.[80] These two documents, together with the inclusion of targets on SRHR and harmful practices in the recently concluded Agenda 2030, are examples of a promising trend in the development of SRHR.

---

[73] Ibid., [3.16].
[74] Ibid., [3.29 (d)].
[75] Ibid., [7.41]. Cf. also United Nations, "Report of the Fourth World Conference on Women" (UN Doc. A/CONF/177/20/Rev.1, 1996), Chapter I, Resolution 1, Annex II (Platform for Action), [108 (k)], which calls for "mutually respectful and equitable gender relations and ... meeting the educational and service needs of adolescents to enable them to deal in a positive and responsible way with their sexuality".
[76] F. Girard, "Taking ICPD beyond 2015: Negotiating Sexual and Reproductive Rights in the Next Development Agenda" (2014) 9 *Global Public Health: An International Journal for Research, Policy and Practice* 607, 608.
[77] Ibid.
[78] Commission on Population and Development, "Adolescents and Youth" (UN Doc. E/CN.9/2012/8, 23–27 April 2012), [7].
[79] Girard, "Taking ICPD beyond 2015".
[80] UNFPA, "Bali Global Youth Forum Declaration" (UN Doc. UNFPA/WP.GTM.1, 10 April 2013).

Global Sustainable Development Agenda

Both the 2005 World Summit Outcome,[81] and the outcome document of the 2010 United Nations Summit on the MDGs, provided ample evidence of international commitment to sexual and reproductive health.[82] In 2012, the outcome document of the UN Conference on Sustainable Development (more widely known as the Rio+20 Conference), The Future We Want, called for "enhancing gender equality, the empowerment of women and equal opportunities for all, and the protection, survival and development of children to their full potential, including through education".[83] The document thus provides further evidence of the linkages between the rights of women and girls, SRHR and sustainable development.

The Rio+20 Conference called for SDGs that would serve as successors to the MDGs, to pursue "focused and coherent action on sustainable development".[84] These goals were adopted as the SDGs in Agenda 2030. Its preamble notes that the vision of the document is a "world in which every woman and girl enjoys full gender equality and all legal, social and economic barriers to their empowerment have been removed".[85] The document goes on to note that gender inequality remains "a key challenge",[86] and that realising gender equality and the empowerment of women and girls "will make a crucial contribution to progress across all the Goals and targets" as "the achievement of full human potential and of sustainable development is not possible if one half of humanity continues to be denied its full human rights and opportunities".[87]

Overall, girls are referenced no less than eleven times throughout the SDGs, and gender equality plays a prominent part in the 2030 Agenda. The International Center for Research on Women note that the agenda in its different facets "include important youth-focused language, so their inclusion in the 2030 Agenda is critical for holding governments accountable for the health and wellbeing of adolescent girls, as well as boys and young people more broadly".[88]

As referenced previously, SDG 5 is devoted to gender equality, and contains provisions both on ending discrimination against women and girls (SDG 5.1), as well as eliminating harmful practices such as the ones described in the preceding text (SDG 5.3). Moreover, the goal contains a target specifically on ensuring universal

---

[81] UNGA, *Sexual and Reproductive Health for All*.
[82] UNGA, "United Nations Millennium Declaration" (UN Doc. A/RES/55/2, 18 September 2000).
[83] UNGA, "The Future We Want", [11].
[84] Ibid., [245] ff.
[85] UNGA, "Transforming Our World", [8].
[86] Ibid., [14].
[87] Ibid., [20].
[88] International Center for Research on Women, *Central or Sidelined? Examining How Girls Fared in the 2030 Agenda for Sustainable Development* (2015), www.icrw.org/wp-content/uploads/2016/10/CentralorSidelined.pdf.

access to sexual and reproductive health and reproductive rights in accordance with the Programme of Action of the ICPD and the Beijing Platform for Action and the outcome documents of their review conferences (SDG 5.6).

It should be pointed out here that universal access to SRHR was already a target as part of MDG 5. Unfortunately, this target was not met by 2015 and was hindered by years of slow progress.[89] As referenced previously, one of the factors highlighted as an obstacle to implementation is the practice of child, early and forced marriages.

For instance, poverty alleviation could be supported through ridding communities of early and forced marriage. Supporting girls and their communities to avoid child marriage and stay in school often translates into greater social and financial opportunities, which can in turn build an economic base for lifting future generations out of poverty.[90] It has also been demonstrated that girls who marry before the age of 18 are more likely to experience violence within marriage than girls who marry later.[91]

Thus, by diminishing economic opportunities, restricting access to education and endangering the opportunity of girls to lead healthy lives, harmful practices such as early and forced marriage hindered the realisation of the MDGs. In addition, the MDGs limited consultation process, framing development within the context of poverty alleviation without referencing broader perspective of sustainable development, and addressed poverty, peace and human rights separately.[92] In fact, as highlighted by Sakiko Fukuda-Parr and others, the MDGs were dubbed the "Minimum Development Goals".[93] This regrettable fact highlights the importance of ensuring effective implementation and access to remedies, which will be discussed in further details in the following text.

Moreover, while the MDGs focused on achieving progress in connection to increased education opportunities for girls, SDG 5 sets out to "empower all women *and girls*". This has been seen as reflecting a shift towards acknowledging that the rights of girls are important in their own right.[94] Importantly, the SDGs also provide implementation targets, such as adopting and strengthening policies and legislation that promotes gender equality and the empowerment of all women and girls at all

---

[89] United Nations, *The Millennium Development Goals Report 2015* (2015), www.un.org/millenniumgoals/2015_MDG_Report/pdf/MDG%202015%20rev%20(July%201).pdf, 43. See also UN Entity for Gender Equality and the Empowerment of Women, *Progress towards Meeting the MDGs for Women and Girls* (2013), www.unwomen.org/en/news/in-focus/mdg-momentum; and Girard, "Taking ICPD beyond 2015", 608.

[90] UNFPA, *Marrying Too Young*.

[91] Ibid., 13.

[92] V. Esquivel and C. Sweetman, "Gender and the Sustainable Development Goals" (2016) 24(1) *Gender & Development*, 1, 3.

[93] S. Fukuda-Parr, "From the Millennium Development Goals to the Sustainable Development Goals: Shifts in Purpose, Concept, and Politics of Global Goal Setting for Development" (2016) 24(1), *Gender & Development* 43. See also Esquivel and Sweetman, "Gender and the Sustainable Development Goals".

[94] International Center for Research on Women, *Central or Sidelined?*

levels, as well as undertaking "reforms to give women equal rights to economic resources, as well as access to ownership and control over land and other forms of property, financial services, inheritance and natural resources".[95]

Other related parts of Agenda 2030 include SDG 3 on health, which contains a target on ensuring universal access to sexual and reproductive health and rights by 2030. SDG 3.7 calls for "ensure universal access to sexual and reproductive health-care services, including for family planning, information and education, and the integration of reproductive health into national strategies and programmes" by 2030. The related indicators to monitor progress focus on the proportion of women of reproductive age (aged 15–49 years) who have their need for family planning satisfied with modern methods (3.7.1) and the adolescent birth rate (aged 10–14 years, aged 15–19 years) per 1,000 women in that age group (3.7.2).

The connection between SDG 4 on education and children's rights has been outlined in the preceding text. In essence, article 24(2) (f) of the UNCRC obligates State Parties to "develop preventive health care, guidance for parents and family planning education and services". Finally, SDG 1 on poverty alleviation is also related to sexual and reproductive rights. Research shows that "poverty and insecurity [is] one of the root causes of child, early and forced marriage. Although the proportion of child brides has generally decreased over the last 30 years, child marriage remains common in rural areas and among the poorest communities".[96]

ACCESS TO REMEDIES AND JUSTICE

To ensure that SRHR are respected and upheld universally, access to remedies and justice is crucial. First, domestic provisions establishing 18 as the minimum age for marriage for both females as males, and on criminalising marital rape, provide an important standard for ensuring the obligations under international human rights law are met.[97] While the UNCRC does not stipulate such an age limit, article 1 defines that a child "for the purposes of the present Convention ... means every human being below the age of eighteen years unless under the law applicable to the child, majority is attained earlier". Thus, such an age limit could be argued to be in the spirit of the Convention. Moreover, the UNCRC Committee "strongly recommends" that the minimum age for marriage should be 18.[98] Similarly, states should ensure that domestic legislations and policies provide for and further access to sexual and reproductive health information, as well as effective remedies for when these rights are violated.[99]

---

[95] UNGA, "Transforming Our World", SDG 5a.
[96] OHCHR, "Preventing and Eliminating Child, Early and Forced Marriage", [17].
[97] UNFPA, *Marrying Too Young*, 52.
[98] UNCRC Committee, "General Comment No. 4 (2003)", [16].
[99] UN Committee on Economic, Social and Cultural Rights, "General Comment No. 22 (2016) on the Right to Sexual and Reproductive Health (article 12 of the International Covenant on Economic, Social and Cultural Rights" (UN Doc. E/C.12/GC/22, 4 March 2016).

Both the Committee on the Rights of the Child as well as the CEDAW Committee have declared that requiring the consent of a third party for access to certain services is contrary to human rights obligations.[100] If third-party consent was always required, that could create a risk for situations in which the consent of adults that are the perpetrators of violence or sexual abuse would be needed for a child to get treatment.[101] For these and other reasons, the Bali Declaration, provides that "parental and spousal consent ... should never prevent access to family planning, safe and legal abortion, and other reproductive health services – recognizing that young people have autonomy over their own bodies, pleasures, and desires".[102] All these examples point to the importance of not requiring parental or spousal consent when providing physical or mental health treatment for girls and boys.

The importance of safeguarding autonomy while respecting the rights of the adolescent child relates to another difficulty reported on by civil society organisations and other stakeholders. If young women are married and become mothers, they need to be regarded as adults to have economic freedom, and be seen as having acquired, for example, the right to enter into contracts under the law. By contrast, it is vital that they are still regarded as children and that their rights under the UNCRC are respected. Striking a good balance for these young mothers in being defined as a woman with full agency, and as a child, with different set of rights, is not always easy. The guiding principle should always be to acknowledge the rights for the girl in question.

Another important pathway towards improved implementation would be through enhancing the economic situation of girls and their families, as well as improving women's access to property rights, housing and land rights more broadly. For instance, formalising land rights and providing access to natural resources such as land can contribute to increased financial security and stability, as can inheritance rights for women and girls.[103] Providing children and girls with school meals as part of their education, mitigates and enhances the economic situation of her entire family, in addition to facilitating her studies through better nutrition.[104] Such developments could assist in breaking the spiral of poverty, and minimise

---

[100] CEDAW Committee, "General Recommendation No. 24 (1999) on Women and Health" (UN Doc. A/54/38/Rev. 1, chap. I, 20 April 1999), [14]; CEDAW Committee, "Concluding Observations on Indonesia" (UN Doc. CEDAW/C/IDN/CO/5, 10 August 2007), [16]; CEDAW Committee, "Consideration of Report Submitted by Turkey" (UN Doc. A/52/38/Rev.1, 12 August 1997), [196]; UNCRC Committee, "General Comment No. 15 (2013)", [31]; UNCRC Committee, "General Comment 4 (2003)", [28].

[101] Cf. UNFPA, OHCHR and Danish Institute for Human Rights, *Reproductive Rights Are Human Rights*, 91.

[102] UNFPA, "Bali Global Youth Forum Declaration", [3.5].

[103] See, e.g., UN Environment Programme, UN Entity for Gender Equality and the Empowerment of Women, UN Peacebuilding Support Office and UN Development Programme, *Women and Natural Resources: Unlocking the Peacebuilding Potential* (2013), www.undp.org/content/dam/undp/library/crisis%20prevention/WomenNaturalResourcesPBreport2013.pdf.

[104] UNFPA, *State of the World Population 2016*, 65.

the incentives for harmful practices.[105] The outcome document of CSW 2016 notes that the "Commission reaffirms that the realization of the right to education contributes to the promotion of gender equality and the empowerment of women and girls, human rights, sustainable development and poverty eradication".[106]

In connection to remedies, be they judicial or nonjudicial, access to information is an important prerequisite to ensure the protection of rights and sustainable development. Access to information and education on sexual and reproductive health has been deemed by the CESCR Committee to constitute a part of the right to health.[107] It is vital that these services are, in addition to being available, affordable,[108] accurate[109] and age-appropriate.[110] For these services to be available, they also have to be comprehensive and understandable. Thus, one way in which such access to information can be ensured is of course through comprehensive sexuality education, particularly as such education can create a "good spiral", in which young people once informed can request that their own rights be upheld and respected.[111] There is clear evidence that comprehensive sexuality education has a positive impact on sexual and reproductive health and helps reduce sexually transmitted infections, including HIV, and unintended pregnancy,[112] and several human rights bodies have emphasised the importance of accessing such education.[113] Regrettably, recent research demonstrates that inequalities between countries and regions are particularly apparent when it comes to access to SRHR services for adolescents.[114]

---

[105] UNFPA, *Marrying Too Young*, 52.
[106] UN Women, *Women's Empowerment*, [9].
[107] UN Committee on Economic, Social and Cultural Rights, "General Comment No. 14 (2000)", [11].
[108] Cf. Barroso, "Beyond Cairo", 640: "The persistent lack of affordable services that are truly responsive to adolescents' and young people's needs and rights is reflected in staggering inequalities between their health indicators and those of their adult counterparts".
[109] UNESCO, *State of the World Population 2014*.
[110] Ibid., 2: "[E]ffective sexuality education can provide young people with age-appropriate, culturally relevant and scientifically accurate information. It includes structured opportunities for young people to explore their attitudes and values, and to practise the skills they will need to be able to make informed decisions about their sexual lives". Cf. also UNFPA, OHCHR and Danish Institute for Human Rights, *Reproductive Rights Are Human Rights*, 83.
[111] Barroso, "Beyond Cairo", 643: "When [comprehensive sexuality education] is accessible, young people gain awareness and become the best defenders of their own sexual rights".
[112] UNFPA, *State of the World Population 2016*, 65. See also UNESCO, *Emerging Evidence, Lessons and Practice in Comprehensive Sexuality Education: A Global Review 2015* (2015), www.unfpa.org/sites/default/files/pub-pdf/CSE_Global_Review_2015.pdf.
[113] See, e.g., UNCRC Committee, "General Comment No. 15 (2013)", [31], [60] and [69]; CEDAW Committee, "Concluding Observations on Eritrea" (UN Doc. CEDAW/C/ERI/CO/3, 3 February 2006), [23]; UNCRC Committee, "Concluding Observations on Antigua and Barbuda" (UN Doc. CRC/C/15/Add.247, 3 November 2004), [54]; UN Committee on Economic, Social and Cultural Rights, "Concluding Observations on Benin" (UN Doc. E/C.12/1/Add.78, 5 June 2002), [42].
[114] Barroso, "Beyond Cairo", 640: "Nowhere are the inequalities in access to services and respect for rights more glaring than when it comes to meeting the needs of adolescents and youth. Young people's sexual rights are regularly violated across cultures, religions and national

Such unfortunate realities, coupled with the challenges posed by a more general lack of access to education, exacerbates the vulnerability of young girls and boys.[115] Ensuring the obligation of all states to implement and uphold the human rights of their citizens is the focus of the next part of this chapter.

When customary law exists in parallel to formal legislation, it is important to ensure that there is not a wide gap between these two systems.[116] While these considerations are, of course, highly context-specific, it can be noted in general that such customary frameworks are often very important for local communities, and thus must be taken into account to provide rights for all.[117] A joint report by UNFPA, OHCHR and the Danish Institute for Human Rights emphasises that national human rights institutions should monitor how customary norms and frameworks can impact and contribute to "the implementation of public policies and programmes" on SRHR.[118]

The possibility of individual complaints under a number of the human rights treaties, including the UNCRC, has been highlighted as a means for individuals to seek redress for violation of their rights.[119] It should nonetheless be noted that such individual complaints often require both access to information about the particular remedy, and the financial resources to pursue such a claim.

Lastly, and as referenced previously, providing an obligation to register birth and marriages contributes to preventing child marriage through increased awareness, and provides evidence regarding the age of a girl and her partner for girls and families seeking legal and financial remedies.[120]

IMPLEMENTATION PROGRESS, PROSPECTS AND CHALLENGES

For the rights described in this chapter to be fully realised and respected, effective implementation is crucial. The multitude of issues and aspects of sustainable development and rights that relate both to gender equality and children's rights demonstrates the interconnectedness of the SDGs. Making progress across a core set of interlinked areas will be "critical and cost-effective, as no sector or intervention can singly achieve the objectives".[121] A key lesson from Cairo is that an excellent Platform of Action

---

borders. ... With the largest generation of young people ever on the planet, meeting their needs and respecting their rights is an urgent priority".

[115] See, e.g., UNFPA, *Marrying Too Young*, 51.
[116] UNFPA, OHCHR and Danish Institute for Human Rights, *Reproductive Rights Are Human Rights*, 39.
[117] Ibid. See also UN Human Rights Committee, "General Comment No. 28 (2000) on the Equality of Rights between Men and Women" (UN Doc. CCPR/C/21/Rev.1/Add.10, 29 March 2000), [23].
[118] UNFPA, OHCHR and Danish Institute for Human Rights, *Reproductive Rights Are Human Rights*, 44.
[119] Ibid., 119.
[120] Girls Not Brides, "How Can We End Child Marriage?" (undated) www.girlsnotbrides.org/how-can-we-end-child-marriage/.
[121] Every Woman Every Child, *The Global Strategy*, 43–46.

backed by government commitments does not automatically lead to results.[122] A number of actors have reported that implementation challenges still persist in the ICPD processes, in the Beijing Platform and to the MDG and SDG processes.[123] While it is important to note that the reasons for the lack of such implementation are highly context-specific, a few general tendencies can be observed.

First, a "lack of awareness and training among law enforcement officials and other relevant professionals to ensure that laws are understood, implemented and enforced" has been highlighted as a hindrance for the full and rights-based implementation of domestic legislation.[124] Training and education efforts, as well as normative transformation through participatory dialogue, have been described as important tools to ensure a shift of minds and action.[125] It has also been demonstrated that the education of girls lead to healthier families and stronger gross domestic product growth.[126] In addition, it has been noted that full participation of women in labour forces "would add percentage points to most national growth rates – double digits in many cases".[127]

Regarding the discrepancies between formal and religious or customary law on the minimum age of marriage, implementation relies on ensuring a stable shift of norms, practices and expectations more broadly. Community leaders, religious leaders, as well as other influential political or social figures play an important role in conveying key considerations and acting as translators between the global and the local, and vice versa.[128] Political figures, such as First Ladies of several countries, have been important actors for promoting and raising awareness about harmful practices, including for example through addressing legislators and policymakers during a panel on harmful practices at the HRC.[129] Working with parents, children, leaders and other stakeholders through community dialogue, education and other

---

[122] Barroso, "Beyond Cairo", 644.

[123] See, e.g., UNFPA, *State of the World Population 2014*, 37: "Although many countries have a comprehensive sexuality education policy and programme, most do not implement it widely or in a way that adhere to international standards".

[124] Girls Not Brides, *Child Marriage and the Rule of Law* (2014), www.girlsnotbrides.org/wp-content/uploads/2014/04/Child-marriage-and-the-rule-of-law.pdf.

[125] Centre for Reproductive Rights, *Substantive Equality and Reproductive Rights*, 19; and CEDAW Committee, "Communication 17 (2011): *Alyne da Silva Pimentel Teixeira v Brazil*" (UN Doc. CEDAW/C/49/D/17/2008, 27 September 2011), [8].

[126] Deliver for Good, *Ensure Equitable and Quality Education at All Levels* (undated) http://womendeliver.org/wp-content/uploads/2016/04/Good_Campaign_Brief_6_092016.pdf.

[127] United Nations, *Gender Equality: Why It Matters* (undated), www.un.org/sustainabledevelopment/gender-equality/.

[128] UNFPA, *Marrying Too Young*, 52; UNFPA, OHCHR and Danish Institute for Human Rights, *Reproductive Rights Are Human Rights*; Girls Not Brides, *Lessons Learned from Selected National Initiatives to End Child Marriage* (2015), http://girlsnotbrides.theideabureau.netdna-cdn.com/wp-content/uploads/2015/07/Lessons-learned-from-national-strategies-Girls-Not-Brides-July-2015.pdf.

[129] OHCHR, "Summary Report on the Panel Discussion on Preventing and Eliminating Child, Early and Forced Marriage" (UN Doc. A/HRC/27/34, 18 July 2014).

efforts has been shown to secure developments that are to the benefit of all.[130] Collaboration between UN agencies and other stakeholders has seen increased progress in countries such as Malawi, where joint efforts by UN Women and the UN Country Team provided joint advocacy which in turn contributed to the passing of the Marriage, Divorce and Family Relations Bill in 2015. The bill stipulates 18 as the minimum age for marriage.[131]

Adolescent girls, both married and unmarried, often face significant challenges in accessing contraception.[132] Age restrictions on access to sexual and reproductive health services is one impediment, while others are fuelled by social norms that hinder young women and girls from seeking out information about their sexuality and their sexual and reproductive health.[133]

Moreover, while the SDGs are not formally binding, they symbolise a commitment on behalf of all states, and a political will and visibility that can be built upon to further the rights of girls and boys worldwide.

The CEDAW Committee and the Committee on the Rights of the Child provide additional visibility and pressure to create and enforce domestic legislation prohibiting harmful practices and providing access to reproductive health services as well as comprehensive sexuality education.[134] A number of the special mandate procedures at the HRC could also ensure that the issue stays on the agenda and attention of policymakers, such as the Special Rapporteur on the right of everyone to the highest attainable standard of health, the Special Rapporteur on violence against women, its causes and consequences and the Special Rapporteur on the right to education.[135]

Gender Disaggregated Data and the Importance of Avoiding Embedding Gender Stereotypes

Collecting data is vital for implementation efforts generally, as measuring ensures visibility and assists in identifying good priorities.[136] UNFPA lists as priorities the collection and analysis of data, as well as identifying geographic "hotspot" areas

---

[130] See, e.g., UNFPA, Marrying Too Young, 52.
[131] UN Entity for Gender Equality and the Empowerment of Women, Annual Report 2014–2015 (2015), 18–19, www.unwomen.org/en/digital-library/publications/2015/6/annual-report-2014-2015.
[132] UNFPA, State of the World's Population Report 2012: By Choice, Not by Chance: Family Planning, Human Rights and Development (2012), www.unfpa.org/sites/default/files/pub-pdf/EN_SWOP2012_Report.pdf, 31.
[133] OHCHR, Information Series on Sexual and Reproductive Health and Rights.
[134] UNFPA, Marrying Too Young, 56.
[135] Cf. UNFPA, OHCHR and Danish Institute for Human Rights, Reproductive Rights Are Human Rights, 184.
[136] See, e.g., Centre for Reproductive Rights, Substantive Equality and Reproductive Rights, 20, and D. Rosche, "Agenda 2030 and the Sustainable Development Goals: Gender Equality at Last? An Oxfam Perspective" (2016) 24(1) Gender & Development 111, 123: "Investing in national statistical capacity to collect, analyse, and use data systematically to inform policymaking is a prerequisite for gathering good data".

where girls are at risk, to design better policies and programmes for the rights of women and girls.[137] In particular, a data gap in regards to indicators on 10- to 14-year-old adolescents has been identified, as many current monitoring mechanisms begin measuring reproductive health at 15, which means that the experiences of younger adolescents are not accounted for.[138]

Ensuring gender-disaggregated data was called for in the development of the SDG indicators,[139] and UN Women estimated in 2015 that at least 50 of the SDG indicators require gender-sensitive data.[140] Such data can serve an important purpose in terms of ensuring education, eliminating violence, and access to SRHR services to fully realise SRHR rights. In certain contexts, existing data such as national censuses could also be further analysed to better understand the rights of children and young adolescents.[141] To support the implementation of Agenda 2030, SDG 17.18 provides that by 2020, capacity-building support to developing countries should be enhanced, "including for least developed countries and small island developing states, to increase significantly the availability of high-quality, timely and reliable data disaggregated by income, gender, age, race, ethnicity, migratory status, disability, geographic location and other characteristics relevant in national contexts".

Nonetheless, while gender disaggregated data is an important tool to analyse whether laws and policies make a difference for individuals within different groups and genders, it is equally important not to limit the potential of women and girls – or men and boys – to act in a different manner than expected by any form of traditional roles. Relying on women to act in accordance with certain characteristics, even if they are considered to be constructive and valuable, could risk binding women and girls to these expectations.[142] In short, adopting traits that are regarded as traditionally female in a particular context should only be a possibility and never an obligation.

---

[137] UNFPA, *Marrying Too Young*, 6: "Each country should collect and analyze its own data to help target geographic 'hotspot' areas where high proportions and numbers of girls are at risk. Policies and programmes should be designed accordingly".
[138] Every Woman Every Child, *Technical Guidance for Prioritizing Adolescent Health*, 21.
[139] UNGA, "Transforming Our World", [48]: "Quality, accessible, timely and reliable disaggregated data will be needed to help with the measurement of progress and to ensure that no one is left behind". See also OHCHR, *SDGs Indicator Framework: A Human Rights Approach to Data Disaggregation to Leave No One Behind*, Draft background note (2015), www.ohchr.org/Documents/Issues/HRIndicators/DataDisaggregation.pdf.
[140] UN Women, *Driving the Gender-Responsive Implementation of the 2030 Agenda for Sustainable Development* (2016), www.unwomen.org/en/digital-library/publications/2016/8/driving-the-gender-responsive-implementation-of-the-2030-agenda-for-sustainable-development.
[141] UNFPA, *State of the World Population 2016*.
[142] UN Secretary-General, "World Survey on the Role of Women in Development: Gender Equality and Sustainable Development" (UN Doc. A/69/156, 18 July 2014) [59]: "First, policymakers should avoid making broad and stereotypical assumptions about women's and men's relationships with the environment. Rather, policies should respond to the specific social context and gender power relations".

FUTURE OUTLOOK AND SUGGESTIONS FOR FUTURE RESEARCH

The year 2015 was important for sustainable development, with the adoption of Agenda 2030 and the SDGs. The implementation of this agenda will prove important for enabling young girls and boys to fully enjoy their sexual, health and reproductive rights. Linking the work on ending harmful practices to a broad and universal agenda could also ensure greater sustainability of the work towards ending early, child and forced marriages, as noted and recommended, for example in a 2015 report from Girls Not Brides.[143]

The Women Deliver conference, organised every three years and aiming to foster a new generation of advocates for gender equality and the rights of women and girls, can serve as an important vehicle in terms of implementation of the post-2015 agenda.[144] Indeed, the focus of the 2016 conference was "on how to implement the SDGs as they relate to girls and women, with a specific focus on health – in particular maternal, sexual, and reproductive health and rights – and the inter-connections with gender equality, education, environment, and economic empowerment".[145] A number of the recommendations stemming from the conference highlight the importance of sustainable development. In addition, the Conference has established a Deliver for Good initiative, which focuses on realising the SDGs for women and girls through twelve specific impact areas, one of which is SRHR.[146]

In the coming years, it will be vital to direct research efforts towards finding examples of how implementation can be achieved, and what lessons can be learned from the processes pertaining to the MDGs and leading to the adoption of the SDGs. It will also be important to continue the work and analysis in forums such as the HRC and the Commission on the Status of Women. The promising developments that have been seen in relation to the panels and resolutions on child, early and forced marriages serve as a vitalising force for the issues where all Member States of the HRC are present and could be built upon and expanded.

Lastly, research efforts should be focused on the agency and rights interface, as mentioned previously, as well as methods for ensuring the dissemination of available information, model legislation for enabling treatments without spousal or parental consent and ways of closing the gap between formal and religious/customary law. Finally, further research could address the ways in which new technology provides opportunities for greater data collection and implementation towards improved gender equality and sustainable development.

---

[143] Girls Not Brides, *Lessons Learned*, 14: "[L]inking child marriage to a broader agenda of girl's empowerment and gender equality in society overall to ensure its sustainability".

[144] Women Deliver, "About" (undated), www.womendeliver.org/about/.

[145] Women Deliver, "2016 Conference" (undated), www.womendeliver.org/conferences/2016-conference/.

[146] Women Deliver, "What Is Deliver for Good?" (undated), http://womendeliver.org/deliver-for-good/faq/.

7

Children with Disabilities, Human Rights and Sustainable Development

Paul Harpur and Michael Ashley Stein

INTRODUCTION

Children with disabilities (CWDs) are among the most vulnerable persons on the planet.[1] They can benefit from human rights protection, non-discrimination laws, social welfare schemes, and international development aid when seeking to fulfill their human potential.[2] Nevertheless, CWDs living in regions that experience poverty or other circumstances requiring foreign-driven assistance are often excluded from those schemes and are thereby disproportionately disadvantaged relative to their non-disabled peers.

The heightened vulnerability of CWDs in recipient regions can be illustrated by considering CWDs and their capacity to exercise their right to education. The education gap between CWDs and children without disabilities is much wider in donor-recipient states than in developed states.[3] Indeed, some estimates indicate that

---

[1] The authors thank Joseph Lelliott for his research assistance. UNCRC Committee, "General Comment No. 9 (2006) on the Rights of Children with Disabilities" (UN Doc. CRC/C/GC/9, 27 February 2007), 2; M. Fineman, *The Autonomy Myth: A Theory of Dependency* (New York and London: The New Press, 2004), 35.

[2] A. S. Kanter and B. A. Ferri (eds.), *Righting Educational Wrongs: Disability Studies in Law and Education* (Syracuse, NY: Syracuse University Press, 2013); R. Dixon and M. C. Nussbaum, "Children's Rights and a Capabilities Approach: The Question of Special Priority" (2012) 97 *Cornell Law Review* 549.

[3] J. Forole Jarso, "Analyzing the Rights of Children and International Human Rights Law: Implementing the Children's Rights Agenda in Kenya: Taking Stock of the Progress, Hurdles and Prospects" (2012) 27 *American University International Law Review* 673. We note that CWDs within donor States continue to experience unequal educational experiences when compared to the wider student cohort. S. Arduin, "Implementing Disability Rights in Education in Ireland: An Impossible Task?" (2013) 36(1) *Dublin University Law Journal* 93; P. Harpur, "Ensuring Equality in Education: How Australian Laws Are Leaving Students with Print Disabilities Behind" (2010) 15(1) *Media and Arts Law Review* 70; J. E. Lord and M. A. Stein, "Social Rights and the Relational Value of the Rights to Participate in Sport, Recreation, and Play" (2009) 27 *Boston University International Law Journal* 249, 265; K. Walker, "Comparing

CWDs in donor-recipient States are three times less likely to be exercising their right to education.[4] In Zimbabwe, for example, 10.1 per cent of children generally have not attended school compared to 27.9 per cent of CWDs.[5] In Malawi and Namibia, CWDs are almost twice as likely to be denied their right to education: 35 per cent of CWDs in Malawi have never attended school relative to 18 per cent of children generally, while in Namibia 38.6 per cent of CWDs have not attended school compared to 16.2 per cent of children generally.[6]

Moreover, many CWDs who are excluded from education in developing states have inconsequential impairments and could attend school if stigma did not prejudice decision makers or if reasonable accommodations were provided.[7] In Uganda, for instance, only 2 per cent of CWDs with deafness or who are hard of hearing attend school.[8] Even where schools in donor-recipient countries try to include CWDs, the lack of resourcing and training means that the education provided can vary in quality.[9] Axiomatically, low-quality education will not enable CWDs to fully realise their right to education, and only inclusive education will enable them to receive quality education.[10]

Denying CWDs their right to education has broader implications for poverty and economic development because that deprivation reduces their prospects for employment and future financial independence.[11] Disallowing CWDs their right to education likewise increases long-term economic costs for the states, communities, and

---

American Disability Laws to the Convention on the Rights of Persons with Disabilities with Respect to Postsecondary Education for Persons with Intellectual Disabilities" (2014) 12 *Northwestern University Journal of International Human Rights* 115.

[4] P. Leia and J. Myers, "Making the Grade? A Review of Donor Commitment and Action on Inclusive Education for Disabled Children" (2011) 15(10) *International Journal of Inclusive Education* 1169.

[5] SINTEF, *Living Conditions among People with Disabilities in Zimbabwe: A Representative Regional Study* (Oslo, Norway: SINTEF, 2003); SINTEF, *Living Conditions among People with Activity Limitations in Malawi: A Representative National Survey* (Oslo, Norway: SINTEF, 2004); P. Thomas, *Disability, Poverty and the Millennium Development Goals: Relevance, Challenges and Opportunities for DFID* (New York: Cornell University, 2005).

[6] Ibid.

[7] S. Peters, *Education Notes – Education for All: Including Children with Disabilities* (Washington, DC: World Bank, 2003).

[8] S. Milesa, L. Waplinga and J. Beart, "Including Deaf Children in Primary Schools in Bushenyi, Uganda: A Community-Based Initiative" (2011) 32(8) *Third World Quarterly* 1515.

[9] C. J. Johnstone and D. W. Chapman, "Contributions and Constraints to the Implementation of Inclusive Education in Lesotho" (2009) 56(2) *International Journal of Disability, Development and Education* 131.

[10] Office of the UN High Commissioner for Human Rights (OHCHR), "Thematic Study of the Rights of Persons with Disabilities to Education" (UN Doc. A/HRC/25/29, 18 December 2013), [3].

[11] D. Filmer, *Disability, Poverty and Schooling in Developing Countries: Results from 11 Household Surveys: World Bank Policy Research Working Paper* (Washington, DC: The World Bank, 2005).

families who provide subsistence to these children when they have grown to adulthood.[12] In sum, the global community and international development programs are failing to address the extreme educational inequalities and consequent human rights violations experienced by CWDs in donor-recipient states, with those states ultimately incurring severe social and financial costs.[13]

The UN Convention on the Rights of Persons with Disabilities (CRPD) precipitated a new disability human rights paradigm[14] by introducing a comprehensive framework for change that includes benchmarks for ensuring the equality of persons with disabilities.[15] Prominently, the CRPD transforms states obligations to promote the rights of CWDs.[16] Progress initiated by the CRPD gained further momentum with the 2015 adoption of the Sustainable Development Goals (SDGs),[17] which acknowledge disability in its programming. Collectively, the CRPD and the SDGs signal a dramatic sea change from the limited protection historically provided to CWDs by international human rights laws.[18] To illustrate: the rights afforded to CWDs in the Preamble and article 23 of the UN Convention on the Rights of the Child (UNCRC)[19] is conditional – "to the extent feasible" – and limited to the exchanging of information.[20] In consequence, international development efforts largely ignored the needs of CWDs, or when recognising the sector merely reinforced welfare dependence.

This chapter critically analyses the extent to which international law and programming, including the SDGs, reflect the disability rights paradigm adopted by the CRPD. Rather than attempting to evaluate development programs and outcomes for every right, we focus on the capacity of CWDs to exercise their right to education. The chapter is divided into four parts. "Disability Rights and the UNCRC" describes the emergence of a disability rights-based approach for CWDs under international

---

[12] Leia and Myers, "Making the Grade?"
[13] Jarso, "Analyzing the Rights of Children and International Human Rights Law".
[14] UN General Assembly (UNGA), *Convention on the Rights of Persons with Disabilities* (UN Doc. A/61/106, 13 December 2006) 2515 UNTS 3; P. Harpur, "Embracing the New Disability Rights Paradigm: The Importance of the Convention on the Rights of Persons with Disabilities" (2012) 27(1) *Disability and Society* 1, 1.
[15] G. Quinn, "The United Nations Convention on the Rights of Persons with Disabilities: Toward a New International Politics of Disability" (2009) 15 *Texas Journal on Civil Liberties & Civil Rights* 33, 33.
[16] R. McCallum and H. Martin, "The CRPD and Children with Disabilities" (2013) 20 *Australian International Law Journal* 17.
[17] UNGA, "Transforming Our World: The 2030 Agenda for Sustainable Development" (UN Doc. A/RES/70/1, 21 October 2015).
[18] G. Quinn and T. Degener, "A Survey of International, Comparative and Regional Disability Law Reform", in M. Breslin and S. Yee (eds.), *Disability Rights Law and Policy: International and National Perspectives* (New York: Transnational, 2002), 3–129.
[19] UNGA, *Convention on the Rights of the Child* (UN Doc. A/RES/44/25, 20 November 1989)1577 UNTS 3.
[20] M. A. Stein and P. J. S. Stein, "Disability, Development, and Human Rights: A Mandate and Framework for International Financial Institutions" (2014) 47 *UC Davis Law Review* 1231, 1242.

law surrounding the UNCRC and also assessing its progress. Next, "The CRPD Paradigm Shift" examines the CRPD's transformation of international human rights law and highlights two of its mandates: the provision by states of inclusive education domestically and the proscription to engage internationally only in disability inclusive cooperation and development. "CWDs and the SDGs" relates the advocacy efforts that resulted in the SDGs including persons with disabilities in its purview, and then enumerates and critiques how CWDs have been included as a targeted and disaggregated population under SDGs Goal 4 relating to inclusive education. "Including CWDs in Future Programming" offers constructive suggestions for operationalising inclusive education in development programs by removing embedded barriers and prioritising the right as a program area in donor-recipient states.

DISABILITY RIGHTS AND THE UNCRC

CWDs' right to education and development has been facilitated by adoption of the UNCRC, subsequent soft law developments, and General Comments and Concluding Observations issued by the UN Committee on the Rights of the Child (UNCRC Committee). Nevertheless, the UNCRC Committee has inadequately advanced the rights of CWDs through Concluding Observations.

The UNCRC

The UNCRC, which came into force in 1990, was the first UN human rights document to expressly enshrine the rights of CWDs.[21] Article 23(3) requires States Parties "to ensure" that CWDs within their jurisdiction have access to "education, training, health care services, rehabilitation services, preparation for employment and recreation opportunities in a manner conducive to the child achieving the fullest possible social integration and individual development".

The UNCRC requires significant efforts from states to promote the right to education for CWDs within their own borders but compels far less from states when promoting the rights and objectives of that treaty in donor-recipient countries. The UNCRC Preamble recognises the general importance of international cooperation for improving the living conditions of children, but its development mechanisms are weak. Article 23(4) of the UNCRC does not require states to mainstream disability equality activities, and instead focuses on sharing information "with the aim of enabling States parties to improve [CWDs'] capabilities and skills". Thus, article 23 recognises that CWDs have rights to education, care, and active involvement in the community but does not require states to enshrine such measures in their

---

[21] V. Torres Hernandez, "Making Good on the Promise of International Law: The Convention on the Rights of Persons with Disabilities and Inclusive Education in China and India" (2008) 17 *Pacific Rim Law and Policy Journal* 497.

development activities. Article 28(3), by contrast, can be read as expanding on extraterritorial obligations by obligating states to "promote and encourage international co-operation in matters relating to education" and thereby contribute "to the elimination of ignorance and illiteracy throughout the world". Conceivably, CWDs ought to have benefited from the requirements of article 28(3), but evidence does not demonstrate significant progress.

Soft Law

Following adoption of the UNCRC, a number of soft laws were promulgated to promote the rights of CWDs. These non-binding measures included efforts to advance the rights of CWDs in development activities. The most significant were the Standard Rules on the Equalization of Opportunities for Persons with Disabilities (Standard Rules)[22] and the Salamanca Statement and Framework for Action on Special Needs Education (Salamanca Statement).[23]

The 1993 Standard Rules enumerate twenty-two guidelines that summarise and make operational the outcomes of the World Programme of Action.[24] Rule 22 focuses on international cooperation and proposes a range of measures to promote rights within state forums and through bilateral activities. In relation to development programs, Rule 22 provides that "States should introduce disability aspects in general negotiations concerning standards, information exchange, [and] development" but conditions that activity to "[w]henever appropriate". Consequently, the Standard Rules made progress towards incorporating the rights of CWDs in development by encouraging their inclusion and by listing some measures. Nonetheless, the Standard Rules also qualified the circumstance of CWDs' inclusion, and thus did not compel the mainstreaming of those children into aid schemes.

The following year, representatives of ninety-two governments and twenty-five international organisations formed the World Conference on Special Needs Education and adopted the Salamanca Statement that introduced a paradigm shift from integrated to inclusive education for CWDs.[25] In doing so, the Salamanca Statement enhanced the role of CWDs on the global development agenda. Clause 77 promotes exchanges of information and research, and arguably reflects the information-sharing focus for development under the UNCRC. Clauses 80 and 81, however, exceeded the promoting of information sharing by integrating

---

[22] UNGA, "Standard Rules on the Equalization of Opportunities for Persons with Disabilities" (UN Doc. A/48/49, 20 December 1993) 202.

[23] UNESCO, *The Salamanca Statement and Framework for Action on Special Needs Education* (Salamanca, Spain: UNESCO, 1994).

[24] UNGA, "The World Programme of Action Concerning Disabled Persons" (UN Doc. A/37/51, 3 December 1982).

[25] F. Kiuppis, "Why (Not) Associate the Principle of Inclusion with Disability? Tracing Connections from the Start of the 'Salamanca Process'" (2014) 18(7) *International Journal of Inclusive Education* 746.

capacity-building measures into development programs concerning CWDs. Clause 80 noted that measures should support advanced training for CWDs professionals at the regional level and "foster co-operation between university departments and training institutions in different countries for conducting comparative studies". Clause 81 encouraged the development and support of regional professional associations that, in turn, are likely to contribute to capacity building. Collectively, these pair of clauses advanced the notion of inclusive development for CWDs.

The UNCRC Committee

Despite the increasing recognition of the rights of CWDs through the Standard Rules and the Salamanca Statement, UNCRC processes have provided limited recognition of the rights of CWDs generally, or the importance of mainstreaming these issues specifically within development programs.[26] Regrettably, the same is true for the UNCRC Committee that was established to monitor progress made by States parties in realising their UNCRC obligations.[27]

The UNCRC Committee's 2001 General Comment on Education (2001 General Comment), the first by the treaty body, recognised that discrimination against CWDs was pervasive in many formal and informal educational systems and settings.[28] At the same time, the 2001 General Comment failed to address global inequalities in education experienced by CWDs, made little effort to combat this discrimination at national levels, and evidenced no effort to combat this iniquity through development programs.

By contrast, the 2006 General Comment on the Rights of Children with Disabilities (2006 General Comment) represents the most significant move by the UNCRC Committee to protect the rights of CWDs and mainstream their development.[29] The 2006 General Comment contains a significant amount of detail on how CWDs' rights should be protected domestically by each state, including the crucial mandate that states provide reasonable accommodations and undertake positive conduct to ensure educational outcomes.[30] In terms of measures within international cooperation and development programming, it is worth quoting at length the 2006 General Comment which:

> strongly recommends States parties to ensure that, within the framework of bilateral or multilateral development assistance, particular attention is paid to children with

---

[26] L. Waddington and C. Toepke, *Moving towards Inclusive Education as a Human Right: An Analysis of International Legal Obligations to Implement Inclusive Education in Law and Policy* (Maastricht, The Netherlands: Maastricht University Faculty of Law, 2014).

[27] UNCRC, article 43(1).

[28] UNCRC Committee, "General Comment No. 1 (2001) on Article 29(1), The Aims of Education" (UN Doc. CRC/GC/2001/,1 17 April 2001).

[29] UNCRC Committee, "General Comment No. 9 (2006)".

[30] Ibid.

disabilities and their survival and development in accordance with the provisions of the Convention, for example, by developing and implementing special programmers aiming at their inclusion in society and allocating earmarked budgets to that effect. States parties are invited to provide information in their reports to the Committee on the activities and results of such international cooperation.[31]

Recognition by the 2006 General Comment of the importance of mainstreaming CWDs' issues in development programs represents relatively dramatic progress. Nevertheless, the obligations placed on states are extremely weak because States Parties are merely invited to share information on how they mainstreamed CWDs-related issues in their development programs. The 2006 General Comment nevertheless provided the basis for the UNCRC Committee to critique state practices when issuing Concluding Observations on periodic reports by individual states.

To analyse the extent to which the UNCRC Committee acted on the opportunity provided by the 2006 General Comment,[32] we reviewed Concluding Observations that followed the adoption of the 2006 General Comment to seven major donor countries:[33] 2012 Australia,[34] 2012 Canada,[35] 2009 France,[36] 2014 Germany,[37] 2010 Japan,[38] 2011 New Zealand,[39] and 2008 and 2016 United Kingdom.[40] The UNCRC Committee raised issues relevant to the rights of CWDs in its Concluding Observations for each of these states. Some of these Concluding Observations noted significant concerns with state practices.[41] However, even when Concluding Observations were critical of domestic practices towards CWDs, there was no mention of international development efforts concerning CWDs. Specifically, when development efforts were mentioned in Concluding Observations, the UNCRC Committee

---

[31] Ibid.
[32] For an assessment of how UN treaty bodies, including the UNCRC Committee, has mainstreamed disability human rights, see K. Skarstad and M. A. Stein, "Mainstreaming Disability in the United Nations Treaty Bodies" (2018) 17 *Journal of Human Rights* 1.
[33] The United States, the United Kingdom, Germany, and Japan are the largest donor countries, but because the United States has not ratified the UNCRC it could not be included in this sample. To replace the United States, we identified states that are State Parties to the UNCRC and have similar CWDs laws to the United States: Australia, Canada, France, and New Zealand.
[34] UN Doc. CRC/C/AUS/CO/4, 28 August 2012.
[35] UN Doc. CRC/C/CAN/CO/3-4, 6 December 2012.
[36] UN Doc. CRC/C/FRA/CO/4, 11 June 2009.
[37] UN Doc. CRC/C/DEU/CO/3-4, 25 February 2014.
[38] UN Doc. CRC/C/JPN/CO/3, 20 June 2010.
[39] UN Doc. CRC/C/NZL/CO/3-4, 11 April 2011.
[40] UN Doc. CRC/C/GBR/CO/5, 3 June 2016; UN Doc. CRC/C/GBR/CO/4, 20 October 2008.
[41] For example, the Concluding Observations for Japan in 2010 were highly concerned with the treatment of CWDs in the Japanese education system. The Committee noted that it remained "concerned that deep-rooted discrimination still exists and that measures for children with disabilities are not carefully monitored. It also notes with concern that children with disabilities continue to have limited access to education due to lack of political will and financial resources for the necessary equipment and facilities" (see UN Doc. CRC/C/JPN/CO/3, 20 June 2010).

did not encourage states to include CWDs, nor did it reference the most relevant international instruments on the rights of CWDs: the 2006 General Comment or the CRPD. Further – and equally astounding – the UNCRC Committee also did not reference the international development provisions in the 2006 General Comment or CRPD when discussing the rights of CWDs across its Concluding Observations despite the considerable guidance contained in those instruments. The 2011 New Zealand Concluding Observation, for instance, does not reference either the 2006 General Comment or the CRPD.[42]

Equally perplexing, where the UNCRC Committee references the 2006 General Comment in the examined Concluding Observations, it does not mention international development or cooperation. The 2009 Concluding Observation for France, to note one example, mentions overseas territories, but this reference is to colonial territories governed directly by that State.[43] Overall, among the Concluding Observations we studied, the UNCRC Committee used the 2006 General Comment merely to critique domestic activities. To illustrate, the 2006 General Comment was used in the Concluding Observations on Australia to identify six issues, including clarifying the definition of disability, strengthening support measures, promoting the social model of disability in laws and policies, improving the availability of resources, ensuring children are able to exercise their right to education, and introducing laws that prohibit non-therapeutic sterilisation of all children.[44] This approach was followed in Concluding Observations for 2016 United Kingdom,[45] 2014 Germany,[46] 2012 Canada,[47] 2010 Japan,[48] and 2009 France.[49]

The impact of the CRPD on development practices is analysed later in this chapter. At this point it is worth observing that the CRPD has been underutilised by the UNCRC Committee.[50] The absence can be partly explained due to the CRPD not having been in operation over the entire period in which we analysed Concluding Observations. This timing might also explain why Concluding Observations nearer the commencement date of the CRPD focused exclusively on encouraging states to ratify the CRPD, as was the case for the United Kingdom in 2008 and Japan in 2010.[51] It does not, however, explain why the UNCRC Committee continued to underutilise the CRPD even after it had been ratified by states, as exemplified by the 2011 New Zealand Concluding Observation noted previously

---

[42] UN Doc. CRC/C/NZL/CO/3–4, 11 April 2011.
[43] UN Doc. CRC/C/FRA/CO/4, 11 June 2009, [70].
[44] UN Doc. CRC/C/AUS/CO/4, 28 August 2012, [58].
[45] UN Doc. CRC/C/GBR/CO/5, 3 June 2016; UN Doc. CRC/C/GBR/CO/4, 20 October 2008.
[46] UN Doc. CRC/C/DEU/CO/3–4, 25 February 2014, [58].
[47] UN Doc. CRC/C/CAN/CO/3–4, 6 December 2012.
[48] UN Doc. CRC/C/JPN/CO/3, 20 June 2010.
[49] UN Doc. CRC/C/FRA/CO/4, 11 June 2009, [70].
[50] Skarstad and Stein, "Mainstreaming Disability in the United Nations Treaty Bodies".
[51] UN Doc. CRC/C/GBR/CO/5, 3 June 2016; UN Doc. CRC/C/GBR/CO/4, 20 October 2008, [53(f)]; UN Doc. CRC/C/JPN/CO/3, 20 June 2010, [59(i)].

(New Zealand ratified the CRPD in 2008).[52] Further, the 2014 Concluding Observation for Germany acknowledged with approval that Germany had ratified the CRPD but then did not reference the CRPD in analysing the rights of CWDs.[53] The 2016 Concluding Observation on the United Kingdom likewise makes no reference to the CRPD[54] despite the CRPD having been ratified by that State in 2009.[55]

When the CRPD was used by the UNCRC Committee to critique state activities, it referenced no more than a very small number of rights. Hence the 2009 Concluding Observation on France uses the CRPD only to critique education;[56] the 2012 Concluding Observation on Australia to critique the full and effective participation of CWDs in society[57] and immigration and migration policies impacting on CWDs;[58] and the 2012 Concluding Observation on Canada to remark on inclusive education,[59] to support parents caring for CWDs so that those parents can exercise their right to work,[60] to encourage data collection on CWDs,[61] and to protect CWDs from violence.[62]

Thus, although the 2006 General Comment and the CRPD provided the UNCRC Committee with the bases for forwarding the rights of CWDs in international cooperation and development through inclusive activities, the treaty body eschewed that course in their Concluding Observations.

THE CRPD PARADIGM SHIFT

The CRPD ushered in a paradigm shift for the rights of persons with disabilities. Notably, the CRPD requires states domestically to provide inclusive education to CWDs, and to engage only in inclusive international cooperation and development activities in the promotion of the rights of persons with disabilities, which include *inter alia* CWDs.

The CRPD's Disability Rights Framework

Prior to the CRPD, international law recognised that persons with disabilities possessed human rights, at least technically, yet treated the group as unequal.[63]

---

[52] In addition to a 2008 ratification date, New Zealand was active in development, drafting, promoting and implementing the CRPD. See www.odi.govt.nz/what-we-do/un-convention/.
[53] UN Doc. CRC/C/DEU/CO/3-4, 25 February 2014, [4(d)].
[54] UN Doc. CRC/C/GBR/CO/5, 3 June 2016; UN Doc. CRC/C/GBR/CO/4, 20 October 2008.
[55] See the map of ratifications of the Convention on the Rights of Persons with Disabilities, produced by the OHCHR: www.ohchr.org/Documents/HRBodies/CRPD/OHCHR_Map_CRPD.pdf.
[56] UN Doc. CRC/C/FRA/CO/4, 11 June 2009, [70].
[57] UN Doc. CRC/C/AUS/CO/4, 28 August 2012, [58(c)].
[58] Ibid., [58(g)].
[59] UN Doc. CRC/C/CAN/CO/3-4, 6 December 2012, [60(b)].
[60] Ibid., [60(c)].
[61] Ibid., [60(a)].
[62] Ibid., [60(d)].
[63] G. Quinn, "A Short Guide to the United Nations Convention on the Rights of Persons with Disabilities" (2009) 1 *European Yearbook of Disability Law* 89, 89–90.

By contrast, the CRPD promotes equal inclusion in society as a fundamental human right[64] and rejects the notion that persons with disabilities should have their rights discounted.[65] In consequence, and for the first time in history, persons with disabilities are now regarded by international law as full and equal citizens,[66] with equal access to rights that non-disabled populations have long assumed as fundamental and assured, including employment, the highest standard of health, access to justice, and living within one's community, to name only a few.[67]

Accordingly, the CRPD substantially transforms how international human rights law approaches persons with disabilities,[68] including its crucial transposition to domestic settings.[69] States Parties are required to help realise the provisions of the CRPD, such that its sweeping human rights agenda should drive domestic law and policy reforms.[70] This includes the obligation under article 4 on adopting all appropriate legislative, administrative, and other measures for the implementation of the rights recognised in the CRPD, and for doing so in active collaboration with civil society, especially persons with disabilities.[71] The CRPD's transformative social

---

[64] R. Kayess and P. French, "Out of Darkness into Light? Introducing the Convention on the Rights of Persons with Disabilities" (2008) 8 *Human Rights Law Review* 1.

[65] A. Lawson, "Accessibility Obligations in the UN Convention on the Rights of Persons with Disabilities: Nyusti and Takacs v Hungary" (2014) 30(2) *South African Journal on Human Rights* 380.

[66] M. Waterstone, "The Significance of the United Nations Convention on the Rights of Persons with Disabilities" (2010) 33 *Loyola International and Comparative Law Review* 1, 2. Professor Quinn heralds the CRPD as the "Declaration of Independence" for persons with disabilities (G. Quinn, "Closing: Next Steps – Towards a United Nations Treaty on the Rights of Persons with Disabilities", in P. Blanck [ed.], *Disability Rights* [Farnham, UK: Ashgate, 2005], 541).

[67] M. Stein and J. E. Lord, "The United Nations Convention on the Rights of Persons with Disabilities: Process, Substance, and Prospects", in F. Gomez Isa and K. De Feyter (eds.), *International Human Rights Law in a Global Context* (Bilbao, Spain: University of Deusoto, 2009), 495.

[68] H. Bielefeldt, "New Inspiration for the Human Rights Debate: The Convention on the Rights of Persons with Disabilities" (2007) 25(3) *Netherlands Quarterly of Human Rights* 397; P. Harpur, "Time to Be Heard: How Advocates Can Use the Convention on the Rights of Persons with Disabilities to Drive Change" (2011) 45(3) *Valparaiso University Law Review* 1271; C. Parker and L. Clements, "The UN Convention on the Rights of Persons with Disabilities: A New Right to Independent Living?" (2008) 4 *European Human Rights Law Review* 508; N. Munro, "Define Acceptable: How Can We Ensure That Treatment for Mental Disorder in Detention Is Consistent with the UN Convention on the Rights of Persons with Disabilities?" (2012) 16(6) *International Journal of Human Rights* 902; Waterstone, "The Significance of the United Nations Convention on the Rights of Persons with Disabilities".

[69] J. E. Lord and M. A. Stein, "Prospects and Practices for CRPD Implementation in Africa" (2014) 1 *African Year Book on Disability Rights* 97.

[70] J. E. Lord and M. A. Stein, "The Domestic Incorporation of Human Rights Law and the United Nations Convention on the Rights of Persons with Disabilities" (2008) 83 *University of Washington Law Review* 449.

[71] E. Flynn, "Ireland's Compliance with the Convention on the Rights of Persons with Disabilities: Towards a Rights-Based Approach for Legal Reform?" (2009) 31(1) *Dublin University Law Journal* 357; P. Gooding, "Navigating the 'Flashing Amber Lights' of the Right to Legal Capacity in the United Nations Convention on the Rights of Persons with Disabilities:

agenda is not, however, limited to law and policy reform. To illustrate: the treaty requires as part of its comprehensive agenda the breaking down of prevailing stereotypes that bolster the exclusion of persons with disabilities from all aspects of society through article 8; likewise, it mandates socially inclusive cultural, sport, and recreational activities through article 30. As persons with disabilities, CWDs are empowered by the human rights mandates of the CRPD. Those rights are comprehensive and designed to be applied holistically.[72] In addition, article 7 specifically highlights CWDs and their full and equal enjoyment of rights and is to be read horizontally across the treaty and be applied to all other articles.[73]

The impact of the CRPD on CWDs is evinced by the significance of the right to education in article 24. The right to education is one of the more strongly worded state duties contained in the treaty. Article 24 contains five sub-articles, all which adopt directive phrases such as "shall"[74] and "ensure".[75] Within these sub-articles, article 24 enumerates eleven paragraphs that provide further detail on what states must do to enable persons with disabilities to exercise their right to education on an equal basis with others. These obligations are extensive, including duties not to exclude persons with disabilities from the general educational system,[76] to provide reasonable accommodations,[77] and to assist with learning orientation skills, braille, and sign language.[78]

In addition, article 24 extends who may benefit from the right to education. Thus, although UNCRC article 23(3) is limited to primary education, CRPD article 24 provides that states "shall ensure an inclusive education system at all levels and lifelong learning". This enables CWDs to access education for a longer period than under the UNCRC where a child is defined as anyone under the age of eighteen, and the right to education is limited to primary school.[79] By contrast, CRPD article 24 maintains that CWDs can exercise their right to education for their entire childhood, and into adult life.

Responding to Major Concerns" (2015) 15(1) *Human Rights Law Review* 45; K. Johnson "The UN Convention on the Rights of Persons with Disabilities: A Framework for Ethical and Inclusive Practice?" (2013) 7(3) *Ethics and Social Welfare* 218; J. E. Lord, D. Samant Raja and P. Blanck, "Beyond the Orthodoxy of Rule of Law and Justice Sector Reform: A Framework for Legal Empowerment and Innovation through the Convention on the Rights of Persons with Disabilities" (2013) 4 *World Bank Legal Review* 41.

[72] M. A. Stein, "Disability Human Rights" (2007) 95 *California Law Review* 75.

[73] M. A. Stein and J. E. Lord, "Future Prospects for the United Nations Convention on the Rights of Persons with Disabilities", in G. Quinn and O. M. Arnardóttir (eds.), *The UN Convention on the Rights of Person with Disabilities: European and Scandinavian Perspectives* (Boston: Brill-Nijhoff, 2009), 17.

[74] CRPD, article 32(1), (3), (4) and (5).

[75] CRPD, article 32(2).

[76] CRPD, article 24(2)(a).

[77] CRPD, article 24(2)(c).

[78] CRPD, article 24(3)(a)–(c).

[79] UNCRC, articles 1 and 28. See also P Harpur & MA Stein, 'Universities as Disability Rights Change Agents' (2018) 10(2) *Northeastern University Law Review* 79.

Arguably the most important measure in article 24 is the right of CWDs to an inclusive education.[80] An observation by the former Chair of the UNCRPD Committee (in conjunction with a co-author) is worth noting at length:

> [The] CRPD Committee has stressed the importance of enabling children with disabilities to obtain education, and preferably inclusive education where children with disabilities are alongside other children in the classroom. Again, owing to their experiences of their own disabilities, the members of the CRPD Committee see the availability of education from kindergarten to university as being crucial for the development of children with disabilities.[81]

The UNCRPD Committee's General Comment No. 4 entitled "The Right to Inclusive Education" (General Comment No. 4) explains the normative content of inclusive education in CRPD article 24.[82] The General Comment provides that education must be available, meaning that there are sufficient places where CWDs can be educated,[83] and that education be affordable.[84] To achieve inclusivity, educational systems need to be accessible at all levels. This includes the built environment, instructional materials, information and communication technologies, teaching techniques, and assessments.[85] One aspect that has attracted particular attention, both in the General Comment and beyond, is the widespread lack of textbooks in formats that are accessible and usable by CWDs.[86] General Comment No. 4 seeks to remedy that situation by encouraging states to implement the Marrakesh Treaty to Facilitate Access to Published Works for Persons Who Are Blind, Visually Impaired, or Otherwise Print Disabled (Marrakesh Treaty).[87] The Marrakesh Treaty reduces the barriers created by copyright, and thereby promotes and enables textbooks that are in accessible formats, such as Braille, to be shared between countries.[88] This will likely have a significant impact on the numbers of textbooks in formats that CWDs in donor-recipient states can use in their education.

---

[80] P. R. Chowdhury, "The Right to Inclusive Education of Persons with Disabilities: The Policy and Practice Implications" (2011) 12(2) *Asia-Pacific Journal on Human Rights and the Law* 1.
[81] McCallum and Martin, "The CRPD and Children with Disabilities".
[82] UNCRPD Committee, "General Comment No. 4 (2016) on Article 24: Right to Inclusive Education" (UN Doc. CRPD/C/GC/4, 2 September 2016), [19].
[83] Ibid., [20].
[84] Ibid., [23].
[85] Ibid., [21].
[86] Ibid.
[87] Ibid., [22]; *Treaty to Facilitate Access to Published Works for Persons Who Are Blind, Visually Impaired, or Otherwise Print Disabled*, Marrakesh (VIP/DC/8, 28 June 2013). See for further analysis of this problem: P. Harpur and N. Suzor, "Copyright Protections and Disability Rights: Turning the Page to a New International Paradigm" (2013) 36(3) *University of New South Wales Law Journal* 745.
[88] P. Harpur, *Discrimination, Copyright and Equality: Law Opening the E-Book for the Print Disabled* (Cambridge: Cambridge University Press, 2017).

Disability Inclusive Development under the CRPD

The CRPD obligates State Parties to promote disability inclusive development, and *inter alia* CWDs' right to education, in international cooperation and development programs. The CRPD implicitly addresses this obligation through a number of provisions. For example, the Preamble draws a link between poverty and disability; the general obligations of article 4 require states to consider disability in all laws, policies, and domestic programs; and article 11 requires states to consider persons with disabilities when responding to risks and humanitarian emergencies.

Yet strikingly, the CRPD goes much further than these indirect references. Unique among all UN human rights treaties, CRPD article 32 provides a standalone international cooperation and development clause. In doing so, and by requiring states to "undertake appropriate and effective measures" to realise the purposes and objectives of the treaty, this provision underscores the impact of development aid and collaboration.

Further, article 32 enumerates a specific road map for disability inclusive development. To assist states, article 32 provides a non-exhaustive list of four measures State Parties may elect to adopt in discharging their obligations. If a state does not adopt these measures, then that state will need to identify other schemes that will achieve the required objective of using international cooperation and development to assist other countries to discharge their CRPD duties. The suggested schemes of article 32 are (1) ensuring that international programming is inclusive of and accessible to persons with disabilities;[89] (2) building and supporting the capacity of persons with disabilities by including them throughout the development scheme,[90] and ensuring the continued viability of the programming beyond the lifetime of the funding;[91] (3) cooperating on research and access to scientific and technical knowledge that leads to more inclusive societies[92] and sustainable results[93] and (4) providing both technical assistance[94] and economic transfers.[95]

---

[89] R. Yeo and K. Moore, "Including Disabled People in Poverty Reduction Work: 'Nothing about Us, without Us'" (2013) 31(3) *World Development* 571.

[90] Thomas, *Disability, Poverty and the Millennium Development Goals*.

[91] E. Karangwa, S. Miles and I. Lewis, "Community Level Responses to DISABILITY and Education in Rwanda" (2010) 57(3) *International Journal of Disability, Development and Education* 267.

[92] E. Le Borgne and S. Cummings, "The Tip of the Iceberg: Tentative First Steps in Cross-Organisational Comparison of Knowledge Management in development organisations" (2009) 5(1) *Knowledge Management for Development Journal* 39; S. van Veen, J. Bunders and B. Regeer, "Mutual Learning for Knowledge Co-Creation about Disability Inclusive Development: Experiences with a Community of Practice" (2013) 9(2) *Knowledge Management for Development Journal* 102.

[93] S. Waddell et al., "Inter-Organisational Learning: A New Frontier" (2013) 46 *Capacity.org*, www.capacity.org/capacity/opencms/en/topics/learning/interorganisational-learning-a-new-frontier.html.

[94] CRPD, article 4(1)(f) and (g).

[95] K. Matshedisho, "The Challenge of Real Rights for Disabled Students in South Africa" (2007) 2(4) *South African Journal of Higher Education* 706.

Requiring states to consider all the provisions of the CRPD in their development programs has the potential to substantially promote inclusivity in circumstances in which equality has not previously been on the agenda. Indeed, evidence demonstrates that state responses to article 32 have "been relatively quick and far-reaching".[96] A range of states, including Australia, Finland, Germany, Italy, Japan, and the United Kingdom, rapidly moved to develop disability inclusive development programs,[97] with other States following suit.[98] It remains, however, very much an uneven work in progress.

CWDS AND THE SDGS

International development programming – including, for fifteen years, the Millennium Development Goals (MDGs)[99] – historically excluded persons with disabilities despite the salience of disability to their stated agendas.[100] In October 2015, the UN General Assembly adopted the successor program to the MDGs, the SDGs, as the centerpiece of the 2030 Agenda for Sustainable Development.[101] Concerted and effective advocacy by international disability rights groups contributed to the SDGs containing references to persons with disabilities. Of signal importance, CWDs are specifically targeted in SDGs Goal 4 as it impacts inclusive education.

Advocacy Efforts

Since the early 1980s, disability rights advocates have lobbied to include persons with disabilities and their needs in the global development agenda.[102] Nevertheless, the MDGs were adopted by the UN General Assembly for implementation from 2000 through 2015 without those interests being included.[103] The globally agreed-on MDGs contained eight goals, eighteen targets, and forty-eight indicators. Each

---

[96] Stein and Stein, "Disability, Development, and Human Rights", 1243.
[97] J. E. Lord et al., *Disability and International Cooperation and Development: A Review of Policies and Practices* (Washington, DC: World Bank, 2010), 18.
[98] M. A. Stein, "Mainstreaming and Accountability: (Really) Including Persons with Disabilities in Development Aid and Humanitarian Relief Programming" (2013) 31 *Nordic Journal of Human Rights* 292.
[99] UNGA, UN Millennium Declaration (UN Doc. A/Res/55/2, 18 September 2000).
[100] Thus, the prescient warning by James Wolfensohn, then-president of the World Bank, that the MDGs would fail if they did not include persons with disabilities in their implementation. See J. D. Wolfensohn, "Editorial, Poor, Disabled and Shut Out" *Washington Post*, 3 December 2002, 25.
[101] UNGA, "Transforming Our World".
[102] A. Ito, "International Legal and Policy Framework on Disability" (1999) 93 *American Society of International Law Proceedings* 334, 334.
[103] G. Mji et al., "Networking in Disability for Development: Introducing the African Network for Evidence-to-Action on Disability (AfriNEAD)", in M. MacLachlan and L. Swartz (eds.), *Disability and International Development: Towards Inclusive Global Health* (New York: Springer, 2009), 75–80.

Goal's provenance was highly relevant to disability. To illustrate: the MDGs sought to halve world poverty, and at the time of their adoption it was believed that 20 per cent of those living below the poverty level had disabilities.[104] Similarly, the MDGs aspired to have every primary age school child attend school, and at the time of their adoption evidence indicated that one-third of primary school age children not in school were CWDs.[105] Thus, even though the MDGs were aimed at combating worldwide poverty and creating a more just social order, the MDGs neglected persons with disabilities – the globe's largest and most disadvantaged minority group.[106]

The decision not to promote disability development in the MDGs, despite the relevance of disability to its programmatic goals, arguably encouraged international cooperation and development programs to likewise elide them from implementation efforts.[107] The fifth review and appraisal of the World Programme of Action concerning Disabled Persons, as well as the desk review of the MDGs country reports, found that disabilities were "invisible" in national development priorities.[108] Similarly, a UN review of the MDG processes found that persons with disabilities were often left out of development interventions.[109] The review likewise determined that persons with disabilities would only be included in future development programs if the MDGs' goals specifically targeted the group.[110] The absence of persons with disabilities from the MDGs, as well as many other development programs, was widely recognised as an error that needed to be remedied in the next round of global development programming.[111]

With the MDGs' end in sight, the disability rights community began to consider how to best ensure that disability issues would be included in any successor global

---

[104] Cf. The "Factsheet on Persons with Disabilities", UN Enable, www.asksource.info/resources/fact-sheet-persons-disabilities.

[105] UNGA, "Status of the Convention on the Rights of the Child: Report of the Secretary-General" (UN Doc. A/66/230, 3 August 2011), [29].

[106] Stein and Stein, "Disability, Development, and Human Rights", 1234.

[107] J. E. Lord and K. N. Guernsey, *Inclusive Development and the Comprehensive and Integral International Convention on the Protection and Promotion of the Rights and Dignity of Persons with Disabilities* (New York: International Development and Disability Consortium, 2005), 6–9.

[108] UNGA, "Realizing the Millennium Development Goals for Persons with Disabilities through the Implementation of the World Programme of Action Concerning Disabled Persons and the Convention on the Rights of Persons with Disabilities: Report of the Secretary-General" (UN Doc. A/64/180, 27 July 2009) 3.

[109] UN Department of Social and Economic Affairs, *Disability and the Millennium Development Goals: A Review of the MDG Process and Strategies for Inclusion of Disability Issues in Millennium Development Goal Efforts* (2011), www.un.org/disabilities/documents/review_of_disability_and_the_mdgs.pdf.

[110] Ibid.

[111] S. Godziek, "MDG 6: What about Disabled People?" (2009) 11(1) *Journal of Health Management* 109.

development agenda.¹¹² Drawing from the experience of the CRPD negotiations and the attendant disability politics that it energised in the form of participatory justice,¹¹³ disabled peoples organisations (DPOs) and their supporters promoted the notion that international development frameworks needed to specifically target persons with disabilities.¹¹⁴ For example, the International Disability Alliance struggled against the invisibility of persons with disabilities by lobbying to have disability referenced in MDGs outcome documents.¹¹⁵ These disability rights lobbying efforts were partially successful with disability being referenced in the 2010 MDGs outcome document; bizarrely, however, disability was not referenced in the 2012 MDGs outcome document.¹¹⁶

In 2012, states agreed at the UN Conference on Sustainable Development to commence a process to develop a set of development goals to replace the MDGs.¹¹⁷ As part of this endeavour, the open group on disabilities recognised that progress within the existing MDGs framework was inequitable for eliding persons with disabilities.¹¹⁸ The 2013 High Level Meeting on Disability and Development accepted that development goals needed to specifically mention disability to ensure that any future development agenda would include their needs.¹¹⁹

In March 2013, the UN Department of Economic and Social Affairs and UNICEF facilitated an online discussion of persons with disabilities and their representatives to inform a subsequent UN High-Level Meeting on Disability and Development. From a worldwide consultation process that encompassed disability rights networks, translations, social media, and physical attendance at key gatherings, well more than 1,000 contributions were received from eighty-eight countries.¹²⁰ This extensive consultation process resulted in publication of a report that identified

---

[112] www.disabledpeoplesinternational.org/DurbanDeclaration.
[113] For a discussion of participatory justice see M. Stein and J. Lord, "Jacobus ten Broek, Participatory Justice, and the UN Convention on the Rights of Persons with Disabilities" (2008) 13(2) *Texas Journal on Civil Liberties & Civil Rights* 167; M. A. Stein and J. E. Lord, "Participatory Justice, the UN Disability Human Rights Convention, and the Right to Participate in Sport, Recreation, and Play", in J. Kumpuvuori and M. Scheinin (eds.), *The United Nations Convention on the Rights of Persons with Disabilities: Multidisciplinary Perspectives* (Helsinki: Vike, 2009), 226.
[114] UNGA, "Report of the Open Working Group of the General Assembly on Sustainable Development Goals" (UN Doc. A/68/970, 2014).
[115] G. Wolbring and B. Burke, "Reflecting on Education for Sustainable Development through Two Lenses: Ability Studies and Disability Studies" (2013) 5 *Sustainability* 2327.
[116] Ibid.
[117] UNGA, "The Future We Want" (UN Doc. A/RES/66/288, 11 September 2012).
[118] https://sustainabledevelopment.un.org/index.php?page=view&type=9502&menu=1565&nr=13.
[119] UNGA, "Outcome Document of the High-Level Meeting of the General Assembly on the Realization of the Millennium Development Goals and Other Internationally Agreed Development Goals for Persons with Disabilities: The Way Forward, a Disability-Inclusive Development Agenda towards 2015 and Beyond" (UN Doc. A/68/L.1, 17 September 2013).
[120] UNICEF and UN Women, *Global Thematic Consultation on the Post-2015 Development Agenda: Addressing Inequalities: Synthesis Report of Global Public Consultation* (New York: United Nations, 2013).

the major obstacles encountered and challenges faced in relation to implementing development policies and programs for persons with disabilities.[121] The nineteen key themes that emerged provided a road map for what a disability inclusive development agenda needed to target to achieve equality.[122]

With additional effort, promotion of the rights of persons with disabilities in the new development goals began to gain official acceptance. This normative transformation led to recognition in both the UN Secretary General's Report "Keeping the Promise: Realizing the Millennium Development Goals for Persons with Disabilities towards 2015 and Beyond",[123] and the report of the High-Level Panel on the Post-2015 Development Agenda.[124] The Outcome Document of the High Level Meeting on the Realization of the MDGs and other internationally agreed development goals for persons with disabilities, entitled "The Way Forward, a Disability-Inclusive Development Agenda towards 2015 and Beyond" adopted values and principles promoting disability inclusive development goals. Specifically, it recognised "the importance of ensuring accessibility for and inclusion of persons with disabilities in all aspects of development and of giving due consideration to all persons with disabilities in the emerging post-2015 United Nations development agenda".[125] Similarly, UN General Assembly Resolution 67/140 called for "realizing the Millennium Development Goals and other internationally agreed development goals for persons with disabilities".[126]

The recognition of the need to include persons with disabilities within the global development agenda resulted in persons with disabilities being distinctly named in the adopted 2015 SDGs (see "The SDGs"). The significant role played by DPOs and their allies that resulted in disability being "included at the heart" of the 2030 development was justly acknowledged by General Assembly President Mogens Ly.[127]

The SDGs

The SDGs were adopted by the United Nations to guide development practices from 2015 through 2030,[128] and to do so with a more ambitious agenda than

---

[121] Ibid.
[122] Ibid.
[123] UNGA, "Keeping the Promise: Realizing the Millennium Development Goals for Persons with Disabilities towards 2015 and Beyond: Report of the Secretary-General" (UN Doc. A/65/173, 26 July 2010).
[124] High-Level Panel of Eminent Persons on the Post-2015 Development Agenda, *A New Global Partnership: Eradicate Poverty and Transform Economies through Sustainable Development* (New York: United Nations, 30 May 2013).
[125] UNGA, "Outcome Document of the High-Level Meeting of the General Assembly", [3].
[126] UNGA, "Realizing the Millennium Development Goals and Other Internationally Agreed Development Goals for Persons with Disabilities towards 2015 and Beyond" (UN Doc. A/Res/67/140, 20 December 2012).
[127] www.un.org/apps/news/story.asp?NewsID=54225#.V7af7fmrhBc.
[128] UNGA, "Transforming Our World", 2–3.

the predecessor MDGs.[129] Accordingly, the SDGs contain seventeen goals, along with 169 associated targets.[130] The indicators have not been released as of this writing.

The SDGs' goals and targets aimed to end poverty; achieve food security; enable the right to health; ensure inclusive and equitable quality education; achieve gender equity; ensure access to water and sanitation; make cities inclusive; promote peaceful and inclusive societies; and combat climate change.[131] From a disability-inclusive perspective, the SDGs represent considerable improvement on the MDGs.[132] Whereas the MDGs were silent as to disability as a programming sector, the SDGs specifically incorporate persons with disabilities within their framework. Seven of the seventeen SDGs goals expressly reference persons with disabilities,[133] a notable improvement on the MDGs.[134] Such is the case with SDGs Goal 4, which specifically if imperfectly targets education. By expressly recognising CWDs, Goal 4 focuses attention on that population for development agents tasked with implementing the SDGs, whereas they could otherwise justify overlooking CWDs under the MDGs.[135]

By the same token, SDGs Goal 4 is uneven relative to the UNCRC and the CRPD, at times matching, falling short, or exceeding their respective mandates. The encouragement in Goal 4 to promote universal design in education, and

---

[129] N. Alreshaid, "Lodging the Sustainable Development Goals in the International Trade Regime: From Trade Rhetoric to Trade Plethoric" (2016) 22(2) *Journal of Environmental and Sustainability Law* 174.

[130] www.un.org/sustainabledevelopment/.

[131] Ibid.

[132] International Disability Alliance and International Disability and Development Consortium, *IDA and IDDC Response to Final Draft of the Outcome Document for the UN Summit to Adopt the Post-2015 Development Agenda* (undated), https://sustainabledevelopment.un.org/content/documents/15718IDA%20and%20IDDC.pdf.

[133] International Disability and Development Consortium and International Disability Alliance, *The 2030 Agenda, The Inclusion of Persons with Disabilities: Introductory Toolkit* (Brussels: International Disability and Development Consortium, 2016).

[134] M. Keogh, "Inclusive Development Aid", in Peter Blanck and Eilionóir Flynn (eds.), *Routledge Handbook of Disability Law and Human Rights* (Oxford: Routledge, 2016), 228.

[135] Parenthetically, although this chapter focuses on Goal 4 and its potential impact on development programs for promoting CWDs' right to education, we note the impact of the other SDGs Goals upon CWDs' capacity to exercise their right to education. Much as the Vienna Declaration characterizes human rights, we would argue that development initiatives are indivisible, interdependent and interrelated. See UNGA, "Vienna Declaration and Programme of Action" (UN Doc. A/CONF.157/23, 12 July 1993), [5]. To provide one example, SDG Goal 1 seeks to end poverty in all its forms everywhere. When CWDs and their families are impoverished, children are often called upon to work and their capacity to seek education is limited. For CWDs, poverty engenders even greater social marginalisation: families in economic straights often prioritise education expenses on their children without disabilities on the notion that they have a better chance to succeed. (K. Lamichhane, *Disability, Education and Employment in Developing Countries: From Charity to Investment* [Cambridge: Cambridge University Press, 2015], 255).

thus ability equality,[136] follows the CRPD's approach to inclusive and universal design.[137] The promotion of equal access to education in the SDGs likewise satisfies the standards posited in the UNCRC that speak of "effective" access within a state's own jurisdiction, but fall short of the duties created by the CRPD that mandate an equal educational experience. Last, the SDGs exceed the UNCRC's much lower obligations as far as disability inclusive education in development programs because the UNCRC is essentially limited to information exchange.

Whether the SDGs meet the standards posited in the CRPD to achieve disability inclusive development by requiring donor bodies "to undergo procedural, substantive, and ultimately institutional cultural changes"[138] may ultimately be determined when the SDG indicators are released. On its face, SDGs Goal 4 lacks the detail and breadth to ensure that development activities will promote disability inclusive education as envisaged by the CRPD. Nothing in that Goal, for instance, would prevent CWDs from being provided equal access to age appropriate education provided in segregated schools, as has been past practice across the globe.[139] By contrast, the CRPD requires states to promote all the rights in the CRPD, including CWDs' right to inclusive education. Moreover, CRPD article 32 requires that states promote those rights outside their boundaries as part of their inclusive international cooperation and humanitarian aid schemes. The SDGs as a development scheme does not contain a parallel legal enforcement measure[140] but can be strongly influential for their prescribed targets, bolstered by resource transfers and programming support, and thereby elicit global reputational considerations and international cooperation.[141] The SDGs can, therefore, help create a framework to promote development and the realisation of the right to education by CWDs.

INCLUDING CWDS IN FUTURE PROGRAMMING

The CRPD, the UNCRC, and SDGs each promote disability empowering development programming and provide tools, jointly and severally, for improving CWDs' right to inclusive education. Nevertheless, operationalising inclusive education in

---

[136] P. Harpur, "From Universal Exclusion to Universal Equality: Regulating Ableism in a Digital Age" (2013) 40(3) *Northern Kentucky Law Review* 529.
[137] For obligations in relation to inclusive and universal design concerning education see, for example, CRPD articles 5(1)(f), 9(1)(a) and 24(2)(b).
[138] Stein and Stein, "Disability, Development, and Human Rights", 1259.
[139] M. A. Stein et al., "Disability", in S. N. Katz et al. (eds.), *The Oxford International Encyclopedia of Legal History* (Oxford: Oxford University Press, 2009), 335.
[140] N. Schrijver, "The Evolution of Sustainable Development in International Law: Inception, Meaning and Status" (2008) *Hague Academy of International Law* 25.
[141] A. Geisinger and M. A. Stein, "A Theory of Expressive International Law" (2007) 60 *Vanderbilt Law Review* 77; A. Geisinger, "A Belief Change Theory of Expressive Law" (2002) 88 *Iowa Law Review* 35.

development programs in a way that removes embedded barriers and is effectively implemented by states remains a pervasive challenge going forward.

Removing Embedded Barriers

The CRPD Committee issued concrete guidance in General Comment No. 4 on what measures states must provide to achieve inclusive education.[142] As an overarching principle, whole systems, education, and person approaches must be adopted.[143] Consequently, disability rights issues need to be embedded in institutional cultures and practices at all levels, with the attendant goal that all actors cooperate to implement flexible learning models that maximise the education of each CWD. To reach this dynamic, appropriate resourcing and support must be provided to schools, teachers, CWDs, and other stakeholders.[144] Likewise, states need to monitor and review their remedial measures.[145] Thus, one immediate lesson to take away is that inclusive education can only be achieved if the rights of CWDs are implemented holistically and coordinated towards a commonly understood goal rather than being left to stakeholders acting in isolation from each other.

Several barriers systemically prevent the realisation of inclusive education. General Comment No. 4 noted that seven such impediments:[146] misunderstandings about disablement,[147] negative stereotypes,[148] lack of political will,[149] inadequate funding,[150] research and development failures,[151] technological barriers,[152] and inappropriate or inaccessible legal remedies.[153] Overcoming these obstacles requires that ministries of education advance the rights of CWDs to education in conjunction with other key ministries by acting across governmental silos.[154] Such cooperative actions were noted by the General Comment as necessary to combat traditional practices of marginalising the educational rights of CWDs into health or disability ministries, practices that resulted in CWDs being excluded from mainstream education.[155]

Accordingly, comprehensive and coordinated regulatory frameworks must be introduced across all government sectors to attain educational flexibility, diversity

---

[142] UNCRPD Committee, "General Comment No. 4 (2016)", 2, [12].
[143] Ibid., [12](a), (b), (c) and (e).
[144] Ibid., [12](d), (f), (g) and (h), [69] and [70].
[145] Ibid., [12](i) and [72].
[146] Ibid., [4].
[147] Ibid.
[148] Ibid.
[149] Ibid.
[150] Ibid.
[151] Ibid.
[152] Ibid.
[153] Ibid.
[154] Ibid., [57].
[155] Ibid.

and equality for CWDs.[156] Legislative frameworks must comply with disability human rights,[157] and contain clear definitions of inclusion and inclusive goals in all laws that impact on inclusive education[158] and against which compliance can be judged.[159] Definitions and obligations must include a duty to provide reasonable accommodations,[160] embracing universal design when developing learning systems and environments,[161] and structures to enable the voices of CWDs to be heard when developing, assessing, implementing, and monitoring these systems.[162] Monitoring and enforcement must involve both government-led "Education Sector Plans," as well as complaint mechanisms that include compensation and sanctions.[163]

In addition to focusing domestically, General Comment No. 4 advises states to mainstream inclusive education within their international activities.[164] To achieve this, all international cooperation "must advance inclusive and equitable quality education".[165] These international activities should include capacity building, information sharing, and facilitating the provision of adaptive technologies. Recognising the diversity of disability, these measures "should be disaggregated by impairment".[166]

When devising inclusive education programs it is important to look beyond the CRPD and the SDGs. The CRPD can do much, but the integration of CRPD rights into mainstream policies can only be achieved when engaging with other rights regimes. For example, the UNCRC promotes the right to education, and the CRPD and SDGs advise that the right to education should be advanced in a way that is inclusive for all children.[167] To ensure that CWDs are not left behind, it is critical to ensure that SDG-based programs are implemented in a manner conducive to realising UNCRC rights to education also consider the rights of CWDs under the CRPD.

General Comment No. 4 demonstrates that promoting inclusive education requires a consideration beyond a single human rights convention and even outside a single state's own jurisdiction. As mentioned previously, General Comment No. 4 identified that implementing the Marrakesh Treaty would promote the realisation of inclusive education in a number of ways, including the availability of accessible textbooks. Whereas the UNCRC and CRPD are UN human rights conventions, the Marrakesh Treaty originated from the World Intellectual Property Organization,

---

[156] Ibid., [61].
[157] Ibid., [61](a).
[158] Ibid., [61](b)–(d).
[159] Ibid., [61](f), (g) and (i).
[160] Ibid., [61](h).
[161] Ibid., [61](e), (j) and (k).
[162] Ibid., [61](l), (m) and (73).
[163] Ibid., [62], [63] and [65].
[164] Ibid., [41].
[165] Ibid.
[166] Ibid.
[167] UNCRPD Committee, "General Comment No. 4 (2016)", 14–15 [41].

which mainly focuses on the protection of intangible property rights. The push in General Comment No. 4 to implement the Marrakesh Treaty demonstrates that disability rights advocates should use every framework available to promote inclusive education and should not think in silos around a particular convention.

The importance of not siloing advocacy to a single international convention should go even further. Bridges should be built between advocacy efforts within donor states and those interested in international development. CWDs are not enjoying equality of education in developed states in a range of areas, such as with respect to inappropriate learning plans or educational environments,[168] access to educational textbooks and materials,[169] access to adaptive technologies,[170] insufficient training on disability-specific technologies or communication techniques,[171] continual overt discrimination and prejudice,[172] problems with enforcement,[173] and the existence of inappropriate punishments and chemical restraints.[174] Presumably, education systems in donor-recipient states experience these problems and more. There also are some barriers to equality that are more unique to donor-recipient states. For example, children with albinism are very vulnerable to attack, kidnapping, mutilation, trafficking, and murder in parts of Africa, where the presence of certain biological differences are constructed as bad omens, yet their body parts are considered beneficial by witch doctors for generating wealth.[175] Thus, although

---

[168] Arduin, "Implementing Disability Rights in Education in Ireland".

[169] P. Harpur and N. Suzor, "The Paradigm Shift in Realising the Right to Read: How ebook Libraries Are Enabling in the University Sector" (2014) 29(10) *Disability and Society* 1658; P. Harpur and R. Loudoun, "The Barrier of the Written Word: Analysing Universities' Policies to Include Students with Print Disabilities and Calls for Reforms" (2013) 33(2) *Journal of Higher Education Policy and Management* 153.

[170] E. Slepak, "No Longer Left to Their Own Devices: Utilizing and Facilitating Mediation to Give Students Access to Assistive Technology" (2013) 15 *Cardozo Journal of Conflict Resolution* 271.

[171] A. R. Ball, "Equal Accessibility for Sign Language under the Convention on the Rights of Persons with Disabilities" (2011) 43 *Case Western Reserve Journal of International Law* 759.

[172] B. Klei, "Two Nations at Different Places: A Comparative Look at Disability Law In United States and Japanese Higher Education" (2008) 3 *Connecticut Journal of International Law* 417; P. M. Secunda, "Overcoming Deliberate Indifference: Reconsidering Effective Legal Protections for Bullied Special Education Students" (2015) *University of Illinois Law Review* 175; A. Todd, "Mandatory HIV Status Disclosure for Students in Illinois: A Deterrent to Testing and a Violation of the *Americans with Disabilities Act*" (2015) 10 *Northwestern Journal of Law and Social Policy* 426.

[173] R. Malhotra and R. F. Hansen, "The United Nations Convention on the Rights of Persons with Disabilities and ITS Implications for the Equality Rights of Canadians with Disabilities: The Case of Education" (2011) 29 *Windsor Yearbook of Access to Justice* 73; T. Walsh, "Negligence and Special Needs Education: The Case for Recognising a Duty to Provide Special Education Services in Australian Schools" (2015) 18(1) *Education Law Journal* 32.

[174] D. Weissbrodt et al., "Applying International Human Rights Standards to the Restraint and Seclusion of Students with Disabilities" (2012) 30 *Law and Inequality* 287.

[175] B. Mulemi and U. Ndolo, *Albinism, Witchcraft, and Superstition in East Africa: Exploration of Bio-cultural Exclusion and Livelihood Vulnerability* (Nairobi, Kenya: Catholic University of Eastern Africa, 2014).

CWDs experience inequalities differently in donor and recipient states, common ground and shared mechanisms exist that could be utilised to enhance equality outcomes.

Domestic Implementation

Despite hard law developments around the UNCRC and CRPD, soft law around the UNCRC, and evolving knowledge and practices related to the SDGs, CWDs will only benefit from inclusive education when laws and policies reflect the new inclusive education and human rights paradigms. Inclusive development programming thus plays a key future role in accomplishing this shift to inclusive education.

Yet, although inclusive education forms part of the development agenda, the educational rights of CWDs remain a second-tier objective in many venues. To illustrate: UNICEF is a UN organisation with a mandate to support child development across the globe.[176] Hence, how UNICEF approaches disability inclusive development will strongly influence how SDG Goal 4 is operationalised by states and international aid agencies. UNICEF recognises that CWDs are one of the most marginalised and excluded groups in society, and that they are often excluded from various rights, including the right to education.[177] UNICEF correctly determined that to enable CWDs to exercise their right to education states should engage in a range of measures. These include promoting accessible and inclusive learning spaces; investing in teacher training for inclusive education; taking a multisectoral approach; involving the community; and collecting data for evidence building and progress monitoring.[178]

Although UNICEF's efforts for promoting a disability inclusive educational agenda within development practices are laudable, CWDs are arguably an overall second-tier priority. Within the broader development space that UNICEF has been promoting,[179] the rights of CWDs remain one of many priorities. UNICEF's Core Commitments for Children in Humanitarian Action (Core Commitments),[180] for instance, advises that programs should enable children to "access safe and secure education and critical information for their own well-being".[181] In doing so, no specific commitment mentions CWDs, and their rights have to be inferred as arising from the omnibus reference to vulnerable populations in Commitment 2 whereby "girls and other excluded children" have a right to access quality education opportunities.[182] UNICEF's delegation of CWDs to second-tier status is likewise reflected among that entity's broader policies. One of UNICEF's leading publications is

---

[176] www.unicef.org/about/who/index_history.html.
[177] www.unicef.org/disabilities/.
[178] www.unicef.org/disabilities/index_65316.html.
[179] www.unicef.org/media/media_24321.html.
[180] UNICEF, *Core Commitments for Children in Humanitarian Action* (New York: UNICEF, 2010).
[181] Ibid.
[182] Ibid.

The State of the World's Children report, which is published each year. The 2016 report includes a list of equity targets.[183] The education equity targets contained in the 2016 report mention girls in poor communities, however they do not mention CWDs.[184]

The status of inclusive education as a second-tier priority is also reflected in state practices. Australia has embraced disability inclusive development programs, and been commended for its efforts by UNICEF, yet continues to construe disability inclusive education as a second-tier priority.[185] Thus, although Australia committed to promoting and implementing disability inclusive programs,[186] and is funding a number of disability inclusive educational interventions across Asia and the Pacific in association with various groups including UNICEF,[187] disability inclusive education is not a priority. Specifically, the Australian government adopted ten high-level targets to assess its aid program and that are used for all aid programs: promoting prosperity; engaging the private sector; reducing poverty; empowering women and girls; focusing on the Indo-Pacific region; delivering on commitments; working with the most effective partners; ensuring value for money; increasing consolidation; and combatting corruption.[188] These ten high-level targets focus on a range of important development objectives, but CWDs and their right to education are nowhere to be found. Indeed, disability is mentioned only once in Australia's performance framework as a priority target related to reducing poverty by promoting persons with disabilities' capacity to work and engage in the economic life of the community.[189]

CONCLUSION

Denying a child an education can reduce or deny them the right to exercise their economic, social, political, and civil rights for the rest of their lives. While education is important for all children, for CWDs education takes on greater urgency, as

---

[183] UNICEF, *The State of the World's Children 2016: A Fair Chance for Every Child* (New York: UNICEF, 2016).

[184] Ibid. To be fair, this absence does not mean that efforts to promote ability equality are not being supported and encouraged by UNICEF. The 2016 report notes with approval efforts to promote the educational rights of CWDs in a number of States, including an intensive public awareness program that has operated since 2010 in Montenegro to alter attitudes that hinder CWDs accessing education. This intervention has been credited with contributing to changes in attitudes and creating opportunities for CWDs.

[185] www.unicef.org/media/media_67727.html.

[186] http://dfat.gov.au/aid/topics/development-issues/disability-inclusive-development/Pages/disability-inclusive-development.aspx.

[187] Ibid.; see also the UNICEF Partnership on Disability: Rights, Education and Protection of children with disabilities 2 (REAP 2) programme.

[188] Australian Government, Department of Foreign Affairs and Trade, *Making Performance Count: Enhancing the Accountability and Effectiveness of Australian Aid* (Canberra: Australian Government, 2014).

[189] Ibid.

disability factors mean that many such children will only ever be able to secure jobs that require an education. Prior to the CRPD, disability inclusive education was governed by the UNCRC. The limited protection afforded to CWDs generally, and to those relying on development programs, was addressed by the CRPD. While other developments, such as the Standard Rules and the Salamanca Statement, increased obligations upon states, these non-binding duties had limited impact. The obligations upon states and non-state actors were transformed with the adoption of the CRPD. The CRPD addresses disability rights in donor programming and has introduced an integrated rights regime. The adoption of the SDGs, and their express recognition of the rights of persons with disabilities, has swept in a regulatory framework that requires states and state actors to promote inclusive education in international cooperation and development programs. Nevertheless, despite the CRPD and SDGs it appears the rights of persons with disabilities remain a second-tier priority. Those who control donor development programs often have a unique opportunity to rebuild much of a society up from the ground. This means that those who control donor development programs have a choice whether they will build school buildings, educational programs, public transport, libraries, and other aspects of society in a way that is inclusive of CWDs, or in a way that excludes them and further marginalises those who are least able to survive when donor assistance is required.

PART III

Children and the Environment

8

Intergenerational Equity and Children's Rights

The Role of Sustainable Development and Justice

Sumudu Atapattu

> *Needless to say, every generation has a responsibility to the next to preserve that rhythm and harmony [of nature] for the full enjoyment of a balanced and healthful ecology.*
> Supreme Court of the Philippines, *Oposa v. Factoran* (1993)

INTRODUCTION

Children are the future of any society and that is why many countries across the world invest in their well-being and provide for their welfare. They need the love and protection of their immediate families and the nurturing and care of their teachers and caregivers. We should take every effort to protect them and ensure that they, among other rights, have a decent standard of living and a good education. Protecting our children is not only a moral issue but is also an investment in the future. However, for most part, children, especially young children, depend on adults for their protection and well-being. The UN Convention on the Rights of the Child (UNCRC) recognises this and provides that "the child, by reason of his physical and mental immaturity, needs special safeguards and care, including appropriate legal protection, before as well as after birth."[1]

The UNCRC also recognises the need to give children special protection and the importance of growing up in a conducive family environment: "the child, for the full and harmonious development of his or her personality, should grow up in a family environment, in an atmosphere of happiness, love and understanding."[2] The Millennium Development Goals (MDGs) had several goals that were applicable to

---

[1] The author would like to thank Maro Kim (3L, UW Law School) for her research assistance.
UN General Assembly (UNGA), *Convention on the Rights of the Child* (UN Doc. A/RES/44/25, 20 November 1989) 1577 UNTS 3, Preamble, which reproduces the provision in the Declaration of the Rights of the Child.
[2] Ibid.

children and their well-being: achieving universal primary education, reducing child mortality, protecting maternal health, eradicating extreme poverty and hunger (equally applicable to adults) and achieving gender equality.[3] Combatting HIV and ensuring environmental sustainability are also relevant to children's well-being. While the global community has made some strides towards reaching these goals, inequalities still persist and the world leaders decided to adopt an ambitious set of sustainability goals to succeed MDGs as part of the post-2015 development agenda. The Sustainable Development Goals (SDGs)[4] embody 17 goals that include some of the MDGs, such as poverty and hunger eradication, but contain new goals such as addressing climate change and adopting affordable and clean energy. Other goals include providing a quality education to children, ensuring gender equality and providing access to water and sanitation.[5] The SDGs are wider than MDGs and reflect all three pillars of sustainable development as articulated by the global community in the Johannesburg Declaration on Sustainable Development:[6] economic development, environmental protection and social development.[7]

One of the integral components of sustainable development is the intergenerational equity principle. This principle requires us to ensure that when taking developmental decisions today, the rights of future generations will not be jeopardised by our actions. However, under contemporary legal principles children (and future generations) do not have direct standing – except in very limited instances and generally through a guardian *ad litem* – and certainly do not have a voice at the table. Climate change is a classic example of a global problem that jeopardises the rights of future generations. As many of these children are yet to be born, they have had no opportunity to voice their concerns about the actions of their elders today.

Because children are affected by the decisions taken by adults but lack a voice at the table to influence these decisions, development activities also implicate justice issues. Justice underlies both sustainable development and intergenerational equity principles, and this chapter will discuss the utility of these different principles and frameworks to protect children as a vulnerable group. They need the protection of their parents and caregivers. They are also vulnerable to health problems caused by environmental pollution – more than adults because their immune system is not as developed as that of adults. Despite the enormous strides we have made with regard to economic development in many parts of the world, the statistics with regard to children are sobering – 17,000 children under the age of five still die *every day* from

---

[3] UNGA, "United Nations Millennium Declaration" (UN Doc. A/Res/55/2, 18 September 2000).
[4] UNGA, "Transforming Our World: The 2030 Agenda for Sustainable Development" (UN Doc. A/RES/70/1, 21 October 2015).
[5] Ibid.
[6] UN World Summit on Sustainable Development, "Johannesburg Declaration on Sustainable Development and Johannesburg Plan of Implementation" (UN Doc. A/CONF.1999/20, 4 September 2002) ("Johannesburg Declaration").
[7] Ibid. Paragraph 5 refers to these three pillars as being "interdependent and mutually reinforcing."

preventable causes.⁸ According to the World Bank approximately 400 million children live in extreme poverty.⁹ Almost 230 million children under the age of five do not have birth certificates, and almost 58 million children of primary school age do not attend school.¹⁰ Moreover, 250 million children have not learned basic literacy or numeracy, whether they have been to school or not.¹¹ They are also the most vulnerable to environmental degradation and climate change impacts:

> In fact, children make up 80% of deaths attributable to climate-related changes. In addition, too many children do not have access to adequate drinking water, sanitation and hygiene (WASH) which globally remains a leading cause of death among children under 5 years of age. Furthermore, almost half of the world's people living in extreme poverty are 18 years old or younger. That is nearly 570 million children who are deprived of their needs, their rights and their dignity. When children's rights are neither recognized nor fulfilled, society bears the burden of not only a moral failing to its children but also a costly reality for its future.¹²

Moreover, we have created many environmental health problems for our children. Of these, climate change is possibly the biggest challenge that we have created that will continue to haunt generations to come. At a time when many children in the Global North cannot imagine life without laptop computers, tablets and smart phones, many of their counterparts in the Global South often have one meal a day, live in squalor and appalling conditions and generally lack access to basic needs that others take for granted. This is not to belittle the disparity within the Global North and the Global South. For example, in the United States, approximately 13.1 million children under the age of 18 years live in food insecure households:¹³ this should be enough to raise red flags and galvanise people into action because "although food insecurity is harmful to any individual, it can be particularly devastating among children due to their increased vulnerability and the potential for long-term consequences."¹⁴

The Independent Expert on Human Rights and the Environment, John Knox, referred to the vulnerability of children to environmental degradation:

> The rights of children, too, may be particularly affected by environmental degradation. The Convention on the Rights of the Child states that environmental

---

⁸ UNICEF, *A Post-2015 World Fit for Children* (UNICEF, 2014), www.unicef.org/agenda2030/files/Post_2015_OWG_review_CR_FINAL.pdf (footnotes omitted).

⁹ World Bank, "Report Finds 400 Million Children Living in Extreme Poverty" (10 October 2013), www.worldbank.org/en/news/press-release/2013/10/10/report-finds-400-million-children-living-extreme-poverty.

¹⁰ Ibid.

¹¹ Ibid.

¹² Ibid.

¹³ Feed America, "Child Hunger Facts" (undated), www.feedingamerica.org/hunger-in-america/impact-of-hunger/child-hunger/child-hunger-fact-sheet.html.

¹⁴ Ibid.

pollution poses "dangers and risks" to nutritious foods and clean drinking water (art. 24, para. 2(c)). In its concluding observations on country reports, the Committee on the Rights of the Child regularly addresses environmental hazards as barriers to the realization of the right to health and other rights. The Special Rapporteur on hazardous substances and wastes has emphasized the harm to children's rights to health caused by exposure to mercury and other hazardous substances in extractive industries.[15]

This chapter seeks to discuss the relevant provisions of the UNCRC within a framework of sustainable development and intergenerational equity. It adopts the intergenerational equity principle as the overarching framework and evaluates its relevance particularly in the context of negative impacts of climate change on children and future generations. It proceeds in six sections. "The Principle of Intergenerational Equity" discusses the salient features of the intergenerational equity principle while "Legal Status of the Intergenerational Equity Principle" discusses its legal status. "The Evolution of Sustainable Development and Intergenerational Equity" discusses the evolution of sustainable development and intergenerational equity and the much-discussed *Minors Oposa* case decided by the Supreme Court of the Philippines. "The UN Convention on the Rights of the Child" surveys the salient provisions of the UNCRC and the Children's Declaration on SDGs. The final section contains a case study of climate change and the chapter concludes with some recommendations. It argues that the worst effects of climate change will be borne by our children and grandchildren, and we need to take mitigation measures today to ensure that their right to a healthy environment and indeed their very survival will not be jeopardised.

THE PRINCIPLE OF INTERGENERATIONAL EQUITY

While the intergenerational equity principle is a rather new addition to the bundle of principles governing environmental issues, it is by no means a new principle. It is at the heart of many ancient legal traditions[16] and, in indigenous societies, it is said that decisions are evaluated to ascertain their impact on seven generations to come.[17]

---

[15] UN Human Rights Council, "Report of the Independent Expert on the Issue of Human Rights Obligations Relating to the Enjoyment of a Safe, Clean, Healthy and Sustainable Environment, John H. Knox" (UN Doc. A/HRC/25/53, 30 December 2013), [28]–[30].

[16] See Separate Opinion of Judge Weeramantry in the *Gabcikovo Nagymaros Project (Hungary v. Slovakia)*, ICJ Reports (25 September 1997).

[17] Fellowship for Intentional Community, "For the Next Seven Generations: Indigenous Americans and Communalism" (undated), www.ic.org/wiki/next-seven-generations-indigenous-americans-communalism/.

Intergenerational equity was first articulated as a principle by Professor Edith Brown Weiss in her seminal work entitled *In Fairness to Future Generations*.[18] She pointed out that the present generation implicates (and jeopardises) the rights of future generations in several ways: the current generation can deplete the resource base in such a way as to limit the choices that the future generation has. In other words, they can exploit the resources at the expense of future generations. Moreover, the current generation can create environmental issues that can cause damage to future generations. Climate change is a good example of an intergenerational environmental problem that the future generations will bear the brunt of. They will be disproportionately affected by a problem that we created without reaping the benefits of the economic development that gave rise to the environmental issue. Finally, accidents can also cause damage to future generations. Nuclear explosions, toxic waste spills and disposal and nuclear waste all have an intergenerational dimension.[19]

To derive the principles of intergenerational equity, Brown Weiss points out that the purpose of sustaining the welfare and well-being of all generations has three aspects: (1) to sustain the life-support systems of the planet; (2) to sustain the ecological processes, environmental conditions and cultural resources necessary for the survival of the human species and (3) to sustain a healthy and decent human environment.[20] To do so, we need to pass on a robust planet to future generations: "The theory of intergenerational justice says that each generation has an obligation to future generations to pass on the natural and cultural resources of the planet in no worse condition than received and to provide reasonable access to the legacy for the present generation."[21] Emphasising that equality among generations is important, she proposes three principles of intergenerational equity: (1) each generation should be required to conserve the diversity of the natural and cultural resource base (*conservation of options*); (2) each generation should pass on the planet in no worse condition than it received it (*conservation of quality*) and (3) each generation should provide its members with equal rights of access to the legacy from past generations and conserve this access to future generations (*conservation of access*).[22]

Stressing that it is important to view the human community as a partnership among nations, Brown Weiss notes that the principles of intergenerational equity form the basis of a set of planetary rights and obligations and each generation acts as the trustee of the planet for present and future generations.[23] Intergenerational equity principle as previously articulated resonates with the call for sustainable development by the World Commission on Environment and Development

---

[18] See E. Brown Weiss, *In Fairness to Future Generations: International Law, Common Patrimony, and Intergenerational Equity* (New York: Transnational, 1988).
[19] Ibid., 5.
[20] Ibid., 37.
[21] Ibid., 38.
[22] Ibid.
[23] Ibid., 45.

(WCED) in 1987. It requires us to act as the trustee of the environment and to ensure conservations of options, quality and access of resources by future generations. It also has an intragenerational dimension that cannot be denied.

Equity and fairness underlie the notion of intergenerational equity and is a general principle common to many legal systems. The International Court of Justice (ICJ) has also discussed this in many contexts. In the seminal Jan Mayen Case,[24] the ICJ discussed the many facets of the role played by equity in international law: it is a basis for individualised justice; it introduces considerations of fairness, reasonableness and good faith; and it is a basis for specific principles of legal reasoning. In addition, equity offers standards to allocate resources and benefits.[25]

The ICJ has also referred to the need protect generations unborn. In its Advisory Opinion on the *Legality of the Threat of Use of Nuclear Weapons*, the Court noted that "the environment is not an abstraction but represents living space, the quality of life and the very health of human beings, including generations unborn."[26] In his dissenting opinion in the *Nuclear Tests Case*,[27] Judge Weeramantry pointed out that the case raised the principle of intergenerational equity as no other case had done before and that it was "an important and rapidly developing principle of contemporary environmental law."[28] Referring to Principle 1 of the Stockholm Declaration, which refers to the solemn duty to protect and improve the environment for present and future generations, Judge Weeramantry noted that the case raises the possibility of damage to generations yet unborn.[29]

Many environmental treaties embody the intergeneration equity principle. The UN Framework Convention on Climate Change,[30] the Convention on Biological Diversity,[31] the Desertification Convention[32] as well as many soft law instruments[33] refer to the need to protect future generations. It has been articulated that the Rio Conference on Environment and Development cemented the intergenerational equity principle in international law:

> Beyond doubt, the 1992 Rio Earth Summit represents the first international effort to safeguard the quality of life of posterity. It is indeed remarkable that the three major

---

[24] *Maritime Delimitation in the Area between Greenland and Jan Mayen (Denmark and Norway)* (1993) ICJ 38.
[25] Ibid.
[26] See (1996) ICJ 226.
[27] Request for an Examination of the Situation in Accordance with Paragraph 63 of the Court's Judgment of 20 December 1974 in the Nuclear Tests (*New Zealand v. France*) Case (1995).
[28] Dissenting Opinion, Judge Weeramantry, ibid., 341.
[29] Ibid., 342.
[30] (9 May 1992) 1771 UNTS 107 ("UNFCCC").
[31] (5 June 1992) 1760 UNTS 79.
[32] UNGA, *Convention to Combat Desertification in Those Countries Experiencing Serious Drought and/or Desertification, Particularly in Africa* (UN Doc. 1/AC.241/27, 12 September 1994) 1954 UNTS 3.
[33] For a discussion of sustainable development see S. Atapattu, *Emerging Principles of International Environmental Law* (New York: Transnational, 2006), ch. 2.

documents signed at Rio, namely, the Rio Declaration, the Convention on Biological Diversity and the Convention on Climate Change incorporate the concept of intergenerational solidarity and responsibilities.[34]

The New Delhi Principles of Sustainable Development adopted by the International Law Association (ILA)[35] in 2002 notes that the principle of equity is central to sustainable development:

> The principle of equity is central to the attainment of sustainable development. It refers to both inter-generational equity (the right of future generations to enjoy a fair level of the common patrimony) and intra-generational equity (the right of all peoples within the current generation of fair access to the current generation's entitlement to the Earth's natural resources).[36]

Elaborating further on the notion of intergenerational equity in the context of exploitation of resources, the ILA principles note:

> The present generation has a right to use and enjoy the resources of the Earth but is under an obligation to take into account the long-term impact of its activities and to sustain the resource base and the global environment for the benefit of future generations of humankind. "Benefit" in this context is to be understood in its broadest meaning as including, *inter alia,* economic, environmental, social and intrinsic benefit.[37]

Reaffirming the formulation in the Rio Declaration on Environment and Development, the New Delhi principles affirm that "the right to development must be implemented so as to meet developmental and environmental needs of present and future generations in a sustainable and equitable manner."[38] Thus, both hard law and soft law including those adopted by private organisations like the ILA and judicial bodies have affirmed the need to sustain the resource base for the benefit of future generations.

That the present generation has an obligation to protect the environment for the benefit of future generations is a rational objective of any society. Put bluntly, we, as adults, should ensure the welfare of our children and grandchildren. But do we as parents owe an obligation to other children and grandchildren? While most parents would not intentionally cause harm to their children, is there a legal obligation to ensure that the next generation inherits a healthy planet? Perhaps 10 years ago, many would have answered this in the negative. However, with consequences of climate

---

[34] See E. Agius, "Obligations of Justice towards Future Generations: A Revolution in Social and Legal Thought," in E. Agius and S. Busuttil (eds.), *Future Generations and International Law* (London: Earthscan, 1998), 3.
[35] ILA New Delhi Declaration of Principles of International Law Relating to Sustainable Development (2 April 2002), http://cisdl.org/tribunals/pdf/NewDelhiDeclaration.pdf.
[36] Ibid., Principle 2.1.
[37] Ibid., Principle 2.2.
[38] Ibid., Principle 2.3.

change looming large over us, the answer may not be so clear cut. If we deliberately act as business as usual knowing very well that our actions will cause damage to the present generation, then we will be held legally accountable for our action. Why should the situation be different if the potential damage is to our children and grandchildren (and many generations to come)? Is it because they lack standing under current legal principles? If that were the case, it may be opportune to revisit these legal principles to accommodate the novel situation created by climate change. Or is it because the consequences have not yet materialised? Current legal principles do not, as a general rule, hold actors accountable for future damage. Foreseeability of harm and reliance on scientific evidence may be necessary to overcome this hurdle. It is interesting to note that in *Taskin v. Turkey*, the European Court of Human Rights found that a gold mine presented an unacceptable risk to the people in the vicinity despite the absence of any accidents or incidents involving the mine.[39]

According to Rawls justice must apply to "all members whether they are living now intratemporally or intertemporally."[40] This means that it applies to not just one group or generation but to all generations. Among the three rights that all generations can claim from their predecessors, Rawls lists conservation of natural resources and the natural environment. Of course, many questions remain: to what extent should the present generation respect the claims of its posterity? How far in time should this duty extend? Are these claims protected? Who can make those claims?[41] Despite these questions and uncertainties, intergenerational equity or justice has wielded considerable influence on international environmental law and policy: "Beyond doubt, the discourse of intergenerational justice marks a fundamental shift in the paradigm of international environmental policy."[42]

Barressi sums up Brown Weiss's proposal on intergenerational justice as embodying three types of rights and duties: (1) intergenerational group rights and duties; (2) intragenerational group rights and duties and (3) intragenerational individual rights and duties.[43] Barresi points out that this theory requires every generation to practice sustainable development but believes that not all countries are *wealthy* enough to practice sustainable development.[44] That sustainable development requires wealth

---

[39] European Court of Human Rights, *Taskin v Turkey (Application no. 46117/99)*, Chamber Judgment, Strasbourg (10 November 2004), as cited by D. Shelton, "Whiplash and Backlash-Reflections on a Human Rights Approach to Environmental Protection" (2015) 13 *Santa Clara Journal of International Law* 11.

[40] Referred to in Agius, "Obligations of Justice towards Future Generations," 5.

[41] See ibid. See also P. Ariansen, "Beyond Parfit's Paradox" in Agius (ed.), "Obligations of Justice Towards Future Generations," 13.

[42] See ibid., 4.

[43] See P. Barresi, "Beyond Fairness to Future Generations: An Intragenerational Alternative to Intergenerational Equity in the International Environmental Arena" (1997) 11 *Tulane Environmental Law Journal* 59.

[44] Ibid., 61.

is a novel argument. In other words, according to Barresi, sustainable development is limited to developed countries. It is precisely the *opposite* argument that developing countries make – that sustainable development is limited to developing countries as developed countries are already developed.[45] He believes relying on non-Western ideologies and concepts is unlikely to appeal to Western societies and it is precisely the Western societies that must address the issue:

> If the most serious environmental threats to future generations are to be alleviated as a practical matter, then the Western industrial democracies will have to assume primary responsibility for doing so, partly by putting their own houses in order and partly by providing less developed countries with the aid that will allow them to do the same. If intergenerational equity in environmental matters is to be justified theoretically by an appeal to the ideological content of existing religious or legal traditions, then those traditions must, to a preponderant extent, be the traditions of the West.[46]

Rejecting the notion of group rights, Barresi suggests that all rights and duties in the new legal order be *intra*national and *intra*generational, and will be individual in nature.[47] He strongly believes that group rights and duties are alien to Western cultural and legal traditions and the support of the Western world would be "essential" if intergenerational equity is to be achieved.[48] Inasmuch as it is incorrect to contend that the Western world does not accept intergenerational rights, it is also incorrect to contend that their support is essential for its realisation. Both the Rio Declaration (non-binding) and the UN Framework Convention on Climate Change (UNFCCC) (binding), which incorporate the intergenerational equity principle, have been widely accepted by the Western world, and there are many examples of principles that have been adopted without the support of the Western world, at times amidst its vehement opposition.[49]

In his report prepared pursuant to paragraph 86 of the Rio+20 outcome document, the UN Secretary-General noted that dedication to future generations "is a universal value shared amongst humanity."[50] He pointed out that while few would question the responsibilities we owe to our children and grandchildren, intergenerational solidarity (or equity) is a relatively new concept in legal and political fields. In the context of sustainable development, the report points out that

---

[45] See D. Hunter, J. Salzman and D. Zaelke, *International Environmental Law and Policy*, 5th ed. (Minneapolis: Foundation Press, 2015), 152.
[46] See Barresi, "Beyond Fairness to Future Generations," 65.
[47] Ibid., 84.
[48] Ibid., 86.
[49] The Resolution on the Right to Development and the New International Economic Order are some examples.
[50] UNGA, "Intergenerational Solidarity and the Needs of Future Generations, Report of the Secretary-General" (UN Doc. A/68/322, 5 August 2013) (hereinafter UN Secretary-General report).

intergenerational solidarity encompasses future generations who do not yet exist and "fairness between generations is embedded in the concept of sustainable development."[51] While we cannot ascertain the precise needs of future generations, we should adopt policies with at least two basic considerations: minimise harm to future generations and adopt policies that will benefit both present and future generations.[52]

LEGAL STATUS OF THE INTERGENERATIONAL EQUITY PRINCIPLE

Many international instruments embody the intergenerational equity principle, particularly since the adoption of the Rio Declaration. Notable among them is the UNFCCC, which embodies a separate article on "principles" that include the intergenerational equity principle:

> The Parties should protect the climate system for the benefit of present and future generations of humankind, on the basis of equity and in accordance with their common but differentiated responsibilities and respective capabilities.[53]

Although couched in soft language,[54] this principle and others included in article 3 are binding on the parties to the Framework Convention. Thus, at least with regard to climate change, this principle has acquired normative status.

Outside the application of treaties that embody the intergenerational equity principle, the question remains whether it has achieved customary international law status. Certainly, a move towards that seems to be emerging given the inclusion in international instruments, court decisions and developments at the national level. Similar to sustainable development, few States would argue that there is no obligation toward future generations but few would accord it customary international law status. Redgewell contends that it has not reached the level of customary international law but:

> [a] process of "creeping intergenerationalisation" may be observed emanating from two processes: First, there is the "spillover effect" of preambular recognition of future generations in the interpretation and application of substantive treaty provisions. Second, other substantive principles of international environmental law embody an intertemporal dimension.[55]

---

[51] Ibid., 8.
[52] Ibid., 18.
[53] UNFCCC, article 3.
[54] Note the word *should* rather than *shall* and the chapeau to article 3, which says that these principles will guide the parties to the Convention in fulfilling their obligations under the Convention. See C. Wold, D. Hunter and M. Powers, *Climate Change and the Law*, 2nd ed. (New York: LexisNexis, 2013), 202.
[55] C. Redgewell, as cited by L. Collins, "Revisiting the Doctrine of Intergenerational Equity in Global Environmental Governance" (2007) 30 *Dalhousie Law Journal* 79, 130.

Redgewell identifies five international environmental law principles that have relevance to the international equity principle: sustainable development, the common heritage of mankind principle, the principle of custodianship or stewardship, the precautionary principle and the common but differentiated responsibility principle.[56] While sustainable development, the precautionary principle and the principle of custodianship embody an intergenerational aspect, the other two principles seem to stem from North-South politics although they too are grounded on the notion of equity.

The UNESCO Declaration on the Responsibilities of the Present Generation towards Future Generations clearly endorses that "the present generations have the responsibility of ensuring that the needs and interests of present and future generations are fully safeguarded."[57] Similarly, the UN Legal Experts Report on Environmental Law includes both intergenerational and intragenerational equity principle[58] while the UN Environment Programme Legal Experts report on International Environmental Law relating to Sustainable Development articulated that "[a]n integrated intergenerational equity approach should constitute an underlying part of any sustainable development strategy in international law."[59] Similarly, the Experts Group on Sustainable Development that was appointed by the Commission on Sustainable Development in 1996 posited that intergenerational equity is well known to international law.

The principle of intergenerational equity reflects the view that as "members of the present generation, we hold the earth in trust for future generations," while "at the same time we are beneficiaries entitled to use it." All generations form a partnership that extends across time in relation to their human environment. The principle includes three components: quality, options and access to the environment. These must be comparable across generations.[60]

While the intergenerational equity principle may not have yet achieved customary international law status, as the preceding discussion revealed, it has certainly been endorsed by the international community in many binding and non-binding instruments. The modalities of using intergenerational equity as a tool are, however, more problematic. Sands critiques the proposal to establish a UN Office of

---

[56] Ibid., 131.
[57] UNESCO Declaration on the Responsibilities of the Present Generation towards Future Generations (12 November 1997).
[58] R. D. Munro and J. G. Lammers, *Environmental Protection and Sustainable Development: Legal Principles and Recommendations* (London: Graham and Trotman, 1986), 9.
[59] UN Environment Programme, "Final Report of the Expert Group Workshop on International Environmental Law Aiming at Sustainable Development" (UNEP/IEL/WS/3/2, 1996), 13–14, [30], [44]–[45], as cited by L. M. Collins, "Revisiting the Doctrine of Intergenerational Equity in Global Environmental Governance" (2007) 30 *Dalhousie Law Journal* 79, 130.
[60] UN Commission on Sustainable Development, "Report of the Expert Group Meeting on Identification of Principles of International Law for Sustainable Development" (26–28 September 1996), [42].

Guardian for Future Generations, even though he accepts the principle that "as members of the present generation, we hold the earth in trust for future generations."[61] He does so not because he disagrees with the legal principle but rather because he questions whether it is the most effective way to ensure that the principle is implemented. He believes that this principle "requires the needs of future generations to be taken into account by present generations in their current activities"[62] and has invoked the principle at both practical and theoretical levels. These practical objections apart, there seems to be consensus among scholars that the intergenerational equity principle is an important principle that *at the minimum* requires the needs of future generations be considered in our decision-making process. What seems contested is *how* this principle should be operationalised.

In addition to many international instruments that refer to future generations[63] and to the intergenerational equity principle[64] in particular, many national constitutions also refer to future generations. Examples include the Constitutions of Bolivia, Ecuador, Germany, Kenya, Norway and South Africa.[65] Of particular interest are the institutions that some countries have established to protect the rights of future generations. Examples include Finland's Committee for the Future, Israel's Commission for Future Generations and the Hungary's Parliamentary Commissioner for Future Generations.[66] These developments seem to have set a new trend in motion that the UN Secretary General proposed to replicate at the international level: by establishing a High Commissioner for Future Generations, a special envoy, a high-level political forum or interagency coordination through the UN Secretary-General.[67]

Another interesting development is the notion of "crimes against future generations" proposed by the World Future Council.[68] According to the draft definition, a crime against future generations means any act within any sphere of human activity "when committed with knowledge of the substantial likelihood of their severe

---

[61] See P. Sands, "Protecting Future Generations: Precedents and Practicalities," in Agius and Busuttil (eds.), *Future Generations and International Law*, 83.
[62] Ibid.
[63] UNGA, "Intergenerational Solidarity and the Needs of Future Generations," 22. These include the *Charter of the United Nations* (24 October 1945) 1 UNTS XVI and the *Declaration of the United Nations Conference on the Human Environment* (UN Doc. A/CONF.48/14/Rev.1, 5–16 June 1972).
[64] Ibid., 23. These include the UNFCCC ([9 May 1992] 1771 UNTS 107) and the Convention on Biological Diversity ([5 June 1992] 1760 UNTS 79).
[65] UNGA, "Intergenerational Solidarity and the Needs of Future Generations," 25.
[66] Ibid., 27.
[67] Ibid., 39. See also J. Anstee-Wedderburn, "Giving a Voice to Future Generations: Intergenerational Equity, Representatives of Generations to Come, and the Challenge of Planetary Rights" (2014) 1(1) *Australian Journal of Environmental Law* 37.
[68] See S. Jodoin, "Crimes against Future Generations: A New Approach to Ending Impunity for Serious Violations of Economic, Social, and Cultural Rights and International Environmental Law" (Working Paper, 15 August 2010, World Future Council).

consequences on the long-term health, safety, or means of survival of any identifiable group or collectivity" and falls within the acts identified in the draft definition. These include causing widespread, long-term and severe damage to the natural environment and unlawfully polluting air, water or soil. The basic premise underlying crimes against future generations is that they are serious violations of economic, social and cultural rights of a particular group or have serious repercussions for the natural environment that have "severe consequences on the long-term health, safety, or means of survival of this group or collectivity."[69] Thus, these are crimes committed against a particular group now that have repercussions for the future. This could create challenges for those issues that do not have a current victim. The proponents note that while crimes against future generations are based on the principle of individual criminal responsibility, some acts or conduct could also give rise to the responsibility of the state under international law.[70]

While the "future" of crimes against future generations remains to be seen, climate change provides a good example of a global issue that has the potential to cause adverse consequences for many generations to come. It will also disproportionately affect the current generation of children who played no part in creating the problem. We now turn to a brief survey of the evolution of sustainable development and its relationship to the intergenerational equity principle.

THE EVOLUTION OF SUSTAINABLE DEVELOPMENT AND INTERGENERATIONAL EQUITY

The WCED appointed by the UN General Assembly in 1983 is credited with popularising the modern concept of sustainable development, although it was by no means a new concept. In its 1987 report titled *Our Common Future*, the WCED defined sustainable development as "development that meets the needs of the present generation without compromising the ability of future generations to meet theirs."[71] This definition, while being rather vague, laid the foundation for the intergenerational equity principle. It clearly acknowledges the responsibility of the present generation not to compromise the ability of future generations to meet their needs. Unfortunately, by creating environmental problems many of which have far-reaching consequences, this is precisely what the current generation has done – not only has it compromised the ability of future generations to meet their needs but it has also created tipping points beyond which life as we know it today will be very

---

[69] Ibid.
[70] Ibid., 8.
[71] See World Commission on Environment and Development, "Our Common Future" (UN Doc. A/42/427, 1987), www.un-documents.net/our-common-future.pdf, 43. Sustainable development has attracted an unprecedented amount of literature that is impossible to analyse here. See generally, A. Boyle and D. Freestone (eds.), *International Law and Sustainable Development: Past Achievements and Future Challenges* (Oxford: Oxford University Press, 1999).

different. In fact, scientists question the ability of human beings to survive on a planet that is heating up and could be at least 4° Fahrenheit warmer in the coming years.[72] Climate change illustrates the negative side of economic development with ramifications for generations to come.

The Rio Declaration on Environment and Development adopted at the Earth Summit in 1992 was a catalyst in elaborating on the components of sustainable development. It elaborated on the substantive components as well as procedural components and also identified linkages and tools to achieve sustainable development. It is now widely accepted that *sustainable development* is an umbrella term that encompasses both substantive and procedural components.[73] The Johannesburg Declaration on Sustainable Development adopted in 2002 took this one step further by identifying the three pillars of sustainable development as economic development, environmental protection and social development.[74] Balancing the three pillars is the challenge that the international community faces.

The Rio Declaration juxtaposes the intergenerational equity principle[75] with the right to development. Principle 3 provides that "[t]he right to development must be fulfilled so as to equitably meet developmental and environmental needs of present and future generations" while Principle 4 embodies the principle of integration: "In order to achieve sustainable development, environmental protection shall constitute an integral part of the development process and cannot be considered in isolation from it."[76] These two provisions taken together means that environmental protection should form an integral part of the economic development process and that development must be fulfilled in such a way to ensure that rights of future generations are not compromised.

While it makes common sense that we should ensure that rights of our children and grandchildren are not affected by our decisions today, giving effect to this

---

[72] See J. S. Hill, "Future Temperatures Could Exceed Human Livability" (Planet Save, 5 May 2010), http://planetsave.com/2010/05/05/future-temperatures-could-exceed-human-liveability/.
[73] See Atapattu, *Emerging Principles of International Environmental Law*.
[74] See Johannesburg Declaration, [5].
[75] The intergenerational equity principle has also attracted considerable scholarly writings, most notable being the seminal work of E. Brown Weiss, *In Fairness to Future Generations: International Law, Common Patrimony, and Intergenerational Equity* (New York: Transnational, 1988). See also, P. Barresi, "Advocacy, Frame, and the Intergenerational Imperative: A Reply to Professor Weiss in 'Beyond Fairness to Future Generations'" (1998) 11 *Tulane Environmental Law Journal* 425; E. Brown Weiss, "The Planetary Trust: Conservation and Intergenerational Equity" (1984) 11 *Ecology Law Quarterly*, 495; L. B. Solum, "To Our Children's Children's Children: The Problem of Intergenerational Ethics" (2001–2002) 35 *Loyola of Los Angeles Law Review* 163; M. C. Wood, "Advancing the Sovereign Trust of Government to Safeguard the Environment for Present and Future Generations (Part II): Instilling a Fiduciary Obligation in Governance" (2009) 39 *Environmental Law* 91; R. Hiskes, "The Right to a Green Future: Human Rights, Environmentalism, and Intergenerational Justice" (2005) 27 *Human Rights Quarterly* 1346.
[76] UNGA, "Rio Declaration on Environment and Development" (UN Doc. A/CONF.151/26 (Vol. I), 12 August 1992), Principle 4.

commonsense ideal within the legal systems has become rather challenging. How do we ensure that the future generations have a voice at the table? Who should ensure that their rights are not violated by our actions today? Some states have established an Ombudsman for Future Generations.[77] Other states have adopted environmental impact assessment laws that require the examination of impacts of our activities into the future.[78] A few states have adopted innovative approaches by relaxing rules relating to standing and allowed children to bring action to protect their rights.[79] Typically, children as minors cannot be part of legal proceedings without a guardian *ad litem* or similar person appointed to act on their behalf.

Some domestic courts have handed down important decisions relating to children, particularly, in relation to legal standing. The groundbreaking *Oposa Minors* case decided by the Philippine's Supreme Court in 1993 achieved celebrity status overnight. In this case, a group of minors, represented by the Philippine Ecological Network, sued on their behalf and on behalf of generations unborn, to stop the logging concessions granted to timber companies by the government. They argued that "continued deforestation would cause irreparable injury to their generation and succeeding ones, and would violate their constitutional right to a balanced and healthful ecology."[80] The plaintiffs argued that they as well as future generations have a right to a healthy environment and that "every generation holds the environment in trust for succeeding generations."[81] They further argued that by issuing timber concessions, the Department of Environment and Natural Resources has violated their duty to protect the environment, and by destroying the life support system of future generations it would commit "generational genocide."[82]

While the respondent sought to have the case dismissed on the grounds that the petitioners lacked standing as well as a proper cause of action, the Court held otherwise:

> This case, however, has a special and novel element. Petitioners minors assert that they represent their generation as well as generations yet unborn. We find no difficulty in ruling that they can, for themselves, for others of their generation and for the succeeding generations, file a class suit. Their personality to sue in

---

[77] The Hungarian Parliamentary Commissioner for Future Generations, see M. Szabó, "The Way Forward: Protecting Future Generations through the Institution of Green Ombudsman" (Future Justice, 24 April 2013), www.futurejustice.org/blog/guest-contribution/an-example-guest-post/.

[78] Environmental impact assessment laws of many countries require the evaluation of the reasonably foreseeable impact of a proposed project on the environment. See, for example, S. Ferrey, *Environmental Law*, 3rd ed. (New York: Aspen Publishers, 2004), 87 for a discussion of environmental impact assessment laws in the United States.

[79] See *Minors Oposa* case, discussed in note 83 and accompanying text.

[80] See T. Allen, "The Philippines Children's Case: Recognizing Legal Standing for Future Generations," (1993–1994) 6 *Georgetown International Environmental Law Review* 713.

[81] Ibid., 715.

[82] Ibid., 716.

behalf of the succeeding generations can only be based on the concept of intergenerational responsibility insofar as the right to a balanced and healthful ecology is concerned. Such a right, as hereinafter expounded, considers the "rhythm and harmony of nature." Nature means the created world in its entirety.[83]

The court further acknowledged not only the right of the present generation to a healthy environment but also their *duty* to protect the environment for the benefit of future generations:

> Needless to say, every generation has a responsibility to the next to preserve that rhythm and harmony for the full enjoyment of a balanced and healthful ecology. Put a little differently, the minors' assertion of their right to a sound environment constitutes, at the same time, the performance of their obligation to ensure the protection of that right for the generations to come.[84]

The Supreme Court thus endorsed both the right to a healthy environment as well the duty of the present generation to preserve the environment for the benefit of generations to come. It further acknowledged that the right to a healthy environment need not even be written in the constitution because it predates constitutions and governments:

> While the right to a balanced and healthful ecology is to be found under the Declaration of Principles and State Policies and not under the Bill of Rights, it does not follow that it is less important than any of the civil and political rights enumerated in the latter. Such a right belongs to a different category of rights altogether for it concerns nothing less than self-preservation and self-perpetuation – aptly and fittingly stressed by the petitioners – the advancement of which may even be said to predate all governments and constitutions. *As a matter of fact, these basic rights need not even be written in the Constitution for they are assumed to exist from the inception of humankind.*
>
> If they are now explicitly mentioned in the fundamental charter, it is because of the well-founded fear of its framers that unless the rights to a balanced and healthful ecology and to health are mandated as state policies by the Constitution itself, thereby highlighting their continuing importance and imposing upon the state a solemn obligation to preserve the first and protect and advance the second, the day would not be too far when all else would be lost not only for the present generation, but also for those to come – generations which stand to inherit nothing but parched earth incapable of sustaining life.[85]

Despite these laudable pronouncements by the Court, it has been pointed out that it did nothing to influence government conduct.[86] Even the lawyer who filed

---

[83] See *Minors Oposa v. Secretary, Ministry of Environment and Natural Resources* (G.R. No. 101083, 30 July 1993).
[84] Ibid.
[85] Ibid. (emphasis added).
[86] See D. B. Gatmaytan, "The Illusion of Intergenerational Equity: *Oposa v. Factoran* as Pyrrhic Victory" (2003–2004) 15 *Georgetown International Environmental Law Review* 457.

the case and whose children were among the petitioners was skeptical about the impact of the case:

> Although hardly known in the country's legal community, the case has been the subject of extensive citation, analysis, and comment in international law circles. Perhaps because it is the first case decided by the highest court of a country which discussed and implemented what had heretofore been rhetorical call for responsibility to future generations for the world's natural resources.[87]

Some contend that the incongruent reception of the case may be because the international legal community misunderstood the case and that the decision is overrated for several reasons: first, the case did not affect government conduct and the timber licenses were not canceled. Second, the Court's statement on standing to sue for future generations is *obiter*. In any event, the court has always adopted a liberal approach to questions relating to standing. Third, the use of intergenerational equity in the case was useless and the protection of rights of future generations was already accepted under the Philippines law:

> The use of "intergenerational equity" – invoking the rights of future generations – while intellectually titillating, is ultimately useless in the resolution of the case. The Philippines Supreme Court would have decided *Oposa* exactly the same way had the children filed the case solely on their own behalf. In cases involving the protection of the environment, the distinction between present and future generations is inconsequential – we cannot protect the rights of future generations without protecting the rights of the present.[88]

Gatmaytan, however, contends that the real impact of the case rests on the Court's pronouncement that the right to a balanced and healthful ecology is a justiciable, self-executory and actionable right that is superior to the Bill of Rights.[89] This important aspect of the judgment has not been exploited by environmental advocates without reducing it to a "rhetorical call for responsibility to future generations for the world's natural resources."[90]

Despite this rather negative account of the case, its influence on advocacy in other parts of the world should not be overlooked. Soon after the judgment, a similar case was filed in Sri Lanka as a test case. Called the *Kotte Kids* case, it involved adverse health effects caused by a power plant on children and the generations unborn. Although it was settled by the parties, the petitioners modelled their case on the *Oposa* case.[91] In the seminal case handed down by the Supreme Court of Sri Lanka in the *Eppawala Phosphate Mining* case, the Court stated: "Decisions with

---

[87] See A. A. Oposa (1997), as cited in ibid.
[88] See Gatmaytan, "The Illusion of Intergenerational Equity," 460.
[89] Ibid.
[90] Ibid., 485.
[91] See S. F. Puvimanasighe, "Towards a Jurisprudence of Sustainable Development in South Asia: Litigation in the Public Interest" (2009) 10 *Sustainable Development Law & Policy* 46.

regard to the nature and scale of activity require the most anxious consideration from the point of view of safeguarding the health and safety of the people, naturally including the petitioners, ensuring the viability of their occupations, and protecting the rights of future generations of Sri Lankans."[92]

The Supreme Court of India has also handed down many decisions that endorse the intergenerational equity principle. In *MC Mehta v. Kamal Nath*, the Supreme Court recognised the need to balance the competing claims of the present generation for development with those of future generations to inherit a healthy environment.[93] Similarly, in the case of *Chinnappa*, the Court reiterated the need to consider the future while providing for the present and stressed that we owed a duty to future generations.[94]

We now turn to a brief survey of the salient provisions of the UNCRC.

THE UN CONVENTION ON THE RIGHTS OF THE CHILD

The UNCRC was adopted by the international community in 1989 and entered into force less than a year later, which is quite unprecedented in international law. It enjoys near universal ratification with 196 states as parties – the United States remains the only country not to have ratified it although it signed the Convention in 1995.

The UNCRC, referring to the Universal Declaration of Human Rights, notes that "childhood is entitled to special care and assistance"[95] and the parties to the Convention have undertaken to respect and ensure that the rights in the Convention are afforded to each child within its jurisdiction without discrimination of any kind. One of the fundamental principles underlying the Convention is the best interest of the child: "In all actions concerning children, whether undertaken by public or private social welfare institutions, courts of law, administrative authorities or legislative bodies, *the best interest of the child shall be a primary consideration.*"[96]

The Convention makes specific reference to adverse effects of environmental pollution in the context of right to health. Under article 24, States Parties recognise the right of the child to the enjoyment of the highest attainable standard of health. In the fulfilment of this right, States Parties are required to take steps, *inter alia*:

> To combat disease and malnutrition, including within the framework of primary health care, through, inter alia, the application of readily available technology and through the provision of adequate nutritious foods and clean drinking-water, taking into consideration the dangers and risks of environmental pollution;[97]

---

[92] See *Bulankulama & others v Secretary, Ministry of Industrial Development & others* (2 June 2000) 3 Sri L.R. 243.
[93] See 1997 (1) SCCC 3886.
[94] See *K. M. Chinnappa v. Union of India*, UP 202/1995 (decided October 30, 2002).
[95] UNCRC, Preamble.
[96] UNCRC, article 3(1) (emphasis added).
[97] UNCRC, article 24.

This is the only human rights convention that refers specifically to the dangers and risks of environmental pollution. While human rights treaty bodies are regularly confronted with human rights violations resulting from environmental pollution, other human rights treaties do not refer to environmental issues or encompass environmental rights. From that perspective, the UNCRC is an exception.

It must be noted here that the UNCRC does not refer to the intergenerational equity principle specifically although that principle had appeared in the international realm then. The fact that environmental pollution was included in the Convention suggests that States Parties were aware of the long-term implications of environmental pollution, including on future generations. Moreover, provisions relating to equality, health, education and non-discrimination all have an intergenerational impact as how the present generation of children is treated and protected very much has an impact on future generations. In this context, the reference to environmental pollution is significant.

In addition, two of the three regional human rights treaties recognise the link between human rights and the environment and embody a substantive right to a healthy environment. These are the African Charter on Human and Peoples' Rights[98] and the San Salvador Protocol to the American Convention on Human Rights.[99] However, only the former treaty confers a justiciable right. Although the European Convention on Human Rights does not specifically embody a similar right, the jurisprudence of the European Court of Human Rights has recognised that rights embodied in the Convention can be violated as a result of environmental pollution and degradation.[100] Many of these cases have affected children and their health. Thus, in *Lopez Ostra v. Spain*[101] the daughter of the petitioner showed symptoms associated with pollution caused by leather industries and the medical practitioner who examined the child recommended that the child be removed from that area.[102] The Court found a violation of article 8 (right to respect for private life) of the Convention.

Children's Declaration on Sustainable Development Goals

In September 2015 a groundbreaking declaration was adopted by children at the Children's Summit held in New York with input from 2,700 children from more than 70 countries who contributed ideas online.[103] Noting that children are the

---

[98] Organisation of African Unity, *African Charter on Human and Peoples' Rights* (OAU Doc CAB/LEG/67/3 rev. 5, 27 June 1981) 21 ILM 58 (1982).
[99] Organisation of American States, *Additional Protocol to the American Convention on Human Rights in the Area of Economic, Social and Cultural Rights* (17 November 1988)
[100] See D. K. Anton and D. L. Shelton, *Environmental Protection and Human Rights* (Cambridge: Cambridge University Press, 2011), 338.
[101] (Appl. No 16798/90), Chamber Judgment, Strasbourg (9 December 1994).
[102] Ibid.
[103] 2015 Children's Declaration on World's Sustainable Development Goals (20 September 2015), http://cisdl.org/public/VOFG/Final_VoFG_Childrens_Summit_Declaration_21_September.pdf.

foundation of future development, the Declaration stressed that children must have their voices heard, on both national and international levels because decisions that the world makes today will define their future. Stressing the importance of education, the Declaration provides that "sustainable development must be included in our educational curriculum, to ensure that all children know about its importance, and ways to achieve it."[104]

The Declaration devotes a separate section to protecting the environment. It recognises the threat that climate change poses to the planet and the future. It provides that everyone has the right to clean air and a clean environment. It stresses the need to preserve the environment and natural resources and that everyone will suffer without healthy ecosystems. The Declaration urges everybody to preserve marine life for future generations and to invest in renewable and clean energy.

In a direct jab at the current generation, the Declaration states that "[c]hildren all over the world should advise our parents, our teachers and all other adults to make the real steps for ensuring sustainable development" because "we are the future." In a further jab, the Declaration states that children should lead the way to make people aware of the need for sustainable development: "This can be done by starting new social movements, creating posters, blogs and radio shows, and even writing our own books." Finally, these brilliant children have pledged to become Child Ambassadors for the UN SDGs in their schools, communities and internationally.

This Declaration should make any right-thinking adult cringe with shame. Rather than rely on adults to protect them, this Declaration clearly shows that children have taken their fate into their own hands because adults have shown at least in the context of climate change that they are not capable of taking the correct course of action, let alone protect them. The adults have shown that they would rather point the finger at somebody else than act. Thus, for example, during climate negotiations, countries like China and India continued to blame the United States for its historic contribution to climate change while the United States gave the non-inclusion of major emitters under the Kyoto Protocol as a reason for its withdrawal from it.[105] This finger-pointing was one of the reasons why the international community was not able to adopt a legal framework to succeed the Kyoto Protocol until the adoption of the landmark Paris Agreement in December 2015. If this shaming is not sufficient to galvanise the current world leaders into action, then it is not clear what would.

The UN General Assembly resolution that adopted SDGs in September 2015 makes a commitment to intergenerational equity. It is based on five "Ps" – people, planet, prosperity, peace and partnership. Elaborating on the section on planet, the resolution proclaims: "We are determined to protect the planet from degradation, including through sustainable consumption and production, sustainably managing

---

[104] Ibid., Paragraph 21.
[105] Hunter et al., *International Environmental Law and Policy*, 667.

its natural resources and taking urgent action on climate change, so that it can support the needs of the present and future generations."[106]

With regard to education, the resolution provided:

> We commit to providing inclusive and equitable quality education at all levels – early childhood, primary, secondary, tertiary, technical and vocational training. All people, irrespective of sex, age, race or ethnicity, and persons with disabilities, migrants, indigenous peoples, children and youth, especially those in vulnerable situations, should have access to life-long learning opportunities that help them to acquire the knowledge and skills needed to exploit opportunities and to participate fully in society. We will strive to provide children and youth with a nurturing environment for the full realization of their rights and capabilities, helping our countries to reap the demographic dividend, including through safe schools and cohesive communities and families.[107]

Several of the SDGs are relevant for children – ending poverty (goal 1); ending hunger and achieving food security and improved nutrition (goal 2); ensuring healthy lives and promoting well-being (goal 3); ensuring inclusive and equitable quality education (goal 4); achieving gender equality and empowering women and girls (goal 5); ensuring availability of water and sanitation (goal 6); ensuring access to sustainable energy (goal 7); and taking urgent action to combat climate change (goal 13). While the intergenerational equity principle is not specifically mentioned in either the General Assembly resolution (except the reference to future generations in relation to protecting the planet) or the SDGs, it can be argued that it underlies the whole endeavor as both inter- and intragenerational equity are integral components of sustainable development.[108] Certainly, the projected consequences of climate change are so far reaching as to affect the right of future generations to a healthy environment and a whole gamut of other rights currently recognised such as water, food, health and adequate standard of living.[109] Thus, the commitment to addressing climate change definitely has an intergenerational reach.

CLIMATE CHANGE AS A CASE STUDY

Perhaps no current global issue brings the intergenerational equity principle into stark reality as climate change.[110] There are other issues that implicate intergenerational equity – abject poverty, war and massive human rights violations such as

---

[106] UNGA, "Transforming Our World."
[107] Ibid., [25].
[108] S. Atapattu, *Emerging Principles of International Environmental Law* (New York: Transnational, 2006), ch. 2.
[109] The link between climate change and human rights has received considerable attention in recent years. See generally, UNGA, "Report of the Office of the High Commissioner for Human Rights on the Relationship between Climate Change and Human Rights" (UN Doc. A/HRC/10/61, 15 January 2009).
[110] See J. Wood, "Intergenerational Equity and Climate Change" (1995–1996) 8 *Georgetown International Environmental Law Review* 293; B. H. Weston, "Climate Change and

genocide and large-scale displacement triggered by war and conflict. However, climate change is unprecedented because it has the potential to unleash forces of nature that are beyond the control of human beings. We are looking at a scenario that could make life as we know it today a thing of the past. Scientists are gravely concerned that if a certain threshold is crossed, the planet will become uninhabitable.[111] Indeed, humans could become an "endangered" species. Thus, if we continue on a business-as-usual path, the consequences for our children and grandchildren will be dire. We owe at a minimum a moral duty to our children and grandchildren to change our course of action now so that they will at least have a habitable planet, let alone the same choices we enjoy today.

UNICEF acknowledges the disproportionate impact of climate change and disasters on children who will have to bear the brunt of their impacts:

> Climate change and natural disasters have a disproportionate impact on today's children, especially the most disadvantaged – and managing the long-term impact will fall on the shoulders of today's youngest generation. The voices, ideas and specific needs of children should be recognized and prioritized in all policies and investments to tackle climate change, reduce greenhouse gases, lessen the impact of disasters and protect an already fragile environment.[112]

Climate change also implicates justice issues both at the interstate level and at the individual/group level.[113] Inasmuch as climate change disproportionately affects certain states and regions (small island states, the Polar regions, etc.), it also affects certain groups and people disproportionately. Indigenous peoples, women, children, "climate refugees," the elderly and the disabled are considered as being particularly vulnerable to climate change.[114] Some include future generations as a vulnerable group and apply a justice framework to them.[115]

A justice framework is based on the notion of fairness and equity and presupposes that certain groups have been historically marginalised or are vulnerable because they have no voice in the decision-making process, due to, *inter alia*, poverty, lack of capacity or subordination. While several definitions of environmental justice have

---

Intergenerational Justice: Foundational Reflections" (2007–2008) 9 *Vermont Journal of Environmental Law* 375.

[111] Intergovernmental Panel on Climate Change, *Climate Change 2014 Synthesis Report: Summary for Policymakers* (IPCC, 2014), www.ipcc.ch/pdf/assessment-report/ar5/syr/AR5_SYR_FINAL_SPM.pdf.

[112] UNICEF, *A Post-2015 World Fit for Children: An Agenda for #EVERYChild* 2015 (UNICEF, 2015), www.unicef.org/agenda2030/files/2pager_everychild_FINAL_web.pdf.

[113] See S. Atapattu, *Human Rights Approaches to Climate Change: Challenges and Opportunities* (London: Routledge, 2016), 93.

[114] See Physicians for Social Responsibility, "Health Implications of Global Warming: Impacts on Vulnerable Populations" (undated), www.psr.org/assets/pdfs/vulnerable-populations.pdf.

[115] See P. Lawrence, *Justice for Future Generations: Climate Change and International Law* (Cheltenham, UK: Edward Elgar, 2015).

been applied, we will adopt the fourfold framework as articulated by Robert Keuhn: distributive justice, procedural justice, corrective justice and social justice.[116]

Climate change clearly implicates the rights of future generations as well as those of children of the current generation who will bear the brunt of the consequences of climate change. These two groups had no hand in creating or exacerbating the problem but will have to bear the burden of coping with the consequences. Moreover, legally they are often not given a voice at the table to object to or shape the decisions that are being taken today and the consequences of climate change will drastically limit the choices they will have to shape their future. Certainly, the present generation had no input into the decisions that our forefathers made with regard to the economic model that they adopted. Clearly, this situation raises justice issues.

Proposing a justice framework with regard to future generations, Peter Lawrence argues that contemporaries have an ethical obligation to take mitigation measures for the protection of future generations.[117] He argues that "this obligation rests on a harm avoidance principle, core human rights to ensure human dignity – to which persons are entitled regardless of when and where they are born – and a transgenerational community extending into the future."[118] The crucial issue, however, is to determine "how the mitigation burden should be fairly distributed between current and future generations."[119] The issue revolves on the basic issue of justice for the current generation in which the vast majority lack access to basic needs that their counterparts in the developed world take for granted. In other words, the issue boils down to intergenerational equity versus intragenerational equity. We could also tie this to mitigation and adaptation measures. While adaptation is crucial for the current generation, mitigation measures become crucial for future generations. The question whether we should expend scarce resources on funding adaptation measures or mitigation measures has become a hotly debated issue.[120] It is obvious that we need to strike a balance between the two to ensure that the current generation can adapt to the consequences of climate change while ensuring that our children and grandchildren and generations to come will inherit at least a liveable planet. Mitigation measures are crucial for this.

Taking their fate into their own hands, a group of children has filed a serious of legal action in all 50 states of the United States against federal agencies and manufacturers claiming that their future is being jeopardised by business interests.[121] The nonprofit *Kids* v. *Global Warming* alleged that these entities failed to give effect to the public trust doctrine and common law that require them to protect nature for

---

[116] R. Keuhn, "A Taxonomy of Environmental Justice" (2000) 30 *Environmental Law Reporter* 10681.
[117] Lawrence, *Justice for Future Generations*, 67.
[118] Ibid.
[119] Ibid.
[120] See Atapattu, *Human Rights Approaches to Climate Change*, ch. 5.
[121] See M. Levitin, "Kids v. Global Warming: The Lawsuit," *Occupy*, 5 October 2012, www.occupy.com/article/kids-vs-global-warming-lawsuit.

future generations. These actions were filed on the basis of the "atmospheric trust doctrine."[122] Although many of the cases have been dismissed, corporations have intervened stating that they have a right to emit pollution into the atmosphere. A member of *Kids* v. *Global Warming* stated that "the fact that huge industry groups have joined this case is a sign of how big this is, because they actually feel threatened.... We stand for the rights of this generation to grow up on a planet that isn't plagued by hurricanes and droughts and corruption and injustice. To have the opportunity to raise our own children on a planet similar to the one we were raised on."[123] While most of the cases were rejected, they scored their first victory when a judge in Washington State ordered the Department of Ecology to consider most recent science on climate change when regulating carbon dioxide emissions.[124]

These litigations are already having a global impact. A case that is likely to become a landmark case, a group of Norwegian children filed legal action against Norway over Arctic Oil Drilling on the basis that it violates the intergenerational equity principle found in the Norwegian Constitution.[125] Paragraph 112 of the Constitution requires legislators to adopt policies that do not harm the planet for the next generation and the children challenged the politicians' decision-making powers with regard to oil drilling in the Arctic. In a case filed by a group of lawyers in the Netherlands, a court in The Hague ordered the Dutch government to reduce its greenhouse emissions by 25 per cent within the next five years.[126] The court held that reducing emissions by just 14 to 17 per cent compared to 1990 levels was unlawful given the scale of the problem. While intergenerational equity was not the basis of the ruling, lawyers who brought the claim stated that "this is the first a time a court has determined that states have an independent legal obligation towards their citizens."[127] Such lawsuits are likely to mushroom around the world if states keep on postponing action on climate change.[128]

---

[122] Ibid.

[123] Ibid.

[124] See Equity for Children, "Case Study: iMatter Kids vs Global Warming" (undated), www.equityforchildren.org/wp-content/uploads/2015/11/iMatter-Casestudy-Desktop-Publishing-1.pdf.

[125] See A. Staalesen, "Lawyers Sue State over Arctic Oil Drilling," *The Barents Observer*, 18 January 2016, www.thebarentsobserver.com/ecology/2016/01/lawyers-sue-state-over-arctic-oil-drilling#.VpoNDpoFYqQ.linkedin.

[126] See A. Neslen, "The Dutch Government Ordered to Cut Carbon Emissions in Landmark Case," *The Guardian*, 24 June 2015, www.theguardian.com/environment/2015/jun/24/dutch-government-ordered-cut-carbon-emissions-landmark-ruling.

[127] Ibid., quoting Dennis van Berkel, legal counsel for Urgenda, the group that brought the lawsuit. A similar case was filed by the youth in Sweden against the state for a coal deal it made (see Press Release, "Youth Sue Swedish State for Coal Deal" [15 September 2016], https://docs.google.com/document/d/1l3pVVZbzRTHe4vg15sCozVIYDuMu9F6AS89B7KViyZg/edit).

[128] Greenpeace filed a petition before the National Human Rights Commission in the Philippines recently against 50 Carbon Majors requesting the Commission to investigate the responsibility of Carbon Majors with regard to human rights violations resulting from the impacts of climate change (petition available at www.greenpeace.org/seasia/ph/PageFiles/105904/Climate-Change-and-Human-Rights-Complaint.pdf).

CONCLUSION

The UNCRC elaborates a set of rights that are applicable specifically to children that complement general human rights law. Starting with the right to life, the UNCRC (which enjoys near universal acceptance with the notable exception of the United States) requires states, *inter alia*, to take the best interests of the child into consideration in all actions relating to the child. Environmental degradation, particularly climate change, has the potential to cause damage not just to the present generation of children but also for many generations to come. Because they lack a voice at the table, the question has arisen as to how their rights can be protected. The intergenerational equity principle is one such tool.

There is a clear link between sustainable development and intergenerational equity. In fact, it will not be wrong to assert that sustainable development requires us to evaluate the impact of our decisions on future generations and to ensure that they have at least the same choices as we have today. As articulated by Collins:

> The close relationship between sustainable development and general concept of intergenerational equity – the notion that the present generation's use of natural resources must be limited to safeguard the ecological needs of future generations – is self-evident and has been widely acknowledged.[129]

Climate change is a given whether or not people accept its existence. The global community is already experiencing its adverse consequences as the Inuit Petition to the Inter-American Commission of Human Rights showed.[130] However, the worst effects are yet to come and "will be felt primarily by today's children and the generations that follow them, especially if they are poor or otherwise lack the capacity to protect themselves."[131] As Weston questions, "What parent, grandparent or great-grandparent would disavow a climate legacy beneficial to their descendants? Which child, grandchild, or great-grandchild will not feel at least a little resentful if such a legacy is denied them?"[132] Climate change brings the intergenerational equity principle into sharp relief as no other issue has in the recent past.

---

[129] See Collins, "Revisiting the Doctrine," 131–132. She, however, contends that sustainable development is notoriously vague and lacks normative specificity. While this is not the place to engage in an elaborate discussion of sustainable development, suffice it to say that sustainable development embodies both substantive and procedural components many of which have achieved normative status under international law. See Atapattu, *Emerging Principles of International Environmental Law*, ch. 2.

[130] Petition to the Inter-American Commission of Human Rights Seeking Relief from Violations Resulting from Global Warming Caused by the Acts and Omissions of the United States (2005) (Petition available at http://earthjustice.org/sites/default/files/library/legal_docs/petition-to-the-inter-american-commission-on-human-rights-on-behalf-of-the-inuit-circumpolar-conference.pdf).

[131] See Weston, "International Equity and Climate Change," 375.

[132] Ibid., 376.

9

Children's Rights and the Environmental Dimension of Sustainable Development

Ellen Desmet

INTRODUCTION

Over the past decades, "sustainable development" has become an overarching policy framework that is widely endorsed, albeit not uncontested as to its precise meaning and implications.[1] Milestones in this process of gaining worldwide policy relevance included the report "Our Common Future" of the World Commission on Environment and Development (WCED) of 1987[2] and the UN Conference on Environment and Development (UNCED, also known as the Earth Summit) held at Rio de Janeiro in 1992.[3] The process recently culminated – as for now – in the adoption of the Sustainable Development Goals (SDGs) by the UN General Assembly in September 2015. During roughly that same time span, the issue of children's rights rose on the international legal and policy agenda, with the adoption of the UN Convention on the Rights of the Child (UNCRC) in 1989 being a key moment.[4]

This chapter explores the interrelation between children's rights and the "environmental dimension" of sustainable development. At least three clusters of factors

---

[1] This research has been funded by the Interuniversity Attraction Poles Programme initiated by the Belgian Science Policy Office, more specifically the IAP "The Global Challenge of Human Rights Integration: Towards a Users' Perspective" (www.hrintegration.be).
    See, for example, B. Giddings, B. Hopwood and G. O'Brien, "Environment, Economy and Society: Fitting Them Together into Sustainable Development" (2002) 10 *Sustainable Development* 187, 187–188; J. Meadowcroft, "Sustainable Development: A New(ish) Idea for a New Century?" (2000) 48 *Political Studies* 370 (focusing on how governments in industrialised countries have engaged with the idea of sustainable development).
[2] World Commission on Environment and Development (WCED), "Our Common Future" (UN Doc. A/42/427, 1987), www.un-documents.net/our-common-future.pdf.
[3] See N. Quental, J. M. Lourenço and F. Nunes da Silva, "Sustainable Development Policy: Goals, Targets and Political Cycles" (2011) 19 *Sustainable Development* 15, 20–21.
[4] UN General Assembly (UNGA), *Convention on the Rights of the Child* (UN Doc. A/RES/44/25, 20 November 1989) 1577 UNTS 3.

justify such a focus. First, the environmental objective of sustainable development can be considered a distinguishing feature of sustainable development compared with other (traditional) development paradigms.[5] The exact weight to be attached to environmental issues within sustainable development policy remains subject to debate though. Giddings, Hopwood and O'Brien have identified three main ways in which sustainable development has been conceptualised.[6] The first, best-known approach understands sustainable development as consisting of three "dimensions" (or "pillars"), namely the environmental, the social and the economic dimension, which are then schematically represented as three interconnected rings.[7] This approach has been criticised for leading to a compartmentalised view, not doing justice to the fundamental links between the environment, society and economy. Based on the starting point that the ecological limits of the planet should provide the boundaries of human action, an alternative, "nested model" of sustainable development has been proposed. This implies that the economy is dependent on society to develop, and both the economy and society should develop within the limits of the ecological carrying capacity of the planet.[8] Finally, Giddings et al. suggest a more integrated model of sustainable development, in which the economy – as a subsector of society – is merged with society, and the boundaries between "human well-being" and the environment are fuzzy, reflecting the constant interaction between them.[9] The point I wish to make is that whichever model of sustainable development one prefers or subscribes to, the "environmental dimension" constitutes a key component of each of them, be it as one of three interconnected dimensions or as the overarching factor constraining and facilitating the development of society and the economy (nested model) or the realisation of human well-being in general (integrated model). Given this centrality of the environmental dimension to sustainable development, it makes sense to analyse how this dimension relates to children's rights.[10]

A second reason for examining the relationship between children's rights and the environmental dimension of sustainable development is that children's health and well-being are strongly dependent upon healthy ecosystems. Children are at greater

---

[5] See T. Waas et al., "Sustainable Development: A Bird's Eye View" (2011) 3 *Sustainability* 1637, 1640.
[6] Giddings et al., "Environment, Economy and Society", 188–194.
[7] In recent years, a fourth dimension is often added, referred to as "democracy" or "governance". See Waas et al., "Sustainable Development", 1651.
[8] Compare with A. Ross, "Modern Interpretations of Sustainable Development" (2009) 36 *Journal of Law and Society* 32 (pleading for ecological sustainability to be recognised as the moral and legal principle underpinning the concept of sustainable development).
[9] Giddings et al., "Environment, Economy and Society", 193–194.
[10] The incorporation of this chapter in a book addressing sustainable development as a whole diminishes the risk of artificially separating the environmental dimension from the other dimensions of sustainable development. This contribution must therefore be read together with the other chapters, to obtain a holistic insight in the complexities of the sustainable development concept.

risk than adults to environmental hazards because of their "physical size, immature organs, metabolic rate, behaviour, natural curiosity and lack of knowledge".[11] The figures are daunting: "Globally, about 43% of the total burden of disease due to environmental risks falls on children under 5 years of age, even though they make up only 12% of the population."[12] There are large regional disparities, with sub-Saharan Africa bearing the largest burden.[13] Also the proportion of deaths attributable to environmental factors among children 0–14 years of age (36 per cent) lies significantly higher than the overall figure (23 per cent).[14] This greater sensitivity of children to environmental degradation and pollution warrants explicit and tailored attention for children in sustainable development policies.

A final rationale underlying this contribution is that in participation processes concerning the environment, children risk being overlooked or only given tokenistic attention.[15] However, children are arguably the most important stakeholders as far as a healthy environment is concerned, not only because of their current heightened vulnerability but also because as adults, they – and their children – will continue to suffer the consequences of unsustainable decisions made today. Although in recent years efforts have been made to address this kind of generational discrimination, as elaborated in the following discussion, much remains to be done.

Different reasons thus underpin this chapter's focus on the interplay between children's rights and the environmental dimension of sustainable development. A few words are needed on how these terms are understood for the purposes of this contribution. To start, "children's rights" are understood as the human rights of children.[16] Children's human rights have been codified most importantly in the UNCRC, which recognises children as rights holders rather than beneficiaries. Intergenerational equity is an important principle of sustainable development. Children are then often seen as representing these future generations. The rights of future generations *as such* are not dealt with in this chapter.[17] Future generations

---

[11] See UNEP, UNICEF and WHO, *Children in the New Millennium: Environmental Impact on Health* (UNEP, UNICEF and WHO, 2002), 7.

[12] K. R. Smith, C. F. Corvalán and T. Kjellström, "How Much Global Ill Health Is Attributable to Environmental Factors?" (1999) 10 *Epidemiology* 573, 582.

[13] Ibid.

[14] A. Prüss-Üstün and C. Corvalán, *Preventing Disease through Healthy Environments: Towards an Estimate of the Environmental Burden of Disease* (World Health Organisation, 2006).

[15] See, for example, M. Liebel, "Discriminated against Being Children: A Blind Spot in the Human Rights Arena", in M. Liebel (ed.), *Children's Rights from Below: Cross-Cultural Perspectives* (New York: Palgrave Macmillan 2012), 103; S. Stephens, "Children and the UN Conference on Environment and Development: Participants and Media Symbols" (1992) *Barn Research on Children in Norway* 44.

[16] See D. Reynaert et al., "Introduction: A Critical Approach to Children's Rights", in W. Vandenhole et al. (eds.), *Routledge International Handbook of Children's Rights Studies* (London: Routledge, 2015), 5–7.

[17] See generally L. Westra, *Environmental Justice and the Rights of Unborn and Future Generations: Law, Environmental Harm and the Right to Health* (London: Earthscan, 2008).

are sometimes mentioned, though, especially when they are the closest reference to children that can be found in a document.[18]

As any concept, the concept of "environment" has been the carrier of a variety of meanings. Whereas it often functions as a shortened reference to "natural environment", in other contexts a broader meaning is attached to the term. This seems especially the case when used in scholarship regarding children and their rights. For instance, a "child's right to a healthy environment"[19] has been interpreted in the literature as including the right to a family environment for children of prisoners as well as other social issues such as violence and slavery.[20] Similarly, a lobby document of UNICEF in the run-up to the 2030 Agenda for Sustainable Development stated: "Children … have the right to survive, live and grow up in a decent environment, with all that implies: attending school, enjoying good health and nutrition, and living and growing in safety and security."[21] In these instances, the concept of "environment" is used in a way that goes beyond its ecological dimensions. Nevertheless, in line with the dominant interpretation given to the term in the context of sustainable development, the notion "environmental dimension" in this chapter relates to all "natural" environmental issues, excluding societal challenges. In addition, the theme of climate change is not touched upon because this is addressed by Karin Arts in Chapter 10 of this volume.

The analysis is undertaken from two perspectives: a children's rights perspective and a sustainable development perspective. First, it is investigated how environmental concerns have been taken up in international children's rights law and policy ("The Environmental Dimension of Sustainable Development in Children's Rights Law and Policy Agendas"). The major part of this chapter enquires whether and how children and their rights are recognised within sustainable development policy agendas, with a focus on environmental issues. After a historical review of the key documents on sustainable development ("Children and Their Rights in Sustainable Development Agendas"), particular attention is paid to the recently adopted 2030 Agenda for Sustainable Development ("Children and Their Rights in the 2030 Agenda for Sustainable Development"). The chapter closes with some final reflections ("Final Reflections").

---

[18] This is for instance the case for the 1972 Stockholm Declaration (see "The Environmental Dimension of Sustainable Development in Children's Rights Law and Policy Agendas").

[19] No general, legally binding "child's right to a healthy environment" is as yet recognised. For a plea in that sense, see D. van Kalmthout, "Out of Isolation: A Claim for Explicit Attention for Children in the Movement toward Recognition of an Environmental Right", in E. Brems, E. Desmet and W. Vandenhole (eds.), *Children's Rights Law in the Global Human Rights Landscape: Isolation, Inspiration, Integration?* (London: Routledge, 2017), 251.

[20] See J. Garbarino and G. Sigman (eds.), *A Child's Right to a Healthy Environment* (New York: Springer, 2010).

[21] UNICEF, "Sustainable Development Starts and Ends with Safe, Healthy and Well-Educated Children" (2013), wwwuniceforg/socialpolicy/files/Sustainable_Development_post_2015pdf.

THE ENVIRONMENTAL DIMENSION OF SUSTAINABLE DEVELOPMENT IN CHILDREN'S RIGHTS LAW AND POLICY AGENDAS

There exists a complex, reciprocal relationship between the environment and human rights, including those of children. On the one hand, a healthy environment is vital for the enjoyment of human rights. As the preamble of the Aarhus Convention of 1998 states, "[A]dequate protection of the environment is essential to human well-being and the enjoyment of basic human rights, including the right to life itself."[22] By contrast, the exercise of certain human rights may be important to maintain or improve the state of the natural environment. In the words of Shelton, "[T]he fulfilment of human rights, especially the right to information and procedural guarantees of participation and access to remedies, is crucial to preventing environmental harm."[23] This reciprocal relationship between human rights and the environment is also apparent from the Draft Principles on Human Rights and the Environment. Its preamble expresses concern that "human rights violations lead to environmental degradation and that environmental degradation leads to human rights violations".[24]

The desirability and feasibility of recognising a substantive human right to the environment has been and continues to be the subject of intense debate. Challenges in recognising such a right include the demarcation of its exact content and scope, the anthropocentrism inherent in recognising a "human" right to environment and the added value of such a right.[25] At the level of the United Nations, various texts have reflected an interest in the idea of a substantive human right to environment,[26] but as of today, no global human rights instrument enshrines this right in a legally binding way. Within the African and Inter-American human rights systems, however, the right to a healthy environment has been recognised.[27] Also at national level, an increasing number of constitutions has incorporated this right.[28]

---

[22] UN Economic Commission for Europe, *Convention on Access to Information, Public Participation in Decision-Making and Access to Justice in Environmental Matters* (25 June 1998) 2161 UNTS 447.

[23] D. Shelton, "Environmental Rights", in P. Alston (ed.), *Peoples' Rights* (Oxford University Press 2001), 186.

[24] UN Sub-Commission on Prevention of Discrimination and Protection of Minorities, "Human Rights and the Environment" (UN Doc. E/CN.4/Sub.2/1994/9, Annex, 6 July 1994).

[25] See E. Desmet, *Indigenous Rights Entwined with Nature Conservation* (Cambridge: Intersentia, 2011), 188–190.

[26] See, for example, UN Sub-Commission on Prevention of Discrimination and Protection of Minorities, "Human Rights and the Environment"; UNESCO General Conference, *Declaration of Bizkaia on the Right to the Environment* (UN Doc. 30 C/INF.11, 24 September 1999).

[27] See article 24 of the Organisation of African Unity, *African Charter on Human and Peoples' Rights* (OAU Doc. CAB/LEG/67/3 rev. 5, 27 June 1981) 21 ILM 58 (1982); article 11 of the Additional Protocol to the American Convention on Human Rights in the Area of Economic, Social and Cultural Rights (Protocol of San Salvador, 17 November 1988) 28 ILM 156 (1989).

[28] See D. R. Boyd, *The Environmental Rights Revolution: A Global Study of Constitutions, Human Rights, and the Environment* (Vancouver: University of British Columbia Press, 2012).

In the preamble of its 2011 Resolution on Human Rights and the Environment, the Human Rights Council recognised that "environmental damage is felt most acutely by those segments of the population already in vulnerable situations".[29] Children were identified as among these vulnerable groups by the Independent Expert on the issue of human rights obligations relating to the enjoyment of a safe, clean, healthy and sustainable environment, John H. Knox.[30]

Turning to children's rights law, the UNCRC contains a balanced image of the child, as being vulnerable (protection paradigm) yet holding agency (liberation paradigm).[31] The Convention does not refer to sustainable development and contains only two mentions of environmental issues. The impact of environmental degradation is referred to in the context of the right to health: to pursue the full implementation of the child's right to the enjoyment of the highest attainable standard of health, State Parties shall take measures "[t]o combat disease and malnutrition, ... through, inter alia, the application of readily available technology and through the provision of adequate nutritious foods and clean drinking-water, *taking into consideration the dangers and risks of environmental pollution*".[32] Moreover, the education of children should be directed to "the development of respect for the natural environment".[33] This limited attention for environmental issues in the UNCRC reflects the lesser urgency of environmental matters at the time of drafting and adopting the Convention. Given the increase in the nature and severity of environmental challenges during the last decades, particularly as regards children, the UNCRC is arguably not well equipped to address these.[34]

At the 1990 World Summit for Children, the political leaders adopted the World Declaration on the Survival, Protection and Development of Children, in which they committed to a 10-point programme to safeguard the rights of children and their living conditions.[35] One point of action was "to work for common measures for the protection of the environment, so that all children can enjoy a safer and healthier future".[36] The Plan of Action for implementing this Declaration in the 1990s contains a separate section on "children and the environment", which

---

[29] UN Human Rights Council, "Human Rights and the Environment" (UN Doc. A/HRC/RES/16/11, 12 April 2011).
[30] UN Human Rights Council, "Report of the Independent Expert on the Issue of Human Rights Obligations Relating to the Enjoyment of a Safe, Clean, Healthy and Sustainable Environment, John H. Knox" (UN Doc. A/HRC/22/43, 24 December 2012).
[31] See W. Vandenhole and J. Ryngaert, "Mainstreaming Children's Rights in Migration Litigation: Muskhadzhiyeva and Others v. Belgium", in E. Brems (ed.), *Diversity and European Human Rights: Rewriting Judgments from the ECHR* (Cambridge: Cambridge University Press, 2013), 71.
[32] UNCRC, article 24(2)(c) (emphasis added).
[33] UNCRC, article 29(1)(e).
[34] See, for example, van Kalmthout, "Out of Isolation".
[35] UNGA, "World Declaration on the Survival, Protection and Development of Children" (UN Doc. A/45/625, 30 September 1990).
[36] Ibid., [20(9)].

commences as follows – explicitly referring to sustainable development: "Children have the greatest stake in the preservation of the environment and its judicious management for sustainable development as their survival and development depends on it."[37] The goals set in the Plan of Action are considered to be "highly compatible with and supportive of environmental protection".[38] A socialisation paradigm, pointing to an image of "children as future citizens",[39] is underlying the provision that "programmes for children ... which inculcate in them respect for the natural environment ... must figure prominently in the world's environmental agenda".

At the special session of the UN General Assembly on children in 2002, the document "A World Fit for Children" was adopted.[40] World leaders stressed their commitment to complete the unfinished agenda of the World Summit and to create a world fit for children. One of the principles and objectives of the agenda is "Protect the Earth for Children". This implies the commitment to "give every assistance to protect children and minimise the impact of natural disasters and environmental degradation on them", which points to an image of a vulnerable child.[41] A socialisation approach is also present in relation to environmental matters, namely in the pledge to "educate all children and adults to respect the natural environment for their health and well-being".[42] In general, an image of children as rights-bearers is noticeable: they are identified as key actors for partnerships, who must be enabled to exercise their right to express their views freely.[43]

Summing up, the main children's rights policy agendas at UN level of the past decades pay considerable attention to environmental issues as being relevant for the realisation of children's rights. When the documents focus specifically on environmental challenges, the paradigms of protection (image of children as vulnerable beings) and, to a lesser extent, socialisation (image of children as future citizens) prevail. This predominance of a protectionist approach when dealing with environmental challenges is confirmed by an analysis of the concluding observations of the UN Committee on the Rights of the Child on natural resource exploitation in Latin America.[44] Also here, the focus was mostly on the protection of children (against economic exploitation, against negative health impacts), viewing them as

---

[37] UNGA, "Plan of Action for Implementing the World Declaration on the Survival, Protection and Development of Children" (UN Doc. A/45/625, Annex, 30 September 1990), [26].
[38] Ibid., [27].
[39] See note 51.
[40] UNGA, "A World Fit for Children" (UN Doc. A/RES/S-27/2, 11 October 2002).
[41] Ibid., [7(10)]. See also [26] (on environmental problems and trends that need to be addressed) and [37(25)] (on the development of legislation, policies and programmes to prevent the exposure of children to harmful environmental contaminants).
[42] Ibid., [28].
[43] Ibid., [32].
[44] See E. Desmet and J. Aylwin, "Natural Resource Exploitation and Children's Rights" in W. Vandenhole et al. (eds.), *Routledge International Handbook of Children's Rights Studies* (London: Routledge, 2015), 401–403.

"in danger" in relation to resource extraction. Only rarely did the Committee refer to the agency and resilience of children in a resource exploitation context.

CHILDREN AND THEIR RIGHTS IN SUSTAINABLE DEVELOPMENT AGENDAS: A HISTORICAL OVERVIEW

Three questions have guided the analysis of the sustainable development policy documents in this and the following section: (1) Which child images seem to underlie these agendas?; (2) How do human rights in general, and children's rights in particular, appear in these documents? and (3) What attention is paid to children and their rights in relation to the environmental dimension of sustainable development in particular? The focus of this chapter on environmental issues implies that other themes in relation to which children are mentioned in these agendas, such as infant and child mortality, education, child labour and HIV/AIDS, are not addressed, unless they are particularly relevant in answering one or more of the three questions previously identified.

According to the Declaration of the United Nations Conference on the Human Environment (UNCHE) of 1972, better known as the Stockholm Declaration, both the natural and the man-made aspects of the environment are essential to the enjoyment of basic human rights.[45] Children are not explicitly mentioned in the Declaration, but implicitly included in the reference to "present (and future) generations". Concretely, man's responsibility to "protect and improve the environment for present and future generations" is laid down in Principle 1, while Principle 2 provides that the natural resources of the earth must be safeguarded for the benefit of present and future generations.

In 1980, the International Union for Conservation of Nature (IUCN), the UN Environment Programme (UNEP) and the World Wide Fund for Nature (WWF) issued the "World Conservation Strategy (WCS) – Living Resource Conservation for Sustainable Development".[46] As the title indicates, the document mainly focuses on environmental matters, and in particular the conservation of living resources, as a way of achieving sustainable development. A "strategy for human rights" is needed next to the proposed conservation strategy to assure human survival and well-being.[47] Human rights thus do not form part of this strategy. The WCS refers to children in the context of the ethical imperative underlying conservation: "We have

---

[45] UN Conference on the Human Environment, "Declaration of the United Nations Conference on the Human Environment" (UN Doc. A/Conf.48/14/Rev.1, 5–16 June 1972), [1].
[46] IUCN, UNEP and WWF, *World Conservation Strategy – Living Resource Conservation for Sustainable Development* (IUCN, UNEP and WWF, 1980). In 1991, these organisations published *Caring for the Earth: A Strategy for Sustainable Living*. The document only refers once to children in relation to malnutrition and preventable disease. IUCN, UNEP and WWF, *Caring for the Earth: A Strategy for Sustainable Living* (Gland, Switzerland: IUCN, UNEP and WWF, 1991), 4.
[47] IUCN et al., *World Conservation Strategy*, [8].

not inherited the earth from our parents, we have borrowed it from our children".[48] It is not clear from the text whether "our children" should be interpreted literally or as a proxy for "future generations".[49] In the remainder of the WCS, "schoolchildren and students" are identified as one of the main target groups of environmental education programmes.[50] The underlying child image in these provisions appears to be one of "children as future citizens": children are to be taught how to behave in an environmentally responsible manner (socialisation paradigm).[51]

The 1987 report "Our Common Future" of the WCED is often referred to as the Brundtland Report, after its Norwegian chair. It contains the probably most known definition of *sustainable development*, as development that "meets the needs of the present without compromising the ability of future generations to meet their own needs".[52] The concept of human rights is only marginally present in the Brundtland Report.[53] Compared to the previous documents on sustainable development, the weight given to children slowly increases. Decision-makers are called upon to act, as "we risk undermining our children's fundamental right to a healthy, life-enhancing environment."[54] This is the first time that children are explicitly recognised as "bearers of rights" in a sustainable development policy agenda. This seems to reflect the zeitgeist, as the drafting process of the UNCRC was coming to a close in the second half of the 1980s. As regards environmental issues, children are mentioned as particularly vulnerable to the consequences of exposure to pesticide and chemical residues[55] and to diseases in cities, most of which are "environmentally based and could be prevented".[56] The Brundtland Report also explicitly links the well-being of "our children" to environmentally unsustainable practices: many such practices "may show profit on the balance sheets of our generation, but our children will inherit the losses. We borrow environmental capital from future generations with no intention or prospect of repaying".[57] In contrast to the WCS, here "our children" seems to be used to refer to "future generations". Finally, the Brundtland Report aptly points to the tension between the interests of decision-makers and young people: "*Most of today's decision makers will*

---

[48] Ibid., [5].
[49] This is different in the Brundtland Report, see following text.
[50] Compare with article 29(1)(e) UNCRC on the aims of education.
[51] See A. T. Kjørholt, "Small Is Powerful – Discourses on 'Children and Participation' in Norway" (2002) 9 *Childhood* 63, 69.
[52] WCED, "Our Common Future", [27].
[53] The Brundtland Report contains only two mentions of the term "human rights", one in relation to population growth (ibid., 8) and one in the speech of a speaker, who refers to the "problems of human rights in Africa" (ibid., [19]). The right to self-determination in the context of family planning, especially for women, is referred to various times (ibid., [6], [43] and [51]).
[54] Ibid., 8.
[55] Ibid., ch. 5, [26].
[56] Ibid., ch. 9, [11].
[57] Ibid., "Our Common Future", [25]. This paragraph ends as follows: "[F]uture generations do not vote; they have no political or financial power; they cannot challenge our decisions".

be dead before the planet feels the heavier effects of acid precipitation; global warming, ozone depletion, or widespread desertification and species loss. *Most of the young voters of today will still be alive.*"[58] Given the reference to young "voters", this will often not include "children" according to the UNCRC definition,[59] unless voting rights are awarded from 16 years onwards. Interestingly, "the young" were heard by the Commission, and clearly spoke out: "*In the Commission's hearings it was the young,* those who have the most to lose, *who were the harshest critics* of the planet's present management."[60] This implies a recognition of the participation rights and agency of "the young", even though it is not clear how this term is to be interpreted here.

At the UNCED, the world's political leaders formally endorsed sustainable development as new development model.[61] The 1992 Declaration on Environment and Development (Rio Declaration)[62] emphasises the environmental dimension of sustainable development: "In order to achieve sustainable development, environmental protection shall constitute an integral part of the development process."[63] The Rio Declaration does not adopt a human rights perspective, only the right to development[64] and the sovereign right of states to exploit their own resources[65] are included. The Declaration does not refer to "children" either, only to "youth": "The *creativity, ideals and courage* of the youth of the world should be mobilized to forge a global partnership in order to achieve sustainable development and ensure a better future for all."[66] Interesting, no reference is made to the *rights* of young people, but they (and especially their creativity, ideals and courage) are rather seen as a *resource* to be used to achieve sustainable development. This approach of youth has also been observed in relation to children. In some participatory projects in Norway, for instance, an image of "children as resources" was present, that is, "as a valuable tool or instrument to realize aims other than children's rights", here sustainable development.[67]

In Agenda 21,[68] the policy agenda accompanying the Rio Declaration, human rights remain at the margins, but children are more present.[69] "Children and youth" are established as one of the Major Groups, and a complete chapter is dedicated to

---

[58] Ibid., [26] (emphasis added).
[59] Article 1 of the UNCRC reads: "For the purposes of the present Convention, a child means every human being below the age of eighteen years unless under the law applicable to the child, majority is attained earlier".
[60] WCED, "Our Common Future", [26] (emphasis added).
[61] Waas et al., "Sustainable Development", 1642.
[62] UN Conference on Environment and Development (UNCED), "Rio Declaration on Environment and Development" (UN Doc. A/CONF.151/26 (vol. I), 12 August 1992).
[63] Ibid., Principle 4.
[64] Ibid., Principle 3.
[65] Ibid., Principle 2.
[66] Ibid., Principle 21 (emphasis added).
[67] See Kjørholt, "Small Is Powerful", 70.
[68] UNCED, "Agenda 21" (UN Doc. A/CONF.151/26 (vols. I–III), 12 August 1992).
[69] The concept "human rights" is only mentioned three times, in a 351-page document (ibid.).

them (chapter 25, "Children and Youth in Sustainable Development"). Agenda 21 hosts a mixture of child images. This is illustrated by the paragraph that provides the "basis for action" of the section on children in sustainable development in chapter 25:

> Children not only will inherit the responsibility of looking after the Earth, but in many developing countries they comprise nearly half the population [children as future citizens]. Furthermore, children in both developing and industrialized countries are highly vulnerable to the effects of environmental degradation [children as vulnerable beings]. They are also highly aware supporters of environmental thinking [children as resources]. The specific interests of children need to be taken fully into account in the participatory process on environment and development in order to safeguard the future sustainability of any actions taken to improve the environment [children as resources].[70]

The absence of the notion of "children as bearers of rights" in this paragraph is striking. Whereas children are conceptualised subsequently as future citizens, vulnerable beings and "resources", they are not seen as bearers of rights. This is particularly evident from the last sentence: the specific interests of children need to be considered, but not because they have an inherent right thereto – as guaranteed however by article 12 UNCRC. The rationale for considering the interests of children seems an instrumentalist one, namely to guarantee the future sustainability of environmental improvement measures. The participation of children is further addressed to some extent in chapter 36 on "Promoting Education, Public Awareness and Training". There, the requirement of children's involvement is mentioned in relation to studies on environmental health drafted by schools and in "relevant activities, linking these studies with services and research in national parks, wildlife reserves, ecological heritage sites etc".[71] Moreover, "support programmes to involve young people and children in environment and development issues" should be developed by UN agencies and nongovernmental organisations.[72]

In the remainder of chapter 25 and in Agenda 21 as a whole, the image of children as vulnerable and in need of protection is predominant. This is especially the case in relation to environmental (health) issues. Chapter 6, on protecting and promoting human health, identifies "infants and children", as younger than 15 years old, and "youth", as younger than 25 years old, as two of the "vulnerable groups" in relation to health.[73] As the link between children and the environmental dimension of sustainable development is concerned, it is recognised that "[t]he health of children

---

[70] Ibid., [25.12].
[71] Ibid., [36.5e].
[72] Ibid., [36.10j].
[73] Ibid., [6.19] and [6.20]. Here, a discrepancy with the UNCRC definition of children is thus noticeable (see article 1 UNCRC). Pursuant to article 24(1) UNCRC, "States Parties recognize the right of the child to the enjoyment of the highest attainable standard of health".

is affected more severely than other population groups by ... adverse environmental factors".[74] To that end, national governments should "[p]rotect children from the effects of environmental and occupational toxic compounds".[75] Also with regard to other environmentally related matters, children are mentioned as groups particularly susceptible to certain threats or risks, mostly together with women through the sentence "in particular women and children". For instance, in chapter 19 on the environmentally sound management of chemical toxics, it is acknowledged that women and children "are at greatest risk" and should therefore be the primary target groups of training and education on chemical risks.[76] Also as regards hazardous waste management, children and women are recognised as particularly vulnerable.[77] Both in chapter 6 on health and regarding other environmental issues, the vulnerability of children thus stands central. This prevalence of the image of the vulnerable child is also evident from the passive manner in which the objectives concerning children in chapter 25 are formulated: governments should take measures to "[e]nsure the survival, protection and development of children" as well as to "[e]nsure that the interests of children are taken fully into account in the participatory process for sustainable development and environmental improvement".[78] Children should thus not necessarily be involved themselves (as is however required by article 12 UNCRC), but their interests should be "taken into account" by others, that is adults. This stands in contrast with the active formulation of the programme area on youth in the same chapter, which reads: "advancing the role of youth and actively involving them in the protection of the environment and the promotion of economic and social development."[79] This subtle difference between the capacity and agency attributed to children and youth in Agenda 21 is confirmed by the following excerpt on capacity building concerning health issues:

> Governments should promote, where necessary... (ii) *women's organizations, youth groups and indigenous people's organizations* to facilitate health and consult them on the creation, amendment and enforcement of legal frameworks to ensure a healthy environment for *children, youth, women and indigenous peoples.*[80]

Whereas the target groups for ensuring a healthy environment are "children, youth, women and indigenous peoples", children are left out when referring to the types of

---

[74] Ibid., [6.19].
[75] Ibid., [6.27, a, iv].
[76] Ibid., [19.22].
[77] Ibid., [20.20].
[78] Ibid., [25.13].
[79] Ibid., [25.1]. On the conceptualisation of "children" and "youth", see E. Desmet, "Implementing the Convention on the Rights of the Child for 'Youth': Who and How?" (2012) 20 *The International Journal of Children's Rights* 3; E. Desmet, "Inspiration for Children's Rights from Indigenous Peoples' Rights" in Brems et al. (eds.), *Children's Rights Law in the Global Human Rights Landscape.*
[80] Ibid., [6.31] (emphasis added).

organisations that should be promoted and consulted to that end: only organisations of women, youth and indigenous peoples are mentioned. Research has shown, however, that also children are very capable of organising themselves.[81] Moreover, according to UNICEF, "[H]undreds of examples are known from around the world where child and youth empowerment has been a catalyst for child-driven change for sustainable development."[82]

This paternalistic attitude of governments towards children, which seems to underlie the language in Agenda 21, is confirmed by Sharon Stephens's account of the actual participation of children in the Earth Summit.[83] Children played a significant role in the opening ceremony, in which a ship arrived with children from various countries, bearing the following UNICEF banner: "Keep the Promise ... For a Better World for All the Children." Children also received much attention in international press coverage. In the actual convention negotiations, however, they felt that their views were not taken seriously. This was evident, for instance, from the fact that only four government officials attended the "Children's Hearing", in which children presented their views. According to Stephens, not only children but also youth were frustrated about their participation in UNCED, even though the texts of the Rio Declaration and Agenda 21 recognise the agency of youth to a somewhat larger extent than that of children, as indicated here in the preceding text.

The Millennium Declaration was adopted by the UN General Assembly at the Millennium Summit in 2000 and formed the basis of the eight Millennium Development Goals (MDGs).[84] "Respect for nature" is one of the fundamental values considered to be essential in international relations in the twenty-first century, in accordance with the precepts of sustainable development. The chapter on environment explicitly recognises the link between children and environmental protection: "We must spare no effort to free all of humanity, *and above all our children and grandchildren*, from the threat of living on a planet irredeemably spoilt by human activities, and whose resources would no longer be sufficient for their needs."[85] Human rights gain in importance in the Millennium Declaration, with a separate chapter on "Human Rights, Democracy and Governance" (chapter V). As children are concerned, the heads of state and government recognise their duty to uphold the principles of human dignity, equality and equity "to all the world's people, especially the most vulnerable and, in particular, the children of the world, to whom the future belongs".[86] This phrase reflects a mixed image of children, as

---

[81] See, for example, M. Liebel, "Working Children as Social Subjects: The Contribution of Working Children's Organizations to Social Transformations" (2003) 10(3) *Childhood* 265.
[82] UNICEF, "Safe, Healthy and Well-Educated Children", 15.
[83] Stephens, "Children and the UN Conference", 44.
[84] UNGA, "United Nations Millennium Declaration" (UN Doc. A/RES/55/2, 18 September 2000).
[85] Ibid., [21].
[86] Ibid., [2].

both vulnerable and future citizens. Age is not mentioned as a possible ground of discrimination in efforts to uphold respect for the equal rights of all; only race, sex, language and religion are.[87] In the remainder of the Declaration, the image of the vulnerable child again prevails. In chapter V on human rights, women and migrants are identified as particular categories of rights holders, and the heads of state and government resolve to implement the Convention on the Elimination of all Forms of Discrimination against Women.[88] Children, in contrast, are not mentioned in this chapter as holding human rights. They are referred to in chapter VI, entitled "Protecting the Vulnerable". Such an approach essentialises children as being "inherently vulnerable". The commitment to encourage the ratification and full implementation of the UNCRC and its (then) two optional protocols is also included in the latter chapter, whereas it would have been more logical to incorporate this in chapter V on human rights. More than a decade after the adoption of the UNCRC, the Millennium Declaration did not recognise children as bearers of human rights but categorised them (only) as vulnerable beings to be protected.

In general, the UN World Summit on Sustainable Development (WSSD) in 2002 was less successful and influential than UNCED.[89] The Johannesburg Declaration on Sustainable Development refers to the "interdependent and mutually reinforcing pillars of sustainable development", namely economic development, social development and environmental protection.[90] Remarkably, the concept of human rights is not mentioned once. With respect to children, however, it is interesting that the Johannesburg Declaration explicitly refers to the participation of children in the summit:

> At the beginning of this Summit, the children of the world *spoke to us* in a simple yet clear voice that *the future belongs to them*, and accordingly challenged all of us to ensure that through our actions they will inherit a world free of the indignity and indecency occasioned by poverty, environmental degradation and patterns of unsustainable development.[91]

The image of children is again mixed, but of a different nature: children are presented as participants (exercising their right to participation under article 12 UNCRC) and as future citizens. The latter image is confirmed by paragraph 4, which emphasises that children "represent our collective future". The importance of the participation of children is again indirectly referred to in the context of "stable partnerships with all major groups"[92] and in the statement that implementation

---

[87] Ibid., [4].
[88] Ibid., [25].
[89] See Waas et al., "Sustainable Development", 1643.
[90] UN World Summit on Sustainable Development, "Johannesburg Declaration on Sustainable Development and Johannesburg Plan of Implementation" (UN Doc. A/CONF.1999/20, 4 September 2002), [5].
[91] Ibid., [3] (emphasis added).
[92] Ibid., [26].

should be an inclusive process, "involving all major groups".[93] In contrast to previous documents, the Johannesburg Declaration does not construct children as vulnerable, but as rights bearers (at least of the right to express their views) and as future citizens.

This shift from viewing children predominantly as vulnerable towards a more nuanced approach is also visible in the Johannesburg Plan of Implementation. According to its introduction, the implementation of the summit's outcomes "should benefit all, particularly women, youth, children *and* vulnerable groups".[94] By juxtaposing vulnerable groups with children and youth, the latter are not automatically presumed to be vulnerable. The change is also noticeable in relation to the environmental dimension of sustainable development, as in chapter VI on "Health and Sustainable Development", it is stated that

> There is an urgent need to address the causes of ill health, including environmental causes, and their impact on development, with particular emphasis on *women and children, as well as vulnerable groups of society*, such as people with disabilities, elderly persons and indigenous people.[95]

The first explicit recognition of the agency of children in a sustainable development policy agenda, occurs in relation to clean drinking water and adequate sanitation in the WSSD Plan of Implementation: education and outreach on these issues should focus on "children, as agents of behavioural change".[96] Although children are included in the major groups and thus in the provisions on the participation of these groups,[97] more emphasis is placed on the role and participation of youth, as in Agenda 21. For instance, all stakeholders are called upon to recognise the "specific role of youth, women and indigenous and local communities in conserving and using biodiversity in a sustainable way".[98] Also, "youth participation" in programmes and activities relating to sustainable development is to be promoted and supported,[99] and the capacity of youth to participate is to be developed.[100] One could imagine similar formulations regarding the participation of children, so as to give effect to the participation provisions of the UNCRC (articles 12–15).

Turning to the environmental dimension of sustainable development, the WSSD Plan of Implementation recognises the particular relationship between children and the environment, referring for instance to the special needs of children in relation to

---

[93] Ibid., [34].
[94] Emphasis added.
[95] Emphasis added, leaving aside here the essentialisation of those included in the category of vulnerable groups (ibid., [55]). However, the vulnerability of children remains emphasised in the context of sustainable development in Africa (ibid., [65]).
[96] Ibid., [8(d)].
[97] Ibid., [168]–[170].
[98] Ibid., [44(k)].
[99] Ibid., [170].
[100] Ibid., [127(e)].

environmental health threats[101] and the particular attention to be paid to children in the "reduction of respiratory diseases and other health impacts resulting from air pollution".[102] The WSSD also launched the Global Initiative on Children's Environmental Health indicators.[103] Finally, data should be disaggregated by sex, age and other factors.[104]

In 2003, the Governing Council of UNEP adopted a "[l]ong-term strategy on engagement and involvement of young people in environmental issues".[105] Under the label of "Tunza",[106] the six-year strategy aimed to increase the participation of young people in environmental issues. *Young people* is used as an umbrella term: young people under the age of 15 years are referred to as "children", whereas "youth" indicates young people between the ages of 15 and 25.[107] Children are represented by the Tunza Junior Board and youth constitute the Tunza Youth Advisory Council. The Tunza strategy comprises four key focus areas for activities: awareness building, participation in decision-making, capacity building and information exchange.[108] Whereas the focus areas of awareness building, capacity building and information exchange are directed towards "young people" (i.e., both children and youth), the facilitation of the involvement in decision-making processes is limited to "youth leaders".[109] In 2009, a second long-term strategy (2009–2014) was adopted, focusing on six thematic priorities: climate change, environmental governance, resource efficiency, ecosystem management, disasters and conflicts, and harmful substances and hazardous waste.[110]

One outcome of the Tunza programme was that the conferences for children and youth that were until then organised separately by UNEP (the International Children's Conference on the Environment and the UNEP Youth Global Forum) were merged into one annual Tunza Conference.[111] Such conferences are not without importance: in interview research, young environmental leaders have indicated the

---

[101] Ibid., [7(f)].
[102] Ibid., [56].
[103] See World Health Organization, *From Theory to Action: Implementing the WSSD Global Initiative on Children's Environmental Health Indicators* (Geneva: World Health Organization, 2004).
[104] WSSD, "Johannesburg Plan of Implementation", [129].
[105] Governing Council of the United Nations Environment Programme, "Policy Responses of the United Nations Environment Programme to Tackle Emerging Environmental Programmes. Report of the Executive Director. Addendum: Long-Term Strategy on Engagement and Involvement of Young People in Environmental Issues" (UNEP/GC.22/3/Add.1/Rev.1, 19 December 2002).
[106] "Tunza" means "to treat with care of affection" in Kiswhahili, an Eastern African language (ibid., n. 1).
[107] Ibid., n. 2. A discrepancy with the UNCRC definition of children is again noticeable.
[108] Ibid., [11].
[109] Ibid. However, in the detailed description of the programme activities on participation in decision-making, this distinction is not upheld consistently. See, for example, [22] ("children and youth representatives") and [23] ("young people").
[110] Governing Council of the United Nations Environment Programme, "Final Review of the Long-Term Strategy on the Engagement and Involvement of Young People in Environmental Issues" (UN Doc. UNEP/GC.25/10, 28 October 2008).
[111] Governing Council of the United Nations Environment Programme, "Policy Responses", [19].

influence of "groups, conferences and gatherings" on their engagement in environmental action.[112] In 2011, the Tunza International Children and Youth Conference took place in Bandung, Indonesia and aimed to provide input to the upcoming UN Conference on Sustainable Development (UNCSD) of 2012. In the Bangdung Declaration, children and youth "[urged] governments to respond and not to ignore the demands of the children and youth".[113] They make a range of commitments in the Declaration, such as to lobby governments and adopt more sustainable lifestyles. They also give their vision on what green economy and governance means for them, and call upon governments and business leaders to "come to Rio and deliver".[114]

The UNCSD, also known as Rio+20, aimed to secure a renewed political commitment for sustainable development, and to address the themes of a green economy, poverty eradication and the institutional framework for sustainable development. In its outcome document, "The Future We Want", human rights and its international law instruments are given more weight than in the WSSD texts.[115] The importance of "respect for all human rights, including the right to development and the right to an adequate standard of living, including the right to food" is emphasised,[116] as well as the responsibilities of all states to respect, protect and promote human rights, without discrimination.[117] It seems, however, a missed opportunity that "age" is not mentioned as a possible ground of discrimination, even though it could fall under "other status".[118] Also, it is to be deplored that data are only to be disaggregated as to sex, not as to age or other factors.[119]

---

[112] In this research, "young environmental leaders" were individuals between 16 and 19 years of age. A serious limitation of the study was the homogeneous sample: all interviewees were from Nova Scotia (Canada), white, not from low-income backgrounds, and mostly female. See H. E. Arnold, F. G. Cohen and A. Warner, "Youth and Environmental Action: Perspectives of Young Environmental Leaders on Their Formative Influences" (2009) 40 *The Journal of Environmental Education* 27.

[113] Tunza International Children and Youth Conference, "The Voice of Children and Youth for Rio+20 (Bangdung Declaration)" (2011), www.unep.org/pdf/Bandung_Declaration_Final.doc.

[114] Ibid.

[115] UNGA, "The Future We Want" (UN Doc. A/RES/66/288, Annex, 11 September 2012).

[116] Ibid., [8]. Compare with article 6 (right to life, survival and development) and article 27 UNCRC (right to an adequate standard of living).

[117] Ibid., [9]. See also the principle of non-discrimination enshrined in article 2 UNCRC.

[118] Paragraph 9 reads: "We reaffirm the importance of the Universal Declaration of Human Rights, as well as other international instruments relating to human rights and international law. We emphasize the responsibilities of all States, in conformity with the Charter of the United Nations, to respect, protect and promote human rights and fundamental freedoms for all, *without distinction of any kind to race, colour, sex, language or religion, political or other opinion, national or social origin, property, birth, disability or other status*". Emphasis added. This paragraph was also included in the 2030 Agenda for Sustainable Development (see UNGA, "Transforming Our World: The 2030 Agenda for Sustainable Development" [UN Doc. A/RES/70/1, 21 October 2015]). This list of discrimination grounds is almost the same as the one in article 2(1) UNCRC, with the exception that "ethnic origin" is included in the convention. "Age" is thus not mentioned in the UNCRC as a separate discrimination ground either.

[119] Ibid., [136] (on sustainable urban planning) and [239] (in general).

A more nuanced construction of childhood appears from "The Future We Want". The images of children as both vulnerable and future citizens seem to underlie the phrase on the need of the "protection, survival and development of all children to their full potential, including through education".[120] Children and youth are explicitly identified as beneficiaries of and participants to sustainable development: "We emphasize that sustainable development must be inclusive and people-centered, *benefiting and involving* all people, including youth and children".[121] In addition, a separate paragraph is dedicated to emphasising the importance of children's and youth's participation, and of their contribution to achieve sustainable development, even though an instrumentalist undertone remains:

> We stress the importance of the active participation of young people in decision making processes as the issues we are addressing have a deep impact on present and future generations, and as the contribution of children and youth is vital to the achievement of sustainable development. We also recognize the need to promote intergenerational dialogue and solidarity by recognizing their views.[122]

Furthermore, in the section on implementation, the importance of the full enjoyment of human rights, in particular for women and children, is emphasised.[123] Regarding the environmental dimension of sustainable development, "harmony with nature" is presented as a precondition to achieve sustainable development.[124] The document calls for "holistic and integrated approaches to sustainable development".[125] Within the chapter on the institutional framework of sustainable development, a separate section is devoted to the "[e]nvironmental pillar in the context of sustainable development", reaffirming the need to strengthen international environmental governance.[126] In the thematic sections, children are mentioned in relation to poverty eradication, food security and sustainable agriculture, sustainable cities, and health and population. It is remarkable, however, that children are not referred to in the more exclusively environmentally related sections (e.g., on oceans and seas, climate change, forests, biodiversity, desertification, mountains, chemicals and waste, sustainable consumption and production, mining).

In conclusion, analysing the key sustainable development policy agendas of the past five decades leads to some interesting observations on the three guiding questions identified in the preceding text. First, as regards the role given to children,

---

[120] Ibid., [11].
[121] Ibid., [31].
[122] Ibid., [50]. "Young people" seems to be used here as an umbrella term, covering both "children" and "youth", in line with the UNEP Strategy (see note 107). This paragraph forms part of the section "Engaging Major Groups and Other Stakeholders", in which the importance of specific groups/actors in advancing sustainable development is recognised.
[123] Ibid., [102].
[124] Ibid., [39].
[125] Ibid., [40].
[126] Ibid., [87].

an evolution is noticeable from no (Stockholm Declaration) or scarce (WCS) mentioning to an increased presence of children in the sustainable development agendas. The child images underlying these references are often mixed. Children are then represented as "future citizens" (e.g., WCS, Agenda 21), as "resources" (e.g., Agenda 21), or as proxies for future generations (e.g., Brundtland Report). In the majority of the agendas, however, the image of the vulnerable child is predominant. Only from the WSSD onwards, a more nuanced approach towards children seems to emerge, in which children are not automatically seen as vulnerable. Moreover, the absence of references to children as bearers of human rights is salient, with the Brundtland Report and "The Future We Want" being notable exceptions. As a consequence, the place given to children's *rights* in the sustainable development agendas is limited. Although the importance of the participation of children is increasingly mentioned, this has been justified referring to an instrumentalist rationale (e.g., Agenda 21, "The Future We Want") rather than on the basis of a rights-based approach in line with the UNCRC. Moreover, greater attention is paid to the agency and participation of youth, compared with those of children (e.g., Rio Declaration, Agenda 21, Johannesburg Plan of Implementation).

Regarding the weight given to human rights in general, no linear evolutions can be discerned. In most documents, human rights are only ephemerally referred to (e.g., Stockholm Declaration, WCS, "Our Common Future"), or even not at all (e.g., Rio Declaration and Johannesburg Declaration). The Millennium Declaration and "The Future We Want" adopt a clearer human rights approach. Finally, as the relationship between children and the environmental dimension of sustainable development is concerned, the environmental sections of the agendas either focus on children's vulnerability in relation to environmental risks (e.g., Agenda 21) or do not mention children (e.g., WCS, "The Future We Want"). The overall tendency in the sustainable development policy agendas to disregard the agency of children thus seems to play out even stronger in relation to the environmental dimension, given the inclination to focus on the vulnerable aspects of being a child in the context of environmental hazards.

CHILDREN AND THEIR RIGHTS IN THE 2030 AGENDA FOR SUSTAINABLE DEVELOPMENT: TRANSFORMING OUR WORLD?

At the UN Sustainable Development Summit, which was held from 25 to 27 September 2015 in New York, the UN General Assembly unanimously adopted the document entitled "Transforming Our World: The 2030 Agenda for Sustainable Development" (2030 Agenda).[127] This document contains 17 SDGs and 169 targets, to follow up on the MDGs. Priority is given to eradicating poverty as "the greatest

---

[127] UNGA, "Transforming Our World".

global challenge".[128] The agenda has come into effect on 1 January 2016 and is to be fully implemented by 2030. After a brief overall appraisal, the three questions that guided the analysis of the previous sustainable development agendas (child images; role of human and children's rights; role of children and their rights regarding the environmental dimension of sustainable development) will also be addressed with respect to the 2030 Agenda.

In general, various positive elements can be noted – without being exhaustive. First, the agenda is the result of a broad consultation process and engagement with civil society and other stakeholders, "which paid particular attention to the voices of the poorest and most vulnerable".[129] Also, the SDGs are directed to all states, whereas the MDGs only focused on developing countries. As the conceptualisation of sustainable development is concerned, the three dimensions of sustainable development – economic, social and environmental – are to be achieved "in a balanced and integrated manner".[130] Such an integrated approach implies "deep interconnections and many cross-cutting elements across the new Goals and targets".[131] Whereas the dimensions of sustainable development are often referred to as the three "Ps," "People, Planet, Profit",[132] the 2030 Agenda refers to "Prosperity" instead of "Profit". This seems to indicate a more holistic perspective on the economic dimension of sustainable development, which is to be applauded.[133] The 2030 Agenda is also very comprehensive, trying to tackle the major challenges of our times.

This comprehensivity is at the same time one of the major weaknesses of Agenda 2030 though: how will efforts be focused and progress be monitored? Furthermore, the emphasis on states' "full permanent sovereignty over all its wealth, natural resources and economic activity" may limit the transformative potential of the SDGs in case of "unwilling" governments, even though the Agenda is to be implemented in a manner consistent with international law.[134] From an ecological perspective, the explicit "people-centred" nature of the SDGs and targets[135] can be criticised. This people-oriented approach is also evident from the order in which the different dimensions of sustainable development are addressed: the social dimension is treated first, then the economic dimension and then the environmental dimension.[136] This seems to subordinate the environmental dimension to

---

[128] Ibid., [2].
[129] Ibid., [6].
[130] Ibid., [2].
[131] Ibid., [17].
[132] See Waas et al., "Sustainable Development", 1651.
[133] Two more Ps are added as "areas of critical importance for humanity and the planet", namely Peace and Partnership (UNGA, "Transforming Our World", preamble).
[134] Ibid., [18].
[135] Ibid., [2].
[136] This is the case in the section "The New Agenda" (ibid., [18]–[38]) as well as in the order of the 17 SDGs.

the interests of human beings, whereas recent conceptualisations of sustainable development suggest that the carrying capacity of the earth should serve as the limiting framework for any human action.[137] The repeated reference to "sustained economic growth"[138] as a goal does not seem to recognise the inherent environmental limits to growth either. However, a more holistic perspective seems to underlie the vision set out in paragraph 7, namely a world "where all life can thrive", as this phrase could be interpreted as including nonhuman life.

Turning to the three main questions guiding the analyses in this chapter, human rights play a prominent role in the 2030 Agenda. In the preamble, the realisation of the human rights of all is explicitly stated as the objective of the SDGs and targets. Gender equality and the empowerment of women and girls also stand central.[139] The pledges that "no one will be left behind" and that "we will endeavour to reach the furthest behind first"[140] are equally in line with a human rights-based approach.[141]

Compared to the zero draft, important provisions recognising the agency and rights of children and young people have been added in the 2030 Agenda. This may at least partly be a consequence of the lobbying of the Major Group of Children and Youth (MGCY), who claimed in a statement responding to the zero draft that "we [children and youth] must be seen as actors and contributors, and beyond just 'vulnerable populations'".[142] In the zero draft, there was only a "token" reference to young people in paragraph 44: "The future of humanity and of our planet ... lies also in the hands of today's younger generation, who will pass the torch to future generations." The MGCY argued that "[t]his [reference] is not good enough in recognising the significant contribution that 'today's younger generation' have already made to the agenda and will continue to make."[143] From a children's rights perspective, the final 2030 Agenda contains stronger language than the zero draft. Two provisions merit particular attention. In paragraph 25 on education, the following sentence was added:

> We will strive to provide children and youth with a nurturing environment for the *full realization of their rights and capabilities*, helping our countries to reap

---

[137] See introduction to this chapter.
[138] Ibid., for example, [3], [9], [13], [21], [27] and Goal 8.
[139] Ibid., for example, [20].
[140] Ibid., [4].
[141] Regarding environmental issues, see R. Bratspies, "Do We Need a Human Right to a Healthy Environment?" (2015) 13 *Santa Clara Journal of International Law* 31, 53: "The human rights approach demands special attention to those groups most vulnerable to environmental harms ... as well as to those already overburdened by environmental harms".
[142] UN Major Group for Children and Youth, "Major Group for Children and Youth (MGCY) Response to the Zero-Draft of the Post-2015 Declaration" (2015), http://childrenyouth.org/2015/07/02/major-group-for-children-and-youth-mgcy-response-to-the-zero-draft-of-the-post-2015-declaration/.
[143] Ibid.

the demographic dividend including through safe schools and cohesive communities and families.[144]

This paragraph recognises children and youth as holders of rights and capabilities, although an emphasis remains on the commitment of governments *to provide* children and youth with a nurturing environment. An agentic approach is more explicitly endorsed in the equally new paragraph 51:

> Children and young women and men are *critical agents of change* and will find in the new Goals a platform to channel their infinite capacities for activism into the creation of a better world.[145]

To a lesser extent, this phrase also reflects an image of children and youth as "resources" for the creation of a better world. Somewhat strangely, the UNCRC is only mentioned as one of the international standards and agreements that the business sector should respect.[146]

The opportunity was missed again to mention "age" as a possible ground for discrimination in the general prohibition of discrimination in implementing international human rights law, a provision copy/pasted from "The Future We Want".[147] Nevertheless, the 2030 Agenda explicitly includes age as a prohibited ground of discrimination regarding particular issues, namely access to lifelong learning opportunities and the promotion of social, economic and political inclusion.[148] Moreover, it is explicitly provided that data collection should be disaggregated by, among other factors, age.[149] Data disaggregation by age was also included in the Johannesburg Plan of Implementation,[150] but was lacking in "The Future We Want".[151] However, the MGCY had recommended to go further in the disaggregation of data, namely towards age groups within the group of children and youth: early childhood (0–5); childhood (5–10); adolescents (10–19) and young people (15–24). This recommendation was thus not taken up.[152]

As regards the reviews of progress by member states at national and subnational levels, the 2030 Agenda provides that these reviews should "draw on contributions from indigenous peoples, civil society, the private sector and other stakeholders".[153] It is a pity that children and youth are not explicitly mentioned here, although they may of course be included in the term "other stakeholders". In this sense, this provision does not live up to the recommendation of the MGCY to provide "legally

---

[144] Emphasis added.
[145] Emphasis added.
[146] UNGA, "Transforming Our World", [67].
[147] See note 118; UNGA, "Transforming Our World", [19].
[148] UNGA, "Transforming Our World", [25] and target 10.2.
[149] Ibid., target 17.18, and [74(g)] (in relation to follow-up and review processes).
[150] See note 104.
[151] See note 118.
[152] MGCY, "Response to the Zero-Draft".
[153] UNGA, "Transforming Our World", [79].

mandated, wellresourced and specifically designated measures for meaningful and effective youth participation in monitoring and review".[154]

Concerning the relationship between children and the environmental dimension of sustainable development, four of the most important environmentally related goals do not mention children.[155] Youth are mentioned once as an important group whose capacity is to be raised in relation to climate change–related planning and management in least developed countries.[156] This confirms the observation of the previous sustainable development agendas that regarding specific environmental issues, the role of children, especially as actors, is not duly acknowledged.

FINAL REFLECTIONS

This chapter has analysed the relationship between children's rights and the environmental dimension of sustainable development from two perspectives: international children's rights law and policy, on the one hand, and sustainable development policy, on the other. Particular attention was paid to the images of children underlying the approaches in these agendas. In recent policy agendas on sustainable development and children, the rights-bearing capacity and agency of children are increasingly recognised at a general level. When looking at the environmental issues addressed in these documents, however, two different scenarios prevail. In a first situation, particularly prominent in the sections on environmental sustainability of the sustainable development agendas, children are not explicitly mentioned or addressed. This does not correspond to the proven particular sensitivity of children to environmental hazards, as indicated in the introduction. If, in a second scenario, children are mentioned in the environmental sections of the sustainable development and children's rights policy documents, then the weight shifts to an image of children as vulnerable beings, which need to be protected. This is, of course, to a certain extent justified, given the more vulnerable situation in which children may find themselves when faced with environmental hazards, due to their physiology and evolving capacities. Another child image that is predominant in environmental sections, especially but not exclusively in the children's rights policy agendas, is that of children as future citizens, to be educated towards being environmentally responsible (socialisation paradigm). In relation to the environmental dimension of sustainable development in particular, it thus seems that the potential

---

[154] MGCY, "Response to the Zero-Draft".

[155] Goal 12. Ensure sustainable consumption and production patterns; Goal 13. Take urgent action to combat climate change and its impacts; Goal 14. Conserve and sustainably use the oceans, seas and marine resources for sustainable development; Goal 15. Protect, restore and promote sustainable use of terrestrial ecosystems, sustainably manage forests, combat desertification, and halt and reverse land degradation and halt biodiversity loss (UNGA, "Transforming Our World").

[156] Ibid., means of Implementation 13.b.

for recognising the rights and agency of children remains to a certain extent untapped. The Tunza programme of UNEP, which aims to enhance the participation of children and youth in environmental issues, is a step in this direction.

Finally, although this chapter focuses on the rights of children in relation to the environmental dimension of sustainable development, it must be emphasised that the human rights of children should not be considered in isolation. Shiva has pointed to the risks associated with artificially separating the environmental interests of children from those of women: "[T]he issue of justice between generations can only be realized through justice between sexes. Children cannot be put at the centre of concern if their mothers are meantime pushed beyond the margins of care and concern."[157] Also more in general, it can be argued that exclusively or mainly focusing on the rights of children without considering the rights of their parents and other adults may turn out to be unfavourable for them.[158] Thus even from a children's rights perspective, it makes sense to consider the rights of children and young people not exclusively separately but also in relation with the rights of other human beings.

---

[157] V. Shiva, "The Impoverishment of the Environment: Women and Children Last", in M. Mies and V. Shiva (eds.), *Ecofeminism* (London: Zed Books, 1993), 84.

[158] See Desmet and Aylwin, "Natural Resource Exploitation", 404 (illustrating this argument in relation to natural resource exploitation).

10

Children's Rights and Climate Change

Karin Arts

INTRODUCTION: CLIMATE CHANGE AND ITS IMPACT ON CHILDREN

Climate change is becoming ever more visible in seriously harmful consequences across the globe.[1] During the last decade, the collective and individual human rights aspects of climate change have gradually gained recognition, among international and national policy makers, law makers and civil society organisations,[2] and within both the UN system[3] and academia alike.[4] Over time, international law too has

---

[1] The work of the Intergovernmental Panel on Climate Change has clearly substantiated this in its numerous reports about the phenomenon of climate change and its effects (see www.ipcc.ch/). Likewise, the World Meteorological Organization is closely monitoring climate change (see, for example, "WMO Statement on the Status of the Global Climate 2015" [Geneva: World Meteorological Organization, 2016]).

[2] See, for example, Oxfam International, *Climate Wrongs and Human Rights: Putting People at the Heart of Climate-Change Policy* (Oxfam briefing Paper 117, September 2008); Human Rights and Climate Change Working Group, "Resources" (undated), http://climaterights.org/resources/; M. Robinson, "Climate Change Is a Human Rights Issue" (5 August 2013), www.themarknews.com/2013/08/05/on-the-brink/#content.

[3] See, for example, Office of the High Commissioner for Human Rights (OHCHR), "Understanding Human Rights and Climate Change: Submission of the Office of the High Commissioner for Human Rights to the 21st Conference of the Parties to the United Nations Framework Convention on Climate Change" (26 November 2015), www.ohchr.org/Documents/Issues/ClimateChange/COP21.pdf; UNEP (in cooperation with Columbia Law School, Sabin Center for Climate Change Law), "Climate Change and Human Rights" (2015), http://web.law.columbia.edu/sites/default/files/microsites/climate-change/climate_change_and_human_rights.pdf.

[4] See, for example, D. Olawuyi, *The Human Rights-Based Approach to Carbon Finance* (Cambridge: Cambridge University Press, 2016); M. Wewerike, "Climate Change (Human Rights Committee, Ad Hoc Conciliation Commission)", in M. Gibney and W. Vandenhole (eds.), *Litigating Transnational Human Rights Obligations: Alternative Judgements* (London: Routledge, 2014); D. Manou, "Climate Change and Human Rights", in A. Mihr and M. Gibney (eds.), *The Sage Handbook of Human Rights* (London: Sage, 2014); D. Bell, "Does Anthropogenic Climate Change Violate Human Rights?" (2011) 14 *Critical Review of International Social and Political Philosophy* 99.

developed such that the arguments in favour of approaching climate change in a human rights-based manner have become plausible, if not unavoidable. According to John Knox, first-ever UN Independent Expert on Human Rights and the Environment (2012–2015) and thereafter the first-ever Special Rapporteur to the UN Human Rights Council on the same topic:

> the belief that human rights is relevant to climate change quickly moved from the fringe to the mainstream. Since 2008, the UN Human Rights Council has unanimously adopted a series of resolutions concluding that climate change can have negative implications for the effective enjoyment of human rights, including the rights to life, health, food, water, housing and self-determination.[5]

The relationship between climate change and human rights can be seen in many different ways. In very general terms, one might distinguish work on establishing the human rights impacts of climate change and developing this into a basis for arguing that action to curb climate change is mandatory and underpinned by human rights norms, from the human rights aspects of mitigating and adapting to climate change. On the latter, Naomia Roht-Arriaza has noted that:

> in a number of places, the climate change regime's single-minded focus on carbon reduction has had negative consequences. These include violations of the rights of farmers or forest peoples, especially indigenous peoples, massive involuntary displacement, or evictions as certain lands become more valuable. The climate change regime may also create undesirable human rights impacts affecting food, water and energy security, increasing the maldistribution of land and resources, and further impoverishing the already poor. Furthermore, when affected people protest against these violations, civil and political rights violations may result.[6]

The use of biofuels as an alternative to fossil fuels is a further, specific example of a climate change measure that may give rise to serious human rights issues including the unavailability of (affordable) food[7] and forced displacement of local populations.[8]

Against this background, this chapter specifically explores some children's rights aspect of climate change. The primary reason for doing so lays in the fact that children are especially affected by climate change. Children – in line with the definition offered in article 1 of the UN Convention on the Right of the

---

[5] J. Knox, "Climate Ethics and Human Rights" (2014) 5 *Journal of Human Rights and the Environment* 22, 25–26.

[6] N. Roht-Arriaza, "Human Rights in the Climate Change Regime" (2010) 1 *Journal of Human Rights and the Environment* 211, 213.

[7] This may occur when crops previously used for human consumption start to be used for fuel production.

[8] For example, as a consequence of hydro-electric projects or conversion of forests to palm oil plantations. See Roht-Arriaza, "Human Rights in the Climate Change Regime", 220.

Child, that is persons between 0 and 18 years old – make up about 30 per cent of the world population.[9] Youth between the ages of 10 and 24 years old count for about a quarter of the world population.[10] Children and youth combined are even the majority of the population in a large number of countries, including the world's 48 least developed countries.[11] One should always operate in an evidence-based manner and thus cannot simply assume the negative consequences of climate change for children. However, there is ample evidence that children are more prone to the harmful health[12] and other negative effects of climate change than adults, and that they are especially vulnerable in climate change–related disasters such as floods. As Suzana Sanz-Caballero has pointed out, climate change also makes "healthcare infrastructures unavailable or scarce. This is a real problem leading, for the first time in centuries, to a decrease in the standard of health, with a shortage of immunization programs and a lack of medicines and surgical instruments".[13] According to Elizabeth Gibbons, "[C]limate change is already having a disproportionate effect on 21st century children".[14] This effect manifests among others in constrained access to clean drinking water, increase of diseases such as diarrhoea and malaria with increase in temperature, reductions in the quantity and nutritional quality of food, flood-related fatality rates of children, undernutrition and mental health effects such as post-disaster trauma, effects on

---

[9] Children make up 2.2 billion of the total world population of 7.3 billion, according to the 2016 data (www.census.gov/population/international/data/idb/worldpop.php).

[10] The exact definition of the category "youth" differs according to purpose and both within and across organisations. For information on this in the UN system, see for example, UN Department of Economic and Social Affairs (UNDESA), "Definition of Youth" (undated), www.un.org/esa/socdev/documents/youth/fact-sheets/youth-definition.pdf. The Office of the Secretary-General's Envoy on Youth, referred to the age range of 10–24 years to underpin its message that at present the world has the largest youth population ever, amounting to about 1.8 billion (www.un.org/youthenvoy/2015/04/10-things-didnt-know-worlds-population/).

[11] Ibid.

[12] See, for example, K. Ebi and J. Paulson, "Climate Change and Children" (2007) 54 *Pediatric Clinics of North America* 213. For more recent material see, for example, M. Miller, M. Marty and P. Landigran, "Children's Environmental Health: Beyond National Boundaries" (2016) 63 *Pediatric Clinics of North America* 149, and UNICEF, *The Challenges of Climate Change: Children on the Front Line* (Florence: UNICEF Office of Research, 2014). The latter is a very useful comprehensive overview of the child-related effects of climate change, presented in contributions by 40 experts who, according to UNICEF, "present the best knowledge from the climate change debate" (ibid., 1). The report conveys among others that "[e]ven leaving aside natural disasters, children are already suffering most from the adverse health consequences of a warmer world, accounting for up to four in five of all illnesses, injuries and deaths attributable to climate change" (ibid.).

[13] S. Sanz-Caballero, "Children's Rights in a Changing Climate: A Perspective from the United Nations Convention on the Rights of the Child" (2013) 13 *Ethics in Science and Environmental Politics* 1, 5.

[14] E. Gibbons, "Climate Change, Children's Rights, and the Pursuit of Intergenerational Climate Justice" (2014) 16 *Health and Human Rights Journal* 19, 20.

access to education, health care and on child protection, involuntary displacement and migration[15] and other "disaster-misfortune".[16]

It is important to note that, perhaps counter-intuitively, at times there may also be positive effects of climate change on particular children's rights. There are, for example, documented instances of positive effects of natural disasters on education, in the sense that "a natural disaster could 'change the opportunity cost of sending children to school, through [reduced] market wages' thus potentially generating larger incentives to send children to school".[17] However, such unexpected positive effects will most probably manifest at a much lower scale than is the case for the negative effects of climate change.

Finally, an additional aspect that makes children especially affected by climate change lies in the fact that they are exposed to the consequences of climate change both at present and in the future. All the preceding combined has led, among others, the UN Children's Fund (UNICEF) to the firm conclusion that "[t]he brunt of the impact of climate change is borne by children".[18] Thus, it is both justified and necessary to take a child-focused approach to climate change. As will be further elaborated in the next section of this chapter, given the existence of the UN Convention on the Rights of the Child, in fact a child rights-based approach to climate change is required. In the remainder of this chapter I will share some ideas about what this means and implies in terms of law, policy-making and implementation. In addition, I will present some relevant practical examples of concrete climate change–related interventions and assess, to the extent possible, their child rights focus and outcomes. This will generate pointers for further strengthening child rights-based responses to climate change in the future. These must include activities

---

[15] An estimated average number of 22.5 million people per year, or 62,000 people every day, have been affected by climate-related displacement. Many of these displaced people are children. See UNICEF, *Unless We Act Now: The Impact of Climate Change on Children* (New York: UNICEF, 2015), 30.

[16] Ibid., 21–23. See also, for example, Ebi and Paulson, "Climate Change and Children"; and K. Arts, "A Child Rights Perspective on Climate Change", in M. Salih (ed.), *Climate Change and Sustainable Development: New Challenges for Poverty Reduction* (Cheltenham, UK: Edward Elgar, 2009), 84–86. Y. Akachi, D. Goodman and D. Parker, in their "Global Climate Change and Child Health: A Review of Pathways, Impacts and Measures to Improve the Evidence Base" (Innocenti Discussion Paper No. 2009–03) (Florence: UNICEF, 2009), presented an overview of the literature on global climate change and child health published before April 2009. For more recent material see, for example, A. Bernstein and S. Myers, "Climate Change and Children's Health" (2011) 23 *Current Opinion in Pediatrics* 221; Z. Xu et al., "Climate Change and Children's Health – A Call for Research on What Works to Protect Children" (2012) 9 *International Journal of Environmental Research and Public Health* 3298; Sanz-Caballero, "Children's Rights in a Changing Climate"; M. Miller, M. Marty and P. Landigran, "Children's Environmental Health: Beyond National Boundaries" (2016) 63 *Pediatric Clinics of North America* 149; UNICEF, *The Challenges of Climate Change*; UNICEF, *Unless We Act Now*.

[17] F. Seballos et al., *Children and Disasters: Understanding Impact and Enabling Agency* (Brighton, UK: Children in A Changing Climate/Institute for Development Studies, 2011), 16.

[18] UNICEF, *The Challenges of Climate Change*, vii and 1.

that, at a minimum, involve children and optimally are child-led; besides being especially affected and often especially vulnerable, children are also important agents of change.

THE NORMATIVE FRAMEWORK: CHILDREN'S RIGHTS, CLIMATE CHANGE AND SUSTAINABLE DEVELOPMENT

All states in the world, except the United States of America, are bound by the UN Convention on the Rights of the Child (UNCRC). This Convention was adopted in 1989 and at present has 196 States Parties.[19] In relation to the problem of climate change, from a legal point of view it is interesting that virtually all these same states are also bound by the UN Framework Convention on Climate Change (UNFCCC), which was adopted in 1991 and at present has been ratified by 197 states.[20] These states also widely support the Paris Agreement (which addresses climate change, was adopted in December 2015 and is in the process of being ratified since) and the Sustainable Development Goals (SDGs). The latter address both climate change in particular and the needs and roles of children in relation to sustainable development more in general.

As will be further specified in the following text, this normative framework makes children's rights an important point of departure both for conceptualising obligations, responsibilities and responses to climate change, and for operationalising adaptation and mitigation measures. This already is the straightforward implication of article 4 of the UNCRC alone, the general implementation article of the Convention. Article 4 indeed prescribes that states "shall undertake all appropriate ... measures for the implementation of the rights recognized" in the UNCRC.[21] Now that it is clear that climate change is both a serious threat to implementation of the UNCRC as a whole, and that it brings concrete health and other risks to children, the implication is that climate change interventions are mandatory and need to be child rights-based. The general implementation principles of the UNCRC – child survival and development as the central substantive objectives, and non-discrimination, best interests of the child and participation as important guidance for both the content and modalities of implementation efforts – provide a useful and practical framework that should inform all relevant climate change–related action.

In line with other UN human rights treaties, none of which include a right to a healthy environment, the UNCRC only scarcely refers to environmental issues directly. It does not refer to climate change at all. In a 2010 journal article, Pamela

---

[19] Status on 11 September 2016, as in UN Treaty Collection, https://treaties.un.org/Pages/ParticipationStatus.aspx?clang=_en.
[20] Ibid.
[21] This was already argued in Arts, "A Child Rights Perspective on Climate Change", 89–90.

Stephens explored whether the then-existing human rights norms in the spheres of the right to life, the rights of indigenous peoples, the right to privacy and socio-economic rights norms encompassed "the impacts of climate change on humans".[22] While she found above-average hold in the UNCRC – given its relevance to future generations and to "the dangers and risks of environmental pollution" in a subsection of article 24 on the right to health[23] – on the whole she concluded that applicable international law on the matter was emerging at the time, but too generic to have concrete legal implications or to provide concrete remedies.

A systematic review of the text of the UNCRC (in terms of relevance in relation to climate change) results in the following picture. In fact, the large majority of UNCRC provisions in one way or another has a (potential) role to play and/or may be seriously affected by climate change, now or in the future.[24] As stated previously, in light of the imminent short-term and long-term negative impacts of climate change on the right to life, survival and development of children (art. 6), and on the child rights to health (art. 24),[25] education (arts. 28 and 29), rest, leisure and play (art. 31) and possibly on the right (art. 30) of minority or indigenous children to enjoy their own culture (e.g., in view of the role of land or traditional livelihoods) states need to take all appropriate measures (art. 4) to counter, if not prevent, such negative impacts. As stated in the preceding text as well, the following general implementation principles of the UNCRC should direct all types of such measures: non-discrimination (art. 2); best interests of the child as "a primary consideration" in "all action concerning children" (art. 3); and participation (in the sense of: the child rights to express her/his views and to be heard in article 12, the freedoms of expression and information according to articles 13 and 17, the freedom of thought according to article 14, the freedom of association and assembly as in article 15).[26]

In situations of disasters related to climate change and resulting situations of displacement or national or international migration, the right to birth registration, to a name and nationality and to know and be cared for by her or his parents (art. 7)

---

[22] P. Stephens, "Applying Human Rights Norms to Climate Change: The Elusive Remedy" (2010) 21 *Colorado Journal of International Environmental Law and Policy* 49, 51.

[23] Ibid., 61–62, analysing article 24(2c).

[24] However, for more restricted lists see UNICEF, *The Challenges of Climate Change*, 48–49, and Our Children's Trust et al., "State Obligations Regarding Children's Rights and Climate Change" (Submission to the UN Committee on the Rights of the Child, 2016 Day of General Discussion), http://static1.squarespace.com/static/571d109b04426270152febe0/t/57bf0ff5ebbd1af b36a4c4e3/1472139275560/OCT+et+al.+CRC+Submission.pdf, 12–13.

[25] In fact, apart from article 6 UNCRC, article 24 is the one provision that connects with the problem of climate change most directly. It refers, among others, to state obligations to diminish infant and child mortality, to ensure the provision of medical assistance and health care to all children, to combat disease and malnutrition, to provide adequate nutritious food and lean drinking water "taking into consideration the dangers and risks of environmental pollution".

[26] See also Our Children's Trust et al., "State Obligations Regarding Children's Rights and Climate Change", 9–10.

may be at particular risk. On the right to a nationality, Sanz-Caballero has already pointed out that in the future the world may even be confronted with the extreme scenario of states whose territories cease to exist because of climate change. This may occur to small-island or other vulnerable states and would cause a complicated situation in terms of the nationality of the citizens of such a state.[27] According to article 7(2) of the UNCRC, in relation to children, States Parties to the UNCRC should find adequate solutions for this situation, "in particular where the child would otherwise be stateless". In this light, article 8(1) of the UNCRC may be relevant as well, to the extent that it provides the right of a child to preserve his or her identity, including nationality, without unlawful interference. Likewise, articles 10 (on the right to enter or leave a state for the purpose of family reunification) and 22 (on refugee children) may be useful.

In disaster and post-disaster situations, the following UNCRC articles might have special significance: article 9 on the child right not to be separated from her or his parent against the child's will; articles 11 and 35 on the illicit transfer of children abroad, and the abduction of, sale of, or traffic in children; article 16 on arbitrary interference with a child's privacy, family or home; article 19 on protection against physical or mental violence, injury, (sexual) abuse, neglect, maltreatment or exploitation while in the care of parents or other caretakers; article 20 on alternative care in case the child cannot stay in her/his family environment; article 21 on adoption; article 23 on the right to special care of children with disabilities; article 25 on children placed in physical or mental health care; article 26 on social security; article 27 on the right of every child to an adequate standard of living; article 32 on economic exploitation and hazardous or harmful work; article 34 on protection from sexual exploitation and sexual abuse; and article 36 on protection against all other forms of exploitation.

Finally, it is important to note that the UNCRC strongly emphasises the need for international cooperation and formulates relatively clear obligations in this regard. At the end of the Preamble, international cooperation is broadly recognised as important "for improving the living conditions of children in every country, in particular in the developing countries". In the UNCRC's main text, international cooperation is specifically featured as a way to realise the Convention's provisions on economic, social and cultural rights (art. 4); the production, exchange and dissemination of information and material of social and cultural benefit to the child (art. 17); protecting and assisting refugee children (art. 22); preventive health care and treatment of children with disabilities (art. 23); health (art. 24); and education (art. 28).[28] In relation to the knowledge, data and other resources needed for combating

---

[27] Sanz-Caballero, "Children's Rights in a Changing Climate", 10.
[28] See, for example, K. Arts, "Twenty-Five Years of the United Nations Convention on the Rights of the Child: Achievements and Challenges" (2014) 61 *Netherlands International Law Review* 267, 281, 300–301.

climate change, international cooperation thus is an essential element of a child rights-based approach.

Since the adoption of the UNCRC in 1989, a few developments have taken place that might provide further context for interpreting and assessing the Convention in relation to environmental issues, and more in particular to climate change, or to get a more informed basis for considering what designated environmental children's rights provisions might look like. In "A World Fit for Children", a non-binding document adopted at the UN General Assembly's Special Session on Children in 2002, heads of states and government pledged to "give every assistance to protect children and minimize the impact of natural disasters and environmental degradation on them".[29] They acknowledged that a "number of environmental problems and trends, such as global warming, ozone layer depletion, [and] air pollution, ... need to be addressed to ensure the health and well-being of children".[30] In addition, they announced that they would take measures to manage their natural resources and protect and conserve their environment in a sustainable manner and help "to educate all children and adults to respect the natural environment for their health and well-being".[31] Finally, they urged

> the private sector to assess the impact of its policies and practices on children and to make the benefits of research and development in science, medical technology, health, food fortification, environmental protection, education and mass communication available to all children, particularly to those in greatest need.[32]

Since 2001, the UNCRC Committee has regularly adopted "General Comments" (GCs). These documents elaborate on specific provisions of the Convention, or address cross-cutting issues,[33] and are generally seen as authoritative views on the substance of the UNCRC and useful sources for interpreting the Convention. While at least 6 of the 19 GCs that have been issued so far address environmental matters in general terms, climate change has been taken up explicitly in one GC only. This occurred in GC No. 15 on the child right to health, adopted in 2013, in which the UNCRC Committee referred to the "growing understanding of the impact of climate change ... on children's health".[34] The Committee presented its specific take on the interpretation of UNCRC article 24 in light of environmental issues, and climate change in particular. According to the Committee, given "the relevance of the environment, beyond environmental pollution, to children's

---

[29] (UN Doc. A/RES/S-27/2, 11 October 2002), [7.10].
[30] Ibid., [27].
[31] Ibid., [28].
[32] Ibid., [57].
[33] Arts, "Twenty-Five Years of the United Nations Convention on the Rights of the Child", 190–191.
[34] UNCRC Committee, "General Comment No. 15 (2013) on the Right of the Child to the Enjoyment of the Highest Attainable Standard of Health (art. 24)" (UN Doc. CRC/C/GC/15, 17 April 2013), 2.

health"; environmental "interventions should, inter alia, address climate change, as this is one of the biggest threats to children's health and exacerbates health disparities. States should, therefore, put children's health concerns at the centre of their climate change adaptation and mitigation strategies".[35]

Six other GCs of the UNCRC Committee contain statements that, although they are formulated in general terms, carry relevance for issues of climate change. The risks of pollution and disasters are underlined respectively in GCs No. 9 and 13. The former, on children with disabilities, explains that "[h]azardous environment toxins also contribute to the causes of many disabilities" and refers to the state's role in preventing environmental pollution.[36] GC No. 13 on violence against children clarifies that "children which are likely to be exposed to violence include ... children ... living in accident- or disaster-prone areas or in toxic environments".[37]

Even though the UNCRC does not contain a directly formulated right to a healthy environment, according to the UNCRC Committee such a right is part and parcel of pursuing the realisation of the Convention. In GC No. 7, on early childhood, the Committee issued the following reminder:

> [T]he right to survival and development can only be implemented in a holistic manner, through the enforcement of all the other provisions of the Convention, including rights to health, adequate nutrition, ... *a healthy and safe environment*, education and play.[38]

This was indirectly reinforced in GCs No. 11, 14 and 16. GC No. 11 points out that "[s]tates parties should closely consider the cultural significance of traditional land *and the quality of the natural environment* while ensuring the children's right to life, survival and development to the maximum extent possible."[39] GC No. 14, on the best interests of the child, clarifies that the term "public and private welfare institutions", which is used in UNCRC article 3, refers among others to institutions that are "related to economic, social and cultural rights (e.g., care, health, *environment*)".[40] GC No. 16, on the right to leisure, play, recreational activities, cultural life and the arts specifies that an "environment sufficiently free from waste, pollution, traffic and other physical hazards" is crucial for allowing children

---

[35] Ibid., 7.
[36] UNCRC Committee, "General Comment No. 9 (2006) on the Rights of Children With Disabilities" (UN Doc. CRC/C/GC/9, 27 February 2007), [54].
[37] UNCRC Committee, "General Comment No. 13 (2011) on the Right of the Child to Freedom from All Forms of Violence" (UN Doc. CRC/C/GC/13, 18 April 2011), [72(g)].
[38] UNCRC Committee, "General Comment No. 7 (2006) on Implementing Child Rights in Early Childhood" (UN Doc. CRC/C/GC/7/Rev.1, 20 September 2006), [10] (emphasis added).
[39] UNCRC Committee, "General Comment No. 11 (2009) on Indigenous Children and Their Rights under the Convention" (UN Doc. CRC/C/GC/11, 12 February 2009), [35] (emphasis added).
[40] UNCRC Committee, "General Comment No. 14 (2013) on the Right of the Child to Have His or Her Best Interests Taken as a Primary Consideration (art. 3, para. 1)" (UN Doc. CRC/C/GC/14, 29 May 2013), [26] (emphasis added).

"to circulate freely and safely within their local neighbourhood" and for allowing them opportunities "to experience, interact with and play in natural environments and the animal world".[41]

Finally, it is relevant to note that GC No. 1, on the right to education, underlined among others the importance of UNCRC article 29(1e) on the role of education in developing respect for the natural environment. According to the UNCRC Committee this entails for example that

> education must link issues of environment and sustainable development with socio-economic, sociocultural and demographic issues. Similarly, respect for the natural environment should be learnt by children at home, in school and within the community, encompass both national and international problems, and actively involve children in local, regional or global environmental projects.[42]

In addition, "[T]he curriculum must be of direct relevance to the child's ... environmental ... context and to his or her present and future needs and take full account of the child's evolving capacities". Obviously, this is a strong plea for climate change education.

Besides global children's rights instruments, clearly environmental instruments too are part of the relevant normative framework for children's rights and climate change. However, while the UNFCCC raises the human impact of climate change here and there, it does not mention children in particular. While children evidently are part and parcel of the terms "humankind" and "present and future generations", which are used in the UNFCCC,[43] the text of this Convention does not pay any explicit attention to children or youth. Human rights or child rights dimensions of climate change are not raised either.[44] In this respect, the latest international climate change instrument, the Paris Agreement adopted in December 2015,[45] is a welcome addition to the normative framework among others because it provides the following:

---

[41] UNCRC Committee, "General Comment No. 17 (2013) on the Right of the Child to Rest, Leisure, Play, Recreational Activities, Cultural Life and the Arts (art. 31)" (UN Doc. CRC/C/GC/17, 17 April 2013), 6.

[42] UNCRC Committee, "General Comment No. 1 (2001) on Article 29(1): The Aims of Education" (UN doc. CRC/GC/2001/1, 17 April 2001), [9].

[43] UNFCCC, article 3(1): "The Parties should protect the climate system for the benefit of present and future generations of humankind".

[44] Rights of states *are* referred to in the UNFCCC. See, for example, preambular paragraph 8 on "the sovereign right [of states] to exploit their own resources pursuant to their own environmental and developmental policies"; and art. 3(4) stipulating that States Parties to the UNFCC "have a right to, and should, promote sustainable development". The only indirect exception to this picture is UNFCCC article 6(a)(ii) and (iii) that refer to the state obligation to promote and facilitate "public participation in addressing climate change and its effects and developing adequate responses" and "public access to information on climate change and its effects". On this matter see also Sanz-Caballero, "Children's Rights in a Changing Climate", 8.

[45] Status on 12 May 2017, as in UN Treaty Collection, see n. 19: 195 signatories and 145 States Parties including China and the United States. The latter might withdraw in the near future due to the new policy directions of the Trump administration.

> [W]hen taking action to address climate change, [States Parties should] respect, promote and consider their respective obligations on *human rights, the right to health*, the rights of indigenous peoples, local communities, migrants, *children*, persons with disabilities and people in vulnerable situations and the right to development, as well as gender equality, empowerment of women and *intergenerational equity*.[46]

However, this explicit commitment is not returned to, and therefore also not further concretised, in the subsequent text of the Paris Agreement. Thus, the latter gives a rather weak follow-up to the growing recognition of the significance of the human rights dimensions of climate change and of the specific relevance of climate change action for children.[47]

The final element of the normative framework that requires attention here is the 2030 Agenda for Sustainable Development, including the SDGs.[48] The text of the SDG document contains no less than 26 references to climate change and 66 relevant references to terms such as child, children, youth, young, girl, boy and age. The term "right" appears in total six times in Agenda 2030, but the terms "child right" or "children's right" do not appear at all.[49] The Convention on the Rights of the Child is mentioned once, in a paragraph addressing the conditions for "a dynamic and well-functioning business sector".[50] While rights discourse as such is hardly present in the SDGs and the associated targets, many important substantive elements of the UNCRC's child rights agenda are nevertheless present. It is especially important that Agenda 2030 sees children and young women and men as

---

[46] Preambular paragraph 11 (emphasis added).

[47] See, for example, the work of the UN Human Rights Council through www.ohchr.org/EN/Issues/HRAndClimateChange/Pages/HRClimateChangeIndex.aspx; the report of the 2010 Cancun Conference of the Parties to the UNFCC (UN Doc. FCCC/CP/2010/7/Add.1, 15 March 2011), especially the last preambular paragraph, paragraphs 8 and 77, Appendix I (2)(c) and footnote 1; and see, for example, Knox, "Climate Ethics and Human Rights" and UNEP, "Climate Change and Human Rights".

[48] UNGA, "Transforming Our World: The 2030 Agenda for Sustainable Development" (UN Doc. A/RES/70/1, 21 October 2015). While this document is a General Assembly Resolution and thus a set of recommendations rather than strictly binding "hard" law, there is enormous political momentum and support behind the SDGs. Their predecessors, the Millennium Development Goals, have already shown that as such this kind of "soft" law commitments can have substantial impact on priorities and implementation practice. Thus, it is relevant to include the SDGs here, alongside human rights and climate change treaties.

[49] See ibid., [7] (on the human right to safe drinking water), [10] and [35] (on the right to development), [29] (on the right of migrants to return to their country of citizenship), [35] (on the right to self-determination of peoples living under colonial and foreign occupation); and a related notion in target 3b (on the right of developing countries to use to the full the provisions in the Agreement on Trade-Related Aspects of Intellectual Property Rights regarding flexibilities to protect public health, and, in particular, provide access to medicines for all).

[50] Ibid. [67].

"critical agents of change" who "will find in the new Goals a platform to channel their infinite capacities for activism into the creation of a better world".[51]

The climate change SDG, Goal 13, specifically underlines the urgency of climate change action. In Target 13(b) the General Assembly draws attention to the need to promote "capacity for effective climate change-related planning and management in least developed countries and small island developing States, including focusing on ... youth". In addition, Agenda 2030 calls for "the widest possible international cooperation" in relation to climate change.[52] Other, more specific targets are included in Agenda 2030 in relation to building resilience and reducing the exposure and vulnerability of poor and vulnerable people "to climate-related extreme events and other economic, social and environmental shocks and disasters"; ensuring "sustainable food production systems and ... agricultural practices that ... strengthen capacity for adaptation to climate change, extreme weather, drought, flooding and other disasters"; and "substantially increas[ing] the number of cities and human settlements adopting and implementing integrated policies and plans towards ... mitigation and adaptation to climate change, [and] resilience to disasters".[53]

All in all, and especially in combination, the legal instruments analysed in the preceding text provide a strong basis for arguing that climate change action is mandatory and should where appropriate be child rights-based. Obviously this has implications for the state and civil society actors that are bound by and/or support the UNCRC, the UNFCC, the Paris Agreement and/or the SDGs. Some of these implications will be discussed in the next section of this chapter.

CHILDREN'S RIGHTS AND CLIMATE CHANGE: A PERSPECTIVE ON PRACTICE

Within the constraints of a short book chapter, this section can only provide a small glimpse of the current practice in developing and implementing child rights-based approaches to climate change. Keeping in mind that such child rights-based approaches are inherently deeply specific and sensitive to the context in

---

[51] Ibid., [51]. Besides in the UNCRC, article 6 of the UNFCC and Agenda 2030, the need for child and youth participation is also recognised in the Sendai Framework for Disaster Reduction according to which governments should engage with children and other stakeholders because "[c]hildren and youth are agents of change and should be given the space and modalities to contribute to disaster risk reduction, in accordance with legislation, national practice and educational curricula". See, Third UN World Conference on Disaster Risk Reduction, "Sendai Framework for Disaster Risk Reduction 2015–2030" (Sendai City, Japan: United Nations, 2015), [36(a)(ii)] and [7].

[52] Ibid., [31].

[53] Respectively in targets 1.5 and 2.4, which both are to be realised by 2030, and target 11(b) which is to be realised by 2020.

which they are developed and applied, there are also common features and challenges that are worthwhile reflecting upon.

First of all, our knowledge base on the specific impact of climate change on children is still relatively thin. Child rights-based approaches typically should start from, and should be backed up throughout, by data and a clear evidence base. This applies in the first place to information about the specific problem, in a specific locality and for children at large as well as for specific groups of children (girls, or boys, children with disabilities, poor children, urban or rural children and so on), so that a proper situation analysis can be made.[54] In general terms, the availability of disaggregated data is one of the weakest elements in the performance record of many States Parties to the UNCRC, as the annually published KidsRights Index has clearly revealed.[55] Obviously, this is not different at all for the subject of climate change, which is a relative newcomer for these purposes. While UNICEF has played an important role in bringing together existing research findings on climate change and children,[56] there still is an immense need for more specific data, including more country level and local level, on what climate change does to children's lives, how children cope or fail to cope, and how their problems – both short term and long term – could be addressed. Participation of children and considering children's voices and inputs is crucial in these processes. There certainly are examples of quality efforts to involve children actively in problematising and addressing climate change,[57] but obviously these have to become more widespread and systematically applied.

---

[54] Save the Children UK, *Getting It Right for Children: A Practitioners' Guide to Child Rights Programming* (London: International Save the Children Alliance, 2007), especially 21–39 on child rights situation analysis.

[55] See www.kidsrightsindex.org/. For this particular aspect, concerning data, the KidsRights Index is based on the assessment of an individual's country's performance on data gathering, handling, analysis and dissemination by the UNCRC Committee, as published in its country-specific COs.

[56] See for example, notes 12, 15 and 16, and UNICEF, *Climate Change and Children* (New York: UNICEF, 2007); UNICEF, *Climate Change and Children: A Human Security Challenge – Policy Review Paper* (Florence: UNICEF Innocenti Research Centre, 2008); and UNICEF UK, *Our Climate, Our Children, Our Responsibility: The Implications of Climate Change for the World's Children* (London: UNICEF UK, 2008).

[57] See for example, Holistic Development India, *Indian Rural Children Speak on the Impact of Climate Change* (Pune, India: Holistic Child Development India, 2009); D. Gautam and K. Oswald, *Child Voices: Children of Nepal Speak Out on Climate Change Adaptation* (2008), www.childreninachangingclimate.org/uploads/6/3/1/1/63116409/child_voices_np.pdf; UNFPA, *At the Frontier: Young People and Climate Change* (New York: UNFPA, 2009); Children in a Changing Climate, *A Right to Participate: Securing Children's Role in Climate Change Adaptation* (Brighton, UK: Institute of Development Studies/Children in a Changing Climate, 2011); United Nations Joint Framework Initiative on Children, Youth and Climate Change, *Youth In Action on Climate Change: Inspirations from Around the World* (Bonn, Germany: United Nations Joint Framework Initiative on Children, Youth and Climate Change/United Nations Framework Convention on Climate Change Secretariat, 2013).

At the level of multilateral human rights and environmental diplomacy, on the whole, children are still involved marginally at best. The UNCRC Committee has a major role in monitoring state performance in realising the Convention, most directly through the regular state reporting procedure. In this procedure governments report about their activities and the children's rights situation in their countries, civil society actors engage with the process by providing additional or alternative information, and the UNCRC Committee comes up with an overall assessment in the form of Concluding Observations (COs). However, as the UNCRC hardly contains environmental provisions, so far environmental concerns have come up relatively infrequently. Reflecting on its practice in this respect in general terms, the UNCRC Committee noted in 2016, in relation to children's rights and the environment that:

> Although children bear the brunt of growing environmental problems, the impact on their lives is rarely addressed as a rights issue. The relationship between children's rights and the environment is still less well-known than it should be. Those concerned with children's rights and those concerned with environmental protection often focus on one to the exclusion of the other. States scarcely address environmental issues in their periodic reports to the CRC, which regularly urges them to collect and submit more information on the matter.[58]

In light of the material presented earlier in this chapter, on both the factual impact of climate change on children and the normative framework in place, it is indeed striking that so far climate change has come up so infrequently in recent UNCRC COs. Of the 24 sets of COs that were adopted in 2015, only 4 explicitly mention climate change. These concern Chile, Jamaica, Mauritius and Turkmenistan. The 2015 COs on Chile, under the general heading "children's rights and the environment", have recommended that the government of Chile increase "children's awareness and preparedness for climate change and natural disasters by incorporating the topic into the school curriculum and teachers' training programmes".[59] In a specifically designated section on the "Impact of Climate Change on the Rights of the Child", the 2015 COs on Jamaica noted "as positive the fact that the State party has established guidelines for child-friendly disaster management and response". However, the UNCRC Committee also expressed concern about "the adverse impact of climate change and natural disasters on the rights of the child, including the rights to education, health, adequate housing, safe and drinkable water and sanitation" and about the potential of natural disasters "to undermine the social safety net of the State party, with negative consequences for children and families exposed to poverty". The UNCRC Committee then recommended that Jamaica

---

[58] UNCRC Committee, "Concept Note Day of General Discussion: Children's Rights and the Environment", www.ohchr.org/Documents/HRBodies/CRC/Discussions/2016/OutlineDGD2016.docx, [12].
[59] (UN Doc. CRC/C/CHL/CO/4-5, 30 October 2015), [64(b)].

develop strategies to reduce the vulnerabilities of and risks for children and families which may be occasioned or exacerbated by climate change, including by mainstreaming child-specific and child-sensitive risk and vulnerability reduction strategies into its national plan on climate change and disaster preparedness and emergency management, and by strengthening its social safety nets and social protection framework so as to mitigate the multiple social, economic and environmental impacts of climate change more effectively.[60]

Also, in the section "Impact of Climate Change on the Rights of the Child", the 2015 COs on Mauritius expressed

concern that policies and programmes addressing climate change and disaster risk management, such as in the case of cyclones, do not address the special vulnerabilities and needs of children, and that data available to formulate policies do not identify the types of risk faced by children.[61]

This was followed up with concrete recommendations for action on these matters. While the 2015 COs on Turkmenistan also contain a section devoted to the impact of climate change on the rights of the child, in fact the text of this section seems to deal with broader issues of child morbidity and environmental pollution. Beyond the title of the section, otherwise climate change is not referred to at all.[62]

Of the 27 sets of COs that were adopted in 2016, only 7 explicitly addressed climate change aspects. The 2016 COs on New Zealand, Samoa, Haiti and Suriname all contain a separate section on the "Impact of Climate Change on the Rights of the Child". In relation to New Zealand, the Committee expressed its concern "about the harmful impact of climate change on children's health, especially for Maori and Pasifika children and children living in low-income settings". While referring to SDG target 13.5, which addresses "mechanisms for raising capacity for effective climate change-related planning and management", the Committee recommended that New Zealand:

(a) Ensure that the special vulnerabilities and needs of children, and their views, are taken into account in developing policies or programmes addressing the issues of climate change and disaster risk management, with special attention to groups of children most likely to be affected by climate change, including Maori and Pasifika children and children living in low-income settings;
(b) Routinely undertake health impact assessments, with particular attention to children, to inform legislation and policies related to climate change.[63]

In relation to Samoa, the UNCRC Committee observed that "more could be done to take into account the special needs of children, including children with disabilities,

---

[60] (UN Doc. CRC/C/ /JAM/CO/3–4, 10 March 2015), [50] and [51].
[61] (UN Doc. CRC/C/MUS/CO/3–5, 27 February 2015), [57].
[62] (UN Doc. CRC/C/TKM/CO/2–4, 10 March 2015), [50]–[51].
[63] (UN Doc. CRC/C/NZL/CO/5, 21 October 2016), [34].

when planning disaster risk reduction preparedness, response and recovery programmes". It also specified an elaborate set of concrete suggestions on taking into account children's views, increasing children's awareness of and preparedness for climate change and natural disasters, and disaggregated data collection, among others.[64] In relation to Haiti, the UNCRC Committee expressed concern "about the significant increase in frequency and intensity of hurricanes and tropical storms, leading to flooding and erosion, as a result of climate change".[65] The specific recommendations refer to the need to take into account special vulnerabilities and the views of children, discontinue deforestation, increase children's awareness and preparedness for climate change and natural disasters, and collect disaggregated data on types of risk faced by children.[66] Concerning Suriname, the Committee did not provide any assessment of the current situation but straight away presented recommendations for climate change action in the form of developing "strategies, including awareness-raising, to reduce the vulnerabilities and risks for children owing to climate change, in particular children in situations of poverty, including Amerindian and Maroon communities" and mainstreaming "child-specific and child-sensitive risk and vulnerability reduction strategies into its national plan on climate change and disaster preparedness and emergency management" and strengthening "its social safety nets and social protection framework so as to more effectively mitigate the multiple social, economic and environmental impacts of climate change".[67]

Three other COs adopted by the UNCRC Committee in 2016 refer to climate change aspects in other, nonspecifically designated, sections. The COs on Kenya contain two references to climate change in the section "Standard of Living", amidst a great deal of different topics. The first one is a reference to the fact that the "negative impact of climate change, combined with population growth and unsustainable development projects, is adding further pressure on children's access to water and sanitation and on their food and nutrition security in arid and semi-arid lands".[68] The second reference relates to policies and programmes to address climate change and disaster risk management that, according to the Committee, should "integrate measures to protect children's rights to housing, sanitation, food, water and health and ensure the full and meaningful participation of communities at risk, including children, at both the national and the county levels".[69] About South Africa, the Committee observed that child food insecurity is among other things caused by climate change.[70] The 2016 COs on the United Kingdom,

---

[64] (UN Doc. CRC/C/WSM/CO/2-4*, reissued for technical reasons on 13 July 2016), [48] and [49].
[65] (UN Doc. CRC/C/HTI/CO/2-3, 24 February 2016), [54].
[66] Ibid., [55].
[67] (UN Doc. CRC/C/SUR/CO/3-4, 9 November 2016), [32].
[68] (UN Doc. CRC/C/KEN/CO/3-5, 21 March 2016), [55(e)].
[69] Ibid., [56(f)].
[70] (UN Doc. CRC/C/ZAF/CO/2, 27 October 2016), [53(b)].

in a section entitled "Environmental Health", called on the UK government to place "children's rights at the centre of national and international climate change adaptation and mitigation strategies, including through its new domestic climate strategy, and in the framework of its international climate change programmes and financial support".[71]

However, the COs on Benin, Brunei, Bulgaria, France, Gabon, Iran, Ireland, Latvia, the Maldives, Nauru, Oman, Pakistan, Peru, Saudi Arabia, Senegal, Sierra Leone, Slovakia, Nepal, Zambia and Zimbabwe contain no references to climate change. It might be useful for the UNCRC Committee to consider, in the future, standardising its approach to raising environmental matters somewhat more systematically in the state reporting process, with climate change prominently included.

The latter might anyway be part of the likely outcome of the "Day of General Discussion" (DGD) on the theme "Children's Rights and the Environment" that the UNCRC Committee held at the end of September 2016. The impact of climate change, at present and in the future, featured prominently in the Concept Note for this DGD.[72] About half of the 48 organisations that submitted written submissions in the run-up to the DGD addressed climate change, next to other issues, or exclusively.[73]

According to UNICEF, at present "climate-impact assessments and policies are generally developed without paying any attention to child-rights issues – and the unique risks to children and the specific responses that they require remain overlooked."[74] Certainly in global climate change deliberations, attention for the specific impact on children, attention for the role of children in tackling climate change, and children's formal participation have been rather limited. If children participated at all, it was so far largely in side events, and in small numbers[75] rather than as participants in the mainstream decision-making process. The risk of tokenism thus is substantial.[76] The 2014 UNICEF report "The Challenges of Climate Change: Children on the Front Line" provides various examples of incomplete, faulty or lacking child participation in the meetings of the Conference of the Parties (COP) of the UNFCCC:

---

[71] (UN Doc. CRC/C/GBR/CO/5, 12 July 2016), [69(b)].

[72] See note 58. For specific remarks on climate change, see [6] and [11].

[73] See www.ohchr.org/EN/HRBodies/CRC/Pages/WSDiscussion2016.aspx for the complete list.

[74] UNICEF, *The Challenges of Climate Change*, 3.

[75] This is the case despite the existence of initiatives such as the UN Joint Framework Initiative on Children, Youth and Climate Change, https://infccc.int/cc_inet/cc_inet/youth_portal/items/61519.php and YOUNGO (UNFCCC observer constituency of youth nongovernmental organisations), https://unfccc.int/cc_inet/cc_inet/youth_portal/items/6795.php. See Plan UK, *Global Warning: Children's Right to Be Heard in Global Climate Change Negotiations* (London: Plan UK, 2009) 10; E. Back, C. Cameron and T. Tanner, *Children and Disaster Risk Reduction: Taking Stock and Moving Forward* (Brighton, UK: Institute of Development Studies, November 2009) 7; and Gibbons, "Climate Change, Children's Rights", respectively, at 23 and 24–25. Gibbons usefully observed that in this respect children are no exception to "other marginalized groups disproportionally affected by climate change. Indigenous people, minority groups, people with disabilities, and the poor have not been granted a voice either" (ibid., 25).

[76] Back et al., *Children and Disaster Risk Reduction*, 21–22.

At COP 17 in Durban, South African and Indonesian child and youth delegates gave cultural performances, interacted with delegates and exhibitors, and were interviewed by Climate Change TV. A special session was also arranged at the Indonesian Pavilion for the children to speak. Unfortunately, however, at COP 18 in Doha last year children were not accredited to attend the talks apart from in exceptional cases or on the dedicated Young and Future Generations Day. Ironically, one side-event that the children could not attend owing to the age restriction was "A Child-centred Approach to Climate-change Adaptation: Opportunities and Challenges". This was organized by the Children in a Changing Climate Coalition comprising Plan International, Save the Children, World Vision and UNICEF.[77]

Like anywhere else, in global environmental diplomacy too, child participation requires a clear support and facilitation structure and straightforward objectives to be(come) meaningful for all concerned, and the process of child participation is as equally important as its outcome. The UNCRC GC on participation presents useful guidelines in this respect, including five steps required for meaningful participation. These steps are preparation (information about the choices at stake and the form of proceedings involved); hearing the child(ren); assessment of the capacity of the child; feedback about the outcome or the impact of the child's view on the decision; and, at the end of the process, a formal possibility of complaints, remedies and redress. According to the UNCRC Committee, meaningful participation requires the process to be transparent and informative, voluntary, respectful, relevant, child-friendly, inclusive, supported by training, safe and sensitive to risk, and accountable.[78]

At the national and local level, many more positive examples can be found of approaching climate change issues in a child-focused and, at times, even in a child-led manner.[79] UNICEF UK has self-reported some interesting examples of such climate change interventions, for example in Vietnam and Zambia. The work in Vietnam focused on increasing the recognition of children's needs, experiences and perspectives in relation to climate change among decision-makers and on enhancing children's participation in "critical national level policy and legal reforms".[80]

---

[77] UNICEF, *The Challenges of Climate Change*, 69. At COP 10 (2010), in Copenhagen, a Children's Climate Forum was organised in the week running up to the COP. A total of 164 participants between 14 and 17 years of age from 44 countries met and compiled a declaration that was presented to the president of the COP (www.unicef.org/infobycountry/denmark_52005.html).

[78] Plan UK, *Global Warning*, 7; Back et al., *Children and Disaster Risk Reduction*, 21–22.

[79] According to UNICEF, *The Challenges of Climate Change*: "Child-focused or child-centred approaches to adaptation fall into two categories: Programmes that focus specifically on children's needs, referred to here as child-targeted policy and programming; and programmes that involve children in the design and delivery, referred to as 'child-led' adaptation" (33).

[80] UNICEF UK, "Children and the Changing Climate: Taking Action to Save Lives" (2015), https://353ld71oiigr2n4p07k4kgvv-wpengine.netdna-ssl.com/wp-content/uploads/2014/10/Unicef_2015childrenandclimatechange_fin.pdf, 31. It is indeed interesting that article 4(2) of Vietnam's 2014 Law on Environmental Protection specifies that "[e]nvironmental protection must harmonize with the economic growth, social security, *assurance about the children's right, promotion of gender equality*, development and conservation of biodiversity,

According to UNICEF UK, this work was successful and resulted in "the incorporation of a child rights approach in ... Vietnam's new national Law on Environmental Protection, approved in 2014".[81] The work in Zambia concentrated on child-led advocacy; peer-to-peer outreach activities; children engaging with government officials, MPs and traditional leaders; and implementing low-cost community projects on climate change.[82]

The child-focused development non-governmental organisation Plan UK has also testified to the great potential of child participation in climate change affairs and interventions. Reportedly, in many of the countries in which the plan works, the organisation "has witnessed how children can effectively challenge adults to better address climate change adaptation at the local level".[83] These experiences have shown that "children's capacity can exceed the expectation of all involved" and that they may have certain important skills (e.g., to locate information on the Internet or to use social media) more than adults do.[84] Thus, they can play a key role in protecting themselves and their communities against some of the adverse effects of climate change, influence the actions of others and seek to transform their environment by tackling the root causes of the problem.[85] However, this will only work to the maximum extent possible if children get the space to make direct inputs into the "real" decision-making processes.

The "Children in a Changing Climate" initiative has also suggested that children must and are able to play a role in various levels of action concerning climate change, respectively in narrowing the current knowledge gap (for example by gathering data on the impact of climate change on children and on appropriate adaptation strategies for children in diverse situations and locations); informing and influencing relevant other actors; learning and adapting so as to protect themselves; and implementing climate change interventions.[86]

---

response to climate changes, in order to ensure the human right to live in a pure environment" (emphasis added). See National Assembly of the Socialist Republic of Vietnam, No. 55/2014/QH13 (Hanoi, 23 June 2014), www.ilo.org/dyn/legosh/en/f?p=14100:503:1898192772154::NO:503:P503_REFERENCE_FILE_ID:172934:NO.

[81] Ibid.
[82] Ibid., 34.
[83] Plan UK, *Global Warning*, 8.
[84] Ibid., 8–9.
[85] This useful typology has been suggested by Back et al., *Children and Disaster Risk Reduction*, 25.
[86] Children in a Changing Climate is "a global initiative spanning research, action, advocacy and learning with the purpose of securing children's influence on tackling climate change at every scale". The participants at the time included Actionaid, Institute of Development Studies, UK National Children's Bureau, Plan International and Save the Children. Some of these organisations dropped out of the initiative later and others joined, such that at present ChildFund Alliance, Plan International, Save the Children, UNICEF and World Vision are involved (see www.childreninachangingclimate.org). See also their "A Right to Participate: Securing Children's Role in Climate Change Adaptation" (2009), www.childreninachangingclimate.org/uploads/6/3/1/1/63116409/ccc_righttoparticipate_2009.pdf, 1 (for the characterisation of the participatory roles of children referred to in this chapter) and 18 (for an explanation of the purpose of the initiative and the organisations involved).

A CHILD RIGHTS-BASED APPROACH TO CLIMATE CHANGE: CONCLUDING REMARKS

Now that the particular effects of climate change on children are starting to become more and more documented, and a normative framework prescribing a child rights approach to climate change has emerged, it is high time to step up practice further. Building a stronger evidence base on the matter, in the form of fact-finding, generating and analysing disaggregated data, impact assessment of policies and other concrete interventions would be greatly helpful in this regard. Equipping states with the required capacity is crucial. According to a 2016 report of the World Meteorological Organization, at present "[s]ome 70 countries around the world do not have the capabilities they need to generate and apply climate information and forecasts with the required timeliness and quality of services".[87] In light of all the preceding, this is clearly unacceptable and has to be redressed. Other keys towards better quality climate change interventions in the future are the dissemination of pertinent information among relevant constituencies (such as policy makers, local communities or children), awareness raising and education. This would help to address the situation that 13-year-old Adeline Tiffanie Suwana (member of the Indonesian child and youth delegation to a UNFCCC COP) sketched so aptly on the basis of her observations during school visits in the suburbs of Jakarta, but that at present is a common state of play across the globe, and for children and adults alike. In 2012 Adeline wrote about her extreme surprise

> that the vast majority of children did not have a clue what climate change is. Most students could learn about it by listening to the news or browsing the internet, but most elementary students or even junior high school students, especially in the outskirt districts, do not have access to both, resulting in their not knowing the term climate change, let alone what it means.[88]

Additional keys towards better quality climate change practice relate to allowing inclusive participation in decision-making, and seeking and providing legal and practical remedies for climate change harm done. In this way only, true child rights-based practices in relation to climate change would come about.

---

[87] WMO, "WMO Statement on the Status of the Global Climate 2015", 3.
[88] UNICEF, *The Challenges of Climate Change*, 71.

11

Inclusion of Indigenous Children's Rights

Informing Water Management in Canada

Carissa Wong

INTRODUCTION

Problems Faced by Indigenous Children

Indigenous people[1] in Canada face severe challenges that are almost unknown to the rest of the Canadian population. For generations, indigenous children have faced a legacy of abuse, mistreatment and neglect, the repercussions of which are seen in the loss of community fabric, and understanding and respect for their own culture. In the wake of colonisation in Canada, indigenous communities have suffered a "loss of culture, loss of identity, loss of economic opportunity, loss of language, loss of family and loss of authority to name a few of the negative impacts".[2] Children have grown up suffering a loss of a physical, spiritual and emotional connection to their natural heritage and land, and a loss of identity, possibly similar to a severe collective condition of medical Alzheimer's.

But indigenous memory, knowledge and languages are not fully lost. Rather they are what the government of Canada now, through its efforts to implement sustainable development, seeks. Without addressing the needs of indigenous

---

[1] I am very grateful for the teaching and support of many indigenous people in Canada. Acknowledging my non-indigenous and non-European descent, I write with deference and humility as one who is concerned about the indigenous experience in Canada but does not purport to represent an indigenous voice. I am open to further dialogue on any of these issues.

"Indigenous communities, peoples and nations are those which, having a historical continuity with pre-invasion and pre-colonial societies that developed on their territories, consider themselves distinct from other sectors of society now prevailing on those territories or parts of them". W. Vandenhole et al. (eds.) *Routledge International Handbook of Children's Rights* (London: Routledge, 2015), 376.

[2] L. Chartrand, "Eagle Soaring on the Emergent Winds of Indigenous Legal Authority" (2013) 18 *Review of Constitutional Studies/Revue d'etudes constitutionelles* 49, 50.

children, their rights to education and to know their own community's language, religion and cultural and natural heritage, Canada cannot fully fulfil the promise of sustainable development.

Government policies "have undermined the ability of knowledge keepers to pass on their understanding of Natural Law and the rules that govern all relationships and, hence, interrupted the flow of knowledge between generations".[3] Today, indigenous children grow up in communities where the adults, who would be a source of customary law knowledge, are disproportionately incarcerated, poisoned, sexually abused and murdered. Canada's colonial and settler policies have attacked the ability of indigenous people to self-determine family, governance and economics, and have left devastating impacts on indigenous families and communities, which are "still mired in social, political, and psychological issues that are complex and difficult to resolve".[4] Indigenous people are overrepresented in the criminal justice system, experience higher rates of being denied bail, spend more time in pretrial detention, and are more than twice as likely to be incarcerated than non-Aboriginal offenders.[5] Once in prison, they are less likely to see their spiritual leaders (elders), who frequently do not receive the same status as prison priests and chaplains.[6] Moreover, indigenous women are overrepresented among Canada's missing and murdered.[7] Aboriginal women experience dramatically higher rates of violent victimisation than non-Aboriginal women.[8] Nearly one-quarter (24 per cent) of Aboriginal women in Canada report having been assaulted by a current or former spouse, compared to 7 per cent of non-Aboriginal women.[9] As well, indigenous children are denied their rights to know their culture because they often *are* the missing and murdered. The Native Women's Association of

---

[3] P. LaBoucane-Benson et al., "Are We Seeking Pimatisiwin or Creating Pomewin? Implications for Water Policy" (2012) 3(3) *The International Indigenous Policy Journal* 1, 1.
[4] Ibid.
[5] The Manitoba Government, *Report of the Aboriginal Justice Inquiry of Manitoba* (Aboriginal Justice Implementation Commission: 1999), vol. 1: *The Justice System and Aboriginal People*, ch. 4: "Aboriginal Over-representation", www.ajic.mb.ca/volumel/chapter4.html.
[6] Ibid.
[7] Canadian Broadcasting Corporation, "Aboriginal Women Still Overrepresented among Canada's Missing and Murdered Women" (20 June 2015), www.cbc.ca/news/aboriginal/aboriginal-women-still-overrepresented-among-canada-s-missing-and-murdered-women-1.3120272.
[8] K. Scrim, "Aboriginal Victimization in Canada: A Summary of the Literature," *Victims of Crime Research Digest No. 3* (Department of Justice, Government of Canada, 7 March 2016), www.justice.gc.ca/eng/rp-pr/cj-jp/victim/rd3-rr3/p3.html. This article is derived from the forthcoming report "A Review of Research on Criminal Victimization and First Nations, Métis and Inuit Peoples 1990 to 2008", which is an update of the original report: L. Chartrand and C. McKay, *A Review of Research on Criminal Victimization and First Nations, Métis and Inuit Peoples 1990 to 2001* (Policy Centre for Victim Issues, Research and Statistics Division, Department of Justice Canada, 2006).
[9] Ibid.

Canada's database of missing and murdered women from 2010 shows that just more than half of the cases (55 per cent) involve women and girls under the age of 31, with 17 per cent of women and girls 18 years or younger.[10] One study found that approximately 30 per cent of youth employed in the Canadian sex trade were Aboriginal.[11]

Not only have government policies affected the relationships among indigenous people, they have undermined their interconnected worldview.[12] They have attacked the relationship between indigenous people and their environment, such that "their ability to teach the process for building and renewing a sacred relationship with water has been compromised".[13] They have also created a "state of disconnectedness from the water" in indigenous communities.[14] Indigenous people are often located in close proximity to areas facing high risk of water contamination.[15] In 2011, 161 water systems in 116 First Nations communities were under Health Canada Drinking-Water Advisories,[16] affecting 18,900 people.[17] In fact, 73 per cent of the inspected water and wastewater systems in First Nations were at high or medium risk of various contaminations.[18] Such contaminants have contributed to higher rates of reproductive health issues including miscarriages, stillbirths and defects.[19]

---

[10] Native Women's Association of Canada, *Fact Sheet Missing and Murdered Aboriginal Women and Girls* (Ottawa, ON: Native Women's Association of Canada, 2015), www.nwac.ca/wp-content/uploads/2015/05/Fact_Sheet_Missing_and_Murdered_Aboriginal_Women_and_Girls.pdf, 4.

[11] Scrim, *Aboriginal Victimization in Canada*.

[12] LaBoucane-Benson et al., "Are We Seeking Pimatisiwin or Creating Pomewin?", 1.

[13] Ibid.

[14] Ibid., 2.

[15] D. Scott and A. Stiver, *Women's Bodies, Men's Bodies: Understanding the Differential Impact of Environmental Contaminants* (unpublished paper, Ottawa, ON, Health Canada, 2009); D. McGregor, "Anishnaabe-Kwe, Traditional Knowledge, and Water Protection" (2008) 3 *Canadian Woman Studies* 26, 27; L. Bruce and K. Harries, "The Anishinabe Kweag Were Bound to Protect the Water for Future Generations: How a Group of Indigenous Women Galvanized a Decades-Old Environmental Battle and Won" (2010) Spring/Summer 82/83 *Women and Environments International Magazine* 6, 6. K. Anderson, B. Clow and M. Haworth-Brockman, "Carriers of Water: Aboriginal Women's Experiences, Relationships and Reflections" (2013) 60 *Journal of Cleaner Production* 11, 12.

[16] Due to any array of specific chemicals, disease-causing bacteria or sediment reaching high enough concentrations to pose a threat to health.

[17] Aboriginal Affairs and Northern Development Canada, *Fact Sheet – The Results of the National Assessment of First Nations Drinking Water and Wastewater Systems* (19 August 2011), www.aadnc-aandc.gc.ca/eng/1313762701121/1313762778061, 1; Neegan Burnside Ltd, *National Assessment of First Nations Water and Wastewater Systems – National Roll-up Report* (Department of Indian and Northern Affairs Canada, 2011), www.aadnc-aandc.gc.ca/eng/1313770257504/1313770328745; as cited by Anderson et al., "Carriers of Water", 12.

[18] Ibid.

[19] Anderson et al., "Carriers of Water", 12.

Problems for Watersheds

Canada holds more than 20 per cent of the world's freshwater supply,[20] covering roughly 755,180 square kilometres (i.e., the area of both California and Nevada).[21] Much of this water is non-renewable and remains in aquifers and glaciers, while more than 60 per cent of Canada's renewable freshwater flows north, in Arctic-bound rivers.[22] Yet, more than 90 per cent of Canada's population lives in southern Canada.[23]

Although Canada "does not have an easily accessible, national system for reporting the health of freshwater ecosystems across the country and the threats they face",[24] the information available shows that water contamination, withdrawal, damming and diversion, and the loss of wetlands and freshwater biodiversity are the national trend.

Water is facing heavy levels of contamination, which places considerable strain on ecosystems and indigenous people in Canada. Based on the Commission for Environmental Cooperation's most recent report on the issue from 2011, an estimated more than 200 million kilograms of pollutants are released into Canada's surface waters annually.[25] The natural hydrological cycle that brings water north has particularly affected the Canadian Inuit, through the bioaccumulation of toxic contaminants in their traditional foods, such as polar bear, seal, fish and caribou.[26]

In addition to water pollution, the flow regimes of Canada's freshwater systems are highly regulated, leading to ecological and sustainable development problems. "Water flow regimes are widely recognised as the 'master variable' for aquatic ecosystem health, however, and are a key factor in sustaining native biodiversity and ecosystem integrity."[27] Scholars recognise that "[j]ust like blood pressure in the

---

[20] K. Bakker (ed.), *Eau Canada: The Future of Canada's Water* (Vancouver: University of British Columbia Press, 2007), 27.

[21] D. Boyd, *Unnatural Law: Rethinking Canadian Environmental Law and Policy* (Vancouver: University of British Columbia Press, 2003), 13; K. Matsui, "Water Ethics for First Nations and Biodiversity in Western Canada" (2012) 3(3) *The International Indigenous Policy Journal* 1, 1.

[22] Boyd, *Unnatural Law*, 13–14.

[23] Ibid.

[24] WWF Canada, *Watershed Reports: Taking the Pulse of Canada's Rivers* (Toronto: WWF, 2017), lwbin-datahub.ad.umanitoba.ca/dataset/wwf-watershed-reports; http://watershedreports.wwf.ca/#canada/by/threat-overall/profile.

[25] Commission for Environmental Cooperation, *Taking Stock: North American Pollutant Releases and Transfers* (Montreal: Commission for Environmental Cooperation, 2011), www.cec.org/Storage/101/9990_CEC-TakingStock13_3n.pdf.

[26] Bakker (ed.), *Eau Canada*, 311.

[27] T. Annear et al., *Instream Flows for Riverine Resource Stewardship* (Cheyenne, WY: Instream Flow Council, 2004); D. M. Carlisle, D. M. Wolock and M. R. Meador, *Frontiers in Ecology and the Environment: Alteration of Streamflow Magnitudes and Potential Ecological Consequences: A Multiregional Assessment* (2010), https://water.usgs.gov/nawqa/pubs/Carlisleetal_FLowAlterationUS.pdf; N. L. Poff et al., "The Natural Flow Regime: A Paradigm for River

human body, the flow and movement of water is a vital indicator and driver of overall aquatic ecosystem health".[28] However, "Canada is one of the largest diverters of water in the world" and by 2010, had 10 of the 40 largest dams in the world, by gross reservoir capacity.[29] "Starting in earnest during the 1950s and progressing into a billion-dollar industry today [2016], hydroelectricity dam construction enables Canada to produce 60 per cent of its power from its waterways, a national hydroelectric production level second only to China".[30]

As a result, Canada's most recent Biodiversity Report, which evaluated the last 40 years from 2010, found "changes in river flows at critical times of the year".[31] It found that "trends over the past 40 years influencing biodiversity in lakes and rivers include seasonal changes in magnitude of stream flows, increases in river and lake temperatures, decreases in lake levels, and habitat loss and fragmentation".[32] "Dams and regulation have significant negative impacts on Ottawa River lake sturgeon populations, blocking migration routes, altering flow regimes, and disturbing spawning habitat".[33] In 2015, of the 155 major fish stocks assessed, only 48 per cent of Canada's fisheries are classified as healthy, 26 per cent were classified as cautious and 10 per cent were classified as critical.[34] A further 25 per cent of stocks were classified as unknown.[35] From at least the 1980s, the number of endangered or threatened fish species has been increasing, and as of 2010, "18 per cent of freshwater fish are listed as endangered or threatened in Canada".[36] Unfortunately, there is no

---

Conservation and Restoration" (1997) 47 *BioScience* 769, 769; L. Nowlan, "CPR for Canadian Rivers – Law to Conserve, Protect, and Restore Environmental Flows in Canada" (2012) 23(3) *Journal of Environmental Law and Practice* 203, 208.

[28] Nowlan, "CPR for Canadian Rivers", 209.

[29] Environment Canada, *Threats to Water Availability in Canada: NWRI Scientific Assessment Report Series No. 3 and ACSD Science Assessment Series, No. 1* (Burlington, ON: National Water Research Institute, 2004), www.ec.gc.ca/inre-nwri/0CD66675-AD25-4B23-892C-5396F7876F65/ThreatsEN_03web.pdf, 9.

[30] National Energy Board, "Market Snapshot: Canada 2nd in World for Hydroelectric Production" (1 December 2016), 1, www.neb-one.gc.ca/nrg/ntgrtd/mrkt/snpsht/2016/06-04cndscndwrld-eng.html?=undefined&wbdisable=true.

[31] Federal, Provincial and Territorial Governments of Canada, *Canadian Biodiversity: Ecosystem Status and Trends 2010* (Ottawa, ON: Canadian Councils of Resource Ministers, 2010), www.biodivcanada.ca/ecosystems, 1.

[32] Ibid.

[33] WWF, *Canada's Rivers at Risk: Environmental Flows and Canada's Freshwater Future* (Toronto: WWF Canada, 2009), http://awsassets.wwf.ca/downloads/canadas_rivers_at_risk.pdf, 21.

[34] Environment and Climate Change Canada, *Canadian Environmental Sustainability Indicators: Status of Major Fish Stocks* (Gatineau, QC: Her Majesty the Queen in Right of Canada, represented by the Minister of Environment and Climate Change, 2016), www.ec.gc.ca/indicateurs-indicators/1BCD421B-E406-44DD-97EC-DD7B23A2859E/StatusOfMajorFish Stocks_EN.pdf, 4; www.ec.gc.ca/indicateurs-indicators/default.asp?lang=en&n=1BCD421B-1.

[35] Ibid.

[36] Federal, Provincial and Territorial Governments of Canada, *Canadian Biodiversity*, 7; Nowlan, "CPR for Canadian Rivers", 212.

current law in Canada stating that either the federal, provincial or territorial governments must protect environmental flows.[37]

Canada, however, has ratified the UN Convention on the Rights of the Child (UNCRC), "the most rapidly and widely ratified human rights treaty in history" – now with 196 countries as State Parties. In this chapter, I argue that by ensuring children's rights to receive information and ideas of all kinds, to be educated to respect their own and diverse cultural identities, values, and religions, and to express their views in matters that affect them, the UNCRC supports children's participation in the practice of indigenous law in Canada. I illustrate that (1) the UNCRC articles 29, 30 support children's rights to learn respect for all living things and to internalise an eco-centric ethic; (2) the UNCRC's preamble and six other articles protect a child's right to understand development and progress in non-material, spiritual terms; and (3) UNCRC article 13 protects a child's right to receive information from nature and participate as a duty-bearer in protecting it. By protecting these rights, the UNCRC requires that Canada include ethnic and intellectual diversity in the path toward a more sustainable future.

HOW CHILDREN'S RIGHTS SUPPORT SUSTAINABLE DEVELOPMENT: HOW DOES THE UNCRC SUPPORT CHILDREN'S RIGHTS TO INDIGENOUS LAW AND CANADA'S WATERSHEDS?

What Is Indigenous Law?

The indigenous, or Aboriginal, people in Canada form three federally recognised groups:[38] First Nations (historically referred to as Indians), Inuit (indigenous peoples inhabiting the global Arctic regions) and Metis (people of mixed First Nations and European heritage).[39] As well, there are many indigenous people in Canada who do not define themselves according to federally recognised categories,[40] but whose rights are nonetheless protected under the UNCRC. Despite differences arising from distinct histories, languages and cultural practices, indigenous legal traditions in Canada share some broad and common understandings, similar to the commonalities found in Western civil and common law traditions already used in Canada.[41]

---

[37] Nowlan, "CPR for Canadian Rivers", 212–213.
[38] There is no requirement for States [party to the UN Convention on the Rights of the Child] to officially recognise indigenous peoples for them to exercise their rights. UNRCR Committee, "General Comment No. 11 (2009) on Indigenous Children and Their Rights under the Convention" (UN Doc. CRC/C/GC/11, 12 February 2009).
[39] S. Kant, I. Vertinsky, B. Zheng and P. M. Smith, "Social, Cultural and Land Use Determinants of the Health and Well-Being of Aboriginal Peoples of Canada: A Path Analysis" (2013) 34 (3) *Journal of Public Health* 462, 462.
[40] Douglas Cardinal, Anishinabek elder, personal communication, Ottawa, ON (26 July 2016).
[41] Chartrand, "Eagle Soaring on the Emergent Winds", 51.

In examining how indigenous law is critical to improving watershed management in Canada, I focus on specific examples from western Canada (British Columbia) and the Prairie Provinces (Alberta, Saskatchewan and Manitoba) in which there is a longer and richer history of water law and planning in the country. Thus, I draw on the indigenous legal traditions of the Cree (whose homeland stretches over a vast area from James Bay to the Rocky Mountains),[42] Haida (indigenous nations along the Pacific coast) and Inuit who share portions of northwestern Canada. I also draw on Anishinabek culture, which has a close connection to the Great Lakes region of southeastern Canada.

Respect for All Living Things

The UNCRC protects the right of a child to enjoy his or her own culture, to profess and practice his or her own religion and to use his or her own language. State Parties are under an obligation to ensure the existence and exercise of this right against violation.[43]

As legal traditions are a cultural phenomenon,[44] by protecting children's cultural rights, UNCRC article 29 and 30 also protect their rights to respect and enjoy the practice of their own legal system. Law is a "culture of argument" that "provides a place and a set of institutions and methods where this conversational process can go on, as well as a second conversation by which the first is criticised and judged".[45] Indigenous legal traditions, like any, are embedded in a culture of argument and require translation.[46] "[T]here is a social practice reflected and contained within the language chosen.... [This] legal coding in itself is bias".[47] By protecting the right to indigenous language and culture, the UNCRC protects the right to indigenous law.

The indigenous people in Canada share land-based cultures that recognise planet Earth as their Mother and the source of everything that they need for survival.[48] Key features of this worldview are collectivism, non-possession, harmony with nature and seeing all things as interconnected.[49] Indigenous law is grounded in

---

[42] J. Borrows, *Canada's Indigenous Constitution* (Toronto, Buffalo and London: University of Toronto Press, 2010), 84.

[43] UNCRC Committee, General Comment No. 11, 4.

[44] AWB Simpson, *Leading Cases in the Common Law* (Oxford: Oxford University Press, 1996), 11; Borrows, *Canada's Indigenous Constitution*, 8.

[45] J. B. White, *Justice as Translation* (Chicago: University of Chicago Press), xiii, 80; Borrows, *Canada's Indigenous Constitution*, 118.

[46] Ibid.

[47] K. Crenshaw et al. (eds.), *Critical Race Theory: The Key Writings That Formed the Movement* (New York: New Press, 1995), 184–185; T. Lindberg, "Critical Indigenous Legal Theory Part 1: The Dialogue Within" (2015) 27 *Canadian Journal of Women and the Law* 224, 237.

[48] Kant et al., "Social, Cultural and Land Use Determinants", 463.

[49] B. Mussell, K. Cardiff and J. White, *The Mental Health and Well-Being of Aboriginal Children and Youth. Guidance for New Approaches and Services* (Vancouver: The Shal'shan Institute,

interrelationships between all animate and inanimate matter.[50] In addition, indigenous legal traditions are diverse and derived from many sources; common elements include sacred law, natural law, deliberative law, positivistic law and customary law.[51]

Spiritual elements are naturally accepted as part of indigenous legal traditions. Law is not perceived to be or preferred in isolation from spiritual and religious beliefs.[52] For example, the Medicine Wheel is a tool for teaching medicine as well as law, as it conveys values and principles of how one is to relate to the environment, to oneself, to others and to the spirit world.[53] To those who understand its teachings, it provides guidance on how to live in a healthy way socially, mentally, spiritually and physically. Indigenous culture allows spiritual and religious beliefs to influence and inform legal thought.[54] Indigenous cultures regard the separation and isolation of reason and law from spirituality and belief as fictitious and unnatural.[55] By protecting an indigenous child's religion and spirituality, the UNCRC protects indigenous law.

Customary Law and Internalising an Eco-Centric Precautionary Principle

But what is the content of this indigenous law, and how does it relate to the achievement of sustainable development? Indigenous law in Canada is largely customary and views the natural world as sacred. It is "an internalised set of understandings for valuing harmonious relationships", and one of many tools for maintaining social and ecological balance.[56]

An example of this can be seen in the practices of the Cree people, who live in the boreal forest and prairies stretching from James Bay to the Rocky Mountains, whose laws are influenced by a range of diverse ecologies.[57] *Wahkohtowin* is the overarching law, which flows from the Creator and governs all relations.[58] Humans are part of this order and exist within the overarching natural law.[59] The consequences for

---

the University of British Columbia, 2004); Kant et al., "Social, Cultural and Land Use Determinants".

[50] Law Commission of Canada (ed.), *Indigenous Legal Traditions*, (Vancouver: University of British Columbia Press, 2007), 118.
[51] Borrows, *Canada's Indigenous Constitution*, 8, 24.
[52] Chartrand, "Eagle Soaring on the Emergent Winds", 49.
[53] Ibid., 60.
[54] Ibid., 58.
[55] Ibid.
[56] Ibid., 66.
[57] F. Berkes, *Sacred Ecology: Traditional Ecological Knowledge and Resource Management* (Philadelphia: Taylor and Francis, 1999); Borrows, *Canada's Indigenous Constitution*, 84.
[58] K. O'Reilly-Scanlon, K. Crowe and A. Weenie, "Pathways to Understanding: Wahkohtowin as a Research Methodology" (2004) 39 *McGill Journal of Education* 1, 29; Borrows, *Canada's Indigenous Constitution*.
[59] Borrows, *Canada's Indigenous Constitution*.

failing to abide by Cree law are *wahkohtowin*, and taking an action against creation or natural law is *pastahowin*.⁶⁰ As also seen in the Anishinabek legal tradition discussed in the following text, the Cree understand that if animals are not treated appropriately, something bad will result.⁶¹ This customary law is internalised and no external enforcement is necessary. The Cree interconnected worldview also sees everything as being alive and that we are all related. Thus, there is a "spiritual dimension of reality" that dictates that "we have a continuing responsibility to our reciprocal relationship with it, whether we are hunting, working, playing or learning".⁶²

Another example is the law of the Haida in Western Canada, which has the unifying value of respect, called *Yah'guudang*. This respect is for all living things. It honours the way our lives and spirits are intertwined, as well as the responsibility we hold to future generations.⁶³ This respect is also for our human place in the web of life and the understanding that our fate runs parallel to that of the ocean, sky and forest.⁶⁴

From the upper Great Lakes and northeast Prairie lakes,⁶⁵ the Anishinabek have a legal tradition that upholds a conservation ethic, as well. They apply stewardship-based enforcement mechanisms (*bimeekumaugaewin*) to the use of land, plants and other animals.⁶⁶ *Bimeekumaugaewin* holds that every being will face, through the laws of nature, the consequences of either failure to perform a responsibility or approbation for proper performance of a duty.⁶⁷ Specifically, they convey that the manner in which plants, animals and people should relate is one of respect.⁶⁸

Similarly, the Inuit's respectful treatment of wildlife is their way of preparing for the future. The Inuit are a circumpolar people who live in Canada's central and western Arctic, High Arctic, Baffin Islands, as well as coastal areas of Hudson's Bay, Quebec and Labrador.⁶⁹ "Because we did not want to experience hardship, we were told not to kill wildlife just for the sake of killing them". In such a way, "A long time ago", one elder explained,

---

⁶⁰ Ibid., 85.
⁶¹ Rupert Ross has observed, "Storytelling as a means of law-giving seems to be based on the ... understanding – that law can be known to everyone through reciting the consequences of acts alone, not through communicating judgment labels for either the act or, worse still, the actor" (*Return to the Teachings: Exploring Aboriginal Justice* [Toronto: Viking/Penguin, 1996], 171); Borrows, *Canada's Indigenous Constitution* , 85–86.
⁶² LaBoucane-Benson et al., "Are We Seeking Pimatisiwin or Creating Pomewin?", 5.
⁶³ S. Quail, "Yah'guudang: The Principle of Respect in the Haida Legal Tradition" (2014) 47 *University of British Columbia Law Review* 673, 676.
⁶⁴ Ibid.
⁶⁵ H. Hornbeck, *Atlas of Great Lakes Indian History* (Norman: Oklahoma University Press, 1982), 58–92; Borrows, *Canada's Indigenous Constitution*, 77.
⁶⁶ Borrows, *Canada's Indigenous Constitution*, 79.
⁶⁷ Ibid., 80.
⁶⁸ Ibid., 79.
⁶⁹ Ibid., 101.

Inuit would prepare for the future. We were told not to make fun of wildlife so we and our children would have a good life.... We were told to take good care of our wildlife and our land. Caribou and beluga [were] abundant. Sometimes when they were too numerous we didn't know how to kill large numbers of them. But now in the winter we use snow machines and we shoot them and they freeze. Some people just take the hindquarters. Some caribou only have the tongues taken and the rest is left behind.... This is something we elders don't like at all. By respecting wildlife, the Inuit culture ensures enough resources in the future. "Animals are thought to be aware of what is done to them. If game is not respected, it will retaliate against the hunter or even the whole community.[70]

"If we are happy and gracious towards wildlife, they will be in great abundance. If we are not thankful and do not appreciate them, they will disappear."[71]

As well, indigenous law upholds the spirit and sacredness in nature that would support a more eco-centric, precautionary approach to water. The indigenous people view water, like the Earth, as being alive, sentient and healing.[72] They believe that water has a spirit and is capable of forming relationships with other life forms, particularly with women. The rush of meltwater in the spring as new life begins is analogous to the breaking of water when a child is born.[73] As the carriers of water as a child gestates and the keepers of water through the transitions and cycles of life, women have a serious and sacred responsibility for respecting and protecting water.[74] They also understand that just like humans, the Earth is mostly comprised of water. Harming or polluting water will cause harm to you.[75] What you do to water, you do to yourself. Caring for one's Earth, one is caring for oneself. This indigenous law supports an eco-centric and precautionary approach to water.

Indigenous customary law is persuasive "not because it is backed by the power of some strong individual or institution, but because each individual recognises the benefits of behaving in accordance with other individuals' expectations [given] that others also behave as [s/]he expects".[76] It derives its binding force not through written agreements, but through sustained, established conduct that arises over time and parties follow out of a sense of legal obligation or *opinio juris*.[77] Although certain

---

[70] J. Oosten, F. Laugrand and W. Rasing (eds.), *Interviewing Inuit Elders: Perspectives on Traditional Law* (Iqaluit, NU: Nunavut Arctic College, 1999), vol. 2, 33.

[71] Ibid., 39.

[72] Anderson et al., "Carriers of Water", 14.

[73] Ibid.

[74] Ibid., 16.

[75] Ibid.

[76] B. Benson, *The Enterprise of Law: Justice without the State* (Oakland, CA: The Independent Institute, 2011), 12.

[77] *Charter of the United Nations and Statute of the International Court of Justice* (26 June 1945) 59 Stat. 1031, 3 Bevans 1153 (drawing on general principles of law shared by nations); J. Currie, *Public International Law*, 2nd ed. (Toronto: Irwin Law, 2008), 100.

customary systems may inform wise resource management policies,[78] but reflect unequal power relations in the distribution and management of water between genders,[79] indigenous traditions in Canada are matriarchal.[80] Thus, when incorporating indigenous customary law to water management in Canada, gender equity would be less of a concern than in other customary jurisdictions.

In addition to the role that indigenous customary laws can play in complementing and informing Canada's laws,[81] their role as ethical principles alone can have a long-term persuasive influence in the country. An example of the strength of ethical principles comes from the Nuremberg Code and the World Medical Association's Declaration of Helsinki, which now form the basis of biomedical ethics in protecting the rights of human subjects in experiments, through the principles of "free prior informed consent".[82] These principles even influenced the Convention on Biological Diversity, especially article 8(j).[83] Similarly, indigenous ethical codes and principles for biodiversity and water management can be used to influence practices over time in Canada.[84]

As Canada agrees on a Federal Sustainable Development Strategy for 2016–2019[85] to reflect the Agenda 2030 Sustainable Development Goals (SDGs)[86] and meet its commitments under the Federal Sustainable Development Act,[87] the country has an opportunity to reflect on indigenous laws. Although the current strategy lacks a

---

[78] P. Ørebech, *The Role of Customary Law in Sustainable Development* (Cambridge: Cambridge University Press, 2006), 435.
[79] B. van Koppen, M. Giordano and J. Butterworth (eds.) *Community-Based Water Law and Resource Management Reform in Developing Countries* (Wallingford, UK, and Cambridge, MA: CAB International, 2007), 23.
[80] Douglas Cardinal, Anishinabek elder, personal communication, Ottawa, ON (26 July 2016).
[81] Law Commission of Canada (ed.) *Indigenous Legal Traditions* (Vancouver: University of British Columbia Press, 2007), 129.
[82] Matsui, "Water Ethics for First Nations", 12.
[83] Ibid.
[84] G. J. Annas and M. A. Grodin (eds.), *The Nazi Doctors and the Nuremberg Code: Human Rights in Human Experimentation* (Oxford: Oxford University Press, 1992), 174–182; Matsui, "Water Ethics for First Nations".
[85] Final tabled in Parliament in October 2016; Environment and Climate Change Canada, *A Federal Sustainable Development Strategy for Canada 2016–2019* (Gatineau, QC: Government of Canada, 2016), www.ec.gc.ca/dd-sd/CD30F295-F19D-4FF9-8E03-EAE8965BE446/3130_FSDS_Eng_FINAL.pdf, www.ec.gc.ca/dd-sd/default.asp?Lang=En&n=CD30F295-1.
[86] UNGA, "Transforming Our World: The 2030 Agenda for Sustainable Development" (UN Doc. A/RES/70/1, 21 October 2015).
[87] At the UN Sustainable Development Summit in September 2015, world leaders, including those from Canada, adopted the 2030 Agenda for Sustainable Development, which consists of 17 SDGs. Canada's main piece of legislation implementing the 2030 Agenda for Sustainable Development is the Federal Sustainable Development Act. It accepts the basic principle that "sustainable development means development that meets the needs of the present without compromising the ability of future generations to meet their own needs and holds as its foundation the precautionary principle". This principle establishes "that where there are threats of serious or irreversible damage, lack of full scientific certainty shall not be used as a reason for postponing cost effective measures to prevent environmental degradation (principe

specific target to protect environmental flow regimes, it contains the goal of Healthy Coasts and Oceans that targets Sustainable Fisheries, the goal of Healthy Wildlife Populations that targets Species at Risk, and the goal of Pristine Lakes and Rivers that targets watershed ecosystems and water quality.[88] To meet its Sustainable Fisheries Target, the Canadian government can incorporate indigenous legal terms to respect wild fisheries, not as a resource, but as an insurance policy for the future, or better yet, as sacred life like a child or sibling or relative, which we do not and cannot own. As one indigenous person said, "If we see water as sacred, how can you expect us to put chemicals in it and shake it to make it pure and safe? That makes no sense".[89]

In particular, indigenous law can support the implementation and interpretation of Canada's existing fisheries and water laws, which, in contrast to US tradition, suffer from a culture of weak enforcement.[90] As seen from the documented enforcement activity and recorded authorisations for habitat destruction from 2012 to 2014 (even before Bill C-38[91] was passed in Canadian Parliament in 2012 to weaken the habitat protection provisions of the federal Fisheries Act),[92] the vast majority of Canada's freshwater and rivers were and are still not benefitting from federal protection, the main jurisdiction responsible for fisheries.[93] The internalised conservation ethic in indigenous law, however, would remove the reliance on federal enforcement and prosecution of environmental offenses. By teaching children that people have a sacred relationship with water, which one must treat with utmost respect as one would a mother, and with responsibility as one would oneself, the government would assist policy makers in achieving better water quality and quantity targets for priority watersheds in Canada.

---

de la prudence)". www.undp.org/content/undp/en/home/sdgoverview/post-2015-development-agenda.html; *Federal Sustainable Development Act*, S.C. 2008, c. 33.

[88] Environment and Climate Change Canada, *A Federal Sustainable Development Strategy for Canada*, ii, 8, 13, 14.

[89] J. White, "Editor in Chief Commentary: Water – Recognizing the Indigenous Perspective" (2012) 3(3) *The International Indigenous Policy Journal* 1, 1.

[90] W. Amos et al., *Getting Tough on Crime? Holding the Government of Canada to Account on Environmental Enforcement* (Vancouver, BC: Ecojustice, 2011), www.ecojustice.ca/wp-content/uploads/2014/08/Getting-Tough-on-Environmental-Crime.pdf, 8–10; M. Olszynski, Assistant Professor, University of Calgary, personal communication (6 March 2016).

[91] Bill C-38, Statutes of Canada 2012 Chapter 19, Assented 29th June 2012, www.parl.gc.ca/content/hoc/Bills/411/Government/C-38/C-38_4/C-38_4.PDF.

[92] *Fisheries Act* (R.S.C., 1985, c. F-14).

[93] "There has been a consistent decline in environmental enforcement activities (including warnings, orders, etc.) since 2005–06 despite an increase in the number of enforcement officers, particularly under the *Canadian Environmental Protection Act*. There are relatively few successful prosecutions under federal environmental legislation. The number of annual convictions, approximately 20 per year under CEPA, is extremely small in relation to the number of inspections, warnings and investigations" (M. Olszynski, "From 'Badly Wrong' to Worse: An Empirical Analysis of Canada's New Approach to Fish Habitat Protection Laws" [2015] 28[1] *Journal of Environmental Law and Practice* 1, 34).

In addition, the government can apply the concept of water ethics, in which "ecological needs are fairly represented in water management systems"[94] and allocate water only after ecological needs are met. Ensuring sufficient water flows in rivers to meet the ecological needs of the river before human uses are allocated would create a "safety valve to deal with the uncertainties of scientific management" and fulfil Canada's commitment to the precautionary principle.[95] Ensuring minimum ecological flows in rivers is part of the customary legal framework of the indigenous in southeastern Ontario.[96] There is strong alignment between indigenous law and Western science on the issue of environmental flows. This is not surprising, given that life, medicine and law are all interconnected in indigenous culture. By incorporating indigenous principles early on, the reliance on science when implementing laws, or later in a battle of expert testimony at court, would be reduced. Further, allocating human water uses only after the ecological needs of the river are met would establish a public trust in the resource, the doctrine for which exists in Canadian water law debates already.[97]

Progress as Balance and Renewal

The UNCRC asserts the right to development in articles 6, 18, 23, 27, 29 and 32, as protecting seven aspects of a child's well-being: physical, moral, mental, spiritual, social, health and normal development.[98] Although the UNCRC does not clarify the meaning of the right to development, scholars suggest that the drafters focused on protecting the "organic process of growing up",[99] and looking to the child's future, as an adult. It suggests that children's future-focused development should centre on physical, moral, mental, spiritual, social, health and harmonious development. These rights of the child to development encompass a suite of aspects that will empower them to be mature and self-actualised adults exercising their own rights.[100] Thus, the UNCRC lays the foundation for sustainable development, by requiring that children develop not merely to acquire material gain or pursue industrial-capitalist aims, but to pursue the seven aspects of well-being.

The UNCRC also clearly stipulates that healthy growing up requires both material and spiritual aspects.[101] Article 27(1) of the UNCRC protects a standard of living

---

[94] Matsui, "Water Ethics for First Nations", 15.
[95] Ibid.
[96] Paula LaPierre, Kichesipirini Algonquin community leader, personal communication, Ottawa, ON (14 December 2016).
[97] W. Amos, "A Refreshing Win for the Public Interest in Ontario" (Ecojustice Blog, 17 February 2015), www.ecojustice.ca/a-refreshing-win-for-the-public-interest-in-ontario/, 1.
[98] F. Malekian and K. Nordlof (eds.), *The Sovereignty of Children in Law* (Newcastle, UK: Cambridge Scholars Publishing, 2012), 151.
[99] Ibid., 46.
[100] Ibid., 152.
[101] Ibid., 146.

adequate for moral and social development. The guaranteed standard of living goes beyond the material aspects of living such as sustenance and shelter, and ensures the conditions for physical, mental, spiritual, moral and social development.[102] This moral development includes how to treat nature and other life. Indigenous well-being and health is linked to their worldview.[103] Understanding indigenous values and morality in contrast to modern Western-industrial views nurtures this multidimensional development. The "Constitution of Canada ... evolved within a market-oriented paradigm",[104] and as a result has limitations in addressing non-market issues, of which the environment is one. The UNCRC can respond to this gap by addressing the importance of nonmaterial, non-market-oriented development goals.

The indigenous principle of progress as renewal encompasses the understanding that a natural harmony exists, in which "no single life force should possess unlimited detached power over others".[105] In contrast to the works of Thomas Hobbes, Jean-Jacques Rousseau or John Locke, indigenous Canadian legal theory[106] is not premised on the belief that living within nature is impossible for human beings without some profound political intervention.[107] Rather, indigenous legal theory in Canada suggests that all nature is in a permeable, interactive, relationship with people.

The sacred relationship between people and the Creator also guides the Cree understanding that certain laws of nature are unchanging and irrefutable. "There are laws that govern the world that do not belong to us, that we cannot overpower, we cannot manipulate or even attempt to have a say over. They have their own way. So what we try to do as people is to fit into that, become part of it. And try not to control it – if we ever try that, then we will bring demise to ourselves".[108]

The interrelatedness of people leads to "an implicit idea of equality among all creation"[109] and the indigenous understanding that people should not try to control nature or face negative consequences. The Anishinabek, for example, believe that

---

[102] A. Eide, *A Commentary on the United Nations Convention on the Rights of the Child: Article 27 the Right to an Adequate Standard of Living* (Leiden, The Netherlands: Martinus Nijhoff Publishers, 2006), 17.

[103] D. L. Morgan, M. D. Slade and C. M. A. Morgan, "Aboriginal Philosophy and Its Impact on Health Care Outcomes" (1997) 21(6) *Australian and New Zealand Journal of Public Health* 597, 597; J. Smylie, J. Williams and N. Cooper, "Culture-Based Literacy and Aboriginal Health" (2007) *Canadian Journal of Public Health* 97 (Supplement 2): S21–S25; Kant et al., "Social, Cultural and Land Use Determinants", 463.

[104] Matsui, "Water Ethics for First Nations", 5.

[105] Chartrand, "Eagle Soaring on the Emergent Winds", 49, 66.

[106] Cree, Inuit, Anishinabee, Nlaka'pamux (Anderson et al., "Carriers of Water", 13).

[107] T. Hobbes, *Leviathan* (London: G. Routledge and Sons, 1887); J. J. Rouseau, *The Social Contract* (London: Dent, 1973); J. Locke, *Two Treatises on Government* (New York: New American Library, 1965); Borrows, *Canada's Indigenous Constitution*, 29.

[108] Fred Campiou, Cree elder, Reconciliation Circles Interview, Alberta, Canada (February 2012) as cited in LaBoucane-Benson et al., "Are We Seeking Pimatisiwin or Creating Pomewin?", 5.

[109] Justice and Solicitor General of Alberta, *Justice on Trial (Cawsey Report)* (Edmonton: Government of Alberta, 1991), c9-2–c9-3.

the land and rocks are alive, and using rocks without their consent is akin to using another person against his or her will.[110] These principles can be applied to oil sands extraction, mining and hydropower developments, which done now without regard for much more than immediate material gain, have created serious water quality and quantity problems to the detriment of people.[111] Water flows through the Earth like the blood in the veins of a person. The rerouting of water is as damaging as rerouting the veins in our bodies.[112] This overstepping the bounds, or going outside the boundaries that you are entitled, *pastahowin* is translated as "sinning against your children".[113] "Clean" hydroelectricity has had a broad impact on First Nations communities across Canada, including increasing methyl mercury contamination in water and fish and creating a fear among the Anishinabek of eating traditional country foods, including whitefish, understood to be good for breast milk.[114] Following Canadian indigenous law would improve water quality, food safety and the sustainability of fisheries.

The indigenous principle of progress as renewal also upholds the cyclical process of adaptive management in sustainable development, as people incorporate lessons from nature through iterations of intervention, assessment and adoption.[115] Adaptive management improves resilience as people can anticipate potential fluctuations in water supply and expressly mandate more conservative use of resources, particularly under climate change.

Life-Wide Legal Agency and Children's Right to Receive Information

Article 13 of the UNCRC guarantees that "[t]he child shall have the right to freedom of expression; this right shall include freedom to seek, receive and impart information and ideas of all kinds, regardless of frontiers, either orally, in writing or in print, or in the form of art, or through any other media of the child's choice."[116]

---

[110] Borrows, *Canada's Indigenous Constitution*, 245.
[111] B. Luby, "From Milk-Medicine to Public (Re) Education Programs: An Examination of Anishinabek Mothers' Responses to Hydroelectric Flooding in the Treaty #3 District, 1900–1975" (2015) 32(2) *Canadian Bulletin of Medical History* 363, 364–367; Environmental Defence, *Realty Check: Water and Tar Sands* (Toronto: Environmental Defence, 2013), http://environmentaldefence.ca/report/report-reality-check-water-and-the-tar-sands/, 3–12; WWF, *Canada's Rivers at Risk*, 2–7, 14–15; Ontario Nature, *Mining in Ontario a Deeper Look* (Toronto: Ontario Nature, undated), www.ontarionature.org/discover/resources/PDFs/reports/mining-in-ontario-web.pdf, 12, 14, 15.
[112] Anderson et al., "Carriers of Water", 14.
[113] Fred Campiou, Cree elder, Reconciliation Circles Interview, Alberta, Canada (February 2012) as cited in LaBoucane-Benson et al., "Are We Seeking Pimatisiwin or Creating Pomewin?", 14.
[114] Luby, "From Milk-Medicine to Public (Re) Education Programs"; Ontario Nature, *Mining in Ontario a Deeper Look*.
[115] H. J. Cortner and M. A. Moote, *The Politics of Ecosystem Management* (Washington, DC: Island Press, 1999), 37.
[116] UNCRC, article 13.

Generally, this right to receive information places an onus on the media and relevant authorities to guarantee that the public is informed on matters of legitimate concern.[117] Additionally, however, matters of legitimate concern include those that relate to a child's environment. Such information is available to children through direct observation, interaction and access to the natural environment because "the medium is the message".[118] The environment is also a source of "ideas of all kinds" to which children are guaranteed, "regardless of frontiers".[119] The Cree, for example, counsel humans to observe other living things for guidance on how to practice their law.[120] Electronic, print media and other authorities are not the only source of information. Nature is an authority that provides vast amounts of information of legitimate concern to children's lives. Thus, the UNCRC protects a child's right to receive information from his or her natural environment.

Although there is little analysis specifically addressing article 13, and it is usually applied with article 12 to support the right to freedom of expression, the "emerging principles are that access to information should be promoted so that children have ways to inform themselves and thus be able to participate in social life".[121] "Information must be varied and diversified, independent, of good quality, and is important on ideological and spiritual matters".[122] There is a positive duty on the state to provide access to this information, as well as a positive right for a child to seek and access it.[123] As well, the state must take measures to acquaint children with different cultures.[124]

---

[117] H. Thorgeirsdottir, *A Commentary on the United Nations Convention on the Rights of the Child Article 13, the Right to Freedom of Expression* (Leiden, The Netherlands: Koninklijke Brill NV, 2006), 21.

[118] M. McLuhan, *Understanding Media: The Extensions of Man* (New York: McGraw-Hill, 1964), 7.

[119] UNCRC, article 13.

[120] Borrows, *Canada's Indigenous Constitution*, 84.

[121] UNCRC Committee, "Summary Record Regarding Portugal" (UN Doc. CRC/C/SR.251, 21 November 1995), [15]. "On one occasion the Committee referred to the right to access appropriate information", see UNCRC Committee, "Summary Record Regarding the Overseas Dependent Territories and Crown Dependencies of the United Kingdom of Great Britain and Northern Ireland" (UN Doc. CRC/C/SR.648, 13 December 2000), [41]; UNCRC Committee, "Concluding Observations on Portugal" (UN Doc. CRC/C/15/Add. 45, 27 November 1995), [16]; S. Langlaude, "On How to Build a Positive Understanding of the Child's Right to Freedom of Expression" (2010) 10(1) *Human Rights Law Review* 33, 38.

[122] UNCRC Committee, "Concluding Observations on Republic of Moldova" (UN Doc. CRC/C/MDA/CO/3, 20 February 2009), [33]–[34]; UNCRC Committee, "Summary Record Regarding Turkmenistan" (UN Doc. CRC/C/SR.1143), [18]: "where the Committee asked how children could obtain access to independent information, considering that the state party had no independent children's associations, that many libraries had been closed and that television was state-run"; UNCRC Committee, "Concluding Observations on Venezuela" (UN Doc. CRC/C/VEN/CO/2, 5 October 2007), [41].

[123] Langlaude, "On How to Build a Positive Understanding", 38.

[124] The UNCRC Committee "takes the example of New Zealand that is located in a remote corner of the world and points out the fact that not many New Zealand children travel as tourists to, for example, Europe" see UNCRC Committee, "Summary Record Regarding New

Under modern circumstances, many First Nations people are not taught to view the land, water and air as sacred gifts from the Creator.[125] According to custom, to ensure children understand the sacred relationship with water, the Cree use a sophisticated, experiential system that involves modelling, ceremonies, living on the land and personal sacrifice.[126] The Anishinabek even encode legal principles on the land.[127] They associate a particular living thing with a particular right and responsibility, transmit legal knowledge through storytelling[128] and are reminded of their role in the world through observations in nature. For example, the wild strawberry in Ontario, called *Odaemin* (heart berry) is a symbol of approbation for the selfless acts of *Odaemin*, who travelled a great distance to make a bridge between the living and the dead to enable the Anishinabek to continue their journey after leaving this life.[129] Seeing the berry reminds people to prepare for their own journey into the land of the dead[130] and is a reminder of their part in life's continuum. Since their law is "written" in the land, an Anishinabek child's right to an education, no less a legal education, is encompassed in the land. The right to education and to respect and thus understand one's culture, values and language includes rights to traverse unmodified land where the heart berry would remind children of their place on the planet.

Thus, through article 13, the UNCRC protects a child's right to information from his or her natural environment. By ensuring that children receive information from naturally vegetated areas, the UNCRC offers protection for undisturbed watersheds that absorb and filter contaminants from rainwater, mitigate flooding and reduce physical soil erosion and siltation that affect water quality. This would support Canada's Sustainable Development Strategy to protect ecosystems, species at risk and fisheries and to meet its climate adaptation goals.[131]

Children as Duty-Bearers, Multi-Stakeholder Participation, Life-Wide Equality

The UNCRC upholds the inclusion of indigenous children as agents of social change and duty-holders who have an important contribution to make to Canada's sustainable development related to water.

Zealand" (UN Doc. CRC/C/SR.364, 23 January 1997), [76], as cited in Langlaude, "On How to Build a Positive Understanding", 38.

[125] LaBoucane-Benson et al., "Are We Seeking Pimatisiwin or Creating Pomewin?", 14.
[126] Ibid., 8.
[127] Borrows, *Canada's Indigenous Constitution*, 81.
[128] Ibid., 79–80.
[129] E. Benton-Banai, *The Mishomis Book: The Voice of the Ojibway* (Hayward, WI: Indian Country Communications, 1988), 57; Borrows, *Canada's Indigenous Constitution*, 81.
[130] Borrows, *Canada's Indigenous Constitution*.
[131] Environment and Climate Change Canada, *A Federal Sustainable Development Strategy for Canada*, 13, 14, 16, 22.

As the first legally binding international instrument to incorporate the full range of human rights from civil and political rights to economic and social-cultural rights, the UNCRC is central to the consolidation of children as human beings and rights holders.[132] Although the lack of implementation of children's rights law is criticised, scholars see the creation of legal standards for children's rights as a process of norm setting that does not need to be top-down and adult-driven, but rather driven by daily realities in different social and cultural contexts that create local and legal meaning.[133] Although the duty-bearer in human rights and children's rights law technically applies to the domestic state that exercises jurisdiction over the child,[134] children have agency over their rights in society and law[135] and are also duty-bearers.[136]

This is consistent with the indigenous legal tradition that values participation and equality and holds that even the smallest and least powerful animals, such as the mole, can contribute to the resolution of issues and the understanding of justice and truth.[137] The indigenous believe that rules and decisions are not the exclusive purview of a select profession of legislators and judges. Although their legal education is not centralised and carried out by an elite, privileged class, but rather exists through informal, oral and uncentralised practices, it is not less legitimate. As well, there is precedent in recognising the supremacy of domestic customary law in conflict with code or statute in Western jurisdictions, such as Germany.[138] Thus, the full expression of children as human beings with civil and political rights and duties resonates very consistently with the indigenous understanding of children's rights and duties. Implementing the UNCRC would strengthen the application and practice of customary law in Canada, as it has been done in other Western countries.

Finally, the application of indigenous law, which recognises that each person and living being has an important role in the practice of law, would support sustainable development by improving dialogue on and review of decisions. In Canada, deference to administrative decision-makers, following *Dunsmuir*,[139]

---

[132] Malekian and Nordlof (eds.), *The Sovereignty of Children in Law*, 139; Vandenhole et al. (eds.), *Routledge International Handbook*, 55.

[133] Ibid., 38–39.

[134] Ibid.

[135] Malekian and Nordlof (eds.), *The Sovereignty of Children in Law*, 139.

[136] Vandenhole et al. (eds.), *Routledge International Handbook*, 55.

[137] See "Story by Phil Lane Jr., Four Worlds Development, University of Lethbridge in Lethbridge, Alberta, as retold by Richard Wagamese" in Royal Commission on Aboriginal Peoples, *The Final Report of the Royal Commission on Aboriginal Peoples* (Ottawa, ON: Supply Services, 1996), vol. 2, 102. As well, animals have legal personality; P. Driben et al., "No Killing Ground: Aboriginal Law Governing the Killing of Wildlife among the Cree and Ojibwa of Northern Ontario" (1997) 1 *Ayaangwaaminzin* 101. Borrows, *Canada's Indigenous Constitution*, 85, 119–121.

[138] U. Mattei, T. Ruskola and A. Gidi (eds.) *Schlesinger's Comparative Law: Cases-Text-Materials*, 7th ed. (New York: Foundation Press, 2009), 608.

[139] *Dunsmuir v. New Brunswick*, [2008] 1 S.C.R 190, 2008 SCC 9.

has created a regulatory regime that diminishes the legal threat to overturning an agency's decision. This increases the likelihood that an agency can successfully avoid compliance without successful review in court.[140] This system is detrimental to the protection of fish and their habitat under section 35 of the Fisheries Act,[141] because required standards are repeatedly renegotiated, resulting in a mandatory regime that bears little resemblance to the "law on the books".[142] By using indigenous law as a source of legal interpretation, however, such a high degree of deference and accommodation to one party in a position of authority would be challenged with a system that better values the contributions of multiple stakeholders in decision-making.

Local Knowledge

This vision of the child as a duty-bearer not only empowers children to express their own rights, and to learn and respect diverse identities, languages and values, but also is aligned with the indigenous principle of life-wide equality and legal agency. This indigenous principle is a model for multi-stakeholder engagement that supports the coordinated planning of river basins and facilitates the use of local knowledge.

The Anishinabek, for example, manage natural resources at a local level, with a close, familial identification with a component of the natural environment.[143] They also allocate resources through a combination of common stewardship and exclusive rights.[144] Family identification with a feature of nature and local leadership over a river basin or component of it is a model for watershed management that can be explored through source-water protection plans and river basin councils. The World Commission on Dams notes, "Locally driven processes to establish the objectives of environmental flows will lead to improved and sustainable outcomes for rivers, ecosystems and the riverine communities that depend on them."[145] These locally driven processes may also hold opportunities for (greater) child involvement where a child and his/her family is intimately familiar with the characteristics of a water flows, flora and fauna of river stretch. Indigenous law and child participation in that law can inform the participatory processes for the identification of environmental flow regimes that dam operators should replicate to ensure downstream ecosystem and livelihood objectives.[146] As well, Canada's

---

[140] Olszynski, "From 'Badly Wrong' to Worse", 39–40.
[141] *Fisheries Act* (R.S.C., 1985, c. F-14).
[142] Olszynski, "From 'Badly Wrong' to Worse", 39–40.
[143] Borrows, *Canada's Indigenous Constitution*, 77–78.
[144] Ibid., 78.
[145] World Commission on Dams, *Dams and Development: A New Framework for Decision-Making – The Report of the World Commission on Dams* (London: EarthScan, 2000), www.unep.org/dams/WCD/report/WCD_DAMS%20report.pdf, 239; Nowlan, "CPR for Canadian Rivers", 207.
[146] World Commission on Dams, *Dams and Development*, 294; Nowlan, "CPR for Canadian Rivers", 217.

2020 Biodiversity Targets and Goals,[147] the Canadian Environmental Protection Act[148] and the Species at Risk Act,[149] which emphasise partnerships and community participation,[150] are potential arenas for child participation and indigenous law to provide local knowledge. Indigenous law can also be used to create water commissions that are appropriate for the region.[151] The Mackenzie River Basin Transboundary Waters Management agreement and Mackenzie River Basin Board already recognise the importance of indigenous peoples' participation in sharing ecological knowledge, however the need for more engagement from youth, women and elders was identified.[152] By supporting education of indigenous knowledge, the UNCRC encourages children to acquire diverse *in-situ* knowledge gained through years of observation and experience[153] to use in future environmental management.

Rehabilitation, Restoration, Relationship-Building

Indigenous legal practices tend to resolve resource disputes in a way that builds relationships because they are "typically ... non-prescriptive, non-adversarial, and non-punitive. They generally promote values such as respect, restoration and consensus and are closely connected to the land, the Creator and the community".[154] Through stories designed to gain the support of the listener, these values are translated into action and decisions about concrete cases. They tend to focus on the process of conflict resolution or reconciliation rather than on norms.[155] For example, the Anishinabek believe that peace and friendship are important values in living a good life and they solve problems through discussion and consensus,[156] emphasising restorative, restitution-oriented solutions. For example, in solving a problem a community will:

1. wait, observe and collect information
2. consult with their friends and neighbours when it is apparent something is wrong

---

[147] Environment and Climate Change Canada, *2020 Biodiversity Goals and Targets for Canada* (Gatineau, QC: Government of Canada, 2016), www.biodivcanada.ca/9B5793F6-A972-4EF6-90A5-A4ADB021E9EA/3499%20-%202020%20Biodiversity%20Goals%20&%20Targets%20for%20Canada%20-%20Final%20Web_ENG.pdf, 2.

[148] *Canadian Environmental Protection Act* (S.C. 1999, c. 33).

[149] *Species at Risk Act* (S.C. 2002, c. 29).

[150] Matsui, "Water Ethics for First Nations", 7.

[151] White, "Editor in Chief Commentary", 2.

[152] Matsui, "Water Ethics for First Nations", 9.

[153] Ibid., 10.

[154] Law Commission of Canada, *Justice Within: Indigenous Legal Traditions: Discussion Paper* (Ottawa, ON: Government of Canada, 2006), 3.

[155] S. Grammond, *Terms of Coexistence: Indigenous Peoples and Canadian Law* (Toronto: Carswell, Thomson Reuters Canada Ltd., 2013), 369

[156] E. J. Danziger Jr., *The Chippewa of Lake Superior* (Norman: University of Oklahoma Press, 1978), 23; Borrows, *Canada's Indigenous Constitution*, 77.

3. help the person who is threatening or causing imminent harm
4. if the person does not respond to help and becomes an imminent threat to individuals or the community, he or she can be removed so that he or she does not harm others [though this is not applied as capital punishment]
5. help those who rely on that person by restoring what might be taken from them by the treatment
6. invite both the community and the individual to participate in the restoration.[157]

These principles support not only the precautionary principle of sustainable development but also focus on maintaining amicable relationships between diverse interests that sustain lasting decisions and balance multiple demands. In contrast to traditional common and civil law litigation, which may lead to polarisation and escalating conflict over time, aboriginal dispute resolution focuses on ensuring harmony in the greater community.

Anishinabek principles of restoration and restitution can be applied in the resolution of modern environmental disputes. Following these principles, individuals who would suffer a loss (e.g., of healthy fisheries) to serve a greater community need (e.g., business development) would receive the respect of the larger community and all parties would be invited to participate in restoration and reconciliation. Relying less on the current weakly applied and poorly enforced punitive measures to protect water and fisheries in Canada, indigenous principles would increase the resilience of environmental decision-making. Solving water resources disputes in a way that is non-adversarial meets multiple interests and is restorative to a community would increase effectiveness in implementing decisions. For example, in the court of Native judges in the Tsuu'T'ina Nation, Alberta, prosecutors work with peacemakers to "resolve [interpersonal] conflicts relying on the traditional concept of healthy human relationships".[158] These processes can also be applied to disputes involving water shortages, contamination, biodiversity and fisheries.

Further, with inter-jurisdictional problems between levels of government and the lack of an effective national approach to water allocation and flow protection requiring regulators from different levels of government to cooperate on water management either informally or formally through a multi-stakeholder plan,[159] the indigenous process of dispute resolution would be helpful. By protecting children's rights to information of all kinds including indigenous law, the UNCRC supports broader stakeholder involvement, the incorporation of local knowledge, as well as and processes of review and restorative dispute resolution that would support sustainable development.

---

[157] Borrows, *Canada's Indigenous Constitution*, 83.
[158] C. Bell and D. Kahane (eds.), *Intercultural Dispute Resolution in Aboriginal Contexts* (Vancouver: University of British Columbia Press, 2004), 213–231; Matsui, "Water Ethics for First Nations", 15.
[159] Nowlan, "CPR for Canadian Rivers", 113.

CONCLUSION

Anthony Lake, Executive Director of UNICEF, stated: "Sustainable development starts and ends with safe, healthy and well-educated children".[160] Indigenous law is a part of indigenous education: they cannot be separated. By guaranteeing a child's right to receive information, to respect his or her own cultural identity and to enjoy his or her own culture, the UNCRC is recognising a child's right to receive and practice his or her own legal traditions. Indigenous law is also dynamic, and it values diverse viewpoints, which are needed to move toward sustainability. By protecting aboriginal children's rights to inherit and practice their own legal traditions in Canada, the UNCRC supports a fuller enunciation and realisation of the country's SDGs.

Children have the right to receive information from nature as well as to their own language, laws and religion. They have a right to healthy development that meets not only material but also psychological and spiritual needs, and to participate in processes as duty-bearers and stakeholders in watershed management. Thus, children's rights as articulated in the UNCRC have an inherent role in achieving sustainable development in Canada. Children of all ethnicities are a part of the global challenges of biodiversity conservation (SDG 15) and water management (SDG 6),[161] and learning the traditional legal systems that cared for our interconnected living systems for millennia will help them in addressing these challenges. By fulfilling its obligation to recognise and teach children the indigenous laws of the land, and by respecting these laws as a critical source for interpreting existing statutes, Canada's government, Parliament and judiciary would expand the country's orientation toward natural harmony, interconnectedness between the natural and human world, and the restorative, rehabilitative and relationship-building methods of dispute resolution. This would improve Canada's capacity to achieve the long-term, multi-sector, and multi-stakeholder goals of clean water, healthy watersheds and sustainable fisheries as enumerated in its sustainable development strategy. Canadians may wonder what it would cost to apply indigenous laws, but the question is what more what they would gain.

---

[160] UNICEF, *A Post-2015 World Fit for Children: Sustainable Development Starts and Ends with Safe, Healthy and Well-Educated Children* (New York: UNICEF, 2013), www.unicef.org/socialpolicy/files/Sustainable_Development_post_2015.pdf, 1.

[161] UNGA, "Transforming Our World".

PART IV

Children's Rights in a Globalised World

12

Children's Rights, International Trade Law and Economic Globalisation

Sébastien Jodoin and Candice Pollack

INTRODUCTION

The concept of sustainable development in international law broadly entails that states have a "collective responsibility to advance and strengthen the interdependent and mutually reinforcing pillars of sustainable development – economic development, social development and environmental protection – at the local, national, regional and global levels".[1] The principle of integration that is inherent in this conception of sustainability thus requires that states should promote synergies and resolve conflicts emerging at the intersections of treaty regimes and related obligations in the fields of international trade and investment law, international environmental law and international human rights and social law.[2]

The integrative pursuit of sustainable development across different spheres of international law is most notably reflected in the efforts of scholars, advocates and policy-makers to reconcile the rights enshrined in the UN Convention on the Rights of the Child (UNCRC)[3] with the regulation of economic globalisation in its various guises.[4] Indeed, the emergence and growth of an international treaty

---

[1] UNDESA, Johannesburg Declaration on Sustainable Development (UN Doc. A/CONF.199/20, 4 September 2002), [5].
[2] See M. C. Cordonier Segger and A. Khalfan, *Sustainable Development Law: Principles, Practices and Prospects* (Oxford: Oxford University Press, 2004), 46–47.
[3] UN General Assembly (UNGA), Convention on the Rights of the Child (UN Doc. A/RES/44/25, 20 November 1989) 1577 UNTS 3. As is discussed elsewhere in this volume, the international instruments that aim to respect, protect and fulfil the human rights of children also include other treaties in international human rights law. Our primary focus in this chapter lies with the UNCRC however.
[4] See, for example, UN Human Rights Council, "Guiding Principles on Business and Human Rights: Implementing the United Nations 'Protect, Respect and Remedy' Framework: Report of the Special Representative of the Secretary-General on the Issue of Human Rights and Transnational Corporations and Other Business Enterprises, John Ruggie" (UN Doc. A/HRC/17/31, 21 March 2011); T. M. Collins and G. Guevara, "Some Considerations for Child Rights

regime focused on the promotion of the rights of children has had to contend with the rise and consolidation of another powerful treaty regime based around the set of multilateral agreements and institutions that make up the World Trade Organization (WTO).[5] A significant majority of states in the world belong to both treaty regimes, with the UNCRC having been ratified by all countries but one (the United States) and the WTO Single Undertaking currently having 164 members.[6] As has been the case in relation to the protection of the environment, public health and human rights more broadly, whether and how the legal obligations of State Parties to both treaty regimes may interact with one another remains a key point of contention for the realisation of sustainable development.[7] For another, the growth in the power and influence of multinational corporations resulting from expanding levels of trade and economic liberalisation has meant that advancing the rights of children largely transcends the capabilities of many governments, especially in developing countries.[8] This new reality has required innovative approaches for monitoring and governing the activities of business actors and ensuring that they contribute to, rather than detract from, efforts to respect, protect and fulfil the rights of children around the world.[9]

This chapter examines the opportunities and challenges for protecting and promoting the rights of children within the field of international trade law and the globalised economy to which it has given rise. In doing so, we adopt a rights-based approach to sustainable development that sees the realisation of human rights as embracing the economic, environmental and social pillars

---

Impact Assessment (CRIAs) of Business" (2014) 44(1) *Revue générale de droit* 153; UNCRC Committee, "General Comment No. 16 (2013) on State Obligations Regarding the Impact of Business on Children's Rights" (UN Doc. CRC/C/GC/16, 7 February 2013); K. McPhail, "Corporate Responsibility to Respect Human Rights and Business Schools' Responsibility to Teach It: Incorporating Human Rights into the Sustainability Agenda" (2013) 22 *Accounting Education: An International Journal* 391.

[5] World Trade Organisation, General Agreement on Tariffs and Trade (30 October 1947) 58 UNTS 187.

[6] United Nations Treaty Collection, https://treaties.un.org/Pages/ViewDetails.aspx?src=TREATY&mtdsg_no=IV-11&chapter=4&clang=_en; World Trade Organisation, www.wto.org/english/thewto_e/whatis_e/tif_e/org6_e.htm.

[7] See, for example, J. M. Diller and D. A. Levy, "Child Labor, Trade and Investment: Toward the Harmonization of International Law" (1997) 91(4) *American Journal of International Law* 66; B. J. Stevenson, "Pursuing an End to Foreign Child Labour through US Trade Law: WTO Challenges and Doctrinal Solutions" (2002) 7 *UCLA Journal of International Law & Foreign Affairs* 129; D. Samida, "Protecting the Innocent or Protecting Special Interests? Child Labor, Globalization, and the WTO" (2005) 33(3) *Denver Journal of International Law & Policy* 411.

[8] UNGA, "Globalization and Its Impact on the Full Enjoyment of All Human Rights" (UN Doc. A/55/342, 31 August 2000), [42]. See also T. M. Collins, "The Relationship between Children's Rights and Business" (2014) 18(6) *International Journal of Human Rights* 583.

[9] The "Respect, Protect, Fulfill" framework and its resulting obligations for states and businesses in the human rights contexts was established in the following: UN Human Rights Council, "Guiding Principles on Business and Human Rights".

of sustainable development.[10] We proceed as follows. In "Children's Rights, International Trade and Economic Globalisation", we review the effects of trade liberalisation and economic globalisation on the rights of children around the world. We outline the benefits and disadvantages of the economic growth emanating from the expansion of international trade, with emphasis on its implications for state and corporate obligations to protect, respect and fulfil the rights of children under the UNCRC. In "The Rights of Children and Trade Liberalisation under International Law", we discuss the relationship between legal obligations relating to the protection of the rights of children and those relating to the liberalisation of trade under international law. We begin by outlining a children's rights approach to international trade based on the UNCRC and then discuss whether and how the promotion of the rights of children could be accommodated within the rules and principles of the WTO. In "Instruments for Protecting the Rights of Children in a Globalising World", we consider two potential instruments for advancing the rights of children at the intersections of these two regimes, namely children's rights impact assessments and non-state market-driven certification programmes. In "Conclusion", we conclude with a broader discussion of the prospects for protecting children's rights in a globalising world and how this may contribute to the realisation of more sustainable forms of development.

CHILDREN'S RIGHTS, INTERNATIONAL TRADE AND ECONOMIC GLOBALISATION

Whether and how the liberalisation of international trade and intensifying levels of economic globalisation have affected the rights of children remains a controversial issue among scholars. Many scholars suggest that globalisation has contributed to the reduction of poverty in developing countries, with related improvements in the welfare of children.[11] Alternatively, critics submit that international trade has engendered a race to the bottom in the protection of basic human and children's rights, as states have lowered their social and environmental standards to attract investment from multinational corporations.[12] The better view, as expressed by the UN Committee on the Rights of the Child, is that the effects of economic globalisation on the well-being of children are much more disparate and nuanced than one-sided, as children are "rights-holders and stakeholders in business as consumers, legally engaged employees, future employees and business leaders and members of

---

[10] See D. McGoldrick, "Sustainable Development and Human Rights: An Integrated Conception" (1996) 45 *International and Comparative Law Quarterly* 796; S. Jodoin, "Rights, Integrity and the Principle of Sustainable Development: Dworkinian Reflections on the Sustainability of International Law" (2012) 56 *Supreme Court Law Review* 703.

[11] J. L. Dunoff, "Does Globalization Advance Human Rights?" (1999) 25 *Brooklyn Journal of International Law* 125, 128.

[12] See, for example, Collins, "The Relationship between Children's Rights and Business".

communities and environments in which business operates".[13] In what follows, we draw on existing scholarly literature and policy documents to review both the positive and negative effects of international trade on the rights of children around the world.

The Positive Implications of International Trade for the Rights of Children

Many observers argue that the liberalisation and expansion of international trade has a marked effect on a nation's wealth. According to standard economic theory, investment and open markets for international trade should lead to economic growth.[14] In turn, as stated by the UN General Assembly, economic growth should normally result in greater respect for children's rights.[15] Indeed, in Vietnam, the UN International Children's Fund (UNICEF) has noted that economic reforms that encouraged foreign investment and trade had a direct, and beneficial, impact on the rights of children, in particular their right under article 27 of the UNCRC to a standard of living that is adequate for their overall development.[16] The underlying rationale of this beneficial impact is twofold. First, greater economic wealth can engender an increase in the resources that are available to the state,[17] which, in the context of children, results in improved access to health-care services, better primary education, affordable housing for their families, and more. Second, the economic growth that results from trade liberalisation can create more employment opportunities, and increase the per capita income in developing countries.[18] As such, parents with improved incomes are better able to meet their children's needs with respect to food, health, shelter and care, and are no longer required to send their children off to work to make ends meet.[19]

Furthermore, many scholars argue that the internationalisation of supply chains generated through trade liberalisation has brought along with it a greater awareness of international human and children's rights abuses in developing countries. Most notably, businesses that fail to undertake their due diligence in their relations with third-party suppliers often have products that are produced in ways that violate the rights of children. The most common such violation relates to the use of child labour, which currently affects approximately 250 million children internationally

---

[13] UNCRC Committee, "General Comment No. 16 (2013)", [2].
[14] J. D. Sachs, "Globalization and Patterns of Economic Development" (2000) 136 *Weltwirtschaftliches Archiv* 579, 579.
[15] UNGA, "Globalization and Its Impact on the Full Enjoyment of All Human Rights", [13].
[16] UN Economic, Social and Cultural Council, "Economic, Social and Cultural Rights: Human Rights, Trade and Investment: Report of the High Commissioner for Human Rights" (UN Doc. E/CN.4/Sub.2/2003/9, 2 July 2003) [10].
[17] UNGA, "Globalization and Its Impact on the Full Enjoyment of All Human Rights", [13].
[18] Ibid., [13]. See also Dunoff, "Does Globalization Advance Human Rights?", 126.
[19] A. Zutshi, A. Creed and A. Sohal, "Child Labour and Supply Chain: Profitability or (Mis)management" (2009) 21(1) *European Business Review* 42, 50.

between the ages of 4 to 15.[20] In addition to child labour, businesses may also infringe on other children's rights, such as their right to a healthy and safe environment or their right to play.[21] Recent scandals involving the use of child labour reveal that market forces can be harnessed by nongovernmental organization (NGOs) to pressure multinational corporations to ensure that their supply chains do not violate article 32 of the UNCRC. Indeed, as a result of negative media attention as well as increased consumer awareness and concern, corporate entities have committed to eliminating child labour in their supply chains and taken action to phase child labourers out of the production line and into the education system.[22] As such, the linkages fostered through the supply chains that have emerged through economic globalisation have helped raised international awareness about certain children's rights violations and offered scope for the adoption of proactive measures to address them.

Finally, the liberalisation of international trade has encouraged the advent of foreign businesses in communities with evolving economies. While some of these businesses may have negative effects on the welfare of children, others may also provide children with essential goods and services that they need to grow and develop.[23] These include things like sports equipment and reading materials, food, training opportunities for employment, emergency relief during natural disasters, and more.[24] Moreover, as highlighted by the UN Committee on the Rights of the Child, many international corporations also "play a role in the provision and management of services such as clean water, sanitation, education, transport, health, alternative care, energy, security and detention facilities that are critical to the enjoyment of children's rights".[25] Accordingly, the establishment of corporate entities in communities that comes as a result of globalisation has shifted some of the onus for the welfare of children away from already overburdened developing States, and businesses have begun to assume a collaborative

---

[20] B. McClintock, "Trade As if Children Mattered" (2001) 28 *International Journal of Social Economics* 899, 899. *Child labour* is defined by UNICEF as the engagement of children in work when they are too young, and/or the work involves activities that are hazardous to the physical, mental, social or educational development of the child. It is distinguished from the term *child work*, which refers to paid or unpaid forms of work that are not harmful or exploitative of a child. See http://data.unicef.org/child-protection/child-labour.html. See also Collins, "The Relationship between Children's Rights and Business", 600–602.

[21] UNICEF, The Global Compact and Save the Children, *How Business Affects Us: A Report of Children's Consultations, Children's Rights and Business Principles* (Save the Children, 2011), 8.

[22] Zutshi et al., "Child Labour and Supply Chain", 57. The UN High Commissioner for Human Rights has noted a need for corporate entities to take preventative measures to address potential human rights violations, due to the increased consumer awareness of international human rights violations (UN High Commissioner for Human Rights, "Business and Human Rights: A Progress Report" [2000], www.ohchr.org/Documents/Publications/BusinessHRen.pdf).

[23] UNICEF, *The Global Compact*, and Save the Children, *How Business Affects Us*, 6.

[24] Ibid., 9.

[25] UNCRC Committee, "General Comment No. 16 (2013)", [33].

role in addressing the complexities that come with the provision and protection of the socioeconomic rights of children.[26]

The Negative Implications of International Trade for the Rights of Children

There are undoubtedly several negative implications that have come along with the liberalisation and expansion of international trade as well. First, Dunoff argues that trade liberalisation has left the economies of emerging markets dependent on those of advanced markets, rendering them defenceless to external shocks and fluctuations.[27] The Asian Financial Crisis of 1997 is one example of the vulnerability of developing nations to market fluctuations; when the short-term capital investment stopped coming in, several states suffered rising private debt, devalued stock markets and near collapses in currency.[28] Therefore, while trade liberalisation may increase economic growth, it can also lead to recession, financial insecurity and poverty,[29] which in turn may make it harder for states to fulfil many of the socioeconomic rights under the UNCRC, including the rights to education, housing, food and adequate health care. Additionally, the intensification of economic globalisation has also contributed to an exacerbation of the gap between the emerging and advanced markets.[30] According to the UN General Assembly, developed states disproportionately benefit from the advantages of trade liberalisation, as developing nations face greater barriers to trade, obtain less investment, and are often forced to adopt economic policies consistent with the values of the investor.[31] The gains from international trade have also not been shared uniformly within many countries and have contributed to increased levels of economic inequality.[32] In his review of the literature on corruption in developing countries, Otusanya found that the combined cost of trade liberalisation in sub-Saharan African countries over the past 20 years could have been used to relieve all debt, as well as vaccinate and educate every child in the region.[33] Instead, the majority of sub-Saharan African people

---

[26] Collins, "The Relationship between Children's Rights and Business", 583.
[27] Dunoff, "Does Globalization Advance Human Rights?", 128.
[28] Ibid.
[29] UNGA, "Globalization and Its Impact on the Full Enjoyment of All Human Rights", [4]. A greater discussion of the economic impacts of globalisation can be found in W. Milberg and D. Winkler, "Economic Insecurity in the New Wave of Globalization" (Working Paper Series of the Schwartz Center for Economic Policy Analysis, 2009).
[30] Dunoff, "Does Globalization Advance Human Rights?", 127.
[31] Numbers indicate that the incidence of child labour in low-income countries is much higher than in low-middle and upper-middle income countries (Y. Diallo, A. Etienne and F. Mehran, Global Child Labour Trends 2008–2012 (Geneva: International Labour Organisation, 2013). See also, UNGA, "Globalization and Its Impact on the Full Enjoyment of All Human Rights", [32]; Dunoff, "Does Globalization Advance Human Rights?"
[32] Dunoff, "Does Globalization Advance Human Rights?", 127.
[33] O. J. Otusanya, "Corruption as an Obstacle to Development in Developing Countries: A Review of Literature" (2011) 14 Journal of Money Laundering Control 30(7), 404–405.

continue to live in poverty, while corrupt political leaders economically thrive. For example, in Kenya in the 1990s, nearly US$8 billion was diverted into foreign bank accounts held by corrupt politicians, including then-president Mobutu.[34] Thus, the benefits from the expansion of international trade can contribute to economic disparity, and often have little to no effect on the poorest and most vulnerable populations of developing nations.

Second, many scholars argue that economic globalisation has, in several instances, caused a race to the bottom in the protection of children's rights, especially in the context of their right to be safe from exploitative work.[35] As multinational corporations grow to unfathomable levels of wealth, the power imbalance in the market increases in their favour.[36] Thus, business entities usually have the upper hand, and sometimes demand that a state turn a blind eye to its human rights violations, in particular its use of child labour, in exchange for further investment.[37] Given that the corporate bottom line is profit maximisation, and that corporations are directing the flow of capital and bringing in high margins of investment, many state actors are unlikely to intervene to enforce their labour laws, thus resulting in long work hours, hazardous conditions and low wages for the children employed.[38] In some cases, states will even surreptitiously lower their labour rights protections to draw in investors.[39] Accordingly, trade globalisation can also result in States neglecting their obligations to protect and respect children's

---

[34] Ibid., 401.
[35] Dunoff, "Does Globalization Advance Human Rights?", 127. With respect to labour exploitation of children, several authors suggest a negative relationship between economic openness in developing countries and child labour, or foreign direct investment and child labour. See in particular: U. Iram and A. Fatima, "International Trade, Foreign Direct Investment and the Phenomenon of Child Labour: The Case of Pakistan" (2008) 35 *International Journal of Social Economics* 809; O. Dagdemir and H. Acaroglu, "The Effects of Globalization on Child Labour in Developing Countries" (2010) 2 *Business and Economic Horizons* 37.
[36] UNGA, "Globalization and Its Impact on the Full Enjoyment of All Human Rights", [42]. See also K. McPhail, "Corporate Responsibility to Respect Human Rights and Business Schools' Responsibility to Teach It: Incorporating Human Rights into the Sustainability Agenda" (2013) 22 *Accounting Education: An International Journal* 391, 392.
[37] UNGA, "Globalization and Its Impact on the Full Enjoyment of All Human Rights", [42]. See also UNCRC Committee, "General Comment No. 16 (2013)", [27]–[28].
[38] UNICEF et al., *How Business Affects Us*, 7. While most states have implemented legislation prohibiting the use of child labour, studies as recent as 2012 indicate that 76 countries "pose extreme child labour complicity risks" (see https://maplecroft.com/about/news/child_labour_2012.html). Moreover, in the last two decades, several media sources have reported the failures of state actors to intervene in child rights violations committed by both local businesses and large multinational corporations. See, for example, K. Collins, "Apple, Samsung and Sony under Fire Over Child Miners in Africa" (CNET, 19 January 2016); J. Burke, "Child Labour Scandal Hits Adidas" (*The Guardian*, 19 November 2000); A. Bezlova, "China: Child Labour Scandal Exposes Gross Corruption" (Inter Press Service, 18 June 2007).
[39] UNGA, "Globalization and Its Impact on the Full Enjoyment of All Human Rights", [42]. General Comment No. 16 of the UNCRC also notes that states have an obligation not to facilitate, aid or abet the infringement of children's rights by businesses either directly or indirectly through lowering human rights standards for investment.

rights, and the competition for investment could theoretically create an international race to the bottom in the name of economic growth.

Finally, globalisation has brought about unregulated industrialisation within states with developing markets, which can have negative effects on the communal well-being of children. International trade has resulted in business enterprises sprouting in communities that were traditionally un-urbanised. As previously noted, these corporations often face little state regulation of their activities, allowing them to negatively affect the environmental and social well-being of the children in these communities. For example, corporations often build their manufacturing plants in areas that children were previously using for play, or so close to these areas that the harmful pollutants released by the business damage the play environment.[40] In the context of social impacts, White submits that the presence and marketing of new industries in developing communities has resulted in a Westernisation of the concept of childhood.[41] In essence, foreign corporations encourage the purchase of products and services particular to a Westernised lifestyle,[42] and the children in developing communities subsequently define their own standard of living according to that of their Western counterparts. The children in these communities do not have access to the same resources and, as a result, seek out labour opportunities to be able to afford to purchase the products and services they think are integral to childhood.[43] Thus, while globalisation can bring economic growth into developing markets, it can also have negative effects on the rights of children and their well-being.

THE RIGHTS OF CHILDREN AND TRADE LIBERALISATION UNDER INTERNATIONAL LAW

Understanding the relationship between legal obligations relating to the rights of children and the liberalisation of trade is ultimately connected to the broader enterprise of uncovering and clarifying the nature and extent of interactions between overlapping treaty regimes,[44] which forms a central concern for the pursuit of sustainable development in international law.[45] As a general rule, international

---

[40] UNICEF et al., *How Business Affects Us*, 8.
[41] B. White, "Globalization and the Child Labour Problem" (1996) 8 *Journal of International Development* 829, 831.
[42] Ibid., 832.
[43] Ibid.
[44] This is a recurring topic in the study and practice of international trade law. See in particular J. Pauwelyn, *Conflict of Norms in Public International Law: How WTO Law Relates to Other Rules of International Law* (Cambridge: Cambridge University Press, 2003); T. Cottier, J. Pauwelyn and E. Bürgi (eds.), *Human Rights and International Trade* (Oxford: Oxford University Press, 2005).
[45] See M. W. Gehring and M. C. Cordonier Segger (eds.), *Sustainable Development in World Trade Law* (The Hague, The Netherlands: Kluwer Law International, 2005).

legal obligations stemming from different treaty regimes are held as having an equal status under international law, with the notable exception of *jus cogens* norms, such as the prohibitions on torture, slavery or genocide.[46]

This proposition has two important corollaries that shape the relationship between the legal norms of the UNCRC and the WTO. First, states are obliged to ensure that they interpret and apply their legal obligations under different international treaties in a consistent manner[47] that avoids normative conflicts whenever and to the extent possible.[48] Second, if conflict between two treaty regimes cannot be resolved through interpretation, legal norms from one regime do not absolve states of their concurrent responsibilities to comply with those of another.[49] Accordingly, regardless of whether a particular measure is permitted under the WTO, states may nonetheless be held in breach of their obligations under the UNCRC for adopting it (and vice versa).[50] In what follows, we discuss the implications of the pursuit of mutual complementarity and the recognition of concurrent responsibilities at the intersections of children's rights and international trade within the context of both treaty regimes, beginning with the UNCRC and then turning to the WTO.

International Trade and the Rights of Children under the UNCRC

As a general matter, the liberalisation of international trade should not be seen as incompatible with the promotion and protection of the rights of children. Neither the objectives nor the provisions of the UNCRC specifically address issues relating to international trade, investment and economic globalisation. Moreover, in practical terms, the expansion of international trade in goods and services can have positive as well as negative implications for children's rights.[51] The argument advanced by the UN High Commissioner for Human Rights in relation to the broader relationship between human rights and international trade applies equally to the UNCRC: "Human rights law is *neutral* with regard to trade

---

[46] M. N. Shaw, *International Law* (Cambridge: Cambridge University Press, 2008), 123–127.

[47] United Nations, Vienna Convention on the Law of Treaties (23 May 1969) 1155 UNTS 331, article 31(3)(c) (providing that the interpretation of a treaty shall consider "any relevant rules of international law applicable in the relations between the parties").

[48] UNGA, "Fragmentation of International Law: Difficulties Arising from the Diversification of and Expansion of International Law: Report of the Study Group of the International Law Commission" (UN Doc. A/CN.4/L.682, 13 April 2006), [37].

[49] See generally B. Simma and D. Pulkowski, "Of Planets and the Universe: Self-Contained Regimes in International Law" (2006) 17(3) *European Journal of International Law* 483. See also G. Marceau, "Conflicts of Norms and Conflicts of Jurisdictions" (2001) 35(6) *Journal of World Trade* 1081.

[50] G. Marceau, "WTO Dispute Settlement and Human Rights" (2002) 13(4) *European Journal of International Law* 753, 802–804.

[51] See "Children's Rights, International Trade and Economic Globalisation". See also UNCRC Committee, "General Comment No. 16 (2013)".

liberalization or trade protectionism. Instead, a human rights approach to trade focuses on processes and outcomes – how trade affects the enjoyment of human rights – and places the promotion and protection of human rights among the objectives of trade reform".[52] This perspective suggests, as has been asserted by the UN Committee on Economic, Social, and Cultural Rights, that international trade "must be understood as a means, not an end" and that it should further "the objective of human well-being to which the international human rights instruments give legal expression".[53]

While the liberalisation of international trade can be reconciled with the objectives and purposes of the UNCRC, this does not mean that this latter treaty does not create legal obligations that should inform the way in which states approach trade and related economic issues. The broad and comprehensive nature of the rights protected under the UNCRC and the duties that they create for states are discussed throughout this volume and will not be reiterated here. We simply highlight two important ways in which children's rights and related obligations may intersect with international trade. First, the UNCRC obliges states to take into account and comply with their obligations to respect, protect and fulfil the economic, social and cultural rights of children in the context of the domestic implementation of their international commitments to trade liberalisation. As highlighted by a variety of international human rights bodies, some of the key rights that might be negatively affected by international trade law most notably include: the right to health (article 24)[54] and the right to an adequate standard of living, including access to food, water and shelter (article 27).[55] As a result of their general obligations under the UNCRC, states are obliged to evaluate the impact of trade agreements on the fulfilment of these rights within their jurisdiction[56] and to adopt appropriate legislative, administrative and other measures to ensure their implementation.[57]

Second, the UNCRC obliges states to cooperate with one another to ensure the full realisation of economic, social and cultural rights around the world, as is the

---

[52] Office of High Commissioner for Human Rights, "Human Rights and Trade" (Statement to the Fifth Ministerial Conference of the World Trade Organization" [2003]), www2.ohchr.org/english/issues/globalization/trade/docs/5WTOMinisterialCancun.pdf, 4 (emphasis in original).

[53] UN Economic and Social Council, "Statement of the UN committee on Economic, Social and Cultural Rights to the Third Ministerial Conference of the World Trade Organization" (UN Doc. E/C.12/1999/9, 26 November 1999), [6].

[54] (UN Doc. CRC/C/15/Add.261, 21 September 2005), [21]: "Committee finally recommends that the State party ensure that Free Trade Agreements do not negatively affect the rights of children, inter alia, in terms of access to affordable medicines, including generic ones".

[55] ICESCR Committee, "General Comment No. 15 (2003) on the right to water (arts. 11 and 12 of the Covenant)" (UN Doc. E/C.12/2002/11, 20 January 2003), [35].

[56] UNCRC Committee, "General Comment No. 5 (2003) on General Measures of Implementation for the Convention on the Rights of the Child" (UN Doc. CRC/GC/2003/5, 27 November 2003), [45]–[47].

[57] Ibid., [24]–[31].

case under the International Covenant on Economic, Social, and Cultural Rights.[58] Article 4 of the UNCRC specifically provides that "[w]ith regard to economic, social and cultural rights, States Parties shall undertake such measures to the maximum extent of their available resources and, where needed, within the framework of international co-operation". This obligation of international cooperation has two important implications for the pursuit of international trade. For one thing, both developed and developing countries should ensure that the conclusion and implementation of international trade agreements takes into account their respective obligations to ensure the full realisation of the rights of children.[59] For instance, in its concluding observations on the implementation of the UNCRC in Nicaragua, the Committee on the Rights of the Child expressed concern that "the free trade agreements currently under negotiation may negatively impact on the allocation of budget for social services" and recommended that "the State party ensure that free trade agreements do not negatively affect the rights of children, e.g. in terms of access to affordable medicines".[60] Likewise, in its concluding observations on the implementation of UNCRC in Australia, the Committee called on the State party to ensure "human rights impact assessment, including child rights impact assessments, are conducted prior to the conclusion of trade agreements with a view to ensuring that measures are taken to prevent child rights violations from occurring".[61] For another, according to the Committee, the obligation of international cooperation should also shape the activities of the WTO:

> In their promotion of international cooperation and technical assistance, all International United Nations and United Nations-related agencies should be guided by the Convention and should mainstream children's rights throughout their activities. They should seek to ensure within their influence that international cooperation is targeted at supporting States to fulfil their obligations under the Convention. Similarly the World Bank Group, the Monetary Fund and World Trade Organization should ensure that their activities related to international cooperation and economic development give primary consideration to the best interests of children and promote full implementation of the Convention.[62]

In sum, the UNCRC requires that State Parties adopt an approach to the negotiation and implementation of international trade agreements that is based on the

---

[58] UNGA, International Covenant on Economic, Social and Cultural Rights (UN Doc. A/6316, 16 December 1966) 992 UNTS 3, article 2(1); See generally, P. Alston and G. Quinn, "The Nature and Scope of States Parties' Obligations under the International Covenant on Economic, Social and Cultural Rights" (1987) *Human Rights Quarterly* 156.

[59] W. Vandenhole, "Economic, Social and Cultural Rights in the CRC: Is There a Legal Obligation to Cooperate Internationally for Development" (2009) 17 *International Journal of Children's Rights* 23, 45–46.

[60] (UN Doc. CRC/C/15/Add.265, 21 September 2005), [16], [17].

[61] (UN Doc. CRC/C/AUS/CO/4, 28 August 2012) [28(c)].

[62] UNCRC Committee, "General Comment No. 5 (2003)", [64]. See also UNCRC Committee, "General Comment No. 16 (2013)", [47]–[48].

fulfilment of the rights of children. As explained by de Schutter, this sort of children's rights-based approach to trade "shifts the perspective from aggregate values – from the benefits of trade for the country as a whole – to the impacts of trade on the most vulnerable and ... insecure".[63] On the whole, a children's rights-based approach to international trade calls for the broad set of interventions that are discussed throughout this volume and that are necessary to respect, protect and fulfil the rights of children in the context of expanding levels of international trade. This would most notably include the adoption of legislative and administrative measures and the development of a national strategy that takes into account and addresses the adverse effects of trade on the rights of children; the establishment of coordinating and monitoring bodies to collect data, raise awareness, provide training and build capacity among public officials, civil society actors and business on the relationship between international trade and children's rights; and the provision of effective remedies for violations of children's rights that occur in the context of economic globalisation.[64] Within the particular context of the development and implementation of trade agreements, such an approach would most notably entail ensuring greater coordination between government bodies responsible for trade and investment issues and those dedicated to the protection of the rights of children[65] and making use of children's rights impact assessments as a key monitoring and decision-making tool for trade-related matters.[66]

The Promotion of the Rights of Children and the Adoption of Trade Measures under the WTO

The purposes and rules of international trade law are likewise not inherently in opposition with those aimed at advancing the rights of children and could thus be read in a manner that is consistent with relevant obligations encapsulated within the UNCRC.[67] Many authors have argued that the references to raising "standards of living" and the principle of "sustainable development" enshrined in the preamble to the WTO offer significant potential for accommodating and avoiding overlaps and conflicts between WTO law and the international protection of human rights.[68]

---

[63] UNGA, "Mission to the World Trade Organization: Report of the Special Rapporteur on the Right to Food, Olivier de Schutter" (UN Doc. A/HRC/10/5/Add.2, 4 February 2009), 5.
[64] UNCRC Committee, "General Comment No. 5 (2003)".
[65] UNCRC Committee, "General Comment No. 16 (2013)", [46], [75].
[66] This instrument is discussed in depth in "Children's Rights Impact Assessments".
[67] Diller and Levy, "Child Labor, Trade and Investment".
[68] See, for example, Marceau, "WTO Dispute Settlement and Human Rights"; M. Mutua and R. Howse, "Protecting Human Rights in a Global Economy: Challenges for the World Trade Organization" (International Center for Human Rights and Democratic Development, Policy Paper, 2002); M. C. Cordonier Segger, "Integrating Social and Economic Development and Environmental Protection in World Trade Law", in Gehring and Cordonier Segger (eds.), *Sustainable Development in World Trade Law*, 133.

In particular, as will be discussed further in the following text, the exceptions related to the protection of "public morals" or "human, animal or plant life or health" set out in article XX of the General Agreement on Tariffs and Trade (GATT) could be interpreted through a flexible and evolutionary approach that takes into account relevant provisions of the UNCRC.[69] In general, as Marceau concludes, "[G]ood faith interpretation and application of WTO provisions, taking into account relevant human rights law, and the exercise of exception provisions will suffice to coordinate WTO and human rights legal systems".[70]

While the WTO treaty regime is not fundamentally incompatible with the protection of the rights of children as such, it does set a number of requirements (known as trade disciplines) that may significantly affect the ability of states to adopt measures to promote these rights. We illustrate this point by discussing whether trade measures adopted for the purposes of eradicating child labour could be found to be WTO compliant. Child labour serves as a useful example for assessing the potential constraints imposed by the WTO on the promotion of children's rights through trade because it constitutes such a clear violation of the UNCRC[71] (as well as international labour law).[72] If the adoption of trade measures aimed at eliminating child labour cannot be reconciled with the provisions of the WTO, the protection of other children's rights through trade measures is unlikely to pass muster either.[73]

We will briefly examine the legality of two types of trade measures within the framework of the WTO. To begin with, a state could ban goods produced through the use of child labour by forbidding the import of such goods across the border or their sale within the country.[74] Such a ban would amount to a *prima facie* violation

---

[69] Diller and Levy, "Child Labor, Trade and Investment", 595–696; Stevenson, "Pursuing and End to Foreign Child Labour", 158–163. In addition to this interpretative argument, a narrower approach has also been advanced to the effect that a state's participation in an international human rights treaty like the UNCRC could serve as evidence of the "necessity" of the adoption of trade measures adopted pursuant to either of these articles. See Marceau, "WTO Dispute Settlement and Human Rights", 789–791.

[70] Marceau, "WTO Dispute Settlement and Human Rights", 802–804.

[71] UNCRC, article 32: "The government should protect children from work that is dangerous or might harm their health or their education. While the Convention protects children from harmful and exploitative work, there is nothing in it that prohibits parents from expecting their children to help out at home in ways that are safe and appropriate to their age. If children help out in a family farm or business, the tasks they do be safe and suited to their level of development and comply with national labour laws. Children's work should not jeopardize any of their other rights, including the right to education, or the right to relaxation and play".

[72] International Labour Organization (ILO), Convention Concerning the Prohibition and Immediate Action for the Elimination of the Worst Forms of Child Labour (ILO No. 182, 17 June 1999) 2133 UNTS 161; ILO, Declaration on Fundamental Principles and Rights at Work (18 June 1988), [2(c)]. However, whether this should be the case is discussed in Chapter 13 of this volume.

[73] Although the following section refers to child labour as taking place in developing countries, child labour also exists in developed countries as well, though to a different extent and better conditions (see White, "Globalization and Child Labour Problem", 831–832).

[74] Stevenson, "Pursuing and End to Foreign Child Labour", 157–158.

of the GATT, with the import embargo running afoul of the prohibition on quantitative restrictions[75] and the restriction on sales contravening the most favoured nation treatment rule (MFN).[76] To be permissible under the WTO, such a ban would need to fall within one of the general exceptions set out in GATT article XX. In its *Reformulated Gasoline* ruling, the WTO Appellate Body set out a two-step process for assessing whether a trade measure that would be otherwise inconsistent with the GATT could be justified under article XX.[77] To begin with, the measure's design and objective must fall properly under one of the exceptions enumerated in article XX. In addition, if an otherwise unlawful measure falls within the ambit of these exceptions, it must also meet the criteria set out in the chapeau to article XX, namely that they not be applied "in a manner which would constitute a means of arbitrary or unjustifiable discrimination between countries where the same conditions prevail, or a disguised restriction on international trade".

The main hurdle for justifying bans on goods produced through child labour pertains to the first step in this test. The general exceptions that could be used to justify bans on goods produced through child labour are those that relate to trade measures "necessary to protect public morals" (article XX(a)) and those that are "necessary to protect human, animal or plant life or health" (article XX(b)). The key question that would need to be further addressed is whether such bans are "necessary" to protect public morals or human health, within the meaning of articles XX(a) or XX(b).[78] Given that the prohibition of child labour is enshrined in both the UNCRC and recognised as part of the International Labour Organization's core principles, we suggest that there is indeed a reasonable fit between a ban on the products of child labour and the protection of public morals within the ambit of article XX(a).[79] The matter is far from clear with respect to article XX(b), however, with scholars unable to agree on the extent to which such a ban would be effective

---

[75] GATT, article XI: "No prohibitions or restrictions ... whether made effective through quotas, import or export licenses or other measures, shall be instituted or maintained by any contracting party on the importation of any product of the territory of any other contracting party".

[76] GATT, article III(2): "The products of the territory of any contracting party imported into the territory of any other contracting party shall be accorded treatment no less favourable than that accorded to like products of national origin in respect of all laws, regulations and requirements affecting their internal sale, offering for sale, purchase, transportation, distribution or use".

[77] WTO Appellate Body, "Report on United States – Standards for Reformulated and Conventional Gasoline" (WT/DS2/AB/R, 12 April 1996), 22.

[78] The WTO Appellate Body has defined the concept of necessity in this context as entailing that a particular trade measure constitutes a plausible way of achieving objectives falling within these general exceptions and that it is less trade-restrictive than reasonable available alternatives that would achieve the same result. See WTO Appellate Body, "Report on United States – Measures Affecting the Cross-Border Supply of Gambling and Betting Services" (WT/DS285/AB/R, 7 April 2005), 101–103; WTO Appellate Body, "Report on Korea – Various Import Measures on Fresh, Chilled and Frozen Beef" (WT/DS161/AB/R, WT/DS169/AB/R, 10 January 2001), [161]–[164].

[79] Stevenson, "Pursuing and End to Foreign Child Labour", 159–165.

in protecting the health of children.[80] Moreover, evaluating the necessity of such bans under either article XX(a) or XX(b) would turn on a factual assessment of whether other less trade-restrictive measures, such as social labelling, preferential trade treatment, or development assistance, would fulfil the same objectives.

Another potential trade measure would entail conditioning access to preferential trade treatment on the basis of whether a developing country has adopted reasonable measures to enforce the prohibition on child labour.[81] Serving as an exception to the MFN rule, the Enabling Clause of the GATT makes it possible for developed countries to grant preferential treatment to developing countries by most notably lowering the tariffs on imported goods from these countries.[82] The possibility of according or denying this sort of status to goods originating in developing countries provides developed countries with the leverage to reward developing country governments who are taking steps to eliminate child labour and to sanction governments that have failed to do so. By way of example, several countries have had their preferential access to the US market withdrawn pursuant to the General System of Preferences Renewal Act[83] for labour rights violations over the last two decades.[84] The European Union has adopted and applied similar conditions in its external trade relations to pressure developing countries that fail to uphold basic norms of international human rights law (including with respect to labour rights).[85] The Enabling Clause does set a number of requirements for the use of preferential tariff treatment in this manner, most notably that any such treatment not discriminate amongst "similarly situated" developing countries,[86] while responding positively to the particular needs of different countries with respect to trade, development and finance.[87]

---

[80] See M. T. Mitro, "Outlawing the Trade in Child Labor Products: Why the GATT Article XX Health Exception Authorizes Unilateral Sanctions" (2002) 51 *American University Law Review* 1223, 1260–1261 (arguing that a ban on the products of child labour would be sufficiently effective in light of alternative measures); Samida, "Protecting the Innocent or Protecting Special Interests?", 427–429 (arguing that the imposition of such a ban would have the perverse effect of increasing the hours worked by children and pushing them toward more dangerous industries and work environments in the informal sector).

[81] M. Trebilcock, R. Howse and A. Eliason, *The Regulation of International Trade* (London: Routledge, 2013), 738–739.

[82] World Trade Organization, "Decision on Differential and More Favourable Treatment, Reciprocity, and Fuller Participation of Developing Countries" (GATT Document L/4903, 28 November 1979).

[83] Pub. L. No. 98–573, 98 Stat. 3019 (1984).

[84] L. Compa and J. S. Vogt, "Labor Rights in the Generalized System of Preferences: A 20-Year Review" (2001) 22 *Comparative Labor Law and Policy Journal* 199.

[85] D. J. Linan Nogueras and L. M. Hinojosa Martinez, "Human Rights Conditionality in the External Trade of the European Union: Legal and Legitimacy Problems" (2001) 7 *Columbia Journal of European Law* 307.

[86] WTO Appellate Body, "Report on European Communities – Conditions for the Granting of Tariff Preferences to Developing Countries" (WT/DS246/AB/R, 7 April 2004), 62.

[87] Ibid., 66–67.

The preceding analysis shows that the WTO offers clear opportunities and challenges for the protection of the rights of children through trade measures such as trade bans and preferential trade treatment. The General Exceptions set out in article XX of the GATT as well as the Enabling Clause can be read in a manner that is consistent with the UNCRC and thus enable developed countries to create incentives for governments in developing countries to act to protect the rights of children. However, the rules conditioning the adoption and design of these measures impose significant burdens on developed countries to demonstrate that they are in line with the fundamental objectives and principles of the WTO, such as non-discrimination and the elimination of unjustified barriers to trade.

INSTRUMENTS FOR PROTECTING THE RIGHTS OF CHILDREN IN A GLOBALISING WORLD

Although they can be interpreted and applied in mutually complementary ways, the UNCRC and the WTO nonetheless impose different and potentially conflicting requirements in how state should approach trade and economic matters, with the former prioritising children's rights and the latter focusing on the liberalisation of trade. We now turn to considering two instruments that could be used to protect the rights of children in the context of an expanding global market:[88] children's rights impact assessments and non-state market-driven certification programmes. In doing so, we describe the nature and take-up of the instrument in question and then address their potential and limitations for avoiding unnecessary (and undesirable) conflicts between the promotion of children's rights and the liberalisation of international trade.

Children's Rights Impact Assessments

Children's Rights Impact Assessments (CRIAs) are tools that identify, analyse and evaluate the possible direct or indirect effects that a policy, legislation or other government decision-making process may have on the rights of children and young people.[89] More specifically, CRIAs exist to introduce the voices of children in decision-making processes; raise awareness and understanding of children's rights; better implement the UNCRC in domestic policy or legislation; and ensure that the

---

[88] For a broader overview of instruments that could be adopted to address the linkages between human rights and international trade, see Trebilcock et al., *The Regulation of International Trade*, 723–731.

[89] L. Payne, "A Children's Government in England and Child Impact Assessment" (2007) 21 *Children and Society* 470, 471. L. Paton and G. Munro, "Children's Rights Impact Assessments: The SCCYP Model" (SCCYP, 2006), www.sccyp.org.uk/uploaded_docs/children's%20rights%20impact%20assessment.pdf.

rights and well-being of children are fully considered throughout decision-making processes.[90] CRIAs may be undertaken *ex ante* or *post facto*, though preference is usually given to evaluating the impacts of a proposal on children's rights before it has been put into effect.[91] Currently, there are very few States that regularly undertake CRIAs; Flanders, Sweden, Norway, Scotland and Northern Ireland have established mandatory CRIA performance, as well as the province of New Brunswick in Canada.[92] While CRIAs were initially conceived of as a tool for State accountability, the United Nations, and several academics, have suggested that it should be translated to the business context to uncover and offset the negative implications of foreign investment and trade on the rights of children.[93] Nonetheless, as of yet, only KUONI Group Corporation is known to have included CRIAs as part of their business assessments policy.[94]

Although awareness of children's rights impacts does not have the same coercive force as statutory-mandated action, CRIAs can be of significant value in a globalised economy. CRIAs help businesses see the big picture; they demand that corporations take a step back from their spread sheets and financial statements and examine the potential impacts that their products and services may have on children and young people.[95] They are a tool for reviewing existing company policies for their effects on children's rights, assessing the potential impact of new products and services before they hit the market,[96] and monitoring current performance in children's rights protection and promotion.[97] They allow corporations to take a preventative approach to children's rights impacts, thereby ensuring that negative effects are mitigated or addressed prior to public scrutiny.[98] In fact, CRIAs are particularly helpful in the context of proposals that do not, on their face, have adverse effects for children's rights. As of yet, CRIAs have been used to assess and mitigate the negative effects of the 2011 National Welfare Reform Bill in Northern Ireland; stop legislation that would have compromised the medical privacy of children in Scotland;

---

[90] See presentation by Lisa Payne at the CRIA Symposium, hosted in Ottawa in 2013: www.unicef.ca/sites/default/files/imce_uploads/BLOG/1._payne_lisa_unicefunitedkingdom.pdf.

[91] Collins and Guevara, "Some Considerations for Child Rights Impact Assessment (CRIAs) of Business", 162; Paton and Munro, "Children's Rights Impact Assessments".

[92] M. Schmidt, "Focusing on Children's Rights to Fight Poverty" (2015), http://bostonfed.org/commdev/c&b/2015/summer/Michael-Schmidt-child-impact-assessment.htm, 5.

[93] Given a new focus on the role of business in the respect, protect and fulfill framework of children's rights, the UN Committee on the Rights of the Child published the *Children's Rights and Business Principles*, and UNICEF, along with Save the Children, has established a Company Assessment Tool for children's rights impacts. See also Schmidt, "Focusing on Children's Rights to Fight Poverty"; Collins, "The Relationship between Children's Rights and Business", 589; and UNCRC Committee, "General Comment No. 16 (2013)", [77]–[80].

[94] Collins, "The Relationship between Children's Rights and Business", 593.

[95] Collins and Guevara, "Some Considerations for Child Rights Impact Assessment (CRIAs) of Business", 163.

[96] Ibid.

[97] Ibid., 164.

[98] Ibid., 166.

and prevent state budget cuts in Tennessee that would have closed down a medical centre serving vulnerable populations of youth.[99] CRIAs are equally important in the business context, as they provide an opportunity for corporations to self-regulate their effects on the full range of rights under the UNCRC and permit socially responsible shareholders and consumers to hold companies accountable. Thus, state-mandated CRIAs can promote transparency and accountability for children's rights in corporate practices, while avoiding breaches of the previously mentioned obligations under the WTO.

While CRIAs are a useful for identifying the implications of a particular policy, service or product, businesses still need a full toolbox to properly ensure that the rights established by the UNCRC are being met. CRIAs face certain inherent limitations when put into practice. First, the lack of awareness of the UNCRC by relevant business actors tends to result in cursory and incomplete evaluations that do not delve deep enough into a proposed initiative to identify all of its potential impacts.[100] Full training on children's rights must be provided to all appropriate members of a corporation to ensure the depth of understanding necessary for a full CRIA.[101] Second, the corporations that are aware of children's rights often lack the resources to commit to a policy that requires regular assessment of their impacts on children.[102] CRIAs require data collection and analysis, staff, technical expertise and financing for consistent and proper implementation. Many businesses lack the economic capacity to dedicate such an extensive amount of resources to an issue that, in their perspective, has little connection with their profit margins.[103] Third, and perhaps the most significant obstacle for CRIAs, is the limited buy-in by key decision-makers.[104] Even when a comprehensive CRIA analysis is completed, there is usually no domestic obligation for the business enterprise to prevent or mitigate the negative effects of their products or services. As such, additional means for protecting the rights of children should be put in place alongside CRIA, such as corporate codes of conduct, human rights policies, state legislation on business impacts, etc.[105] In short, conducting a CRIA is a necessary first step for any business enterprise seeking to advance the rights of

---

[99] Schmidt, "Focusing on Children's Rights to Fight Poverty", 5.
[100] Collins and Guevara, "Some Considerations for Child Rights Impact Assessment (CRIAs) of Business", 179.
[101] Ibid. Children's rights impact assessments require technical expertise in the UNCRC. Governments implementing mandatory CRIA assessments also provide training for employees whose work has consequences for children to enhance their competency in children's rights, as is done under the "Strategy for Implementation of the CRC in Sweden"; see L. Sylwander, "Child Impact Assessments" (*Ministry of Health and Social Affairs*, Sweden, 2001), 10. Training sessions were also offered for all government employees when the province of New Brunswick made CRIA a mandatory policy assessment.
[102] Ibid., 180–181.
[103] Ibid., 179.
[104] Ibid., 180.
[105] Ibid., 187.

children in the context of their activities, however, they must be complemented by other measures and systems to be truly effective.[106]

Non-State Market-Driven Certification Programmes

Non-state market-driven certification programmes are created by NGOs, corporations or some combination thereof to steer the behaviour of actors operating in a particular market.[107] These programmes typically perform three principal functions: they set voluntary standards of behaviour addressed to a particular set of actors; create a process for monitoring and verifying compliance with these standards; and possess mechanisms to reward compliance and/or sanction non-compliance (most frequently through a labelling scheme).[108] Although there are no certification programmes that focus on the realisation of the full set of children's rights as such, numerous schemes have been created to eliminate the use of child labour in several industries, such as carpet manufacturing and garments and textiles.[109] The best known of these schemes is the one operated by GoodWeave International (formerly known as Rugmark). GoodWeave works with a network of NGOs in three supplier countries (Afghanistan, India and Nepal) to monitor and inspect carpet supply chains, rescue children working in carpet manufacturing and provide children with alternative educational opportunities. It provides a label that certifies that a rug was produced without child labour and is present in three consumer countries: Germany, the United Kingdom and the United States.[110] Since 2005, more than 11 million carpets certified by GoodWeave have been sold and more than 4,000 children have been directly rescued as a result of inspections conducted by GoodWeave.[111]

These certification programmes have two important advantages for protecting the rights of children in a context of economic globalisation. The first is that they are not subject to the same sort of legal scrutiny that might apply to trade measures falling within the purview of the WTO provided that they are not made compulsory by a market regulation adopted by a government.[112] While the Agreement on Technical

---

[106] UNICEF, "Child Rights Impact Assessment Discussion Paper on Bringing Children in from the Margins: Symposium on Child Rights Impact Assessments" www.unicef.ca/sites/default/files/imce_uploads/TAKE%20ACTION/ADVOCATE/DOCS/child_rights_impact_assessment_discussion_paper.pdf, 3.

[107] B. Cashore, G. Auld and D. Newsom, *Governing through Markets: Forest Certification and the Emergence of Non-State Authority* (New Haven, CT: Yale University Press, 2004).

[108] S. Bernstein and B. Cashore, "Can Non-State Global Governance Be Legitimate? An Analytical Framework" (2007) 1 *Regulation and Governance* 347.

[109] J. Hilowitz, "Social Labelling to Combat Child Labour: Some Considerations" (1997) 136(2) *International Labour Review* 215, 223–228.

[110] GoodWeave International, "Child-Labor-Free Certification", www.goodweave.net/about/child_labor_free_rugs.

[111] Skoll Foundation, "GoodWeave", www.skollfoundation.org/entrepreneur/nina-smith/.

[112] Trebilcock et al., *The Regulation of International Trade*, 312.

Barriers to Trade[113] obliges State Parties to take "reasonable measures" to ensure that voluntary certification programmes comply with the Code of Good Practice for the Preparation, Adoption, and Application of Standards included in Annex III, this provision has yet to give rise to a dispute among WTO members and its scope of application is unclear. In any case, the criteria applicable to voluntary certification schemes are unlikely to be problematic in the case of a certification scheme focusing on the implementation of the UNCRC.[114] The second advantage of such programmes pertains to their transformative potential. In the immediate stages of the development of such programmes, their acceptance and effectiveness largely depends on the value that suppliers and retailers accord to the benefits of certification, particularly whether it provides or denies them access to particular client or consumer segments or important foreign markets.[115] In the long term, these programmes (or the norms that they instantiate) may achieve a particular level of legitimacy through which its effectiveness may no longer be beholden to the cost-benefit calculations of market actors. Instead, compliance may become taken for granted by producers, consumers and other actors operating in a particular market as a result of mechanisms of social influence.[116]

Certification programmes are not without their limitations, however. Given that the market incentives for such programmes typically come from retailers and consumers in developed countries, they tend to apply to export-oriented economic sectors in developing countries and neglect other, less "visible" sectors that may also employ children.[117] Until there is more market demand within developing countries and emerging economies for goods that are certified as having been produced without child labour, certification will continue to cover a narrow range of industries and products, with limited effects on the broader use of child labour across the economies of the poorest countries in the world.[118] This resembles the main impediment that the enforcement of labour laws in developing countries face more generally. Child labour is most common in the informal sector, which is generally not adequately regulated by developing country governments.[119] The other, related limitation with certification programmes is that while many existing programmes

---

[113] Article 4(1). World Trade Organisation, Agreement on Technical Barriers to Trade (15 April 1994) 1868 UNTS 120.

[114] C. Lopez-Hurtado, "Social Labelling and WTO Law" (2002) *Journal of International Economic Law* 719, 738–742.

[115] M. Potoski and A. Prakash, "A Club Theory Approach to Voluntary Programs", in M. Potoski and A. Prakash (eds.), *Voluntary Programs: A Club Theory Approach* (Cambridge, MA: MIT Press, 2006), 17.

[116] Bernstein and Cashore, "Can Non-State Global Governance Be Legitimate?"

[117] R. J. Liubicic, "Corporate Codes of Conduct and Product Labeling Schemes: The Limits and Possibilities of Promoting International Labor Rights through Private Initiatives" (1998) 30 *Law and Policy of International Business* 111, 140.

[118] Hilowitz, "Social Labelling to Combat Child Labour", 229.

[119] A. Kolk and R. Van Tulder, "The Effectiveness of Self-Regulation: Corporate Codes of Conduct and Child Labour" (2002) 20(3) *European Management Journal* 260, 263.

focus on the problem of child labour, they do not address the broader range of children's rights that may be affected by the activities of multinational corporations and expanding levels of trade liberalisation.[120] This speaks to an enduring challenge for certification schemes – whether they can go beyond piecemeal effects and exert influence on the broader systematic challenges that underlie social problems and injustices.

CONCLUSION

This chapter offers a nuanced account of the complex relationship between the protection of the rights of children and the liberalisation of international trade. We began by arguing that the pursuit of economic globalisation has both positive and negative implications for the rights of children. In general, international trade can generate economic growth and thus contribute to reducing poverty among children and expanding the range of goods, services and opportunities available to them. At the same time, it is clear that the liberalisation of trade and the activities of multinational corporations can also have negative repercussions, both direct and indirect, on the rights and welfare of children.

We then addressed whether and how countries could grapple with the multifaceted intersections between children's rights and trade liberalisation and abide by their corresponding legal obligations under both the UNCRC and the WTO. For one thing, the development and implementation of a rights-based approach to international trade offers a country with a proactive set of methodologies and tools of enhancing the benefits of trade for the welfare of children, while mitigating its negative effects. For another, the WTO offers some scope for adopting trade measures that promote the rights of children, albeit in a manner that is constrained by trade disciplines that preserve some of the general principles of the multilateral trading system such as non-discriminatory treatment or the requirements of necessity and proportionality that are embedded into its general exceptions provisions.

Lastly, we turned to the potential as well as the limitations of two key instruments that could be used for avoiding conflicts between the promotion of children's rights and the liberalisation of international trade: CRIAs and non-state market-driven certification programmes. Both instruments have the virtue of not attracting the sort of scrutiny that would normally attach to the adoption trade measures within the context of the WTO and offer a way of changing business practices in a fundamental way. At the same time, the current take-up of these instruments is highly variable and is limited to sectors where there is significant demand for corporate social responsibility and improved performance in the protection of children's rights.

This chapter ultimately speaks to the broader set of lessons that should guide efforts aimed at protecting the rights of children in the context of the realisation of

---

[120] See "Children's Rights, International Trade and Economic Globalisation".

sustainable development. One key lesson has to do with adopting a sophisticated approach that considers the variety of ways that economic globalisation may intersect with the welfare of children and recognises that it offers multiple pathways of influence that can reinforce as well as undermine the promotion of children's rights.[121] Another key lesson concerns the limitations inherent in the legal principles and practices that are often used to resolve conflicts between treaty regimes as part of an integrated approach to the pursuit of sustainable development. Although states have the ability to interpret and apply their obligations under the WTO and the UNCRC in mutually complementary ways, the opportunities for doing so impose significant legal burdens on states and economic realities on the ground too often reflect the subordination of children's rights to the objectives of trade liberalisation and economic growth. This calls for the use of a mix of regulatory tools and instruments such as rights-based approaches, CRIAs and certification programmes that can enable public and private actors to evaluate and address the linkages between children's rights and economic globalisation in a proactive manner.[122] One final lesson pertains to the transformation of international human rights law away from its historical focus on state sovereignty towards greater concern with non-state actors and private forms of regulation.[123] This necessitates acknowledging the respective spheres of influence of governments, corporations and civil society and seeking to foster cross-sectorial collaboration that advances the rights of children in new and innovate ways.[124] By taking on board some of these important lessons and moving beyond traditional debates opposing trade and the rights of children, the advocates of children will thus be better positioned to ensure that the best interests of children are recognised as being central to the realisation of sustainable development in our globalised world.

---

[121] On pathways of influence through which international trade, may affect environmental issues, see S. Jodoin, "Pathways of Influence in the NAFTA Regime and Their Implications for Domestic Environmental Policy-Making in North America", in H. Kong and K. Wroth (eds.), *NAFTA and Sustainable Development: The History, Experience and Prospects for Reform* (Cambridge: Cambridge University Press, 2015), 329.

[122] This is consistent with the broader conception of public-private integrative linkage developed by Kolben ("Integrative Linkage: Combining Public and Private Regulatory Approaches in the Design of Trade and Labor Regimes" [2007] 48[1] *Harvard International Law Journal* 203).

[123] D. Shelton, "Protecting Human Rights in a Globalized World" (2002) 25 *Boston College International & Comparative Law Review* 273.

[124] UNCRC Committee, "General Comment No. 16 (2013)"; UN Human Rights Council, "Guiding Principles on Business and Human Rights".

13

Present Needs and Future Prospects

Exploring the Policy Conundrum of Working Children in Developing Nations

Jenny Driscoll

INTRODUCTION

Article 32 of the UN Convention on the Rights of the Child (UNCRC) imposes an obligation on States Parties to protect children "from economic exploitation and from performing any work that is likely to be hazardous or to interfere with the child's education, or to be harmful to the child's health or physical, mental, spiritual, moral or social development".[1] To that end, states are required under article 32(2) to provide (1) "for a minimum age or minimum ages for admission to employment"; (2) "for appropriate regulation of the hours and conditions of employment"; and (3) "for appropriate penalties or other sanctions" to ensure effective enforcement of children's rights under article 32. Other international conventions are more prescriptive. The International Labour Organisation (ILO) Minimum Age Convention (MAC)[2] stipulates a general minimum age of child employment of not less than the age at which compulsory schooling ends and in any event not less than 15,[3] with provision for an initial lower limit of 14 in nations where educational provision and economic development are particularly weak.[4] *Child labour* is not specifically defined in the ILO Conventions, but domestic work and unpaid work in family enterprises appear to be excluded from their scope, the terminology of which suggests that they are concerned with economic activity.[5] *Light work* (defined as

---

[1] UN General Assembly (UNGA), Convention on the Rights of the Child (UN Doc. A/RES/44/25, 20 November 1989) 1577 UNTS 3.
[2] International Labour Organisation (ILO), Convention concerning minimum age for admission to employment (MAC) (ILO No. 138, 26 June 1973) 1015 UNTS 297.
[3] MAC, article 2(3).
[4] MAC, article 2(4).
[5] E. V. Edmonds, "Defining Child Labour: A Review of the Definitions of Child Labour in Policy Research" (Working paper, Geneva: International Labour Organisation [ILO]/International Programme on the Elimination of Child Labour [IPEC]/Statistical Information and Monitoring Programme on Child Labour [SIMPOC], 2008).

work not likely to be harmful to children's health or development, and "not such as to prejudice their attendance at school, their participation in vocational orientation or training programmes approved by the competent authority or their capacity to benefit from the instruction received") may be permitted for children aged 13 to 15.[6]

The goal of eradicating child labour was adopted in the MAC and affirmed in 2010 at the Hague Global Child Labour Conference, which culminated in a "Roadmap for Achieving the Elimination of the Worst Forms of Child Labour by 2016".[7] This document includes an "acknowledgement" that "the effective abolition of child labour is a moral necessity" and an explicit consideration that "action to eliminate the worst forms of child labour is most effective and sustainable when it is situated within action to eliminate all child labour".[8] The commitment to abolish child labour is reiterated in the Post-2015 Sustainable Development Goals (SDGs), which were adopted by the UN General Assembly in September 2015 and include a target to "end child labour in all its forms" by 2025 (Target 8.7).[9] This commitment arises from the assumption that child labour holds back economic development as well as from concerns to protect children from exploitation and harm.[10] Analysis of the responses of 63 UN member states to a preliminary questionnaire to inform development of the SDGs elicited general agreement that the eradication of poverty continues to be the most important goal, and that economic growth in developing nations is a prerequisite for attaining it.[11] The target contributes to Goal 8, the aim of which is to "[p]romote sustained, inclusive and sustainable economic growth, full and productive employment and decent work for all". Juxtaposition of target 8.7 with 8.5 ("by 2030 achieve full and productive employment and decent work for all women and men, including for young people and persons with disabilities, and equal pay for work of equal value") and 8.6 ("by 2020 substantially reduce the proportion of youth not in employment, education or training") reveals a vision of employment as exclusively a function of adulthood, a Westernised assumption that will be interrogated in this chapter. Alliance 8.7, which describes itself as a "global multi-stakeholder initiative designed to assist all countries to achieve a world free from forced labour, modern slavery, human trafficking and all forms of child

---

[6] MAC, article 7.
[7] ILO-IPEC and Ministry of Social Affairs and Employment of the Netherlands, "The Hague Global Child Labour Conference 2010 – Towards a World without Child Labour, Mapping the Road to 2016" (Conference report, Geneva: International Labour Office, IPEC, Ministry of Social Affairs and Employment of the Netherlands, 2010), www.ilo.org/ipec/Campaignandadvocacy/GlobalChildLabourConference/lang—en/index.htm, 33–38.
[8] Ibid., 33.
[9] UNGA, "Transforming Our World: The 2030 Agenda for Sustainable Development" (UN Doc. A/RES/70/1, 21 October 2015), Target 8.7.
[10] See, for example, ILO Governance and Tripartism Department, "Marking Progress against Child Labour: Global Estimates and Trends 2000–2012" (IPEC, 2013), which refers to child labour as "compromising [children's] individual and our collective futures" (3).
[11] UNGA, "Initial Input of the Secretary-General to the Open Working Group on Sustainable Development Goals" (UN Doc. A/67/634, 17 December 2012).

labour", claims that achieving target 8.7 is prerequisite to meeting Goal 8 and that it will also contribute to SDG goals 1 (ending poverty), 4 (provision of education), 5 (gender equality), 10 (the reduction of inequalities) and 16 (the promotion of peaceful and just societies).[12]

This chapter questions the assumptions underpinning the international goal to eradicate child labour,[13] an issue that exemplifies the complexity of the effects of development programmes at the individual, community and national levels. The principle of sustainable development, defined as "development that meets the needs of the present, without compromising the abilities of future generations to meet their own",[14] is applicable to the life trajectory of the individual working child and to the welfare of their family and community, as well as to economic development at national and supranational levels. This chapter considers three issues: the relationship between poverty reduction and children's work at each of these levels; the extent to which children can and/or should contribute to family income and community activities through paid and unpaid work when that work may have the potential to undermine both the developmental aims of the society in which they grow up and their own future prospects; and whether the ILO's abolitionist agenda is congruent with the aims of the SDGs. These issues are addressed first through a review of the available international evidence on the nature and context of children's work and its impact on their health and development in "Children's Work, Child Employment and Child Labour", which concludes with consideration of factors affecting the assessment of children's best interests in relation to children's work. Next, in "Development, Education and Children's Work", the interrelationship between education and work is discussed to examine the short and longer-term implications of removing children from the workforce for children, their families and communities. A broader rights-based analysis is brought to bear on these debates in "Human and Children's Rights Perspectives" to provide greater insight into how concerns as to the immediate well-being of children can and should be balanced against considerations of their future prospects. These insights are used in the final section to demonstrate the need for reconsideration of international policy in relation to children's work.

---

[12] www.sdg-alliance8-7.org/.
[13] It is not concerned with the uncontentious call for the abolition of the "worst forms of child labour" as identified in the Worst Forms of Child Labour Convention 1999 (Convention concerning the Prohibition and Immediate Action for the Elimination of the Worst Forms of Child Labour [ILO No. 182, 17 June 1999] 2133 UNTS 161). The term *work* is used here to cover all result-oriented activity undertaken by children that is neither education nor leisure, whether paid or unpaid, and *employment* or *productive labour* refers to work for which the child or their family is paid.
[14] World Commission on Environment and Development (WCED), "Our Common Future" (UN Doc. A/42/427, 1987), www.un-documents.net/our-common-future.pdf.chpt 2, [1].

CHILDREN'S WORK, CHILD EMPLOYMENT AND CHILD LABOUR

Social, Cultural and Economic Contexts of Children's Work

The extent of children's work is difficult to establish, and prevalence rates are likely to be underestimates[15] because data are patchy, often unreliable as a result of under-reporting of work that is illegal, and are gathered using different definitions and age boundaries. The ILO estimates that 16.7 per cent of children are employed, a fall from 23 per cent in 2000, with 5.4 per cent, or 85 million, undertaking hazardous work.[16] In contrast, UNICEF data – which includes 5- to 14-year-olds undertaking at least 28 hours of household chores – suggest that 24 per cent of children in the least developed nations work.[17] There has been considerable criticism of the exclusion from international policy initiatives of domestic or unpaid work because the majority of working children are engaged in domestic chores or work for the family farm or other business.[18] The importance of agriculture, which is the biggest employment sector for children,[19] may account for higher involvement in family business work for children, and particularly boys, in rural areas in both Africa and Asia,[20] yet this work is often unpaid.[21] Nicola Ansell points out that young carers also fall outside the remit of the ILO's attention, although they may well undertake many hours of onerous and harmful work at cost to their education.[22] Despite the potentially harmful nature of these informal types of work, domestic work and that of AIDS-affected or orphaned children are significantly under-represented in the literature.[23] Regions with the highest proportion of working children are in Africa and the least developed nations, but although ILO statistics suggest low levels of child employment in high-income countries, some studies suggest that the ILO conventions may

---

[15] A. Admassie, "Child Labour and Schooling in the Context of a Subsistence Rural Economy: Can They Be Compatible?" (2003) 23(2) *International Journal of Educational Development*, 167; S. Dessy and J. Knowles, "Why Is Child Labor Illegal?" (2008) 52 *European Economic Review* 1275.

[16] ILO Governance and Tripartism Department, "Marking Progress against Child Labour".

[17] See https://data.unicef.org/topic/child-protection/child-labour/ for May 2016 data.

[18] For example, E. Webbink, J. Smits and E. de Jong, "Hidden Child Labor: Determinants of Housework and Family Business Work of Children in 16 Developing Countries" (2012) 40(3) *World Development* 631; E. Edmonds and N. Pavcnik, "Child Labor in the Global Economy" (2005) 19(1) *The Journal of Economic Perspectives* 199.

[19] P. P. Emerson, "Understanding Child Labour: The Economic View of Child Labour", in H. D. Hindman, *The World of Child Labour: An Historical and Regional Study* (Hoboken, NJ: Taylor and Francis, 2009); Edmonds and Pavcnik, "Child Labor in the Global Economy"; ILO Governance and Tripartism Department, "Marking Progress against Child Labour".

[20] Webbink et al., "Hidden Child Labor".

[21] See, for example, D. DeGraff, D. Levison and M. Robison, "Child Labour and Mothers' Work in Brazil" (2009) 29(3/4) *International Journal of Sociology and Social Policy* 152.

[22] N. Ansell, *Children, Youth and Development* (Oxford: Routledge, 2005).

[23] T. Abebe and S. Bessell, "Dominant Discourses, Debates and Silences on Child Labour in Africa and Asia" (2011) 32(4) *Third World Quarterly* 765.

be flouted to a significant degree even in wealthy nations.[24] The proportion of children working increases with age in both developed and developing nations.[25]

The work carried out by children remains highly gendered and gendered differences in the work undertaken increase with children's age;[26] boys are therefore more likely to suffer illness and injury as a result of the nature of the work undertaken.[27] Cultural or traditional divisions of family labour frequently allocate domestic chores to girls to release other members of the family for jobs outside the home.[28] Consequently, studies in which unpaid work in the home is taken into account produce considerably higher figures for the hours of work undertaken by children and in some cases eliminate or reverse the impression given by statistics relating to paid employment that boys engage in more work than girls.[29] DeGraff et al.'s research in Brazil found that children whose mothers were employed in the labour market were close to twice as likely to work as those whose mothers were not employed[30] and the nature of mothers' work may influence that of their daughters in particular.[31] But children's work – and particularly that of girls – most usually substitutes for women's activities, thereby freeing women for more specialised employment but contributing ultimately, as Tatek Abebe and Sharon Bessell argue, to the maintenance of gendered and generational patterns of patriarchy.[32] There is some reason to suppose that eradicating girls' work may be more challenging than freeing boys from labour: improvements in access to water, the educational attainment of mothers, and income are less likely to result in reduction in girls' work than in that of boys,[33] and in communities in which girls will leave the family on marriage and boys will

---

[24] For example, Portugal (P. Goularta and A. S. Bedi, "Child Labour and Educational Success in Portugal" [2008] 27 *Economics of Education Review* 575) and New Zealand, which has not ratified the MAC (N. R. Gasson and C. Linsell, "Young Workers: A New Zealand Perspective" [2011] 19 *International Journal of Children's Rights* 641).

[25] Dessy and Knowles, "Why Is Child Labor Illegal?" (Latin America); L. Ersado, "Child Labor and Schooling Decisions in Urban and Rural Areas: Comparative Evidence from Nepal, Peru, and Zimbabwe" (2005) 33(3) *World Development* 455; Goularta and Bedi, "Child Labour and Educational Success in Portugal".

[26] L. Guarcello et al., *Child Labour in the Latin America and Caribbean Region: A Gender-Based Analysis* (Washington, DC: ILO-IPEC, 2006).

[27] For example, Guarcello et al., ibid.; S. Okyere, "Are Working Children's Rights and Child Labour Abolition Complementary or Opposing Realms?" (2013) 56(1) *International Social Work* 80; P. Tetteh, "Child Domestic Labour in (Accra) Ghana: A Child and Gender Rights Issue?" (2011) 19 *International Journal of Children's Rights* 217.

[28] For example, Guarcello et al., *Child Labour in the Latin America and Caribbean Region*.

[29] See Webbink et al., "Hidden Child Labor"; Admassie, "Child Labour and Schooling in the Context of a Subsistence Rural Economy"; Guarcello et al., *Child Labour in the Latin America and Caribbean Region*; Edmonds and Pavcnik, "Child Labor in the Global Economy"; K. Basu, S. Das and B. Dutta, "Child Labor and Household Wealth: Theory and Empirical Evidence of an Inverted-U" (2010) 91(1) *Journal of Development Economics* 8.

[30] DeGraff et al., "Child Labour and Mothers' Work in Brazil".

[31] Ibid.

[32] Abebe and Bessell, "Dominant Discourses, Debates and Silences".

[33] Ibid.

take responsibility for supporting ageing parents, families are incentivised to prioritise boys' education over that of girls.[34] Moreover, Gayatri Koolwal hypothesises that an increase in the potential earnings of girls may be protective to an extent against the practice of son preference, while an outright ban on child labour is liable to exacerbate son preference, undermining attainment of target 4.5 of the SDGs (gender equality in education).[35] In this context, the ILO's narrow focus on paid employment is blind to issues of gender discrimination, although gender equality is the focus of Goal 5 of the SDGs and non-discrimination is one of the core principles of the UNCRC, set out in article 2.

Although poverty is regarded as the primary reason for children to engage in productive labour and there is a negative correlation between the gross domestic product (GDP) per capita and the proportion of school-aged children in work,[36] the relationship between poverty and children's employment is complex. Child labour is higher in rural than urban areas[37] for a number of reasons, including migration by men from rural to urban settings to gain work (leaving women and children at home); the prevalence of agricultural work as the main means of earning a living; higher levels of poverty in rural areas and less access to adequate schooling; the likelihood that parents are more highly educated in urban communities and therefore more likely to value education themselves; and the greater preservation of traditional customs and ways of life in rural areas.[38] Short-term use of child labour may protect against penury or facilitate economic growth. For example, child employment rates may rise significantly in response to transitory income shocks such as crop loss,[39] while Basu et al. demonstrate that as landownership rises, so does child labour, until a level of wealth is reached that no longer requires the family to rely on child labour.[40]

Michael Bourdillon et al. caution that causal relationships need to be specifically determined in each context[41] and household-level factors are the most significant determinants of "hidden" or informal work.[42] A high proportion of children appear

---

[34] Edmonds and Pavcnik, "Child Labor in the Global Economy"; Tetteh, "Child Domestic Labour in (Accra) Ghana".
[35] G. B. Koolwal, "Son Preference and Child Labor in Nepal: The Household Impact of Sending Girls to Work" (2007) 35(5) World Development 881.
[36] Dessy and Knowles, "Why Is Child Labor Illegal?"
[37] Edmonds and Pavcnik, "Child Labor in the Global Economy"; M. Fafchamps and J. Wahba, "Child Labor, Urban Proximity, and Household Composition" (2006) 79(2) Journal of Development Economics 374.
[38] E. Neumayer and I. De Soysa, "Trade Openness, Foreign Direct Investment and Child Labor" (2005) 33(1) World Development 43.
[39] K. Beegle, R. H. Dehejia, and R. Gatti, "Child Labor and Agricultural Shocks" (2006) 81(1) Journal of Development Economics 80.
[40] Basu et al., "Child Labor and Household Wealth".
[41] M. Bourdillon et al., Rights and Wrongs of Children's Work (New Brunswick, NJ: Rutgers University Press, 2010).
[42] Webbink et al., "Hidden Child Labor".

to work at the behest of their parents,[43] with parental factors associated with the practice including low educational and socio-economic status, large family size and polygamy.[44] The decisions made by parents as to their children's use of time depend on many factors, including cultural and traditional norms; the family's financial standing; the mother's education; the age and gender of the child and their position in the family; the availability of childcare (in urban areas); the cost and quality of schooling; and the nature of the work available, including adults' opportunities in the labour market.[45] In general, rising living standards tend to lead to a fall in children's productive work[46] and most families withdraw their children from work if their financial circumstances improve sufficiently to enable them to do so.[47] Given the context-specific nature of factors involved in such decisions, the principle that the best interests of the child shall be a primary consideration in all actions concerning children, enshrined in article 3 of the UNCRC, is far preferable to the imposition of a universally applicable regime. Assessing children's best interests in this regard requires consideration of the family and community context as well as the effect of their work on children's health, well-being and education, and appropriate weight to be given to the child's own views and capacities in accordance with articles 12 and 5. The following section explores the evidence on children's attitudes to work and its impact on their health and well-being, illustrating the wide range of considerations that may affect where the best interests of an individual child lie in their particular circumstances.

Children's Work and Their Best Interests

Work may be regarded in some African communities as an irrefutable duty owed to parents,[48] but children may also be motivated by a desire to earn money to support their family, gain experience, learn a trade and/or help their parents.[49] Work may

---

[43] Ibid.; Edmonds and Pavcnik, "Child Labor in the Global Economy".

[44] Ersado, "Child Labor and Schooling Decisions in Urban and Rural Areas"; F. O. Omokhodion and O. C. Uchendu, "Perception and Practice of Child Labour among Parents of School-Aged Children in Ibadan, Southwest Nigeria" (2010) 36(3) *Child: Care, Health and Development* 304; S. Chakrabarty and U. Grote, "Child Labor in Carpet Weaving: Impact of Social Labeling in India and Nepal" (2009) 37(10) *World Development* 1683.

[45] Webbink et al., "Hidden Child Labor"; Ersado, "Child Labor and Schooling Decisions in Urban and Rural Areas".

[46] Edmonds and Pavcnik, "Child Labor in the Global Economy"; E. Edmonds and N. Pavcnik, "The Effect of Trade Liberalization on Child Labor" (2005) 65(2) *Journal of International Economics* 401.

[47] Edmonds and Pavcnik, "Child Labor in the Global Economy".

[48] R. V. B. Okoli and V. E. Cree, "Children's Work: Experiences of Street-Vending Children and Young People in Enugu, Nigeria" (2012) 42 *British Journal of Social Work* 58; K. Orkin, "In the Child's Best Interests? Legislation on Children's Work in Ethiopia" (2010) 22 *Journal of International Development* 1102.

[49] E. Al-Gamal et al., "The Psychosocial Impact of Child Labour in Jordan: A National Study" (2013) 48(6) *International Journal of Psychology* 1156; F. Omokhodion, "School Attendance and Attitude to Child Labour: A Comparison of In-School and Out-of-School Working Children in

also be a source of fun and/or pride, a way of passing time and a means of boosting young people's marriageability.[50] Vegard Iversen's study of child labour migrants[51] found that boys leaving home to seek work often did so against their parents' wishes, but would nonetheless send money back home to support their family, although migration to find work was also associated in this study with escape from domestic discord or abuse. Adolescents may choose to work to be seen as contributing to their community, to gain greater independence from their parents or to access consumer goods.[52] Work may also provide younger children with a sense of self-respect, community belonging and competence.[53] The young Nigerian street-hawkers in Rosemary Okoli's study[54] preferred market trading (illegal under the Nigerian Child Rights Act of 2003) to domestic chores, as being more fun, sociable and interesting. These examples illustrate the engagement of a range of UNCRC rights in issues pertaining to children's work, including engagement in cultural and community life (articles 30 and 31); achievement of an adequate standard of living (article 27); involvement in decisions affecting them (article 12); and the exercise of autonomy in accordance with children's evolving capacities (article 5). They also highlight the extent to which judgements as to where the best interests of children lie are ambiguous and even, to some extent, subjective.

Surprisingly little is known about the effect of children's work on their health and well-being.[55] Karen Wells concludes that there is "little concrete evidence"[56] that work is necessarily damaging to children's future prospects and health. Where there is evidence of harm to children, strict regulation may protect children better than the invisibility arising from rendering the employment of children illegal. Madhura Swaminathan studied 5,631 children in the Indian city of Bhavnagar, Gujarat, at a time of rapid economic growth accompanied by labour deregulation.[57] She found that children were subjected to physical and verbal abuse, given insufficient water to

---

Southwest Nigeria" (2015) 23(1) *Journal of Public Health* 63; M. Liebel, "Do Children Have a Right to Work? Working Children's Movements in the Struggle for Social Justice", in K. Hanson and O. Nieuwenhuys, *Reconceptualising Children's Rights in International Development: Living Rights, Social Justice, Translations* (Cambridge: Cambridge University Press, 2013); Okyere, "Are Working Children's Rights and Child Labour Abolition Complementary or Opposing Realms?"

[50] V. Morrow and K. Pells, "Integrating Children's Human Rights and Child Poverty Debates: Examples from Young Lives in Ethiopia and India" (2013) 46(5) *Sociology* 906.

[51] V. Iversen, "Autonomy in Child Labor Migrants" (2013) 30(5) *World Development* 817.

[52] Bourdillon et al., *Rights and Wrongs of Children's Work*.

[53] E. T. Sackey and B. O. Johannesen, "Earning Identity and Respect through Work: A Study of Children Involved in Fishing and Farming Practices in Cape Coast, Ghana" (2015) *Childhood*, 1–13.

[54] Okoli and Cree, "Children's Work".

[55] E. Turner-Moss, "Child Labour Must Be on the Post-2015 Agenda" (2013) 382(9910) *The Lancet* 52; Abebe and Bessell, "Dominant Discourses, Debates and Silences".

[56] K. Wells, *Childhood in Global Perspective* (Cambridge: Polity Press, 2009), 109.

[57] M. Swaminathan, "Economic Growth and the Persistence of Child Labor" (1998) 26(8) *World Development* 1513.

drink and lacked access to toilet facilities. They suffered tiredness and ill-health and the stress of job insecurity as well as being exposed to a swathe of physical risks arising from the hard physical work undertaken. Nigerian children in Omokhodion's study[58] regarded road traffic accidents, bad company, poor attainment at school and ill health as the most significant disadvantages of work, while those participating in Okoli's research with Nigerian child street vendors highlighted carrying heavy burdens in the hot sun and occasional fights with competing groups.[59] A study of more than 4,000 children aged 6 to 16 in Jordan[60] found higher reports of psychosocial problems in children who worked and attended school than in those who either worked or attended school, but not both, but the children juggling work and school worked on average nearly 34 hours a week.

There is general consensus that engagement in work has a deleterious effect on children's attendance and attainment in school,[61] with Silvian Dessy and John Knowles concluding from their study of representative household surveys from 12 Latin American countries that the effect of children's work on their educational attainment is both "large and significant".[62] A survey of nearly 1,500 rural households in Ethiopia[63] found that more than 90 per cent of parents considered education to be an important investment for their children but only one in five children attended school, while nearly a half engaged in domestic or agricultural work. Child respondents aged 11 to 14 in that study cited work as the main underlying reason for non-attendance at school, and in Okoli's study of Nigerian street hawkers the need to work or care for siblings affected both their attendance and attainment,[64] yet children often work to fund essentials for school attendance.[65]

The provision of education is central to international development goals. Target 4.1 of the SDGs aims to provide all children with free high-quality primary and secondary education by 2030 and target 4.6 includes ensuring all youth achieve literacy and numeracy by 2030.[66] Issues as to the nature, quality and value of the education afforded to children in developing countries are complex and contested. Although it is beyond the scope of this chapter to address these issues in any depth, it

---

[58] Omokhodion, "School Attendance and Attitude to Child Labour".
[59] Okoli and Cree, "Children's Work".
[60] Al-Gamal et al., "The Psychosocial Impact of Child Labour in Jordan".
[61] Webbink et al., "Hidden Child Labor"; Admassie, "Child Labour and Schooling in the Context of a Subsistence Rural Economy"; L. Guarcello, S. Lyon and F. Rosati, "Child Labour and Education for All: An Issue Paper" (Understanding Children's Work Project, University of Rome "Tor Vergata": Rome, 2008), www.researchgate.net/publication/272300404_Child_Labour_and_Education_For_All_An_Issue_Paper; C. Heady, "The Effect of Child Labor on Learning Achievement" (2003) 31(2) *World Development* 385–398.
[62] Dessy and Knowles, "Why Is Child Labor Illegal?", 1298.
[63] Admassie, "Child Labour and Schooling in the Context of a Subsistence Rural Economy".
[64] Okoli and Cree, "Children's Work".
[65] For example, Okyere, "Are Working Children's Rights and Child Labour Abolition Complementary or Opposing Realms?"; Orkin, "In the Child's Best Interests?"
[66] UNGA, "Transforming Our World".

is important to note their significance in weighing up the extent to which short-term benefits from children's work for children and their families may be off-set in the longer term by poor educational outcomes. Poor quality schools are associated with lower attendance, while policies to improve access to school and raise the standard of education,[67] as well as reductions in the cost of education,[68] can help reduce child labour.

Working children not attending school were found to have lower career aspirations than those attending school in Omokhodion's research with working children in Nigeria,[69] but many children understand and accept the sacrifices to their future that they are making for the sake of their families' current subsistence. For example, although children in Enoch Sackey and Berit Johanssen's ethnography valued fishing and farming work as integral to community life and cultural identity and practice in Ghana, they were likely to have aspirations beyond the traditional means of subsistence in the community and consequently missed school to fulfil their expected duties only reluctantly.[70] Similarly, the street vendors in Okoli's study[71] aspired to further education and professional careers and hoped to leave vending behind in their adult lives, although some regarded it as useful experience for a career in business.[72] Such insights are a reminder that even children in very poor communities may have ambitions for their future that are inspired by a vision of life beyond the confines of their childhood experiences. These should be a critical factor in consideration of their best interests, although the international community and some researchers appear to take a more pragmatic approach. Target 4.4 of the SDGs includes a substantial increase in youths' relevant skills for employment by 2030,[73] while Webbink et al.[74] argue that, in some communities, work experience may be more important than formal education for access to the types of work available, and Sackey and Johanssen[75] argue that community livelihoods are undervalued by schools, as a consequence of which what is learnt in school is often irrelevant to community work and vice versa. The following section takes a closer look at the role of education in the development agenda and the inter-relationships between education and work to examine the short- and longer-term implications of removing children from the workforce for children, their families and communities.

[67] Ersado, "Child Labor and Schooling Decisions in Urban and Rural Areas"; Guarcello et al., "Child Labour and Education for All".
[68] Edmonds and Pavcnik, "Child Labor in the Global Economy".
[69] Omokhodion, "School Attendance and Attitude to Child Labour".
[70] Sackey and Johannesen, "Earning Identity and Respect through Work".
[71] Okoli and Cree, "Children's Work".
[72] See also Okyere, "Are Working Children's Rights and Child Labour Abolition Complementary or Opposing Realms?"
[73] UNGA, "Transforming Our World".
[74] Webbink et al., "Hidden Child Labor".
[75] Sackey and Johannesen, "Earning Identity and Respect through Work".

DEVELOPMENT, EDUCATION AND CHILDREN'S WORK

In the Western world in particular, the worlds of work and school are sharply delineated. Some commentators argue that international policy in relation to child labour is influenced by "[g]lobal ideologies of work-free childhoods".[76] The vision of childhood as a space for education and play reflects Westernised romantic notions of childhood, which have been "globalised" through the construct of the "world's children" promoted by international NGOs and agencies,[77] despite the fact that, as Virginia Morrow points out, the extension of education to a full-time occupation throughout childhood is a relatively recent phenomenon in developed nations.[78] Moreover, this view of childhood disregards cultural contexts in which "children's work is seen not as a defect but as a contribution to shared responsibilities, something to be appreciated".[79] Paul Close controversially suggests that compulsory school should be regarded as forced labour and should be recognised as contributing to social production in a similar way to women's domestic work.[80] Diane Elson also draws on parallels between the status of children and that of women in her analysis of the way in which children are subordinated through hierarchies of seniority in the same way that women have been subordinated through hierarchies of gender.[81] She points out that the shift away from work in favour of education for children has preserved children's subservient status in Western nations through strengthening their economic dependence on adults. Further, there are arguably some valid parallels to be drawn between an abolitionist stance in relation to child labour and historic policies that banned or restricted women from certain areas of work on the grounds of their physical weakness; the risk that their work would undermine the status and income of men; and the fear that work would distract women from their proper duties in the home.[82] Abolition of child labour was supported by many adult trade unions, some of which opposed women's employment in the past,[83] and that position reflects concerns in some quarters that children's work might displace that of adults and/or drive down wages and thereby threaten to reduce adult incomes.[84]

---

[76] Abebe and Bessell, "Dominant Discourses, Debates and Silences", 766.
[77] Ibid., 767.
[78] V. Morrow, "Should the World Really Be Free of 'Child Labour'? Some Reflections" (2010) 17 (4) *Childhood* 435, 437.
[79] Liebel, "Do Children Have a Right to Work?", 237.
[80] P. Close, "Making Sense of Child Labour in Modern Society", in J. Qvortrup (ed.) *Sociological Studies of Children and Youth Volume 12: Structural, Historical and Comparative Perspectives* (Bingley, UK: Emerald Group Publishing Limited, 2009).
[81] D. Elson, "The Differentiation of Children's Labour in the Capitalist Labour Market" (1982) 13 (4) *Development and Change* 479.
[82] See, for example, T. C. Leonard, "Protecting Family and Race: The Progressive Case for Regulating Women's Work" (2005) 64(3) *American Journal of Economics and Sociology* 757.
[83] Ansell, *Children, Youth and Development*.
[84] D. M. Post, "Conceiving Child Labour in Human Rights Terms: Can It Mobilize Progressive Change?", in B. H. Weston (ed.), *Child Labor and Human Rights: Making Children Matter* (Boulder, CO, and London: Lynne Rienner Publishers, 2005).

However, the enhanced focus on education in childhood (and beyond) also reflects a developmental – human capital – perspective that highlights the importance of education in ensuring children are prepared for full economic productivity in high-skills economies in adulthood, and the potential threat that this process may be undermined by children's work.[85] Greater foreign investment and open international trade is associated with lower child labour rates in developing countries,[86] which appear to be attributable to the increased income generated.[87] Research shows that entry into the workforce at a very early age does not furnish children with a head start in relation to the development of skills and earning capacity; rather, early entrants are likely to find themselves trapped in low-skilled, poorly paid jobs.[88] Sen argues that economies such as Japan have demonstrated the efficacy of the universal expansion of education as a precursor to development and, comparing India and China, he attributes China's greater success in the market economy to its pre-existing education infrastructure, compared with high levels of illiteracy in India.[89] Sen points out that education is cheap in the early stages of development because it is a labour-intensive service. His analysis challenges critics of education systems that do not prepare children directly for work in the communities in which they live and suggests that children with the aspirations and skills to move beyond the confines of traditional community livelihoods are integral to the economic development of their nation.

National-level effects such as those set out in the preceding paragraph may not benefit all families equally, however. Dessy and Knowles theorise that, because the returns from investment in education are not reaped until adulthood, education rather than work may be a good long-term investment for parents with intermediate incomes, but not beneficial for the very poor.[90] Other research suggests that restricting child labour, sanctions against exports from countries with a child labour force, imposing compulsory education and banning the importation of goods made by children or labelling the products of child labour appear effective in removing children from labour where their families are above the subsistence level, but for poorer families, risk the removal of children to informal or unregulated sectors, likely to be more harmful to their health and well-being.[91] Kaushik Basu and Homa

---

[85] J. Ennew, W. E. Myers and D. P. Plateau, "Defining Child Labor as if Human Rights Really Matter", in B. H. Weston (ed.), *Child Labor and Human Rights: Making Children Matter* (Boulder, CO, and London: Lynne Rienner Publishers, 2005).

[86] A. Cigno, F. Rosati and L. Guarcello, "Does Globalization Increase Child Labor?" (2002) 30 (9) *World Development* 1579; Neumayer and De Soysa, "Trade Openness, Foreign Direct Investment and Child Labor".

[87] R. B. Davies and A. Voy, "The Effect of FDI on Child Labor" (2009) 88 *Journal of Development Economics* 59.

[88] Swaminathan, "Economic Growth and the Persistence of Child Labor".

[89] A. Sen, *Development as Freedom* (Oxford: Oxford University Press, 1999), 41.

[90] Dessy and Knowles, "Why Is Child Labor Illegal?"

[91] S. Chakrabarty and U. Grote, "Child Labor in Carpet Weaving: Impact of Social Labeling in India and Nepal" (2009) 37(10) *World Development* 1683; Dessy and Knowles, "Why Is Child

Zarghamee theorise that product boycotts cause children's wages to drop as demand for the product decreases, forcing children to work harder and/or drawing more children into work.[92] Thus policies to eliminate child labour may in the short term at least undermine Goal 10 of the SDGs, the reduction of inequality within countries.[93]

Abebe and Bessell argue that the international emphasis on education "is less about the needs, interests and/or human rights of children than about the requirements of a particular economic and political agenda"[94] and concerns as to the appropriateness of the abolitionist agenda are more than merely ideological objections. Primary amongst them is evidence that removing children from the formal labour market without addressing the underlying poverty that drives families to put their children to work will merely shift their labours into informal or illegal markets where they are unprotected and invisible.[95] Admassie considers that total elimination is "neither feasible nor desirable" in the context of subsistence agricultural communities in Ethiopia,[96] while Burns H. Weston concludes that minimum age legislation "has in many cases proved more disastrous for children than was the work in which they were engaged prior to the exclusion".[97] Liebel's research with working children's groups in Latin America, Africa and Asia found that working children are opposed to the fixed aged limits and to boycotts of products made by children.[98] Salvador Contreras argues that outlawing child labour increases the differential between adult and child earnings and reduces poor families' ability to invest in education.[99] He suggests that policies should aim to reduce the gap between adult and child wages while offering universal access to schooling, which, although increasing child work in the short term, in the longer term can be shown to promote movement away from child employment in favour of schooling.

Labor Illegal?" (Latin America); Neumayer and De Soysa, "Trade Openness, Foreign Direct Investment and Child Labor"; Emerson, "Understanding Child Labour"; Edmonds and Pavcnik, "Child Labor in the Global Economy".

[92] K. Basu and H. Zarghamee, "Is Product Boycott a Good Idea for Controlling Child Labor? A Theoretical Investigation" (2009) 88(2) *Journal of Development Economics* 217.

[93] UNGA, "Transforming Our World". Target 10.1 reads: "By 2030, progressively achieve and sustain income growth of the bottom 40 per cent of the population at a rate higher than the national average".

[94] Abebe and Bessell, "Dominant Discourses, Debates and Silences", 769.

[95] N. Howard, "On Bolivia's New Child Labour Law" (Open Democracy, 6 November 2014), https://www.opendemocracy.net/beyondslavery/neil-howard/on-bolivia's-new-child-labour-law.

[96] Admassie, "Child Labour and Schooling in the Context of a Subsistence Rural Economy", 183.

[97] B. H. Weston, "Bringing Human Rights to Child Labor: Guiding Principles and Call to Action", in B. H. Weston (ed.), *Child Labor and Human Rights: Making Children Matter* (Boulder, CO, and London: Lynne Rienner Publishers, 2005), 428.

[98] Liebel, "Do Children Have a Right to Work?".

[99] S. Contreras, "Child Labor Participation, Human Capital Accumulation, and Economic Development" (2008) 30 *Journal of Macroeconomics* 499.

It was considerations such as these that led to Bolivia explicitly rejecting an abolitionist approach to children's work in favour of regulation through the Code for Children and Adolescents (Law No. 548) of July 2014, under which children may work in a self-employed capacity from the age of 10, provided they attend school, and they may undertake employment from the age of 12, subject to parental agreement and continued school attendance.[100] The revised law lays down conditions for the protection of working children, with strong sanctions for breach by employers, and has the support of Bolivia's Union of Child and Adolescent Workers (UNATSCO), which was among the groups campaigning for the change in the law.[101] Although UNICEF objected to the new law on the grounds that it is contrary to Bolivia's obligations under the ILO Conventions,[102] the move was supported by the population and justified by the government as necessary to meet the goals of its Poverty Reduction Strategy.[103] World Bank figures suggest that more than 65 per cent of Bolivia's population live below the national poverty line and that Bolivia is one of the most unequal nations on earth.[104] The SDGs aim to eradicate extreme poverty (defined as living on less than $1.25 a day) and reduce by half the proportion of the population living in poverty judged by national standards by 2030,[105] as well as to reduce inequality within and between nations.[106] Despite prompting international outrage in the media, Bolivia's action chimes with concern in the academic community as to the appropriateness and efficacy of the international drive to eradicate child labour. Some commentators are strongly in favour of the legislation, on the grounds that it reflects the reality of work as a necessity for the many poor children in Bolivia, provides protection through regulation and respects children's agency and voice in ascertaining where their best interests lie.[107] As a member of a global group of academics and child rights practitioners calling on the UN Committee on the Rights of the Child not to reference ILO Convention 138 in the General Comment on the Rights of Adolescence in 2016, I endorse the group's submissions to the Committee, which applaud the involvement of children and young people in development of the legislation and the use of a human and children's rights framework to protect children from exploitation and harm.[108]

---

[100] Estado Plurinacional de Bolivia/Asemblea Legislativa Plurinacional, *Codigo del Nino, Nina y Adolescente* (Ley No. 548 de 17 de Julio de 2014).
[101] Howard, "On Bolivia's New Child Labour Law".
[102] UNICEF Press Release, "Bolivia's New Code on Children Welcome, but Concerns Remain" (Panama City, 23 July 2014), www.unicef.org/media/media_74569.html.
[103] Republic of Bolivia, "Poverty Reduction Strategy Paper" (La Paz: Bolivia, 2001), www.preventionweb.net/english/professional/policies/v.php?id=9310.
[104] World Bank, *World Development Indicators* (Washington, DC: World Bank, 2009).
[105] Target 1.1: UNGA, "Transforming Our World".
[106] Goal 10: Ibid.
[107] Howard, "On Bolivia's New Child Labour Law".
[108] See "Open Letter: A Better Approach to Child Work" (27 January 2016), www.opendemocracy.net/open-letter-better-approach-to-child-work and "Why ILO Convention 138 Should Not Be Referenced in the General Comment on the Rights of Adolescents: An Argument from

The following section utilises a rights-based analysis to inform consideration of the appropriateness and value of children's work in circumstances in which children's immediate and long-term interests may appear to conflict.

HUMAN AND CHILDREN'S RIGHTS PERSPECTIVES

While international development perspectives are primarily concerned with issues of education and children's work at the macro-economic level, a rights analysis facilitates examination of the impact of political and legislative actions on individual children's well-being not only in the present but also for their future. It brings to the fore children's own views and ambitions as to the shaping of their adult lives and enables consideration of the appropriate balance to be struck between their claims to protection and autonomy.

The principle of the right to work is set out in article 23 of the Universal Declaration of Human Rights (UDHR),[109] which provides that:

1. Everyone has the right to work, to free choice of employment, to just and favourable conditions of work and to protection against unemployment.
2. Everyone, without any discrimination, has the right to equal pay for equal work.
3. Everyone who works has the right to just and favourable remuneration ensuring for himself and his family an existence worthy of human dignity, and supplemented, if necessary, by other means of social protection.
4. Everyone has the right to form and to join trade unions for the protection of his interests.

The International Covenant on Economic, Social and Cultural Rights (ICESCR)[110] provides greater elaboration of the right to work in articles 6 through 8. The ICESCR recognises the "right of everyone to the opportunity to gain his living by work which he freely chooses or accepts" (article 6(1)), and imposes an obligation on State Parties to provide "technical and vocational guidance and training programmes, policies and techniques to achieve steady economic, social and cultural development and full and productive employment under conditions safeguarding fundamental political and economic freedoms to the individual". Article 7 provides for "the enjoyment of just and favourable conditions of work", including "equal remuneration for work of equal value without distinction of any kind"; "[s]afe and

---

Human Rights Principles: Submission to the United Nations Committee on the Rights of the Child" (13 August 2016), www.opendemocracy.net/beyondslavery/open-essay-better-approach-to-child-work.

[109] UNGA, Universal Declaration of Human Rights (UN Doc A/810, 10 December 1948).
[110] UNGA, International Covenant on Economic, Social and Cultural Rights (UN Doc. A/6316, 16 December 1966) 992 UNTS 3.

healthy" working conditions; and reasonable opportunities for rest and leisure. Article 8 requires State Parties to protect the right to form and join a trade union.

While not drafted with children in mind, both the UDHR and the ICESCR explicitly refer in their respective preambles to the principle that "recognition of the inherent dignity and of the equal and inalienable rights of all members of the human family is the foundation of freedom, justice and peace in the world". This principle would be wholly undermined by the exclusion of children from the protected rights, yet demands by Peruvian children's working movements for explicit recognition of children's right to work in an amendment to the UNCRC were not met: labour organisations were opposed to the representation of working children in discussions about child labour and the children's call was regarded as "a distraction rather than a contribution" by IPEC Peru.[111] Arguably, the protective focus of article 32 of the UNCRC and the UN Committee on the Rights of the Child's endorsement of ILO Convention 138 in its General Comment on Adolescence[112] support academic criticism that the UNCRC tends to a Western protectionism in its view of children. The following sections consider the inter-relationship and tensions between the notion of the right to free choice of employment as conceptualised in the UDHR and the ICESCR and children's rights to protection from harm to their future prospects, using Sen's concept of ethical universalism between as well as within generations; articles 3, 5 and 12 of the UNCRC; and Hollingsworth's notion of foundational rights.

Free Choice of Employment and the Evolving Capacities of the Child

Given that the reality for many children is that they work because they have to, and that the work-education dichotomy is a fallacy, an abolitionist approach to child labour is not always in children's best interests, nor that of the family and community of which they are a part.[113] Eric Edmonds draws attention to the fact that although the international policy agenda assumes child labour to be work that it would be better for the child not to undertake, given the nature or the circumstances of the work, evidence does not allow for clear generalisations about the balance of harm for children in these situations.[114] Children are often best positioned to evaluate the least harmful solution to their individual situations themselves, as demonstrated by research such as that of Samuel Okyere in Ghana's artisanal gold mines.[115] In Okyere's study, children chose

---

[111] Post, "Conceiving Child Labour in Human Rights Terms".
[112] UNCRC Committee, "General comment No. 20 (2016) on the implementation of the rights of the child during adolescence" (UN Doc. CRC/C/GC/20, 6 December 2016).
[113] See, for example, Orkin, "In the Child's Best Interests?"; Okyere, "Are Working Children's Rights and Child Labour Abolition Complementary or Opposing Realms?"
[114] Edmonds, "Defining Child Labour".
[115] Okyere, "Are Working Children's Rights and Child Labour Abolition Complementary or Opposing Realms?"

relatively hazardous work that meets the criteria to be targeted for immediate abolition by the ILO in preference to alternative opportunities because it was sufficiently lucrative that work in the school holidays could fully fund their expenses for the forthcoming term and offered significant autonomy for the children to choose the nature and hours of the work undertaken. Application of the principles underpinning article 5 of the UNCRC as set out in Gerison Lansdown's analysis for UNICEF's Innocenti Research Centre suggests that children should be empowered to make decisions for themselves in matters affecting them when they reach sufficient competence to do so.[116] Since competence increases with maturity and experience as well as age, children in the contexts under consideration here will often display high levels of competence and capacity for autonomous decision-making. Lansdown proposes that to promote both children's competence and respect for their autonomy rights, a proportionality framework should be used to determine in what circumstances children should be empowered to make their own decisions. Under such a framework, children's decisions would only be overruled where it can be shown that "the child is not competent to understand the implications of the choice *and* that the consequent risks associated with the choice would be counter to the child's best interests".[117] A capabilities approach is consistent with this framework because the centrality of agency in a capabilities approach "means that children should be afforded the maximum scope for decisional freedom consistent with their actual – or potential – capacity for rational and reasoned forms of choice, or judgement".[118] Such an approach would potentially open up decisions as to their participation in harmless activities to very young children. In relation to children's work, Kate Orkin advocates regulation in keeping with this approach, whereby work that causes no or minimal harm is not limited, to avoid withholding the advantages of work from children.[119] These advantages may be not only immediate, in alleviation of the effects of present poverty and by enabling access to schooling, but may in some contexts also enhance children's evolving capacities further by providing valuable skills for their future employment. Orkin stresses the importance of children's participation in locally specific definitions of harmful work in environments best understood by the local community.

Yet further consideration of the varied social, economic and cultural contexts of children's lives reveals the complexities and potential pitfalls of this approach. In her analysis of article 5 of the UNCRC, Lansdown also discusses the need to consider the extent to which children may be vulnerable to coercion or manipulation

---

[116] G. Lansdown, *The Evolving Capacities of the Child* (Florence, Italy: Save the Children/UNICEF Innocenti Research Centre, 2005).
[117] Ibid., 56 (emphasis added).
[118] R. Dixon and M. Nussbaum, "Children's Rights and a Capabilities Approach: The Question of Special Priority." Chicago Public law and Legal Theory Working Paper No. 384 (2012) 97 *Cornell Law Review* 549, 560.
[119] Orkin, "In the Child's Best Interests?"

when assessing their competence to make any particular decision for themselves.[120] Although a child's best interests are "a primary consideration" in all actions affecting the child under article 3 of the UNCRC, pressures to conform to cultural and gendered expectations and to contribute to their family's income may be intense on children who have not experienced other lifestyles or roles. Manfred Liebel points out that children may not be well able to judge risk, to determine their own best interest or to balance the short-term benefits of work against their interests in the longer term.[121] For example, it may not be realistic to expect children imbued with a strong notion of a "dutiful" child[122] to be able or willing to disentangle consideration of their personal best interests from those of their wider family and community, or for girls to aspire to a career in the face of gendered expectations of domestic servitude. These concerns are reflected in the capabilities approach through consideration of what Nussbaum refers to as "preference-deformation".[123] And the question arises here as to whether, or to what extent, an individual child's best interests can or should be regarded as subsumed within those of their family and/or community and/or in what circumstances they should cede priority to those other or broader interests.

Children's Foundational Rights and Access to an Open Future

Kathryn Hollingsworth uses the term "foundational rights" to encompass the group of rights that operate in childhood to support the development of the capacities required for the child to exercise "full" autonomy when she or he reaches the age of legal majority.[124] Hollingsworth distinguishes "full" autonomy from the more limited liberal definition of autonomy, which comprises no more than adequate capacity to exercise agency and freedom from external constraints on doing so. "Full" autonomy, in contrast, incorporates consideration of the way in which a person's exercise of autonomy may be affected by social relationships and context, such as the cultural traditions and expectations discussed briefly in the preceding text. Foundational rights represent explicit recognition of the legal function of childhood in the development of the child's potential to the fullest extent possible (as articulated, for example, in article 29 of the UNCRC), and thereby of what distinguishes the rights of children from those of adults. School attendance is one

---

[120] Lansdown, *The Evolving Capacities of the Child*, 55.
[121] Liebel, "Do Children Have a Right to Work?"
[122] See Organisation of African Unity, African Charter on the Rights and Welfare of the Child (OAU Doc CAB/LEG/24.9/49, 11 July 1990) article 31 and for a discussion of the concept, see J. Sloth-Nielsen and B. D. Mezmur, "A Dutiful Child: The Implications of Article 31 of the African Children's Charter" (2008) 52 *Journal of African Law* 159.
[123] M. Nussbaum, *Women and Human Development: The Capabilities Approach* (Cambridge: Cambridge University Press, 2000).
[124] K. Hollingsworth, "Theorising Children's Rights in Youth Justice: The Significance of Autonomy and Foundational Rights" (2013) 76(6) *The Modern Law Review* 1046, 1039.

issue that Hollingsworth cites as an example of an area in which curtailing a child's current exercise of autonomy may be justified in the interests of maximising their future potential as a fully autonomous adult. A liberal account of autonomy might justify assuring to a child only the minimum competences required to function independently in adulthood, so that the rights of children growing up in a rural subsistence economy would arguably be significantly different from those that might be claimed on behalf of children for whom a university education may be regarded as a necessary precondition to access the "skilled economy". But an account founded on notions of a child's foundational rights would reject such unequal claims based upon a child's social and cultural context.

The notion of foundational rights is premised on the concept of human capabilities, proposed by Sen and developed further by Martha Nussbaum.[125] The capabilities approach rejects models of development that focus on economic indicators as failing to give adequate attention to inequality and to significant aspects of people's lives, such as education and health.[126] It stresses instead the importance of creating "conditions in which people have real opportunities of judging the kind of lives they would like to lead".[127] The notion of full autonomy incorporates this vision of assuring to people the freedom to "lead the kind of lives they value – and have reason to value".[128] In *Development as Freedom*, Sen asserts that freedom is the "preeminent objective of development".[129] Development, in his analysis, "consists of the removal of various types of unfreedoms that leave people with little choice and little opportunity of exercising their reasoned agency".[130] He describes the move from forced or bonded labour to free contract systems of employment as one of the most important changes in the development process of many economies and points to the lack of freedom of choice for children from poor families being forced into exploitative work as a poignant example of the constraints of poverty on freedom.

Sudhir Anand and Amartya Sen have coined the term "ethical universalism" to denote "recognition of a shared claim of all to the basic capability to lead worthwhile lives".[131] The concept was developed in a paper devoted to the issue of sustainable human development, and is defined specifically to incorporate the

---

[125] The relationship between the capabilities approach and human rights is beyond the scope of this chapter but see A. Sen, "Human Rights and Capabilities" (2005) 6(2) *Journal of Human Development* 151, for a discussion of the extent to which they are complementary. Nussbaum stresses the "very close connection between the account of central capabilities and an account of basic human rights", describing the capabilities approach as "one way of further fleshing out an account of human rights" (Nussbaum, *Women and Human Development*, 148–149).
[126] Dixon and Nussbaum, "Children's Rights and a Capabilities Approach".
[127] Sen, *Development as Freedom*, 63.
[128] Ibid., 18.
[129] Ibid., xii.
[130] Ibid.
[131] S. Anand and A. Sen, "Human Development and Economic Sustainability" (2000) 28(12) *World Development* 2029, 2030.

principle of "impartiality between as well as within generations".[132] Although Anand and Sen had in mind the challenge of promoting economic development in the present without prejudicing the prospects of future generations, the principle applies equally well to the life trajectories of children growing up in very poor communities, whose future prospects are constrained by the short-term needs and expectations of families and communities. Children's longer-term interests may conflict with those of their parents, who may be unable to look beyond their own immediate needs or to prioritise investment in their children's future. Sen, addressing the objections of developmentalists that economic development may be harmful to communities' cultures and traditional way of life, concludes that this issue raises a question of values and that the people directly involved must have the freedom to choose whether to adhere to traditional customs or sacrifice or adapt them for developmental advantages.[133] Although Sen is considering here the rights of communities to collectively determine their priorities, in relation to children who are reared within a particular framework of expectations, application of this principle implies allowing children sufficient understanding of alternative lifestyles and gendered or generational roles to reject traditional models in adulthood should they choose to do so. Perhaps, therefore, we should be slow to criticise education that appears not to be directly relevant to the world of work to which children will be exposed within their own communities if it opens their eyes to the prospect of a wider world of opportunity in the globalised economy.

RECONCILING THE INTERESTS OF THE CHILD IN THE PRESENT AND THE FUTURE, AND THE RIGHTS OF THE CHILD WITH THE NEEDS OF THE COMMUNITY OF WHICH THEY ARE A PART

In this chapter I have argued that children have a right to work, but that they also have a right to an "open" future and to the development of their capabilities to the fullest extent to allow them to take advantage of opportunities that might exist in the globalised and developing world, should they choose to do so. Children's rights-based objections to the international agenda to eradicate child labour challenge the assumption of a universal determination that employment is contrary to children's best interests. This challenge arguably applies to children in high-income countries as much as to those in the poorest nations. In the context of New Zealand, for example, Ruth Gasson et al. argue that the MAC limits children's life chances, including through denying poorer children access to equal opportunities to those available to wealthier peers.[134] As others do in the context of developing nations,

---

[132] Ibid.
[133] Sen, *Development as Freedom*.
[134] N. R. Gasson et al., "Young People's Employment: Protection or Participation?" (2015) 22(2) *Childhood* 154.

Gasson et al. argue that rather than banning all children under a certain age from employment, government policy in New Zealand should be concerned with fair treatment and conditions for those that do work. Work experience is also a powerful means by which children's evolving capacities may be enhanced and in the context of developed nations, as Morrow puts it, "turning children into 'learners', and excluding them from work, leaves governments with the problem of converting young people into 'earners'".[135]

Children's participation in decisions affecting their working lives in the particular local contexts in which they grow up is critical to the promotion of their best interests and to protect them from exploitation and harm, both to their immediate health and well-being and to their future prospects.[136] However, as discussed previously, overemphasis on children's competence to make decisions in relation to the work they undertake risks underestimating the extent to which children may feel bound by the constraints of cultural and natural loyalty, gendered expectations and community traditions. This may be particularly the case for girls involved in domestic work in their own home or that of another family because of the hidden and unregulated nature of the work and because of the weight of gendered expectations as to the appropriate conduct of girls and the narrow prospects for their future in some communities. Working children's movements offer a powerful means by which children may collectively challenge their status and working conditions, but implementation of children's article 12 rights in family businesses and in the home, where children's work goes unrecognised and unregulated, presents a significant challenge. This must be addressed through parental education[137] and community discussion as well as through the principles of article 29, which expects that states provide education directed, *inter alia*, to the "development of respect for human rights and fundamental freedoms". Children's participation in research is also key to understanding the factors that draw children into work and that place them at risk of exploitation.[138]

Children's fight for the "right to work" – that is, to choose for themselves whether to work and the work that they do – has arisen from the failure of international measures to protect them from poverty and exploitation, or even the tendency for such interventions to worsen their plight.[139] In all contexts, the literature demonstrates that an outright ban on children's employment is liable to result in moving children's work into informal and/or illegal economies and that the way forward to

---

[135] Morrow, "Should the World Really Be Free of 'Child Labour'?", 437.
[136] In response to feedback, the final version of the ILO Roadmap was revised to include in the Guiding Principles that government responsibility to enforce the right to education and eliminate the worst forms of labour should be assumed "with the best interests of children in mind and 'taking into consideration the views of children and their families'" (ILO, *Roadmap for Achieving the Elimination of the Worst Forms of Child Labour* [2010], 2).
[137] DeGraff et al., "Child Labour and Mothers' Work in Brazil".
[138] Abebe and Bessell, "Dominant Discourses, Debates and Silences".
[139] Liebel, "Do Children Have a Right to Work?".

protect children from exploitation lies in legal recognition for and regulation of their labour to ensure that it meets the present needs of the child, their family and community without prejudicing children's future prospects. To this end, working children's movements and organisations developed from informal support groups of children in Latin America in the late 1970s, spreading to Africa and Asia from the early 1990s.[140] Working children's movements seek dignity for their members through and at work; respect for the work they do; safe conditions; education and professional training appropriate to their situation; and participation in relevant policy decisions at all levels. These demands represent no more than the fulfilment of the rights laid down by the UDHR and the ICESCR (which include the right to form and join trade unions for the protection of workers' interests) and of children's participation rights under article 12 of the UNCRC.

The international focus on child labour addresses a genuine, widespread and severe global problem of the exploitation of children. But the claim that the elimination of the worst forms of child labour is best addressed through eradication of all child labour does not withstand scrutiny and the term should be redefined in line with the UNCRC article 32. Further, the abolitionist agenda endorsed in the SDGs is not specifically or even primarily child-focused. The ILO claims that the elimination of child labour "can yield high social and economic returns, and that eradicating child labour – and providing the alternative of education and training, and decent work for adults and children of working age – contributes to households breaking out of the cycle of poverty, and helps countries advance human development".[141] Yet closer scrutiny demonstrates that international policy disregards the risk of children being forced into informal or illegal labour markets and families plunged into outright destitution through removal of lawful opportunities for children to work, while failing to address the plight of children in domestic servitude. It also suggests that the abolitionist agenda may conflict in some cases with achievement of SDG goals 1 (eradication of poverty), 4 (universal education), 5 (gender discrimination) and 10 (reduction of inequalities) and sacrifice the life chances of individual children and families in the name of global economic development. The approach of the UNCRC is to be preferred to that of the ILO not only because it focuses on protection from harm rather than imposing an arbitrary ban but also because of the holistic scheme of rights under the UNCRC. This enables a child-centred assessment of the best interests of children in the particular context of children's lives, taking into account their own views and respecting children's evolving capacities.[142] The decision of the UN Committee on the Rights of the Child to endorse ILO 138 in the General Comment on the implementation of the

---

[140] Ibid.
[141] ILO-IPEC and Ministry of Social Affairs and Employment of the Netherlands, "The Hague Global Child Labour Conference 2010", 33, point iv.
[142] See "Why ILO Convention 138 Should Not Be Referenced in the General Comment on the Rights of Adolescents".

Rights of the Child during Adolescence represents a significant failure by that body to uphold children's article 3 and article 12 rights in particular.[143]

The fundamental strength of a rights-based approach lies in its accordance of dignity and equal value at a personal level. Combining insights from recent developments in children's rights theory and the concept of ethical universalism facilitates an analysis that balances children's protection against their autonomy interests, as well as their immediate well-being and autonomy against their future prospects, and that recognises children as individuals with unique histories and aspirations. If we aspire to a world in which all children have equal freedom to choose their own future, this must be the way forward.

---

[143] UNCRC Committee, "General Comment No. 20 (2016) on the Implementation of the Rights of the Child during Adolescence" (UN Doc. CRC/C/GC/20, 6 December 2016).

14

Advancing the Right to Play in International Development

Tara Collins and Laura H. V. Wright

"The right to play is the right to be yourself" (14-year-old male).
"When you're younger it allows you to form who you are" (17-year-old male).
"It's human to express yourself" (18-year-old male).
"Knowing that every child has to have the opportunity to play, explore and be a kid" (15-year-old female).
"The right to play is being able to express yourself without being judged" (17-year-old female).[1]
"Play is having fun for the rest of your life" (7-year-old female).[2]
"Play is the exultation of the possible" (Bruber).[3]

INTRODUCTION

Play is not simply a desire or need of children. Play is a human right of children recognised by international law. In article 31 of the 1989 UN Convention on the Rights of the Child (UNCRC),[4] the international community promotes and protects the child's right to play to affirm its essential role in children's lives.

---

[1] The co-authors are grateful to Emma Colucci, Christina Brinco and Faith Lee for their valuable research support in this chapter.
   Young people consulted and quoted in Hon. L. Pearson and L. Akbar, *Shaking the Movers VII: Standing Up for Children's Right to Play* (Ottawa, ON: Landon Pearson Resource Centre for the Study of Childhood and Children's Rights, Carleton University, Ryerson University, Provincial Advocate for Children and Youth, 2013), 13.

[2] Seven-year-old quoted in J. Nicholson et al., "Listening to Children's Perspective on Play across the Lifespan: Children's Rights to Inform Adults' Discussion and Contemporary Play" (2014) 3 *International Journal of Play* 136, 136.

[3] M. Bruber, *Pointing the Way: Collected Essays* (New York: Harper, 1957).

[4] UN General Assembly (UNGA), Convention on the Rights of the Child (UN Doc. A/RES/44/25, 20 November 1989) 1577 UNTS 3

Play is often considered an integral part of our humanity as *homo ludens*, the playful human being as described by Huizinga.[5] Nevertheless, there are diverging perspectives on how play is understood and appreciated. While some international actors and agencies may consider play as an integral part of human experience, others understand play as "nuisance ... [or] privilege" as Mullen critiques.[6] In the serious business of supporting children's development and redressing the humanitarian problems caused by natural disasters and conflict around the world, the child's right to play is often minimised as an afterthought or even ignored. Play is often conceived as less important by individuals and organisations placing priority on such urgent essential requirements of human life as clean water, adequate nutrition, disease control and so on. Since Yordi et al. describe that "rights are also expressed through everyday attitudes and practices",[7] where is play in relation to international development and humanitarian efforts?

The child's right to play is an integral element in sustainable development in relation to international development and humanitarian programming, which is deemed to instrumentally support children's healthy development and well-being in the present and future, as well as having intrinsic value as part of childhood. Sustainable development describes the international approach *inter alia* to realising "the human rights of all" in an integrated and indivisible manner.[8] This chapter explores the role of the right to play in the lives of children and young people across cultures and contexts. We argue that children's right to play should be respected and supported, not belittled or manipulated through adult or organisational influence or control. This chapter also discusses how play can be advanced and how international development and humanitarian work can strengthen intentionality for more effective contributions to children's current and future well-being and development. As noted in the opening quotations, young people are clear about play's importance when consulted, and their voices should be given "due weight" in decision-making around the advancement of play in accordance with UNCRC article 12.

Access to more programming and infrastructure to support this right is a problem within countries and across countries around the world in "Minority" and "Majority" world countries. In the Minority world countries, a lack of quality play spaces and a reduction in opportunities to play infringes on children's ability to actualise this right. For example, 14-year-old Wes Prankard created Northern Starfish focussing on indigenous First Nations reserves that do not have playgrounds because

---

[5] J. Huizinga, *Homo Ludens* (London: Routledge and Kegan Paul Ltd., 1949); and B. Sutton-Smith, *The Ambiguity of Play* (Cambridge, MA: Harvard University Press, 1997).

[6] See, for example, M. Mullen, "Getting Serious about the Human Right to Play" (2014) 3 *Asia Pacific Journal of Sport and Social Science* 130, 130.

[7] R. Yordi et al., "Making Rights Work: Exploring Rights Based Programming to Enhance Education Opportunities for Children Working in Egyptian Micro-enterprises" (PPIC-Work, 2009), www.ppic-work.org/download/manuals/PPIC_Work_LTW_Paper.pdf, 8.

[8] UNGA, "Transforming Our World: The 2030 Agenda for Sustainable Development" (UN Doc. A/RES/70/1, 21 October 2015), preamble.

"playgrounds are a way for kids to be kids but most northern communities do not have playgrounds. My mission is to build a playground in every northern community in Canada that doesn't have one".[9] In another example, young people associated with the Child Rights Alliance in Ireland identified the lack of recreational spaces as one of the top three critical issues in a film they developed on about children's rights in Ireland.[10] Although limitations in the realisation of the right to play exist across countries, this chapter will focus on play in development and humanitarian contexts. Further, this chapter will focus on play in article 31 only and will not focus on other elements in article 31 namely cultural life and rest due to limited scope; it does not elaborate upon the role of organised sport, which has already been more extensively discussed in the sport for development and peace literature.[11]

This chapter relies upon three main influences for its conceptual framework: children's rights, sociology of childhood, and an anti-colonial discursive framework. First, children's rights are multidisciplinary and reflect the scope in, and breadth of, international and regional instruments. This chapter relies upon the primary instrument: the UNCRC, which is the most successful human rights treaty ever with 196 States Parties,[12] that must reflect the specific contexts and realities of children around the world. As described later, a child rights-based approach (CRBA), stemming from several UNCRC provisions, informs the exploration of the role and realisation of the right to play in international development and humanitarian efforts. Second, the sociology of childhood considers children as social actors or agents, influencing their own lives, the lives of others as well as the societies in which they live.[13] Third, an anti-colonial discursive framework critiques the ongoing realities of colonised peoples, and imagines what other possibilities exist, and is rooted in the perspective and experiences of those subordinated through colonisation.[14]

---

[9] Northern Starfish, "About", http://northernstarfish.org/about-2/.
[10] The other young people identified poverty and bullying as the other two issues: Children's Rights Alliance (Ireland), "Do Children's Rights Matter?" film (Dublin: Children's Rights Alliance, 2013), www.childrensrights.ie/.
[11] E. Colucci, "Sport as a Tool for Participatory Education – The Grassroot Soccer Methodology", in K. Gilbert and W. Bennett (eds.), *Sport, Peace, and Development*, (London: Common Ground Publishing, 2012), 341–354; E. Donnelly, S. Darnell and J. Coakley, "The Use of Sport to Foster Child and Youth Development and Education", in *Literature Reviews on Sport for Development and Peace* (Toronto: Sport for Development and Peace International Working Group, 2007).
[12] UNGA, Convention on the Rights of the Child (UN Doc. A/RES/44/25, 20 November 1989) 1577 UNTS 3.
[13] G. Dahlberg, P. Moss and A. Pence, "Constructing Early Childhood: What Do We Think It Is?", in *Beyond Quality in Early Childhood Education and Care: Languages of Evaluation*, 2nd ed. (London and New York: Routledge, 2007), 43, 49.
[14] G. J. S. Dei and A. Asgharzadeh, "The Power of Social Theory: The Anti-colonial Discursive Framework" (2001) 35(3) *The Journal of Educational Thought* 297.

To define play, this chapter relies upon the influential theoretical work of Huizinga, which is defined and summarised in the following section. The common terminology of "international development and humanitarian" work – whether activities, efforts or settings – is also utilised to reflect the common vocabulary of international discourse, but it is important to note that development is occurring all over the globe. The terms of *Majority world(s)* and *Minority world(s)* from international development studies are used to distinguish the majority of countries considered to have economic, political and social challenges, while the Minority world includes those countries considered industrialised and economically and politically stable.[15]

This chapter is organised in the following manner. First, we explore the definition of play and how the right to play has developed. Second, the relationship is discussed between the right to play and children in the international development and humanitarian settings. In the final section, we introduce the CRBA to analyse and advance right to play in this sector, before concluding with recommendations for future actions at the advocacy, implementation and monitoring and evaluation level to support the child's right to play.

PLAY DEFINED AND THE RIGHT TO PLAY

"Child's play" is an all too common expression denoting simplistic activities with a pejorative connotation in terms of societal priorities.[16] Yet, play is a complex activity. In *Homo Ludens*, Huizinga explains that

> play is more than a physiological phenomenon or a psychological reflex. It goes beyond the confines of purely physical or purely biological activity. It is a *significant* function – that is to say, there is some sense to it. In play there is something "at play" which transcends the immediate needs of life and imparts meaning to the action. All play means something.[17]

Huizinga explains that play is not simply a psychological task of childhood, or a developmental phenomenon through the stages of childhood but rather defines play as a cultural construct of human life.[18] Play has four necessary factors for participants according to Burghardt: "sufficient metabolic energy, buffered from severe stress,

---

[15] See, for example, O. Nieuwenhuys, "Global Childhood and the Politics of Contempt" (1998) 23(3) *Alternatives: Global, Local, Political* 267.
[16] Play is described as "enjoyment" according to the Cambridge English Dictionary, that is, "activity that is not serious but done for enjoyment, especially when children enjoy themselves with toys and games" (http://dictionary.cambridge.org/dictionary/english/play).
[17] Huizinga, *Homo Ludens*, 1.
[18] Ibid.

need for stimulation, [and] a lifestyle that involves complex sequences of behaviour in varying conditions".[19]

According to Huizinga, play is defined as "a voluntary activity or occupation executed within certain fixed limits of time and place, according to rules freely accepted but absolutely binding, having its aim in itself and accompanied by a feeling of tension, joy and the consciousness that it is 'different' from 'ordinary life'".[20] Play has several characteristics. First, "it is free, is in fact freedom"; and second, "play is not 'ordinary' or 'real' life. It is rather a stepping out of 'real' life into a temporary sphere activity with a disposition all of its own. Many children are aware that play is a time and space for 'pretending', and/or 'fun'".[21] "Play is distinct from 'ordinary' life both as to locality and duration. This is the third main characteristic of play: its secludedness and its limitedness. It is 'played out' with certain limits of time and place. It contains its own course and meaning".[22] Fourth, play also "creates order, *is* order. Into an imperfect world and into the confusion of life it brings a temporary, a limited perfection. Play demands order absolute and supreme. The least deviation from it 'spoils the game', robs it of its character and makes it worthless".[23]

Further, there have been additional understandings of the nature of play distinguished between intrinsic and instrumental play as described in the following text.

> *Intrinsic Play*: Intrinsic play recognises how play is "an extremely important and basic characteristic of a person or thing".[24] In other words, play is understood and appreciated for what it contributes to a child's life and its enjoyment. Further to Huizinga's aforementioned descriptions of play, Doddridge succinctly describes the role and significance of the intrinsic value of play: "Live, while you live".[25]
>
> *Instrumental Play*: Intrinsic play is often contrasted with the instrumental play, which recognises the role of how play serves a specific or several objectives to reach intended outcomes. Instrumental play acknowledges how play contributes to a child's development, education, socialisation and so on. For instance, the instrumental element reflects inter alia the fact that neuroplasticity that helps us "to recover from developmental traumas is itself a product of play – since play is known to produce neurotrophins".[26] Instrumental play recognises that: "Therapies in

---

[19] As cited by S. Lester and W. Russell, "Children's Right to Play: An Examination of the Importance of Play in Children's Lives Worldwide" (The Hague, The Netherlands: Bernard Van Leer Foundation, 2010), 36.
[20] Ibid., 28.
[21] Ibid., 8.
[22] Ibid., 9.
[23] Ibid., 10.
[24] Cambridge English Dictionary, "intrinsic" (http://dictionary.cambridge.org/dictionary/english/intrinsic).
[25] As cited by J. Orton, *Memoirs of the Life, Character and Writings of the Late Reverend Philip Doddridge, D.D. of Northampton* (London: J. Cotton and J. Eddowes, 1766), 171.
[26] O. Ouidon, "Well Played. The Origins and Future of Playfulness" (2014) 6 *American Journal of Play* 234, 252.

children almost universally incorporate play because the play drive is so strong in children, it can be considered the natural language of childhood".[27]

Our literature review conducted in this chapter in 2015 and 2016 reveals that there is a gap in the literature on the topic of intrinsic and spontaneous play in the Majority world. Most of the literature is based on instrumental play focusing on play approaches, pedagogy in preschools and so on.

The established tension between instrumental basis and intrinsic value of play is resolved from a child rights framework. Child rights are not only concerned about the future of the child and reaching full potential, as instrumental play emphasises, but also how they are respected in the present. In other words, we cannot simply consider children as "our future", even though such understanding is very pervasive because children are also part of our present.[28] Consequently, the either/or binary dichotomy between intrinsic and instrumental understandings of play must be abandoned to embrace the full complexity and value of the child right to play in and of itself and how it relates to other rights. In general, Stammers outlines that consistent with the work of Hanson and Nieuwenhuys, there is a need to move beyond "sterile binaries – those strong ontological and epistemological assumptions found in so much academic and popular thought that describe and analyse the world in terms of polarities or dichotomies".[29] Children's rights and the sociology of childhood inform the understanding that children's agency should determine what play is and should be.

In exploring the right to the play, this section describes the provision of play in international human rights law. It then describes why play is a human right. Subsequently, the diversity of childhood in relation to play is explored.

Play in International Human Rights Law

Play has a long history in international human rights law. Prior to the UNCRC, "leisure" is recognised in: the Universal Declaration of Human Rights in article 24, which states that "[e]veryone has the right to rest and leisure"; and in the International Covenant on Economic, Social and Cultural Rights, "the right of everyone to the enjoyment of just and favourable conditions of work" includes in article 7(d) the provision for "[r]est, leisure and reasonable limitation of working hours and periodic holidays with pay, as well as renumeration for public holidays".[30]

---

[27] Ibid., 253.
[28] T. M. Collins and C. Gervais, "Children's Rights: Their Role, Significance and Potential", in G. DiGiacomo (ed.), *Current Issues and Controversies in Human Rights* (Toronto: University of Toronto Press, 2016), 168–197.
[29] N. Stammers, "Children's Rights and Social Movements: Reflections from a Cognate Field", in K. Hanson and O. Nieuwenhuys (eds.), *Reconceptualizing Children's Rights in International Development* (Cambridge: Cambridge University Press, 2013), 275–292, 275.
[30] UNGA, Universal Declaration of Human Rights (UDHR), (UN Doc A/810, 10 December 1948); UNGA, International Covenant on Economic, Social and Cultural Rights (ICESCR) (UN Doc. A/6316, 16 December 1966) 992 UNTS 3.

A provision for the child to "have full opportunity for play and recreation" was also included in Principle 7 of the Declaration on the Rights of the Child adopted in 1959.[31] As Mullen describes, the "1959 Declaration of the Rights of the Child positioned play as a right that 'should be directed to the same purposes as education', which 'society and public authorities shall endeavour to promote'".[32]

The most significant elaboration of play is article 31 of the UNCRC, which outlines:

1. States Parties recognize the right of the child to rest and leisure, to engage in play and recreational activities appropriate to the age of the child ...
2. States Parties shall respect and promote the right of the child to participate fully in cultural and artistic life and shall encourage the provision of appropriate and equal opportunities for cultural, artistic, recreational and leisure activity.

David highlights the fact that "the right to play is a new type of right which was for the first time recognised in the UNCRC and thereafter in the African Charter. It is therefore a right only acknowledged under international law for persons below 18. No other human rights instruments do recognise this right, though some soft law instruments do promote the right to play".[33] The African Charter of the Rights and Welfare of the Child provides for the child's right to play in article 12, using the same influential language as the UNCRC's provision.[34]

According to the UN Committee on the Rights of the Child (UNCRC Committee), the right to play is important in itself but also in relation to other rights in the UNCRC.[35] The UNCRC Committee has adopted a General Comment to elaborate the significance of the child's right to play, which acknowledges and advances "the unique and evolving nature of childhood" and how play supports

> the quality of childhood, to children's entitlement to optimum development, to the promotion of resilience and to the realization of other rights. Indeed, environments in which play and recreational opportunities are available to all children provide

---

[31] UNGA, Declaration of the Rights of the Child, (UN Doc. A/RES/14/1386, 20 November 1959).
[32] Mullen, "Getting Serious about the Human Right to Play", 131.
[33] P. David, Article 31 The Right to Leisure, Play and Culture: A Commentary on the United Nations Convention on the Rights of the Child (Leiden, The Netherlands: M. Nijhoff Publishers, 2006), 3.
[34] Organisation of African Unity, African Charter on the Rights and Welfare of the Child (OAU Doc CAB/LEG/24.9/49, 11 July 1990); and David, Article 31 The Right to Leisure, Play and Culture, 6.
[35] UNCRC Committee, "General Comment No. 17 (2013) on the Right of the Child to Rest, Leisure, Play, Recreational Activities, Cultural Life and the Arts (art. 31)" (UN Doc. CRC/C/GC/17, 17 April 2013), 2.

the conditions for creativity; opportunities to exercise competence through self-initiated play enhances motivation, physical activity and skills development.[36]

As such, duty bearers are obligated to respect children's right to play. However, the UNCRC Committee

> is concerned by the poor recognition given by States to the rights contained in article 31. Poor recognition of their significance in the lives of children results in lack of investment in appropriate provisions, weak or non-existent protective legislation and the invisibility of children in national and local-level planning.[37]

In line with the UNCRC Committee's concern, David outlines that article 31 is likely the UNCRC Committee's most overlooked provision.[38] David outlines that a UNICEF "analysis of the 98 country-based concluding observations adopted by the Committee between 2000 and 2004 shows that only in 15 countries the UNCRC Committee addressed the contents of article 31 (less than 15 per cent), often even in a very brief and scattered manner".[39] David posits that perhaps this lack of addressing article 31 exists because States Parties under-report in this area, and child advocacy groups and non-governmental organisations (NGOs) often neglect to report on this right specifically. Another reason offered by David is that rest, play, leisure and culture may be regarded "as a luxury in comparison to other rights whose violations bear [crueller], visible, and spectacular consequences".[40] Since then, article 31 has been promoted to the "2004-Day of General Discussion on 'Implementing Child Rights in Early Childhood'"[41] and, more recently, the aforementioned General Comment. Further support is needed from the main international treaty monitor.

Mullen also highlights how the UNCRC Committee has called upon State Parties to commit to ensuring the right to play internationally but that it also inadequately supports this emphasis since there is room to improve upon the UNCRC Committee's reporting on children's play. He notes that in 10 Lists of Issues submitted to States Parties during the monitoring process to request more information, play is only referred to one time in relation to St. Lucia.[42] Although the UNCRC Committee has adopted the critical General Comment to elaborate the obligations related to the right to play, additional support to garner international recognition as a human right in practice and monitoring is essential for further attention and dedicated efforts.

---

[36] Ibid.
[37] Ibid., 1.
[38] David, *Article 31 The Right to Leisure, Play and Culture*, 17.
[39] Ibid.
[40] Ibid.
[41] Ibid., 18.
[42] Mullen states that "The List published on 25 November 2013, asked St Lucia to consider using sport as a means of protecting children from high levels of crime and violence" (footnote omitted) ("Getting Serious about the Human Right to Play", 132).

As a human right of children, it is not sufficient to simply acknowledge negative obligations where the state must not interfere unduly in children's play. Human rights also involve a positive state duty to do what is possible to support the right. As Van Bueren notes in reference to Lowy: "In truth human rights, from which many of the rights of the child are derived, are concerned with both the protection of the individual from the state and the creation of societal conditions by which all individuals can develop to their fullest potential".[29] Hence, the state should not only respond to the concerns of the UNCRC Committee about play, as there may not be adequate attention to this particular right in the international monitoring process. The state must develop its approach to the right to play, recognising local contexts and realities and buttressed by international support and insights as appropriate.

The right to play, enshrined in article 31, continues to be one of the most neglected of all children's rights, particularly in the international development and humanitarian sector, often due to a lack of awareness and understanding of the benefits of play.[43]

Why Is Play a Human Right?

As a human right in international law, the international community recognises the fundamental role that play has in children's lives. While still undervalued by many, play is found in all cultures and is increasingly seen as a cornerstone of children's well-being, and full and healthy development (cognitive, social, emotional, physical and spiritual) across disciplines.[44] Play is often thought of as an integral part of our humanity as *homo ludens*, the playful human,[45] and has emerged as a serious focus of study in the last century.[46] Classic play theorists, namely Mead, Freud, Bateson, Piaget and Vygotsky, argue that play supports cognitive, social, emotional and language development.[47]

Thus, the affirmation of play as a child right reflects years of influential work. Numerous authors including Bruner, Vygotsky, Piaget, Sutton-Smith, Baer and others have established the long-standing understanding that play builds strong

---

[43] International Play Association (IPA), *IPA Global Consultations on Children's Right to Play: Summary Report* (2010), www.childwatch.uio.no/projects/activities/Article31/globalreportsummary-201010.pdf.

[44] UNCRC Committee, "General Comment No. 17 (2013)".

[45] Huizinga, *Homo Ludens*; and Sutton-Smith, *The Ambiguity of Play*.

[46] Huizinga, *Homo Ludens*.

[47] S. Gaskins, "Pretend Play as Culturally Constructed Activity", in M. Taylor (ed.), *Oxford Handbook of the Development of Imagination* (Oxford: Oxford University Press, 2013); A. Göncü and S. Gaskins, "Comparing and Extending Piaget's and Vygotsky's Understandings of Play: Symbolic Play as Individual, Sociocultural, and Educational Interpretation", in A. D. Pellegrini (ed.), *Oxford Handbook of the Development of Play* (Oxford: Oxford University Press, 2011).

affective, cognitive, social, motor development; communication; emotional self-awareness and self-regulation; peaceful citizenship and divergent thinking.[48] More recently, for example, Fiorelli documents in doctoral work that dramatic play can often inform healthy early childhood development and serves as a protective factor and, over time, supports children's acquisition of more effective responses to stress; "children who express their emotions either positive or negative in play generally feel happier, more energetic, and more cheerful than children who are more constricted in their play".[49]

Realisation of the right to play is fundamental to the quality of childhood, to children's entitlement to optimum development and to the promotion of resilience and realisation of all children's rights.[50] Play contributes to other children's rights including health, education and so on. Mullen outlines how play is fundamental to the realisation of all rights and aiding in full developmental potential – which has been evidenced by work in the field of psychology and neuroscience.[51] For instance, learning through play is highlighted in the early years.[52] Lester and Russell outline that:

> Play has an essential role in building children's resilience across adaptive systems – pleasure, emotion regulation, stress response systems, peer and place attachments, learning and creativity. These benefits arise from play's unpredictability, spontaneity, nonsense and irrationality, and also from children's sense of control. Adults need to ensure that the physical and social environments in which children live are supportive of their play; otherwise their survival, well-being and development may be compromised.[53]

Moreover, the UNCRC Committee enunciates in its General Comment how the provision is "mutually linked and reinforcing" in children's lives and that:

> Together, they describe conditions necessary to protect the unique and evolving nature of childhood. Their realization is fundamental to the quality of childhood, to children's entitlement to optimum development, to the promotion of resilience and to the realization of other rights. Indeed, environments in which play and recreational opportunities are available to all children provide the conditions for creativity; opportunities to exercise competence through self-initiated play enhances motivation, physical activity and skills development; playful interactions

---

[48] Gordon, "Well Played".
[49] J. A. Fiorelli, "Pretend Play, Coping, and Subjective Well-Being in Children: A Follow-Up Study" (unpublished PhD thesis, Case Western Reserve University, 2011), 100.
[50] UNCRC Committee, "General Comment No. 17 (2013)".
[51] See, for example, Mullen, "Getting Serious about the Human Right to Play".
[52] See following for further discussion about tensions; F. S. Baker, "Tensions in Policy and Practice: Influences on Play in Abu Dhabi's New School Model KG framework" (2014) 184 *Early Child Development and Care* 1830.
[53] Lester and Russell, "Children's Right to Play", 52.

through immersion in cultural life; necessary energy and motivation to participate in play and creative engagement.[54]

The UNCRC Committee's articulation is helpful to highlight the interdependence of play in relation to other children's rights.

Diversity of Childhood

As a human right, play should be respected around the world, but the diversity of childhoods can influence understandings of this right. How play and its characteristics are respected differ around the world just as implementation of this right varies depending upon the context and worldview.

According to article 1 of the UNCRC, a child is everyone up to the age of 18 years unless the age of majority in the jurisdiction is attained earlier. Yet, there is a great diversity of childhood and of children around the world. For instance, the right to play of a 12-week-old baby will vary dramatically from a 12-year-old. Moreover, a child in a refugee camp in Jordan may desire different outlets for play than a child in inner city Addis Ababa. Childhood can also be considered a social and cultural construction because a young person may be considered "ready" for marriage at the age of 13 in some contexts including Iran, and children can be held criminally responsible for their actions at the age of eight in Antigua and Barbuda, yet a "youth" in certain countries in Africa can include people up to the age of 35 years.[55] Due to this diversity, it is critical to question whether there is such thing as a global childhood, and deconstruct the predominant normative understanding.

Accordingly, play is understood differently across cultures. The discrepancy in this understanding between the Minority world and Majority world is evident in the debate about the need for greater efforts to support children's play outside due to the declining rate of outdoor play and increasing time spent on technological devices around the world.[56] The push for greater outdoor play in Western nations is well documented,[57] but Lester and Russell note: "When natural space is accessible for play, children will appropriate this, and children indicate that these are among their favourite play sites. For many children in large cities, contact with 'natural space' may be restricted, and children's main priority for place selection is

---

[54] UNCRC Committee, "General Comment No. 17 (2013)", 2.
[55] Right To Education Project, "Comparative Table on Minimum Age Legislation" (2013), www.right-to-education.org/page/comparative-table-minimum-age-legislation; and "youth or young people shall refer to every person between the ages of 15 and 35 years" in African Union Commission, African Youth Charter (2 July 2006), 3.
[56] J. L. Roopnarine and J. E. Johnson, "Play and Diverse Cultures: Implications for Early Childhood Education" in R. S. Reifel and M. H. Brown (eds.), *Early Education and Care, and Reconceptualising Play* (Amsterdam, The Netherlands, and New York: JAI, 2001), 234.
[57] Karsten and Van Gils, as cited in Lester and Russell, "Children's Right to Play", ix.

more akin to whether the space supports their play rather than a consideration of whether the space is natural or manufactured".[58]

Lester and Russell enunciate that in Minority countries, play is valued in the development of children because it provides important opportunities for children's learning. As a contrast to this, in certain spaces in the Majority world, adults and children share spaces. "Play is an integral part of daily patterns and is closely linked with the demands of household tasks and other chores. The temporal demands on children to carry out tasks become extended by combining play with work".[59] For example, as Nieuwenhuys describes, play occurs in South India in "places such as paths, fallow lands, the beach, the river bank, the wells and the public taps".[60] Lester and Russell then explain that: "Such mundane, everyday spaces become children's places for play in between the performance of daily tasks and routines".[61] In these spaces children are free from the regulations of adults. They can play as they wish and create "as if" behaviours, representing "fields of free action".[62] Thus, play is varied and influenced by the culture and values of the individuals within the community.[63]

Play serves many purposes depending upon the context. Finnegan points out that while oral traditions are used over time with children and can support understanding of solidarity, there is also societal division through different African songs, for example, that are paired to specific jobs to delineate children from youth and from adult work.[64] Nsamenang also outlines that "African parents, caregivers, and peer mentors use tacit cultural techniques and strategies that provoke the cognitive faculties to induce behavioural and affective changes and adjustment to knowledge and skills acquisition and social situations".[65] Hence, pretend play is not common in many African communities, and these adults engage children in daily responsibilities as a means of "productive play", also as a means of learning and growing as part of the community "often within the peer groups of neighbourhood and school. These ubiquitous developmental spaces have not been well researched".[66]

However, play is not always widely embraced and can be part of a general critique of the perceived challenge of international human rights and their universal framing in relation to cultural, religious and national relativism. Consequently, some actors are concerned that play only reflects the Western cultural imperative and that the

---

[58] As cited by Lester and Russell, "Children's Right to Play", 38, footnote omitted.
[59] Ibid., 29, footnotes omitted.
[60] Nieuwenhuys, as cited in ibid., 29.
[61] Lester and Russell, "Children's Right to Play", 29.
[62] Ibid., 31.
[63] Ibid., 33.
[64] R. Finnegan, "Child Play Is Serious: Children's Games, Verbal Art and Survival in Africa" (2014) 3 *International Journal of Play* 293, 296.
[65] A. B. Nsamenang, "Chapter 2 Dilemmas of Rights-Based Approaches to Child Well-Being in an African Cultural Context", in D. J. Johnson, D. L. Agbényiga and R. K. Hitchcock (eds.), *Vulnerable Children: Global Challenges in Education, Health, Well-Being, and Child Rights* (New York: Springer, 2013), 15.
[66] Ibid., 16.

conception of play as championed by international NGOs across the world ignores local realities.[67] Some recent research challenges this assumption. For instance, it was assumed that the influence of many theoretical and pedagogical ideals from Western education, and Western English-speaking teachers hired to work in Abu Dhabi schools, would lead to the role of play as a key element in the kindergarten program. In a case study approach with purposive sampling of 60 teachers from various countries and ethnicities there, Baker finds that play is limited in practice due to three themes from teachers: unanimous teacher focus on academic performance; a deficit view of children's ability to engage in play; and parents' emphasis upon literacy and numeracy skills in schools instead of play.[68] If play is considered "nuisance" and/or "privilege" as Mullen describes,[69] it is no wonder that parents rejected these efforts favouring play. Consequently, these challenges are likely pertinent in Gulf countries and "developing" countries that are implementing education reform.[70] This research highlights various questions including the potential discrepancy in understanding the role of play across actors including organisations, teachers, guardians and children. In addition, how do we rectify the challenge of children's perceived inability to play in the schools? What implications does the influence of Western valuing have on the understanding of play and what impacts does this have on the intrinsic and instrumental values of play? These issues are discussed later in the chapter.

Despite the differences, research has found that play has an important role to play in diverse cultures. Participation in play interactions, especially with parents, helps children to develop socially acceptable interactions within the context of their communities with some noted differences across cultures. For example, Turkish mothers socialise their children to be more autonomous, while English-speaking Caribbean mothers emphasise warmth and behavioural control.[71] It is critical "to underscore the culture-specific beliefs and the seminal properties of parent-child activities endemic to a particular community or diverse communities within a society".[72] In small-scale comparisons, mothers were play partners with their children in the United States 47 per cent of the time, 7 per cent in Guatemala and 24 per cent in India as examples.[73]

Yet there are also consistencies. For instance, across all countries that Bornstein and Putnick studied (127,000 families in 28 countries), parents invest considerable

---

[67] For example, ibid., 17.
[68] Baker, "Tensions in Policy and Practice", 1830.
[69] For example, see Mullen, "Getting Serious about the Human Right to Play", 130.
[70] Baker, "Tensions in Policy and Practice", 1839.
[71] Davidson, "Parent-Child Play across Cultures: Advancing Play Research" (2015) 7(2) American Journal of Play 228, 230.
[72] J. L. Roopnarine and K. L. Davidson, "Parent-Child Play across Cultures: Advancing Play Research" (2015) 7(2) American Journal of Play 228, 230.
[73] B. Rogoff et al., "Firsthand Learning through Intent Participation" (2003) 54 Annual Review of Psychology 175.

time taking their children outdoors and playing, where 60 per cent of mothers reported playing with their children under the age of five years, 64 per cent took them outdoors, 25 per cent read to their children and 47 per cent spent time pursing academic activities.[74]

These differences in the practice of play may lead critics of play to assert that play cannot be a human right of children. However research, practice and advocacy by academics and organisations elaborate the critical importance of play and why it is a right.[75] Lester and Russell, for example, highlight how play is the central way in which children interact with the world around them and "contribute to family life". "Play does not take place in a vacuum; it appears in the cultural, social and physical fabric of everyday life".[76] The diversity of childhoods demands a more complex understanding of the right to play.

THE CHILD'S RIGHT TO PLAY IN SUSTAINABLE DEVELOPMENT IN THE INTERNATIONAL DEVELOPMENT AND HUMANITARIAN SECTOR

In the international development and humanitarian sector, play is frequently deprioritised as frivolous and "silly" and of limited importance. Play continues to be one of the most neglected rights of the child in this sector. This is further exemplified by the lack of its explicit inclusion in the new Sustainable Development Goals (SDGs).[77] The International Play Association (IPA) global consultations found that these negative perceptions of play have deep roots in the socio-cultural construction of play as a concept in many different societies, where play is defined in opposition to work and, by implication, is not necessary and therefore not important.[78] Research, however, has increasingly highlighted the critical role of play in the healthy development of children.[79] Rather than being deemed a mere luxury, play can contribute to the realisation of children's rights to survival, development, participation and protection when properly utilised. Play can also contribute to the realisation and implementation of the SDGs. For instance, the 8th Commonwealth Sports Ministers Meeting in August 2016 recognised how sport, which is a

---

[74] Bronstein and Putnick as cited in ibid., 232.
[75] See, for example, Mullen, "Getting Serious about the Human Right to Play"; UNICEF (2014), "Why Sport?" www.unicef.org/sports/23619_23624.html.
[76] Lester and Russell, "Children's Right to Play", 27.
[77] UNGA, "Transforming Our World"; R. Shackel, "The Child's Right to Play: Laying the Building Blocks for Optimal Health and Well-Being", in A. B. Smith (ed.), *Enhancing Children's Rights: Connecting Research, Policy and Practice* (Basingstoke, UK: Palgrave Macmillan, 2015).
[78] IPA, *IPA Global Consultations on Children's Right to Play*.
[79] K. Hirsh-Pasek and R. Michnick Golinkoff, *Why Play = Learning* (2008), www.child-encyclopedia.com/play/according-experts/why-play-learning; R. Marantz Henig, "Taking Play Seriously" (*The New York Times Magazine*, 17 February 2008), www.nytimes.com/2008/02/17/magazine/17play.html?pagewanted=all; J. Ratey, *Spark: The Revolutionary New Science of Exercise and the Brain* (New York: Little, Brown and Company, 2008).

component of play, can contribute to the new global sustainable development agenda, and "welcomed recognition in the 2030 Agenda that sport can be 'an important enabler of sustainable development'. They committed to align sports architecture, and sport-based policy and strategy, to the Sustainable Development Goal (SDG) framework and associated targets".[80] This meeting acts as a critical entry point into the dialogue of sport and play in SDG implementation globally, recognising that play is an essential activity in a child's life.

While we do not see play explicitly identified in organisational mandate or programmatic priorities, in numerous international development and/or humanitarian organisations, play is used as a tool/method/approach in many child-centred organisations to support children's well-being and development outcome areas. These organisations recognise that intentional efforts in relation to play contribute to other children's rights including to health, education and so on. Our mapping of 19 international child-centred NGOs' use of play-based learning in their programs confirms that the majority use play at some level, namely: Plan International, Child Fund, Equitas: International Centre for Human Rights Education, IPA, Terre des hommes, Oxfam, Red Cross, War Child, World Vision International, Care, Women Win, Keeping Children Safe Coalition, Aga Khan Foundation and Right To Play. Our grey literature review revealed that these organisations integrate various forms of play into child-centred programs including the establishment of child-friendly spaces in refugee camps and conflict-affected communities,[81] play-based learning activities integrated into non-formal and formal learning,[82] play-based activities integrated into the education sector[83] and child and youth initiatives.[84] A few

---

[80] The Commonwealth, "8th Commonwealth Sports Ministers Meeting Communique" (4 August 2016), http://thecommonwealth.org/sites/default/files/inline/8CSMM%20Communiqué%20-%20FINAL%20-%2004.08.16.pdf, 1.

[81] For example: Plan International, "Haiti Recovery: Child-Friendly Spaces" (undated), https://plan-international.org/what-we-do/emergencies/haiti-recovery/priorities/child-protection/child-friendly-spaces; Janice Babineau, "Video Dispatch from the Philippines: Smiles Inside Children's Play Tent" (Red Cross, 16 December 2013), www.redcross.ca/blog/2013/12/video-dispatch-from-the-philippines–smiles-inside-children-s-play-tent; War Child Holland, "The Story of Yara" (undated), www.warchildholland.org/story-yara.

[82] For example: Care, "Empowering Girls to Learn and Lead" (2 October 2013), www.care.org/impact/stories/empowering-girls-learn-and-lead; Aga Khan Early Learning Centre, "Investing in Early Childhood Development" (undated), www.agakhanschools.org/akelc/downloads/akelc_brochure.pdf; Keeping Children Safe, Resource Centre (undated), www.keepingchildrensafe.org.uk/resources.

[83] For example, Right To Play International, "What We Do" (undated), www.righttoplay.com/Learn/ourstory/Pages/What-we-do.aspx; World Vision International, "Turning Sports Dreams into Reality" (undated), www.wvi.org/albania/article/turning-sports-dreams-reality.

[84] For example, Child Fund International, "Supervised Neighborhood Play in the Philippines" (2016), www.childfund.org/articles/Supervised-Neighborhood-Play-in-the-Philippines.aspx; Women Win, "The Work: What We Do" (undated), https://womenwin.org/work; Terre de hommes, "Sri Lanka: Sport for Development and Peace" (26 February 2014), www.tdh.ch/en/news/sri-lanka-sport-for-development-and-peace; Oxfam, "Football Breaks Down Barriers in Jordan Refugee Camp" (July 11, 2014), www.oxfam.org/en/multimedia/video/2014-football-

organisations explicitly identify play in their vision statements, such as Right To Play, which intends to create a healthy and safe world through the power of sport and play, or in their programmatic priorities, such as Equitas International Human Rights Organization Play it Fair Program.[85] Indeed, as discussed in the next section, the child's right to play can be valuable to realise the majority of the SDGs including Good Health and Well-Being, Quality Education, Peace and Justice and Gender Equality.

Yet, international development and humanitarian organisations generally do not see play identified in their organisational mandate or programmatic priorities. For example, UNICEF affirms the child's right to play "as fundamental to the health and growth of children everywhere", but it is not included in the Strategic Framework 2014–2017 or the final results framework for this plan.[86] However, play is consistently identified as a tool that is central to many organisations' activities used to achieve their intended outcomes. So while play is recognised, its impact has the potential to be far greater if it is explicitly and intentionally including in organisations' programmatic structure, such as theory of change, logic models and monitoring, evaluation and learning tools. With intentionality, the international community can strengthen quality of programs for children and build a strong evidence base in relation to play in international development and humanitarian efforts, and long-term sustainability.

The literature and international practice are rife with numerous examples of the need for, and role and influence of, play in children's lives and in society generally. For instance, there is a challenge for humanitarian work to "respond to children's immediate needs for safety and psychosocial well-being on the large scale that is needed" and to "help to strengthen sustainable child protection supports that have positive, long-term outcomes for children".[87] Child Friendly Spaces (CFSs) is one solution in camps for internally displaced persons and refugees. For example, for Syrian children in Jordan CFSs serve as safe spaces to play, to safeguard children from attacks and crime and to support rebuilding of

---

breaks-down-barriers-jordan-refugee-camp; and related policy initiatives: IPA, "The Child's Right to Play" (undated), http://ipaworld.org/childs-right-to-play/the-childs-right-to-play.

[85] Right To Play, "Partners" (undated), www.righttoplay.com/Learn/keyplayers/Pages/Partners.aspx; and Equitas, "Play It Fair! International" (undated), https://equitas.org/en/what-we-do/children-and-youth/play-it-fair-international

[86] UNICEF, "Why Sport?" (2014), www.unicef.org/sports/23619_23624.html; UNICEF, "The UNICEF Strategic Plan, 2014–2017" (UN Doc. E/ICEF/2013/21, 11 July 2013), www.unicef.org/strategicplan/files/2013-21-UNICEF_Strategic_Plan-ODS-English.pdf; UNICEF, "Final Results Framework of the UNICEF Strategic Plan, 2014–2017" (UN Doc. E/ICEF/2014/8, 4 April 2014), www.unicef.org/strategicplan/files/2014-8-Final_results_framework_of_strategic_plan-ODS-EN.pdf.

[87] M. Wessells and K. Kostelny, "Child Friendly Spaces: Toward a Grounded, Community-Based Approach for Strengthening Child Protection Practice in Humanitarian Crises: Natural Helpers Play a Critical Role in Ensuring Children's Safety during and in the Aftermath of Crises" (2013) 37 *Child Abuse and Neglect* 29, 30.

trust in community.[88] "CFSs make their greatest contribution when they are implemented in a manner that supports community mobilization and the engagement of informal resources that are contextually appropriate and well-positioned to support children and families [sustainably] over the long term, well beyond the crisis and recovery periods".[89]

As Burr and Montgomery outline, it is clear there is "tension at the heart of all human rights legislation … between universal acceptance of such rights and how different cultures understand them".[90] This tension is often even more evident in the children's rights discussion due to the perceived misconception that the UNCRC focuses solely on children as autonomous beings, which is foreign to many belief systems and contextual realities.[91] Moreover, there is a critique that rejects the UNCRC and the Western contemporary development discourse that childhood is characterised largely or solely by play, which is inherently limited in international development settings.[92] For instance, Nsamenang identifies intervention as the means for how Western organisations attempt to enforce Western ideas on African people: The "[d]iscourse on child development and the 'quality' of childhood care and services inspired by and framed within the dominant mainstream narratives generally pathologize African forms of childrearing and child guidance", therefore requiring a different perspective about human development there.[93]

The differing perceptions of "injustice" across cultures and understandings of childhood, as well as views on "participation at different levels",[94] can result in tension across children's spheres of influence and contexts. This difficulty is evident, for instance, in relation to the issue of child work that some influential actors and agencies, including the International Labour Organisation, critique as child labour. However, the significant efforts of children's movements and some researchers have challenged the common conclusion that child work must be eliminated from their lives.[95] The "growing imposition of a particularly Western conceptualization of childhood"[96] on starkly different

---

[88] Ibid., 30.
[89] Ibid., 31.
[90] R. Burr and H. Montgomery, "Children and Rights", in M. Woodhead and H. Montgomery (eds.), *Understanding Childhood: An Interdisciplinary Approach* (Chichester, UK: Wiley Publishing, 2003), 141.
[91] Ibid.
[92] See, for example, N. Ansell, "Chapter 1: Global Models of Childhood and Youth", *Children, Youth and Development* (London: Routledge, 2004).
[93] Nsamenang, "Chapter 2 Dilemmas of Rights-Based Approaches", 17.
[94] Ibid., 19.
[95] Examples include Concerned for Working Children, www.concernedforworkingchildren.org/, in India and M. Bourdillon et al., *Rights and Wrongs of Child Work* (New Brunswick, NJ, and London: Rutgers University Press, 2010); T. M. Collins, "The Relationship between Children's Rights and Business" (2014) 18(6) *International Journal of Human Rights*, 582–633. On this point, see Chapter 13 of this volume.
[96] A. Prout and A. James, "A New Paradigm for the Sociology of Childhood? Provenance, Promise and Problems", in A. James and A. Prout (eds.), *Constructing and Reconstructing*

circumstances around the world not only pathologises and disavows children but also (re)constructs a pejorative static image of childhood in the different contexts. Therefore, the necessity to "always contextualize our study findings, our policies, our programs in the socio historical and cultural contexts from which they arise"[97] acknowledges that "human development always occurs in a specific cultural context".[98] For example, Long's doctoral study of Jamaican children's understandings of play highlights that play must be understood from the context in which it comes from; and play must be seen in its historical context and meanings associated to it by the cultural beliefs and the historical impact on its development. This is meaningful to understand play in cultures around the globe and implication of "pushing" play in areas where play is not prioritised as a meaningful way to learn, grow or contribute to society.[99] "It underscores the significance of context and culture and the need to notice, accept and be inclusive of the huge variety of childhoods that international child rights instruments appear to subvert".[100] Similar to Heron,[101] we acknowledge that by merely denouncing generic conceptions of privileged Western concepts of play in the development sector, we do automatically unsettle the operation of development and privilege. Intentional action is necessary.

In sum, international development and humanitarian play activities with children must reflect the deconstruction of international paradigms and generic conceptions of play through an anti-colonial discursive framework. This is critical to develop quality sustainable local initiatives that respect the role of children and their spheres of influence in their particular socio-historical contexts. Through an anti-colonial framework we therefore aim to disrupt dominant ways of knowing that perpetuate the social, political and economic inequalities that persist today and affect the way play is realised across communities.[102]

A CRBA TO THE RIGHT TO PLAY IN SUSTAINABLE DEVELOPMENT AND ITS RELEVANCE TO CHILDREN AND INTERNATIONAL DEVELOPMENT AND HUMANITARIAN SETTINGS

This section explores the advancement of the right to play in sustainable development in relation to development and humanitarian contexts through an

---

Childhood: Contemporary Issues in the Sociological Study of Childhood (London, New York, and Philadelphia: Falmer Press, 1990), 7, 9.

[97] M. Hoskyn et al., "Letters from the Editors" (2007) 1 *Child Development, Health and Education* i, ii.

[98] P. R. Dasen and G. Jahoda, "Editorial Preface" (1986) 9 *International Journal of Behavioural Development* 413, 413.

[99] C. A. Long, "A Case Study of Jamaican Children's Lived Play Experiences" (unpublished PhD thesis, University of South Florida, 2013).

[100] Nsamenang, "Chapter 2 Dilemmas of Rights-Based Approaches", 22.

[101] B. Heron, *Desire for Development: Whiteness, Gender and the Helping Imperative* (Waterloo, ON: Wilfrid Laurier University Press, 2007).

[102] G. J. S. Dei, *Anti-Colonialism and Education: The Politics of Resistance* (Rotterdam, The Netherlands: Sense of Publishers, 2006).

interdisciplinary CRBA[103] based on the UNCRC's four general principles of non-discrimination, best interests of the child, maximum survival and development and child participation (articles 2, 3(1), 6 and 12, respectively) and the sociology of childhood. A CRBA is important in "describing actions not only in terms of responding to needs but as obligations to protect or provide for the fulfilment of every child's rights, and to remedy situations where they are violated".[104] "Accordingly, rights demand and inspire approaches, which are neither reflections of generosity, nor vagaries of political whims, resources constraints or other excuses. Rights should involve responses to established legal obligations and duties to human beings".[105]

Accordingly, for the right to play to be actualised, a CRBA should be used to advance article 31, particularly the right to play, and ensure effective measurement processes exist for sustainable efforts. How do we understand play through these UNCRC principles? How do the principles inform sustainable processes and results in the international development and humanitarian sector? The CRBA is critical to support duty bearers and states to respect, protect and fulfil their responsibilities for children's right to play. The UNCRC should be seen as a work in progress and be understood as "a beginning rather than the final word on children's rights".[106] We seek to deconstruct the perception of the CRBA as a "one-size-fits-all" Western model and explore the ways in which it contributes to respect for children and communities' diversity and expertise. As such, we do not presume to have concrete answers to "solve" the lack of recognition of play through a CRBA. We do, however, hope to begin a conversation on how a CRBA can be used to transform the current state of the realisation of article 31, particularly the right to play, globally.

Throughout this section, we affirm that play has both intrinsic and instrumental value that is mutually reinforcing and contributes to children influenced by the international development and humanitarian sector.

Non-Discrimination

Non-discrimination is an expansive child rights principle that requires consideration of every child and his/her group identity(ies),[107] and play is an important means by which necessary challenges to discriminatory and exclusionary norms can be

---

[103] T. M. Collins, "The Monitoring of the Rights of the Child: A Child Rights-Based Approach" (unpublished PhD thesis, University of London, 2007).

[104] T. M. Collins and L. Wolff, "Canada's Next Steps for Children's Rights? Building the Architecture for Accountability through the General Measures of Implementation of the CRC", in E. Murray (ed.), *Children Matter – Exploring Child and Youth Human Rights Issues in Canada* (Calgary, AB: Mount Royal University, 2012), 18.

[105] Collins, "The Monitoring of the Rights of the Child", 17.

[106] M. Liebel, *Children's Rights from Below: Cross-Cultural Perspectives* (New York: Palgrave MacMillan, 2012), 15.

[107] Collins, "The Monitoring of the Rights of the Child", 17.

explored and enacted by children. Consistent with the SDGs for Quality Education and Gender Equality, through play, children can be engaged in the interrogation of power relations structured along lines of gender, class, ethnicity, religion, language, ability and sexuality.[108] Play supports the critique of ongoing circumstances of discriminatory practices and supports children to imagine other possibilities of interaction across cultures, that are rooted in their own knowledges, perspectives and understandings, and can contribute to positive community dialogue. The academic and grey literature contains much evidence about the role that play has in strengthening intercultural communication and inclusion amongst children. For example, children in CFSs in camps for internally displaced persons and refugees frequently have diverse backgrounds and are engaged in psychosocial support play-based activities that attempt to rebuild trust in community and reduce barriers to cultural conflict.[109] Through conflict resolution, cooperation and inclusion activities, children begin to value one another's diversity and encourage those around them to settle conflicts. This proclamation was confirmed in a recent evaluation by Right to Play in Mali. Ghak, a 15-year-old Tuareg boy who had recently arrived in Ségou, was invited to join a local Frisbee club but was met with resistance from others who "don't like that he is a Tuareg as they are associated with starting the conflict. Also, he is from the North; he may be a security risk; he could be dangerous".[110] The youth involved discussed the matter and realised the importance of children's rights including non-discrimination and eventually welcomed him to their Frisbee team. The youth identified this experience as "their most significant change" due to the "deep-rooted nature of cultural stereotypes in Mali and the challenges in changing these strongly held beliefs ... [and *inter alia*] they shared the power of play in crossing cultural boundaries".[111]

While play can be used to reduce discriminatory practices, it also has the potential to reinforce discriminatory practices, such as lack of engagement of females and persons with disabilities, and to contribute to discrimination and violence against children. Mullen describes that play can become a platform for violence (commonly understood as "bullying"),[112] especially in the case of sports, where it can

---

[108] G. J. S. Dei, "Global Education from an 'Indigenist Anti-colonial' Perspective" (Keynote speech presented at Concordia University, Montreal, QC, 2012).
[109] Wessells and Kostelny, "Child Friendly Spaces", 30.
[110] P. Cook, "Monitoring Right to Play's Child Protection Impact on War Affected Children in Mali" (unpublished report, International Institute for Child Rights and Development and Right to Play, 26 May 2015), 30.
[111] Ibid.
[112] See further M. Paré, T. M. Collins and M. Ranjbar, "Taking Stock of Bullying and Cyberbullying Research and Introducing a Child Rights Perspective", in T. Liefaard and J. Sloth-Nielsen (eds.), *The United Nations Convention on the Rights of the Child: Taking Stock after 25 Years and Looking Ahead* (Leiden, The Netherlands: Brill/Nijhoff Publishers, 2016).

"bring out the worst in people"; and as such, play must be guided to achieve the positive outcomes that are possible for future benefits.[113]

Furthermore, there is discrimination with inequality of play among child populations including girls and children with disabilities, among others.[114] Mullen outlines that in some places play is reserved to the "physically gifted, affluent males", and others, including girls, are not permitted to play (under the guise of protecting females), and children with disabilities do not have access; this exclusion of certain groups of children in play "undermines human dignity, human development, and the interdependent human rights formula".[115] For instance, safety is a serious issue as Brady found in the study of an NGO in Nairobi and an experimental pilot in Upper Egyptian villages where various forms of harassment by boys of more than three-quarters of the girls when they venture outside the home poses a serious problem, and "often girls are held responsible for boys' behaviour".[116] In response, Brady recommends that practitioners support safe mobility in several ways including scheduling of the program to appropriate times of day, as determined by the communities; suitable arrangements for transportation, escorting girls to and from the programs and the organisation taking the responsibility for the cost; teaching girls to recognise potential threats in their surroundings; girls walking together and meeting up with other girls from other communities and privacy walls for girls to play in Egypt; and consulting with parents and community to accommodate schedules and mobility considerations.[117] Additionally, integration of positive masculinity and knowledge, attitude and behaviour shift for the whole community on gender equality is necessary to address gender inequality in play-based programming. It is paramount that a CRBA is actualised so that play is a right that can be practiced by all children, not just a privileged few.

Through play, children are able to recognise the links between cultural diversity, power and belonging, and can become conscious players in negotiating the cultural politics of identity in their lives and community.[118] This is a valuable life skill to equip children with, particularly in locations where cultural conflict is high. Further, play supports intergenerational cultural learning and transmission through the world of play, from oral traditions to games.[119] Recent perspectives on play in the early years of childhood[120] underscore the importance of understanding children's

---

[113] Mullen, "Getting Serious about the Human Right to Play", 134.
[114] Ibid., 132.
[115] Ibid., 133.
[116] M. Brady, "Creating Safe Spaces and Building Social Assets for Young Women in the Developing World: A New Role for Sports" (2005) 33 *Women's Studies Quarterly* 35, 43.
[117] Ibid., 43.
[118] A. James and A. James, *Constructing Childhood: Theory, Policy and Social Practice* (London: Palgrave, 2004), 25.
[119] Finnegan, "Child Play Is Serious", 295.
[120] See L. Brooker, M. Blaise and S. Edwards (eds.), *The Sage Handbook of Play and Early Learning in Childhood* (London: Sage Publications, 2012), 98.

play not only as subject to the social contexts and conditions within which they are situated but also as a means of children's participation in the production of contemporary culture and their implication in the operations of power and change.[121] Education is a key contemporary site of social construction where difference can be ignored, suppressed or taken up.[122] Play is a valuable tool for children to engage in experience and dialogue of the child rights of non-discrimination in a safe learning environment.

Best Interests

The best interest principle demands a focus on the child, rather than political, financial and societal constraints.[123] The best interest principle can be used to consider how play acts as a vital tool for self-protection and resilience in children. This intersects with the sociology of childhood model, which recognises children as unique social actors.[124] Providing opportunities for play hones innate play skills, which are critical resources that can support children's self-determination by preparing them for what life delivers, as well as helping them to develop coping mechanisms and skills for their own well-being[125] and developing self-protection skills.[126] This plays an integral part to support individual children as well as groups of children in their families, communities and society at large to actualise the SDG on Good Health and Well-Being, for example. Exposure to trauma and toxic stress during early years has detrimental effects on the organisation and development of the brain, which can result in developmental delay and other health-related problems – such as heart disease, substance abuse and depression – later in life.[127] Psychosocial play programs aim to restore children's social well-being and psychological health within their communities through group-focused practices, tailored to fit the context of local culture, traditions, needs and resources.[128] Children are able to enhance adaptive capabilities and resilience in a supportive environment.[129]

---

[121] W. A. Corsaro, *The Sociology of Childhood* (Thousand Oaks, CA: Pine Forge Press, 2005), 19.
[122] L. H. V. Wright, "Transforming Canada's Hegemonic Global Education Paradigm through an Anticolonial Framework", in G. J. S. Dei and P. B. Adjei (eds.), *Emerging Perspectives on "African Development": Speaking Differently* (New York: Peter Lang, 2014).
[123] Collins, "The Monitoring of the Rights of the Child".
[124] A. James, C. Jenks and A. Prout, *Theorizing Childhood* (Cambridge: Polity Press, 1998).
[125] J. Bradshaw, P. Hoelscher and D. Richardson, "An Index of Child Well-Being in the European Union" (2007) 80 *Social Indicators Research* 133.
[126] R. Hart, *Children's Participation* (New York: Earthscan, 1997).
[127] K. Covell and R. B. Howe, *Children, Families and Violence: Challenges for Children's Rights* (London: Jessica Kingsley Publishers, 2009).
[128] See R. Henley et al., "How Psychosocial Sport and Play Programs Help Youth Manage Adversity: A Review of What We Know and What We Should Research" (2007) 12 (1) *International Journal of Psychosocial Rehabilitation* 51–58.
[129] G. M. Burghardt, *The Genesis of Animal Play: Testing the Limits* (Cambridge, MA: MIT Press, 2005).

Opportunities for play support development, empower children to meet challenges, help them recover from adversity and enable them to come to terms with life experiences.[130] Through regular ongoing interactions between children and favourable features in their surroundings, children can further develop resiliency competencies when facing adversity.[131] Children throughout difficult lived circumstances, such as Nazi concentration camps[132], and the Rwandan refugee context show evidence of commitment and interest to engage in free play in oppressive contexts.

Maximum Survival and Development

The maximum survival and development principle must be regularly considered and implemented over time and the child's right to play supports all aspects of development, inclusive of cognitive, social, emotional, physical and spiritual development. Cognitively, play supports the enhancement of the learning process, which can for instance advance the SDG on Quality Education. Play helps to boost neurological growth and the development of complex, skilled, responsive and cognitively flexible brains, and can also enhance the development of concepts and ideas.[133] Through play, children can build their executive functioning and critical thinking skills, and can generate ideas of their own while exercising their imaginations.[134] The healthy holistic development of children is a key contributing factor to success in education at all stages of learning.[135] Research from countries globally highlights the positive contribution that sport and play can make to life skills development.[136] Problem solving and critical thinking skills are valuable tools

---

[130] M. Fearn and J. Howard, "Play as Resource for Children Facing Adversity: An Exploration of Indicative Case Studies" (2012) 26 *Children and Society* 456.

[131] Ibid.

[132] G. Eisen, *Children and Play in the Holocaust: Games among the Shadows* (Amherst: University of Massachusetts Press, 1990).

[133] J. Duncan and M. Lockwood, *Learning through Play: A Work-Based Approach for the Early Years Professional* (New York: Continuum International Publishing Group 2008); Marantz Henig, "Taking Play Seriously"; Ratey, *Spark*.

[134] Colucci, "Sport as a Tool for Participatory Education", 341–354; Duncan and Lockwood, *Learning through Play*; Hirsh-Pasek and Michnick Golinkoff, *Why Play = Learning*; E. Miller and J. Almon, "Crisis in the Kindergarten: Why Children Need to Play in School (Summary of Recommendations)" (2009), www.allianceforchildhood.org/publications; Ratey, *Spark*.

[135] B. J. Zimmerman, "A Social Cognitive View of Self-Regulated Academic Learning" (1989) 81 *Journal of Educational Psychology* 329; G. W. Ladd, "Having Friends, Keeping Friends, Making Friends, and Being Liked by Peers in the Classroom: Predictors of Children's Early School Adjustment?" (1990) 61 *Child Development* 1081; S. Normandeau and F. Guay, "Preschool Behavior and First-Grade School Achievement: The Mediational Role of Cognitive Self-Control" (1998) 90 *Journal of Educational Psychology* 111; S. B. Miles and D. Stipek, "Contemporaneous and Longitudinal Associations between Social Behavior and Literacy Achievement in a Sample of Low-Income Elementary School Children" (2006) 77 *Child Development* 103.

[136] Hirsh-Pasek and Michnick Golinkoff, *Why Play = Learning*; Ratey, *Spark*; R. Bailey, "Physical Education and Sport in Schools: A Review of Benefits and Outcomes" (2006) 76 *Journal of*

developed through play that contribute to children's immediate and long-term cognitive development. Furthermore, problem-solving skills have found to be a strong predictor of improved resilience in children, and they can enhance the possibility that life's challenges will be resolved successfully.[137]

Accordingly, Mullen recommends a public health approach to play because the lack of play poses huge risks to overall health of entire populations; and universal policies are needed because play "cannot be mainstreamed by isolated initiatives", as in the case of state or school board policies.[138] Respect and implementation of the human right to play should lead to stronger, smarter and happier children.

According to the International Network for Education in Emergencies, a critical component of the education response in conflict-affected areas is setting up child-friendly spaces to play and learn. Connecting play-based learning to education in unstable environments further increases children's success in education through regular participation in active learning and student-centred pedagogy as well as emotionally and physically safe spaces for learning and play. Furthermore, training for teachers in play-based methodologies, supports them to use child-centred participatory methods, as an alternative to corporal punishment, which supports children to have a positive association with school, resulting in increased attendance and quality education outcomes, as well as demonstrating a respect for children's human dignity and integrity.[139]

Play in the international development and humanitarian sector can be a powerful entry point for protecting children and can support the SDG on Peace and Justice with particular emphasis of target 16.2 on ending "abuse, exploitation, trafficking, and all forms of violence against and torture of children".[140] Opportunities to access play are threatened significantly in times of conflict, violence and disaster and children and youth are most vulnerable, especially girls. As previously mentioned, article 31 is often given lower priority than provision of

---

School Health 397; F. Trudeau and R. Shephard, "Physical Education, School Physical Activity, School Sports and Academic Performance" (2008) 5 International Journal of Behavioural Nutrition and Physical Activity 10.

[137] J. Boyden and G. Mann, "Children's Risk, Resilience, and Coping in Extreme Situations", in M. Ungar (ed.), Handbook for Working with Children and Youth: Pathways to Resilience across Cultures and Contexts (Thousand Oaks, CA: Sage Publications, 2005); M. S. M. Fok and D. Y. S. Wong, "A Pilot Study on Enhancing Positive Coping Behaviour in Early Adolescents Using a School-Based Project" (2005) 9 Journal of Child Health Care 301; and M. Place et al., "Developing a Resilience Package for Vulnerable Children" (2002) 7 Child and Adolescent Mental Health 162.

[138] Mullen, "Getting Serious about the Human Right to Play", 136.

[139] S. Vohitio, "Prohibiting Corporal Punishment in Schools – A Requirement for Realizing Children's Rights to Education" (London: Global Initiative to End All Corporal Punishment, 2014).

[140] Global Partnership to End Violence Against Children, "Global Partnership to End Violence against Children Zero Draft Strategy" (September 2015), 6; UNGA, "Transforming Our World".

food, shelter and traditional health care. Play, however, can be used as a contextual tool for therapeutic and rehabilitative benefit to help children recover their sense of normalcy and joy after experiences of loss, dislocation and trauma,[141] which supports in the treatment, recovery and social reintegration of children who are victims of conflict (UNCRC article 39). Play can help displaced children, and children who have experienced bereavement, violence, abuse or exploitation, to overcome emotional pain and regain control over their lives.[142] Additionally, play can intrinsically act as a healing experience for children affected by war and conflict. This assertion can be exemplified by evaluation results from Right To Play Mali, which found that play in a conflict-affected community benefited children and community through mind-body connection and harmonious conjoining of joy and creativity, that offers important opportunities for broadening the range of emergency options available to children in the humanitarian context.[143] Settings for play also provide opportunities for practitioners to identify children suffering from the harmful impact of conflict and to refer children requiring additional psychosocial support. Moreover, this assertion is not just about play in isolation, as a process in which the individual child takes part. It is also about play as part of the social fabric of a community and as a dynamic exchange between the child and their world. Play can return children of conflict to enjoyment of their childhoods.[144]

Participation in play and recreation, offers children an opportunity to engage in a shared experience, to rebuild a sense of personal value and self-worth, to explore their own creativity and to achieve a sense of connectedness and belonging with peers, family and community. It supports children to "get to explore [their] surroundings and to know [themselves]" as a consulted 17-year-old female expresses.[145] Such activities can restore a sense of identity, help make meaning of their lives and enable them to experience fun and enjoyment. In the humanitarian sector, findings suggest that play is reinforcing protection and the resulting social well-being is contributing to children's education in multiple ways including enhancing mind-body connection, social bonding, learning and creative thinking to solve problems; overcoming social challenges; and fostering agency, community engagement and social activism.[146]

---

[141] UNCRC Committee, "General Comment No. 17 (2013)".
[142] Ibid.
[143] International Institute for Child Rights and Development (IICRD) and Right To Play (RTP), "Monitoring Right To Play's Child Protection Impact on War Affected Children in Mali" (unpublished paper, IICRD and RTP, 2015) 38.
[144] T. Hyder, *War, Conflict and Play* (Berkshire, UK: Open University Press, 2005).
[145] As quoted in Pearson and Akbar, *Shaking the Movers VII*, 14.
[146] IICRD and RTP, "Monitoring Right To Play's Child Protection Impact on War Affected Children in Mali", 7.

Views of the Child

This principle must inform how the right to play should be protected and advanced to contribute to all other aspects of children's lives and support the actualisation of all children's rights. Child participation is defined as "ongoing processes, which include information-sharing and dialogue between children and adults based on mutual respect, and in which children can learn how their views and those of adults are taken into account and shape the outcome of such processes".[147] Since the ratification of the UNCRC, emerging theory and research in both the sociology of childhood and children's rights studies have recognised children as social actors who contribute to shaping and changing families, communities and society.[148] Learning through play contributes to children's ability to participate as active agents of change in their lives, communities and world.

Skills acquired through play contribute to children's meaningful participation (child-led, collaborative and consultative) in decision-making processes and has had a significant impact on children to be active social agents in their own development.[149] In Rwanda, youth engaged in play-based leadership initiatives are being elected in different institutions such as the National Youth Council, as well as sector, cell and village administration.[150] In Ethiopia, where only 4.3 per cent of children are currently enrolled in Early Childhood Education Centres, Plan Ethiopia supports establishment of early learning centres where children have the opportunity to learn through play with trained educators.[151] Furthermore, in Save the Children programs across the globe, children are participating in conflict and post-conflict peace-building initiatives through child clubs whereby they utilise songs, dance and play to strengthen awareness amongst peers, family, schools and community on child rights and peace. As proclaimed by children in Bosnia-Herzegovina, they want to be "the generation that is capable of thinking of change".[152] Thus through play, children are able to acquire core

---

[147] UNCRC Committee, "General Comment No. 12 (2009) on the Right of the Child to Be Heard" (UN Doc. CRC/C/GC/12, 20 July 2009), 5.

[148] B. Mayall, "The Sociology of Childhood in Relation to Children's Rights" (2000) 8 *The International Journal of Children's Rights* 243; E. K. M. Tisdall, "Children and Young People's Participation: A Critical Consideration of Article 12", in W. Vanderhole et al. (eds.), *Routledge Handbook on Children's Rights Studies* (London and New York: Routledge, 2015); A. James, C. Jenks and A. Prout, *Theorizing Childhood* (Cambridge: Polity Press 1998).

[149] P. Jones and G. Walker (eds.), *Children's Rights in Practice* (London: Sage Publications Limited, 2011); E. Uprichard, "Children as 'Being and Becomings': Children, Childhood and Temporality" (2008) 22 *Children and Society* 3.

[150] D. Lavan, G. Massart and C. Monseur, "Independent Evaluation Report: Right To Play's Play to Learn Program in Benin and Rwanda" (unpublished paper, Ottawa, ON: Lavan Consulting, 2013).

[151] Plan International Canada, "Playing Hard and Dreaming Big in Ethiopia" (2016), https://plancanada.ca/the-right-to-play-in-ethiopia.

[152] C. Feinstein, A. Giertsen and C. O'Kane, "Children's Participation in Armed Conflict and Post Conflict Peace Building", in B. Percy-Smith and N. Thomas (eds.), *A Handbook of Children and Young People's Participation* (New York: Routledge, 2009).

life skills to strengthen their leadership competencies and use play as a tool to communicate critical issues pertaining to children in their communities. For example, poverty could be better understood and responded to if children have opportunities to express their views about the realities of poverty in their communities through such playful communication as skits, thereby supporting the SDG on No Poverty.

While play contributes to children's leadership and ability to express their views and be engaged in decision-making, it is paramount that the views of children are recognised to inform how the right to play should be protected and advanced to contribute to aspects of their lives. While participation should not be romanticised,[153] it can contribute to the further development of capacities and support mutual learning of the subjects and others in the process.[154] Furthermore, children should be engaged in the dialogue on the pitfalls of play and challenge the normative adult-centric discourses that dominant the global conversation. A significant feature of the present-day childhood paradigm is the attention paid to the evolving agency of children and their subjectivity experiences, meaning and content of their everyday life from multiple perspectives.[155] Although the participatory rights within the UNCRC reflect a paradigmatic shift in the conceptualisation of children, children are too often positioned as "passive objects of adults' agency" instead of competent, capable and active social stakeholders who are treated equitably with adults.[156] During the drafting process and in the outcome of Millennium Development Goals (MDGs), children were not engaged meaningfully. As such, for the drafting of the SDGs, the United Nations developed a plan of action for a "participatory, inclusive and bottom up process" to depart from the expert, technocrat original design of the MDGs for "the voices of the people [to] be heard".[157] Although the United Nations was lauded for its attempt to operationalise a meaningful participatory approach that includes multiple voices and sources of knowledge, there is still criticism that results of these consultations were not effectively integrated into the final SDGs and the associated targets.[158] One useful participatory consultation involving academics, NGOs and international organisational representatives to identify 100 questions to support the development agenda included

---

[153] J. Ennew, "Preface", in V. Johnson et al. (eds.), *Stepping Forward: Children and Young People's Participation in the Development Process* (London: Intermediate Technology Publications, 1998).

[154] T. M. Collins, "Children's Participation in Monitoring the United Nations Convention on the Rights of the Child", in T. Gal and B. F. Duramy (eds.), *International Perspectives and Empirical Findings on Child Participation* (Oxford: New York, 2015), 419

[155] M. Graham, "Changing Paradigms and Conditions of Childhood: Implications for the Social Professions and Social Work" (2011) 41(8) *British Journal of Social Work* 1532–1547.

[156] Liebel, *Children's Rights from Below*, 15.

[157] United Nations Development Group, *Post-2015 Development Agenda: Guidelines for Country Dialogues* (New York: United Nations, 2012).

[158] C. Enns, B. Bersaglio and T. Kepe, "Indigenous Voices and the Making of the Post-2015 Development Agenda: The Recurring Tyranny of Participation" (2014) 35(3) *Third World Quarterly* 358–375.

consideration of children in relation to such areas as "governance, participation and rights" and "social and economic inequalities".[159] In advancing the understanding of sustainable development as a complex process of social change, this exercise highlights the need to question who benefits through SDG development and who determines the agenda for development to investigate the paradigms and shifts in the discourse about international development and human rights perspectives.[160] To effectively create policies and programming in sustainable development, children's meaningful participation and an actual shift in power dynamics, instead of participation as a "fashionable rhetoric" or false myth of equal opportunity, is critical.[161] Child participation is valuable because "[c]hildren are the primary source of knowledge about their own views and experiences".[162] We argue that children's perspectives will reinforce, challenge and/or expand adults' narratives on play[163] and improve children's play-based experiences and the advocacy to support access to quality play experiences.

In summary, a CRBA supports understanding and implementation of the right to play. Child rights inform not only what our objectives should be but also how these efforts should be undertaken in international development and humanitarian contexts.

CONCLUSION AND KEY RECOMMENDATIONS

The human right of play for children is critically important and requires further attention across countries and in international development and humanitarian efforts as part of sustainable development. Despite strong evidence that play is beneficial to children's development, article 31 continues to be one of the most neglected rights of the child.[164] For the CRBA to support the realisation of play, regular monitoring, evaluation and learning to assess the process and outcomes and to support sustainable progress in the future is vital. Through bottom-up and top-down processes, the local to global community should continue to implement sustainable quality development and humanitarian programs, and strengthen the evidence base in relation to the right to play. Both process and outcome-oriented research in collaboration with children, caregivers, community, government, organisations, international bodies and others is needed to learn and strengthen practice.

---

[159] J. A. Oldekop et al., "100 Key Research Questions for the Post-2015 Development Agenda" (2016) 34(1) *Development Policy Review*, 55–82, 64, 65, 67, 70–71.
[160] Ibid., 74.
[161] R. Lund, "At the Interface of Development Studies and Child Research: Rethinking the Participating Child" (2007) 5(1–2) *Children's Geographies* 131, 134.
[162] P. Alderson, "Children as Researchers: The Effects of Participation Rights on Research Methodology", in P. A. Christensen and A. James (eds.), *Research with Children: Perspectives and Practices* (London and New York: Falmer, 2000), 243.
[163] Nicholson et al., "Listening to Children's Perspective on Play across the Lifespan", 138.
[164] Shackel, "The Child's Right to Play".

The lessons from the development of indicators for General Comment No. 7, General Comment No. 12 and General Comment No. 13[165] by expert working groups can be used to support in the development of strong monitoring tools for General Comment No. 17. In accordance with UNCRC article 45(a), various actors monitor the national situation and then contribute to international UNCRC monitoring. By request of the UNCRC Committee, a group of experts entitled the "General Comment No. 7 Indicators Group" developed an Early Childhood Rights Indicators Framework that was presented to the UNCRC Committee in 2008.[166] Pilot tools were developed by this group using a website to support the international community to effectively utilise the indicators in their monitoring.[167] Furthermore, in the same vein, the Global Reference Group on Accountability, which has been leading indicator development for General Comment No. 13, can be engaged in supporting the Committee to streamline article 31 into the international child rights monitoring process. Utilising General Comment No. 17, "indicators for compliance, as well as mechanisms for monitoring and evaluating implementation need to be developed to ensure accountability to children and the fulfilment of obligations" of states to respect, protect and fulfil children's right to play.[168] Further to the issue of indicator development, the connections between these General Comments and the SDGs should be recognised. For instance, mechanisms for effectively monitoring the components of SDGs that pertain to children are critical to their realisation and that of children's rights as outlined in the General Comments. Yet there is concern among commentators due to the "moderate" human rights language and the framework's voluntary nature,[169] and while human rights principles are identified within the text of the preamble and larger declaration, there is limited explicit reference to rights in SDG metrics.[170] There is also criticism from a human rights perspective that the SDGs have not explicitly translated into human rights-based goals and countries must determine their own plans to implement them.[171]

---

[165] Human Early Learning Partnership and International Institute for Child Rights and Development, "Early Childhood Rights Indicators: GC 13 Indicators" (Vancouver and Victoria, BC: Human Early Learning Partnership and International Institute for Child Rights and Development, 2013), http://iicrd.org/learning-hub/gc13-indicators.

[166] Z. Vahgri et al., "CRC General Comment 7 Indicators Framework: A Tool for Monitoring the Implementation of Child Rights in Early Childhood" (2011) 10(2) *Journal of Human Rights* 178.

[167] Human Early Learning Partnership, "Early Childhood Rights Indicators: A Global Monitoring Tool to Implement the United Nations Convention on the Rights of the Child" (Research Brief, 2012) http://earlylearning.ubc.ca/media/documents/international_research_brief_14nov2012.pdf.

[168] UNCRC Committee, "General Comment No. 17 (2013)", 9–11.

[169] M. Langford, "Lost in Transformation? The Politics of the Sustainable Development Goals" (2016) 30(2) *Ethics and International Affairs* 173.

[170] C. E. Brolan, "A Word of Caution: Human Rights, Disability, and Implementation of the Post-2015 Sustainable Development Goals" (2016) 5(2) *Laws* 22, 12.

[171] K. Buse and S. Hawkes, "Health in the Sustainable Development Goals: Ready for a Paradigm Shift?" (2015) 11(1) *Globalization and Health*, 1.

Nevertheless, there is moderate progress in incorporating rights. Actors leading and supporting global initiatives and laws for children's rights namely the SDGs and UNCRC, generally share complementary visions for children's rights and wellbeing. The SDG indicators provide an opportunity to realise children's rights.[172] Collaboration between these actors fosters opportunity for collectively moving forward interconnected agendas to meet the best interest of children. Further, the lessons learned and best practices in indicators should be acknowledged to support cross learning based on different strengths and expertise of those involved. Actors must become committed in practice, and mechanisms and processes must be developed to ascertain the situation of the human rights of all including to play and support progress over time.

Additionally, implementation tools are central to support civil society to strengthen local, national and international capacity in play. Similar to the General Comment No. 13 Implementation Resource Program plan, a comprehensive plan for policy, practice and research at the global, regional, national and community level will support the realisation of article 31 through a CRBA.[173] The global community needs to strengthen knowledge dissemination of promising programs, increase advocacy for child rights to play and develop quality education, training and tools to support implementation. Furthermore, programmes and tools that are developed from a CRBA can and should be developed by a plethora of diverse groups to ensure that they are in the best interest of the child and meet contextual needs.

For sustainable development in the international development and humanitarian sector, NGOs and UN bodies can play an enormous role in the promotion, actualisation and monitoring of the right to play. In the last 30 years, the global community has witnessed a large increase in children's rights–focused organisations and collaboration across organisations. The period from 1979, when drafting of the UNCRC began, to 1989, has been considered a period of significant collaboration across NGOs. NGO networks played and continue to play a crucial role in the conception and realisation of children's rights.[174]

It is essential that children be engaged in decision making at the implementation and monitoring level. Consequently, it is important to move away from limited assumptions of children as if they are objects identical across time and space because children are individuals with multiple ways of knowing.[175] Children's lived

---

[172] B. A.-M. O'Hare, D. Devakumar and S. Allen, "Using International Human Rights Law to Improve Child Health in Low-Income Countries: A Framework for Healthcare Professionals" (2016) 16(1) *BMC International Health and Human Rights* 1, 4.

[173] K. Svevo-Cianci et al., "The New UNCRC General Comment 13: 'The Right of the Child to Freedom from All Forms of Violence' – Changing How the World Conceptualizes Child Protection" (2011) 35 *Child Abuse and Neglect* 979, 988.

[174] B. C. Edmonds and W. R. Fernekes, *Children's Rights: A Reference Handbook* (Santa Barbara, CA: ABC-CLIO, 1996).

[175] Graham, "Changing Paradigms and Conditions of Childhood".

experiences and expertise are critical to advancing the right to play. "[W]ithout children's engagement, the monitoring process and results would reflect a limited picture with restricted impact".[176] Children's participation rights, are in fact "the most elusive" for children, and are in described as "the most difficult to define, to implement and to monitor".[177] Internationally vetted tools and documents, such as Lansdown and O'Kane's *A Toolkit for Monitoring and Evaluating Children's Participation*, can be used to ensure children are engaged in quality monitoring, evaluation and learning of the right to play.[178]

Although the UNCRC has been critiqued for promoting Western conceptions of childhood, it is important to recognise the cultural and community values embedded in the instrument. A critical reframing of the child's human right to play can serve to generate a contextually tailored discourse on how to better support the actualisation of play across cultures.[179] It is time for the international development and humanitarian community not only to acknowledge the significance of the right to play but also ensure that it is followed up on effectively with a view of moving sustainably forward together with children.

---

[176] Collins, "Children's Participation in Monitoring the United Nations Convention on the Rights of the Child", 406 footnote omitted.

[177] M. Black, "Monitoring the Rights of Children: Innocenti Global Seminar Summary Report" (Florence: UNICEF International Child Development Centre 1994), 28.

[178] G. Lansdown and C. O'Kane, *A Toolkit for Monitoring and Evaluating Children's Participation* (London: Save the Children UK, 2014), www.savethechildren.org.uk/resources/online-library/toolkit-monitoring-and-evaluating-childrens-participation.

[179] A. Gerlach, A. Browne and M. Suto, "A Critical Reframing of Play in Relation to Indigenous Children in Canada" (2014) 21(3) *Journal of Occupational Science* 253.

15

Rapid Development and the Child's Future Right to the City

Liam Magee, Amanda Third and David Sweeting

INTRODUCTION

Rapid urbanisation is one of the arresting features of late-twentieth- and early-twenty-first-century human development. The commonly cited statistic of the UN Development Programme, signaling as of 2008 that 50 per cent of the world's human population now resides in cities and towns,[1] marks a monumental relocation of people away from rural and small settlements towards dense and bustling metropolitan centres. The vast majority of this migration has taken place away from the famed "global cities" of New York, London, Paris and Tokyo and the emergent East Asian global centres of Hong Kong, Singapore, Shanghai and Beijing. Rapidly growing cities are instead often those that remain relatively anonymous and invisible to the global gaze. The *City Mayors* website catalogues the fastest-growing urban areas in the world, measured by population; leading in percentile terms are cities such as Beihai, Gaziabad and Sana'a.[2] Of the top 100 catalogued, only two are part of the recognisably "developed" world: Austin and Atlanta, markers of the US' internal economic migratory patterns. Similar patterns emerge when measured by rates of economic growth; again, inconspicuous cities feature heavily. According to the Brookings Institute, drawing from a sample of 300 metropolitan areas, Macau, Izmir, Istanbul, Bursa and Dubai recorded the highest combined rates of GDP per capita and employment growth in 2014.[3] Of the top 30 metro areas, the only "developed" city to feature is London (26th). Reflecting a form of urban diasporic

---

[1] UN Population Division, "World Urbanization Prospects: The 2007 Revision Population Database" (Brussels, Belgium: UN Population Division, Department of Economic and Social Affairs, 2007).
[2] City Mayors, "The World's Fastest Growing Cities and Urban Areas from 2006 to 2020" (undated), www.citymayors.com/statistics/urban_growth1.html.
[3] Brookings Institute, "Global Metro Monitor 2014: An Uncertain Recovery" (2015), www.brookings.edu/research/reports2/2015/01/22-global-metro-monitor.

migration from prominent centres to lesser known satellites such as Kunming, Hangzhou, Xiamen and Fuzhou, China houses the majority of the remaining cities.

The locations of urban growth contrast markedly with the geographic preoccupations of celebrated urbanism discourses since the 1990s. Three key texts published in the past 25 years highlight a continued fascination with cities that, in relative terms, show decidedly less dramatic growth in demographic and financial terms. Sassen's *The Global City* acknowledged the concentration of wealth and agglomeration of service industries in critical nodes – New York, London, Tokyo, Paris – of the global economic network. Florida's "The Creative City" emphasises the rise of a professional technical and creative elite, revitalising inner city warehouses and tenements in cities such as San Francisco.[4] Glaeser's *Triumph of the City*, more recently, enthused over the city as a human achievement, one that acts as an intensifying crucible to other achievements in education, politics, science, technology and the arts.[5] More geographically distributed in its attentions, Glaeser nevertheless emphasises familiar references of global urban discourse: Bangalore, Detroit, Rio de Janeiro.

These discourses are often and increasingly transposed and interwoven with the burgeoning attention on sustainable development. The city is the locus of waste production, energy consumption and heat generation; at the same time, it increasingly serves as a container for human activity, potentially insulating some of the corrosive effects of that activity from the surrounding environment and generating significant potential for mass energy reduction, smarter forms of resource management, efficient transport of both goods and people and sustainable construction practices that lower collective emissions and carbon footprints. Shrinking cities such as Detroit emphasise new green practices of urban agriculture and ecotourism to compensate partially for loss of employment and industry. Gleaming new metropolises like Songdo in South Korea are announcing themselves as "green cities", developing according to "principles of New Urbanism" and complying with LEED rating systems in design and construction.[6] Discursively at least, the city functions as cause of, as well as remedy to, many of the world's ecological challenges.

This recent enthusiasm can tend to obscure, however, the threats posed by rampant development in fast-growing cities both to people and to the planet. Such threats impact particularly upon the child populations of these cities. Children's rights are often impinged immediately and directly by, for example, the continuation of exploitative and harmful child labour practices and the lack of free and high-quality schooling. The long-term environmental consequences of

---

[4] R. Florida, *The Rise of the Creative Class and How It's Transforming Work, Leisure, Community and Everyday Life* (New York: Basic-Perseus, 2002).

[5] E. Glaeser, *Triumph of the City: How Our Greatest Invention Makes Us Richer, Smarter, Greener, Healthier and Happier* (London: Pan Macmillan, 2011).

[6] Gale International, "One of the World's Greenest Cities" (2015), www.songdo.com/songdo-international-business-district/why-songdo/sustainable-city.aspx.

growing congestion, high pollution, lack of water, high temperatures and loss of flora and fauna species also risk obstructing the exercise of their future rights. Immediate effects of accelerated urban growth risk contravening a number of rights established under the UN Convention on the Rights of the Child (UNCRC): article 32, concerning hazardous forms of work; articles 28 and 29, concerning the rights to free primary and available secondary education, and the development of a child's "personality, talents and mental and physical abilities to their fullest potential"; article 24, concerning the right to the "highest attainable standard of health", considering both the availability of "adequate nutritious foods and clean drinking-water" and "the dangers and risks of environmental pollution"; and article 31, the right of the child to "rest and leisure" – including the leisure associated with exploring green spaces and ecological biodiversity.[7] To reframe Henri Lefevbre's famous phrase through the lens of children, their "right to the city" becomes doubly refused, in future as well as present tenses.

Demographic distribution intensifies the impacts of this double refusal. As Parnell and Walawege note,[8] much rapid growth can be the product of sustained high birth rates as much as rural migration. Seeking work and education, a considerable proportion of migration is undertaken by young families, youth and children. High fertility rates also continue to contribute strongly to population growth – though not always with a commensurate "demographic dividend".[9] Economic growth in the urban centres of Africa, Latin America and Asia flows only partly and unevenly into the critical infrastructures to support sustainable child development. In these centres, schools are frequently overcrowded, under-resourced and in deteriorating physical condition. Meanwhile areas for play are often informally eked out in slum alleyways or alongside congested roads. As others have noted,[10] the rise of a perpetual youth underclass in fast-expanding cities also correlates strongly with the development of alternate authorities such as gangs and rebel armies, able to recruit from vulnerable youth and child populations otherwise uncared for by the state or by stable communitarian structures.

Yet rapid urban growth also presents forms of ambivalence. As much as the sudden escalation of high-density apartment or tenement housing and the sprawl of informal tent and makeshift slum housing seems to defy the prescriptions of sustainable development, the dynamic pressures of these urban forms, along with the political and economic exuberance that seems to accompany them, generate possible

---

[7] UN General Assembly (UNGA), Convention on the Rights of the Child (UN Doc. A/RES/44/25, 20 November 1989) 1577 UNTS 3.

[8] S. Parnell and R. Walawege, "Sub-Saharan African Urbanisation and Global Environmental Change" (2011) 21 *Global Environmental Change* 12.

[9] S. Fox, "Urbanization as a Global Historical Process: Theory and Evidence from Sub-Saharan Africa" (2012) 38(2) *Population and Development Review* 285.

[10] R. Muggah, "Deconstructing the Fragile City: Exploring Insecurity, Violence and Resilience" (2014) 26(2) *Environment and Urbanization* 345.

alternative arrangements. Children and youth are thrown into what is configured by some as a kind of premature adulthood born of necessity; they organise, police, regulate and patrol urban spaces, adopting roles that in more stable and mature cities presume formal qualifications, training and education. Accordingly, much of the conceptual apparatus that accompanies discussions of rights needs pragmatic calibration to the conditions that prevail in these fast-changing environments.

We examine and seek to intersect with three of the more influential of these conceptual tools here. The first, the "child-friendly city", has become a tagline of aspiring cities, a kind of brand label that now sits alongside other modifiers like "livable", "vibrant", "resilient" and indeed "sustainable". Yet at its core, it seeks to articulate how the rights of the child might be accommodated within the frequently hostile and severe confines of urban forms.[11] Though the relevant literature references sustainable objectives obliquely, the concept nonetheless serves as a useful starting point that might with some refinement work both to accommodate practices of sustainable development, and to serve as a normative framework for cities undergoing rapid growth. The second conceptual tool is the prolific and influential work of Amartya Sen and Martha Nussbaum on capabilities. In Nussbaum's recent articulation of capabilities as they relate to children, it is possible to see opportunities for a kind of charter for the developing city that might ensure children's *full* capabilities, both actual and potential, are nurtured and encouraged. We then turn to more explicitly political theorisations of the city, to connect what has come to be termed "critical urbanism" to considerations of the rights of the child and sustainable development. Through these theoretical lenses, we draw out a series of five provocations that bring to the fore the uncomfortable contradictions seemingly embedded in the intersections between discourses on child-friendly cities and sustainable development, and the realities of rapidly expanding informal urban settlements. In voicing these provocations, we draw upon various experiences working in and on behalf of several international non-governmental organisations (INGOs) in such spaces, particularly in the two Indian cities of Kanpur and Siliguri. We conclude the chapter by arguing a more attenuated definition of sustainability and sustainable development is required to take stock of the complex and chaotic conditions of rapidly developing cities, and how these necessarily must be negotiated and rearranged around the pivotal figure of the child.

SUSTAINABLE URBAN DEVELOPMENT AND THE CHILD-FRIENDLY CITY

The Sustainable Development Goals (SDGs) released by the United Nations in 2014 offer a broad and deep array of aspirations. Many of these clearly mention or

---

[11] UNICEF Innocenti Research Centre, "Building Child Friendly Cities: A Framework for Action" (Florence: UNICEF Innocenti Research Centre, 2004).

relate to aspects of child well-being, stretching from poverty alleviation (Goal 1) to better educational opportunities and the elimination of child labour (Goals 4, 8). Goal 11 refers specifically to sustainable cities and urban development, and also lists targets that relate to children, including safe, accessible and affordable housing, transport systems and public spaces. Not mentioned in those targets are any reference to the pressures of rapid development, which often contrast with principles of sustainable development either because urban planning is not present at all or is undertaken in a context of aggressive capital investment, and accordingly, is under pressure to respond with approvals that ignore broader and future implications of development. These pressures are further exacerbated when such development is accompanied with sudden, temporary, intermittent or sustained high growth in migrants and refugees. The movement of people and children into cities also highlights another omission from the SDGs: a specific positive sense in which the city is an active agent in welcoming and fostering children on the move, and whose emerging capabilities therefore require special attention.

The "child-friendly city" moniker has gained considerable attention in recent urban literatures and seems to supplement the SDGs in many productive ways.[12] Its benign invocations conjure images of quaint playgrounds, designer spaces and open-air environments where children's creativity, health and education are nurtured. Encompassing a broad set of definitions, policies, practices and recommendations, its use has been embraced by local governments, non-governmental organisations (NGOs) and academics. Considerations of the spatial conditions under which children's rights are adumbrated is in many respects a welcome one. In its contemporary articulations, the city is increasingly viewed as an unstable and endlessly shifting entity, a *dispositif*[13] or an assemblage,[14] a host of networks, relations, links, and structures. These more supple understandings of urban space can also enable new possibilities for thinking about and addressing the needs, desires, dreams and rights of children. Alongside this theoretical reorientation, the child-friendly city has also motivated specific interventions of urban designers and planners, intended to refashion public space as safe and enjoyable for children to live.[15]

Yet enthusiasm for the rights-enforcing capabilities of the child-friendly city needs also to be tempered. Uncritical adoption of the "child-friendly cities" label

---

[12] See, for example, M. Racelis and A. D. M. Aguirre, "Child Rights for Urban Poor Children in Child Friendly Philippine Cities: Views from the Community" (2002) 14(2) *Environment and Urbanization* 97; E. Riggio, "Child Friendly Cities: Good Governance in the Best Interests of the Child" (2002) 14(2) *Environment and Urbanization* 45; UNICEF Innocenti Research Centre, "Building Child Friendly Cities".

[13] B.P. Braun, "A New Urban Dispositif? Governing Life in an Age of Climate Change" (2014) 32(1) *Environment and Planning D: Society and Space* 49.

[14] C. McFarlane, "The City as Assemblage: Dwelling and Urban Space" (2011) 29(4) *Environment and Planning D: Society and Space* 649.

[15] J. Wilks, "Child-Friendly Cities: A Place for Active Citizenship in Geographical and Environmental Education" (2010) 19(1) *International Research in Geographical and Environmental Education* 25.

risks comfortably metamorphosing into yet another empty and generic platitude; such terms can also serve as convenient covers for networks of exploitation and extraction. Like the "Land of Toys", the fabled city of endless play that eventually entraps Pinocchio in servitude, actual lived-in cities also exhibit contradictory features. Acknowledging cities need concepts, rubrics and metrics for improving policy, intervention and action, there is nonetheless a risk that the wanton use of these terms only serves the interests of particular urban actors. It is easy to imagine the "child-friendly city" being used as the latest brand to boost family tourism, entice executive migration or redirect unwanted attention away from urban pockets of neglect. Other dangers exist: In the rush to develop definitions, frameworks and evaluations of the child-friendly city, it becomes all too tempting to trumpet a form of abstract and general universalism about what constitutes friendliness. What works for a set of paradigmatic cities is assumed to work, *pari passu*, in every other. Yet children's needs and desires vary city to city. Against these temptations we suggest that it is vital to develop an approach that is critical, contextual and participatory.

The role and rights of children in directing their own growth and development, including influencing their spatial surroundings, has generated considerable critical debate in a diverse set of fields, extending from developmental psychology to urban planning and international development, with considerable and growing intersection. Discourses on the child-friendly city represent one vibrant strand of this broader discussion. As Woolcock and Gleeson argue, since at least the 1970s there has been an increasing recognition that the health and well-being of children are strongly correlated to features of urban development.[16] The idea of the child-friendly city began to receive prominence following the Rio Earth Summit in 1992, Habitat II in Istanbul in 1996,[17] and the UN Special Session on Children in 2002.[18] Italian scholars and practitioners did much to develop this concept initially in the 1990s and early 2000s, formulating working principles of the child-friendly city,[19] which culminated in the publication of "Building Child Friendly Cities" by the UNICEF Innocenti Research Centre in Florence.[20]

In the decade since, the term has been broadly applied. It has been used to describe attempts by cities to address concerns about participation[21] and

---

[16] G. Woolcock and B. Gleeson, "Child-Friendly Cities: Critically Exploring the Evidence Base of a Resurgent Agenda", (2007) *Proceedings of the State of Australian Cities Conference*, Adelaide, 28–30 November.

[17] M. Corsi, "The Child Friendly Cities Initiative in Italy" (2002) 14(2) *Environment and Urbanization* 169.

[18] Riggio, "Child Friendly Cities".

[19] Corsi, "The Child Friendly Cities Initiative in Italy".

[20] UNICEF Innocenti Research Centre, "Building Child Friendly Cities".

[21] K. L. Knowles-Yánez, "Children's Participation in Planning Processes" (2005) 20(1) *Journal of Planning Literature* 3.

citizenship,[22] security,[23] physical[24] and mental well-being, environmental quality,[25] macro-economic impacts[26] and both housing[27] and urban forms.[28] Geographically, the preponderance of the literature focuses on developed cities in North America, Europe, Australia and New Zealand, with specific case studies centred on cities such as Waterloo,[29] Denver,[30] Rotterdam,[31] Florence[32] and Sydney.[33] Such work is to be applauded in showcasing the challenges and opportunities inherent in creating urban spaces in which children can develop and thrive. However, the developed world's prominence in formulating the principles, measures and methods for implementing the child-friendly city raises questions about the relevance and applicability of the concept in the developing world. This is especially true given the aggressive rate of urbanisation in South and South East Asia, Africa and parts of Latin America. There, arguably, the need for spaces that nurture children's capabilities is even more acute.

A further dilemma stems from the fact that unfriendly cities can generally be impervious to the best intentions of planners and practitioners. On the one hand, it can be argued that urban planning ought to assume much of the responsibility for child friendliness and greater social inclusion in urban development – not least of which would include promoting the role of children in shaping positive and negative freedoms of the built environment.[34] But on the other hand, the speed

---

[22] Wilks, "Child-Friendly Cities"; M. Nordström, "Children's Views on Child-Friendly Environments in Different Geographical, Cultural and Social Neighbourhoods" (2010) 47(3) *Urban Studies* 514.

[23] Racelis and Aguirre, "Child Rights for Urban Poor Children"; C. McAllister, "Child Friendly Cities and Land Use Planning: Implications for Children's Health" (2008) 35(3) *Environments* 45.

[24] P. Wridt et al., "A Qualitative GIS Approach to Mapping Urban Neighborhoods with Children to Promote Physical Activity and Child-Friendly Community Planning" (2010) 37(1) *Environment and Planning B: Planning and Design* 129; M. Oliver et al., "Kids in the City Study: Research Design and Methodology" (2011) 11(1) *BMC Public Health* 587.

[25] P. J. Tranter and S. Sharpe, "Escaping Monstropolis: Child-Friendly Cities, Peak Oil and Monsters, Inc." (2008) 6(3) *Children's Geographies* 295.

[26] M. E. Warner and L. Morken, "Building Child and Age Friendly Communities in Tight Fiscal Times" (2013) *The Municipal Year Book* 47.

[27] H. Easthope and A. Tice, "Children in Apartments: Implications for the Compact City" (2011) 29(4) *Urban Policy and Research* 415.

[28] G. Woolcock, B. Gleeson and B. Randolph, "Urban Research and Child-Friendly Cities: A New Australian Outline" (2010) 8(2) *Children's Geographies* 177.

[29] McAllister, "Child Friendly Cities and Land Use Planning".

[30] Wridt et al., "A Qualitative GIS Approach to Mapping Urban Neighborhoods".

[31] M. Berg, "City Children and Genderfied Neighbourhoods: The New Generation as Urban Regeneration Strategy" (2013) 37(2) *International Journal of Urban and Regional Research* 523.

[32] Nordström, "Children's Views on Child-Friendly Environments".

[33] Easthope and Tice, "Children in Apartments"; Woolcock et al., "Urban Research and Child-Friendly Cities"; H. Little, S. Wyver and Fr. Gibson, "The Influence of Play Context and Adult Attitudes on Young Children's Physical Risk-Taking during Outdoor Play" (2011) 19(1) *European Early Childhood Education Research Journal* 113.

[34] Knowles-Yánez, "Children's Participation in Planning Processes".

with which developing cities are developing can run ahead of the best intentions of planners and urban authorities to include, consult, and encourage participation. For children working 14-hour days in domestic servitude, in factories as menial labour, on the streets or in home businesses, the "child-friendly" discourse of green spaces, consultative exercises or "surplus safety"[35] can seem literally a world away. Making sure that a developing city grows as one that is child friendly, then, is not an exhortation to planners and other professionals to add another item – "include children" – to some imagined development checklist. Instead it is a political imperative – in the very direct and spatial sense as it concerns the *polis* – to allow children to help shape the spaces they inhabit, work in and play in.

This political dimension ought to translate to a specific binding legal appeal: as a series of rights to exercise specific capabilities. The connection between friendliness and universal rights needs to be taken seriously. A mere critique of the child-friendly city as somehow overly Western, prescriptive or part of a humanitarian whitewash of urban poverty would miss the chance to continue the significant research and results already accumulating under its banner. We argue instead that the term can be conceptually embellished to provide a more nuanced and rigorous framework for urban improvement. The blueprint for implementing the child-friendly city, UNICEF's "Building Child Friendly Cities",[36] explicitly links the project of constructing the child-friendly city to the task of protecting and promoting children's rights: "The building process is synonymous with implementation of the Convention on the Rights of the Child in a local governance setting".[37] Indeed that blueprint asserts that building child-friendly cities is a legal obligation of State Party signatories to the UN Convention for the Rights of the Child,[38] explicitly linking the potentials for cities to be child friendly with the necessity for robust legal rights protections.

This is especially critical for cities that continue to be described with the problematic label "developing", and that are, in practice, often developing very rapidly. The growth of East and South Asian, African and Latin American economies has resulted in sudden and drastic agglomerations of populations in cities. This growth continues to take place in peripheral areas of major centres as well as in emergent urban zones that constitute second- and third-tier cities: population clusters of 100,000 to 3 million that seem to sprout from what were once anonymous townships.[39] The rate of urbanisation in such places is as significant as the scale. Rapid change creates conditions that make it difficult to imagine how these cities could be considered child-friendly, even under very elastic definitions. Labour practices are

---

[35] Shirley Wyver et al., "Ten Ways to Restrict Children's Freedom to Play: The Problem of Surplus Safety" (2010) 11(3) *Contemporary Issues in Early Childhood* 263.
[36] UNICEF Innocenti Research Centre, "Building Child Friendly Cities".
[37] Ibid., 4.
[38] Ibid.
[39] B. H. Roberts and R. P. Hohmann, "Secondary Cities: Managing Urban Land Governance Systems", World Bank Conference on Land and Poverty (2014).

often poorly monitored, informal and hazardous; schooling standards are uneven; and urban planning, including the allocation of places for play and recreation, is frequently either haphazard or non-existent. As others have noted, conditions for children in these rapidly developing cities mirror those first diagnosed by critics of industrialisation in nineteenth-century England – but now on a vastly greater global urban canvas.[40] In spite of recent legal frameworks for child education and protection in countries,[41] the numbers of children exposed to unsafe and exploitative work have overwhelmed the efforts of governments and non-government agencies alike to address basic concerns about safety, fairness, health, sexual predation and forced migration. The cities that house these children under such conditions are hard to judge, on any set of criteria, as friendly.

As we argue though, there are opportunities precisely in the massive upheaval and disruption that have followed recent global waves of urbanisation and urban development. Cities make visible conditions that might otherwise be obscured behind the big numbers and vast geographies of China, India and other new economies. In a contradictory fashion they engender the worst forms of child labour and simultaneously make those forms conspicuous to a growing middle class. In cities, people, including children, speak: through the images of informal waste collectors, as well as through those of schoolchildren playing, through the sights and sounds of young suffering bodies, through the decrepit conditions of slums left behind in the race towards ever greater and more conspicuous affluence. Dense populations allow discomfited responses to these conditions to percolate and disseminate.

Even the unfriendly city, then, has its affordances or, in the language of Sen and Nussbaum, capabilities: the proximity and visibility of inequality, the accelerated communication channels and the greater access to nodes and linkages of power allow for the potential interruption of childhood oppression. These capabilities are not merely those that derive from a guilt-ridden middle-class class consciousness finding itself all too close to dire poverty. As recent scientists of the city emphasise, they manifest in the systemic properties of a structured mass of people, where small perturbations to health, education, law and public sentiment can quickly spread.[42] Or, in de Certeau's terms, the space of the city *strategically* organises time, space and its inhabitants, and in this sense the city's momentum can be seen as oppressive:

---

[40] M. Bourdillon et al., *Rights and Wrongs of Children's Work* (New Brunswick, NJ: Rutgers University Press, 2010); N. Odendaal, "Reality Check: Planning Education in the African Urban Century" (2012) 29(3) *Cities* 174.

[41] For example, The Right of Children to Free and Compulsory Education Act, 2009: Gazette of India, "The Right of Children to Free and Compulsory Education Act, 2009" (2009), http://indiacode.nic.in/amendmentacts2012/The%20Right%20to%20Free%20and%20Compulsary%20Education%20Act.pdf.

[42] L. M. A. Bettencourt et al., "Growth, Innovation, Scaling, and the Pace of Life in Cities" (2007) 104(17) *Proceedings of the National Academy of Sciences* 7301; M. Batty, *Cities and Complexity: Understanding Cities with Cellular Automata, Agent-Based Models, and Fractals* (Cambridge, MA: MIT Press, 2007).

It seeks to solidify the social, political and economic relations that perpetuate inequities.⁴³ However, this totalising impulse simultaneously opens up opportunities for the *tactical* disruption of the ordering and organising operations of everyday urban space. Paradoxically, the city is both a site for the reproduction of dominant order and one of potential contestation, subversion and transformation. As such, small and larger disruptions to the sequencing of the everyday can lead in turn to the active promotion of children's rights and material changes to children's lives. Perhaps precisely in its many spatial overlays, condensations and intensifications, then, lies the transformational potential of the city – the capacity to find friends, and the possibilities and mechanisms for change, in unusual places.

A CAPABILITIES APPROACH TOWARDS THE CITY

In this third part we turn towards examining how a developmental agenda for the "child-friendly city" might be composed. To do so, we introduce one prominent line of inquiry: the capabilities approach (CA) put forward by Amartya Sen, and further elaborated by Martha Nussbaum and others. Our discussion of CA does not presuppose an uncritical adherence; there are limitations, particularly in its individualist emphasis, that become especially constraining when considering large-scale and communitarian systems such as cities.⁴⁴ In spite of these concerns CA presents a more rigorous way of considering how the rights of children, in particular, can be supported in diverse environments. Notably Nussbaum has sought to identify CA with questions of social justice, equity and rights, rather than any form of libertarianism.⁴⁵

Much as we argue the concept of the child-friendly city elaborates the SDGs, similarly CA can act to enrich, extend and strengthen understandings of the UNCRC. While we will not rehearse those rights in detail, we argue CA allows for those rights to be translated into practical actions that can be observed, quantified and measured. Whereas capabilities express positive freedoms, through the choice of "combinations of functionings", rights are more often observed solely in their breach, as violations that inhibit what and how capabilities are exercised. As Sen has acknowledged, rights nonetheless form the basis under which capabilities become available as choices and become expressed. In the case of the child, clearly many of their capabilities, including the ability to learn, play and develop physically, mentally and emotionally, are conditional upon a background of rights entitlement, or what Sen terms "process aspect of freedom".⁴⁶ These capabilities become

---

⁴³ M. De Certeau, *The Practice of Everyday Life: Living and Cooking*, vol. 2 (Minneapolis: University of Minnesota Press, 1998).
⁴⁴ See, for example, D. Gasper, "Sen's Capability Approach and Nussbaum's Capabilities Ethic" (1997) 9(2) *Journal of International Development* 281.
⁴⁵ M. Nussbaum, "Capabilities as Fundamental Entitlements: Sen and Social Justice" (2003) 9(2–3) *Feminist Economics* 33.
⁴⁶ A. Sen, "Human Rights and Capabilities" (2005) 6(2) *Journal of Human Development* 151.

unthinkable as choices, and inexpressible as realities without, for instance, the various rights to life (UNCRC article 6), to naming and identity (7–8), freedom of expression, thought and assembly (12–15), protection from violence (19), health (24), social security and living standards (26–7), education and development (28–29) and protection from forms of economic, physical and sexual exploitation (32–28). Equally, it is through the concrete evidence of children developing and exercising a wide and dynamic range of capabilities that a city is able to exhibit its adherence to the obligations of the UNCRC and other children's rights frameworks.

CA has been highly influential in the construction of various general rights-based developmental frameworks and measurement tools, including the "Human Development Index", and both Sen and Nussbaum have argued for their close connection.[47] This is in part because it develops in deliberate opposition to what Nussbaum describes as the "dominant emphasis on economic growth as an indicator of a nation's quality of life".[48] Specifically, capabilities are possible courses of action that humans and other agents can be entitled to pursue,[49] and further imply the ability for these agents choose rationally and act upon such courses.[50] For Sen, this broad definition cuts across many assumed distinctions between, for example, needs and wants, means and ends and compulsions and freedoms.[51] More so than for Nussbaum, Sen's capabilities are essentially free-floating; they must be sensitive to the specific affordances of time and place. Hence, for example, it is justifiable that in 1947 the Indian government prioritised the creation of opportunities for exercising health and education capabilities, and it is similarly justifiable that only much more recently the capability of long-distance communication has been prioritised.[52] In both cases, the type and priority of contending capabilities must be determinable by the specific conditions that rational actors can assess. This does not rule out that lists such as Nussbaum's "Central Human Capabilities"[53] have a pragmatic value; it is rather that, for Sen, their unflinching universality must be held in question.

Sen's own involvement in developmental issues with children extends back to his early research on fertility rates.[54] However, his interests have been more directed towards questions of macro-economic policy than with children's rights. More recently, scholars have attempted to take up CA in relation to children specifically. Harreveld, Singh and Li productively engage CA's emphasis on freedom with

---

[47] Ibid. M. C. Nussbaum, "Capabilities, Entitlements, Rights: Supplementation and Critique" (2011) 12(1) *Journal of Human Development and Capabilities* 23.
[48] Nussbaum, "Capabilities as Fundamental Entitlements".
[49] Ibid.
[50] Sen, "Human Rights and Capabilities".
[51] A. Sen, "The Ends and Means of Sustainability" (2013) 14(1) *Journal of Human Development and Capabilities* 6.
[52] A. Sen, "Capabilities, Lists, and Public Reason: Continuing the Conversation" (2004) 10(3) *Feminist Economics* 77.
[53] Nussbaum, "Capabilities as Fundamental Entitlements".
[54] A. Sen, "Missing Women" (1992) 304(6827) *BMJ* 587.

empirical findings on young indigenous people transitioning from work to school.[55] Unsurprisingly, they found that "physical, social, emotional and economic" constraints limited those people's choices. However, they also found that CA could be used to better articulate where systemic shortfalls could be found.[56] Similarly, Robertson has recently argued CA provides a useful fit for a more holistic perspective on career development, and accordingly develops a list of "career capabilities".[57]

Most notably in this context, Dixon and Nussbaum have recently put forward an argument directly addressing "children's rights and the capabilities approach".[58] In this article they suggest CA offers distinct advantages over social contractual approaches to the question of rights. They further argue that such contractual theories of rights assume fully capable and mature adults who, critically, have the legal as well as the moral right to be parties to contracts. One consequence of this framing is that there exist less capable individuals who, due to illness, disability, imprisonment or, crucially in this context, age, are necessarily excluded from exercising their rights in toto. By contrast, Dixon and Nussbaum suggest that rights for children can be specified in a variety of ways, in line with the various capabilities that younger and older children can be said to possess. They posit that CA instead allows for a more negotiable and variable set of rights; for Dixon and Nussbaum, "CA also does better ... in accounting for the extension of rights to young children, and the denial of various rights to older children".[59] Their discussion of children's rights avoids the kinds of libertarian pitfalls Sen's position might arguably fall into; in their argument, rights involve inviolable positive freedoms to exercise some minimum set of capabilities. Critically, the state has a specific role to ensure these freedoms can indeed be exercised by the vulnerable. CA foregrounds the protection of "weak" parties in the essentially asymmetric power relations that constitute rights deliberation; conversely, "theories grounded in the classical social contract cannot adequately incorporate children's unusual vulnerability and their needs for care".[60] For Dixon and Nussbaum, then, children represent, in some sense, bundles of capabilities that can be more or less expressed, and to a greater or lesser degree need nurturing. Their variant of CA assumes "human beings come into the world with a variety of inchoate capacities that need development".[61] They cite as a case Adam Smith's example of

---

[55] R. B. Harreveld, M. Singh and B. Li, "A Capability Approach to Cultural Diversity in School-to-Work Transitions: Amartya Sen and Young Adults' Diversely Different Education and Work Communities", in G. Tchibozo (ed.), *Cultural and Social Diversity and the Transition from Education to Work* (Dordrecht, The Netherlands: Springer, 2013).

[56] Ibid.

[57] P. J. Robertson, "Towards a Capability Approach to Careers: Applying Amartya Sen's Thinking to Career Guidance and Development" (2015) 15(1) *International Journal for Educational and Vocational Guidance* 75.

[58] R. Dixon and M. C. Nussbaum, "Children's Rights and a Capabilities Approach: The Question of Special Priority" (2012) 97(3) *Cornell Law Review* 549.

[59] Ibid., 553.

[60] Ibid., 563.

[61] Ibid.

children in eighteenth-century Scotland receiving schooling, while their English counterparts were sent directly to work. The tragedy in the English case is that such children are denied seeing their potential capabilities – to learn, to acquire new ways of doing and being – come to fruition. A child's immediate capability to work is exploited, and the freedom to (eventually) choose to exercise other capabilities – to work in different occupations for example – are heavily circumscribed.

If, together with Sen's groundwork, Dixon and Nussbaum's account provides significant impetus for articulating and defending children's capabilities and rights, it is also critical to consider how the urban geographies children inhabit might support these capabilities. In line with the idea that capabilities can be potential as well as actual, and can be variable according to the age and maturity of the child, the child-friendly city must support the nurturing of those capabilities-yet-to-be. Yet the geographic, economic and political diversity of cities renders difficult the prescriptions of substantive rights that pertain to child friendliness. Even Dixon and Nussbaum's apparently unambiguous case of child education cited in the preceding text is not clear-cut in many of today's cities. As Bourdillon et al. note, the ability for children to work is often a necessary "freedom" that must be exercised before education can become a possibility.[62] Simply stipulating that children's work, in all its forms, has no place in the child-friendly city ignores the economic conditions that pertain in many contexts, which necessitate that children contribute to the family income.

What can be prescribed is an idea of procedural rights: the right to be involved in self-determining decision-making, or what Robertson calls the "meta-capability to choose".[63] Sen has frequently acknowledged the need for a suitable political process to house the development and exercise of capabilities: "capabilities and the opportunity aspect of freedom, important as they are, have to be supplemented by considerations of fair processes and the lack of violation of people's right to invoke and utilize them".[64] Following Dixon and Nussbaum, we can see how these rights could be partially but unequivocally extended to children, to ensure they have a role in determining what capabilities, including potential or future capabilities, might matter for them. The city, with its intensity and localisation of power relations, offers an ideal space in which children could – and indeed often do – learn to exercise their political rights. While specific design recommendations for how such spaces could be constructed clearly vary, obvious examples include public places – schoolyards, shopping malls, transport stations – where children can safely congregate, socialise and organise. But more saliently, the city needs an equivalent political infrastructure to support dialogue between children and its other citizens.

---

[62] Bourdillon et al., *Rights and Wrongs of Children's Work*.
[63] Robertson, "Towards a Capability Approach to Careers".
[64] Sen, "Human Rights and Capabilities", 157.

The child-friendly city, then, would be one in which children are entreated to join the broader urban bestiary of Aristotelian "political animals" – animals, also, of the *polis*.

THE RIGHTS OF THE CHILD IN AN AGE OF SUSTAINABLE URBAN DEVELOPMENT

So far, we have advanced the argument that the child-friendly city must be one that supports children exercising a broad range of capabilities, including, to some degree, the "meta-capability to choose". The concept of a *right* includes, in this context, a right to exercise those capabilities. In this section, we further pursue this idea with respect to the spatial and temporal scales of the city and its forward-going sustainable development. While space seems self-evidently caught up in developments of the city, *time* also matters here, in two specific respects. First, as Dixon and Nussbaum's work has suggested, children's capabilities must be understood both as *actual* – as functionings that be exercised in the present – and as *potential* – as functionings that cannot be exercised in the present but can be anticipated or expected to be exercised in the future. Accordingly, constraints upon those capabilities can then be understood to be actions that prohibit their exercise today, as well as actions that prohibit their exercise at some future time. Second, the city is increasingly the scene or setting in which these capabilities are exercised. How the city develops, unfolds and expands sustainably over time becomes an accompanying requirement for ensuring the potential capabilities of the child can be exercised in the future.

It is in this temporal sense that we consider the specific political rights of the urban child to their surroundings. The "child-friendly city" develops, under this interpretation, as one that seeks to preserve and sustain spaces for the present and future exercising of capabilities – and instantiates this sense of sustainability not merely as an altruistic exhortation, but as an embedded political and legal right. This interpretation further connects both notions of the child-friendly city and the CA with what Lefebvre has referred to as the "right to the city", which includes a *future* right to enjoy the city as spaces for exercising potential capabilities. In a minimal, limiting sense, this corroborates the second key clause of the Brundtland Commission's well-known definition of *sustainability*, "the ability of future generations to meet their own needs".[65] A fuller conception of sustainable urban development must move beyond one that is needs-based, however; consideration of a wider range of capabilities, framed within a politically oriented "meta-capability", provides one means for doing so. We further interpret sustainable urban development along lines suggested by James's recent recasting of the Triple Bottom Line into four domains of

---

[65] World Commission on Environment and Development, "Our Common Future" (UN Doc. A/42/427, 1987), www.un-documents.net/our-common-future.pdf.

economic, ecological, cultural and political domains.[66] Adopting this recast form here serves as a reminder that the sustainable city is a place where political life, the active and engaged life of the polis, must be continuously enacted and exercised. In the language of rights, this translates into a demand that both present and future rights to the city must be respected and enforced. Pursuing this interpretation further, sustainable urban development invokes not only, then, questions of economic rectitude, ecological protections and preservation of cultural heritage but it must consider also how children's political capabilities can be nurtured and given institutional structures through which they are progressively exercised in line with their maturation.

From this premise, we consider here five provocations that might orient how the child's future rights to the city – including the right to exercise a political "meta-capability" – might be framed. As we have argued, the sustainable development of child-friendly cities in rapidly growing urban contexts appears oxymoronic, an impossibly normative claim that flies in the face of spiraling informal settlements, waste and emissions production, intractable conflicts over land use and ownership, widespread child labour and irregular sanitation and education standards. Simple exhortations to become "sustainable" or "child-friendly" are unlikely to shift substantively patterns of fast urban development; responding instead to the complexity of these cities, the provocations have similarly oxymoronic or disjunctive characteristics. These mark the implicated contradictions that attend how rapidly emergent spaces evolve to meet a more nuanced interpretation of sustainability, as shifting overlays of present and future needs, demands, rights and capabilities stretched out across economic, ecological, cultural and political fields.

We have labelled the five provocations "Complex Participation", "Multiplicitous Cartographies", "Open Development", "Organised Serendipity", and "Live Laboratories". These we imagine as ways of describing and documenting complex and sustainable urban spaces that enable children's rights and give full force to their exercise of actual and potential capabilities. In the context of rapid urban growth, where considerable charge for the protection of children's rights often falls to non-state actors, these also can be translated into rubrics for the monitoring and evaluation of NGO projects. Though we raise these provocations with particular attention to rapid informal urban development contexts, we argue they also function as open-ended questions to ask of any urban space, irrespective of particular patterns of informality, development, rate of growth or ecological footprint.

In discussing these provocations, we draw upon fieldwork conducted by two of the authors in the Indian cities of Kanpur and Siliguri, during evaluations of INGO projects in 2013. Specific observations of children's life in those cities are presented as concluding vignettes to the theoretical points that follow.

---

[66] P. James, *Urban Sustainability in Theory and Practice: Circles of Sustainability* (Abingdon, UK: Routledge, 2015), 6.

Kanpur is a medium-sized Indian city of more than 6 million residents in the state of Uttar Pradesh. Known as the "Manchester of India", it has a noted industrial heritage, specialising in the production of leather and textile goods. In recent decades, industrial output has declined, and economic growth has been focused in tertiary sector areas such as banking, information technology and higher education.

Siliguri is a rapidly growing city located in the narrow stretch of land connecting the North East to mainland India. Close both to the borders of Nepal (80 km) and Bangladesh (10 km), it also provides a rail and road transit point from mainland India to China, Bhutan and South East Asian neighbours. The increased trade within India and with its neighbours has led to the city growing considerably in the past 20 years. According to local informants, it has grown from a population of approximately 250,000 in the 1990s to somewhere in excess of one million in the 2010s.

As the brief vignettes that follow suggest, there are examples of what might be termed "insurgent urban friendliness" – ways in which children adapt the urban fabric to express at least some capabilities. These must be measured though against the vast challenges many children face in these and other developing cities.

Complex Participation

Cities are complex, and they ferment dissent; they must protect the political rights of children to protest.

In India, 12 million children are officially involved in some form of labour. Unofficial estimates range from 60 to 100 million. Children's work includes paid domestic help, waste collection, factory and retail work and prostitution. National legislation bans work for children aged 14 and younger and mandates universal education. For many children living in urban slums, however, the choice between school and work is a false one. As adult manufacturing labour has declined in former industrial cities like Kanpur, unskilled labour is often the only form of income poor households can draw upon. Not infrequently this falls to the children of the family, to either supplement or provide for the household entirely. Sometimes work is a precondition rather than an alternative to education. Merely legislating away the right to work is therefore overly simplistic. Instead – and extending the existing stipulations of article 32 of UNCRC – children's rights to fair working conditions, which include rights to sufficient income, safety, the time and energy for study, on-the-job training and to collectivise and negotiate, need to be protected. In the language of the CA, such conditions must both aim to develop certain capabilities, and not inhibit nor curtail the development of others.

Global cities are often perceived as facing large-scale, intractable and irretrievably complex challenges: entrenched poverty, climate change, economic recessions, youth unemployment, political unrest and overlapping and sometimes conflicting cultural structures. Sustainable development must negotiate this complexity, as both a practical phenomenon and a pervasive "structure of feeling".[67] In rapidly growing cities, this complexity manifests itself in relation to children's rights in numerous ways.

One example is the question of child labour. Children's need to work and support their families as a matter of survival often exists in stark tension with their right to an education, which might enable them to find ways out of poverty traps. Goal 4 of the SDG demands universal "inclusive and equitable quality education" that provides "literacy and numeracy" and also increases opportunities for "employment, decent jobs and entrepreneurship".[68] In support of this, Goal 8.7 aims "by 2025 [to] end child labour in all its forms".[69] Yet as Bourdillon et al.[70] discuss in relation to teenage women in Morocco, in some cases depriving such children of the right to work – including mandatory and inflexible schooling methods – may not be adequate to the immediate demands and desires of children. Their participation in relation to legal and political questions of rights to education must here negotiate the complexity that unfolds particularly in fast-growing urban spaces, where precarious and informal labour are often the norm. Safe paid work offers forms of skills development, training, socialisation and, in certain cases, political empowerment. Ignoring the work of children also serves to further entrench structures that exploit this work. Children require, in such instances, the right to balance present economic needs with future aspirations. SDG goals 4 and 8 therefore remain subordinate and dependent upon the eradication of the endemic poverty that today makes work a necessity and a priority over education for many children – subordinate, that is, to the realisation of Goal 1: "End poverty in all its forms everywhere".[71] To this we might qualify "poverty" to include precisely those conditions that limit education and necessitate labour.

This translates to a broader political imperative: In line with article 12 of the UNCRC, children must feel they can talk to the city, and that they can speak to, be listened to and have effect upon its systems and structures of power. This includes those represented by INGOs who work more and more in urban contexts, often acquiring statelike authority and responsibilities. Adapting the language of de Certeau, child-friendly cities must remain open to dissent and tactical disruption.[72] Harnessing dissent in the service of the continual refinement of the child-friendly city will render them vital places that the child might want to

---

[67] I. Ang, "Navigating Complexity: From Cultural Critique to Cultural Intelligence" (2011) 25(6) *Continuum* 779.
[68] UNGA, "Transforming Our World: The 2030 Agenda for Sustainable Development" (UN Doc. A/RES/70/1, 21 October 2015).
[69] Ibid.
[70] Bourdillon et al., *Rights and Wrongs of Children's Work*.
[71] UNGA, "Transforming Our World".
[72] De Certeau, *The Practice of Everyday Life*.

befriend. A process-oriented CA is crucial: The child-friendly city must develop dedicated processes for channeling dissent into child-centred innovations that respond to the tensions inherent in children's everyday lives.

How can children's capabilities be identified, activated and prioritised? Children's participation in the city is not merely a matter of bureaucratic consultation; it requires dedicated attention to developing tailored modes of engagement that resonate in specific contexts. Children need to be involved in designing these interfaces of dialogue and input; not to cede control but to mobilise them in ongoing conversations with other urban actors, in which they become co-authors of the child-friendly city.

Alternative Cartographies

The city must see itself also through children's eyes; they must be able to explore alternative cartographies of value and meaning.

On the fringes of Siliguri, the horizon is littered with apartment building construction. As with similar constructions in Kanpur, it was unclear when they might be completed, and who would occupy them. The inner areas of the city featured relatively established slums, with brick buildings and some semblance of communal infrastructure – running water, basic schooling facilities and religious buildings. Others, particularly those near the main NJP railway station, are far more basic still. Nevertheless, street children are attracted to the station. They earn money from the constant traffic of passengers, enjoy the presence of other children and receive often equivocal forms of protection from NGOs, police and railway staff. The railway is an urban space that develops the economy of the city; it is also a place where a child's livelihood capabilities develop. Apparently "rehabilitated" children, taken back to their rural homes by well-intentioned NGOs and authorities, frequently return to the relative comfort of concrete floors and the sociability of their peers.

The child-friendly city sees itself through the eyes of its children. Children's agency must be acknowledged and mobilised, and children must be called upon to participate in the conceptualisation, design and implementation of child-friendly cities. Article 12 of UNCRC enshrines children's right to be heard and participate in the decision-making processes that affect them, in accordance with the child's age and maturity. In doing so, the UNCRC constructs children as people with the right to express their opinion in matters that concern them, emphasising participation rights alongside those of protection and provision. As the UNICEF child-friendly cities framework states, "[C]hildren are seen and heard in a Child Friendly City ... The process of building a Child Friendly City must involve children as active, informed participants".[73]

---

[73] UNICEF Innocenti Research Centre, "Building Child Friendly Cities", 7.

In practice, however, the speed of development in cities of the Global South has tended to sideline the role of children in planning policy and creation of the urban form. This has occurred despite, and alongside, efforts by UN agencies and civil society organisations lobbying for safer, more sustainable and resilient cities to meet the needs of the most vulnerable including women and children. Other processes are also at play: severe poverty, the apathy of state and private city actors and globalised capital that restlessly seeks new markets and new reserves of labour all join to create an inhospitable form of urbanism for many children.

Yet in the midst of this swirling medley of forces, children refabricate the city in ways that respond to their demands. As with the case of the railway station, as well as profit and excitement they find places that strangely offer harbour, sanctuary and safety. Against other criteria, these places may exhibit none of these qualities. But other urban actors need to look, observe, ask and listen: What motivates children to go where they go? What are the features they look for, and what capabilities are they exercising? And how could new spaces be created that also nurture their other capabilities? Adopting UN conventions and frameworks involves not only lip service to general principles but also it means paying attention to how children warp the fabric of the city to exercise certain capabilities. And it also means examining how the city can help develop other capabilities – even in its infrastructural spaces, like railway stations, shopping malls and factories, that are not built for housing, education or play.

Open Development

The city must restlessly imagine and continue to develop its own capabilities; it is never fully "developed".

The streets of Kanpur are a sensory patchwork of color, odor, dust and sound. Despite their colonial origins, today they follow no evident order; the city instead has accreted horizontal and vertical layers of sporadic and unplanned development since its heyday as a centre of textile manufacturing. Children sell tea on the side of the road, run alongside cars creeping forwards in a perennial traffic jam, tag along behind a mother carrying goods back home and play cricket in the liminal spaces between where the cars drive and where the fences demarcating private property begin. The heavy and humid air seems to carry the potential for an infinite array of activities; children are visibly part of how the city is developing.

From the perspective of child friendliness, the usual distinctions between "developed" and "developing" worlds no longer work. Seen through the eyes of the child – and given that today planning policy rarely addresses the needs of children adequately – all cities may be considered to be developing. Children must feel the city continues to develop its capabilities to house and nurture them. As we previously discussed, the CA foregrounds the importance of processes for achieving the child-friendly city, thus emphasising continual practical and material transformation. However, it is equally crucial that the aspirational and imaginative dimensions of such projects are explicitly recognised as a necessary terrain of action if we are to build cities that children willingly befriend and act upon. Rather than an immutable and impassive entity, the child-friendly city needs to be one where its own capabilities are continually developed alongside those of the children it houses.

This is an imaginative, creative imperative for all actors in the city. Urban authorities and experts must begin to develop mechanisms for enabling the rights and capabilities of children to dialogue productively with the rights and capabilities of others as they jostle for position within the space of the city; institutions must actively centre children and their rights and capabilities as routine practice; and city inhabitants must be provided with provocations, resources and spaces to imagine children as both integral to securing better futures and as a site of attention and action in the present. This imaginative work is a crucial pillar of the success of the child-friendly city. It underpins the institutional and everyday transformations that are necessary for the child-friendly city to materialise as a phenomenon with widespread currency and impact.

The child-friendly city has been embraced most enthusiastically in the developed world. Nonetheless, its uptake is, to date, far from widespread, and its material impacts on the everyday lives of children continue to fall a long way short of meeting its aspirations, even where individual cities have committed to the key principles and have developed an actionable plan. This is in part because the principles of child friendliness frequently have limited and highly particularised visibility within both the lived spaces and infrastructures of the city. Instead of conspicuous "child-friendly" branding, and without regard for its GDP or economic standing, the city must weave imagination and creativity into its unfolding social and physical fabric.

Organised Serendipity

The city must allow for both planning and discovery; to be child-friendly requires, paradoxically, organised serendipity

Siliguri has doubled its population in each of the past two decades. Fueled by migration from surrounding rural areas and neighboring countries, its growth is largely represented by a young demographic. It exhibits some of the worst characteristics of rampant development: deteriorating air quality, chaotic traffic patterns, ungainly, unplanned construction and a lack of conspicuous spaces and activities for children. A large and central shopping area, Siliguri City Centre Mall, has emerged as an iconic representation of what the future city might be for children. It is safe, with metal detectors, security guards and surveillance, is clean, is modern and provides connectivity with both Indian and Western commercial worlds. Far from being a "non-place"⁷⁴ (Augé), the shopping mall represents the metonymic condensation of expectations, a place where children's capabilities might achieve their proper expression. This does not obviate its problematic status as site for capitalist consumerism. Rather, it suggests such spaces can be overdetermined in terms of their symbolic value, operating at once as places of consumption, aspiration, safety, pleasure and socialising.

Child-friendly cities must critically engage with epistemes of power and ethics in city planning. This begins with framing and redefining different realities and subsequent planning decisions. Moreover, we argue for planning authorities to evolve with greater ethical grounding, such as a code of practice, to reconfigure planning systems, knowledge and practice. A critical question becomes how planning decisions and choices can be disentangled from political and ethical dilemmas and struggle, to build in child friendliness – conceptually and in practice – as part of a broader urban planning regime. As Michael Safier notes, "[P]lanning and its place in the urban world of yesterday, today and tomorrow are viewed, sometimes simultaneously, as examples of progressive public learning and of oppressive and mystified manipulation".⁷⁵ This contradictory condition argues in part for understanding how urban places take on roles that are not envisaged during the processes of planned "manipulation": how they develop their own publics, including a public of children. This can take place even in spaces abjured by "good" urban planning and design. The gleaming shopping mall is a frequent target of jaundiced urban aesthetes and critics of consumerist capitalism. Yet it offers a space for children, including those from the slums, to imagine alternative urban futures. Urban planning must equally be a process of urban discovery.

In a related context, noted aid critic William Easterly highlights this distinction between planning and discovery: "[T]welve-cent medicine is supplied by Planners while Harry Potter is supplied by Searchers".⁷⁶ Urban planning equally needs to be attentive to the discovered use of space, even if these cut against the political or aesthetic grain of disciplinary training. If the city is "the soil in which democracy lives"⁷⁷ – a strategic place for interaction, exchange, conflict and crisis necessary for transformation to occur – then the public spaces in which this democracy is enacted cannot always be proscribed. For children, it may coincide with the architectural trophies of a rampant global capitalism, such as plazas, shopping malls and transit places. Observing where, how and why young people go where they go, and

---

⁷⁴ M. Augé, *Non-places: Introduction to an Anthropology of Supermodernity* (London: Verso, 1995), 75.
⁷⁵ M. Safier, "On Estimating 'Room to Manoeuvre'" (2002) 6(1) *City* 118.
⁷⁶ W. Easterly, *The White Man's Burden: Why the West's Efforts to Aid the Rest Have Done So Much Ill and So Little Good* (London: Penguin, 2006), 5.
⁷⁷ J. Borja, "Democracy in Search of the Future City", in A. Sugranyes and C. Mathivet (eds.), *Cities for All: Proposals and Experiences towards the Right to the City* (Santiago: Habitat International College, 2010).

without simply succumbing to free marketism, planners and other urban professionals must be attentive to these counter-intuitive impulses in urban rhythms. The child-friendly city needs a professional class that can engage in reflexive and research-oriented practice, understanding that "as a researcher in practice, the practice can be a source of renewal".[78]

Live Laboratories

Cities are now clusters of physical and digital infrastructures; their intersections must be child-friendly as well as user-friendly.

In the slums of Siliguri, children use mobile phones to connect with each other. Their use blends play with the gradual and invisible reinforcement of a child protection network. A young woman saw children on a train accompanied by an adult who did not appear to be a guardian or parent. She called the police, who intercepted the group at the next station, revealing that the children were being smuggled to another location by a child trafficking ring. The caller had been trained by an NGO to identify and respond to instances of trafficking. In urban spaces where "networks" include powerful trafficking mafia, where children can be easily isolated before being exploited and where the official surveillance mechanisms of the state are far from being pervasive, mobile media can continuously signal the fluid locations of children: at school, at play or at work.

More and more the child-friendly city embraces the possibilities afforded by digital media for supporting children's rights and capabilities. Across the globe, the space of the city is increasingly overlaid by the space of the digital. Access to technology is now a commonly accepted and widely integrated condition for the performances of everyday life. Mobile media, in particular, has avoided the obvious dichotomies between developed and developing, permeating cities without particular distinction for their GDP. This permeation has ambiguous effects. Claims about the potential for the latest information technologies to produce unprecedented levels of engagement and participation must be carefully measured against progress on issues of access and digital literacy. Yet investment in wireless infrastructure and the increasing affordability of mobile technologies has opened new prospects for the child-friendly city.

Children are early and enthusiastic adopters of digital technologies across social, political economic and cultural fields of practice. They are at home with the rise of user-generated content and social media. This creates risks: child trafficking networks, for instance, are increasingly adept at recruiting children via online forums. However, a city can equally leverage the agile character of mobile infrastructure to develop its own capabilities to support the growth and development of its children. These capabilities include those of "delivering educational outcomes; facilitating supportive

---

[78] D. Schön, *The Reflective Practitioner: How Professionals Think in Action*, vol. 5126 (New York: Basic Books, 1984), 299.

relationships; identity formation; and, promoting a sense of belonging and self-esteem".[79] Constant online connectivity can be leveraged to grow and promote children's awareness of their rights and their capacity to enact them.[80] Even where access is patchy or where hardware is basic, children and their communities are using digital technologies to envisage and enact their rights in highly inventive and effective ways.[81] Examples include: 24-hour help lines like India's nationwide "Childline" service; websites that offer advice on children's legal rights; messaging apps that connect children to each other in informal networks; photo-sharing apps that alert authorities to dangers in the city and local governance online form lodgement processes that reduce bureaucratic red tape. Each of these can protect children's rights and exercise their capabilities in potentially cost-effective, large-scale and impactful ways. Importantly, digital media provide a medium through which to undertake some of the imaginative work that, as we argue in the preceding text, necessarily underpins the child-friendly city.

CONCLUSION

The language of sustainable urban development has often, and understandably, focused on the balance of environmental, social and economic aims. How can economic growth be managed alongside protection of environmental goods and pursuit of social goals? And what specific affordances of the city lend themselves to establishing or promoting this balance?

We have looked to pursue a related but different line of inquiry. In our interpretation, sustainable development becomes instead a process of continued remaking of the city as a space where actual capabilities are exercised in the present, and potential capabilities are anticipated, and planned for, for the future. Continuing this thread, we have also sought to indicate how the CA might intersect with formulations of the child-friendly city: as an exhortation to include children, at various stages and in different ways, in the political life of the city, as well as in the framing of the capabilities they can choose to exercise, both now and in the future. We also introduced five provocations that could help shape the critical capabilities of the city with respect to children. These provocations reflect different dimensions of an urban fabric that can be seen as enfolding – rather than suffocating – the children who inhabit it. In no particular order or priority, these include political, humanitarian, developmental, planning and technological strands of that fabric. Extending Sen and Nussbaum's approach, these reflect the capabilities of the city – what it must do for children to want to befriend it. We conclude here with thoughts

---

[79] P. Collin et al., "The Benefits of Social Networking Services" (Melbourne, Cooperative Research Centre for Young People, Technology and Wellbeing, 2011), 7.
[80] A. Third et al., "Children's Rights in the Digital Age" (Melbourne, Cooperative Research Centre for Young People, Technology and Wellbeing, 2014).
[81] Ibid.

on how these might translate for urban practitioners working in the NGO sector on child-centred development programs.

First among these is to recognise the many ways cities are capable of being child-friendly and promoting the rights of children. The density of populations, communications and transport means messages of child protection, safety, inclusion and participation can be rapidly disseminated and distributed. This creates virtuous networks that can be exploited, for instance, to promote education, reduced work and safer working conditions for a city's children. Second, to be child-friendly, a city must offer specific instruments for including children in its politics and planning. These include school visits and consultations; shared adult-child forums that lead to decision-making; online polling or voting; public displays of children's art and stories on the walls and windows of the city; and listening and observing the revealed preferences of children – where they prefer to go, how they travel, in what groups and formations. Related to this, the grievances of children must be registered as legitimate voices of dissent and protest. Children must be able to establish and join political organisations that have representation within the city. Such rights, alongside those of rights to education, fair working conditions and access to public health and housing services, must be enshrined in a city's legislature and ways of life. Fourth, the digital capabilities of the city need to support how children navigate the physical, and vice versa. In particular, online child-child as well as child-adult networks can be used to offer protection, identify of safe and unsafe spaces, provide advice and information and connect with others. Finally, while we hope "child-friendliness" does not become yet another empty adjective that adheres to cities, we do see merit in cities continuing to advertise their efforts to comply with the complex criteria we and others have promoted. Child-friendliness must be seen as an integral and universal civic virtue, even if its implementation varies from city to city.

Many of these characteristics exist in several of today's cities. Nor is it an exclusive list. However, they go some way to increasing options for how the current and future capabilities of children can be exercised within them. As we discussed at the outset, rapidly developing cities face challenges to child protection and safety most acutely. They are also well poised to capitalise on the fast pace of change, in terms of both hard and soft infrastructures, to build in capacities for inclusion and participation. New corridors for transport, new types of housing and schooling, new spaces for meeting and conversing, and new digital meshes for communication and collaboration – the flow-on effects of development – represent new options or capabilities. The developing city can appear hostile and alien to those wandering its streets, working its factories or restlessly inhabiting its run-down housing. But it can open itself up to being befriended too, inviting children to become political actors in its unfolding elaboration. Under this interpretation, sustainable urban development could be reoriented conceptually, turned from a fixation on the built environment toward the sustained development of children's present and future capabilities, alive to the possibilities these capabilities might express.

16

Healthy Diet as a Global Sustainable Development Issue

Reasons, Relationships and a Recommendation

Lucia A. Reisch and Wencke Gwozdz

> The world is facing a nutrition crisis, with malnutrition responsible for a large proportion of premature death and disease. Poor diets now underlie over 11 million deaths annually and are the leading risk factor for death. Cancer, cardiovascular disease, diabetes, and other noncommunicable diseases (NCDs) killed more than eight million people before their sixtieth birthdays in low and middle-income countries in 2013 alone. Furthermore, stunting and wasting continue to be a major cause of death and disability in many low- and middle-income countries, creating a double burden of malnutrition. All of these conditions are highly influenced by diet and could be addressed by a healthy food system. The global economic impact from obesity is roughly $2.0 trillion, or 2.8 percent of global GDP, roughly equivalent to the global impact from smoking or armed violence, war, and terrorism. Rates of prevalence are rising far faster in developing economies. Premature illness and disability from diet-related NCDs impoverish families, hurt productivity and bankrupt health systems. Something transformative needs to be done.
>
> World Obesity/Consumers International[1]

WHY CHILDHOOD OBESITY MATTERS

The Evidence: Markedly High with Harmful Consequences

Obesity and overweight, rising in every region and nearly every country, are now a staggering global challenge. The number of children under five years of age who are overweight is approaching the number who suffer from wasting.[2] Within the last two

---

[1] World Obesity and Consumer International, "Why We Need a Global Convention to Protect and Promote Healthy Diets" (2015), www.worldobesity.org/site_media/uploads/convention_briefing_may15.pdf.

[2] International Food Policy Research Institute (IFPRI) (ed.), *Global Nutrition Report 2016: From Promise to Impact: Ending Malnutrition by 2030* (Washington, DC: International Food Policy Research Institute, 2016).

decades, obesity has spread from the United States, the United Kingdom and other high-income consumption societies to the world. Today, 2.1 billion people – nearly 30 per cent of the world's population – are either obese or overweight.[3] The rise in global obesity rates over the last three decades has been substantial and widespread, presenting a major public health epidemic in both the developed and the developing world. Unhealthy diets now rank as high as alcohol and tobacco smoking as a global cause of preventable non-communicable diseases (NCDs).[4] Recent large-scale studies have shown that the body mass index (BMI) has increased globally and is the leading health risk in Australasia and southern Latin America; it also ranks high in newly high-income regions such as North Africa, Middle East and Oceania.[5] On a global scale, the BMI has risen from rank 10 in 1990 up to rank 6 in 2010 on a scale of 67 risk factors identified as attributable to diseases.[6] In the developing world and the BRICS countries, there is a general trend towards both overweight and malnutrition at the same time, closely linked to income level.[7]

Particularly alarming is the fact that globally, children's overweight and obesity rates and numbers of children affected are still rising; notably, the number of overweight children in lower-middle-income countries has more than doubled since 1990, from 7.5 million to 15.5 million.[8] One of the fastest-growing childhood obesity rates can be found in those countries where the Western food style has been introduced and mass marketed recently, such as China and Russia, as well as African and Arabic islands of wealth (such as Egypt and the United Arab Emirates). In contrast with the early days of the obesity pandemic, the vast majority of obese children today live in low- and middle-income countries, where the rate of increase has been more than 30 per cent higher than that of high-income countries. For instance, in the WHO African Region alone, the number of overweight or obese children increased from four to nine million between 1990 and 2013. And even the smallest children suffer: The number of overweight or obese children

---

[3] M. Ng et al., "Global, Regional, and National Prevalence of Overweight and Obesity in Children and Adults during 1980–2013: A Systematic Analysis for the Global Burden of Disease Study 2013" (2014) 384 *The Lancet* 766.

[4] World Health Organisation (WHO) (ed.), *Global Action Plan for the Prevention and Control of Noncommunicable Diseases 2013–2020* (Geneva: World Health Organisation, 2013), www.who.int/nmh/events/ncd_action_plan/en/, 7.

[5] S. S. Lim et al., "A Comparative Risk Assessment of Burden of Disease and Injury Attributable to 67 Risk Factors and Risk Factor Clusters in 21 Regions, 1990–2010: A Systematic Analysis for the Global Burden of Disease Study 2010" (2012) 380 *The Lancet* 2224, 2260.

[6] Ibid., 2224.

[7] WHO, *Nutrition* (undated), www.who.int/nutrition/challenges/en/; IFPRI (ed.), Global Nutrition Report 2016.

[8] UNICEF, WHO and World Bank Group (2015), *Levels and Trends in Child Malnutrition: UNICEF – WHO – World Bank Group Joint Child Malnutrition Estimates*, key findings of the 2015 edition, September 2015. OECD (Organization for Economic Co-operation and Development), *Health at a Glance: Europe 2012* (Paris: OECD Publishing, 2012).

under five years increased from 32 million globally in 1990 to 42 million in 2013.[9] This general trend is expected to continue: The World Obesity Federation estimates that, assuming no effective policy interventions, by 2025 about 270 million children aged 5–17 years may be overweight, including 91 million obese[10] (see Figure 16.1).

It is the many harmful effects of obesity on children's physical and emotional health that underlies policy makers' concern:[11] Children who are overweight or obese are at greater risk of asthma, high blood pressure, musculoskeletal disorders, fatty liver disease, insulin resistance and Type 2 diabetes – even when excess weight is lost in adulthood.[12] These children are more likely to be obese in later life and are more at risk of developing a range of NCDs. Moreover (less visible and more difficult to measure, yet highly relevant) these children suffer from pronounced social, mental and emotional disadvantages and have a markedly lower level of well-being than non-obese children.[13]

The right of children to a healthy diet was recognised in the UN Convention on the Rights of the Child (UNCRC) in 1989. Article 24, which deals with the right to health, refers to the need to "combat malnutrition" and the "provision of adequate nutritious foods". While many may consider "malnutrition" only to refer to those children who are underweight and lack sufficient food, the Global Nutrition Report has emphasised that it must be conceived in a much wider manner. It states that "[m]alnutrition manifests itself in many different ways: as poor child growth and development; as individuals who are skin and bone or prone to infection; as those who are carrying too much weight or whose blood contains too much sugar, salt, fat, or cholesterol; or those who are deficient in important vitamins or minerals".[14] As such, the UNCRC places a clear imperative on States to take action to combat

---

[9] World Obesity Federation, *World Map of Obesity* (undated), www.worldobesity.org/aboutobesity/world-map-obesity. For, e.g., girls see www.worldobesity.org/data/map/overview-girls
[10] World Obesity Federation, www.worldobesitydata.org, based on T. Lobstein and R. Jackson-Leach, "Planning for the Worst: Estimates of Obesity and Comorbidities in School-Age Children in 2015" (2016) 11 *Pediatric Obesity* 321.
[11] World Health Organisation Europe (WHO Europe) (eds.), *Prevalence of Overweight and Obesity in Children and Adolescents: Fact Sheet No. 2.3* (Geneva: European Environment and Health Information Systems, 2009).
[12] T. Lobstein and R. Jackson-Leach, "Estimated Burden of Pediatric Obesity and Co-morbidities in Europe. Part 2: Numbers of Children with Indicators of Obesity-Related Disease" (2006) 1 *International Journal of Pediatric Obesity* 33; M. M. Kelsey et al., "Age-Related Consequences of Childhood Obesity" (2014) 60 *Gerontology* 222; WHO (ed.), *Report of the Commission on Ending Childhood Obesity 2020* (Geneva: World Health Organisation, 2016), 7.
[13] M. Tsiros et al., "Health-Related Quality of Life in Obese Children and Adolescents" (2009) 33(4) *International Journal of Obesity* 387, 400; L. J. Griffiths, T. J. Parsons and A. J. Hill, "Self-Esteem and Quality of Life in Obese Children and Adolescents: A Systematic Review" (2010) 5(4) *International Journal of Pediatric Obesity* 282, 304; M. Buttita et al., "Quality of Life in Overweight and Obese Children and Adolescents: A Literature Review" (2014) 23 *Quality of Life Research* 1117.
[14] IFPRI (ed.), *Global Nutrition Report 2016*, 20.

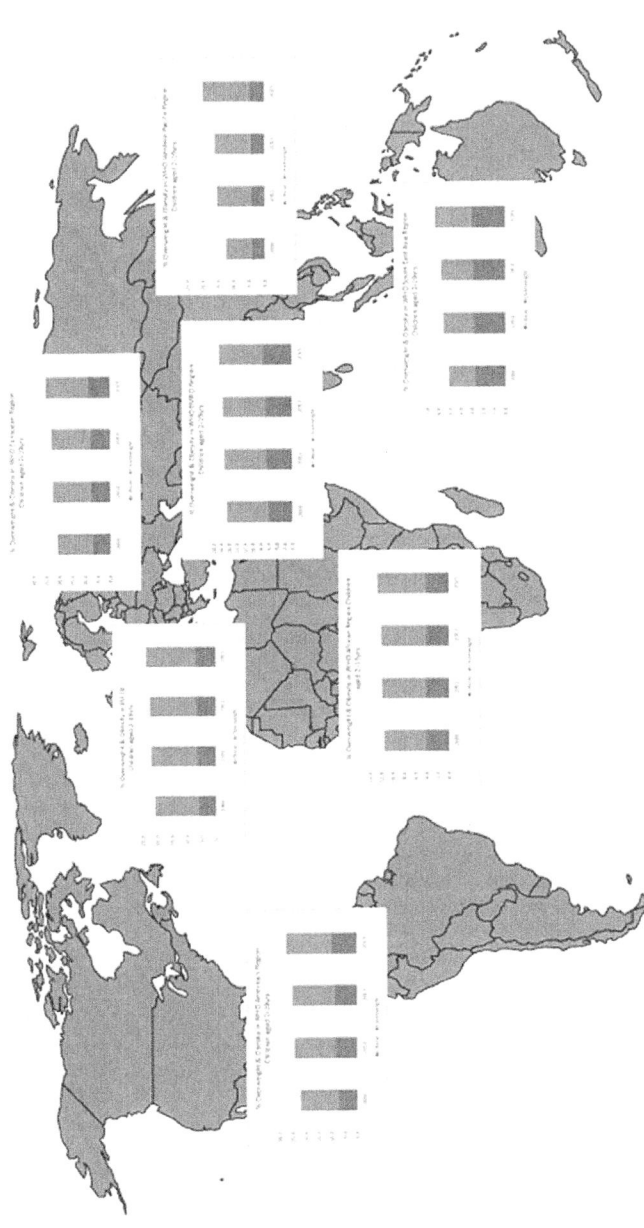

FIGURE 16.1 Percentage of childhood overweight and obesity

obesity, and ensure that all children have access to food that is not only sufficient in quantity but in quality also.

After decades of worsening diets and sharp increases in obesity worldwide, there is finally some hope on the horizon: The increase in adult obesity in many developed countries has slowed down.[15] Of all nations, in the United States – the premier export nation of the unhealthy Western diet and lifestyles, and typically blamed for the obesity pandemic – Americans' eating habits have begun changing for the better. The good news is that the changes in diets have been the most substantial in households with children.[16] Calories consumed daily by the average American child have fallen by 9 per cent since the late 1990s.[17] This decline cuts across most major demographic groups, including higher- and lower-income families and ethnic groups, though it varies somewhat by group. In the most striking shift, the amount of full-calorie soda drunk by the average American child has dropped significantly in the last decade.[18] This could be the beginning of a transformative trend because sugar sweetened beverages have long been identified as a major cause of excessive calorie intake with low nutritional value.

Similar improvements can be witnessed in other developed countries that typically share a history of "McDonaldisation" of their national diets, for example, many Arabic countries.[19] However, these nations also have introduced consumer and health policy measures to fight the obesity challenge already years ago. The reversal appears to stem also from growing realisation that health is seriously harmed by eating and drinking along the Westernised diet, i.e., a diet that is high-fat, high-calorie, easily palatable and heavily processed food, paired with sugar sweetened beverages ubiquitously available and typically served in big portion sizes.[20] This is backed by increasing evidence that the economic, social and ecological costs of high obesity rates are putting an immense pressure on societies struggling to become more resilient and sustainable.[21]

In the United States, the largest and "heaviest" consumer market of the Western world, the awareness began to build in the late 1990s. This is largely due to a burst of scientific research about the risks and costs of obesity and, based on this research,

---

[15] Ng et al., "Global, Regional, and National Prevalence".
[16] US Department of Agriculture, Centers for Disease Control and Prevention, University of North Carolina food research program analysis of Nielsen Homescan Services data, as cited by Margot Sanger-Katz, "Americans Are Finally Eating Less" (*New York Times*, 24 July 2015), http://mobile.nytimes.com/2015/07/25/upshot/americans-are-finally-eating-less.html?rref=upshot&smid=tw-upshotnyt&_r=2&referrer=.
[17] Ibid.
[18] Ibid.
[19] G. Ritzer, *The McDonaldization of Society* (Thousand Oaks, CA: Pine Forge Press, 2004).
[20] L. Cordain et al., "Origins and Evolution of the Western Diet: Health Implications for the 21st Century" (2005) 81(2) *The American Journal of Clinical Nutrition* 341, 354.
[21] L. A. Reisch and W. Gwozdz, "Chubby Cheeks and Climate Change: Childhood Obesity as a Sustainable Development Issue" (2011) 35(1) *International Journal of Consumer Studies* 3. This book chapter draws in part on this article.

dedicated public health campaigns. One of the recent and most influential ones was Michele Obama's "Let's Move! Campaign".[22] Indeed, the Obama administration increased political pressure on companies and has improved consumers' access to health supporting food and information. The Affordable Care Act passed in 2010 requires chain restaurants to publish the calorie content of their meals. The US government has also changed requirements, making school lunches healthier. Several American cities have gone further: New York limits the kind of food available in day care centres.[23] Berkeley, California, is taxing sugar-sweetened beverages.[24] While the evidence for the effectiveness of these interventions is mixed,[25] their popularity reflects public health officials' emphasis on diet and obesity. Similar initiatives and developments of increased regulation and careful design of the nation's food system can be found in many developed countries; these can be assumed to have spurred the reported slight improvements.

Clearly, the encouraging data does not mean an end to the obesity epidemic. Adults and children in high-income countries are still eating far too few fruits and vegetables (though increasing)[26] and too much high caloric food (though somewhat less).[27] But the changes in eating habits suggest that what once seemed an inexorable decline in health may finally be changing course. Since the mid-1970s, when American eating habits began to rapidly change, calorie consumption had been on a near-steady incline – as was the case in other developed countries where the triumph of Westernised diets has led to similar developments, albeit with some years' delay. Hence, this recent sign of a possible shift, however small it may be, is encouraging news.

The Influencing Factors: Many and Interrelated

While the focus on caloric intake is useful, the issue of obesity is a highly complex and multifaceted one. Many interdependencies between a wide variety of factors related to individual biology (e.g., microbiome, genes), eating behaviours

---

[22] Let's Move, https://letsmove.obamawhitehouse.archives.gov.

[23] New York City, "Nutrition and Physical Activity Regulations in Child Care Centres" (undated), www1.nyc.gov/assets/doh/downloads/pdf/dc/childcare-phys.pdf.

[24] City of Berkley, "Imposing a General Tax on the Distribution of Sugar-Sweetened Beverage Products" (undated), www.cityofberkeley.info/uploadedFiles/Clerk/Elections/Sugar%20Sweetened%20Beverage%20Tax%20%20-%20Full%20Text.pdf.

[25] J. Gil, G. López-Casasnovas and T. Mora, "Taxation of Unhealthy Consumption of Food and Drink: An Updated Literature Review" (2013) 207 *Review of Public Economics* 119, 140.

[26] G. W. Evans et al., "Family Income and Childhood Obesity in Eight European Cities: The Mediating Roles of Neighborhood Characteristics and Physical Activity" (2012) 75(3) *Social Science and Medicine* 477, 481; E. Kovacs et al., "Adherence to the Obesity-Related Lifestyle Intervention Targets in the IDEFICS study" (2014) 38 *International Journal of Obesity* 144, 151.

[27] S W Ng, M. M. Slining and B. M. Popkin, "Turning Point for US Diets? Recessionary Effects or Behavioral Shifts in Foods Purchased and Consumed" (2014) 99(3) *American Journal of Clinical Nutrition* 609, 616.

(e.g., low fruit and vegetable intake) and physical activity (e.g., sedentary lifestyles, media use) do play a role. These internal and external factors are set within a social, cultural and environmental landscape, and further complicate the identification of single causes.[28] The British Foresight "Tackling Obesities" project report[29] has visualised these relationships of factors in a system map, which charts 108 internal and external factors that influence weight gain, each supported by bodies of empirical evidence.[30]

In consumer research, childhood obesity is best captured in so-called ecological models[31] that incorporate all those factors within and around an individual, and groups them in several social and physical "environments": individual, group/family, neighbourhood/city, as well regulatory framework and respective markets.[32] In an earlier contribution, we have focused on the influence of interrelated internal and external factors such as individual behaviour, the influence of parents as gatekeepers, the role of maternal employment, the increased purchasing power of children, today's ("toxic") food environment supplied by the food industry, retailers and restaurants, as well as food marketing to children suggesting products and food styles.[33]

In a nutshell, obesity evolves whenever the calorie intake exceeds calorie consumption over a long period. This long-term energy imbalance is largely determined by characteristics of lifestyle, food intake and level of physical activity. While it is ultimately the individual who chooses these three, choice in the real world might be more limited than assumed: In fact, individuals are embedded in general trends of development such as less physically demanding labour, urbanisation, increasing purchasing power, sedentary lifestyles and highly efficient food marketing.[34] Unhealthy and unsustainable lifestyles are hence also

---

[28] Reisch and Gwozdz, "Chubby Cheeks and Climate Change".
[29] Foresight, *Foresight Tackling Obesities: Future Choices – Modelling Future Trends in Obesity and Their Impact on Health*, 2nd ed. (London: Department for Innovation, Universities and Skills, Government Office for Science, 2007).
[30] A. Darnton, "The Determinants of Obesity", unpublished manuscript, British Department of Health, London (2009), www.gov.uk/government/uploads/system/uploads/attachment_data/file/296290/obesity-map-full-hi-res.pdf.
[31] L. Brennan et al., "Socio-Cultural Ecological Models", in L. Brennan et al. (eds.), *Social Marketing and Behaviour Change* (Cheltenham, UK: Edward Elgar, 2014), 121.
[32] For instance, M. Story et al., "Individual and Environmental Influences on Adolescent Eating Behaviors" (2002) 102(3) *Journal of the American Dietetic Association* 40, 51; T. H. Witkowski, "Food Marketing and Obesity in Developing Countries: Analysis, Ethics, and Public Policy" (2007) 27(2) *Journal of Macromarketing* 126, 137; G. Rayner et al., "Sustainable Food Systems in Europe: Policies, Realities and Futures" (2008) 3 *Journal of Hunger and Environmental Nutrition* 145, 168.
[33] Reisch and Gwozdz, "Chubby Cheeks and Climate Change", 3.
[34] Witkowski, "Food Marketing and Obesity in Developing Countries", 126. K. D. Brownell et al., "Personal Responsibility and Obesity: A Constructive Approach to a Controversial Issue" (2010) 29(3) *Health Affairs* 379, 387.

an issue for health and consumer policy because the external effects of private consumption are reflected in social costs now and particularly for the life chances of future generations. While governments' influence on changing individual consumption behaviour is limited, both ethically and practically, a more promising approach is to actively design the consumption contexts people live in: the food and drinks offered in canteens and supermarkets, the content of marketing and advertisements broadcasted, the walkability and bike-ability of cities and so forth. Consumption environments today have been coined as "obesogenic",[35] containing stimuli that encourage obesity, or even as "toxic",[36] promoting toxiclike food and lifestyles. If these factors impact the lifestyle of adults, environmental factors will be even more crucial for children who have typically limited opportunity and ability to "exit" their food environments – such as their schools and neighbourhoods. This approach is in line with article 24(e) of the UNCRC, which requires states to take all appropriate measures to "ensure that all segments of society, in particular parents and children, are informed, have access to education and are supported in the use of basic knowledge of child health and nutrition". Without this information and the creation of environments in which it can be exercised, it is difficult for children to achieve their right to a healthy, sustainable, lifestyle.

The remainder of this chapter is organised as follows: In the next part, we argue that obesity, in general, and childhood obesity, in specific, has become a major factor jeopardising the sustainable development of societies, in a social, economic and ecological perspective. While this is true for all countries, it is particularly impactful for low- and middle-income countries that have neither a financial nor societal "buffer" to cope with such (avoidable) costs. We further argue that both conceptually and politically, it is useful to apply a systems or "nexus" perspective of sustainable development and childhood obesity because they are both closely interrelated. Based on this, we then go on to suggest policy implications in the nexus of consumer, public health and sustainability policy.

WHY (CHILDHOOD) OBESITY IS UNSUSTAINABLE

Increasingly, curtailing and preventing obesity already in childhood has become recognised as a goal of a sustainable and resilient society. In the 2000s, some

---

[35] See B. Swinburn, G. Egger and F. Raza, "Dissecting Obesogenic Environments: The Development and Application of a Framework for Identifying and Prioritizing Environmental Interventions for Obesity" (1999) 29 *Preventive Medicine* 563, 570; Darnton, see n. 30.
[36] Harvard School of Public Health Obesity Prevention Source Web, "Toxic Food Environment: How Our Surroundings Influence What We Eat" (undated), www.hsph.harvard.edu/obesity-prevention-source/obesity-causes/food-environment-and-obesity/.

countries such as Germany,[37] Ireland,[38] England,[39] Spain,[40] the Maltese Islands[41] and Switzerland,[42] as well as the European Union,[43] have integrated levels of obesity as one measurable indicator in their respective sustainability strategies with a focus on young consumers. Against the backdrop of the Brundlandt Commission,[44] which defined *sustainable development* as "development that meets the needs of the present without compromising the ability of future generations to meet their own needs", high levels of childhood obesity are clearly unsustainable because they put current as well as future generations in a worse position to meet their needs. In the following, we explain in more detail why this is the case.[45]

[37] Bundesregierung, "Perspektiven für Deutschland – Unsere Strategie für eine nachhaltige Entwicklung" (2002), www.bundesregierung.de/Content/DE/_Anlagen/2006-2007/perspektiven-fuer-deutschland-langfassung.pdf?__blob=publicationFile; Bundesregierung, "Nationale Nachhaltigkeitsstrategie: Fortschrittsbericht 2012" (2012), www.bundesregierung.de/Content/DE/Publikation/Bestellservice/2012-05-08-fortschrittsbericht-2012.pdf?__blob=publicationFile.

[38] Irish Ministry for Environment, Heritage and Local Government, "Making Ireland's Development Sustainable – Review, Assessment and Future Action" (2007), www.environ.ie/en/Publications/Environment/Miscellaneous/FileDownLoad,1839,en.pdf; Irish Ministry for Environment, Heritage and Local Government, "Our Sustainable Future: A Framework for Sustainable Development for Ireland" (2012), www.environ.ie/en/Environment/SustainableDevelopment/PublicationsDocuments/FileDownLoad,30452,en.pdf.; Irish Ministry for Environment, Heritage and Local Government, "Our Sustainable Future: A Framework for Sustainable Development for Ireland – Progress Report 2014" (2014), www.environ.ie/en/Environment/SustainableDevelopment/PublicationsDocuments/FileDownLoad,41918,en.pdf.

[39] Cross-Government Obesity Unit, Department of Health and Department of Children, Schools and Families, "Healthy Weight, Healthy Lives: A Cross-Government Strategy for England" (2008), http://webarchive.nationalarchives.gov.uk/20130401151715/www.education.gov.uk/publications/eOrderingDownload/DH-9087.pdf.

[40] Government of Spain, "Spanish Sustainable Development Strategy" (2007), www.sd-network.eu/pdf/country_profiles/Spain_EEDS.pdf.

[41] National Commission for Sustainable Development of Malta, "A Sustainable Development Strategy for the Maltese Islands 2007–2016" (2006), www.um.edu.mt/__data/assets/pdf_file/0003/64812/SD_Strategy_2006.pdf.

[42] Swiss Federal Council, "Sustainable Development Strategy: Guidelines and Action Plan 2008–2011" (2012), www.are.admin.ch/dokumentation/publikationen/00014/00271/index.html?lang=en&download=NHzLpZeg7t,lnp6I0NTU042l2Z6ln1ad1IZn4Z2qZpnO2Yuq2Z6gpJCDflR4gmym162epYbg2c_JjKbNoKSn6A--; Swiss Federal Council, "Sustainable Development Strategy 2012–2015" (2012), www.are.admin.ch/themen/nachhaltig/00262/00528/index.html?lang=en&download=NHzLpZeg7t,lnp6I0NTU042l2Z6ln1ad1IZn4Z2qZpnO2Yuq2Z6gpJCEd319gGym162epYbg2c_JjKbNoKSn6A--.

[43] European Commission, "Review of the EU Sustainable, Development Strategy (EU SDS) – Renewed Strategy" (2006), http://eur-lex.europa.eu/LexUriServ/LexUriServ.do?uri=COM:2009:0400:FIN:EN:PDF; European Commission, "Mainstreaming Sustainable Development into EU Policies: 2009 Review of the European Union Strategy for Sustainable Development" (2009), http://eur-lex.europa.eu/legal-content/EN/TXT/PDF/?uri=CELEX:52009DC0400&from=EN.

[44] World Commission on Environment and Development, "Our Common Future" (UN Doc. A/42/427, 1987), www.un-documents.net/our-common-future.pdf.

[45] The following part 2 is largely based on W. Gwozdz, "Obesity, Sustainability and Public Health", in J. Thøgersen and L. A. Reisch (eds.), *Handbook of Research on Sustainable Consumption* (Cheltenham, UK: Edward Elgar Publishing, 2015).

Development experts have traditionally focused on undernutrition. The recent UN Sustainable Development Goals (SDGs)[46], however, which cover both developed and developing countries, have tried to correct this imbalance. SDG 2: "End hunger, achieve food security and improved nutrition and promote sustainable agriculture" separates poverty and hunger and takes a more holistic view of food and nutrition security. Also, nutrition and NCDs receive more attention in the SDGs than they did before. Although cutting obesity is not mentioned in the SDGs as a distinct goal, one of the 169 proposed targets is to reduce premature deaths from NCDs by one-third; another is to end malnutrition in all its forms. A closer reading of the 17 goals reveals that healthy diets and healthy lifestyles, in particular for children, are seen as one pillar of sustainable development. After all, at least 12 of the 17 SDGs contain indicators that are highly relevant for nutrition, reflecting its central role in sustainable development. The most recent Global Nutrition Report 2016 "From Promise to Impact; Ending Malnutrition by 2030" summarises its analysis of the SDGs accordingly: "Improved nutrition is the platform for progress in health, education, employment, female empowerment, and poverty and inequality reduction. In turn, poverty and inequality, water, sanitation and hygiene, education, food systems, climate change, social protection, and agriculture all have an important impact on nutrition outcomes".[47]

Hence, only focusing on SDG 2 is not enough: While it includes three of the World Health Assembly indicators for undernutrition – namely, stunting, wasting and overweight among children under five, the Global Nutrition Report 2016 rightly points to the fact that out of all 242 indicators proposed for the 17 SDG goals, about 50 are of potential nutrition relevance, and that SDG 2 contains only seven of those.[48] In policy terms, this means that there is still leeway for the research and policy community to pick those indicators that should be focused on and hence tracked most closely. Rates of childhood obesity should certainly be one of them.

Obesity and Social Sustainability

The consequences of obesity are socially unsustainable because they threaten social cohesion, equity and fairness;[49] that is, obesity is closely linked to deteriorating health, reduced mobility, stigma, lower socio-economic status (only in developed countries), income inequality and premature mortality resulting in an overall poorer quality of life.[50]

---

[46] UN General Assembly (UNGA), "Transforming Our World: The 2030 Agenda for Sustainable Development" (UN Doc. A/RES/70/1, 21 October 2015).
[47] IFPRI (ed.), *Global Nutrition Report 2016*, 19.
[48] Ibid., 96–97, fig. 8.1.
[49] Reisch and Gwozdz, "Chubby Cheeks and Climate Change .
[50] Foresight, *Foresight Tackling Obesities*.

Above all, obese individuals experience deteriorating health, such as a 7 (men) or 12 (women) times higher risk of diabetes than normal weight individuals.[51] Obesity is also associated with cardiovascular diseases, including coronary heart disease (32 per cent increased risk over normal weight individuals), stroke (64 per cent increased risk) and cardiovascular death (53 per cent increased risk).[52] Overweight and obesity are also linked to respiratory diseases like asthma, with a 50 per cent higher risk for the obese.[53] Although the link between obesity and cancer remains unclear, there is evidence for increased risk for some kinds of cancer. Obesity is, however, linked to lower fertility, being possibly responsible for about 25 per cent of cases of infertility in the United States.[54] Obesity is also co-morbid with mobility-reducing conditions like osteoarthritis, lower back pain and chronic generalised pain[55] and results in reduced functional mobility that impairs general mobility and rewarding participation in everyday life.[56] This is also relevant for children as obese children are likely to become obese adults because behaviour learned in childhood is likely to be transferred into adulthood.[57] As habits are not yet formed as solidly as in adults, it is easier to develop new healthy eating habits among children than adults.[58] Research has shown that preventive actions in early life have a better chance of being successful and effective.[59]

Because of these increased health risks and impairments, obesity is also related to premature mortality. In fact, obesity and its co-morbidities are currently the second most frequent cause of death (after tobacco consumption) in the United Kingdom, where obesity has decreased the average life expectancy for men by two years.[60]

---

[51] D. P. Guh et al., "The Incidence of Co-Morbidities Related to Obesity and Overweight: A Systematic Review and Meta-Analysis" (2009) 9(88) *BMC Public Health*, 1.

[52] P. Strazzullo et al., "Excess Body Weight and Incidence of Stroke: Meta-Analysis of Prospective Studies with 2 Million Participants" (2010) 41(5) *Stroke*, 418.

[53] D. A. Beuther and E. R. Sutherland, "Overweight, Obesity, and Incident Asthma: A Meta-Analysis of Prospective Epidemiologic Studies" (2007) 175(7) *American Journal of Respiratory and Critical Care Medicine* 661.

[54] J. W. Rich-Edwards et al., "Physical Activity, Body Mass Index, and Ovulatory Disorder Infertility" (2002) 13(2) *Epidemiology* 184.

[55] V. H. Taylor et al., "The Impact of Obesity on Quality of Life" (2013) 27(2) *Best Practice and Research Clinical Endocrinology and Metabolism* 139.

[56] M. Forhan and S. V. Gill, "Obesity, Functional Mobility and Quality of Life" (2013) 27(2) *Best Practice and Research Clinical Endocrinology and Metabolism* 129.

[57] T. Lobstein, L. Baur and R. Uauy, "Obesity in Children and Young People: A Crisis in Public Health" (2004) 5(1) *Obesity Reviews* 4, 104; C. F. Lowe et al., "Effects of a Peer Modelling and Rewards-Based Intervention to Increase Fruit and Vegetable Consumption in Children" (2004) 58(3) *European Journal of Clinical Nutrition* 510.

[58] J. Klein-Hessling, A. Lohaus and J. Ball, "Psychological Predictors of Health-Related Behaviour in Children" (2005) 10 *Psychology, Health and Medicine* 31.

[59] K. L. Procter, "The Aetiology of Childhood Obesity: A Review" (2007) 20(1) *Nutrition Research Reviews* 29, 45.

[60] UK Government, "Healthy Weight, Healthy Lives: A Cross-Government Strategy for England" (London: Cross-Government Obesity Unit, Department of Health and Department of Children, Schools and Families, 2008).

Moreover, if forecasted trends hold true, this two-year decrease will rise to five years by 2050.[61] Such an association between BMI and cause-specific mortality was the subject of an analysis by the Prospective Studies Collaboration,[62] which observed the lowest mortality for a BMI between 22.5 and 25.0 kg/m^2. At a BMI of 30 to 35 kg/m^2, life expectancy is already reduced by two–five years, while a BMI of 40 to 45 kg/m^2 shortens the expected age by as many as 6–10 years. This latter is comparable to the expected mortality of smokers.

Social sustainability is further jeopardised by "weight-related stigma", defined as negative attitudes and discriminatory behaviours directed towards obese individuals.[63] In the United States, the prevalence of weight-related discrimination is believed to be equal to that of race-related discrimination.[64] These discriminatory behaviours, which stereotypically attribute such characteristics as laziness, lack of self-control or motivation, incompetence and/or non-compliance to obese people,[65] include insulting comments, social exclusion, discrimination in the school environment and health-care settings and depreciatory representation in the media. Wardle and Cooke state, for instance, that children as well as adults stereotype the obese as lazy, ugly and stupid, and weight related teasing is commonplace.[66] Similarly, Strauss and Pollack find that overweight/obese adolescents are more likely to be at the periphery of social networks and, thus, more socially isolated compared to normal weight adolescents. They thus make obese individuals vulnerable to social injustice, unfair treatment and impaired quality of life.[67] Job discrimination, for example, is induced through disadvantages in hiring, wages, promotions and job termination.[68] Likewise, obese individuals receive around 18 per cent lower wages than their non-obese counterparts even given equal occupation, education and job experience.[69] According to McCormick and Stone, the lower employment rates of obese individuals result from an assumption that their productivity will be lower because they will need more sick days or will die prematurely.[70] In fact,

---

[61] D. W. Haslam and W. P. T. James, "Obesity" (2005) 366 The Lancet 1197.
[62] Prospective Studies Collaborations, "Body-Mass Index and Cause-Specific Mortality in 900,000 Adults: Collaborative Analyses of 57 Prospective Studies" (2009) 373 The Lancet 1083.
[63] R. M. Puhl and C. A. Heuer, "The Stigma of Obesity: A Review and Update" (2009) 17(5) Obesity 941.
[64] R. M. Puhl, T. Andreyeva and K. D. Brownell, "Perceptions of Weight Discrimination: Prevalence and Comparison to Race and Gender Discrimination in America" (2008) 32 International Journal of Obesity 992.
[65] Ibid.
[66] J. Wardle and L. Cooke, "The Impact of Obesity on Psychological Well-Being" (2005) 19(3) Best Practice and Research Clinical Endocrinology and Metabolism 421.
[67] R. S. Strauss and H. A. Pollack, "Social Marginalization of Overweight Children" (2003) 157 Archives of Pediatrics and Adolescent Medicine 746, 752.
[68] Puhl and Heuer, "The Stigma of Obesity", 941.
[69] F. Sassi (ed.), Obesity and the Economics of Prevention: Fit Not Fat (Paris: OECD Publishing, 2010).
[70] B. McCormick and I. Stone, "Economic Costs of Obesity and the Case for Government Intervention" (2007) 8(S1) Obesity Reviews 161, 164.

research does show a correlation between obesity and sick leave days, as well as decreased productivity.[71] According to Sassi, however, such a link should be seen not as a justification for discrimination but rather as an alert for public health actors.[72]

Poorer employment opportunities are also associated with lower socio-economic status. Yet there is ample empirical evidence that, in developed countries, members of low socio-economic status groups are more likely to be obese than any other social group.[73] Even in developing countries, such as those in Central and Southern America, where the opposite used to be true, a shift has been observed.[74] One explanation for this higher prevalence of obesity in lower socio-economic status groups is the poor access to and the higher prices for healthy food, as well as fewer opportunities for physical activity.[75] Nevertheless, the relation between obesity and socio-economic status is bidirectional: belonging to a lower socio-economic status group increases the probability of becoming obese, while being obese decreases the opportunities to improve socio-economic status.[76] In developed countries, obesity is also related to income inequality; that is, the higher the income inequality, the higher the prevalence of obesity.[77]

All these factors – deteriorating health, reduced mobility, premature mortality, stigmatisation, poorer employment opportunities and lower socio-economic status – affect the overall quality of life. Despite the various studies on overweight/obesity and quality of life, little research has been done on the association between socio-economic status and overweight/obesity and quality of life, while the association between socio-economic status and overweight/obesity is well established.[78] A British study on adults shows that overweight/obese adults with low socio-economic status reported lower levels of quality of life compared to their normal weight counterparts and the same is true when comparing overweight/obese adults with low and high socio-economic status; overweight/obese adults with low socio-economic status experience lower quality of life levels than overweight/obese adults with high socio-economic status.[79] Also, household stressors can contribute to both

---

[71] Ibid.
[72] Sassi, *Obesity and the Economics of Prevention*.
[73] L. McLaren, "Socioeconomic Status and Obesity" (2007) 29(1) *Epidemiologic Reviews* 29.
[74] C. A. Monteiro, W. L. Conde and B. M. Popkin, "Income-Specific Trends in Obesity in Brazil: 1975–2003" (2007) 97(10) *American Journal of Public Health* 1808.
[75] A. Robertson, T. Lobstein and C. Knai, *Obesity and Socio-Economic Groups in Europe: Evidence Review and Implications for Action* (Brussels: DG SANCO, 2007).
[76] Reisch and Gwozdz, "Chubby Cheeks and Climate Change", 4.
[77] K. E. Pickett et al., "Wider Income Gaps, Wider Waistbands? An Ecological Study of Income Inequality and Obesity" (2005) 59(8) *Journal of Epidemiology and Community Health* 670.
[78] McLaren, "Socioeconomic Status and Obesity"; K. Bamman et al., "Socioeconomic Factors and Childhood Overweight in Europe: Results from the Multicentre IDEFICS Study" (2012) 8 (1) *Pediatric Obesity* 1; Evans, "Family Income and Childhood Obesity", 477.
[79] J. M. Kinge and S. Morris, "Socioeconomic Variation in the Impact of Obesity on Health-Related Quality of Life" (2010) 7(10) *Social Science and Medicine* 1864.

weight outcome and quality of life.[80] When all these factors are linked to obesity, it is no surprise that research has found a negative, bidirectional relation between obesity and quality of life,[81] including poorer self-image and social ostracism for individuals and routine difficulties (like finding suitable seating) in daily life.[82]

Obesity and Economic Sustainability

Economic sustainability means maintaining or increasing current standards of living without decreasing the living standard of others, especially that of future generations. The economic consequences of obesity, however, are severe with regard to both health-care systems and labour markets. As regards the first, national health systems are burdened by obesity's many co-morbidities, which make public spending on health care and long-term care a challenge for Western policy makers. In Europe, since 2010, health spending has experienced severe cuts following a trend of steady increases, with health expenditures remaining stable or declining an average 9 per cent of GDP.[83] Yet on average, less than 3 per cent of health expenditures are used for preventative measures such as vaccinations or campaigns against alcohol abuse, smoking and obesity.[84]

In particular, health-care costs have increased because of obesity-related chronic diseases. According to Finkelstein et al. obesity is responsible for approximately 1 to 3 per cent of total health expenditures in most countries, except in the United States where it was responsible for 9 per cent of total health expenditures (~US$86 billion) in 2006.[85] On the individual level, health-care expenditures for an obese person are on average about 30 per cent higher than those for a normal weight person.[86] Hence, projections for the United States and United Kingdom, assuming a continued rise in obesity, foresee costs of US$48 to 66 billion per year in the United States and £1.9 to 2 billion per year in the United Kingdom in 2030.[87]

In addition to the health expenditures, resources forgone because of health conditions also generate indirect costs, most notably, perhaps, the losses in productivity. These indirect costs, however, are harder to trace and nowhere coherently defined, although the National Obesity Observatory suggests that they include

---

[80] C. Gundersen et al., "Linking Psychosocial Stressors and Childhood Obesity" (2011) 12(5) *Obesity Reviews* 54.
[81] Taylor, "The Impact of Obesity on Quality of Life", 139.
[82] Witkowski, "Food Marketing and Obesity in Developing Countries", 126.
[83] OECD, see n. 8.
[84] Ibid.
[85] E. A. Finkelstein et al., "Annual Medical Spending Attributable to Obesity: Payer- and Service-Specific Estimates" (2009) 28(5) *Health Affairs* 822.
[86] D. Withrow and D. A. Alter, "The Economic Burden of Obesity Worldwide: A Systematic Review of the Direct Costs of Obesity" (2010) 12(2) *Obesity Reviews* 131.
[87] Y. C. Wang et al., "Health and Economic Burden of the Projected Obesity Trends in the USA and the UK" (2011) 378 *The Lancet* 815.

labour market-related lost earnings from attributable sickness and premature mortality.[88] Depending on the calculation method, these indirect costs are estimated to be up to twice the direct costs. In the United States for example, in 2008, the estimated obesity-related lost working days and costs of absenteeism amounted to a loss of 1.7 to 3.0 productive person-years in the working population, with a corresponding cost of US$390 to 580 billion.[89] Nevertheless, these indirect costs are very much dependent on the actual labour market situation and on the structure of the welfare system.

The long-term costs of obesity over a lifetime have been little researched, and the few studies that do exist offer no consistent findings. Whereas some suggest that health-care costs for obese individuals are lower than for normal weighted individuals because of premature mortality, others claim that the costs of obesity outweigh the health-care expenditures of the longer life expectancy of non-obese individuals.[90] The more important observation might be that the costs of obesity for a health-care system arise in a certain period, so during that period, an obese population costs more than a lean population.[91] Nevertheless, although such an economic modulation could be policy makers' strongest argument for prevention and intervention, basing intervention decisions on calculated costs over a lifetime of normal weighted versus obese individuals raises serious ethical questions.

Obesity and Ecological Sustainability

Finally, obesity is closely connected to ecological unsustainability because current food production and consumption are characterised by an excessive use of energy and water.[92] This is also the approach of the SDGs that clearly focus on the nexus between social, ecological and economic sustainability issues. Globally, food production accounts for about one-fifth of greenhouse gas (GHG) emissions, while food-related transport accounts for an additional 14 per cent.[93] In the European Union, food and non-alcoholic beverages account for 21 per cent of the GHG emissions of private consumption, with meat, meat products and dairy being the largest contributors.[94] In fact, with the earlier mentioned changes in food

---

[88] National Obesity Observatory, "The Economic Burden of Obesity" (2010) www.noo.org.uk/uploads/doc/vid_8575_Burdenofobesity151110MG.pdf.
[89] Wang et al., "Health and Economic Burden of the Projected Obesity Trends", 815.
[90] Sassi, *Obesity and the Economics of Prevention*.
[91] Wang et al., "Health and Economic Burden of the Projected Obesity Trends", 815.
[92] L. A. Reisch, U. Eberle and S. Lorek, "Sustainable Food Consumption: An Overview of Contemporary Issues and Policies" (2013) 9(2) *Sustainability: Science, Practice, and Policy* 7.
[93] A. Haines et al., "Public Health Benefits of Strategies to Reduce Greenhouse-Gas Emissions: Overview and Implications for Policy Makers" (2009) 374 *The Lancet* 2104.
[94] European Environmental Agency (EEA), *Environmental Pressures from European Consumption and Production* (EEA Technical Report No 2/2013, 2013).

production and supply,⁹⁵ local farmers have become more likely to feed their products into the large industrial food system instead of trading them locally, thereby increasing transportation or food miles. This tendency, in turn, increases transport distances between farmers, industry and consumers.

Food production also requires masses of fresh water, accounting for about 75 per cent of total water use in Germany, 40 per cent directly consumed within the country and 60 per cent consumed indirectly through production elsewhere (virtual water consumption).⁹⁶

Another important aspect is food waste, primarily during food manufacturing and consumption. Around 90 megatons of food are wasted in the European Union every year, 39 per cent generated from food manufacturing and 42 per cent of consumption, which later accounts for 170 megatons of GHG equivalent emissions (about 3 per cent of the European Union's total GHG emissions), 45 per cent directly from consumers.⁹⁷ The overall effect on GHG emissions of rising obesity is estimated by Edwards and Roberts.⁹⁸ They show that compared to a normal population with about 3.5 per cent obese and a mean BMI of 24.5 (equivalent to the United Kingdom in the 1970s), a population with 40 per cent obese and a mean BMI of 29.0 (equivalent to the United Kingdom in the 2010s) requires 16 per cent more food energy. In a population of one billion people, such an increase would result in a 0.4 to 1.0 gigaton rise in carbon dioxide equivalents per year in GHG emissions from food production and transportation. Hence, reducing the BMI should have equally beneficial effects for the environment.

In fact, changes in current diets could substantially reduce environmental impacts, as clearly shown by studies on the effects of diet changes on GHG emissions⁹⁹ and water use.¹⁰⁰ The point of departure for such investigation is diets high in meat and low in vegetable consumption versus healthier diets in which consumers adhere to current food-based dietary guidelines or move towards vegetarian diets that have greater potential to reduce not only obesity but also GHG emissions and water use. Changes in purchasing behaviour – that is, better planning – could also reduce food waste by about 13 per cent.¹⁰¹ Hence, shifting consumer behaviour towards healthier diets (decreased animal product

---

[95] Reisch et al., "Sustainable Food Consumption", 25.
[96] World Wide Fund for Nature (WWF), *Der Wasser Fußabdruck Deutschlands: Woher stammt das Wasser, das in unseren Lebensmitteln steckt?* (Berlin: WWF Germany, 2009).
[97] European Commission, *Preparatory Study on Food Waste Across EU-27* (European Communities, 2011), http://ec.europa.eu/environment/eussd/pdf/bio_foodwaste_report.pdf.
[98] P. Edwards and I. Roberts, "Population Adiposity and Climate Change" (2009) 38(4) *International Journal of Epidemiology* 1137, 1140.
[99] E. Stehfest et al., "Climate Benefits of Changing Diet" (2009) 95(1) *Climatic Change* 83.
[100] D. Vanham and G. Bidoglio, "A Review on the Indicator Water Footprint for the EU28" (2013) 26(0) *Ecological Indicators* 61.
[101] C. E. Delft, Fraunhofer Institute for Systems and Innovation Research and LEI Wageningen, *Behavioural Climate Change Mitigation Options and Their Appropriate Inclusion in Quantitative Longer Term Policy Scenarios* (2012), www.cedelft.eu/publicatie/behavioural_climate_

consumption, increased vegetable and fruit consumption) could have a substantial impact both on obesity reduction and environmental sustainability.

PROMOTING HEALTHIER LIFESTYLES THROUGH POLICY ALLIANCES

The Power of a Healthy Supporting Environment

Children are vulnerable consumers in many respects. Due to their limited resources and mobility, they are much more on the mercy of their immediate social and physical environment than adults. While they have the same fundamental consumer rights as adults – codified, for example, in the Charter of Fundamental Rights of the European Union[102] – child consumers enjoy a higher level of protection and allegedly more responsible marketing practices from industry. For some years, child consumers have had the special attention of consumer and health policy makers. Following the European Commission's Recommendation "Investing in Children: Breaking the Cycle of Disadvantage" of 2013, "children are more at risk of poverty or social exclusion than the overall population in a large majority of EU countries; children growing up in poverty or social exclusion are less likely than their better-off peers to do well in school, enjoy good health and realize their full potential later in life".[103] While the reasons and forms of economic and social disadvantage are manifold, overweight and obesity are clearly linked to a lower socio-economic status of their families.[104]

On a global scale, a range of environmental risk factors threatens the health of children: inadequate water and sanitation, unsafe home and recreational environments, lack of spatial planning for physical activity, indoor and outdoor air pollution, and hazardous chemicals, pesticides and environmental pollutants.[105] Recent developments – including financial constraints, widening socio-economic and gender inequalities and more frequent extreme climate events – amplify these threats, in particular for the socially disadvantaged children. While these challenges have been put on the global agenda by the World Health

---

change_mitigation_options_and_their_appropriate_inclusion_in_quantitative_longer_term_policy_scenarios/1290.

[102] European Union, Charter of Fundamental Rights of the European Union (2012/C 326/02, 12 December 2007).

[103] European Commission, "Investing in Children: Breaking the Cycle of Disadvantage" (2013/112/EU, 20 February 2013).

[104] For instance, Robert Koch-Institut, *Gesundheit in Deutschland* (Berlin: Robert Koch-Institut, 2015), 206.

[105] US Environmental Protection Agency, *National Agenda to Protect Children's Health from Environmental Threats* (EPA 175-F-96-001, 2006), www2.epa.gov/sites/production/files/2014-05/documents/national_agenda_to_protect_childrens_health_from_environmental_threats.pdf; WHO Europe, "Parma Declaration on Environment and Health" (EUR/55934/5.1 Rev. 2, 11 March 2010), www.euro.who.int/__data/assets/pdf_file/0011/78608/E93618.pdf?ua=1.

Organization (WHO) and its allies,[106] an important challenge has been missing until recently: childhood obesity. We hence suggest that national and international efforts to protect children's health from environmental threats should extend their area of application to create health-supporting environments in schools, neighbourhoods, as well as virtual spaces such as gaming sites and online places they typically visit on the Internet. If children are not protected and empowered within those contexts where they spend most of their daytime, governments should not expect improvement.

A strategic alliance between the environment and health sectors is essential and highly recommended because there are quite some synergies: for instance, most of the actions that reduce levels of carbon dioxide (CO_2) emissions benefit health. While this is obvious on a macro level, there are also many benefits on household level. To illustrate, changes in the home that increase energy efficiency, such as improved insulation and ventilation control, have the potential to reduce indoor air pollution.[107] Good starting points are efforts to create healthy and sustainable cities, with a clear sustainability agenda for urban planning and sustainable buildings. Cities and neighbourhoods have a perfect size and governance systems to test and implement all kinds of policy tools, in particular, choice architecture, as controlled field experiments.

Article 5 of the UNCRC requires States to respect the responsibilities, rights and duties of parents to provide appropriate direction and guidance to children. While we agree that parents have the main responsibility for their children, responsibility can only be asked for if these parents have the competence and the time to make informed choices and transfer their knowledge to their offspring. For some groups of vulnerable consumers – the money poor, the time poor, those with limited consumer competence – this might prove difficult, if not impossible.[108] Other socialisation agents, in particular preschools and schools, are hence called into action. While education for healthy diets and lifestyles has a tradition in many countries and decades of experience of application, there has been a lack of focus on the choice architecture they provide to children regarding food styles and options for physical activity. Only a handful of nations (e.g., Sweden) have binding dietary guidelines and quality standards for public schools. Messages are quite difficult to be put into action if barriers are high, opportunities are low and access to the healthy choice is complicated, time consuming, expensive or otherwise cumbersome or tagged with prohibitive costs.

---

[106] WHO Europe, *Protecting Children's Health in a Changing Environment: Report of the Fifth Ministerial Conference on Environment and Health* (2010), www.euro.who.int/__data/assets/pdf_file/0004/123565/e94331.pdf.

[107] J. Milner et al., "Housing Interventions and Health: Quantifying the Impact of Indoor Particles on Mortality and Morbidity with Disease Recovery" (2015) 81 *Environment International* 73.

[108] S. Mullainathan and E. Shahr, *Scarcity: Why Having Too Little Means So Much* (London: Macmillan, 2013).

Major attention should be given to the design of the immediate environment in which children live, play and study: While the factors influencing overweight and obesity are manifold, and their interrelations are still hardly understood, the evidence of the impact of the immediate food and drink environment, strongly determining the access, availability and affordability (also called the "triple A") of healthier food choices, is overwhelming. This holds true for all population groups, but in particular to vulnerable consumers such as children. The "triple A" of unhealthy food environments, paired with strong media influence and advertising from early ages, seems to be at least as influential as educational campaigns and rising awareness.[109]

The impact of the immediate environment, providing specific "affordances" – i.e., the perceived utility of objects in, or features of, one's surroundings – has been studied by environmental and perceptual psychology. In particular, the pioneering work of James J. Gibson showed that cognitive biases are partly due to affordances that provide immediate and not necessarily reflected opportunities for action.[110] This view has been applied to many fields designing user-environment interfaces such as software user interface and usability engineering, environmental psychology and the psychology of architecture (including store architecture). Building on the groundbreaking work of psychologists Daniel Kahneman and Amos Tversky,[111] behavioural economics and behaviourally based regulation have focused on what has been coined "choice architecture".[112] In the early 2000s, the US law professor Cass Sunstein and the economist Richard Thaler started an influential debate on how and when to design choice environments that softly "nudge" behaviour quasi-automatically in more beneficial, self-promoting and welfare-increasing directions.[113] Today, there is an increasing and well-funded research field applying and testing "nudges" to stimulate healthier food and lifestyles.[114]

Recent overviews of intervention practices for healthier eating and lifestyles showed that different policy measures – both hard and soft instruments – may bear fruits.[115] One of the key success factors seems to be a flexible design that is

---

[109] Ibid.
[110] J. J. Gibson, "The Theory of Affordances", in R. Shaw and J. Bransford (eds.). *Perceiving, Acting, and Knowing: Toward an Ecological Psychology* (Hillsdale, NJ: Lawrence Erlbaum, 1977), 67.
[111] A. Tversky and D. Kahnemann, "The Framing of Decisions and the Psychology of Choice" (1981) 211 *Science* 453.
[112] R. H. Thaler and C. R. Sunstein, *Nudge: Improving Decisions About Health, Wealth, and Happiness* (New Haven, CT: Yale University Press, 2008).
[113] R. H. Thaler and C. R. Sunstein, "Libertarian Paternalism" (2003) 93(2) *The American Economic Review* 175. Behavioural economics does not use the concept of affordances, however.
[114] B. Wansink, *Slim by Design: Mindless Eating Solutions for Everyday Life* (New York: Harper Collins, 2014).
[115] M. T. Gorski and C. A. Roberto, "Public Health Policies to Encourage Healthy Eating Habits: Recent Perspectives" (2015) 7 *Journal of Healthcare Leadership* 81.

co-developed by target groups, health professionals and other relevant actors boosting the policies' potential adaptability, due to its built-in customisation. With regards to "diverse target segments", involving whole families instead of children alone is crucial for success. The policy design should also stress a realistic mix of short- to long-term objectives that are comprehensively targeted. Another key success factor is committed institutional and political support. The more committed political and legislative institutions are as regards securing the relevant resources for the design, implementation, monitoring and evaluation of the measures, the better the results. Moreover, the sustainability and effectiveness of a policy measure is also increased if it is backed by an interdisciplinary, cross-professional and multilevel stakeholder coalition. Assessment of success factors and barriers also made clear that deficient or unsuitable monitoring and assessment often prevents learning curves, which are so important for the improvement, further development and transferability of programmes. Further, there is evidence that interventions are more successful if they are designed empirically informed, if they work with and not against people's biases and heuristics, provide simple ways to choose the healthier alternative, include the whole food system and are designed for a longer time frame and not just short-term interventions.[116]

There is increasing evidence from consumer research that behavioural change is not necessarily motivated by knowledge and intentions, but at least as strongly by simple opportunity and access.[117] On a social level, benefits clearly outweigh potential higher costs: Research has shown that the quality of food provided in schools – based on high-quality nutritional standards and guidelines – can have a significant impact on a child's health and development. Eating a healthy school meal can have a positive impact on academic performance.[118]

In general, there are three main strategies promoting healthier life and food styles: raise awareness of the risks of obesity, reduce energy intake and increase energy output.[119] Clearly, the classical instruments of consumer policy, consumer information, education and advice are ideal for raising awareness; however, they proved to not be far-reaching enough. The "information paradigm" of consumer policy has clearly shown its limits, particularly when it comes to influencing the energy intake-output balance, which is the bigger challenge. For behavioural changes to take place and to eventually become habits, one of the most effective instruments is a form of soft paternalism, or "nudging", in the sense of steering consumption gently towards healthier choices by shaping the consumption context accordingly. As explained previously, access, availability and affordability play a role, as do default settings and

---

[116] Wansink, *Slim by Design*.
[117] F. Ölander and J. Thøgersen, "Understanding of Consumer Behaviour as a Prerequisite for Environmental Protection" (1995) 18(4) *Journal of Consumer Policy* 345.
[118] M. L. Anderson, J. Gallagher and E. R. Ritchie, "School Lunch Quality and Academic Performance" (Working paper for the National Bureau of Economic Research No. 23218, 2017).
[119] Witkowski, "Food Marketing and Obesity in Developing Countries", 126.

smart choice architecture in places where children choose and eat.[120] Healthy canteens, choice-edited vending machines and tuck stops in schools, simplified food guidelines and easy-to-grasp simple labelling are tools worth testing.[121] The general aim is to make healthy food choices simpler and hassle-free – echoing the mantra of the WHO: "To make the healthy choice the easy choice".

A popular, yet not highly effective, tool is cooperative approaches such as voluntary codes of conduct, self-commitments or "pledges" by industry.[122] For instance, the international soda industry has promised to decrease the calories of their product assortment in the coming years.[123] Such pledges and self-commitments work typically best if there is an independent monitoring by, for example, a consumer group. In particular, the role that children can play in monitoring should be advanced, in line with children's right to participation and recognition of their status as rights holders, not merely recipients of protection.[124] Hence, strengthening consumer organisations focused on children as consumers, and involving them in a dialogue on effective measures as well as in the monitoring of programmes and commitments can have broad benefits.[125]

Beyond voluntarism, economic incentives and disincentives – discussed as fat and soda taxes, on the one hand, and value-added tax reductions for fruit and vegetables, on the other – can be powerful tools, even though the experiences are mixed.[126] In addition, laws and hard regulation, such as banning unhealthy food and drinks, banning supersized portion sizes or limiting advertising and sponsoring in children's television programmes might be supportive of protecting children from constant overexposure. There is a well-established connection between food marketing and children's food preferences, purchase requests and consumption patterns.[127] Television is still the predominant media, but techniques have moved on to now

---

[120] Thaler and Sunstein, "Libertarian Paternalism".
[121] Wansink, *Slim by Design*.
[122] In the United States, the Council of Better Business and the National Advertising Review Council implemented self-regulated limits to unhealthy advertisements, see D. M. Desrochers and D. J. Holt, "Children's Exposure to Television Advertising: Implications for Childhood Obesity"(2007) 26 *Journal of Public Policy and Marketing* 182. In Denmark, a voluntary code of responsible food marketing communication to children has been implemented (see Forum of Responsible Food Marketing Communication, Code of Responsible Food Marketing Communication to Children [2008]).
[123] For instance, an agreement between the US Alliance for Healthier Generation and America's Beverage Association on a reduction of beverage calories (www.ameribev.org/news-media/news-releases-statements/more/334/).
[124] See article 12, UNGA, Convention on the Rights of the Child (UN Doc. A/RES/44/25, 20 November 1989) 1577 UNTS 3.
[125] M. Viswanathan and R. Gau, "Functional Illiteracy and Nutritional Education in the United States: A Research-Based Approach to the Development of Nutritional Education Materials for Functionally Illiterate Consumers" (2005) 25 *Journal of Macromarketing* 187.
[126] See for example, J. D. Jensen and S. Smed, "The Danish Tax on Saturated Fat – Short Run Effects on Consumption, Substitution Patterns and Consumer Prices of Fats" (2013) 42 *Food Policy* 18.
[127] G. Hastings et al., *Review of the Research on the Effects of Food Promotion to Children* (Glasgow: Centre for Social Marketing, University of Glasgow, 2003).

also include product placement using toys, educational materials, songs and movies; character licensing and celebrity endorsements; and word-of-mouth campaigns, text messages, website-, and "advergames". US fast food restaurants alone spent US$4.6 billion on advertising to children and teens in 2012. Worldwide, most of the television food advertising to which children are exposed is for foods high in energy sugar, salt or fat.[128]

The Role of International Bodies and Initiatives

The significance of the impact of marketing on children's diets has been recognised by the World Health Assembly (WHA) – the decision-making body of the WHO. In 2010, the WHO urged Member States to address the exposure and power of marketing foods to children: "Settings where children gather should be free from all forms of marketing of foods high in saturated fats, trans-fatty acids, free sugars, or salt. Such settings include, but are not limited to, nurseries, playgrounds, family and child clinics and pediatric services and during any sporting and cultural activities that are held on these premises".[129] The implementation of the WHO Recommendations on the Marketing of Foods and Non-Alcoholic Beverages to Children was a key policy action contained in the WHO Global Action Plan 2013–2020 for the Prevention and Control of Noncommunicable Diseases, which was endorsed by the WHA in 2013. However, most governments have yet to implement these agreed recommendations. To date, they are largely still only on paper.

At the World Consumer Rights Day 2015, the worldwide consumer organisation Consumers International (CI) put a spotlight on consumers' right to healthy food with a focus on young consumers. To make schools healthier food environments, CI suggested a package of measures required to protect and promote healthy diets, including schools to be free from unhealthy food marketing; the provision of safe, free drinking water in all schools; rules on nutritional content of food sold in canteens, vending machines and similar; and purchasing and commissioning activities to promote the consumption of healthier foods and limit the consumption of unhealthy foods.[130] Together with a broad range of like-minded allies such as Global Obesity, CI is campaigning for a Global Convention on Healthy Diets to protect and promote healthy diets, using a similar mechanism to the Framework Convention on Tobacco Control (Figure 16.2). Such a Global Convention would commit

---

[128] D. M. Desrochers and D. J. Holt, "Children's Exposure to Television Advertising: Implications for Childhood Obesity" (2007) 26(2) *Journal of Public Policy and Marketing* 182; D. J. Holt et al., "Children's Exposure to TV Advertising in 1977 and 2004 – Information for the Obesity Debate" (2007) *Bureau of Economics Staff Report* 133.

[129] WHO Europe, *Set of Recommendations on the Marketing of Foods and Non-Alcoholic Beverages to Children* (2010), www.who.int/dietphysicalactivity/publications/recsmarketing/en/.

[130] World Obesity and Consumer International, "Why We Need a Global Convention to Protect and Promote Healthy Diets".

Targets to be asserted	Government initiative
Improve global state of nutrition, protect economic security and stability of health systems	Implement a package of multisectoral policies, as recommended by UN General Assembly, which assures that their food supplies can protect and promote public health.
Prevent obesity and non-communicable diseases	Food marketing should favour foods recommended for increased consumption in national food-based dietary guidelines.
	Food marketing should be strictly limited for those foods for which decreased consumption is recommended.
Prevent hunger and under-nutrition	Foods recommended in national food based dietary guidelines need to meet minimum standards of nutritional quality, be equitably accessible, sustainable and affordable.
Prevent food waste and increase sustainability	Food supplies should aim to match population nutritional requirements, determined by national dietary guidelines.
Strengthen food and nutrition security	Ensure food markets and food marketing support healthy dietary patterns.
Strengthen national food sovereignty	Protection of a legally binding Global Convention (by all types of governments, also those within regional economic areas and smaller nations).
Promote consumer rights and protect public health	Initiate robust government wide legislation which permits and requires public health action to promote food and nutrition security.
	Define minimum nutritional standards and ensure that those standards help to drive commercial food markets and the operation of global food trade.
Promote consumer rights and protect public health	Initiate robust government wide legislation which permits and requires public health action to promote food and nutrition security.
	Define minimum nutritional standards and ensure that those standards help to drive commercial food markets and the operation of global food trade.

SOURCE: World Obesity and Consumer International (2015), *Why we need a global convention to protect and promote healthy diets*.

FIGURE 16.2 Draft for a global convention on healthy diets

governments to a package of policy measures designed to help consumers eat more healthily. This would include restrictions on food marketing to children; nutrition labelling; provision of better food in schools and public institutions; and consideration of fiscal tools to promote healthier eating such as taxes and subsidies.

Such an initiative is surely welcome. As argued in the preceding text, to be effective, it should be designed with a systems view and be closely tied to the debate of globally sustainable consumption and production patterns in the food sector – and hence with the SDGs. Latest initiatives such the Global Convention Initiative do indeed point to a nexus approach, which is a sign of hope – particularly for the most vulnerable group of consumers, our children.

CONCLUSION

In this chapter, we have attempted to show how and why healthy diets and health-supporting environments are basic preconditions for children to develop and a fundamental right of all children. We have also shown that both malnutrition and overweight affect millions of children, both in the developed and less developed world. Besides the SDG of ending hunger and malnutrition, there is today an equally important goal of ending overweight and obesity that comes with a major impact on life chances. The obesity pandemic is still on its rise, overall, and constitutes a major burden and development barrier for many children. We do welcome the fact that, increasingly, in politics, academia and practice, the issues of obesity, climate change and economic disparity and discrimination are thought of and brought together under the umbrella of SDGs and that a more systemic public health approach is gaining ground. A systemic view and "nexus thinking" in both analysis and politics is needed to provide not only the future generations but also today's youngest generation with the opportunity to live a healthy and meaningful life and to develop their talents. With an ageing population in most developed countries, it is more important than ever before to invest in the children's health.

PART V

Concluding Observations

17

The Future Research Agenda

Where to from Here?

Claire Fenton-Glynn

Sustainable development has been described as being like motherhood, and God – "difficult not to approve of".[1] For this reason, it is a concept that has been invoked in support of numerous different agendas, and has come to mean all things to all people. Likewise, children's rights are a difficult concept to disagree with – and invoking the "best interests of the child" can give legitimacy to a wide variety of claims.

This volume has sought to bring together these two concepts, viewing sustainable development through the lens of children's rights, while also examining how children's rights can be viewed in the context of sustainable development. In doing so, it has endeavoured to provide a greater understanding of how children's rights are affected by, and can affect, sustainable development. The importance of a rights-based approach is both principled and pragmatic. From a principled perspective, a rights-based analysis helps us to understand the power dimensions in sustainable development processes. It provides a framework for examining the operation of structures of power and authority, and, in particular, lays bare the asymmetry in vertical power relationships that shape children's lives. On a practical level, the negotiating capabilities of children are strengthened by using rights-based language. The human rights discourse, and the systems that surround it, has a global legitimacy, especially in the case of the UN Convention on the Rights of the Child (UNCRC), the most widely ratified human rights treaty in the world.

While this book has the UNCRC at its heart, it has not limited itself to this framework. The Convention has been viewed as a starting point, rather than the final word on children's rights. In doing so, it has shown that while the UNCRC has significant potential, it also has discernible gaps, and must be interpreted in a

---

[1] M. Redclift (ed.), *Sustainability: Critical Concepts in the Social Sciences* (New York: Routledge, 2005), 191.

dynamic manner to provide adequate protection and promotion of children's rights in our rapidly developing world.

This concluding chapter attempts to bring together the various strands of the UNCRC explored throughout the book – first looking at the core principles of the UNCRC, and how these elide with the sustainability agenda, then moving on to consider where the gaps in the UNCRC lie. Finally, it will consider how sustainable development requires expanding our understanding of human rights frameworks, looking beyond State responsibility to non-state actors and international cooperation.

ENFORCING THE UNCRC

As has been discussed throughout the preceding chapters, the UNCRC is founded on four core principles: non-discrimination (art. 2), best interests (art. 3), life, survival and development (art. 6) and participation (art. 12). While each being vital substantive rights on their own, they are also interpretative principles that direct the implementation of all other children's rights. They are thus central considerations for any action involving sustainable development, instrumental in ensuring that this is achieved in a way that promotes and enhances children's rights.

Non-Discrimination

One of the criticisms of the Millennium Development Goals (MDGs) was the unequal progress across regions, and amongst groups of people. The MDGs created targets to provide fundamental rights to one-half of the population, which falls short of the pre-existing obligations enshrined in human rights treaties.[2] Such an approach allows for unequal progress, meaning that goals can be "met" whilst still leaving the most vulnerable behind.

This has been a pervasive problem facing global development. Development patterns have allowed some countries to thrive, while others have been excluded from accessing opportunities. Even within countries, power differences between groups can result in inequalities of access – rich rather than poor, men rather than women, urban rather than rural, adults rather than children. At its heart, sustainable development can be characterised as a tool for achieving equity and enforcing the "equitable accountability" of the state, to all of its citizens – current and future.

As Haughton has set out, sustainable development invokes five equitable claims: intergenerational, intragenerational, geographical, procedural and inter-species.[3]

---

[2] See Save the Children's Submission to the Sixth Session of the General Assembly Open Working Group on Sustainable Development Goals, 9–13 December 2013.

[3] G. Haughton, "Environmental Justice and the Sustainable City" (1999) 18 *Journal of Planning Education and Research* 233–243.

It requires that development is inclusive, and involves all people – rich, poor, male, female, old, young and unborn. It is this last aspect that this volume has focused on, trying to reverse the priority given to adult interests and ensure that the drive for sustainable development is seen through a child rights lens.

The importance of article 2 of the UNCRC, however, is that even amongst children many vulnerabilities and disparities continue to exist. And while some groups continue to be left behind, truly sustainable development cannot be achieved. This was clearly articulated by UN General Assembly in relation to gender equality, which recognised that "sustainable development is not possible if one half of humanity continues to be denied its full human rights and opportunities".[4]

Throughout this volume, authors have analysed various groups of children who have been left behind in global development: in particular, girl children (Chapter 6), children with disabilities (Chapter 7), indigenous children (Chapter 11) and children in humanitarian situations (Chapter 14). While this list is not exhaustive, they serve as important reminders of the ways in which children can be subjected to intersecting vulnerabilities.

Non-discrimination under article 2 is not just a negative obligation – to treat all children equally – but a positive obligation, to make sure all children have equal opportunities to achieve their full capacities. This may require differentiated treatment to achieve substantive equality. An important foundation for this is the collection of up-to-date, reliable, disaggregated data. Such data is vital for implementation efforts – as Kron argued in Chapter 6, it ensures visibility of the most vulnerable and assists in identifying priorities. Without such data, we cannot determine where development priorities should be focused, or how needs should be addressed.

Best Interests of Children

Article 3 of the UNCRC plays a vital role in ensuring children's rights in all areas of sustainable development. It is not only a substantive right but also a fundamental interpretative legal principle and a rule of procedure, ensuring children are at the centre of decision-making processes.

The importance of prioritising children's interests can be seen in every chapter throughout this volume, from health to education, water management to climate change, trade to urban development. Despite having been a central principle of the nearly universally ratified UNCRC for nearly 30 years, legislations and administrations continue to fail to consider the rights and interests of children. Children cannot use the democratic process as other groups can, meaning that without a clear rights-based framework, their interests can go unheeded.

---

[4] UN General Assembly (UNGA), "Transforming Our World: The 2030 Agenda for Sustainable Development" (UN Doc. A/RES/70/1, 21 October 2015), [20].

One important tool for ensuring that the best interests of children are identified and taken into consideration was discussed by Jodoin and Pollock in Chapter 12, when they discussed child rights impact assessments (CRIAs). These tools identify, analyse and evaluate the possible direct or indirect effects that a policy, legislation or other government decision-making process may have on the rights of children and young people, and ensure that the best interests of the child are fully considered throughout decision-making processes. While currently there are only a few jurisdictions that regularly undertake CRIAs – Flanders, Sweden, Norway, Scotland, Northern Ireland and New Brunswick – this is an important next step in the child rights agenda. As children are often not in a position to identify, investigate or enforce their own rights, it is up to government authorities to scrutinise carefully their own actions, and ensure accountability and transparency. This is also a tool that can be translated into the private sector and used to uncover and offset the negative implications of corporate decision-making on the rights of children.

Life, Survival and Development

The third fundamental principle under the UNCRC is the inherent right of every child to life, and the obligation on states to ensure to the maximum extent possible the survival and development of the child (art 6). The environmental dimension is a distinguishing feature of sustainable development compared with other (traditional) development paradigms, and in Part III, the authors stressed the interaction between a healthy environment and the healthy development of children. Children are at greater risk than adults to environmental hazards because of their "physical size, immature organs, metabolic rate, behaviour, natural curiosity and lack of knowledge".[5] The World Health Organisation estimates that 26 per cent of under-five child deaths every year are associated with environment-related causes and conditions.[6] Nearly a quarter of the global disease burden is attributable to environmental factors, and of this, 43 per cent falls on children under the age of five, despite this demographic making up only 12 per cent of the population.

The right to life, survival and development are also closely linked with the right to health under article 24 and the impact that unsustainable development patterns and lifestyles have on children's well-being. In its General Comment No. 7, on early childhood, the UN CRC Committee issued the following reminder:

> [T]he right to survival and development can only be implemented in a holistic manner, through the enforcement of all the other provisions of the Convention,

---

[5] See UNEP, UNICEF and WHO, *Children in the New Millennium: Environmental Impact on Health* (Nairobi, Kenya: UNEP, UNICEF and WHO, 2002), 7.
[6] See A. Prüss-Üstün et al., "Preventing Disease through Healthy Environments, A Global Assessment of the Burden of Disease from Environmental Risks" (WHO, 2016).

including rights to health, adequate nutrition, ... a healthy and safe environment, education and play.[7]

But the right to health is a contested notion, as was explored by Ferraz in Chapter 5. Here he highlighted the "rights resources dilemma" – in the context of limited resources, prioritisation is necessary, and difficult decisions have to be made concerning what treatment and services will, and will not, be available. In examining the case of Brazil's "butterfly children", he articulates the difficult questions and policy dilemmas that governments are faced with when asked to provide the "highest achievable standard of health" for all children.

Survival and development relies not just on medical care, however, but also on healthy lifestyles. Chapters in this volume have emphasised the importance of play for children's development (Chapter 14), as well as measures to combat obesity (Chapter 16). These are areas that are often overlooked when considering international sustainable development, and one in which the UNCRC can play an important role in bringing to the fore.

Participation of Children

One of the key themes running through every chapter in this book has been the importance of the participation of children in development processes, governmental decision-making and in simply directing their own lives. People are the principal agents of sustainable development, and it is vital that children are empowered to play their part. They must be seen not merely as beneficiaries of this development but also active agents of change. This is particularly important in terms of sustainable development, not only because of their current heightened vulnerability but also because they will continue to suffer the consequences of decisions made today for decades to come.

Unfortunately, as Davis pointed out in Chapter 3, many attempts to include children in decision-making are more concerned with process than product and serve to replicate and exacerbate existing patterns of power and privilege. Desmet, in Chapter 9, also catalogued the ways in which children risk being overlooked, or only given tokenistic attention, thus remaining largely invisible in debates relating to sustainable development. She showed that the main children's rights policy agendas at the UN level focus on paradigms of protection – that is, the image of children as vulnerable beings – rather than as active stakeholders, who are bearers of human rights.

This is highlighted by Davis in Chapter 3, where she calls for children's participation rights to be expanded beyond their current conception to include active and agentic participation to be the norm. She argues that children's participation requires reformulation, as current conceptualisations are outmoded for the times

---

[7] UNCRC Committee, "General Comment No. 7 (2006) Implementing Child Rights in Early Childhood" (UN Doc. CRC/C/GC/7/Rev.1, 20 September 2006), [10].

in which we live. In this way, the UNCRC is of vital importance – viewing children as citizens with rights obliges recognition of children as social actors and agents of change, able to make contributions to decision-making concerning not only their own lives but also the world they live in.

As Magee, Third and Sweeting discuss in Chapter 15, participation is not merely a matter of bureaucratic consultation – it requires developing modes of engagement that resonate in specific contexts. As the UNCRC Committee has emphasised, meaningful participation requires the process to be transparent and informative, voluntary, respectful, relevant, child friendly, inclusive, supported by training, safe and sensitive to risk and accountable.[8] Moreover, with sustainable development, we are not only talking about the participation of children today but also of future generations. Atapattu, in her chapter on the intergenerational equity principle (Chapter 8), asked the key question: How do we ensure that future generations have a voice at the table? Some states have tried to achieve this by creating an Ombudsman for Future Generations – an adult who is empowered to speak for those who are yet to come. Others have relaxed their rules on standing for bringing legal challenges, allowing arguments to be brought on behalf of future generations. It is vital that states continue to innovate in this area and develop new ways to approach traditional questions. This necessarily involves challenging the existing paradigms, ensuring that children's rights are seen as more than theoretical, but a practical reality.

DEVELOPING THE UNCRC

Although the concept has been around for some years now, the law and practice of sustainable development is in its infancy, with the international community only now starting to actively engage with its concepts. Likewise, children's rights are a relatively new phenomenon, emerging in the late twentieth century. However, unlike our constantly advancing understanding of sustainable development on an international level, the codification of children's rights in the UNCRC has meant that these rights have become somewhat static, and that some new and evolving rights are not adequately recognised.

This is particularly the case for rights concerned with development. When the UNCRC was drafted nearly 30 years ago, the world was only just starting to understand the implications of rapid development, and the impact this would have on children's rights. As Davis points out in Chapter 3, twenty-first-century societies are already vastly different from those that framed the UNCRC, leaving the instrument as a "historical and political artefact, requiring interrogation and updating, and not a document that sets children's rights 'in stone'".

---

[8] UNCRC Committee, "General Comment No. 12 (2009) on the Right of the Child to be Heard" (UN Doc. CRC/C/GC/12, 1 July 2009).

This can be seen on two levels. The first level focuses on principle and whether there are gaps in the rights articulated in the UNCRC that reflect a lack of adequate consideration of sustainable development concerns in the drafting. The second level looks at practice and how the rights that are incorporated have been interpreted and implemented in a way that can accommodate the changing world we live in.

Textual Gaps in the UNCRC

On the first level, over the course of this book, several authors have identified areas in which the UNCRC does not go far enough in elaborating specific rights for children. The first and most significant of these criticisms relates to the limited attention to environmental issues, which is a core component of sustainable development. Although the UNCRC is the only international human rights treaty that refers specifically to the dangers and risks of environmental pollution, this is only mentioned in the context of combating disease and malnutrition. The protection of the environment, as a right in and of itself – as opposed to a component of the child's right to the highest attainable standard of health – is not recognised. This limited attention to environmental issues reflects the lesser urgency of environmental matters at the time of the drafting of the Convention. However, given the increase in the nature and severity of environmental challenges during the last decades, coupled with the advances in our understanding of the interdependency of human and environmental well-being, this is an area where the UNCRC seems sadly anachronistic.

A second problem with the text can be seen in its individualistic nature. This ties in with Vandenhole's concern, expressed in Chapter 2, about the individualistic character of human rights law in general. As he has highlighted, there is a clear tension between "the anthropocentric, here-and-now, individualistic focus of children's rights (law) and the non-anthropocentric, intergenerational and arguably more collective DNA of sustainable development law". Even where the UNCRC is referring to the risks of environmental pollution, there is an inherent anthropocentrism to this "human" right to a healthy environment.

This individualism is also apparent in the way in which the majority of rights are articulated in the UNCRC. With a few notable exceptions,[9] rights in this document focus on the individual independent of social groupings. It presents the child as an isolated human being, rather than recognising the idea of collective rights, with a view of children as they really are – social beings, interconnected with the world around them. This interconnectedness needs to be recognised, not only in relation to *the present* but also with future generations. Despite having appeared in the international realm at the time of drafting, the intergenerational equity principle is not referenced in the text. The intergenerational equity principle moves the

---

[9] See, for example, article 5, article 30.

discussion away from simply state responsibilities in relation to identifiable individuals with legal personality, towards a more holistic understanding of responsibilities concerning the human community as trustees of the planet and environment. In Chapter 8, Atapattu discusses this principle and emphasises the necessity of providing legal standing to these future generations, as well as recognising this as an enforceable and justiciable right. This has already been recognised in some domestic jurisdictions, but this will necessarily be a piecemeal approach without the force of the UNCRC behind it.

These examples highlight areas where international children's rights law has a great deal to learn from the evolving field of sustainable development. While the text of the Convention is now not easily amended, there have now been three Optional Protocols, which expand on the rights considered in the main text.[10] Given the fundamental importance of environmental rights, the necessity of which will only become more urgent as time goes on, and of the rights of future generations, there is a need for the international community to come together to consider the best way to incorporate these developing challenges into international children's rights law.

Expanding Definitions

Even in areas where the UNCRC *has* explicitly set out relevant rights for children, viewing these rights from the perspective of sustainable development necessitates revisiting accepted understandings of how they should be interpreted and applied. Throughout this book, authors have shown that some prevailing mainstream approaches are inadequate to deal with new challenges, while others need updating based on new understandings of the rights and interests in question. This can particularly be seen in three areas: the right to education, the right to work and the rights of children with disabilities.

In Chapter 3, Davis shows how mainstream approaches fail to appropriately deal with the challenges imposed by sustainable development. She argues that current educational paradigms are increasingly based in neoliberal individualism, market-based scientism, competitive outcomes and reductionist specialisms rather than whole-of-systems, relational learning and critical, restorative and participative alternatives. As such, they are inadequate for enabling children to understand and deal with the realities, uncertainties and complexities of modern issues now confronting them – including economic instability, climate change, population migrations, inequalities, loss of biodiversity, rapid resource consumption and urbanization.

---

[10] UNGA, Optional Protocol to the Convention on the Rights of the Child on the Sale of Children, Child Prostitution and Child Pornography (UN Doc. A/RES/54/263, 25 May 2000) 2171 UNTS 227; UNGA, Optional Protocol to the Convention on the Rights of the Child on the Involvement of Children in Armed Conflict (UN Doc. A/RES/54/263, 25 May 2000) 2173 UNTS 222; UNGA, Optional Protocol to the Convention on the Rights of the Child on a Communications Procedure (UN Doc. A/RES/66/138, 27 January 2012).

For this reason, she presents the UNCRC as only the starting point of an updated children's rights framework, which must be supplemented by four additional layers of rights – agentic participation rights, collective rights, intergenerational rights and bio/ecocentric rights.

Moreover, in relation to the right to work, Driscoll questions the assumptions underpinning article 32 of the UNCRC, as well as the international goal to eradicate child labour. Applying the principle of sustainable development – "development that meets the needs of the present, without compromising the abilities of future generations to meet their own" – to the life trajectory of the individual working child, she suggests that this goal is incongruent with other goals of sustainable development, such as poverty reduction, gender discrimination, reduction of inequalities and national economic development. She argues that the immediate well-being of the child must be balanced against considerations of future prospects, and an approach developed in accordance with the child's evolving capacities that protects children's long-term, and not just short-term, interests.

This analysis also highlights a further structural flaw in the UNCRC, namely the Western-centric conceptualisation of childhood and well-being. Although non-Western states were involved in the drafting of the Convention, the concept of childhood endorsed by the final instrument centres on a romantic Western understanding. In this case, this is exemplified by a global ideology of a work free childhood, and where education and schooling is sharply delineated from work. This not only fails to recognise developmental differences between countries and communities but also ignores individual realities of children's lives. It rests on an assumption of a universal determination that employment is contrary to children's best interests, without recognising children's agency in deciding, in their local context, where their long-term interests lie.

The final area that this book has highlighted as an area of concern for the UNCRC is in the context of children with disabilities. As Harpur and Stein note in Chapter 7, the scope of the rights for children with disabilities in article 23 of the UNCRC is extremely limited, forcing children to look beyond this Convention to engage with other rights regimes. While this is not necessarily a fatal flaw – on a general level, not siloing advocacy to a single international convention is important – the differences between the UNCRC and the Convention on the Rights of Persons with Disabilities (CRPD) is telling. One example of this is the right to education for children with disabilities, limited to primary education under the UNCRC while the CRPD provides a more substantive requirement of an inclusive education at all levels. Moreover, in terms of international development, we can see in the CRPD a more comprehensive and advanced understanding of the interdependence of the international community in promoting children's rights, leaving the UNCRC looking limited and dated.

Of course, this is not to say that the UNCRC has no value, either in these areas or as a whole. Nor is it to suggest that the Convention is not capable of evolving, to a certain extent, over time. Rather, it is an indication that the UNCRC should only be seen as a starting point, a beginning for our conceptualisation of what rights children hold, rather than the "final word" in how these should be conceived.[11] Moreover, and despite its flaws, what this book has hopefully shown is that the UNCRC is still an extremely powerful tool for the progression and enforcement of children's rights in relation to sustainable development. It may not be perfect, but given the importance of rights-based language, and the power this can give to any agenda, it continues to remain the primary mechanism for promoting children's rights.

EXPANDING COMPETENCES BEYOND THE STATE

Non-State Actors

One of the key limitations of a human rights perspective of sustainable development is the central role traditionally give to the state as the focus of accountability. However, the process of development and globalisation has undermined the position of the nation-state and, increasingly, we are seeing the necessity of reconceptualising international human rights law towards greater concern with non-state actors – corporations, non-governmental organisations (NGOs) and international bodies – and private forms of regulation. This was highlighted by the UNCRC Committee in its General Comment No. 16, regarding the impact of the business sector on children's rights.[12]

The impact of non-state actors, and the power that they have in relation to children's rights, has been analysed in several chapters in this volume. Corporations play an unavoidable role in enforcing children's rights in the context of the labour market (Chapter 13), as well as in relation to child obesity (Chapter 16). In the context of international trade, Jodoin and Pollock in Chapter 12 recognise the multiple pathways of influence through which corporations can reinforce as well as undermine children's rights. They note that the establishment of corporate entities in communities that comes as a result of globalisation has shifted some of the onus for the welfare of children away from developing states and led to businesses assuming a greater role in the provision and protection of socio-economic rights of children. This necessitates acknowledging the respective spheres of non-state actors in regulating and enforcing children's rights and developing new and innovative ways of responding to the resulting paradigm shift.

This applies not only to corporations but also to all non-state actors – including civil society. In Chapter 2, Vandenhole advocates a shift of perspective away from

---

[11] M. Liebel, *Children's Rights from Below: Cross-Cultural Perspectives* (New York: Palgrave MacMillan, 2012), 15.
[12] UNCRC Committee, "General Comment No. 16 (2013) on State Obligations Regarding the Impact of Business on Children's Rights" (UN Doc. CRC/C/GC/16, 7 February 2013).

the state as the key actor, towards social action groups and the legal strategies that these adopt. Likewise, Magee et al. (Chapter 15) note that in the context of rapid urban growth, protection of children's rights often falls to non-state actors – particularly NGOs.

The UNCRC Committee has started responding to these new challenges – both in its General Comment and in Concluding Observations. But to achieve the goals of sustainable development, it is important approaches continue to evolve, and that we integrate these new actors into a rights-based framework.

International Cooperation

A second important shift that is driven by globalisation is the extent to which responsibility for enforcing – or violating – children's rights is no longer confined within one state's borders. This is important when considering not only transnational trade (see Chapter 12) but also humanitarian assistance (Chapter 14). Moreover, in Chapter 7, Harpur and Stein emphasise the importance of including children's rights within programmatic development goals. Focusing specifically on the rights of children with disabilities, they note that such children living in regions requiring foreign-driven assistance are often excluded from those schemes and are thereby disproportionately disadvantaged relative to their non-disabled peers. This is an area where the UNCRC sets low standards for states – requiring only information sharing – in contrast to the more robust provisions of the UN Convention on the Rights of Persons with Disabilities, which includes a standalone development and cooperation clause, requiring States to "undertake appropriate and effective measures" to realise the purposes and objectives of the treaty, thus underscoring the impact of development aid and collaboration.

This is particularly important in the context of sustainable development. Sustainable development cannot occur in a vacuum and requires international cooperation to ensure that its goals become a reality. The international human rights system must take concrete steps to ensure that States are not only fulfilling their obligations within their own jurisdictions but within all actions that they take on the international stage.

Role of the Committee on the Rights of the Child

The Committee on the Rights of the Child plays a vital role in promoting, and monitoring, sustainable development within a child rights framework. It sets the agenda for States, as subjects discussed in General Comments, Concluding Observations and Days of General Discussion have greater visibility, and a greater likelihood of change. A number of contributors in this volume have discussed the extent to which various aspects of children's rights and sustainable development have been considered in such instruments, and the impact that this has had on the recognition and implementation of certain rights.

For example, Harpur and Stein in Chapter 7 note that the UNCRC processes have provided limited recognition of the rights of children with disabilities generally, or the importance of mainstreaming these issues specifically within development programmes. This has rendered such children less visible and meant that States have less of an impetus to rectify their practices.

Likewise, in relation to the right to play, there has traditionally been a lack of discussion by the UNCRC Committee of this right, described as the Convention's most overlooked provision. This has meant that negative perceptions of the significance of this right – dismissed and de-prioritised as frivolous and of limited importance – have been allowed to prevail. The UNCRC Committee's recent General Comment on the right to rest, leisure, play, recreational activities, cultural life and the arts[13] has placed these rights back on the international agenda, highlighting the influence that this Committee can have in agenda setting.

This is a role that cannot be overlooked and must be strengthened to provide a strong international review and restraint on the interpretation of children's rights, and how these must be implemented in the context of our developing world.

CONCLUSION

One of the primary achievements of the UNCRC was to situate children as human beings, capable of holding rights, rather than simply "human becomings". As Collins and Wright made clear, "[W]e cannot simply consider children as 'our future', even though such understanding is very pervasive, because children are also part of our present." This challenge must also be met in relation to sustainable development. Children's rights cannot be respected simply because they are going to be the most affected by our decisions in the future, but we must recognise their present role as individual agents of change.

For this reason, we must recognise that although sustainable development has the power to address fundamental questions and challenges facing humanity, it cannot be interpreted in isolation. The potential of the UNCRC must be harnessed to inform and strengthen policy frameworks when implementing sustainable development.

This volume has sought to provide an insight into the various issues facing children and sustainable development today, and those that will continue to challenge us in the future. While it has not attempted to comprehensively discuss all rights of children, or all aspects of sustainable development, it is hoped that it has given readers a starting point for thinking about sustainable development through a child-rights lens, and a reminder that children are not only our future but also they are our present.

---

[13] UNCRC Committee, "General Comment No. 17 (2013) on the Right of the Child to Rest, Leisure, Play, Recreational Activities, Cultural Life and the Arts (art. 31)" (UN Doc. CRC/C/GC/17, 17 April 2013).

Index

A world fit for children, 198, 223
Aarhus Convention, 196
abduction of, sale of, or traffic in children, 222
African Charter of the Rights and Welfare of the Child, 312
African Charter on Human and Peoples' Rights, 125, 185
Agenda 21, 201–204, 210

Bangdung Declaration, 208
Beijing Platform for Action, 115, 122, 126–127, 130, 135
best interests of the child, 184, 191, 220–221, 285, 289–297, 300, 302, 312–327, 387, 389–390
birth registration, 121, 221
Brundtland Report, 3, 45, 179, 192, 200–201, 210, 350, 369

CEDAW Committee, 116, 121, 136
CEDAW General Recommendation No. 24, 132
CESCR Committee, 270
CESCR General Comment No. 14, 133
child friendly cities, 342–357
child labour, 9, 222, 263–272, 283–305, 322–323, 338, 341, 345, 349, 352–353, 395–396
child participation, 5, 8, 10, 20, 25, 37, 39, 43, 48–50, 52–77, 109–110, 120, 122, 168, 180–184, 189–190, 194, 198, 201–209, 212–213, 220–221, 228, 232–235, 241, 252–255, 298–300, 303–304, 307, 327, 331–333, 336, 353–355, 359, 391–392
child rights impact assessment, 9, 235, 263, 271, 276–279, 281–282, 390

child-friendly cities, 10, 337–360
child-friendly spaces, 320–321
children with disabilities, 6, 126, 139–163, 188, 222, 325–326, 389, 395, 398
Children's Declaration on Sustainable Development Goals, 185–187
civil society, 229, 335, 355
climate change, 7, 41, 168–169, 171, 173–174, 179–180, 186–191, 214, 252
collective rights, 37, 42–45, 48, 174–175, 393
Convention on Biological Diversity, 172, 246
customary law, 134–135, 237, 243–247

data collection, 117–136, 213, 228, 230, 235, 272, 278, 389
Declaration on the Rights of Indigenous Peoples, 44
Declaration on the Rights of the Child (1924), 57
Declaration on the Rights of the Child (1959), 39, 57, 312
Desertification Convention, 172
Draft Principles on Human Rights and the Environment, 196

early and forced marriage, 6, 114, 116, 121, 126, 130–131, 138
ecocentric rights, 34–46, 49, 245
economic development, 5, 8, 13–14, 26–28, 115, 121, 140, 168, 193, 211, 263–264, 266, 281, 284–285, 302
EU Charter of Fundamental Rights, 377
European Convention on Human Rights, 125, 174, 185
evolving capacities, 21, 125, 225, 290, 298–300, 332, 349, 395

Index

female genital mutilation, 116
future citizens, 198, 200, 202, 205, 209–210, 214
future generations, 199–200, 205, 210, 221, 392–393

GATT, 272–276
gender equality, 6, 10, 114–138, 187, 285, 287–288, 304, 324–326, 389
Global Convention on Healthy Diets, 382

Human Development Index, 347

ICPD Beyond 2014 Conference, 124, 128
indigenous children, 8, 221, 236–257, 307, 389
indigenous peoples, 16, 37, 44–45, 49–50, 170, 188, 213, 217, 221, 236–257
Inter-American Commission of Human Rights, 191
intergenerational equity principle, 4, 7, 22–23, 27, 29, 167–191, 194, 302, 392–393
intergenerational rights, 37, 45–46, 48
International Conference on Population and Development, 115, 122, 127–128, 130
international cooperation, 7, 144, 151–152, 160, 163, 222–223, 271, 397
International Covenant on Civil and Political Rights, 39, 44, 60, 125
International Covenant on Economic, Social and Cultural Rights, 39, 123, 271, 297–298, 304, 311
International Labour Organization, 9, 274, 284–285, 296, 298, 304–305

Johannesburg Declaration on Sustainable Development, 180, 205–207, 210

Kyoto Protocol, 174–186

Marrakesh Treaty, 150, 159
Millennium Development Goals, 118–119, 129–130, 135, 138, 152–155, 167–168, 204–205, 210–211, 332, 388

New Delhi Principles of Sustainable Development, 173
non-discrimination, 6, 20, 39, 114, 205, 208, 213, 220–221, 388–389

Paris Agreement, 220, 225–226
precautionary principle, 4, 22, 177, 245, 256
private sector, 223, 262, 264–268, 276–282, 396–397

right not to be separated from parents, 222
right to a healthy environment, 185, 195–196, 202–204, 265, 390, 393
right to a name, 347
right to access information, 8, 125–126, 128, 221, 241, 250–252, 257
right to an adequate standard of living, 222, 249, 264, 270, 290, 347
right to culture, 242, 257
right to development, 12
right to education, 5–6, 9–10, 37–51, 119–120, 124, 129, 131–134, 139–163, 186–187, 198, 212, 219, 221–222, 225, 241, 257, 285, 291–296, 324, 328, 339, 347, 352–353, 394–395
right to freedom from exploitation, 265, 267, 283, 304, 347, 352
right to freedom of assembly, 347
right to freedom of association, 221
right to freedom of expression, 221, 347
right to freedom of thought, 221
right to health, 6, 10, 78–113, 116, 120, 125, 131, 184, 194, 197, 202–204, 207, 218–219, 221–223, 270, 290–291, 327, 347, 361–384, 390–391
right to identity, 222, 347
right to know and be cared for by parents, 221
Right to life, survival and development, 27, 39, 194, 220–221, 328–330, 347, 391
right to nationality, 221–222
right to play, 9, 221, 265, 268, 306–336, 339, 398
right to privacy, 222
right to protection from abuse and neglect, 222, 347
right to recovery and reintegration, 330
right to water, 236–257
right to water and sanitation, 124
Rio Conference on Environment and Development, 172–173, 175–176, 192
Rio Declaration on Environment and Development, 180, 201–204
Rio+20 Conference, 129, 175, 208–209

Salamanca Statement and Framework for Action on Special Needs Education, 143
San Salvador Protocol to the American Convention on Human Rights, 185
sexual and reproductive health rights, 6, 114–116, 120–134, 136, 138
Stockholm Declaration, 172, 199, 210
Sustainable Development Goal, 53
Sustainable Development Goals, 3, 7, 53, 81, 115–116, 120, 122, 130–131, 134, 136–138, 141, 152, 154–157, 159, 161, 168, 186–187, 192, 195, 210–214, 220, 226–227, 246, 284–285, 288, 291–292, 296, 304, 321, 325, 327–329, 332, 334–335, 340, 353, 370

The Future We Want, 129, 210, 213

UN Convention on the Elimination of All Forms of Discrimination Against Women, 122, 125, 205
UN Convention on the Rights of Persons with Disabilities, 7, 126, 141, 146–152, 156–157
UN Development Programme, 337
UN Environment Programme, 199, 207
UN Framework Convention on Climate Change, 172, 175–176, 220, 225, 232–233
UN Population Fund, 118, 136
UN Women, 115, 136
UNCRC Committee, 8, 53, 56, 60, 64–66, 70, 116–117, 136, 144–147, 198, 223, 229–232, 271, 296, 298, 312–314, 334, 392, 397–398
UNCRC General Comment
  No. 1, 144, 224–225
  No. 11, 224
  No. 12, 66–67, 71–72, 334
  No. 13, 224, 334–335
  No. 15, 132, 223–224
  No. 16, 224–225, 264–265, 396
  No. 17, 312–315, 334, 398
  No. 18, 117
  No. 19, 66–67
  No. 20, 296, 298, 305
  No. 4, 123
  No. 5, 56–77
  No. 7, 66, 224, 334
  No. 9, 144–147, 224
UNCRPD General Comment
  No. 4, 150, 158–161
UNESCO, 34
UNESCO Declaration on the Responsibilities of the Present Generation towards Future Generations, 177
UNICEF, 34, 161–162, 188, 204, 232–233, 264, 296, 313, 321
Universal Declaration of Human Rights, 37, 184, 297, 304, 311
universal health coverage, 81–82, 98–101

Vienna Convention on the Law of Treaties, 53, 61–64, 68

water management, 8, 236–257
World Commission on Environment and Development, 172, 192, 200
World Conservation Strategy, 199–200, 210
World Declaration on the Survival, Protection and Development of Children, 197
World Health Organization, 81–82, 98–102, 105, 111, 113, 378, 382
World Population Conference, 123
World Summit for Children, 197
World Trade Organization, 9, 262, 269, 272–276, 279, 281
World Wide Fund for Nature, 199

Made in the USA
Monee, IL
03 May 2026